JR

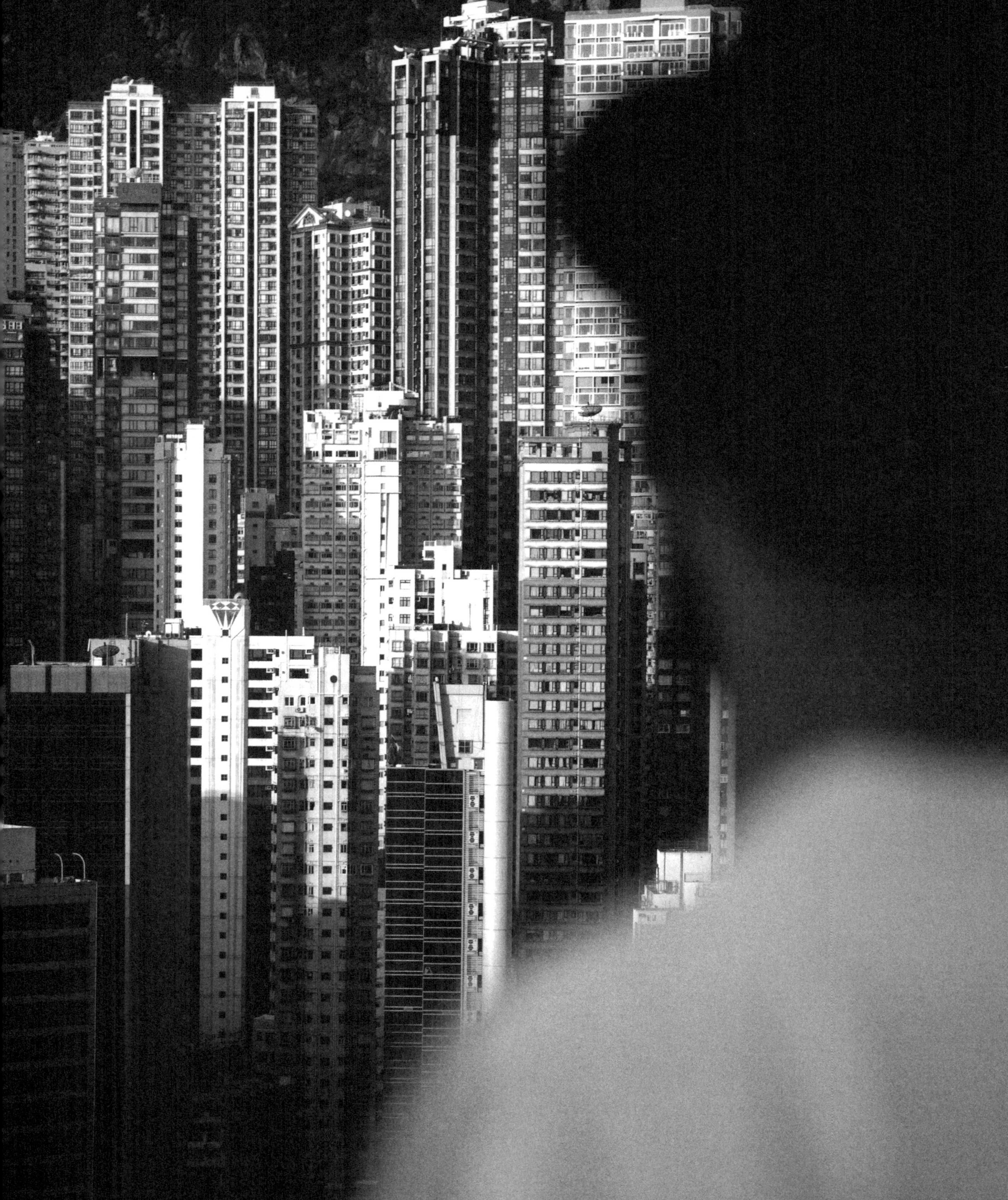

JR

CAN ART CHANGE THE WORLD?

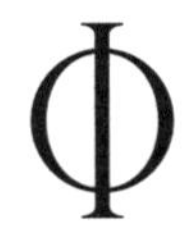

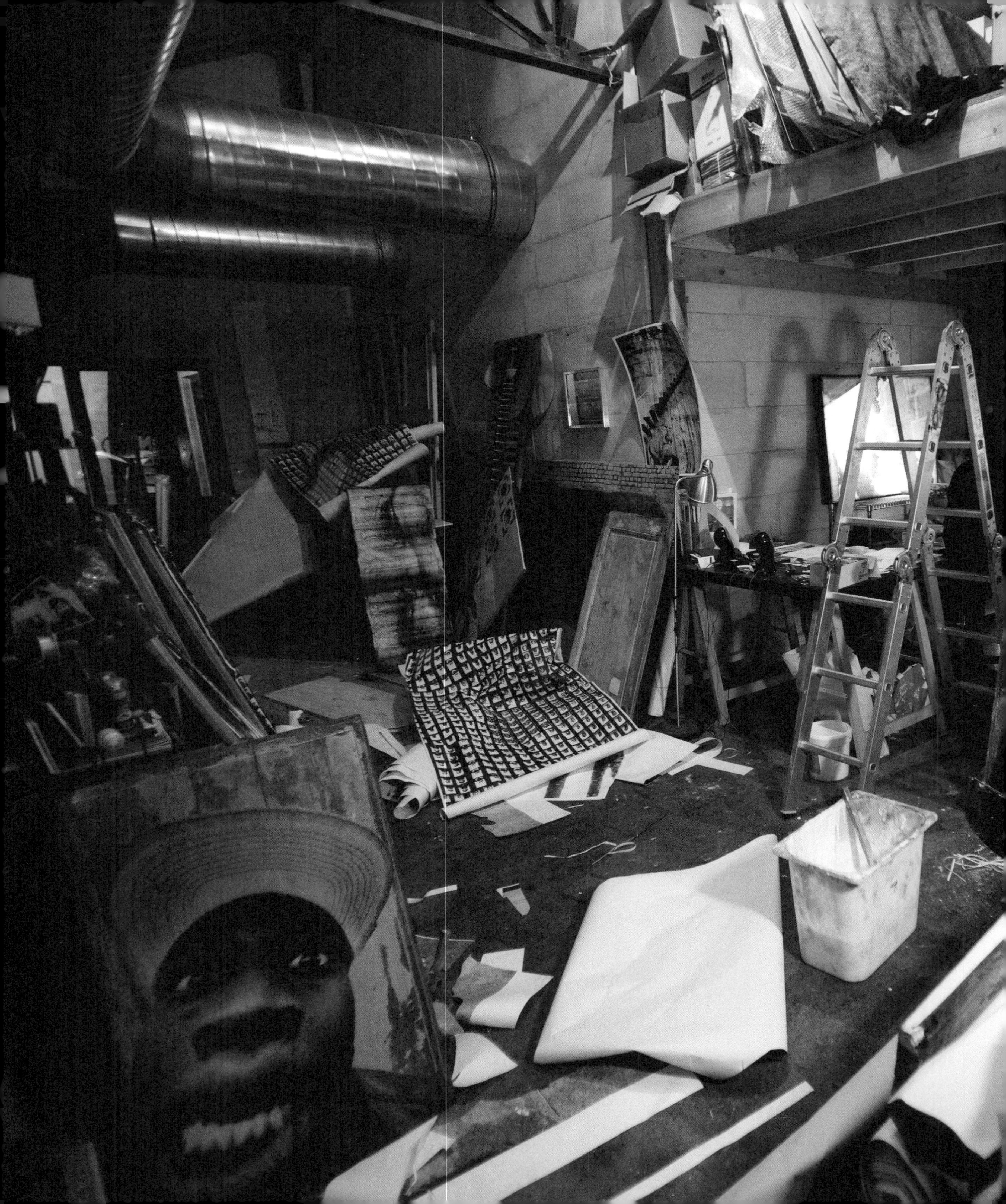

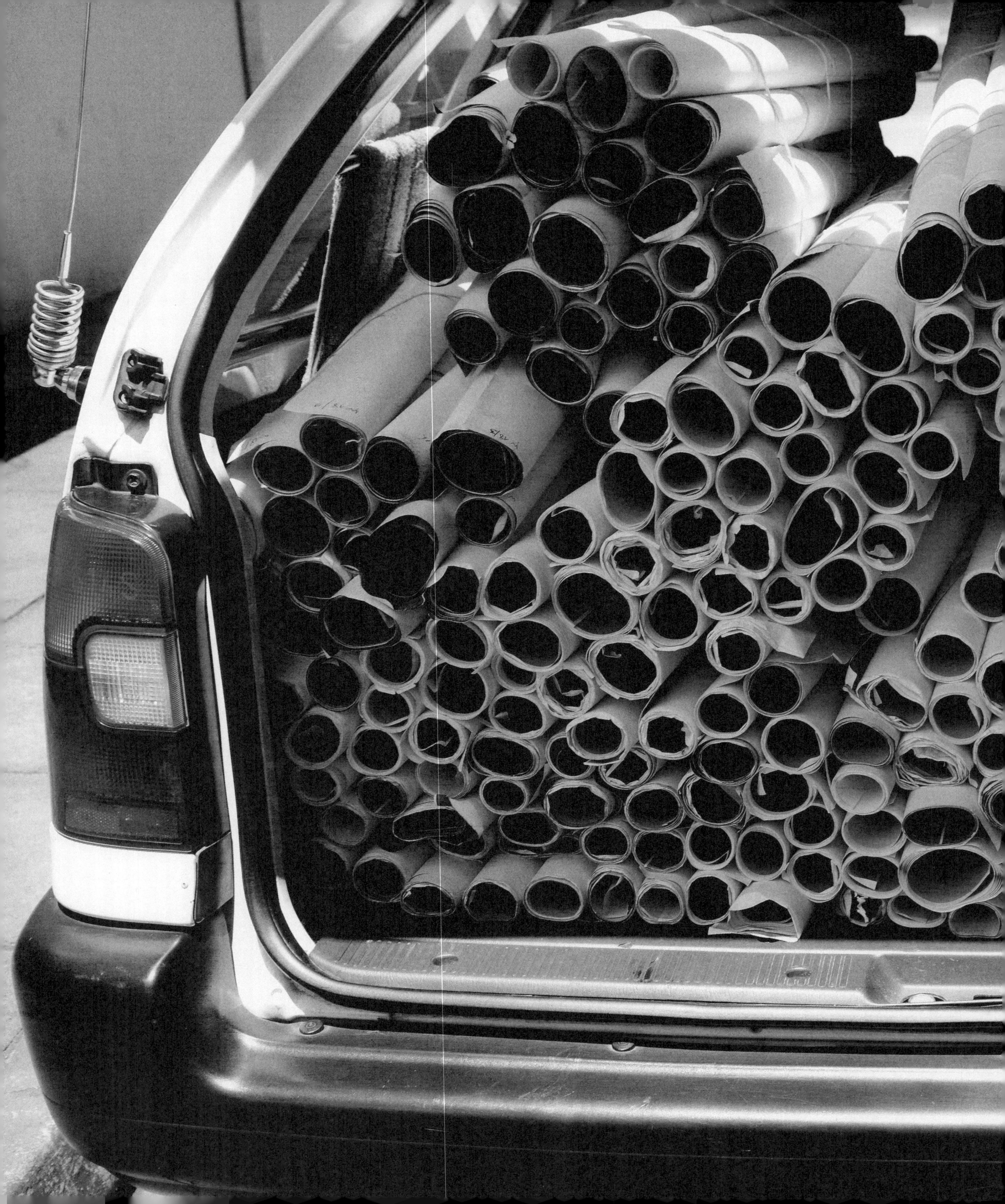

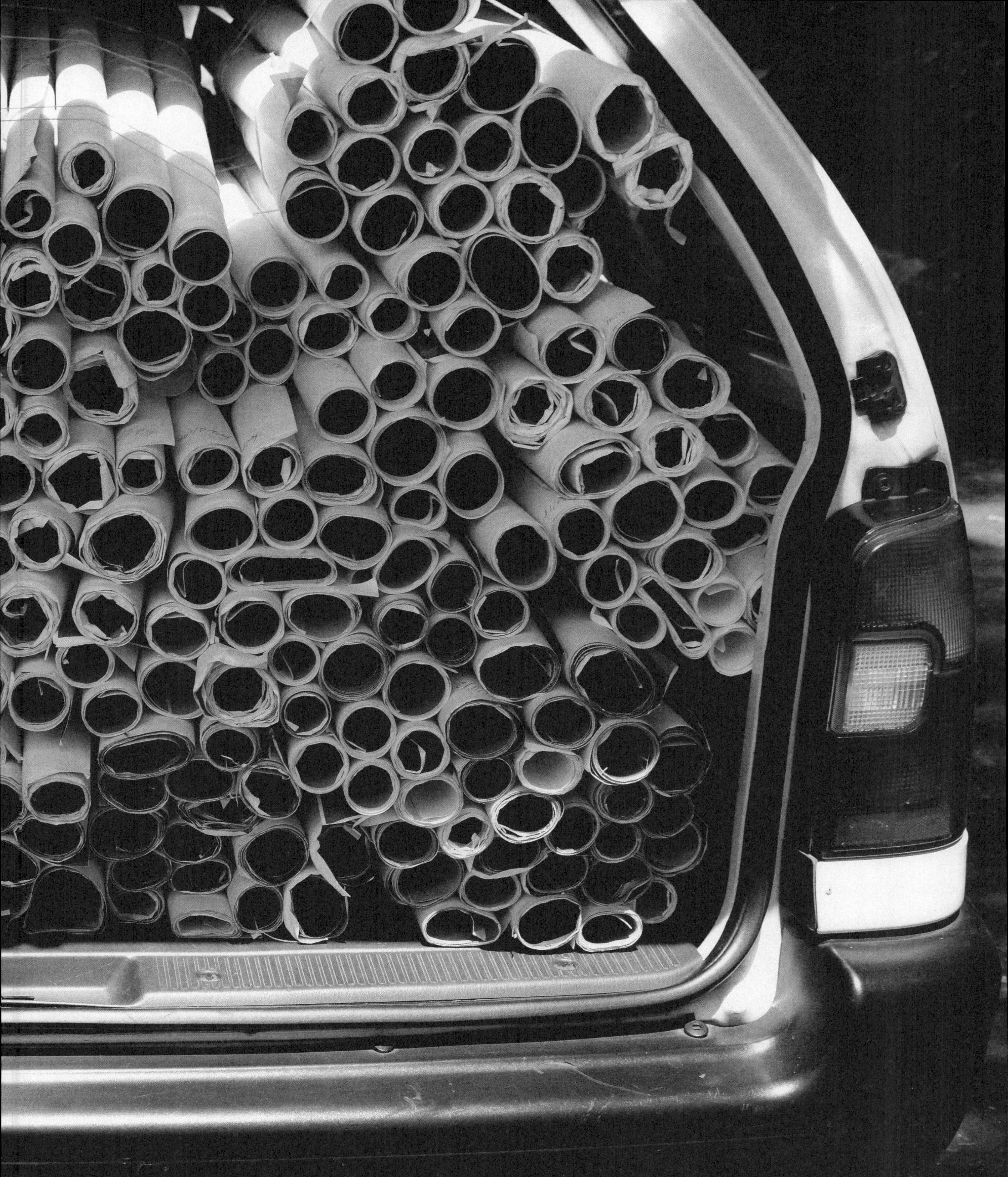

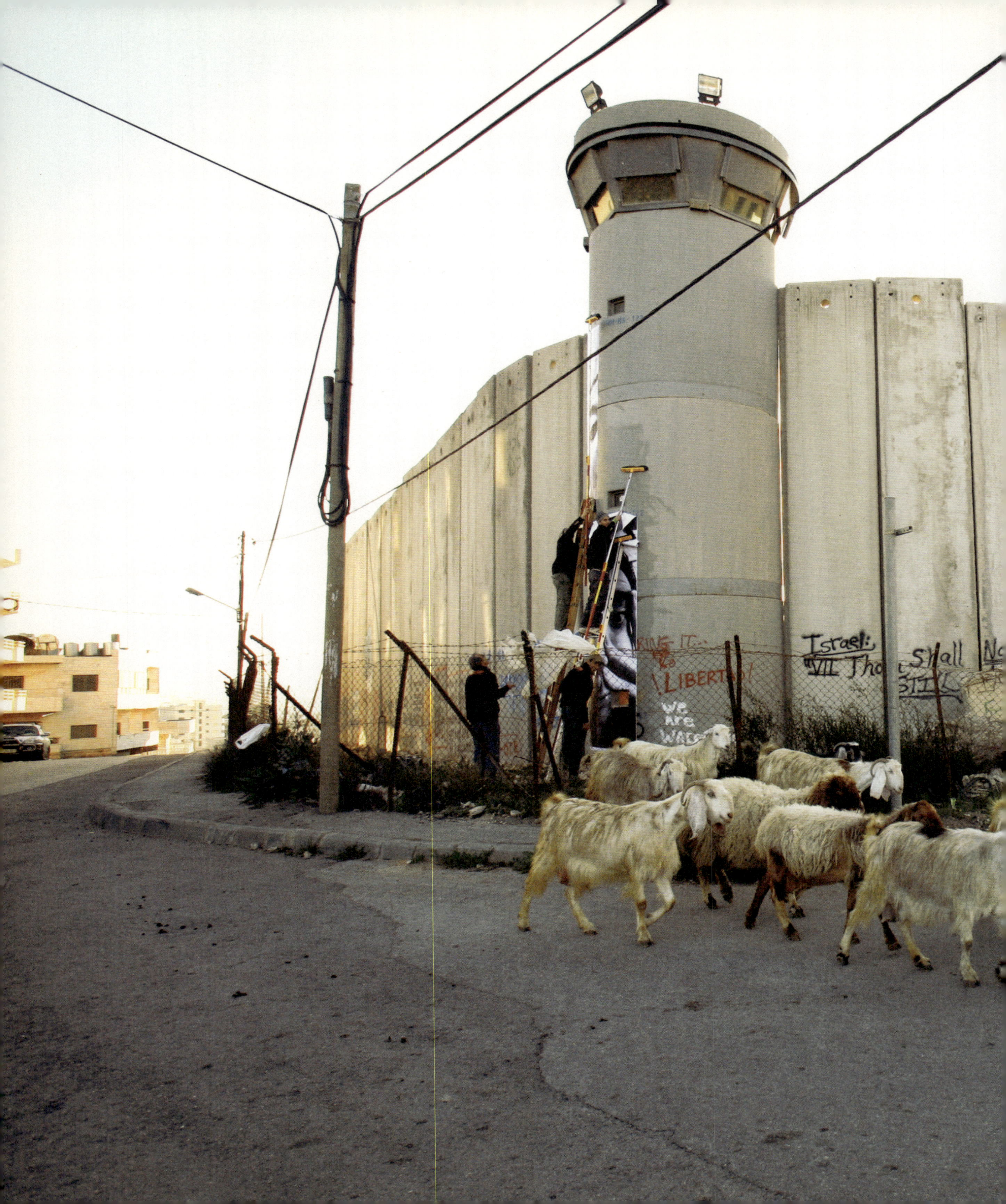
Israel:
Shall
We
Are

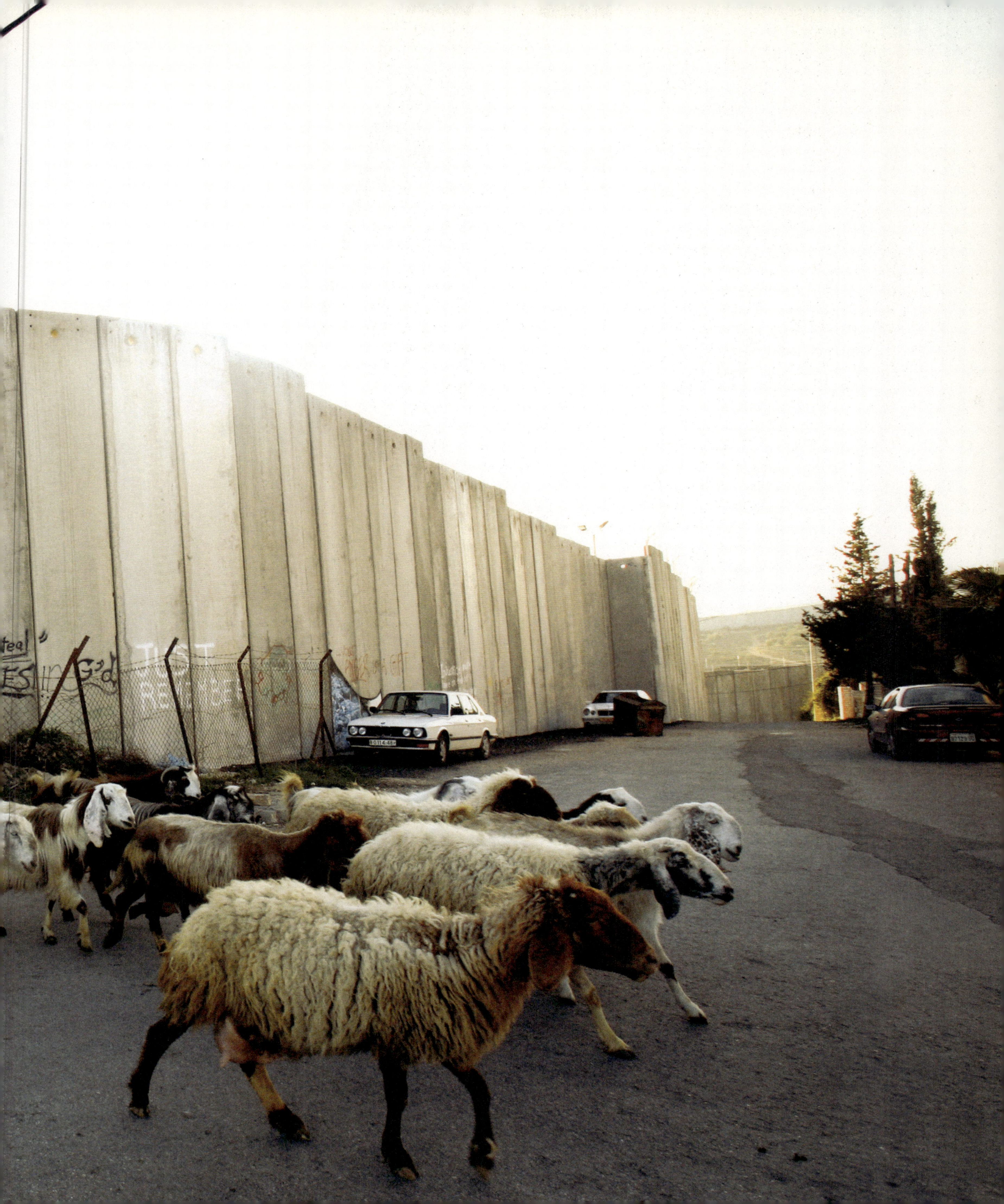

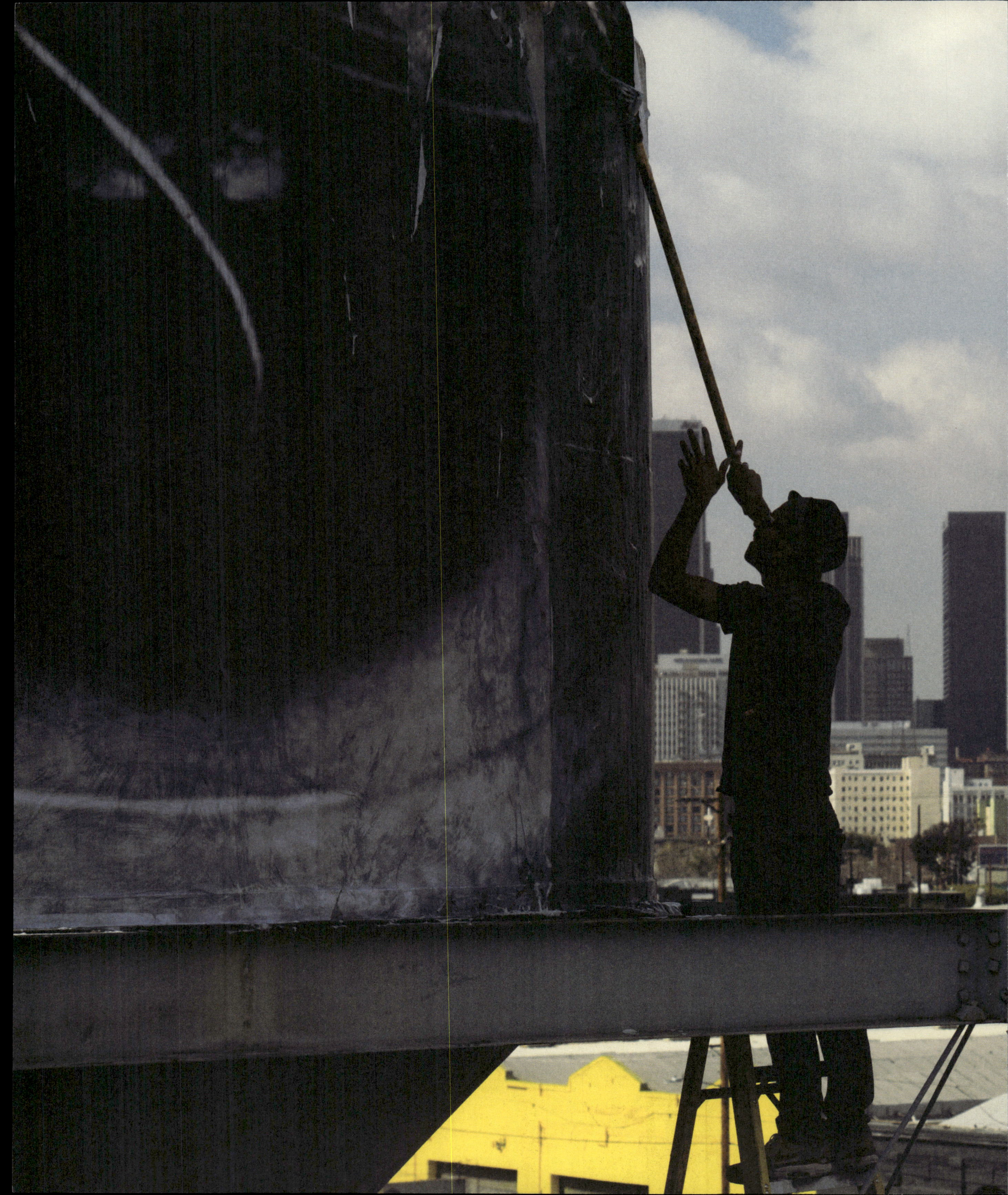

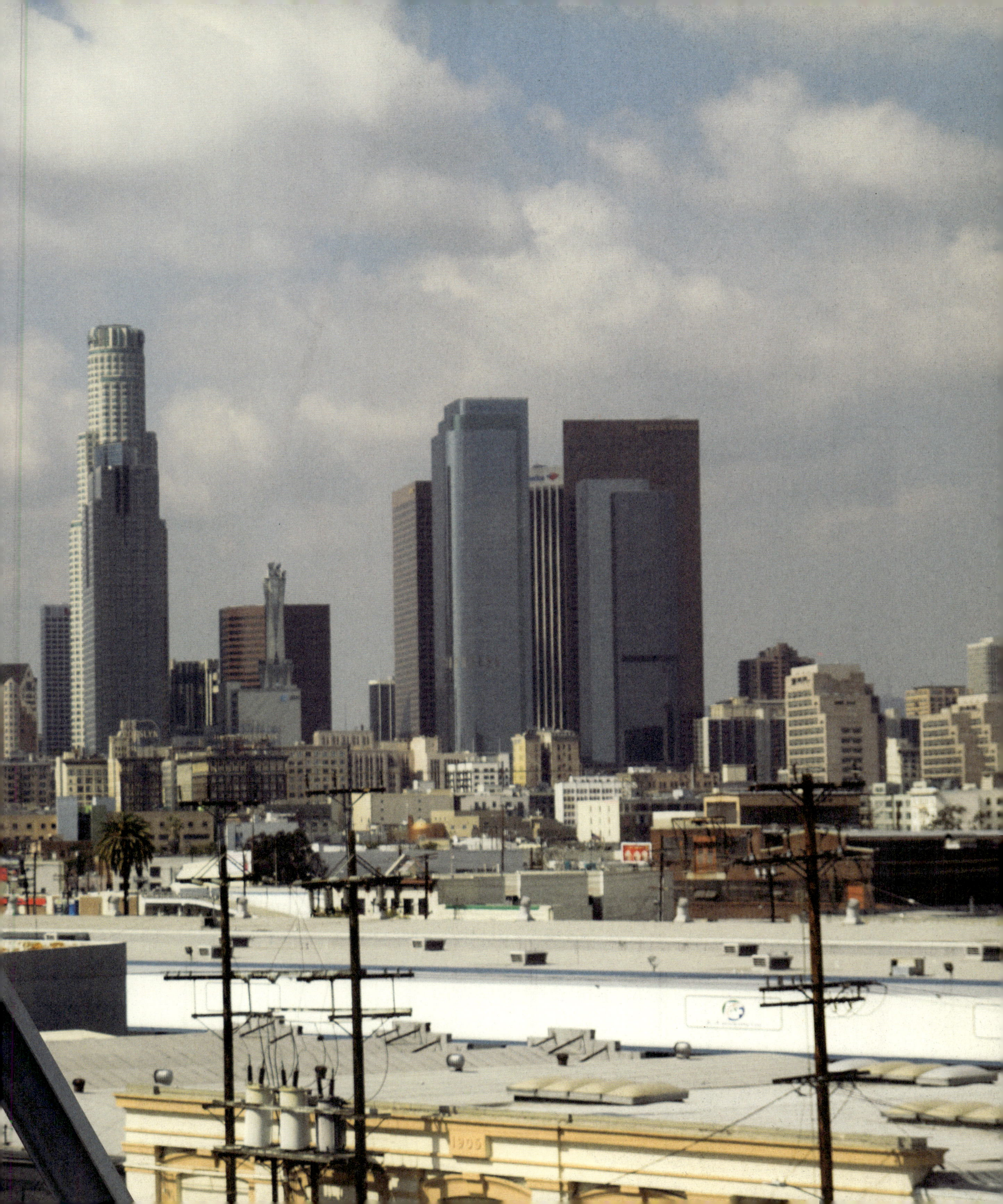

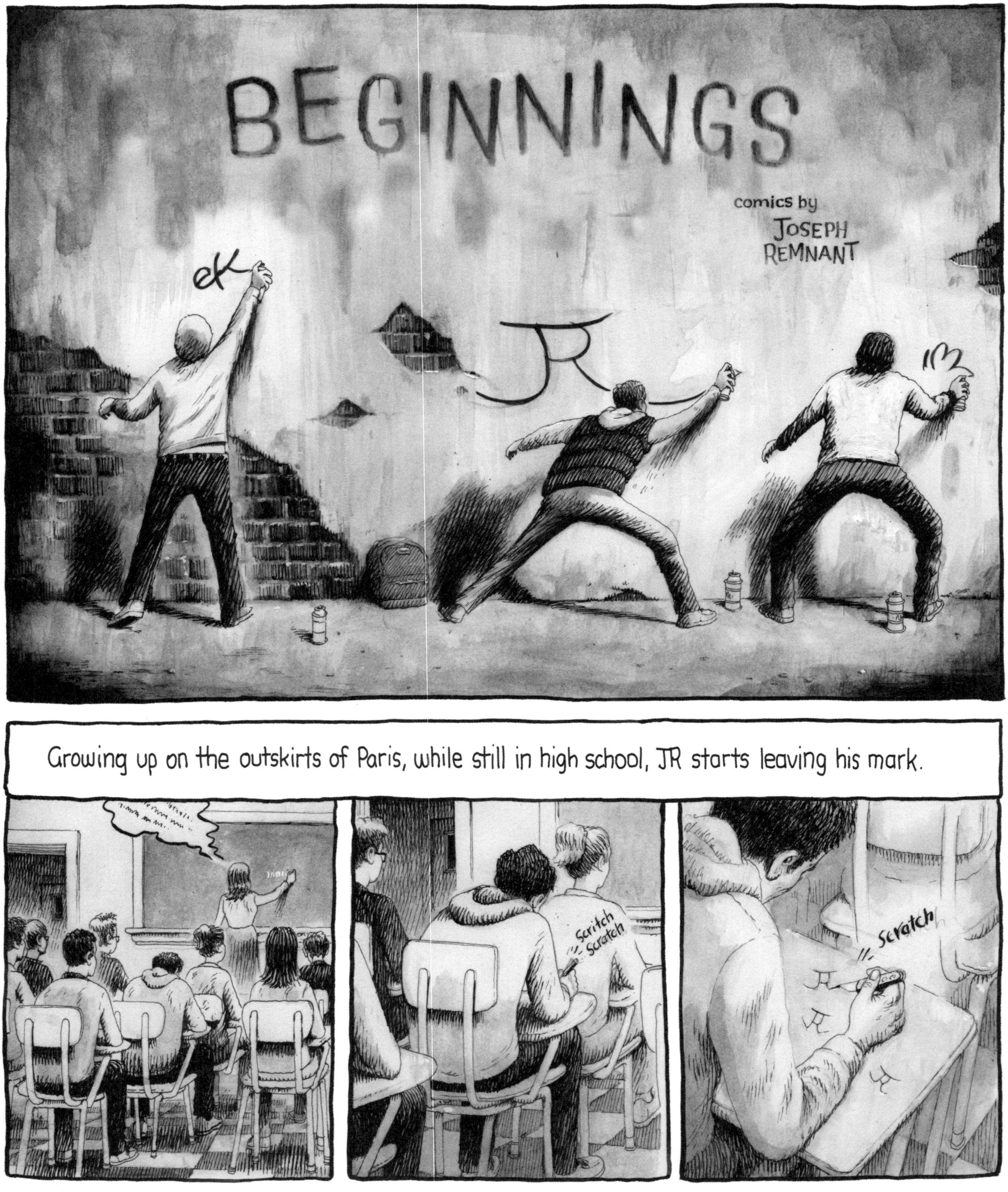

BEGINNINGS

comics by JOSEPH REMNANT

Growing up on the outskirts of Paris, while still in high school, JR starts leaving his mark.

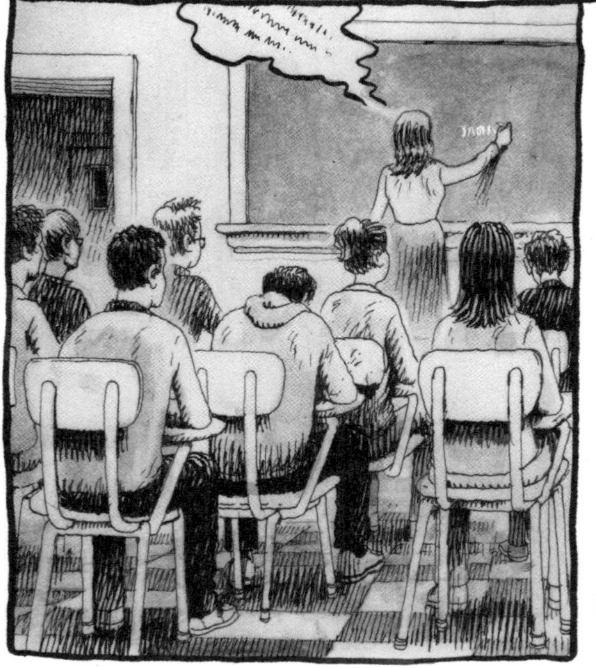

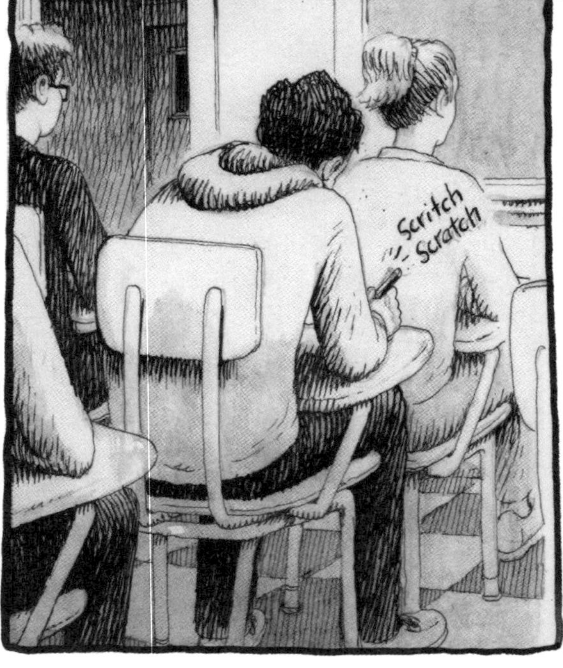

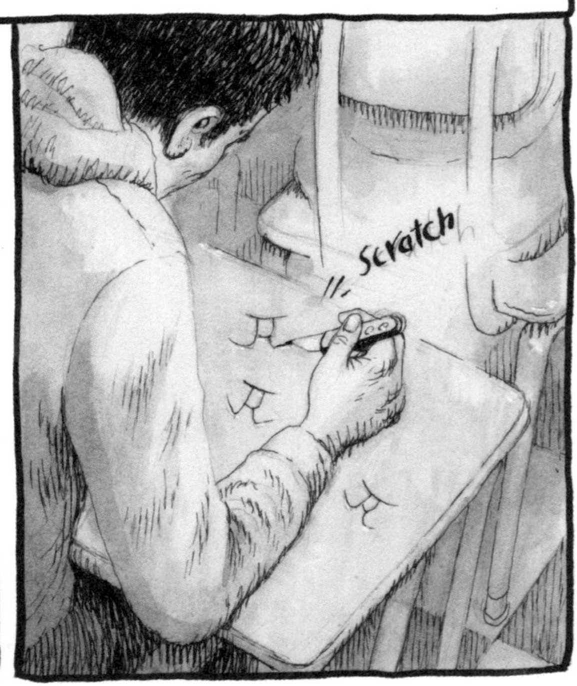

At 14/15 years old, he and his friends just tag their names on walls everywhere.

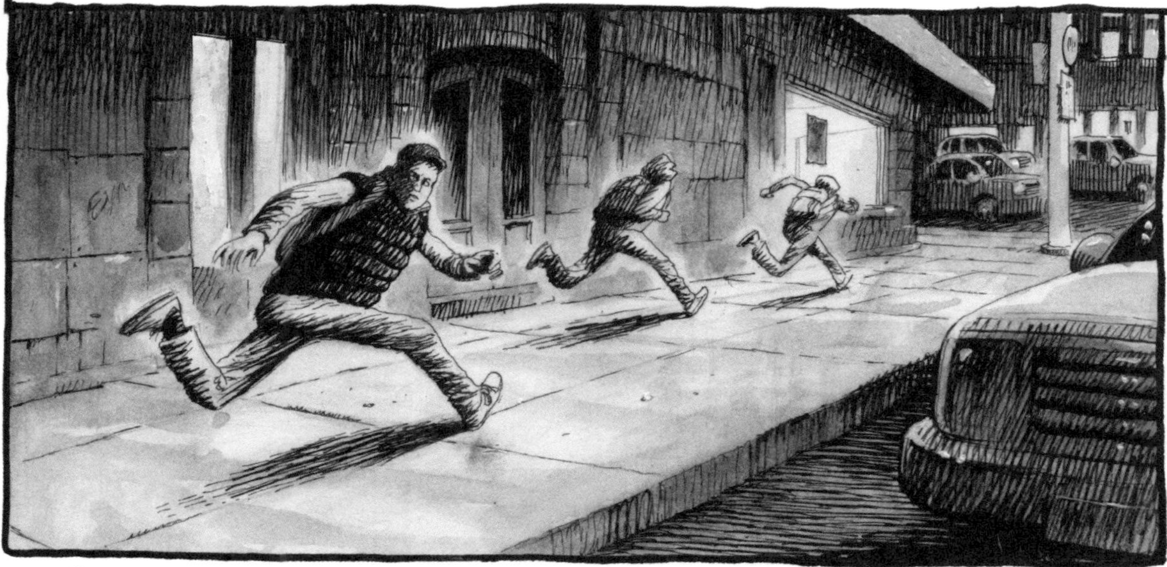

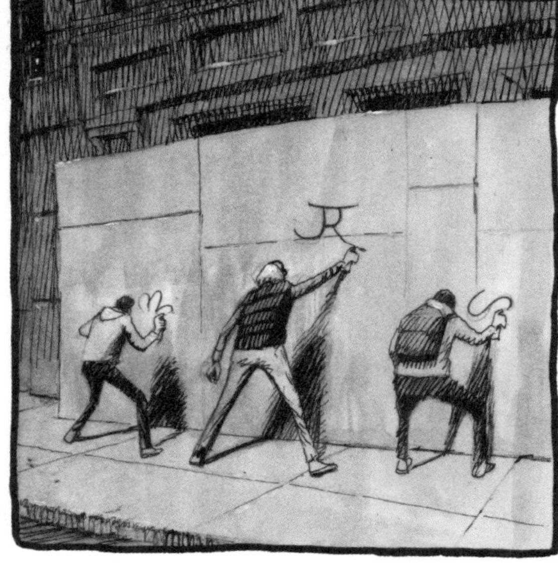

It's about the adventures – climbing up to rooftops, crawling through tunnels, seeing the city from a different angle to the people on the streets – and then leaving a little mark there.

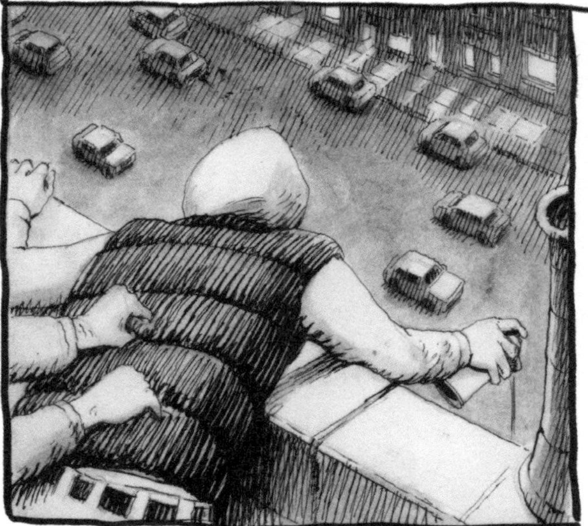

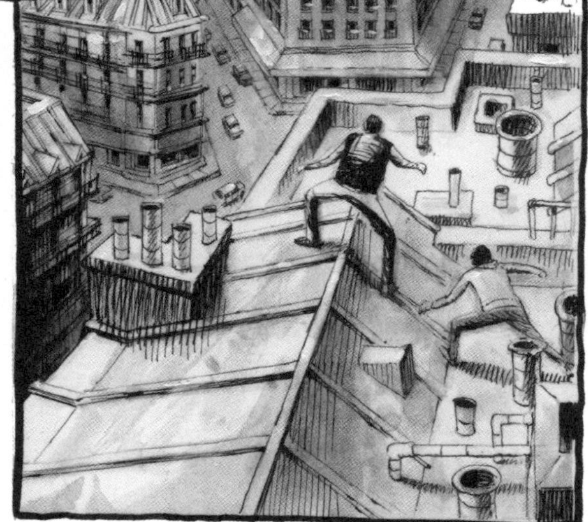

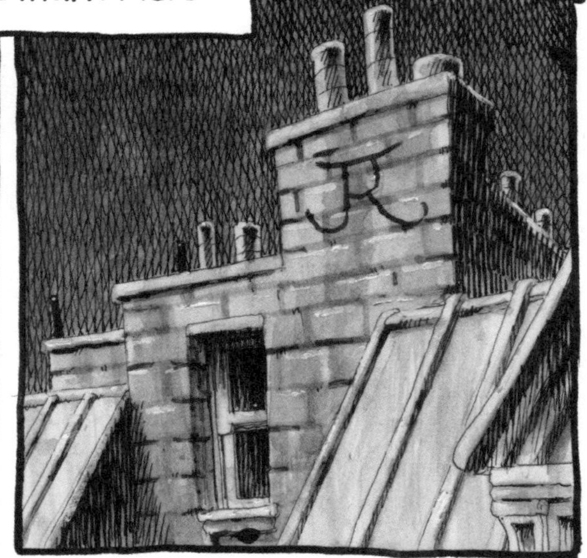

Waiting for a train home at the Charles De Gaulle–Étoile RER station in Paris, he finds an abandoned film camera.

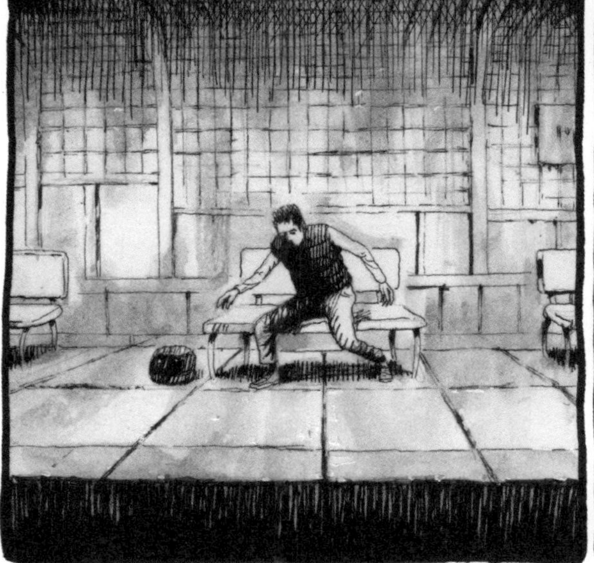

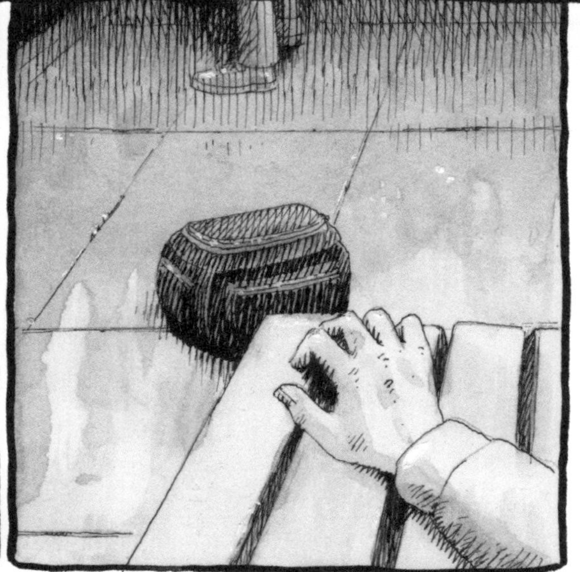

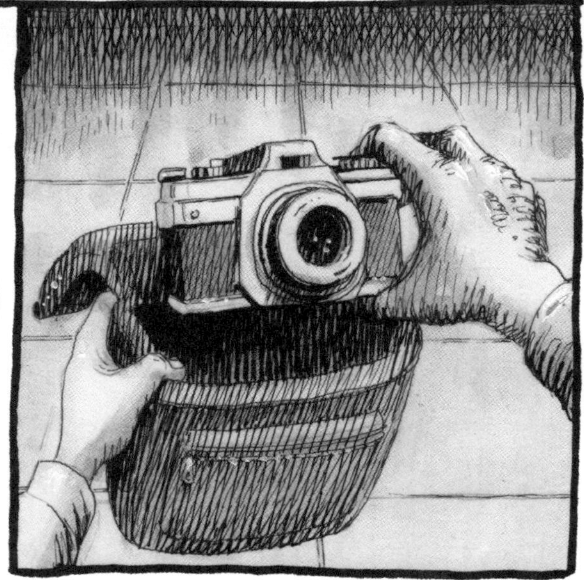

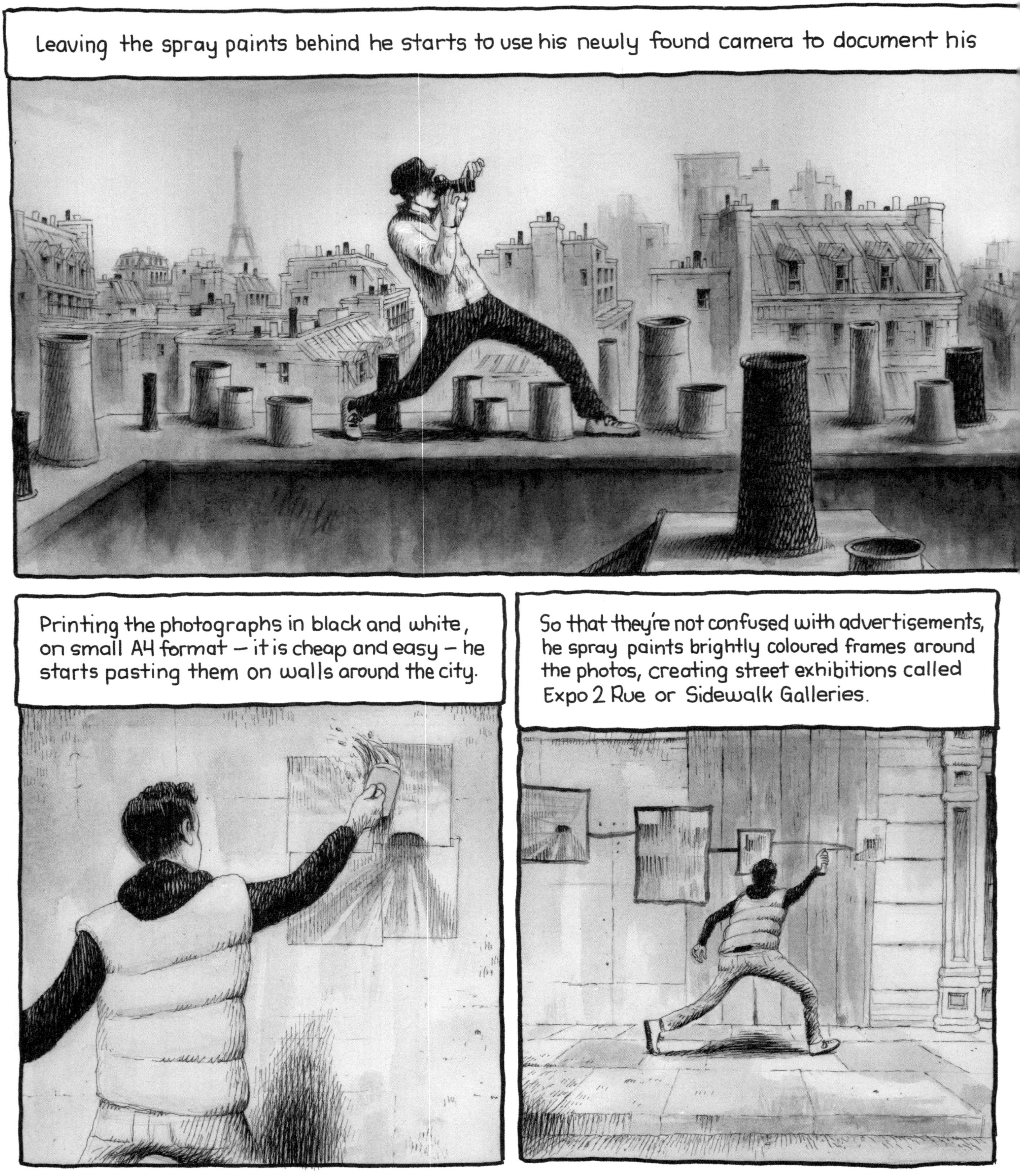

Leaving the spray paints behind he starts to use his newly found camera to document his

Printing the photographs in black and white, on small A4 format – it is cheap and easy – he starts pasting them on walls around the city.

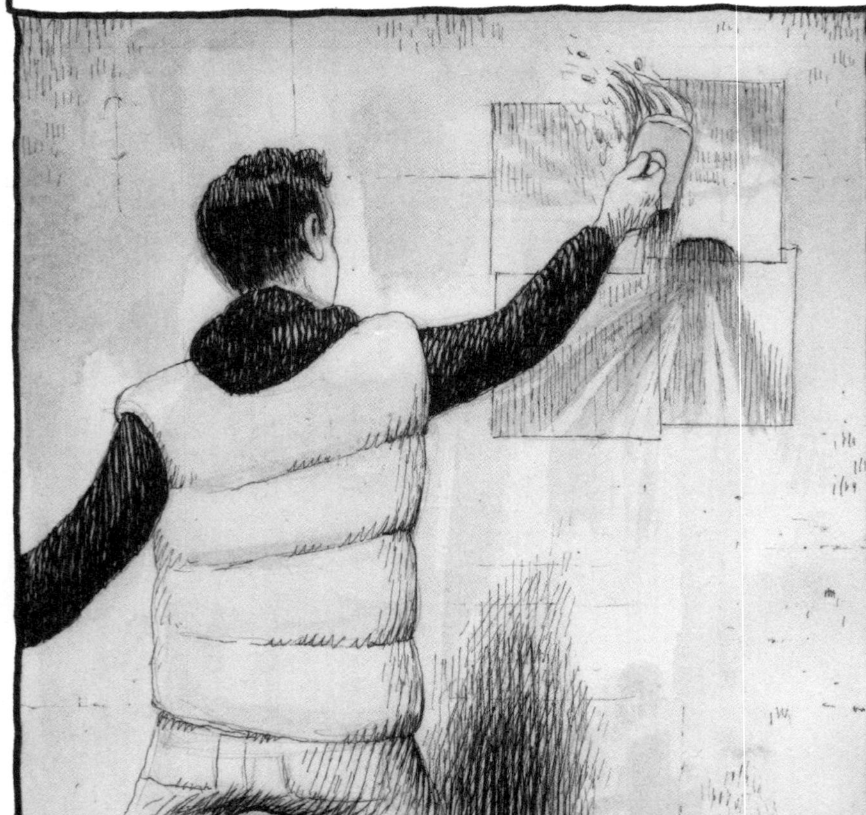

So that they're not confused with advertisements, he spray paints brightly coloured frames around the photos, creating street exhibitions called Expo 2 Rue or Sidewalk Galleries.

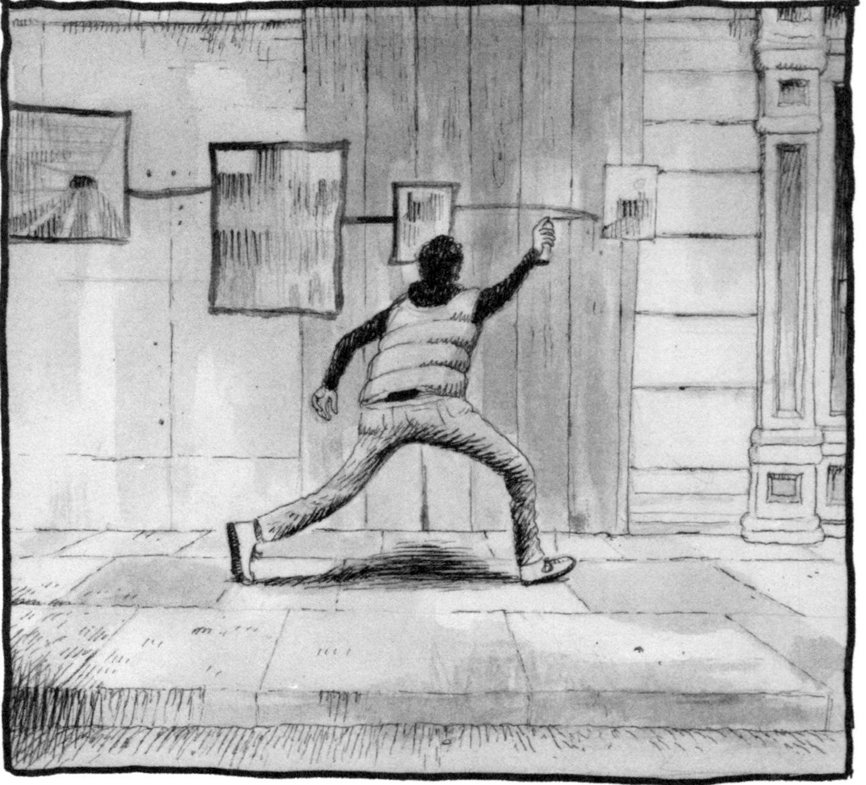

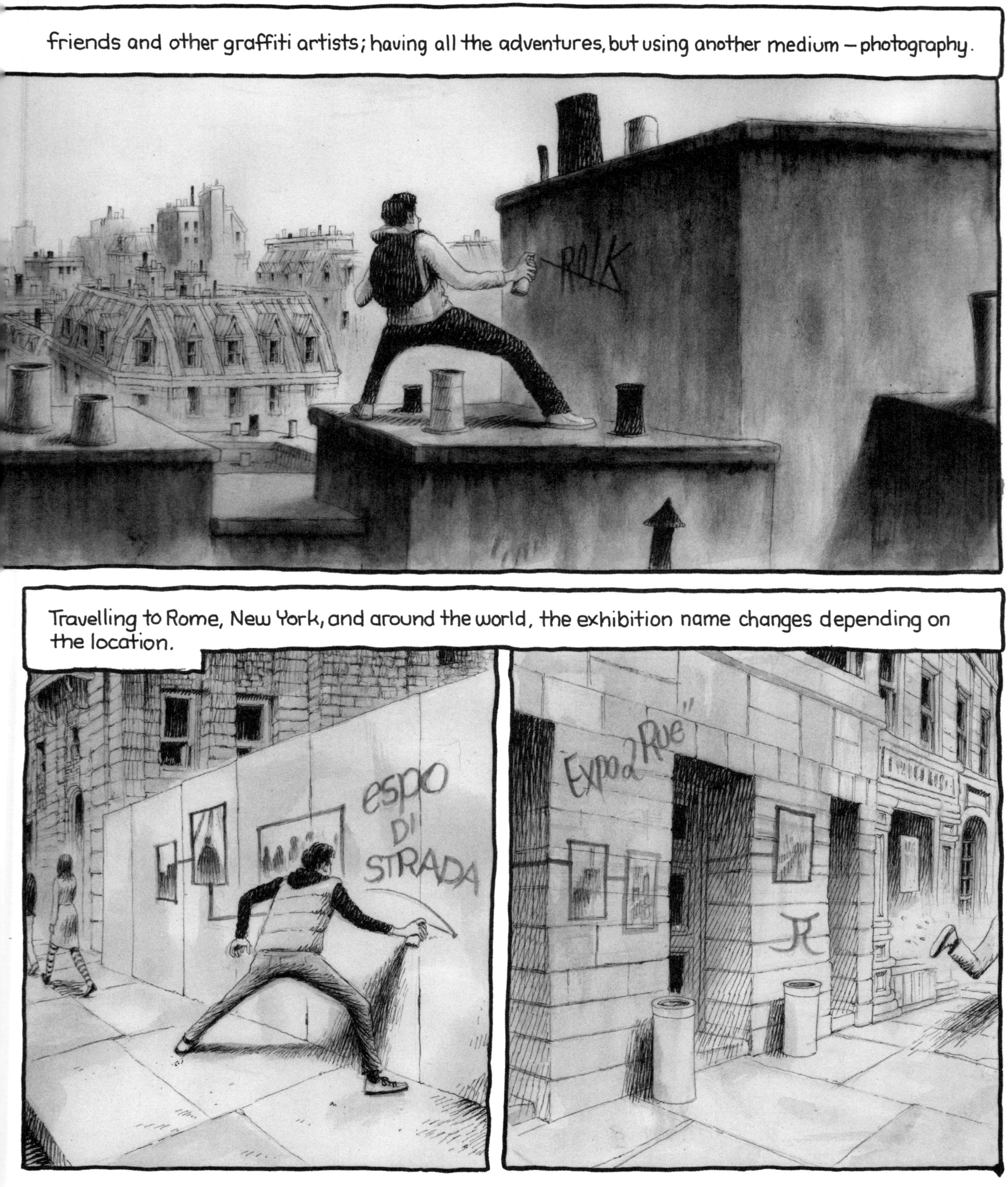

friends and other graffiti artists; having all the adventures, but using another medium – photography.

Travelling to Rome, New York, and around the world, the exhibition name changes depending on the location.

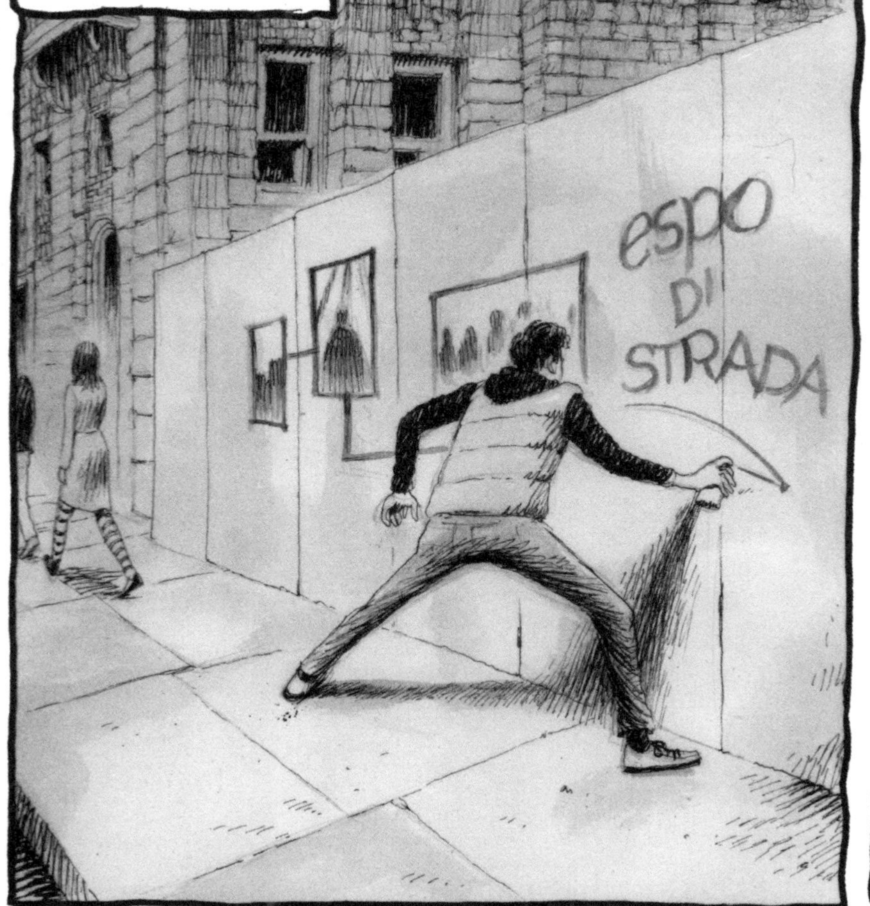

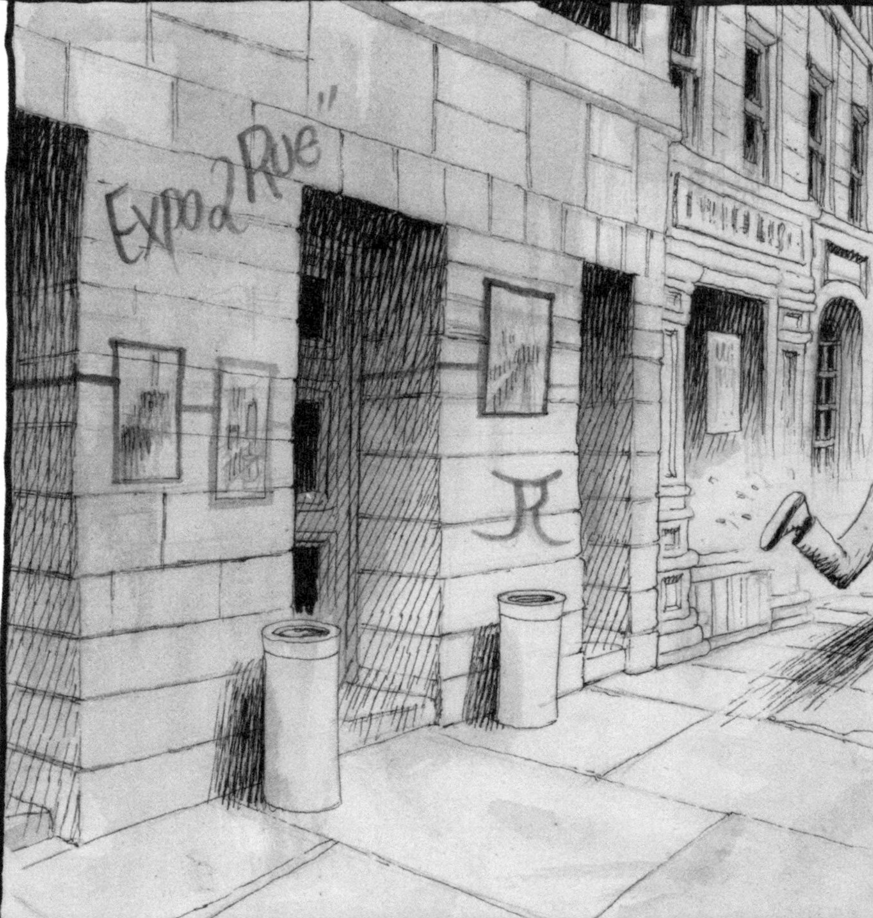

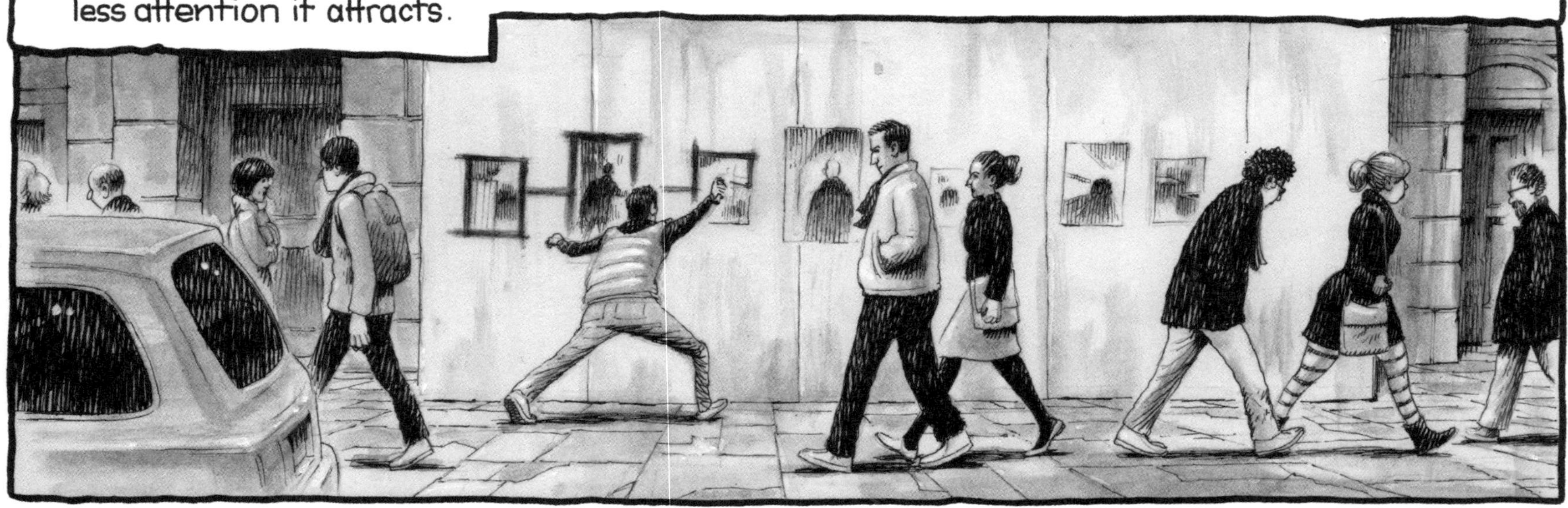
He pastes in broad daylight and in densely trafficked areas. The more obvious it is, the less attention it attracts.

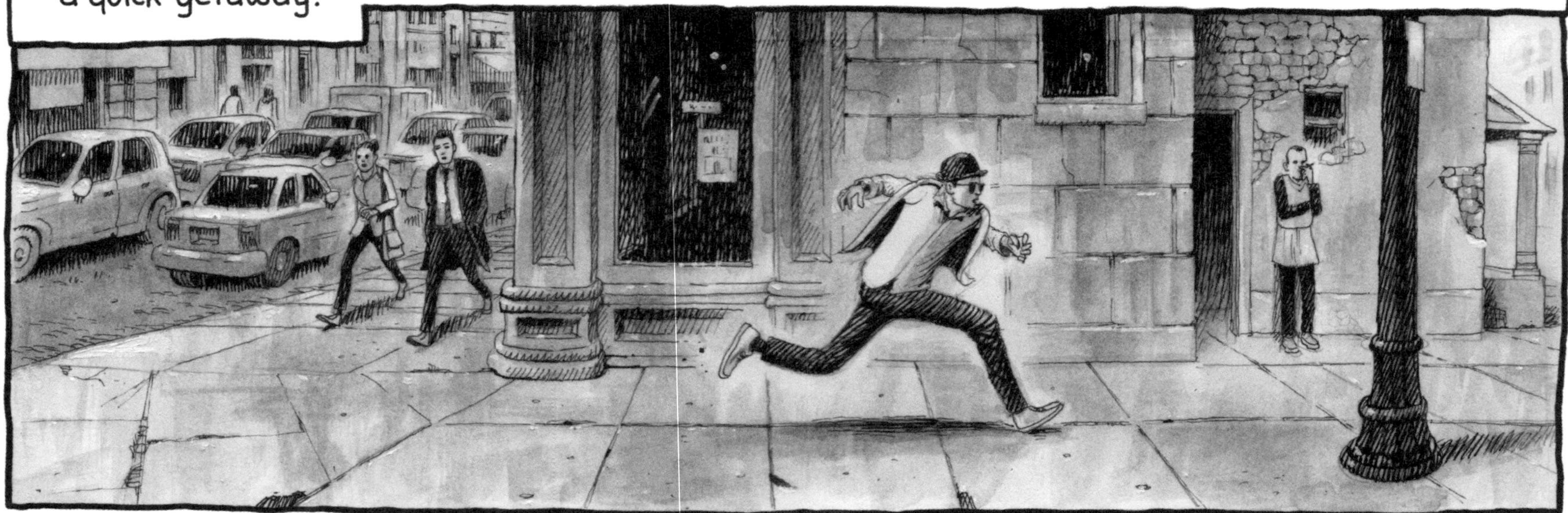
Wearing a reversible jacket, he can change immediately after finishing a pasting and make a quick getaway.

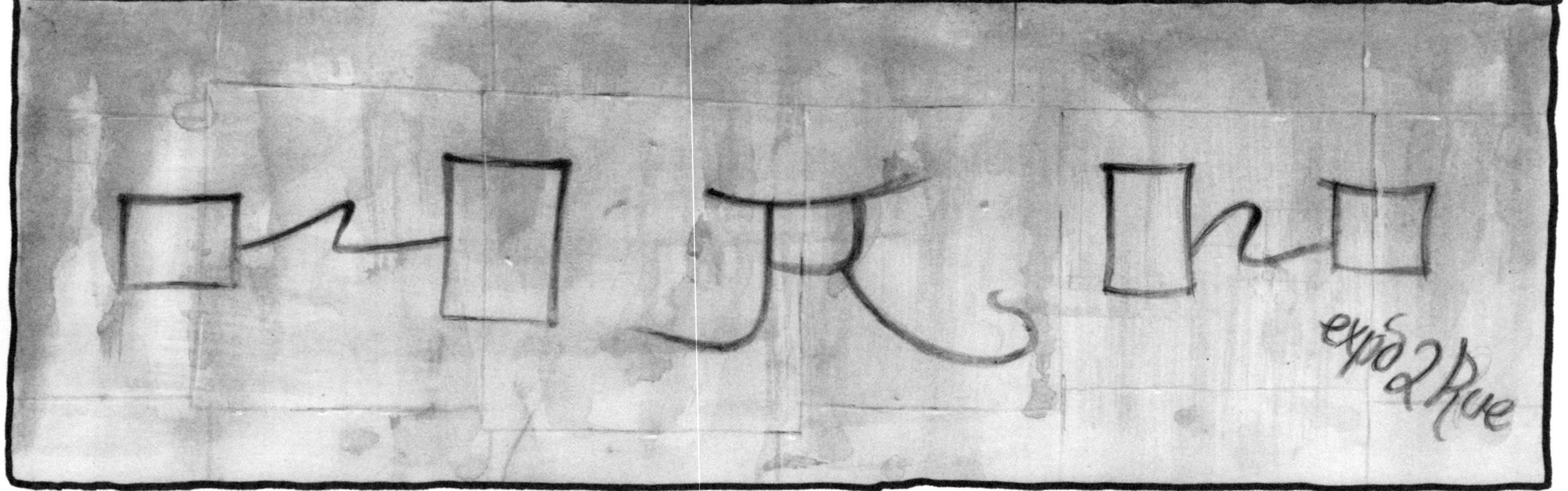
Even when the pastings are removed the spray painted frames remain – reminders that JR was there.
JR
expo2Rue

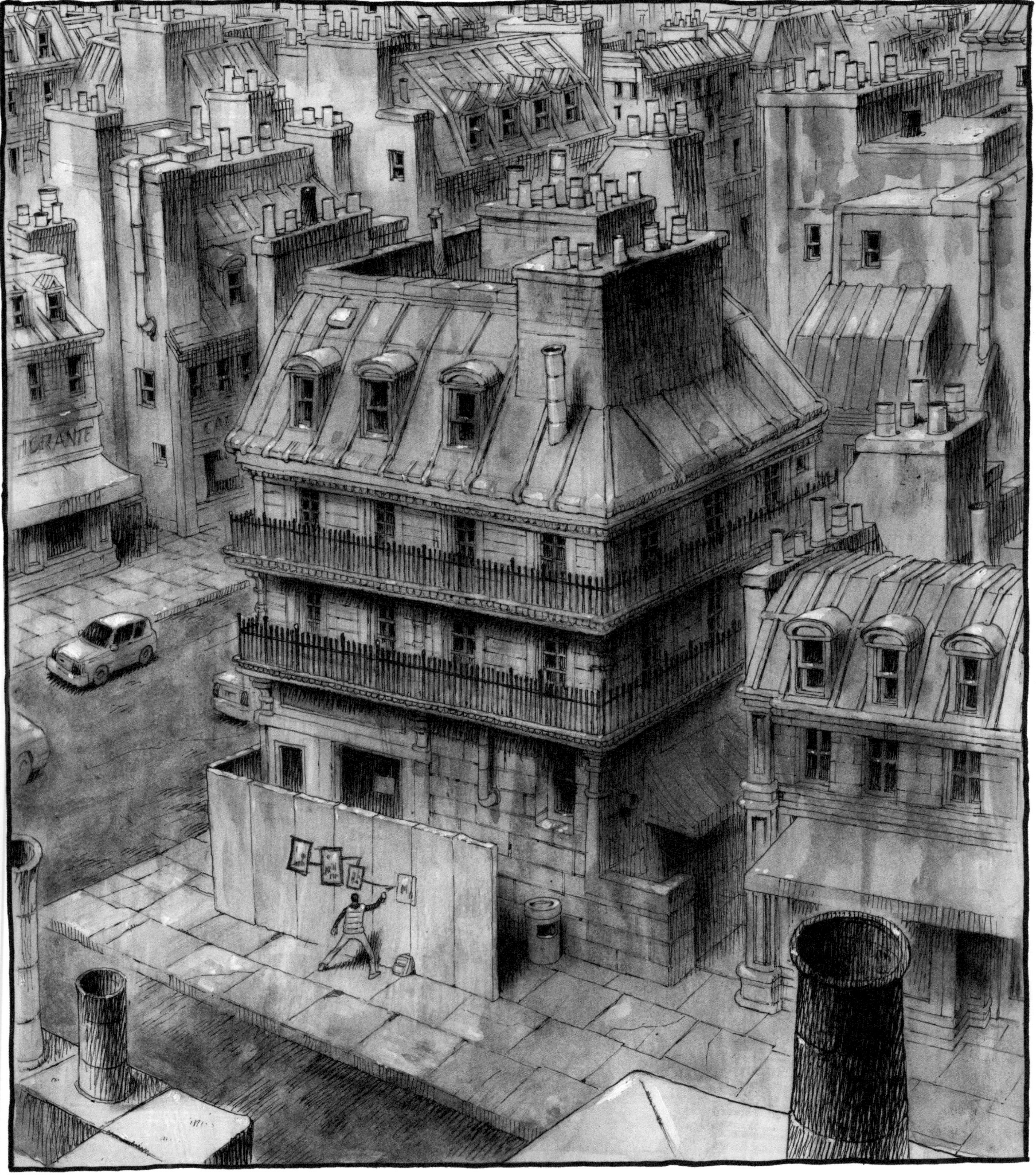

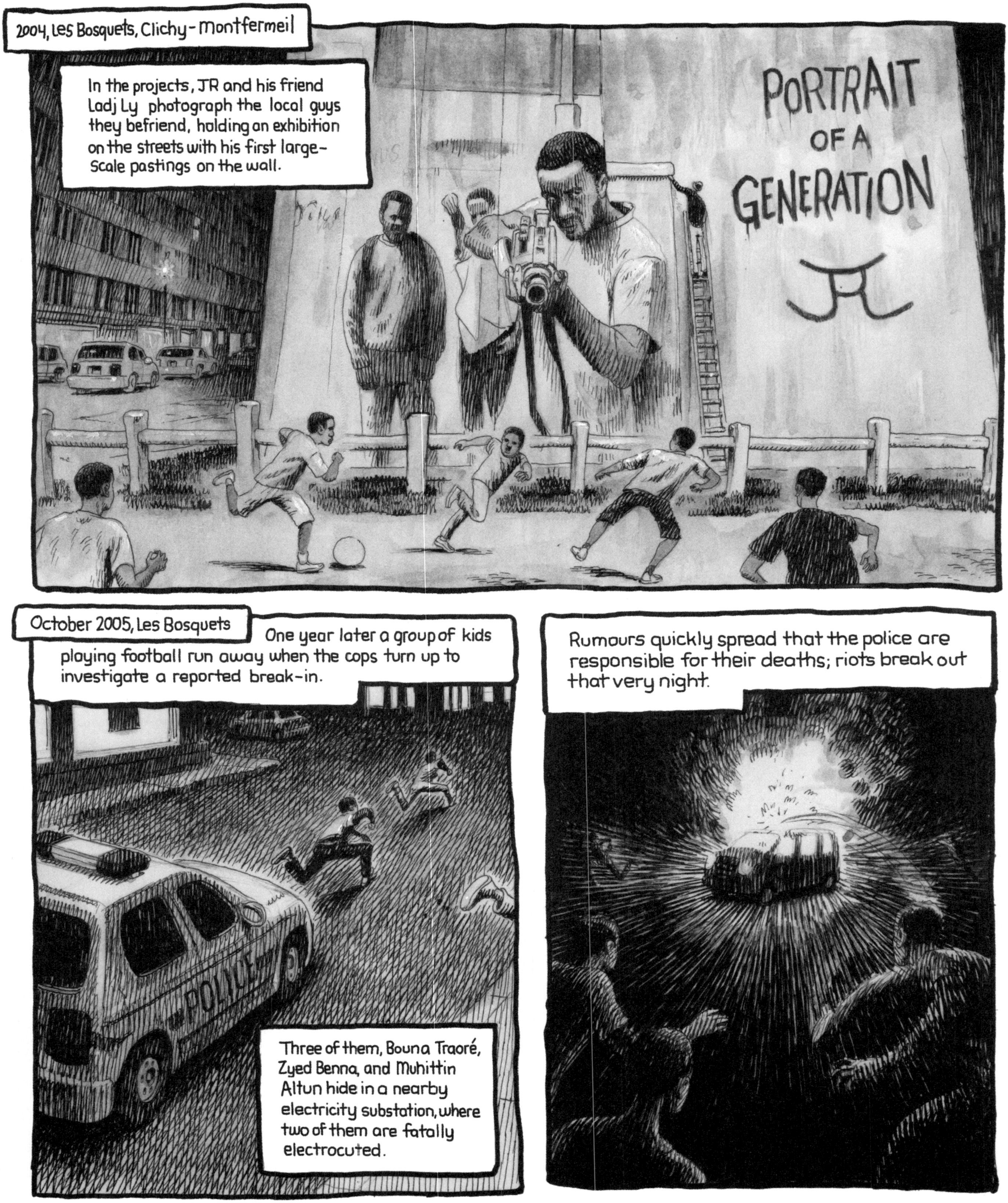

2004, Les Bosquets, Clichy-Montfermeil

In the projects, JR and his friend Ladj Ly photograph the local guys they befriend, holding an exhibition on the streets with his first large-scale pastings on the wall.

PORTRAIT OF A GENERATION

JR

October 2005, Les Bosquets

One year later a group of kids playing football run away when the cops turn up to investigate a reported break-in.

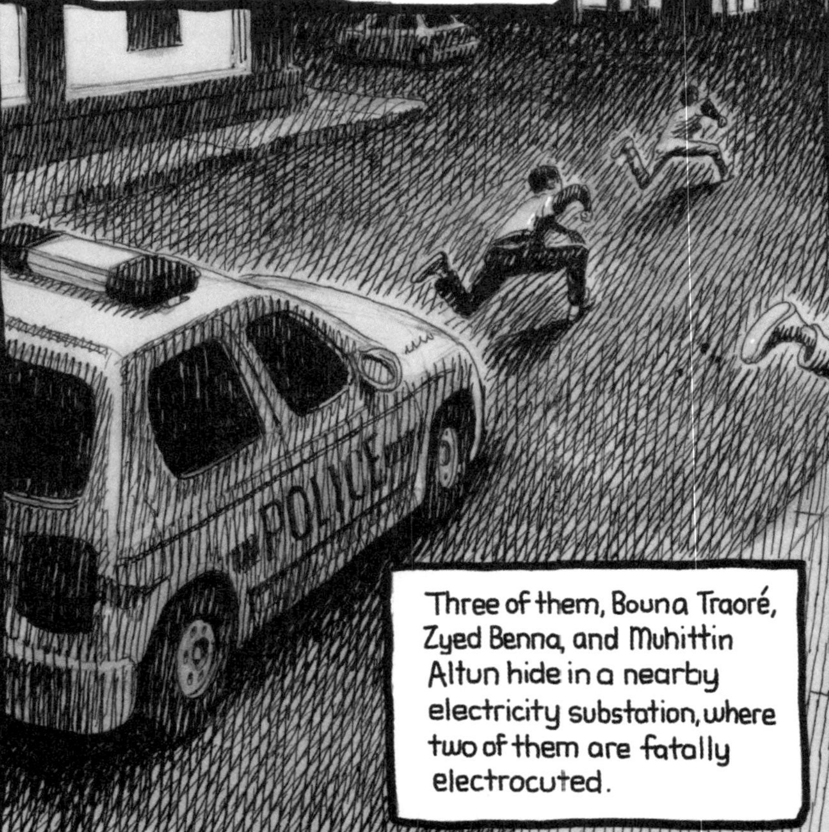

Rumours quickly spread that the police are responsible for their deaths; riots break out that very night.

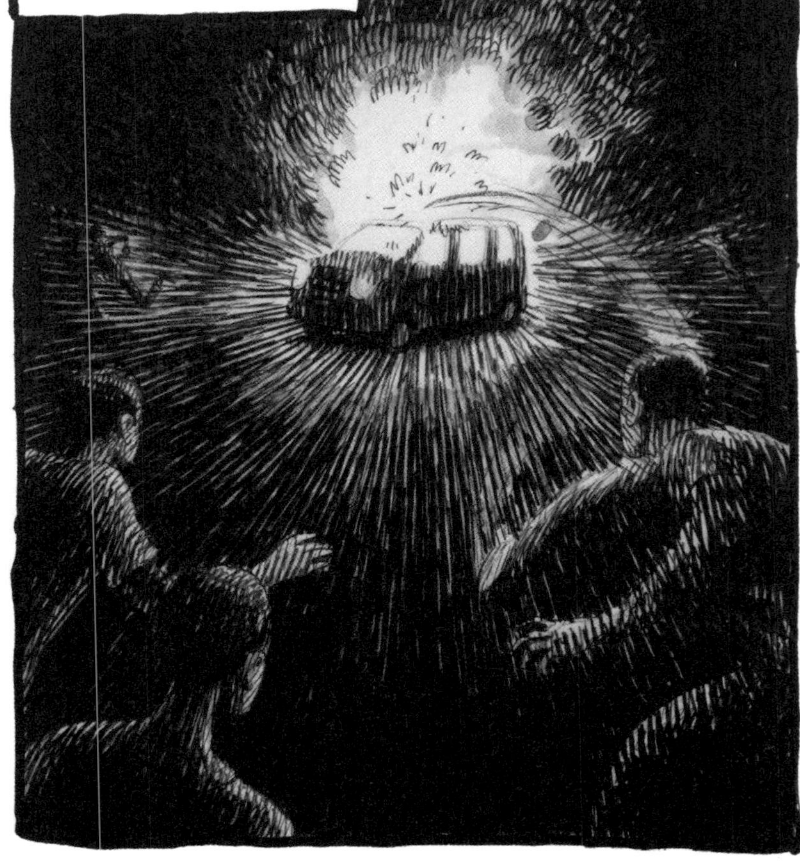

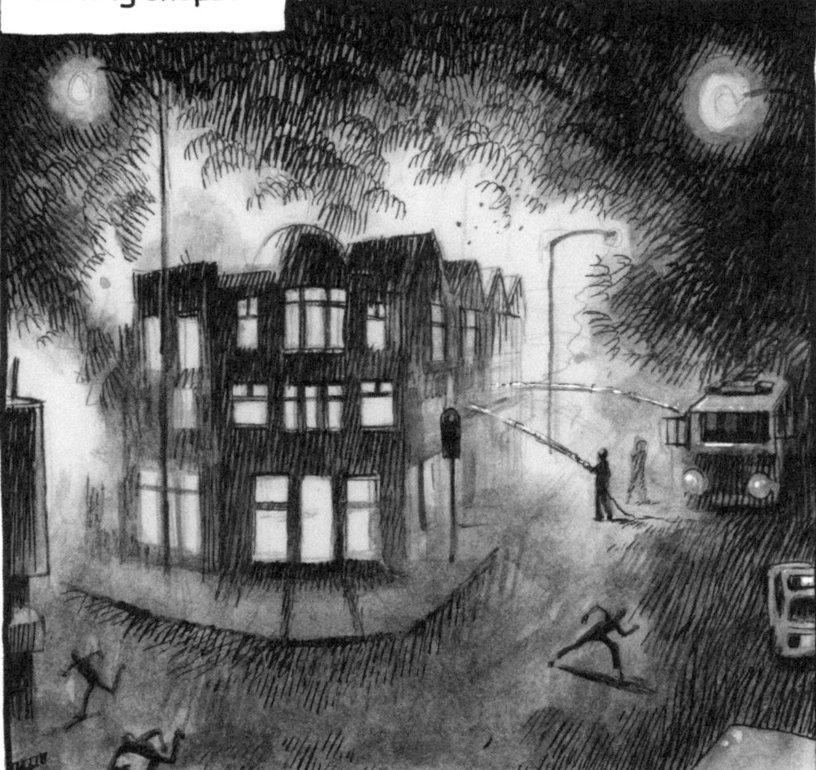
November 2005, Paris
The riots take over the suburbs and kids are shown on TV, out of control, throwing molotov cocktails, attacking cops and looting shops.

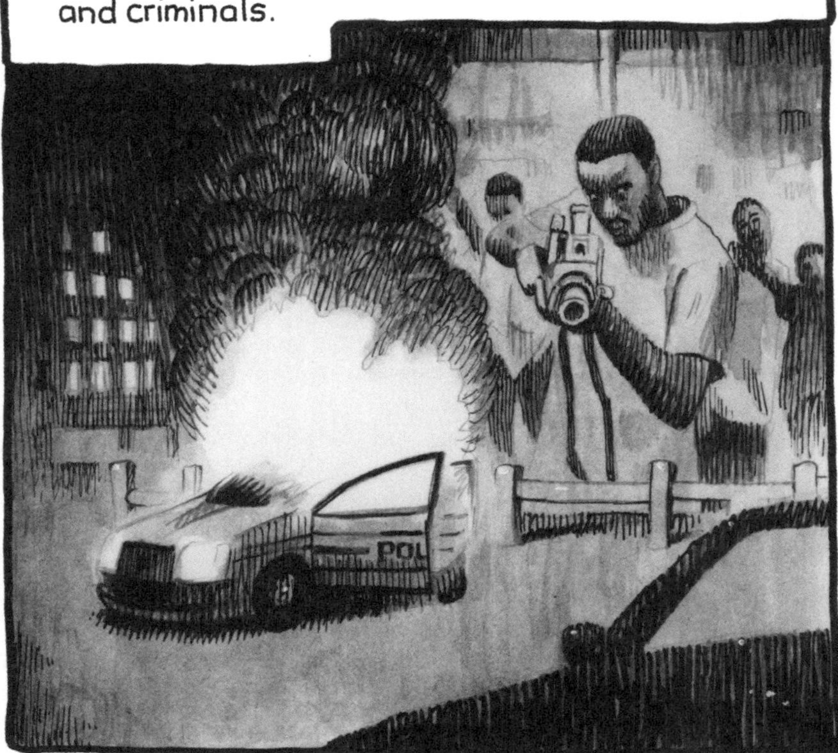
Watching the riots unfold on TV, to JR's surprise, he sees a pasting he did a year earlier, still there, on a wall behind a burning car, and he realizes they are his friends on TV, shown as thugs and criminals.
POL

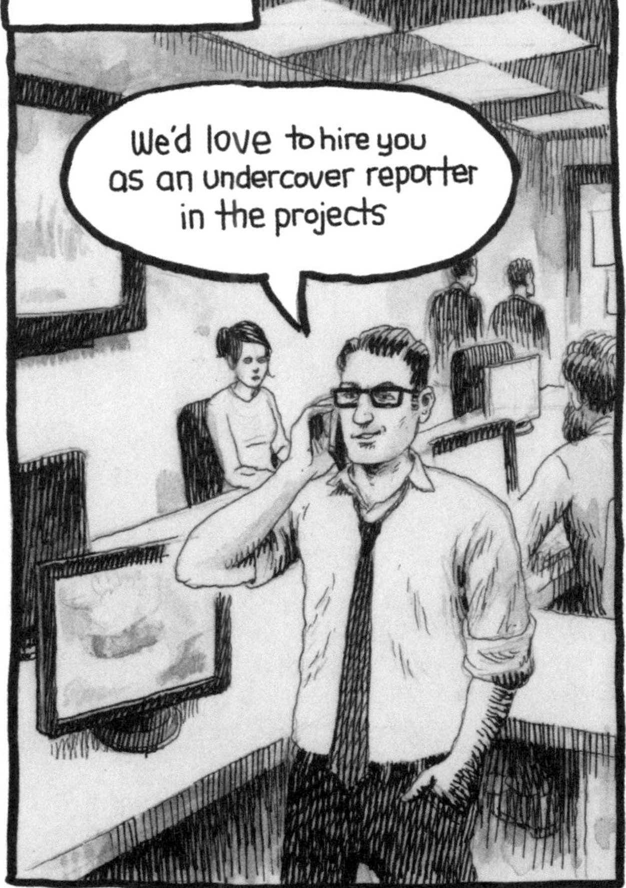
Journalists soon contact JR, investigating what the pasting is all about.
We'd love to hire you as an undercover reporter in the projects

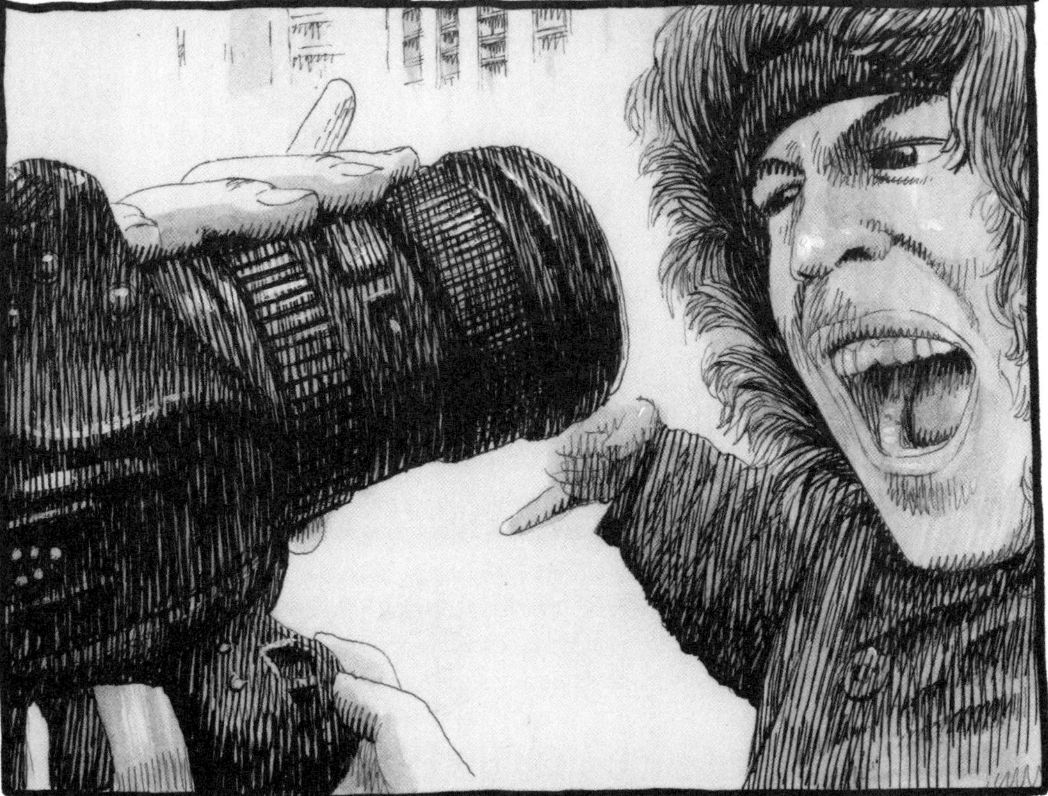
Les Bosquets
JR turns down the offer but returns to Les Bosquets, this time equipped with a 28mm lens – requiring him to get close up and gain the trust of his subjects – and an artistic agenda; to show the world the real side of these guys misrepresented in the media – not angels, but not monsters either.

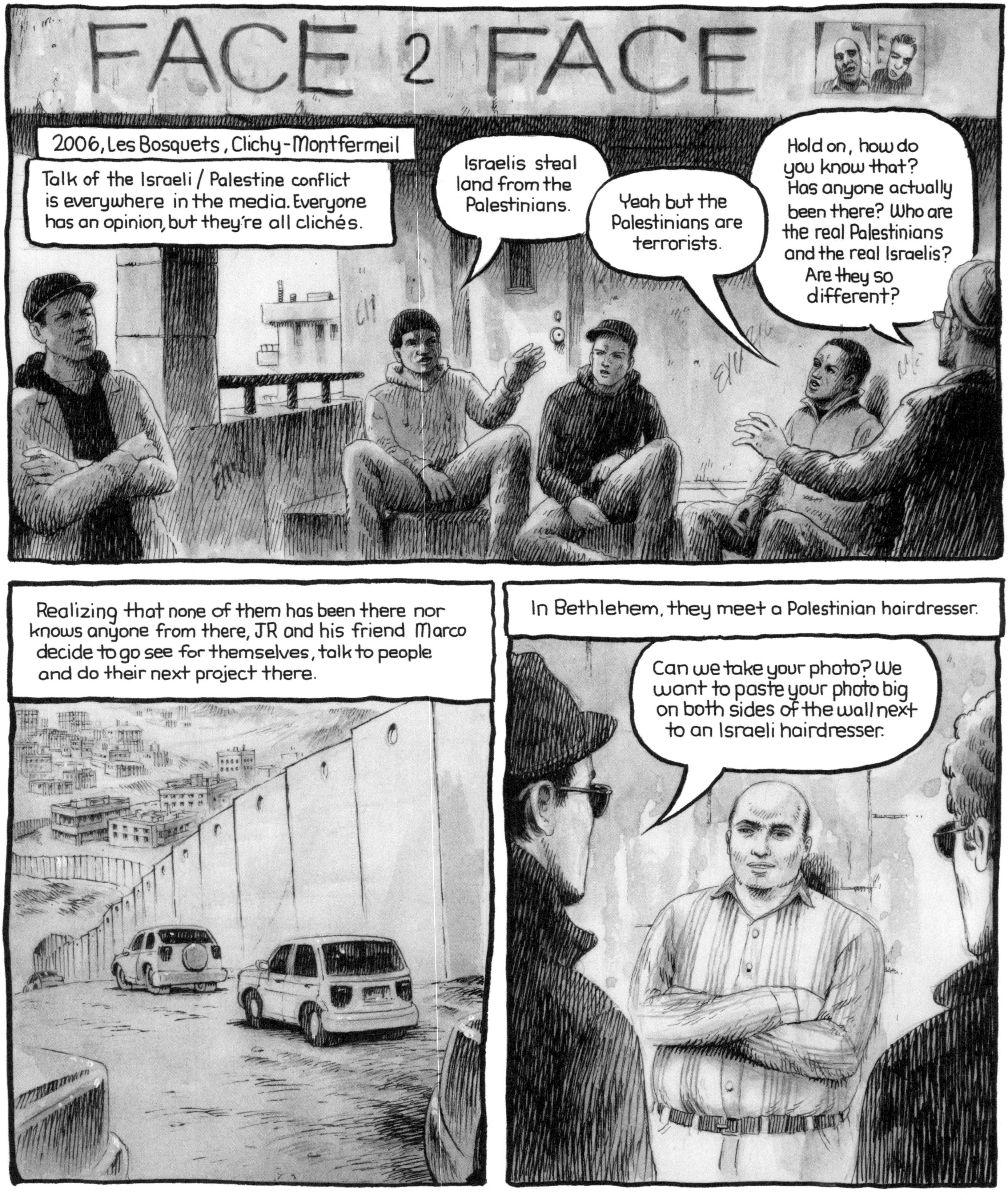

FACE 2 FACE

2006, Les Bosquets, Clichy-Montfermeil

Talk of the Israeli / Palestine conflict is everywhere in the media. Everyone has an opinion, but they're all clichés.

Israelis steal land from the Palestinians.

Yeah but the Palestinians are terrorists.

Hold on, how do you know that? Has anyone actually been there? Who are the real Palestinians and the real Israelis? Are they so different?

Realizing that none of them has been there nor knows anyone from there, JR and his friend Marco decide to go see for themselves, talk to people and do their next project there.

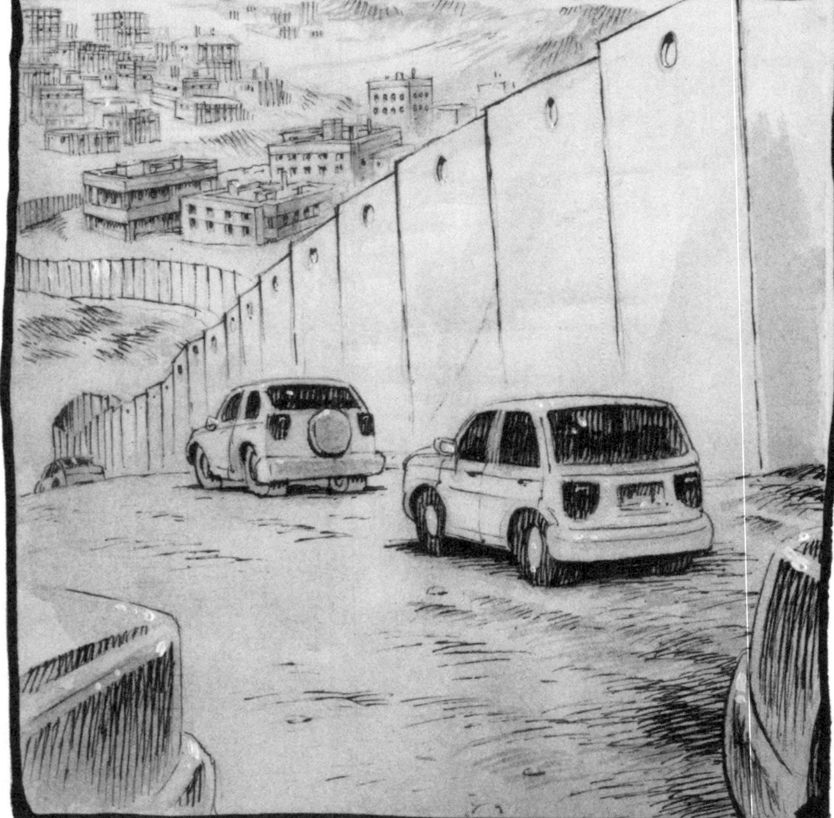

In Bethlehem, they meet a Palestinian hairdresser.

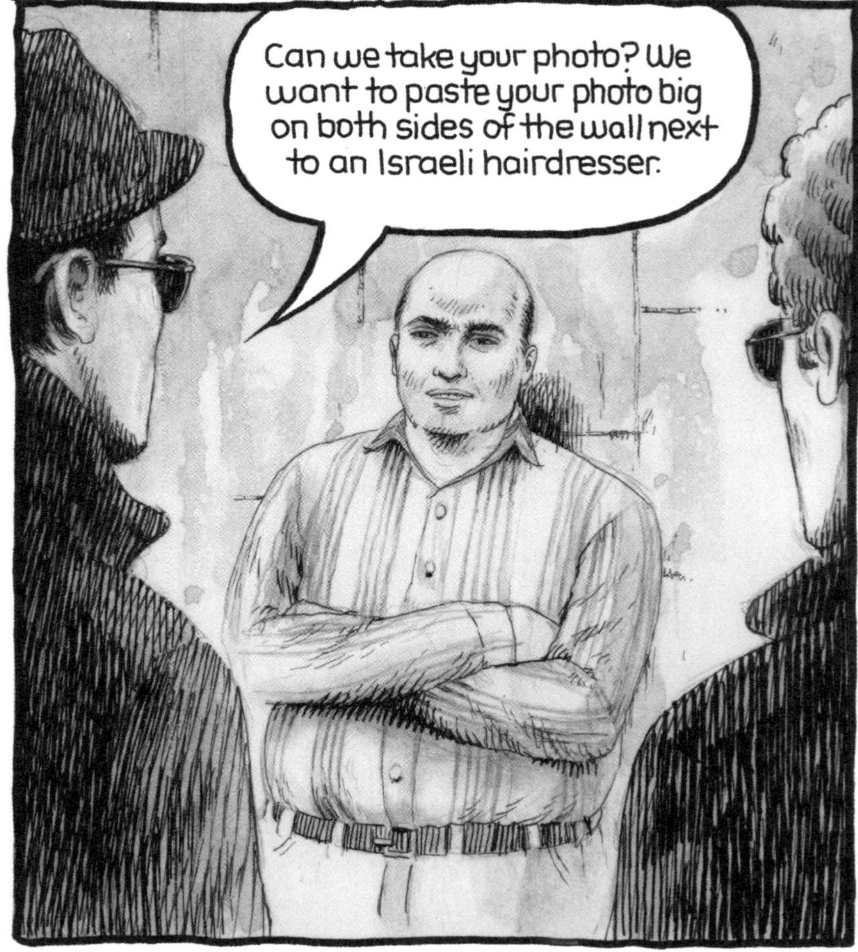

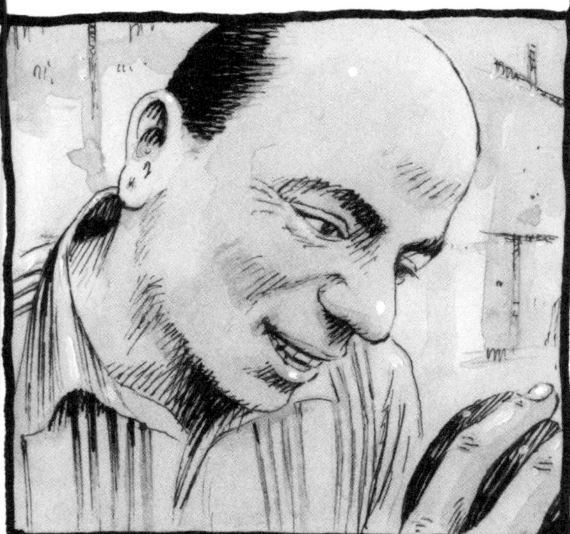
Sceptical that they'll actually paste the photo, he agrees to pose anyway.

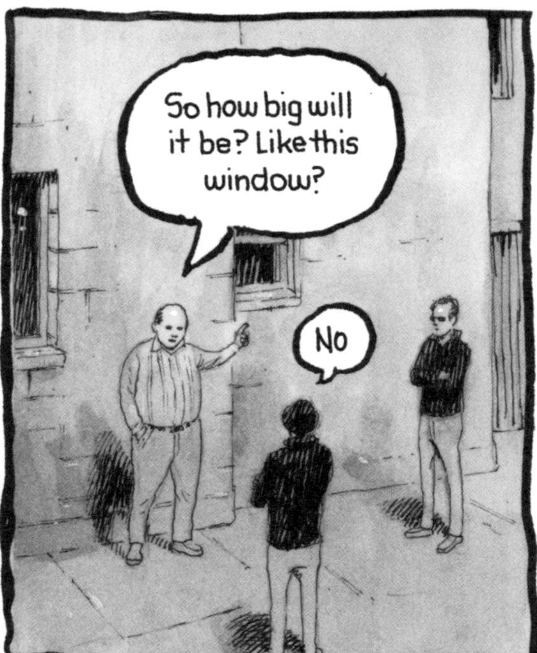
So how big will it be? Like this window?
No

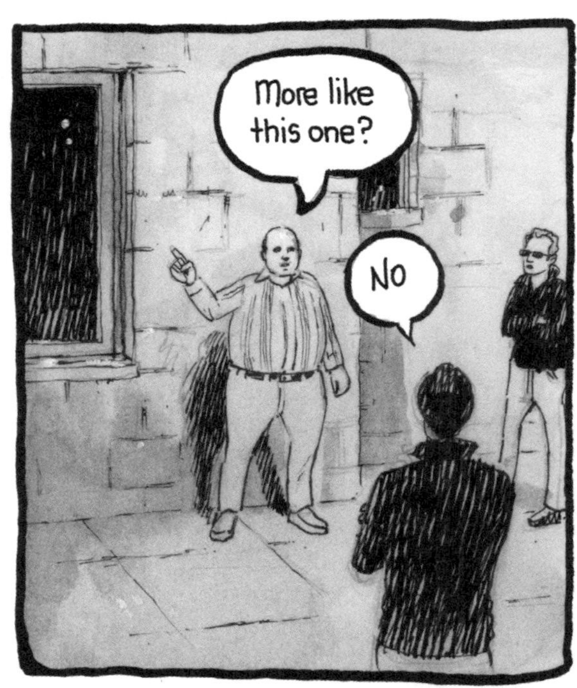
More like this one?
No

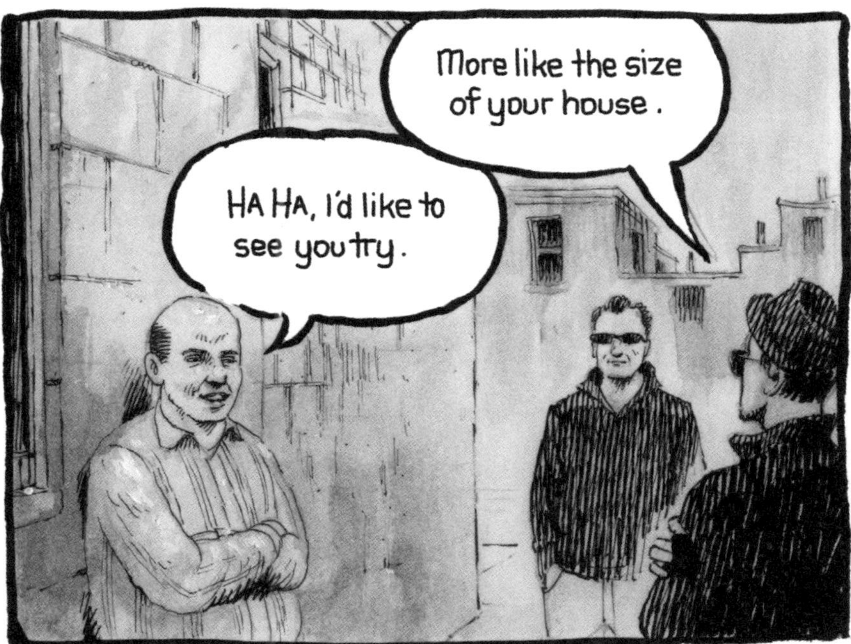
More like the size of your house.
HA HA, I'd like to see you try.

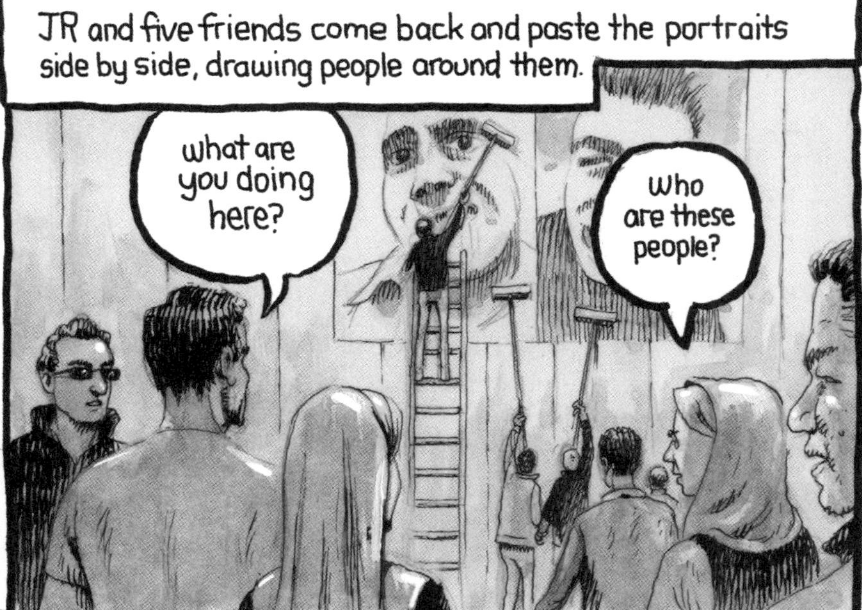
JR and five friends come back and paste the portraits side by side, drawing people around them.
what are you doing here?
Who are these people?

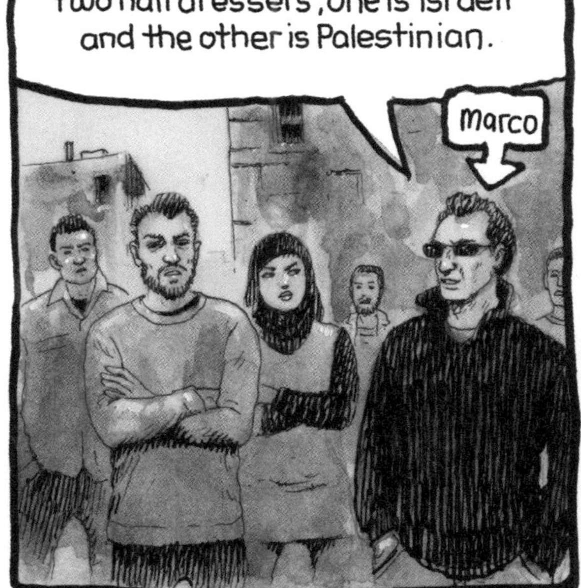
Oh, it's an art project – those are two hairdressers, one is Israeli and the other is Palestinian.
marco

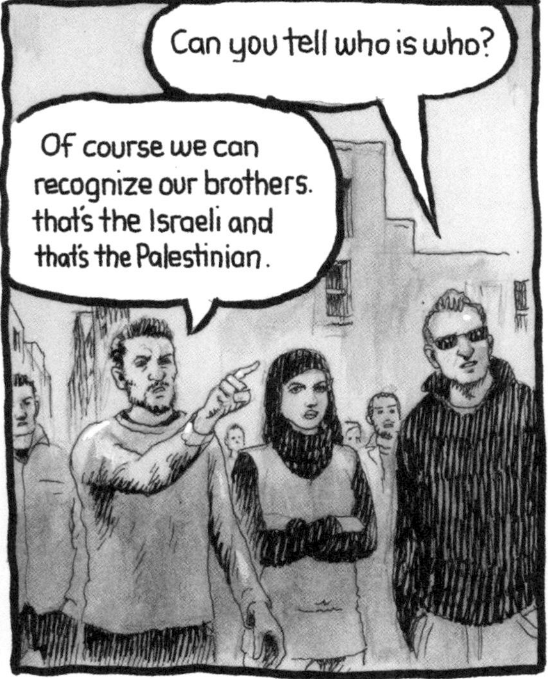
Can you tell who is who?
Of course we can recognize our brothers. that's the Israeli and that's the Palestinian.

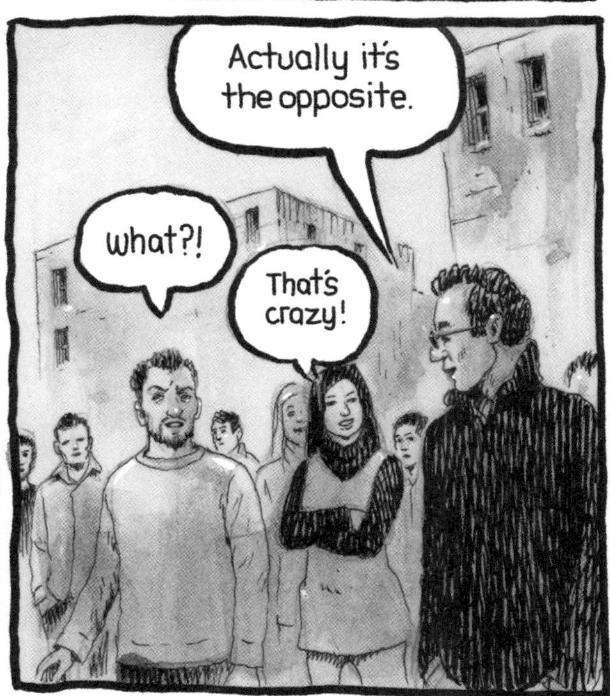
Actually it's the opposite.
what?!
That's crazy!

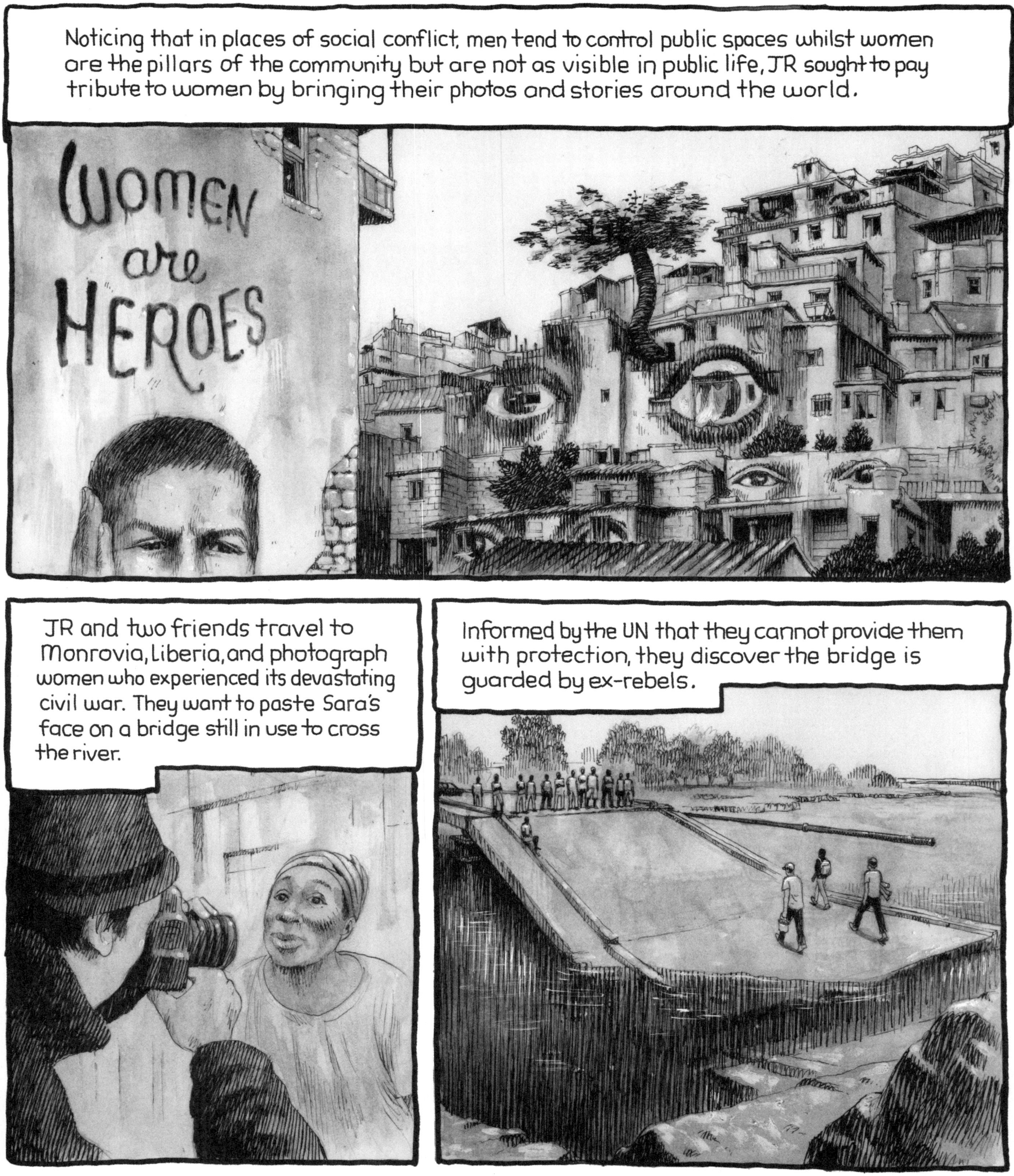

Noticing that in places of social conflict, men tend to control public spaces whilst women are the pillars of the community but are not as visible in public life, JR sought to pay tribute to women by bringing their photos and stories around the world.

Women are Heroes

JR and two friends travel to Monrovia, Liberia, and photograph women who experienced its devastating civil war. They want to paste Sara's face on a bridge still in use to cross the river.

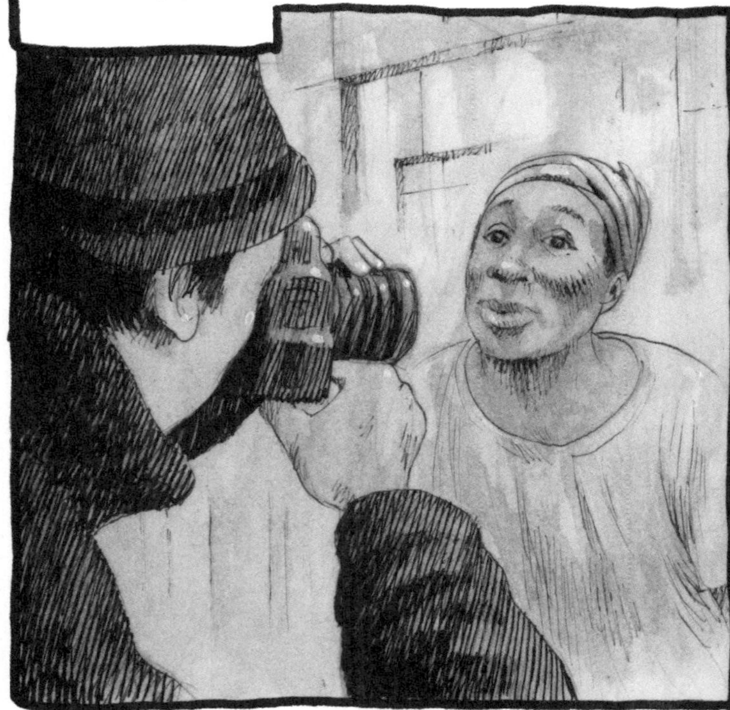

Informed by the UN that they cannot provide them with protection, they discover the bridge is guarded by ex-rebels.

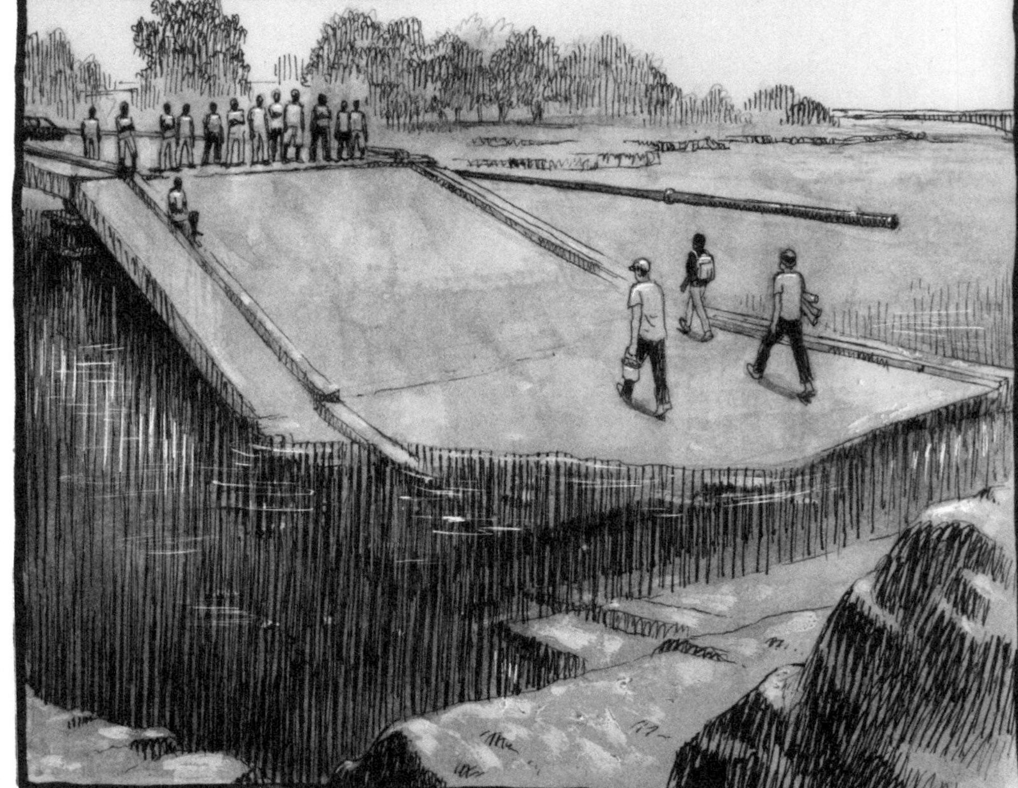

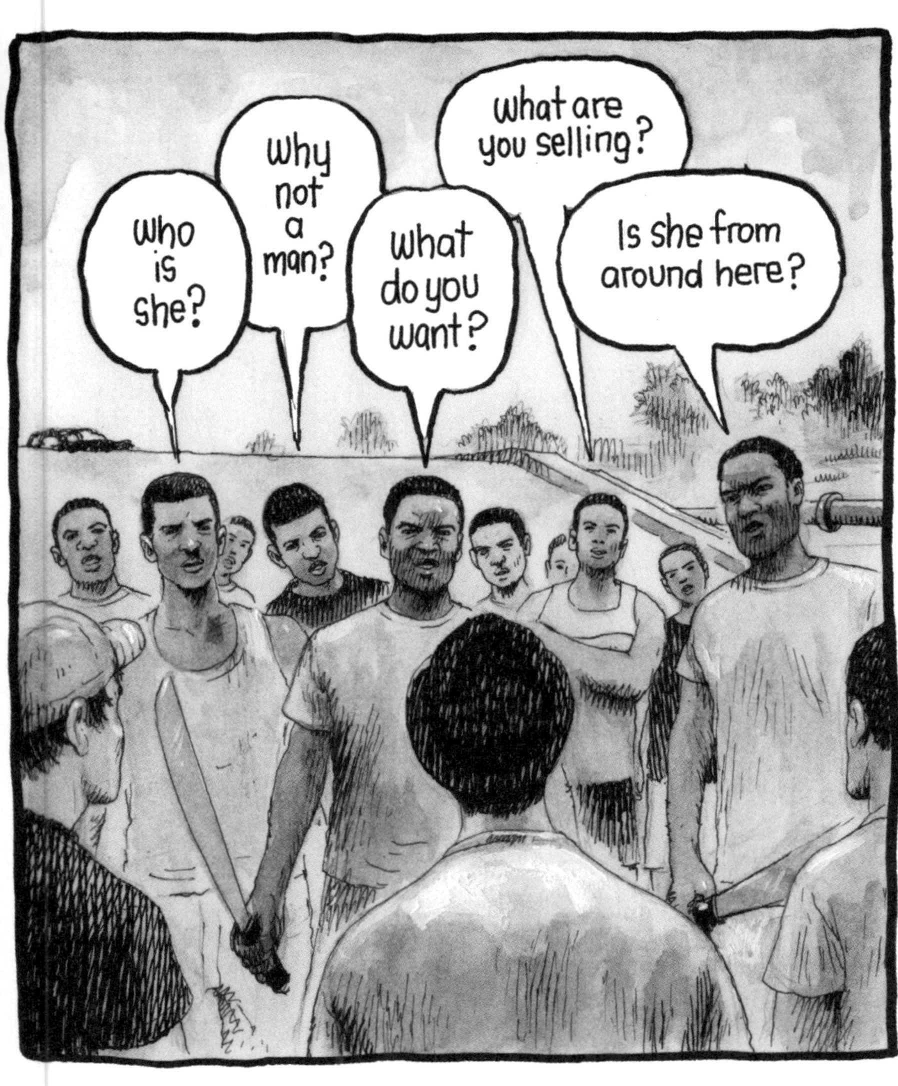

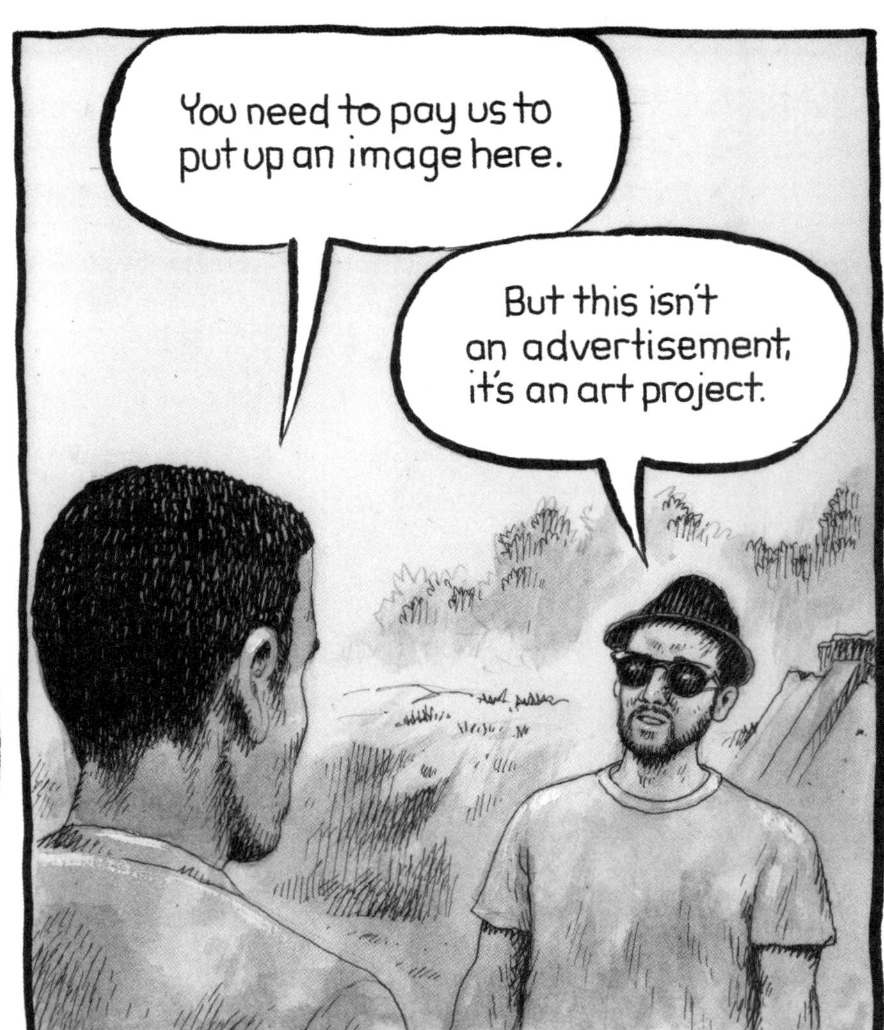

Persuaded, they let JR and his friends paste, but the bridge is wet and they keep slipping.

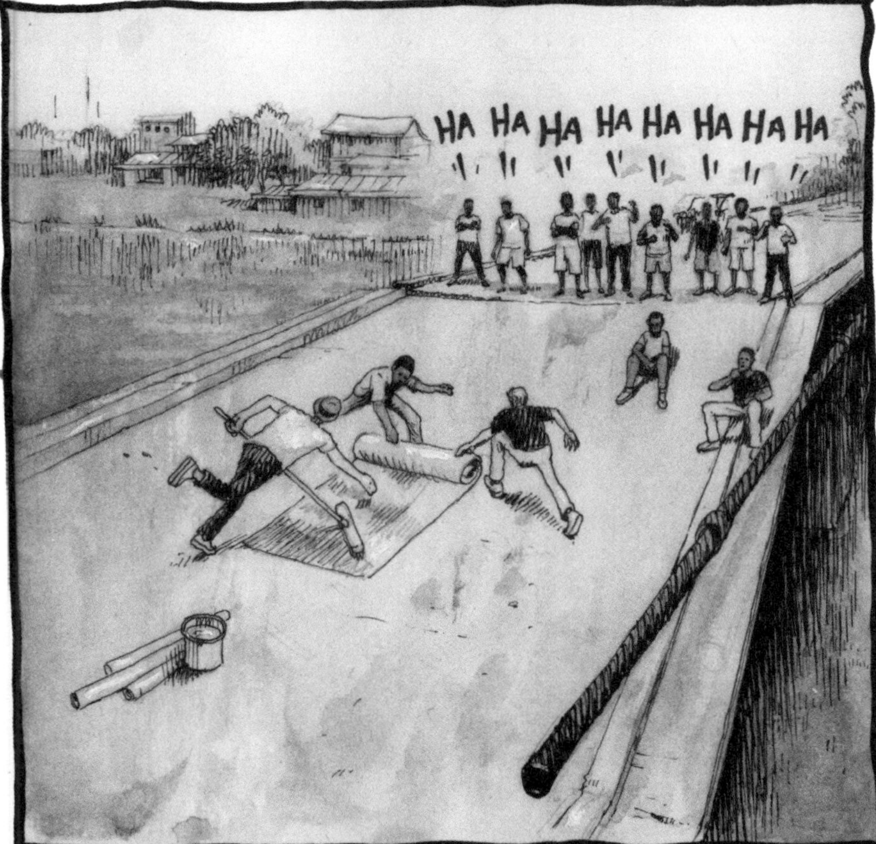

Eventually, the ex-rebels take the brushes and join in, helping to paste Sara's photo – someone they could have attacked during the war.

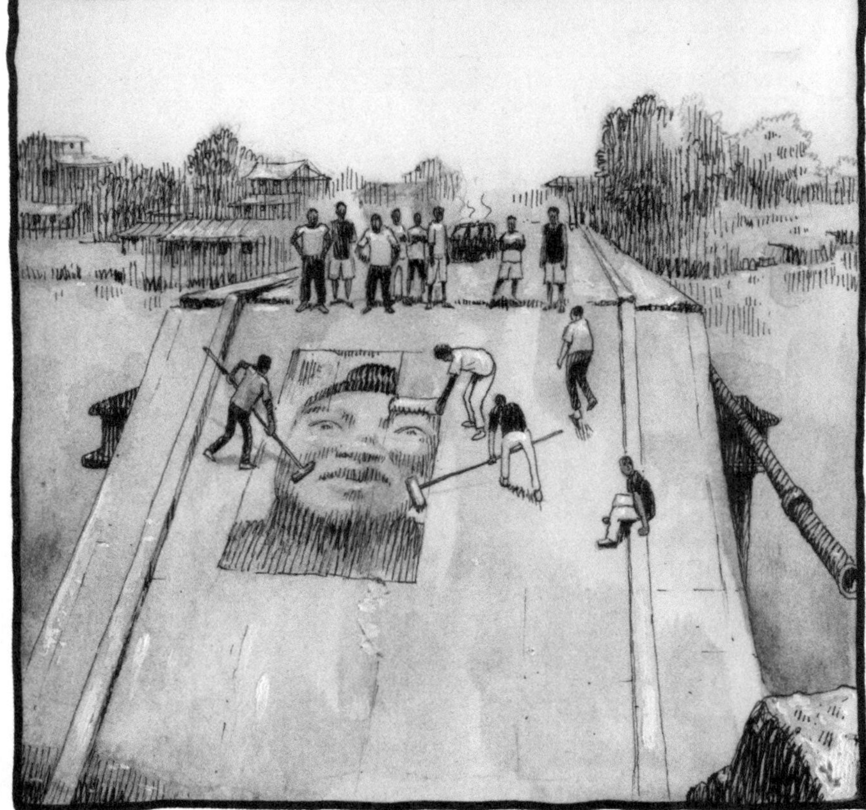

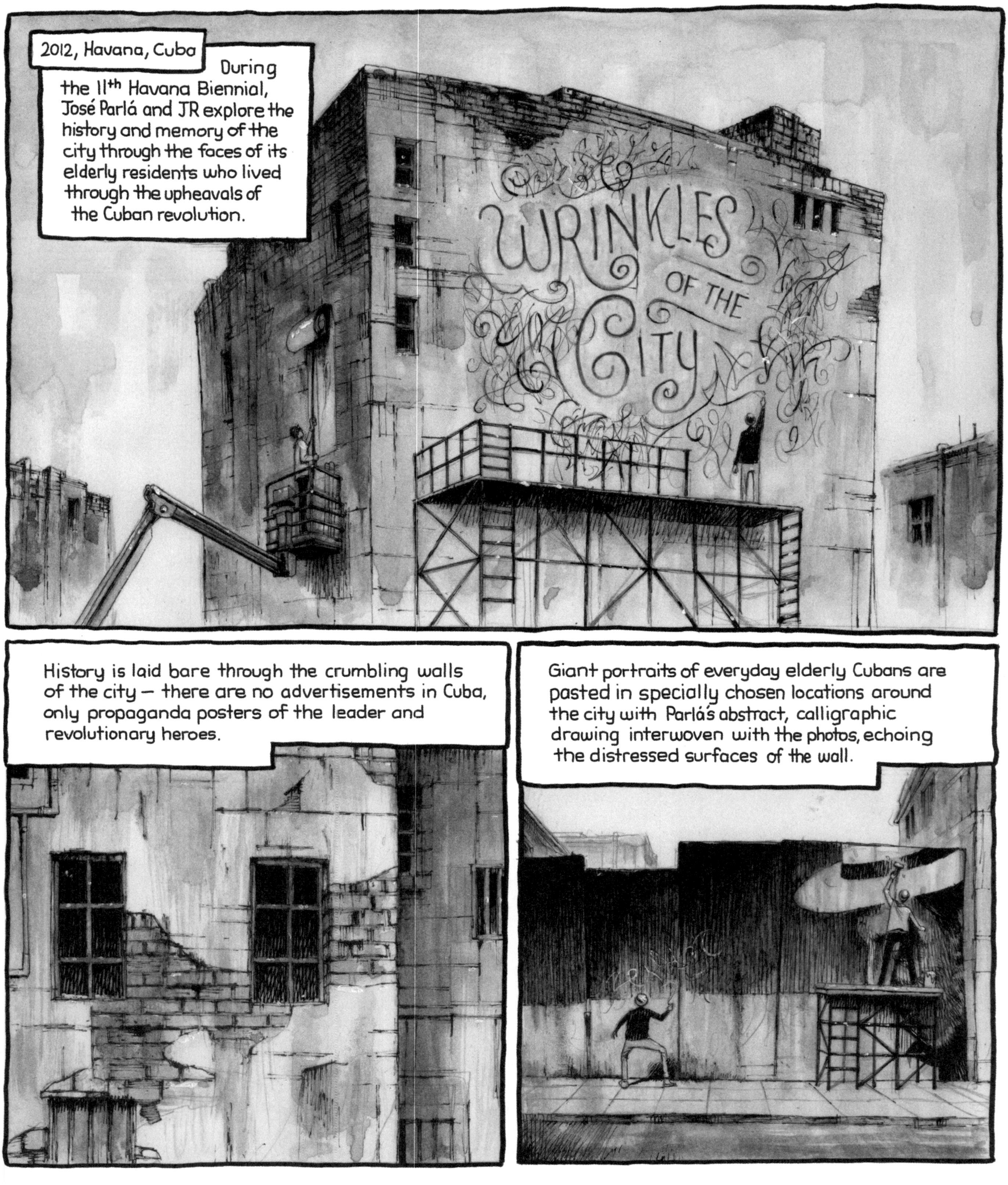

2012, Havana, Cuba

During the 11th Havana Biennial, José Parlá and JR explore the history and memory of the city through the faces of its elderly residents who lived through the upheavals of the Cuban revolution.

History is laid bare through the crumbling walls of the city – there are no advertisements in Cuba, only propaganda posters of the leader and revolutionary heroes.

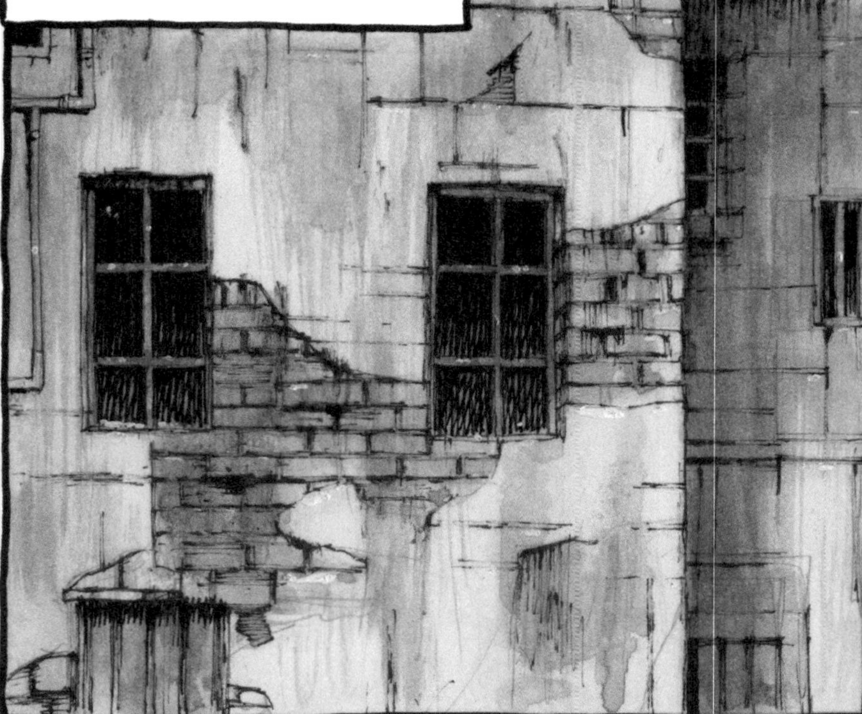

Giant portraits of everyday elderly Cubans are pasted in specially chosen locations around the city with Parlá's abstract, calligraphic drawing interwoven with the photos, echoing the distressed surfaces of the wall.

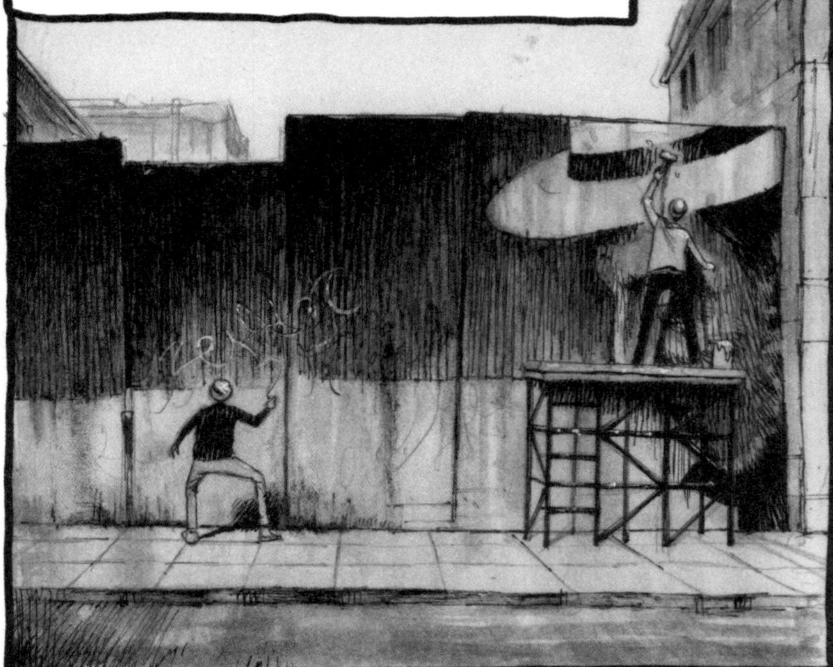

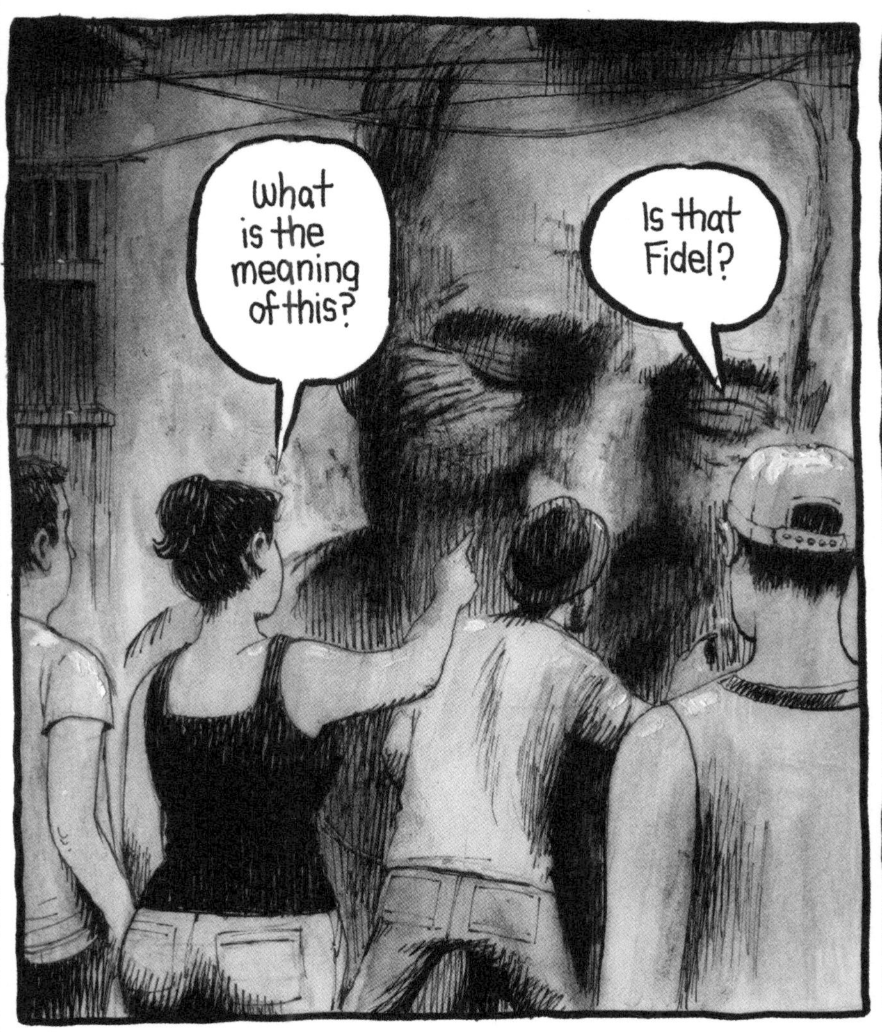

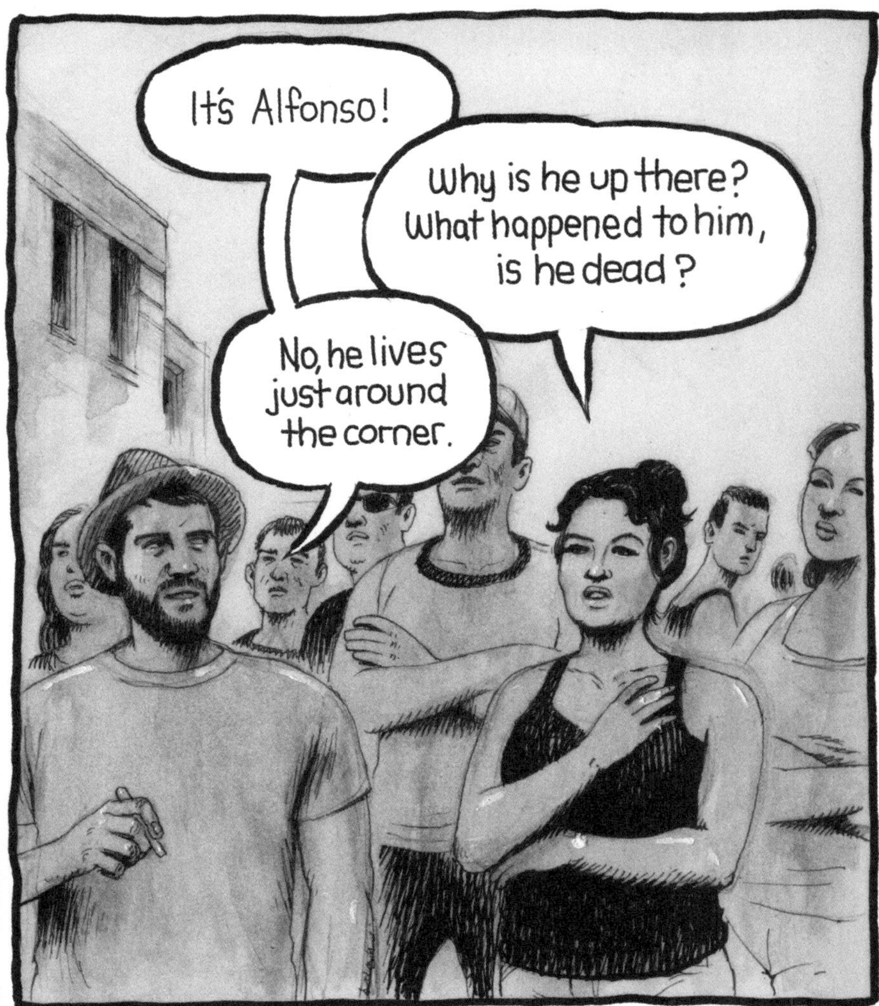

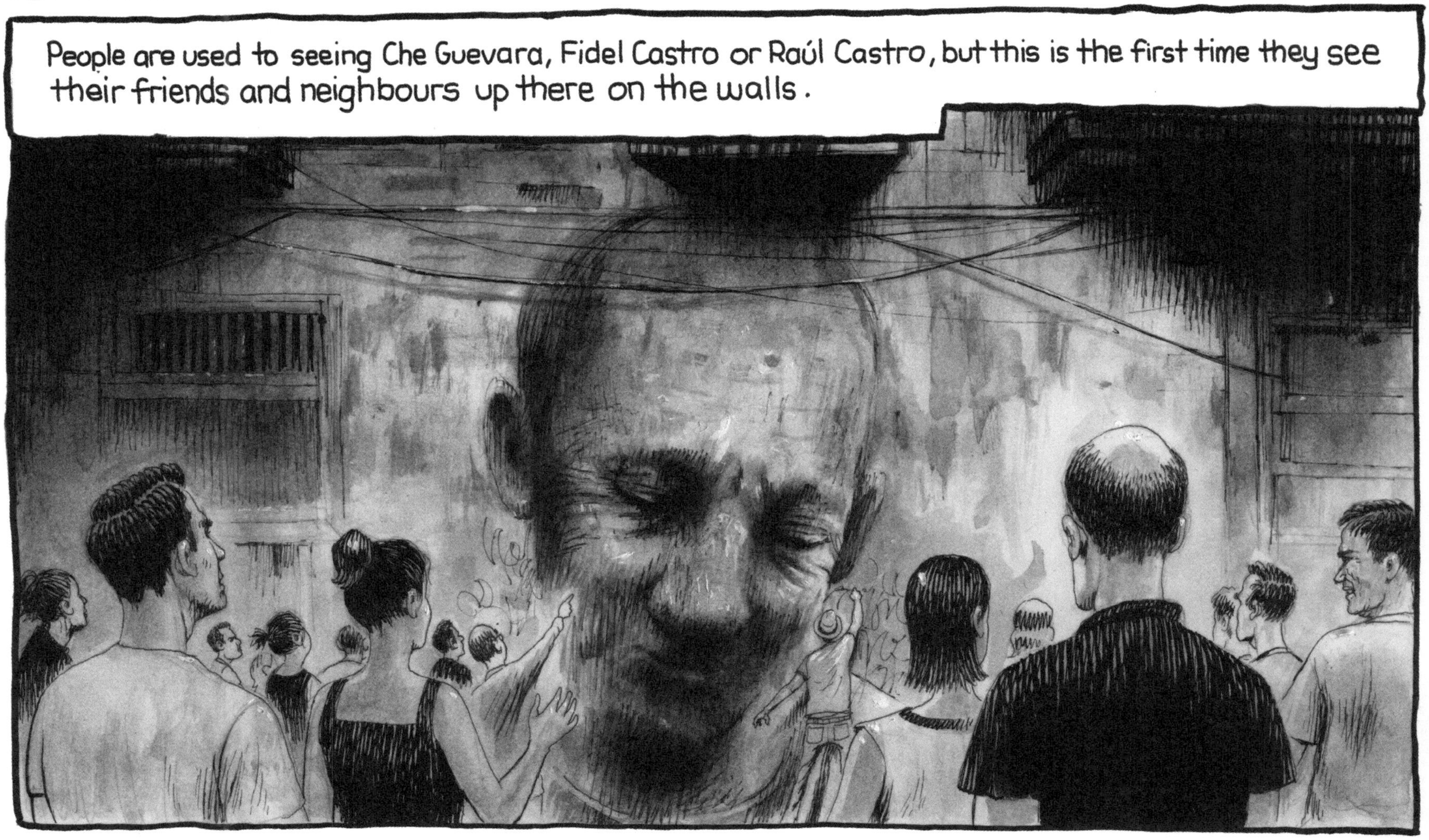

People are used to seeing Che Guevara, Fidel Castro or Raúl Castro, but this is the first time they see their friends and neighbours up there on the walls.

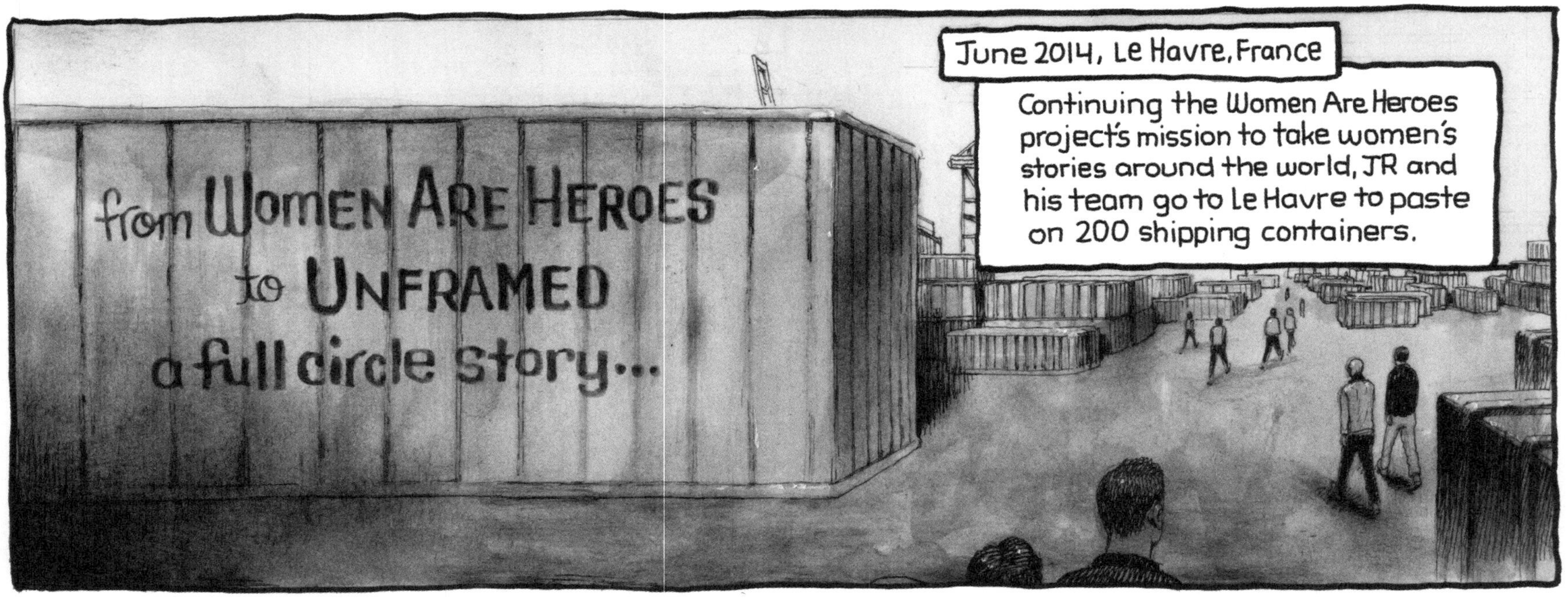
June 2014, Le Havre, France
Continuing the Women Are Heroes project's mission to take women's stories around the world, JR and his team go to Le Havre to paste on 200 shipping containers.
from WOMEN ARE HEROES to UNFRAMED a full circle story...

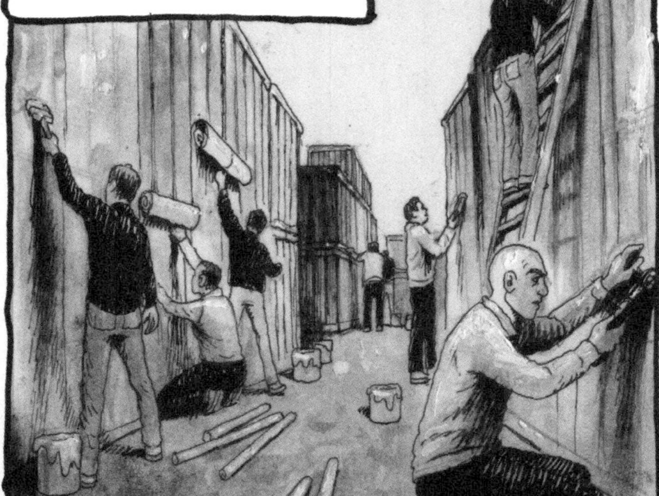
With the help of the dockers, over 2500 strips of paper are pasted in just a few days.

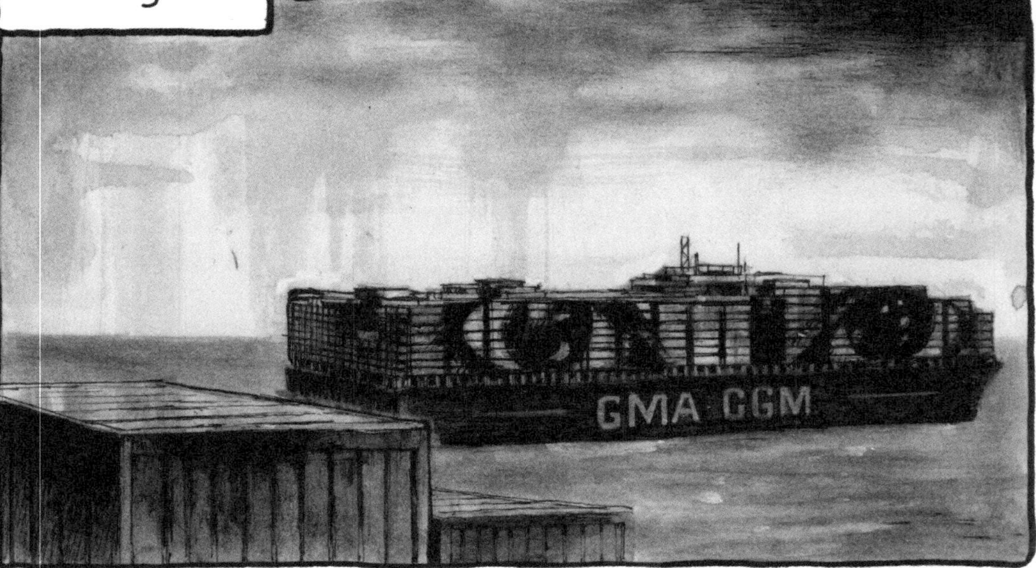
The huge container ship sets sail across the globe to Malaysia.
GMA CGM

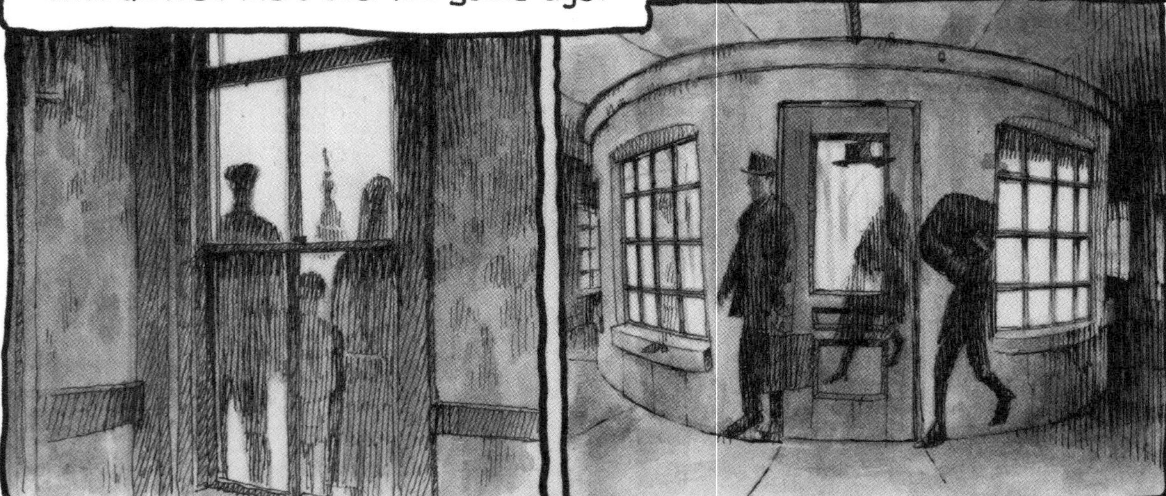
In the meantime... August 2014, Ellis Island, New York, USA
Ellis Island was once the gateway to the USA. 12 million immigrants passed through from 1892 to 1954. JR is invited by 'Save Ellis Island' to work in the abandoned hospital on the south side of the island. He pastes life-size archival images of immigrants who arrived there over 100 years ago.

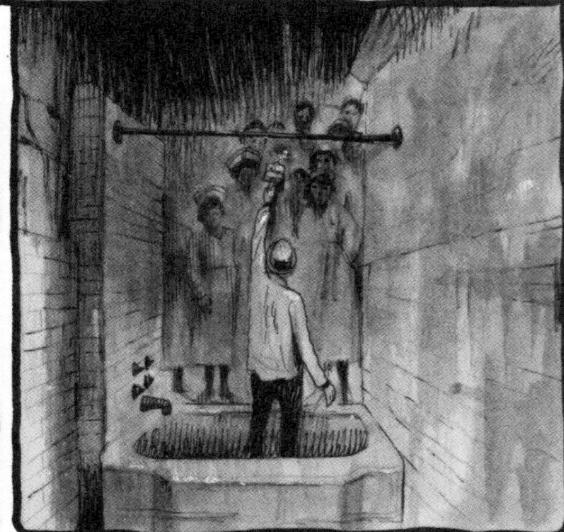

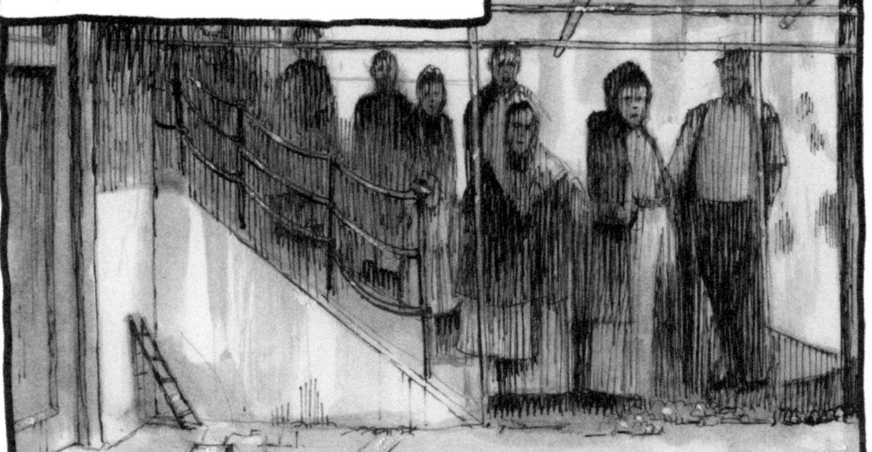
Sick or mentally ill immigrants were not permitted to enter the country and over one million people had to go through the hospital.

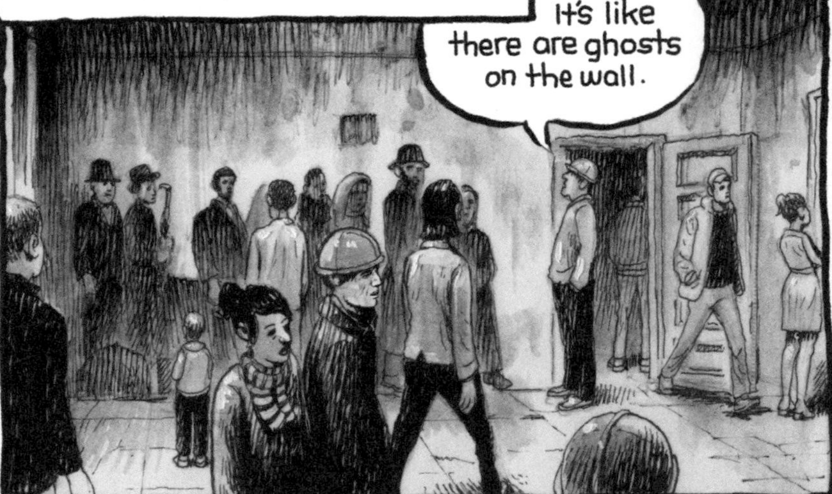
October, 2014
For the first time since it closed in 1954 the hospital opens to the public.
It's like there are ghosts on the wall.

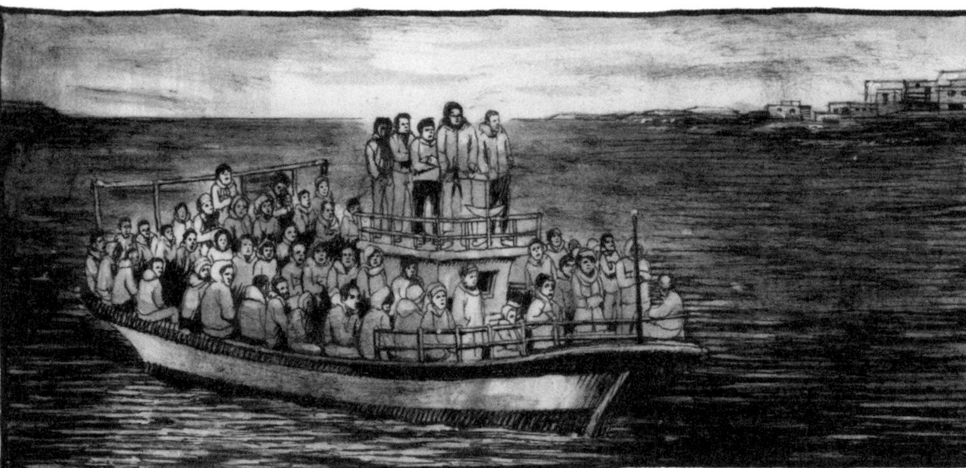
November 2014, Lampedusa, Italy
Intrigued by Ellis Island's stories, JR goes on a research trip to Lampedusa, an island off the coast of Sicily where immigrants try to enter Europe, and he sees boats arriving packed with Syrian refugees.

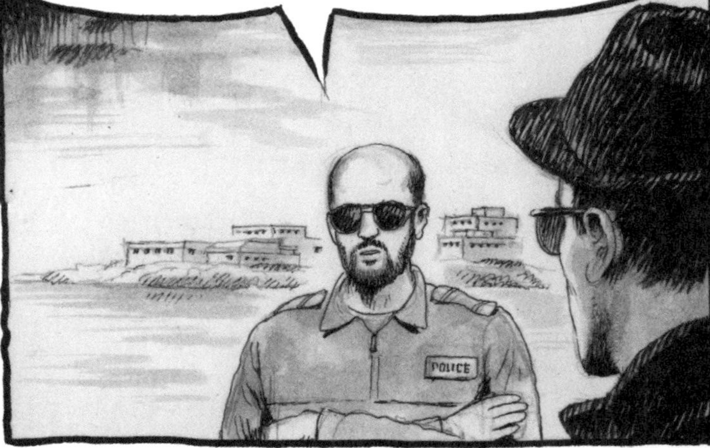
Many die in their attempt to come to Lampedusa so a new law has come in – now ships have to assist any boat of immigrants that may be in danger.
POLICE

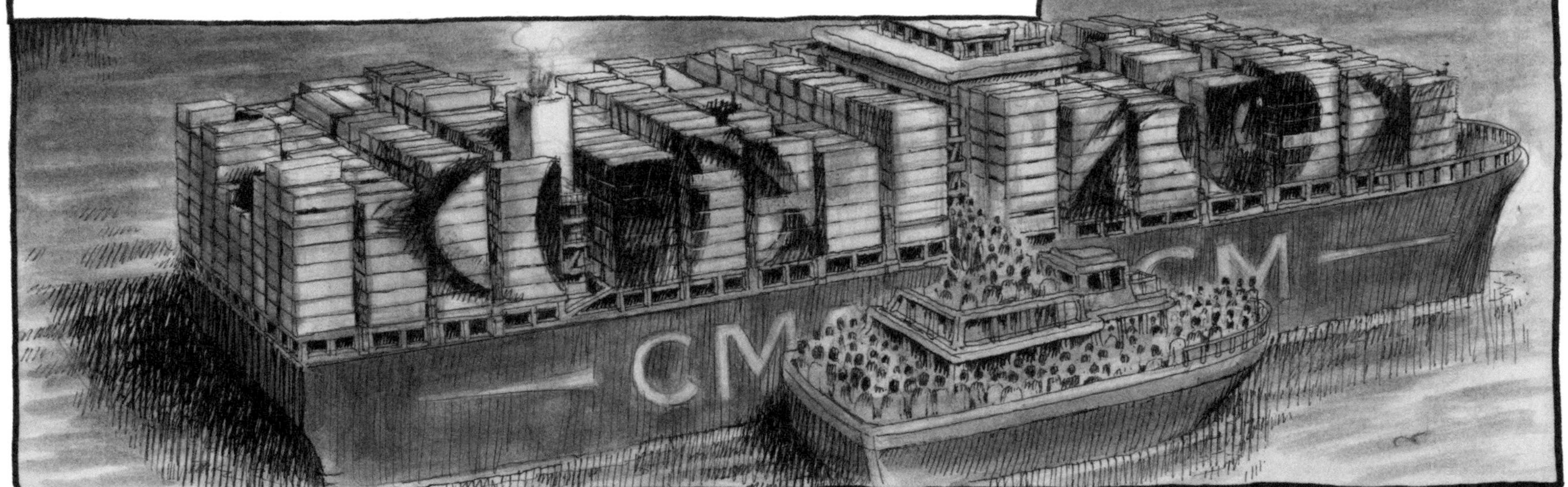
A week later, he learns that in September, on its way to Europe, the very container ship on which he had pasted the eyes stopped to rescue a boat full of Syrian refugees.

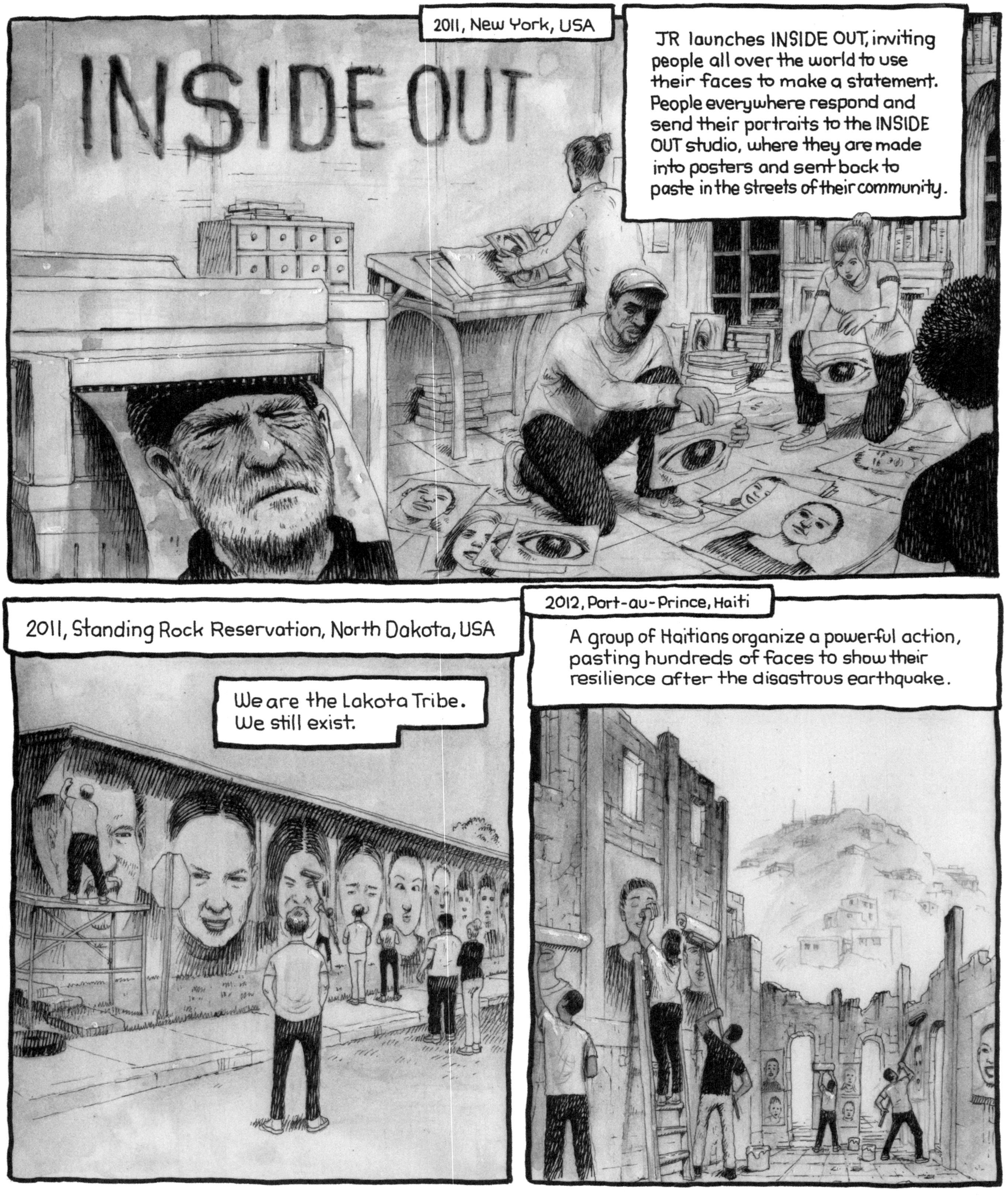

2011, New York, USA

INSIDE OUT

JR launches INSIDE OUT, inviting people all over the world to use their faces to make a statement. People everywhere respond and send their portraits to the INSIDE OUT studio, where they are made into posters and sent back to paste in the streets of their community.

2011, Standing Rock Reservation, North Dakota, USA

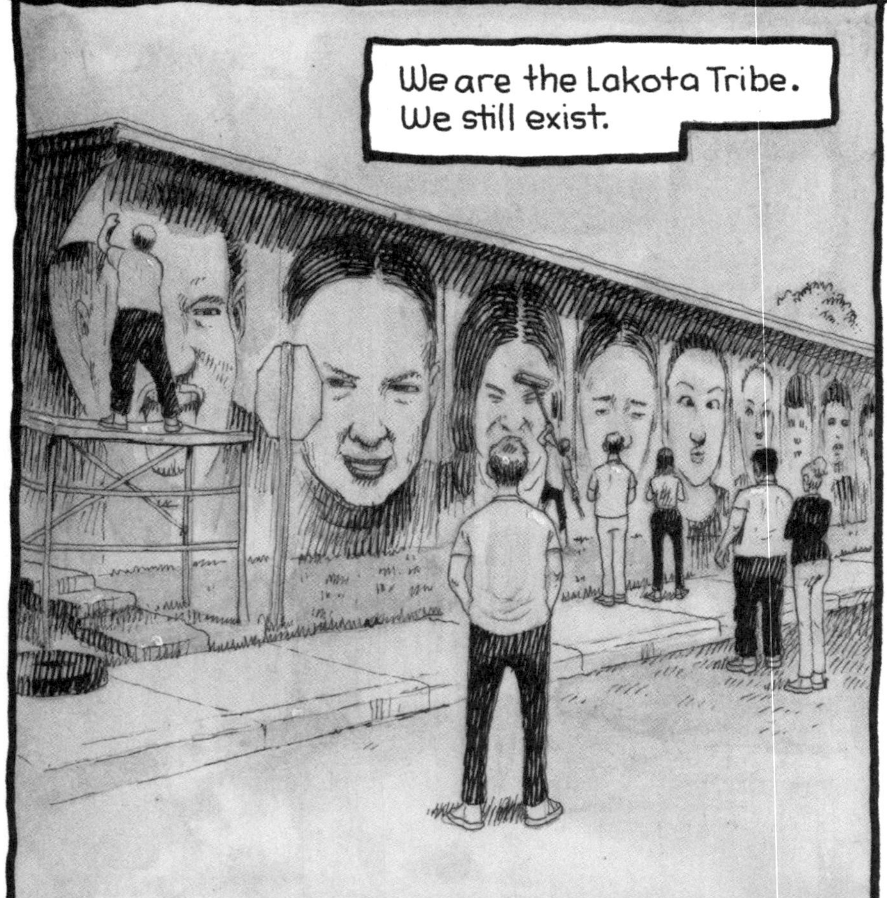

2012, Port-au-Prince, Haiti

A group of Haitians organize a powerful action, pasting hundreds of faces to show their resilience after the disastrous earthquake.

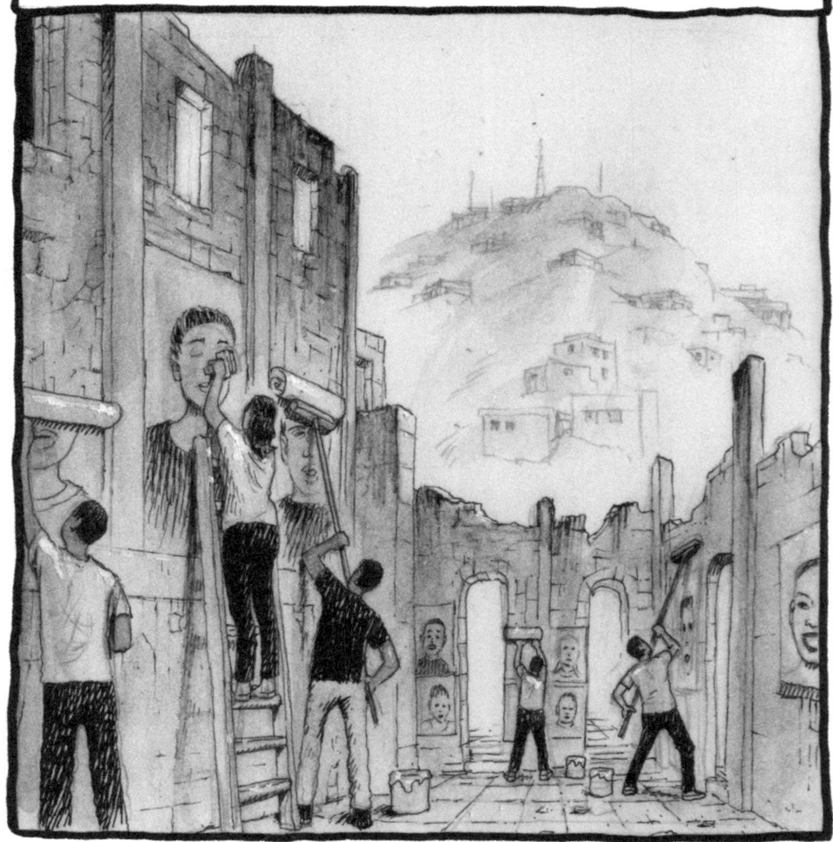

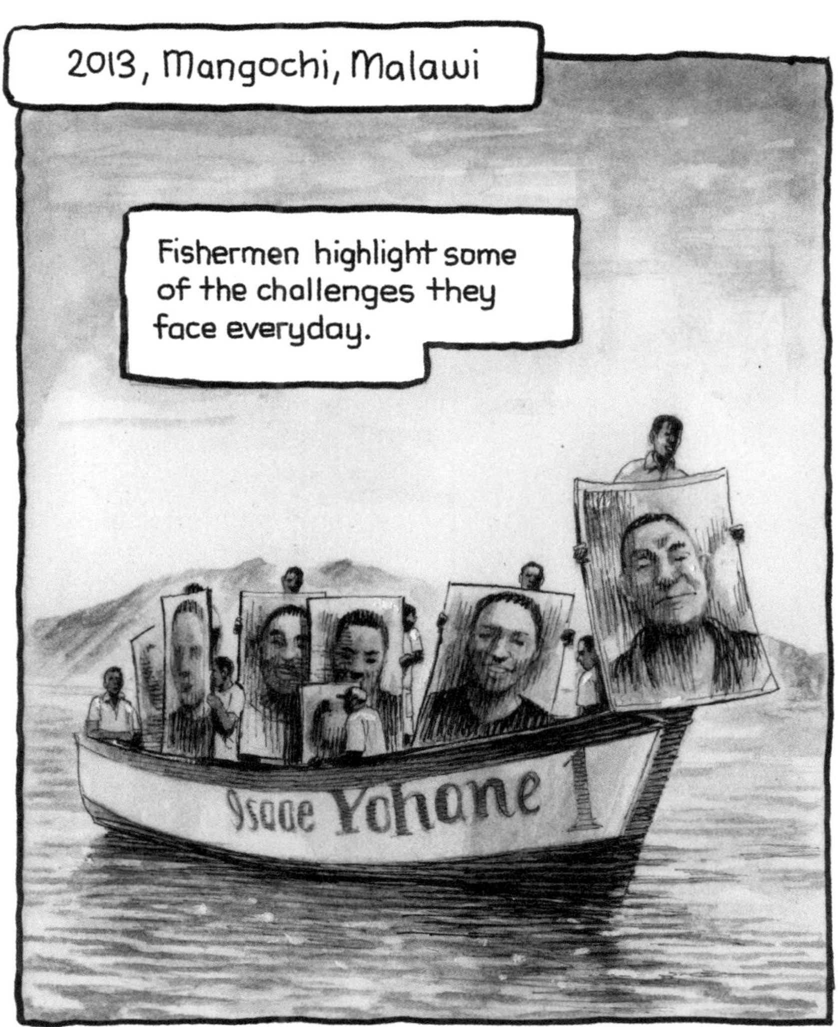

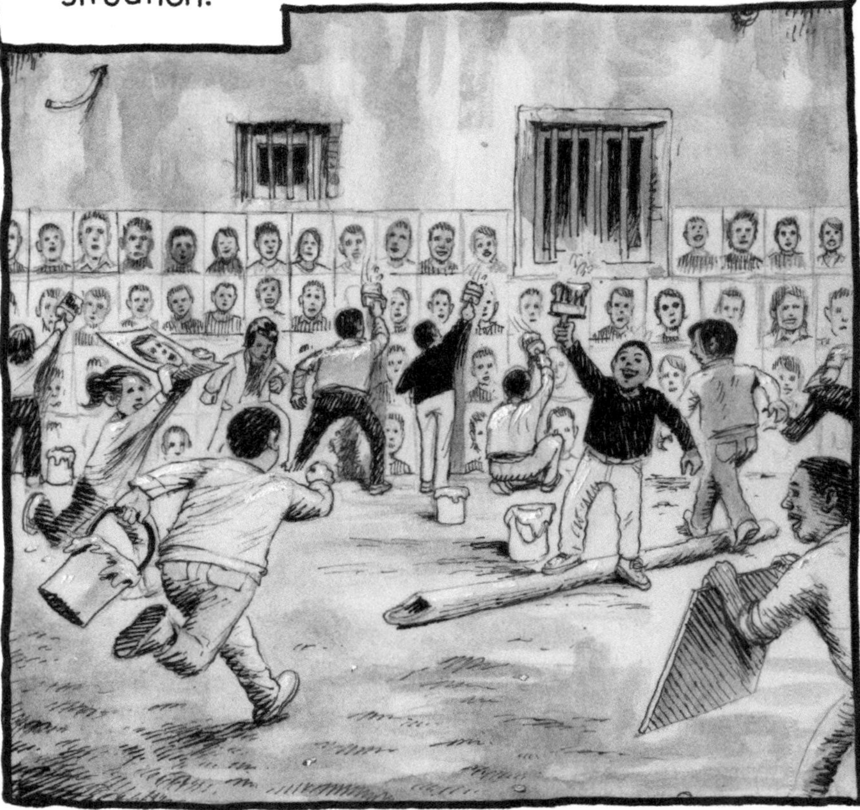

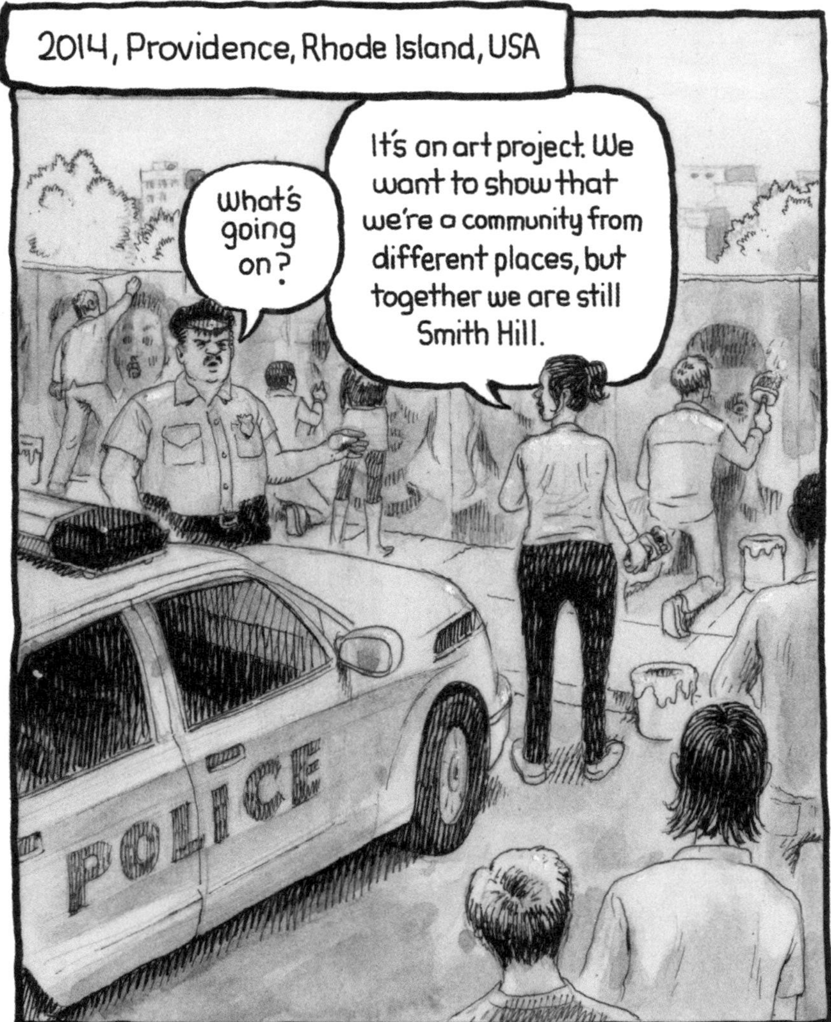

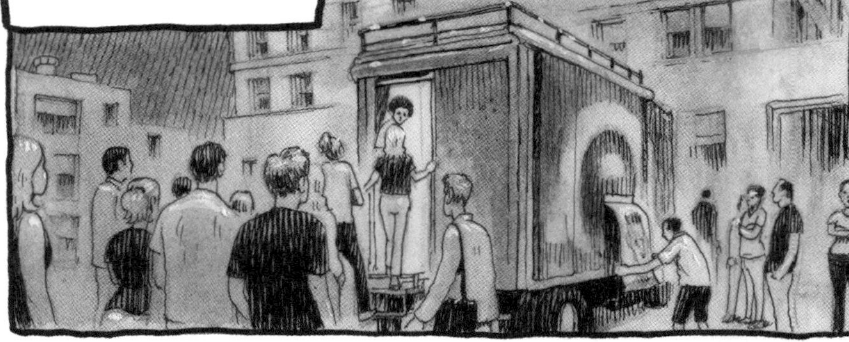

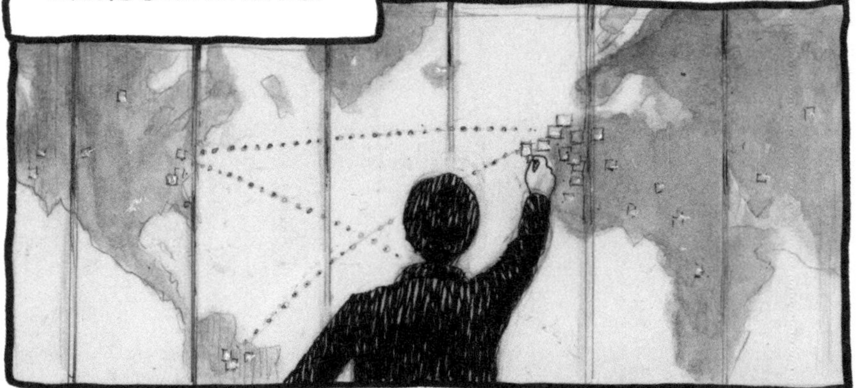

Joseph Remnant '15

IF A SM

IS A W

LE

THE ART OF JR

NATO
THOMPSON

EAPON

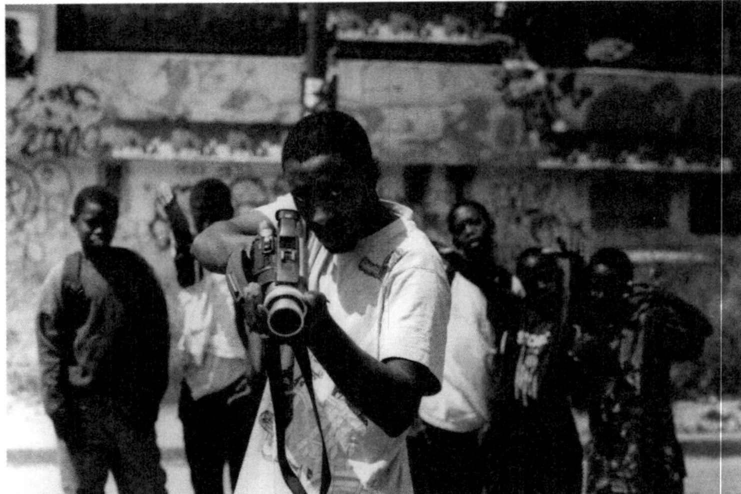

Ladj Ly, Les Bosquets, Montfermeil, France, 2004
from *Portrait of a Generation*

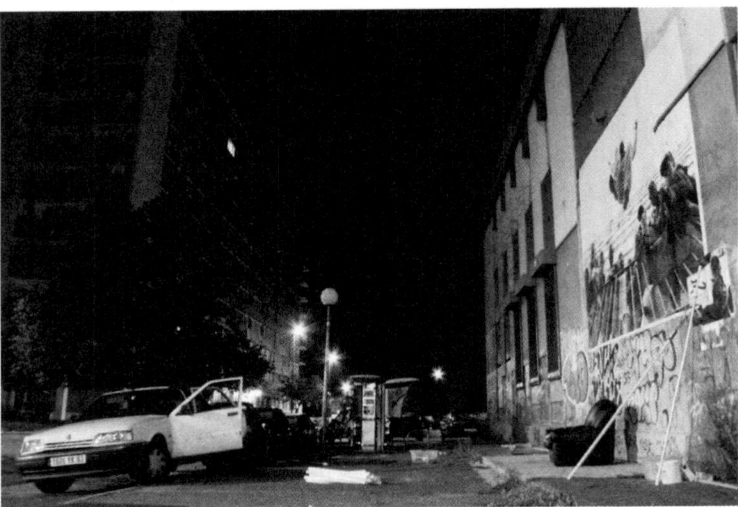

Pasting in Les Bosquets, Montfermeil, France, 2004
from *Portrait of a Generation*

'With a bullet, you can get one man;
with a photo, you can get a hundred.'
- Lucas, Women Are Heroes project participant,
Morro da Providência, Brazil

Let's begin with an image. A French–Malian man in his mid-twenties stands in front of a crumbling concrete building adorned in graffiti, with several young children throwing hand gestures as well as staring curiously at the camera taking the photograph. It's a black-and-white photograph from 2004, shot in one of the *banlieues* – suburban French housing projects – called Les Bosquets. The man points what appears to be a gun at the camera, his eyes looking directly at us. This is the first read.

Looking more closely, we realize that the man – his name is Ladj Ly – points a video camera and not a gun. The eyes of the children and the man change as we realize that the expressions on those depicted in the image can be read differently. Everyone in the photograph seems to be aware of what is going on except us, the viewers, who have to take a second look. This is the second read.

Upon realizing that what appears to be a gun is, in fact, a camera, we become aware how we, as viewers, easily let images fall into our assumptions of what they provide. Due perhaps to the media or to clichés of visual culture, we might initially assume that the object in the hands of a black man is a gun. Not only are we guilty of making this assumption, but both Ly and the photographer seem to be calling us out by pointing the 'gun' back at us. The image itself is, in fact, a weapon. This is the third read.

JR took this photograph as part of the project *Portrait of a Generation*, photographing the residents of Les Bosquets. At twenty-one years old, JR was already an experienced street artist – he had been doing graffiti since he was thirteen – who had begun to use photocopies of his photographs as a street medium. He included *Portrait of a Generation* and his other first projects in the series *28 Millimetres,* the title of which is not only

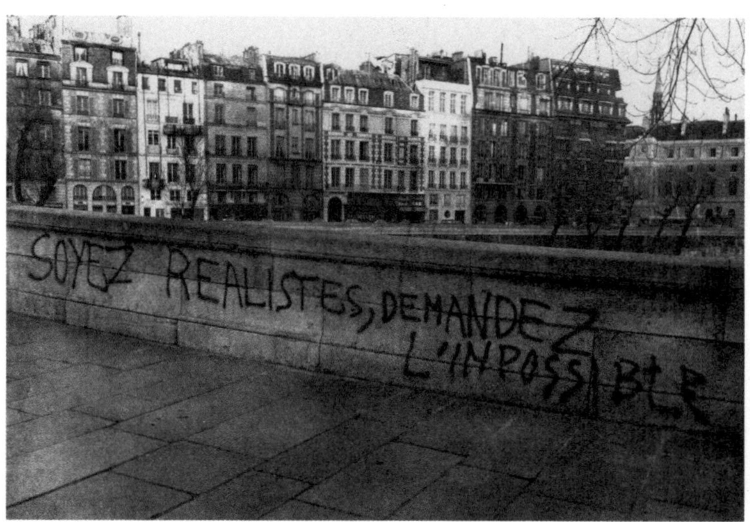

'Be realistic, demand the impossible',
Situationist International graffiti, Paris, May 1968

a reference to the lens he used in the photographs but also to the proximity between photographer and subject. These images presented carnivalesque, sympathetic, fun-house images of the locals, reminiscent of photographs taken in black-and-white photobooths – intimate and yet self-aware. Unlike the distanced and threatening portrayals in the media, these images were personal and extremely close up.

One year later, the Paris riots of 2005 broke out in these very suburbs. The trigger for the violence was the death of two teenage boys, Bouna Traoré and Zyed Benna, who were electrocuted while hiding from police in an electricity substation. News of the teenagers' deaths quickly spread among the mainly first and second-generation immigrant residents of Les Bosquets, releasing a collective sense of anger at institutional racism and its attending impoverishment that had been growing for the previous fifty years and sparking a historic uprising. The photographs JR had pasted throughout the neighbourhood were suddenly broadcast on news reports as the backdrop to the riots.

JR has stated presciently, 'Images are not special. It is what you do with them.' This insight holds true not only for his practice but also for those who participated in the riot. 'The media had to stop reporting how many cars were being torched because it quickly became a competition between different suburbs. Television played an important role. People I know would participate in the riots so they could go home later that day and see themselves on the news and say, "That is me!"'

That is me. The words carry a primary sense of existence that translates into mediums of representation, be they television or, in the case of JR's work, a hybrid format of photography with the street as its gallery. Andy Warhol notoriously quipped that in the future every person would be famous for fifteen minutes, but in the case of the world's most disenfranchised, not only is it rare to have their fifteen minutes of fame, but when they do, they are often reduced to clichés, to mediated stereotypes, to abstractions of the individual, intimate person. The news images of the riots reduced the rioters to something they felt they were not. What JR provides is a self-aware lens that demonstrates the mediated nature of everyone. We are all both famous and alienated, the viewer and the subject alike.

THE CAMERA AND THE STREET

'In the decor of the spectacle, the eye meets only things and their prices'
- May 1968 graffiti, Paris

There is no doubt that JR works with keen awareness of a deeply mediated urban environment. Like Ly holding that video camera, JR shoots and pastes amidst a larger spectrum of images ranging from branding to news media and advertising. For a person walking down the street, to encounter JR's smiling, wide-eyed portraits at eye level, staring from building façades, is jarring in many ways. The images are not advertisements, but it is unclear what their intention is. Perhaps they simply say hello. In his innovative manoeuvres to make intimate gestures come to life against a backdrop of commercialism, JR has a historically important antecedent in the work and protest art of the Situationist International of the 1950s and 1960s. The tone has shifted – JR's work does not espouse any analysis or critique – but JR shares an interest with the Situationists in countering the world of advertising by producing intimate encounters.

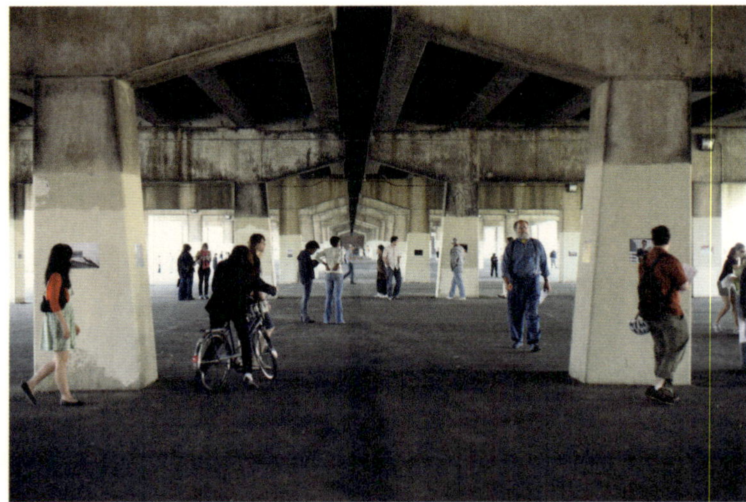

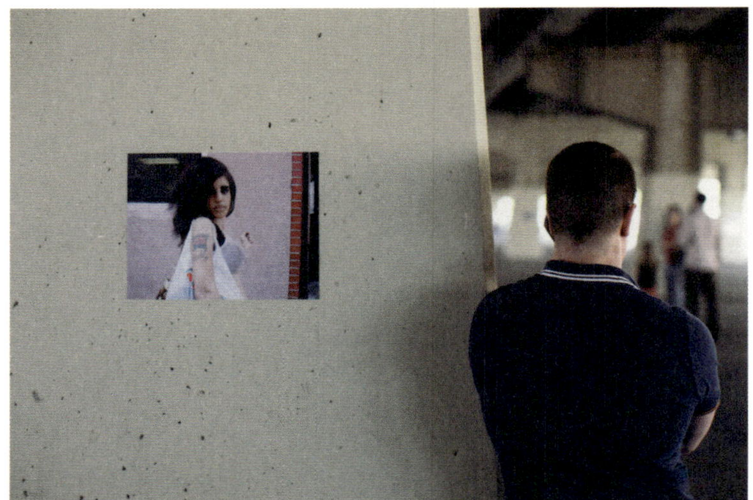

(above and right) Zoe Strauss, 'Under I-95' exhibition, Philadelphia, USA, 4 May 2008

The Situationists were the inspiration of the slogans that appeared in the streets of Paris during the student riots of May 1968, such as 'Never work' and 'Under the paving stones, the beach'. A worldwide avant-garde collective initiated in the 1950s, the Situationists were concerned with poverty, daily life and the way the everyday world was mediated by images. They focused their analysis of capitalism on the alienation of daily life produced by cinema, television, radio, consumerism and advertising. They strongly believed that the cultural machines of capitalism produced problematic relationships between people that were alienating and deadening. They early on advocated what they termed *détourné*, a reorganization of advertisements to say something else – to turn the culture of power against itself. In essence the Situationists advocated a form of cultural trespassing, a transgression that has everything to do with the desires of graffiti itself.

Fast forward from 1968 to 2001, when JR was seventeen and already four years into his life as a graffiti artist. In the graffiti tradition, JR pasted his images directly at the eye level of the street, demonstrating an impressive invasion of the tightly controlled urban space. Adventure, frankly, is an historic and essential part of graffiti culture. Trespassing and a bold confrontation with illegality are graffiti's calling card. Using a can of spray-paint, JR connected the series of images with spray-painted frames and aggressive lines. He subsequently called this early work *Expo 2 Rue*, or *Sidewalk Galleries*.

In a sense JR's important shift as an artist was to turn the subject of the graffiti from a position of 'this is me' to a position of 'this is us'. His work moved past the demonstration of a style that merely demonstrated the artist's individual aesthetic skill and instead used his art to put into motion a relationship between his audiences. By pasting portraits of locals on the walls of their immediate environments, JR's photography makes a shift to the local and public, emphasizing the dynamic of people living in the city together. In making this aesthetic and political shift, JR joins a number of artists who are finding formats to put the local into contact with the photographic image. His work shares a resonance with Philadelphia photographer Zoe Strauss. In 2001, Strauss began displaying her colour photographs of local residents beneath the Interstate 95 overpass. The photographs focused on the residents whose lives embodied the struggle, hardship and joy experienced by many in the working-class community. In her version of the street as gallery, Strauss would hang her exhibition on the concrete supports of the freeway. When the exhibition closed, visitors could take a print of the photographs directly off the walls. If attendees could not get a print off the supports – attendances grew over the ten years Strauss engaged in the project – she would sell and sign additional copies for $5.

It is no coincidence that the shifts towards the local and public seen in the work of both JR and Strauss came at the very beginning of mass use of the internet and the rise of social networking in the early 2000s. If artists have a role as soothsayers or visionaries of social change, the artistic move to localized and participatory forms of engagement occurred in reaction to a mass media that dehumanized people, rendering them abstract, while anticipating a move to the mass sharing of local experience. Of course, social networking also provided an antidote to the alienation traditionally produced by mass media, while the rise of social networking and blogging allowed artists to scour the internet for inspiration and for like-minded people. JR's work reflects the art of photography in the public sphere as documentation in the age of the internet. In the age of mass photography, with such a simple low-cost medium and the ability to snap a picture in any part of the world and share it with

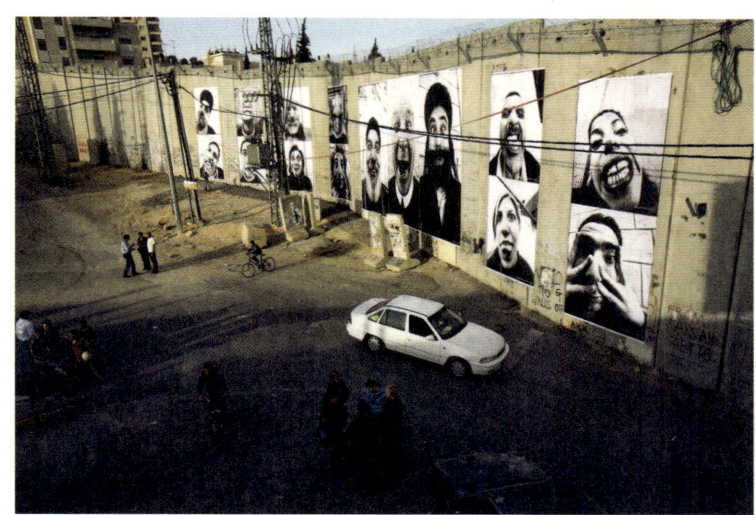

Pasting on the Separation Wall, Israeli side, Abu Dis, Jerusalem, 2007
from *Face 2 Face*

enthusiasts from around the world, what has been called Street Art grew tremendously in audience and participants. The artistic use of public space on a local level gained an international audience – and JR was there to lead the charge.

THE DIFFICULTY OF SEEING

'Seeing is more than a physiological phenomenon ... We see not only with our eyes but with all that we are and all that our culture is. The artist is a professional see-er.'
- Dorothea Lange

Working in a long history of documentary photographers that stretches back to realist painters, JR's work continues the story of making human those who are typically not taken into consideration. This long tradition in the arts reaches from Jean-Francois Millet's *The Gleaners* of 1857 – where the painter turned his brush to the labours of peasants in the French countryside – to the Depression era photography of Dorothea Lange, who captured the faces of those living in poverty in the United States, and the work of David Goldblatt, who photographed the faces of those living under Apartheid in South Africa.

In 2005, JR talked to his friend Marco Berrebi, whom he has since referred to as his *consigliere*. After the two artists discussed Israel/Palestine and how the media abstracts individuals in the region, they decided to coordinate an illegal art exhibition on the wall built by Israel along its border with Palestinian territory in 2007. The barrier is both a physical and metaphorical embodiment of a region embroiled in disputes over land and, through that land, an exacerbation of cultural animosity. In terms of its geopolitical symbolism and the kind of surface perfect for street artists, the wall held out new possibilities and challenges.

The period of this project, like many in the region, was both turbulent and specific. JR and Marco arrived in October 2006 and worked until March 2007, a time when intense factional fighting broke out in the Gaza Strip between Hamas and the Fatah-run Palestinian Security Forces. The unrest made it a more difficult time to do an art project, but also made it all the more urgent. The premise for *Face 2 Face* was simple. As French citizens, JR and Marco were able to travel to both sides of the wall, where JR photographed Israeli and Palestinian residents on either side. On each side of the wall, the team had conversations with individuals. They discussed politics. As part of the work, the participants signed a letter declaring they were for peace and a two-state solution to the Palestinian–Israeli conflict. And, as each participant had their photo taken, he or she also became a public ambassador, taking on the responsibility of becoming an advocate for their position by having their images presented in such a bold fashion. Using the same photographic techniques as he used in *Portrait of a Generation*, JR captured personal yet funny portraits and then pasted large-scale printouts on the wall: the crossed eyes and big smiley grins – faces full of humour and humanity – stand in stark contrast to the severity of a wall that separates the very people portrayed. The images themselves again were double-images. As goofy as the images were, they were also taken with an awareness by the subjects of how they were presented in the media and how they would appear on the wall. The images were sincere portraits of humanity engulfed in a complex array of self-aware photography.

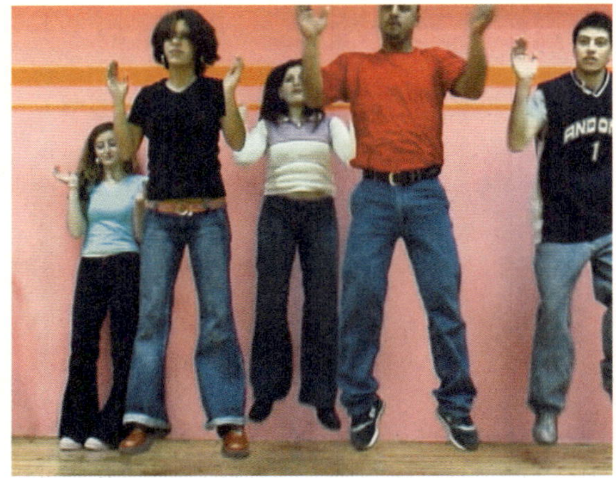

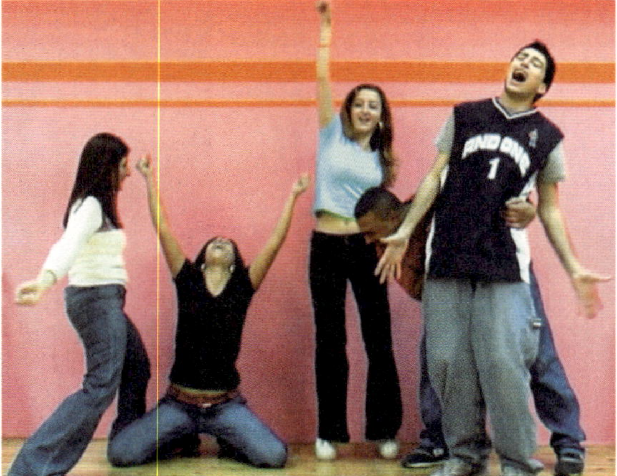
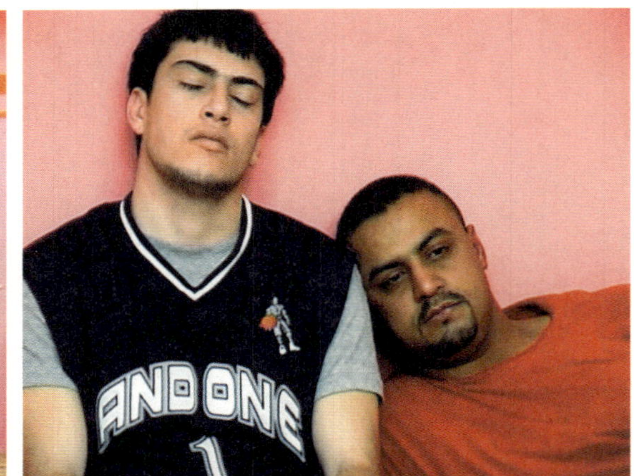

Phil Collins, *they shoot horses*, video, two projections, colour and sound, 7 hours

Face 2 Face not only presented the faces of those living on one side of the wall to those living on the other but, again, also provided a non-sensationalized image of the humanity of the 'other'. Pasting the images on the wall further demonstrated to an international community of street artists that the Occupied Territories were a place where artists could work. The British artist Banksy had been to the wall five months previously (operating on only one side, it should be noted) and by 2008 artists such as Ron English, Swoon and many others had used the wall as an opportunity to raise concerns about issues ranging from peace to solidarity and humanity. The wall became not only a symbol but also a profound, geopolitically loaded canvas.

Unlike *Portrait of a Generation*, the subjects of *Face 2 Face* were neither friends nor acquaintances of the artist. JR trusted his instinct that what made his work resonate in the suburbs of Paris would resonate in many conditions around the world – the basic assumption that, even in the harshest conditions, people deserve to be presented to the world with their humanity intact. It is not an easy thing to do without falling into the traps of cliché or stereotypes – both Palestinians and Israelis could easily argue that their problems are more complicated than merely recognizing each other's humanity – but the conflict, and the way it is presented to the world, reduces people to abstractions who neither seem to have a location (in an actual place) nor to be personal, in the sense of relating to an actual individual. It is a similar awareness that compelled British artist Phil Collins to enact and film a day-long dance contest with young Palestinians in the city of Ramallah. Entitled *they shoot horses*, the video follows the day. As we watch Palestinians dance to pop music, gradually becoming fatigued, we become deeply aware of their humanity and familiarity. Like *Face 2 Face*, the work becomes an opportunity to humanize a people who have typically been presented as villains or victims in the media. Not only do JR and Collins share an interest in similar subject matter, they both also use highly familiar tools to close the distance between situations that appear removed from daily life in the West. And humanization need not flatten an individual. In fact, it does just the opposite, adding depth to the complexity of what a person is. Laughter, joy, depression, volatility and perversity are all part of what makes up an individual. To humanize someone is not necessarily to make someone more appealing, but instead to make them as strange and wonderful as we are ourselves.

In subsequent projects, JR continued this desire to allow his subjects to become agents of their own public identity within their local communities, but also strove to present them to the attention of a growing global audience. Travel across the globe increasingly became an integral part of his photo-documentary medium.

In 2008, JR tackled two regionally specific projects, *Women Are Heroes* and *Wrinkles of the City*, both addressing sectors of communities often excluded from mainstream dialogues: women and the elderly. He initiated the first, *Women Are Heroes*, after hearing a story about three children who were captured by the police and then left for dead in the Brazilian favela of Morro da Providência in Rio de Janeiro. Following a series of conversations with mothers in the favela, he realized that these women were the backbone of the community but also often the victims of violence. Setting out to highlight their position in the community, JR engaged members of the whole neighbourhood to help paste posters of the women's eyes and faces throughout the favela: intense eyes stared from the sides of buildings; a woman's face stretched up along the bricks of a hillside stairway; the black-and-white image of children appeared alongside a shanty. Later, JR and his team pasted the images in locations around the world.

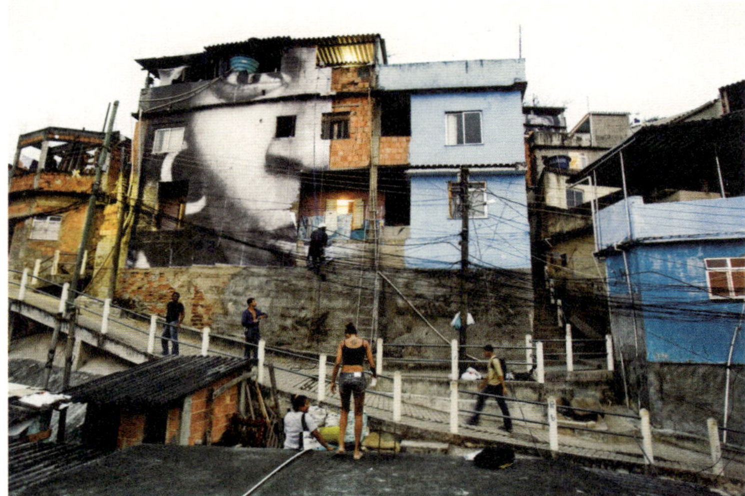

Pasting in Morro da Providência favela, Rio de Janeiro, Brazil, 2008
from *Women Are Heroes*

Women Are Heroes also took JR to Kibera in Kenya, the largest slum in Africa, where he again spoke to mothers and residents. In Kibera, JR noticed that men dominated the public spaces but women bore the brunt of social violence, whether it was domestic violence, violence from political persecution or sexual violence. Following close dialogue within the community, JR printed images of women's eyes on rain-resistant tarpaulins and pasted them on rooftops (thus providing a secondary benefit of weather protection for the rainy season). He also pasted three large-scale images of the mouths of women along the hillside above the slum and had the eyes pasted on the side of a commuter train that regularly passed. The two parts of the faces would come together at a particular time as the train passed, and the artwork would become a regular, small-scale event. JR recounts how the effect of the photographs could be redemptive. For some women who were raped and then shamed in the slum, having their faces pasted large near the church, for example, lent a powerful sense of self that challenged both the violence and the perspective of the community. These images were not simple. They were complex depictions of the oppressed and their positioning in space, among the structures of Kibera, provided a re-negotiated arrangement of what meant what. As JR often notes, his images, while important, are also souvenirs of vast social projects. The images can act as a device to put social relationships into motion.

The project continued in more locations: Cambodia, Sierra Leone, Sudan, Liberia and India. Each site offered another opportunity to introduce the smiling, wild and funny faces of the women of the community to a public sphere. The film documenting the project became an official film selection at Cannes in 2010. And thus another element was born as part of the myriad of outlets that accompany JR's localized projects; subject, camera, public space, internet and, now, film.

Using encounters and dialogues with local participants, JR's collaborative working style touches upon elements associated with what might be called community arts, social practice or socially engaged art. A burgeoning field in and of itself, social practice emphasizes relationships with groups of people as part of the aesthetic quality of an artwork. That is to say, the experience for local participants becomes an emphasized part of the artwork. For JR, his work with communities becomes an element of the narrative and provides, ideally, a meaningful engagement for people ranging from Cambodia to New York to Liberia.

In 2008, JR initiated his *Wrinkles of the City* project in Cartagena, Spain, focusing on the elderly residents, some of whom could still recall the Spanish Civil War. Cartagena was the stronghold of the Republican Government that held out against General Franco's Nationalists. JR was struck not only by the memories of the city's elderly but also by how their thoughts resonated with the impressive but decaying architecture of the city itself. Here were the last people who could remember the resistance to Franco and the city, it seemed, bore the wrinkles and scars of its citizenry. As JR's large-scale images began to dominate the actual surfaces of an urban environment, the people of the city rose out of the shadows and, for a few months or longer, became visible: the actors within a city's history rose up to take ownership of that history. The engagement with public space is critical to the images' aesthetic. Literally taking over the architecture of the city, JR's art, while presenting a sweet face, is deployed in an aggressive, anti-private property, way. Like graffiti, JR's artworks cannot be appreciated without appreciating their relationship with the body of the city itself.

In 2010, JR's aesthetic took another turn as he tried using archival photographs rather than pasting his own images.

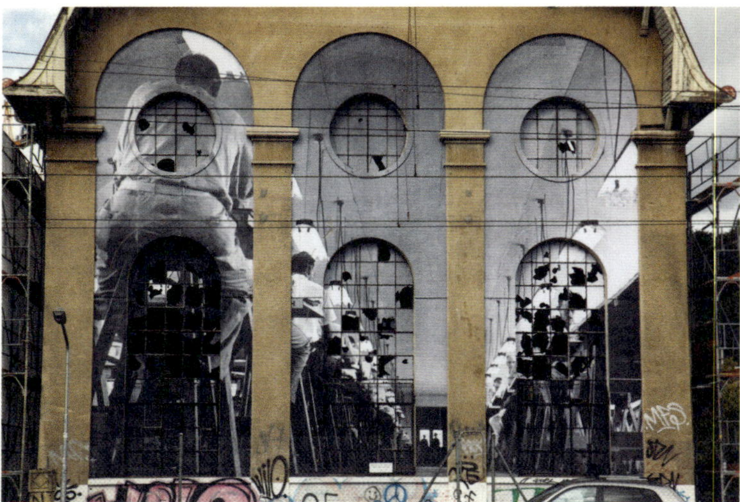

John Phillips, Workshop in Corpus Christi, 1940, seen by JR, Vevey, Switzerland, 2010, from *Unframed*

Moving away not only from close-up portraiture but also from the rectilinear wheat-pastes, this new style of working allowed JR the freedom to apply historical references with a sensitive dynamism adapted to a building's surface and context. Working from the collection of the Musée de l'Élysée, JR reworked the buildings of Vevey, Switzerland, with photographs by Man Ray, Robert Capa, Helen Levitt and Mario Giacomelli. A young woman's face adorns a clock tower with her hair flying sky high. Troops waving goodbye as they make their way to the military front in 1936 near Barcelona, adorn an abandoned railway car.

JR titled the project *Unframed* and the venture took him, again, to far reaches of the planet over the following years, including São Paolo, Washington DC, Baden Baden, Atlanta, Marseille, Vevey and Grottaglie. As with each of JR's umbrella projects, each site provides a unique opportunity to re-interpret the possibilities of a project's parameters. With *Unframed*, for example, JR worked with a museum collection in Vevey, Switzerland; instigated an intervention about toxic waste featuring a photograph from Chernobyl in Grottaglie, Italy; worked with images of deforestation in São Paolo; and highlighted archival images from Ellis Island on Ellis Island.

In 2013, as part of the celebrations of Marseille being chosen as the City of European Culture, JR was invited to do a project in the working-class neighbourhood of La Belle de Mai. He took the opportunity to explore the *Unframed* project in an altogether different manner by asking residents to supply images from their own collections. The open call received thousands of images for JR to sort through. Acknowledging that La Belle de Mai is a neighbourhood of historic and contemporary immigration, he turned it into a veritable black-and-white scrapbook highlighting its complex ethnic citizenry. A 1966 classroom photograph stretched across the facades of five buildings, a mustached man in a cowboy hat played the game pétanque, a pair of eyes from a woman's lost father from Algeria welcomed visitors at the train station and an Afghani man named Ali chose a photograph of people on a boat in homage to his own harrowing trip to Marseille in 2010. These images spread across the urban architectural landscape – each rich in its own right but also in conversation with the next, thus developing a complex narrative of who actually resides in the city.

FLIPPING THE SCRIPT

'My wish: use art to turn the world inside out.'
- JR, 2011

In 2011, JR received the TED Prize for his works. It was a first in many ways, as JR was not only the youngest recipient of the $100,000 prize but also the first artist. The prize offered the opportunity for JR to launch *Inside Out*, a massive global participatory project. As *Unframed* provided the conceptual space for JR to step outside the role of direct photographer, so *Inside Out* magnified the potentialities by encouraging the audience to become the producers of the images themselves. The idea was simple and the results unpredictable. As opposed to JR being the instigator of his documentary-style 'street' work, he would turn the camera over to a global audience. He set a few simple rules: potential participants had to organize themselves into a group of at least five; they would need a statement; the images would need to be individual portraits, ideally expressive ones, and the photographers would need the permission of those they photographed. Participants would send the portraits electronically to JR's studio in New York and, if they lacked

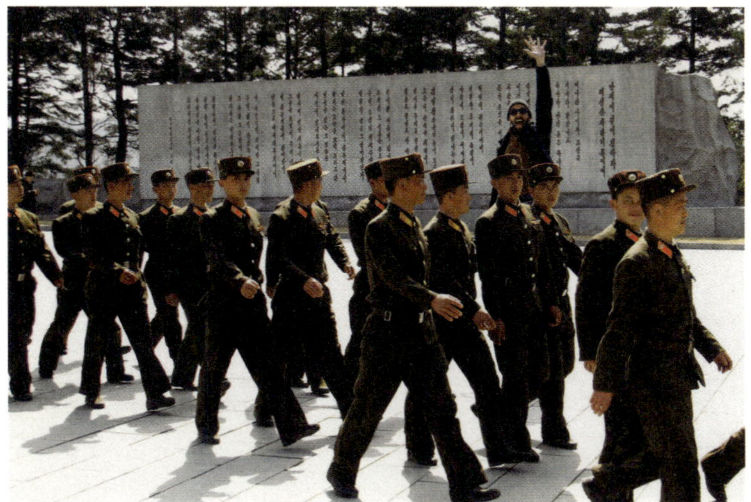

JR in Pyongyang, North Korea, 2012

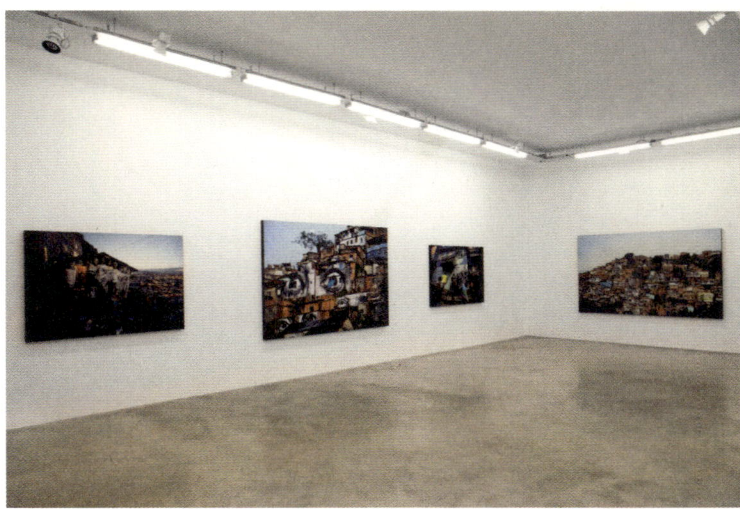

'Encrages' exhibition, Galerie Perrotin, Paris, 2011

money for materials, the *Inside Out* project would send the large-scale printouts in bulk for them to paste in their own 'actions'. Finally, the results would be published on the *Inside Out* website. The visibility and access to sources of funding provided by the TED Prize allowed JR to spread the word. In the first few months results came in from across the globe, from Medellin in Colombia to Seoul, Korea, from Johannesburg, South Africa, to Whanganui in New Zealand.

JR's images, of course, are not without their own economy; there must be money to pay for JR to hop on a plane and paste large-scale images across an urban landscape. It is neither unreasonable nor beside the point to wonder what the nuts and bolts finances are behind any project. In essence, JR makes his living on a gallery-based model, in which his images have a value that is exchanged on the market, and is proud that this economic model allows him the freedom not only to make whatever artwork he wants but also not to have to brand his images in corporate logos or sell them in retail chains. He retains a marked independence even from his galleries, and this independence has provided a freedom to work. As JR's reputation has grown over the years, so too have the prices for his artworks – lithographs and works on wood, for example – which he exhibits internationally and sells through his galleries in Paris, London, Shanghai, Geneva, Berlin, Hong Kong and New York. With the *Inside Out* project, JR could not only use the gallery model but also manipulate the economy of participation by having those who could afford it pay to assist those who could not afford the materials on their own. In a sense, *Inside Out* became a work that also provided an alternative economy as part of its overall approach.

Inside Out spread like wild fire. No longer limited by JR actually having to be at each site, and instead acting as a facilitator of mass participation, the project appeared across the globe simultaneously. A global network emerged, with participants able to both act locally and share an international platform. In essence, the project reveals that communities around the world seem to be wrestling with similar battles about media representation and the uses of public space. To reference back to *Portrait of a Generation*, the participants seemed to be saying, 'Hello. I am here.' Using the website as a platform to share particular concerns produced a sense of a global community as participants saw their work alongside that of others.

JR is neither the first nor the last artist to embrace participation as a form of aesthetic. Participatory artworks became popular in the contemporary art world in the 1990s and 2000s. But while contemporary art often focuses on the immediate experience in a gallery or in a public space, JR took the concept one step further with a global audience. And, as in many participatory artworks, JR used a relatively straightforward concept (the portrait) as a method for engagement. Those participating did not need to know anything about contemporary art as long as they understood a universal language of image making in order to appreciate and participate in the work. This sense of a universal language of image making is perhaps not only what has allowed JR's work to gain global appreciation but also what has encouraged the participation from people from every walk of life, from every corner of the globe.

Increasing the participatory nature of the project, JR and his team developed photobooth trucks that provide the opportunity for the curious to have their photograph taken and receive an instant, large-format, black-and-white printout to take and paste. The photobooths have travelled the globe and also provided an opportunity to partner with art exhibition sites and public art exhibitions. JR's images – whether shot by him or taken in a photobooth or by participants in *Inside Out* – sit within an

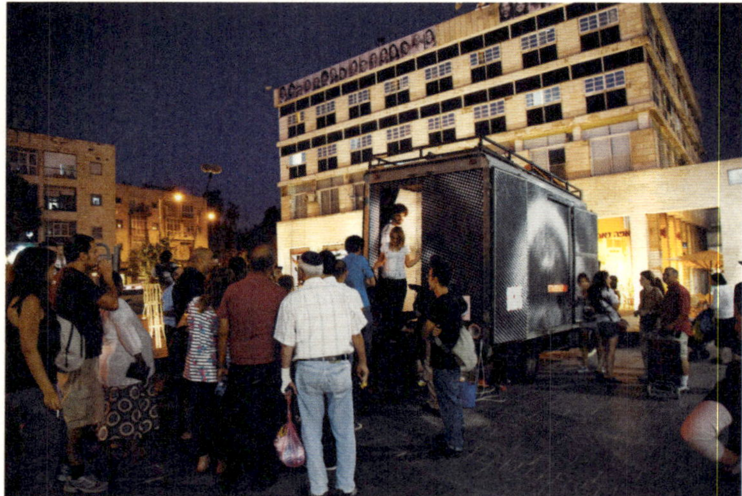

Photobooth truck in Jerusalem, Israel, 2011
from *Inside Out*

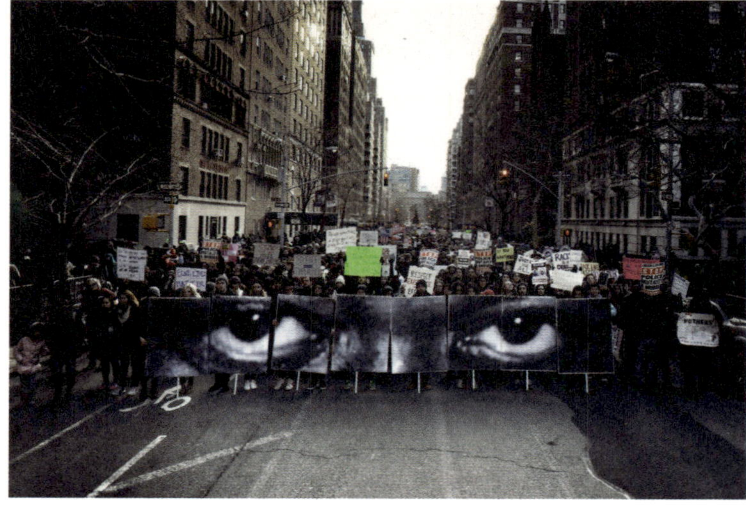

JR's image of Eric Garner's eyes leads the protest march in New York over Garner's death in police custody, 2014

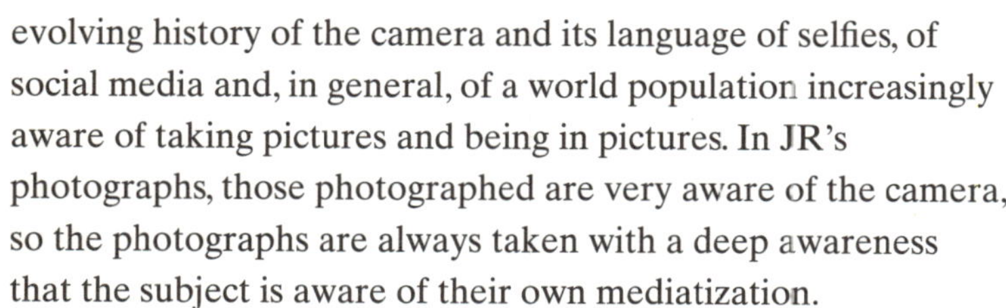

evolving history of the camera and its language of selfies, of social media and, in general, of a world population increasingly aware of taking pictures and being in pictures. In JR's photographs, those photographed are very aware of the camera, so the photographs are always taken with a deep awareness that the subject is aware of their own mediatization.

While many participants used *Inside Out* as an opportunity to highlight members of a community or express solidarity around narratives of peace or tolerance, at times the project came up against unexpected opposition. Public space is a contested space and community is, more often than not, a series of various contradicting opinions. In an illuminating section of the *Inside Out* film, for example, JR visits a group in Tunisia in the aftermath of the Arab Spring. A sense of potential was in the air as society could re-invent itself after years of surveillance and paranoia. Banners of the deposed president Zine el Abidine Ben Ali had previously covered every surface in Tunisia's major cities, and the organizers were excited to be able to replace them with the portraits of Tunisian citizens, which they planned to paste in the former presidential palace. But in a hobbled post-Arab Spring Tunisia, suspicion of outsiders and their motives dominated the reception of the images. The organizers were shocked as community members tore down the new posters – an ethically ambiguous episode that JR nevertheless retained in the film. At times, the question of what the uses of public space should be and who should be represented there is a subject of debate.

JR's work continues not only to grow but also to find itself inside the heart of large-scale social movements with images as part of the conversation. On 13 December 2014, JR printed photographs to support a march against police violence in New York. The images were of the eyes of Eric Garner, a man who died in police custody in Staten Island after being subjected to a chokehold that was caught on camera. The video went viral but the officer concerned was found innocent of killing Garner just days after another officer was found innocent of killing an unarmed black teenager named Michael Brown in St Louis. Protests erupted and, as they reached New York, JR's placards of Garner's eyes found their way to the front of the march – piercing, looking for justice – as protesters moved through the streets of the city. The images represented a man caught in the violence perpetrated on him by a police force that clearly had begun to confuse the mediated images of black men as criminals with the actual humanity of a man full of laughter, joy and sadness. The eyes that marched across the city said something about people needing to be heard and needing the global community to march with them. These eyes said everything about photography, about art, about the cities we all live in and, ultimately, about humanity.

Over a decade, JR's expansive oeuvre has managed to both capture the imagination of the globe and to expand the medium of photography and public art itself. JR's desire to touch people's lives allowed him to become a photographer who was willing to let go of everything that constitutes photography in order to re-invent the medium itself with a much more expansive capability. Mobilizing participation, working site-specifically, finding new forms of economy, deploying archival images and catalyzing a global community seem to have come naturally to a body of work that has travelled the globe many times over. But the simple aesthetic innovations that have propelled JR's iconic black-and-white images onto the cracked walls of cities the world over have touched upon a sense of meaning that resonates widely, and portends the future for photography, public art, street art, contemporary art and citizenry worldwide.

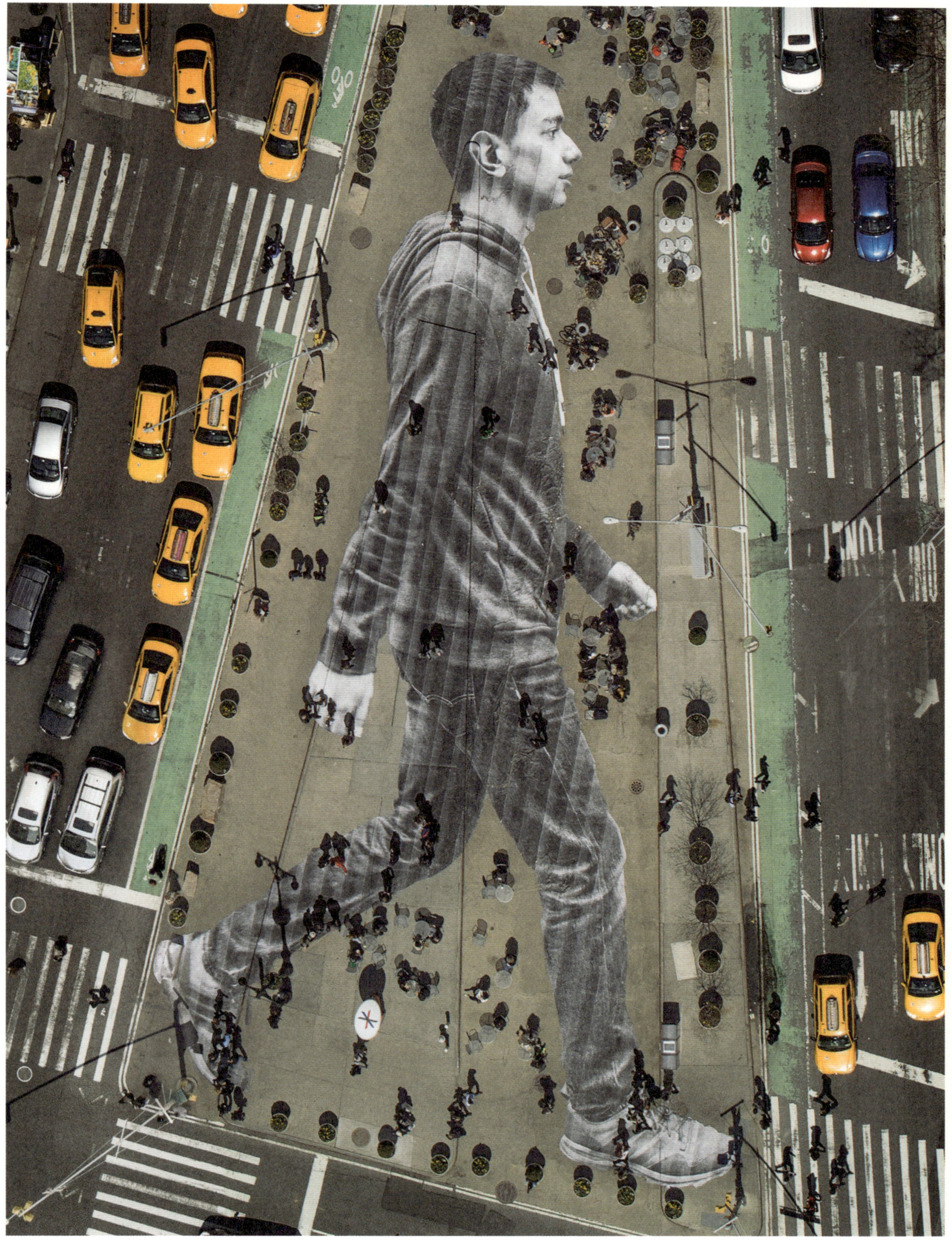

Elmar, Flatiron Plaza, New York, 2015

'This was a project on anonymous immigrants who arrive everyday in New York. All day long people walked on this pasting without realizing what it was – it was over 50 metres (150 feet) long. It was only when I photographed it from a helicopter and the image was published on the cover of *The New York Times Magazine*, that people noticed it; then the focus flipped – the guy in the photo, Elmar, a recent immigrant from Azerbaijan, was in the spotlight, and the pedestrians walking over it became the shadows.' – JR

EXPO

2RUE

As a teenager, JR began his career as a graffiti artist wanting to make his mark on public space and society. His graffiti often targeted precarious places such as rooftops and subway trains. He enjoyed the adventure of painting in these hard-to-reach spaces.

After finding a camera in the Paris Metro, JR began to photographically document his own graffiti painting and other graffiti artists in action. When he was seventeen years old, he started pasting photocopies of these photographs onto outdoor walls, creating *Expo 2 Rue,* or *Sidewalk Galleries*, that turned city streets into open galleries for everyone to see.

Wanting to explore the vertical limits, walls and façades that form the structure of cities, JR travelled extensively in Europe and the United States to meet artists who used outdoor walls. After observing the people he met and listening to their motivations and stories, JR pasted photos of their actions in the streets.

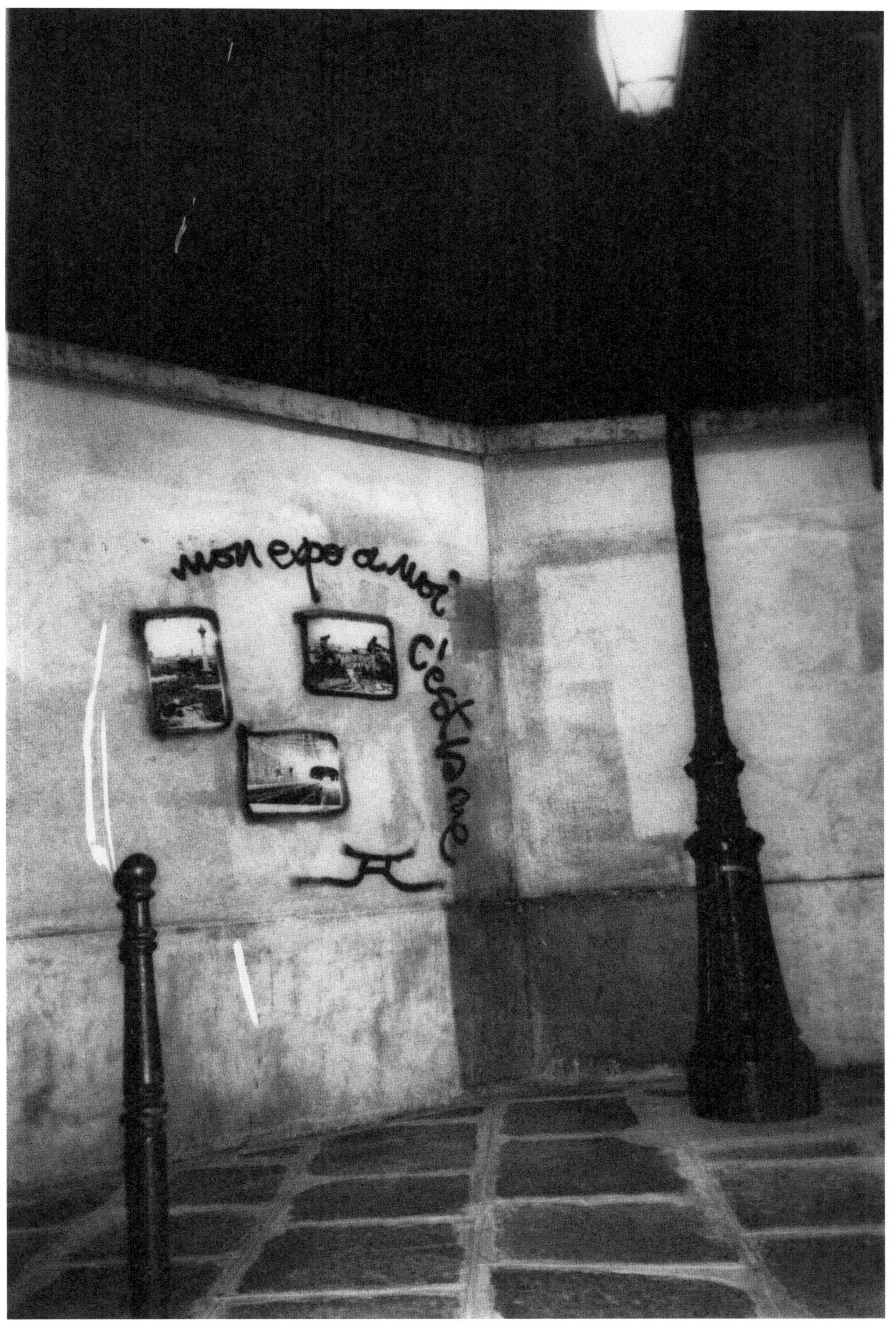

Expo 2 Rue exhibition, Paris, 2001

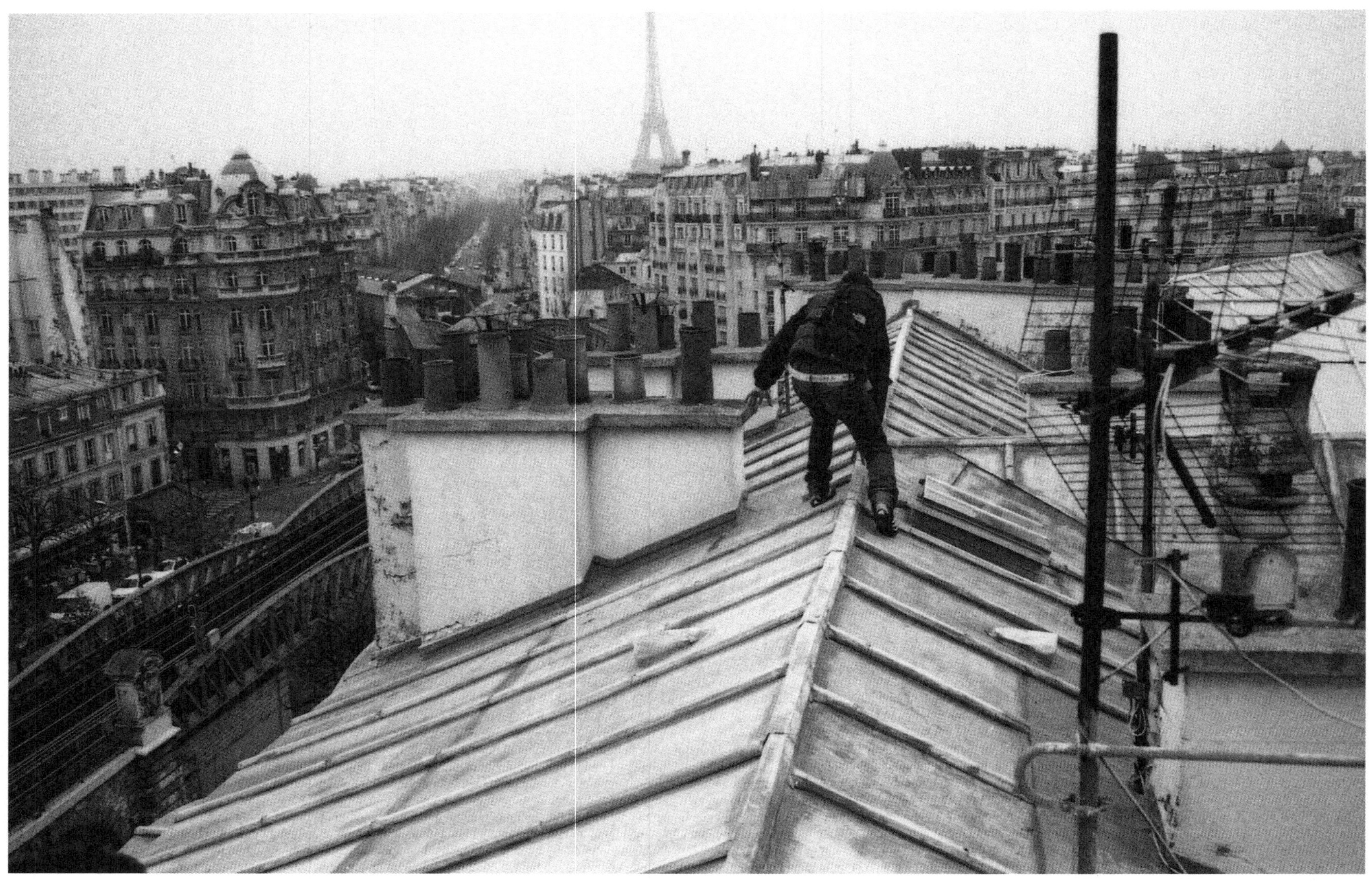

Paris, 2001

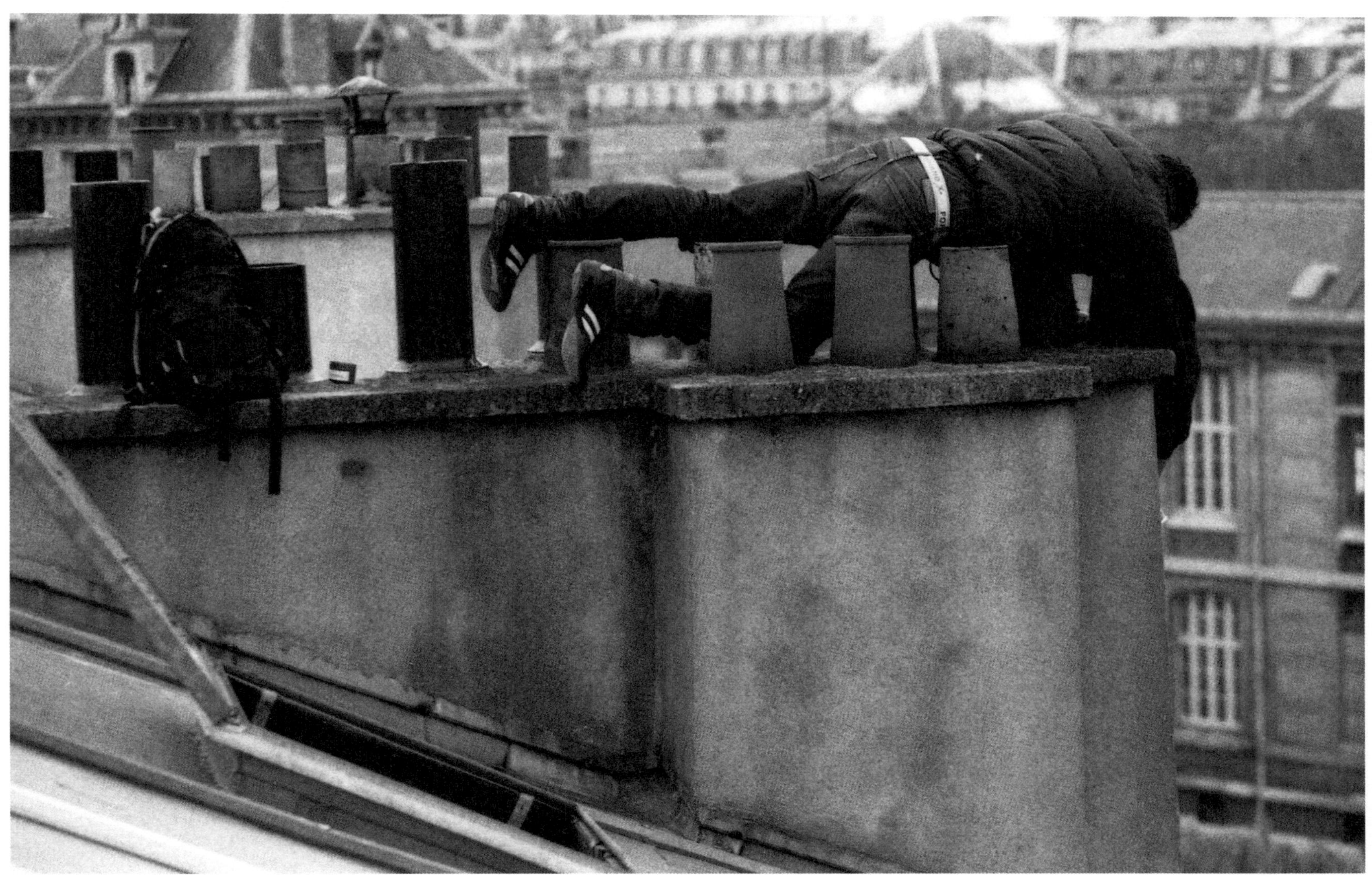

Paris, 2001

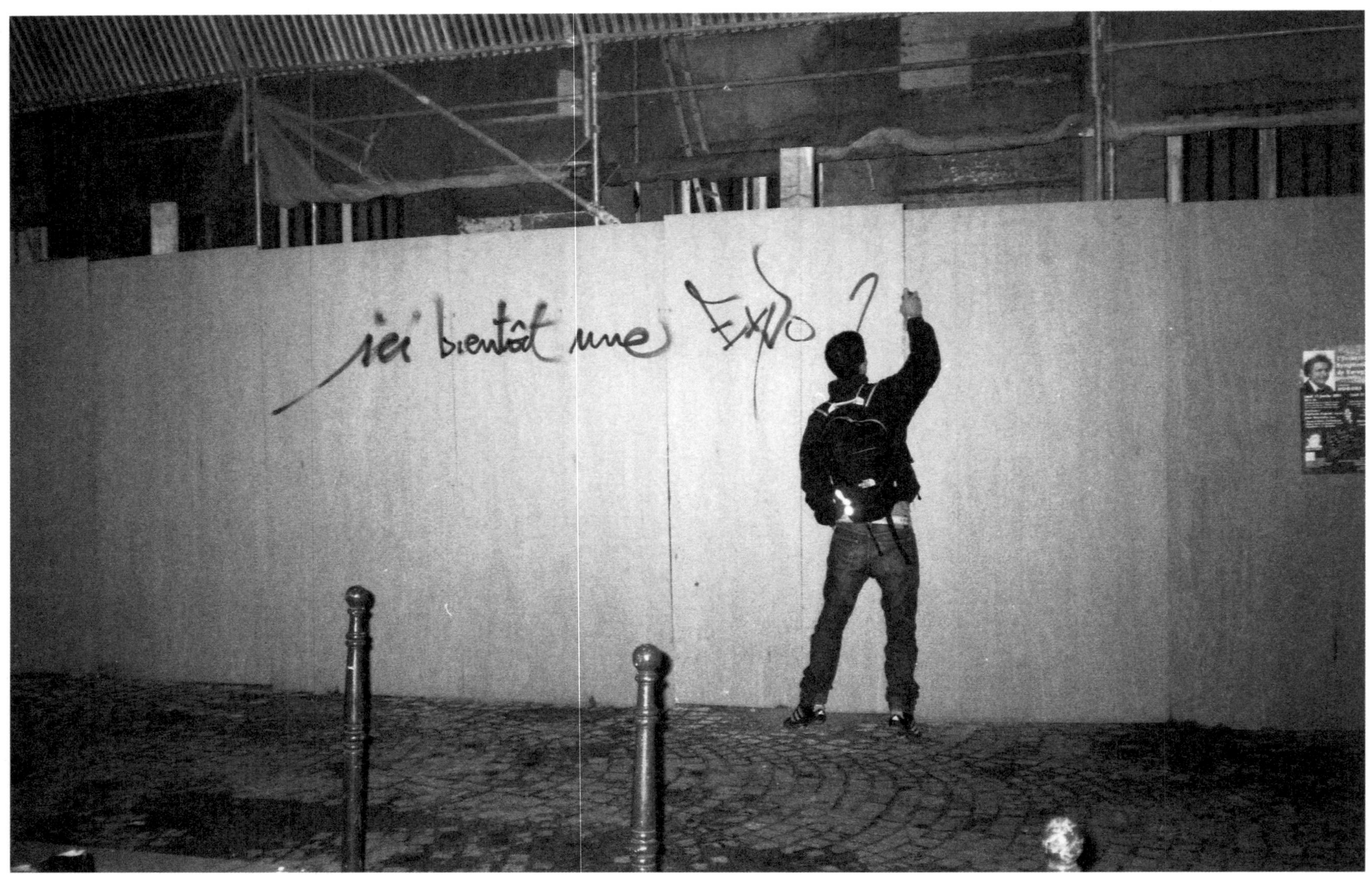

Paris, 2002

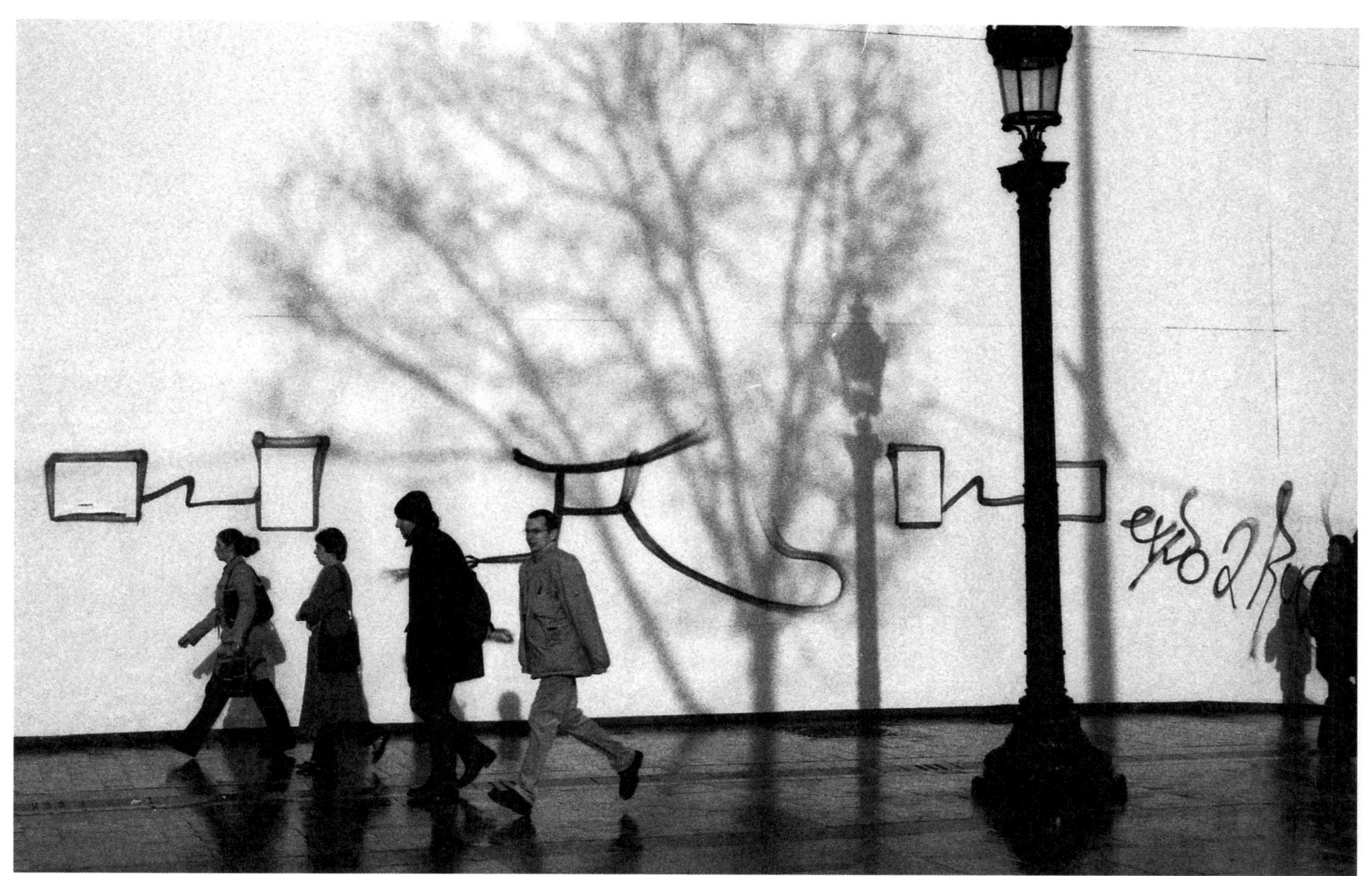

Paris, 2002

PORTRAI

GENER

T OF A

ATION

In 2004, in search of places where no-one would expect to see art, JR held his first exhibition on the walls of Les Bosquets, the 'ghetto' of Montfermeil, a suburb of Paris. He photographed its young inhabitants and pasted enlarged photocopies to the walls.

In November 2005, in the very same place, in a climate of social discontent triggered by the deaths of two teenage boys who were hiding from police in an electricity substation, riots broke out and quickly spread through the city. More than 10,000 cars were burnt by inhabitants of the suburbs in one month alone. Rather than only disrupting other neighbourhoods of Paris, the rioters destroyed their own environment, breaking the only toys left in their backyard.

Across France, people watched frightening images of the events on television. The media portrayed out-of-control kids throwing Molotov cocktails, attacking cops and firemen and looting anything they could. Political leaders from all sides – who had failed to make things any better – were on air every day, juggling buzzwords: prevention, repression, integration, immigration, youth, assimilation, education, citizenship, respect, language, generation, soccer. They discussed the symptoms of this sudden fever without looking at the causes behind it.

In reaction to the media treatment of people who had become his friends, in 2006, JR returned to the heart of the district and, with his friend Ladj Ly, a local artist, began a project with the young people of Les Bosquets. Aware, of course, that they were not all angels, JR nevertheless wanted to challenge the term *racaille*, or 'scum', the then Minister of the Interior had used to describe the rioters. Using a 28 mm lens, he shot full-frame portraits of young people pulling scary faces to caricature themselves and pasted the enlarged posters onto the walls of both Les Bosquets and 'bobo' (bourgeois bohemian) districts of the city.

Portrait of a Generation invited us to look into the eyes of men playing bad boys. With a certain 'in your face' rudeness, the portraits provoked passers-by to question the media representation of them. Were they promising students or thugs? France's future or a threat to national identity? What were their dreams and their nightmares? Should they be punished or motivated? Were the riots an eruption of violence or the beginning of a revolution? Most importantly, should we close our doors to them – or open our arms?

In 2013, JR learned that the buildings that featured the original pastings in Les Bosquets were soon to be demolished, so he revisited the *Portrait of a Generation* project. Using the photographs from the original series, JR and his team secretly pasted two-storey-high portraits in the buildings before they were knocked down. During the demolition, the portraits were exposed, creating a new dialogue between the recent history of Paris, its suburbs and their inhabitants.

(top) Lady Ly, B12, Les Bosquets, Montfermeil, 2004
(middle) P'tit Zé, Les Bosquets, Montfermeil, 2004
(bottom) B12, Les Bosquets, Montfermeil, 2004

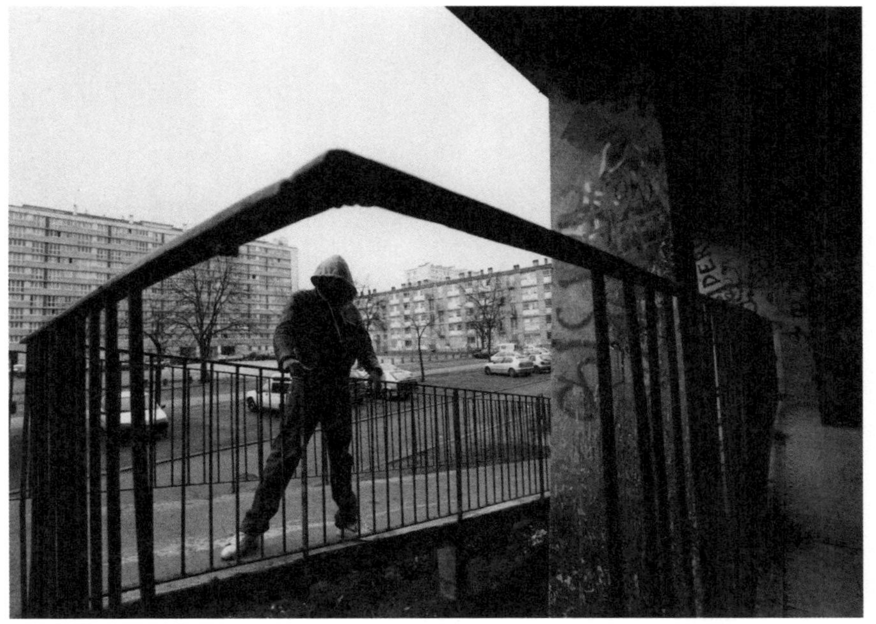

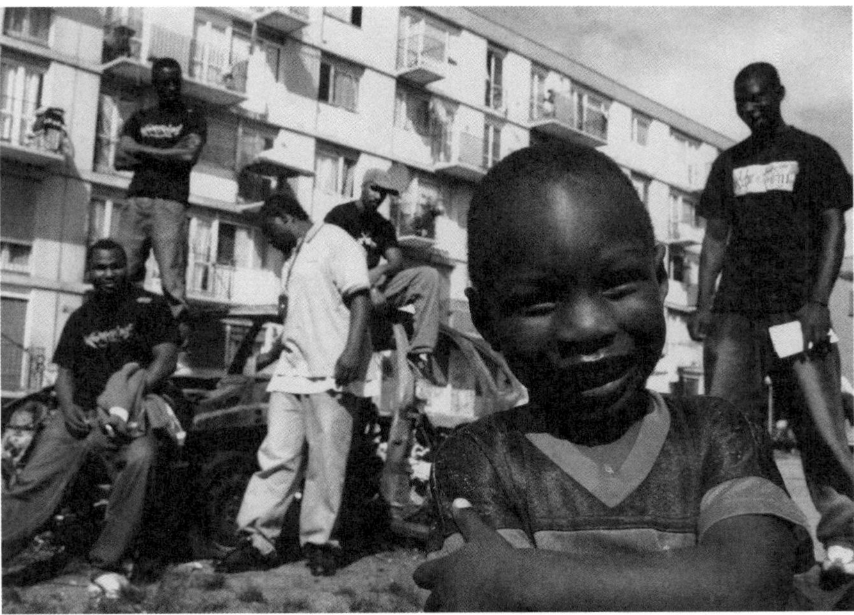

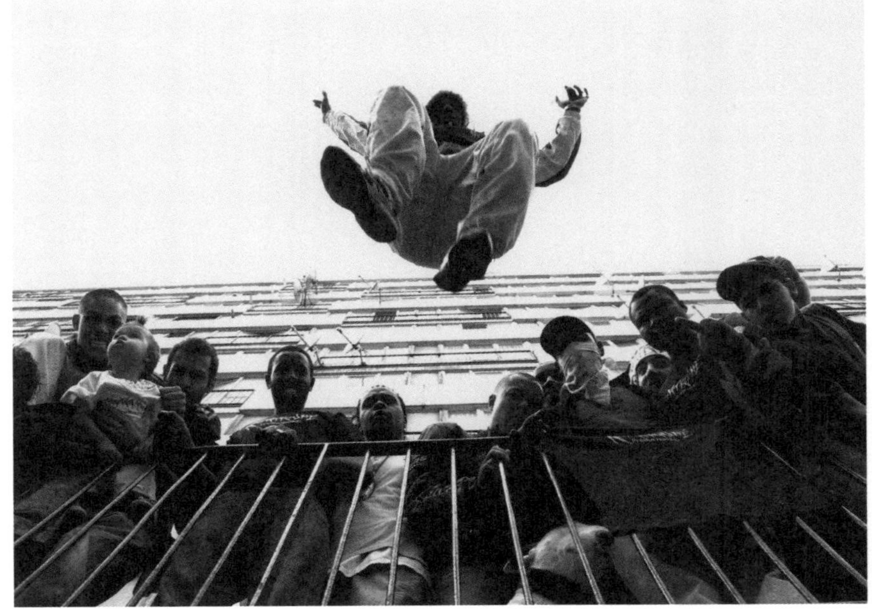

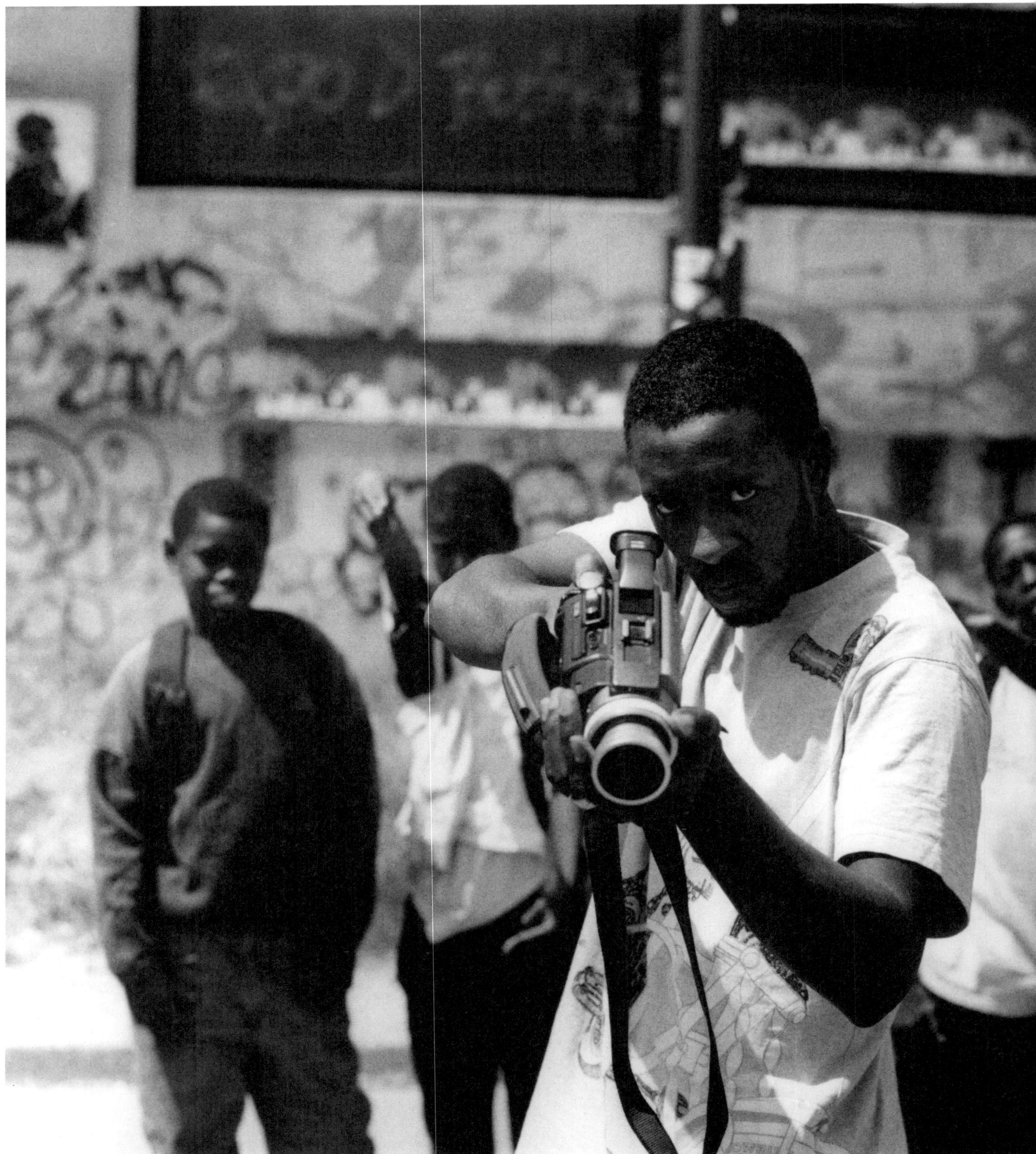

(left) *Braquage*, Ladj Ly, Les Bosquets, Montfermeil, 2004

'I took this picture when I was eighteen. It was the first time I went to Les Bosquets. If you look carefully in the back, you can see small posters from *Expo 2 Rue* – and I wrote "Expo D Boske". The kids asked me if I could take a picture of them. This photo of Ladj Ly filming me was the first one on the roll of film, and I felt something special had happened. This image is very emblematic of my work and of the message we portrayed with this project with Ladj.' – JR

(overleaf) Place des Husler, B23/24, La Forestière, Clichy-sous-Bois, 2004

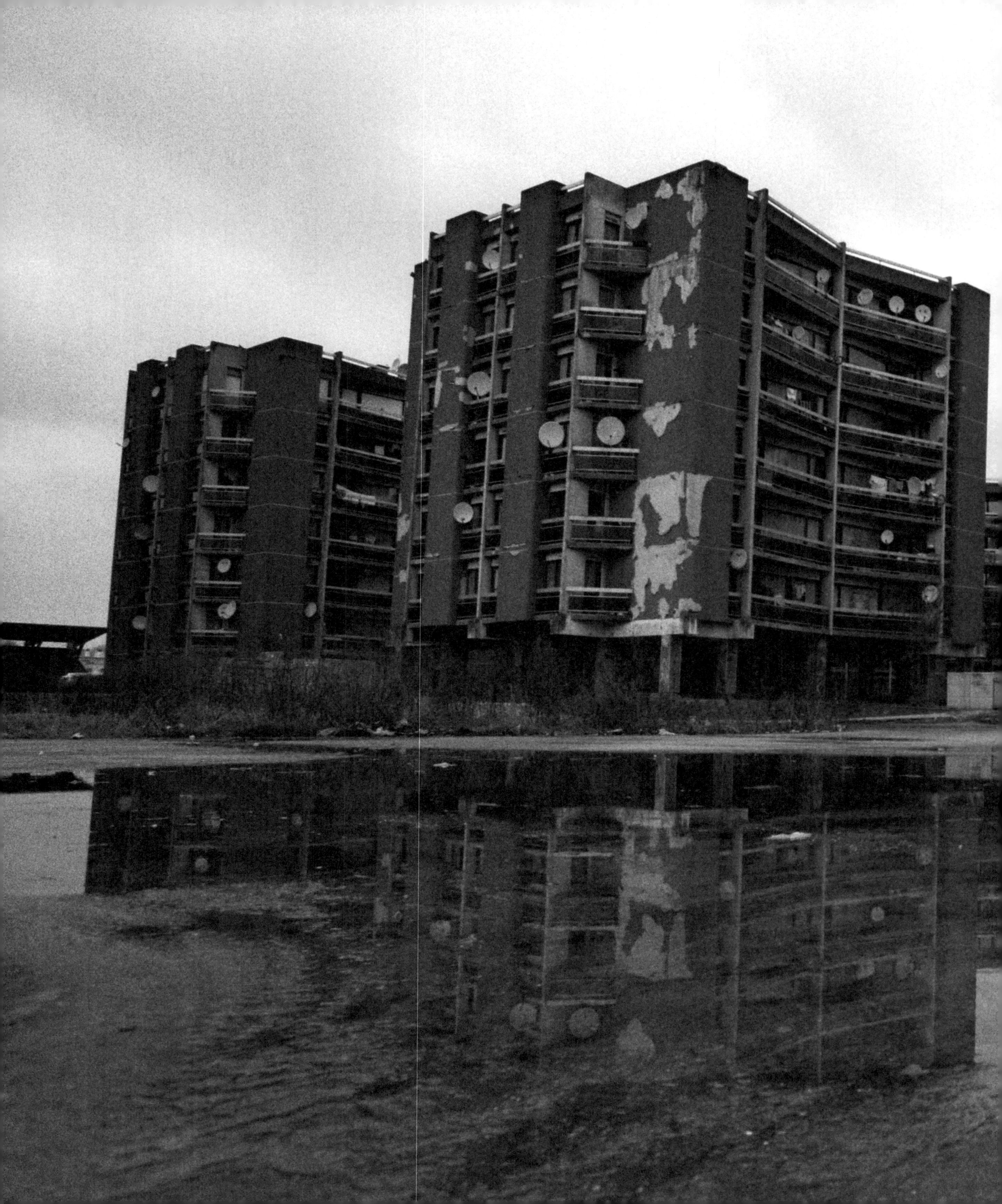

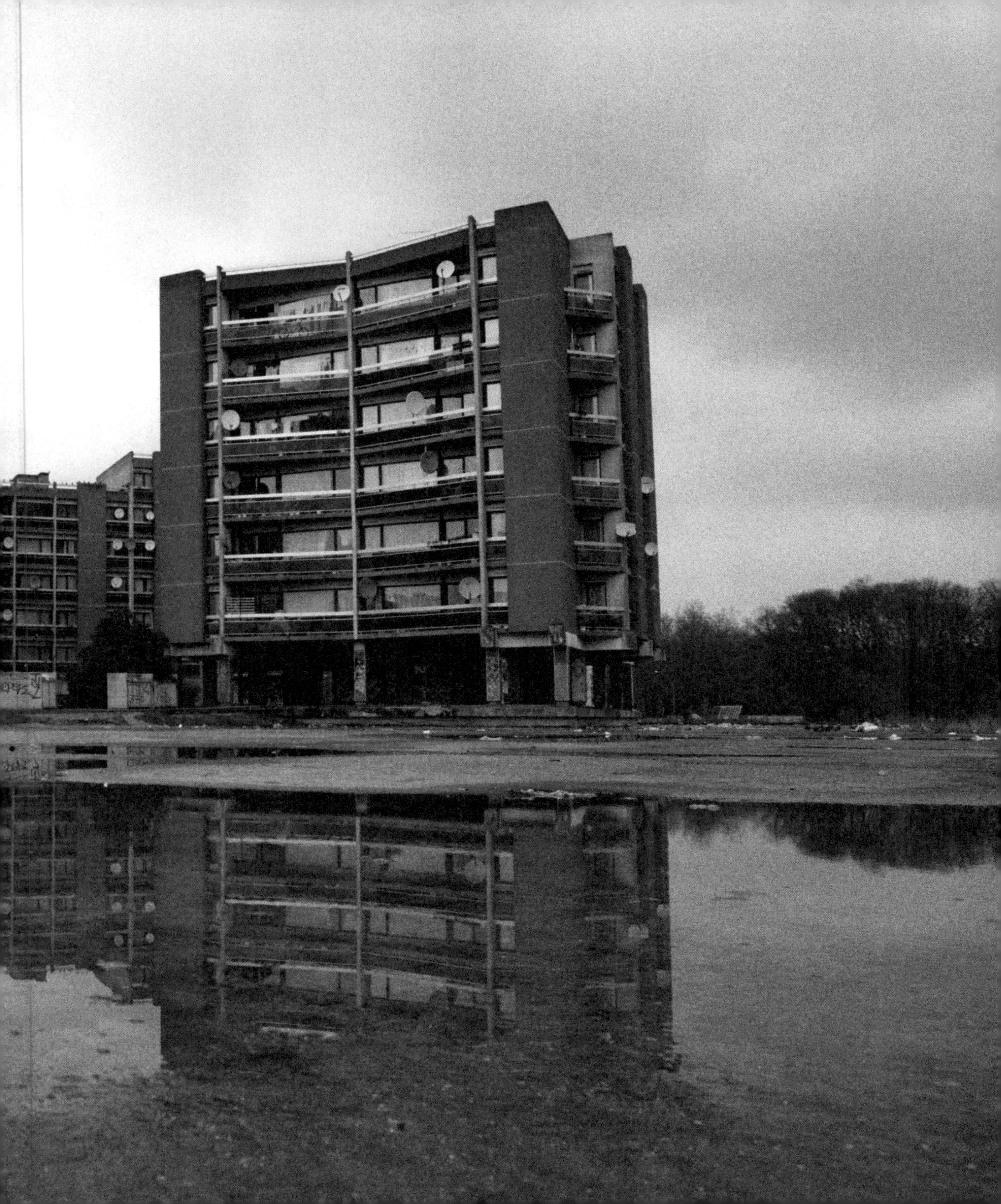

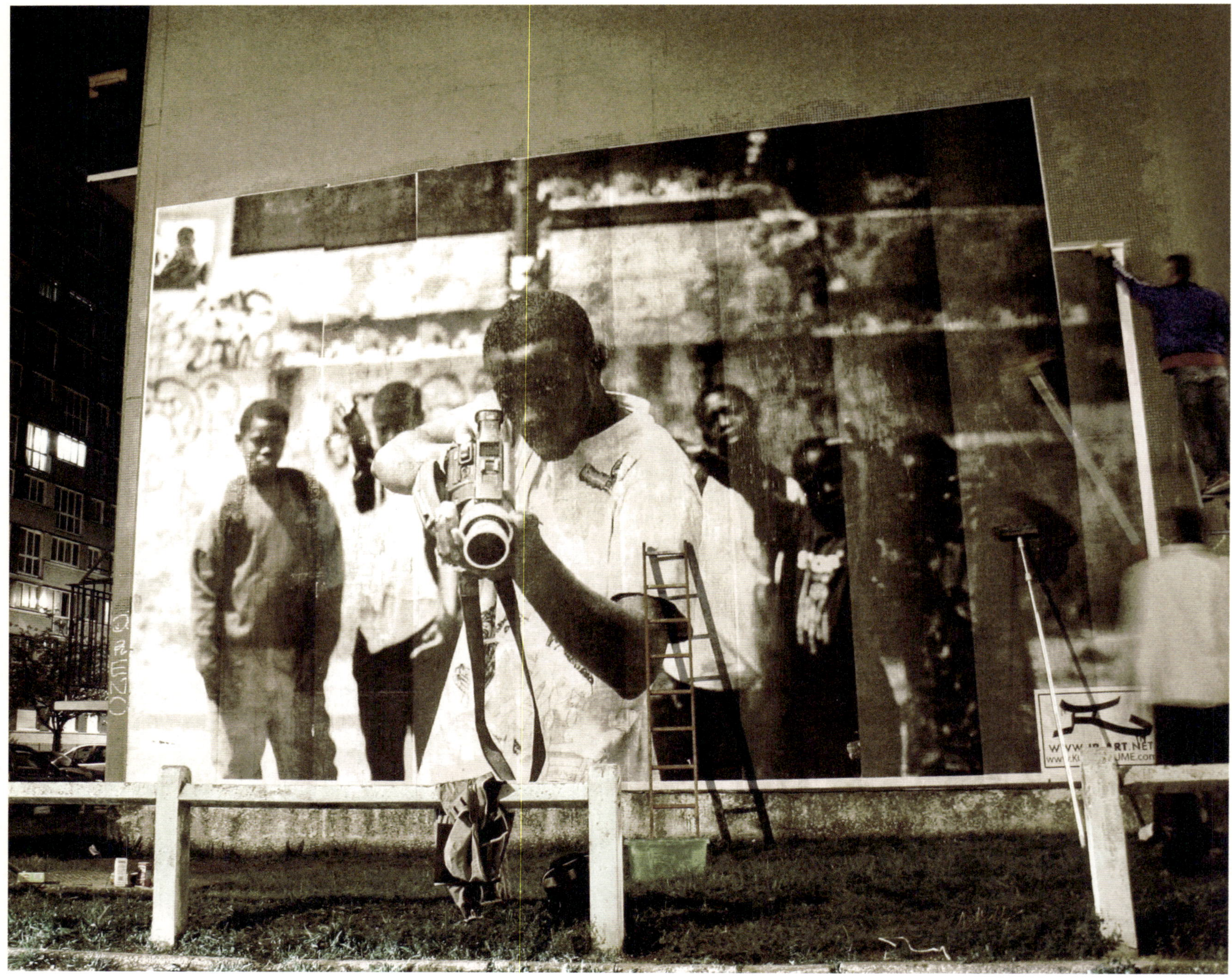

Pasting of Ladj Ly in Les Bosquets, Montfermeil, 2004

'This image was my first large-scale pasting using strips created on a large-format printer. We pasted at night and asked kids from the neighbourhood to wait at the bottom of the ladder in order to create a crowd and avoid the police. I was pasting the second strip when we realized we made a mistake. We had to come back the next night! The pasting took eight hours with the help of all the community. Today, a pasting like this would only take us a couple of hours.' – JR

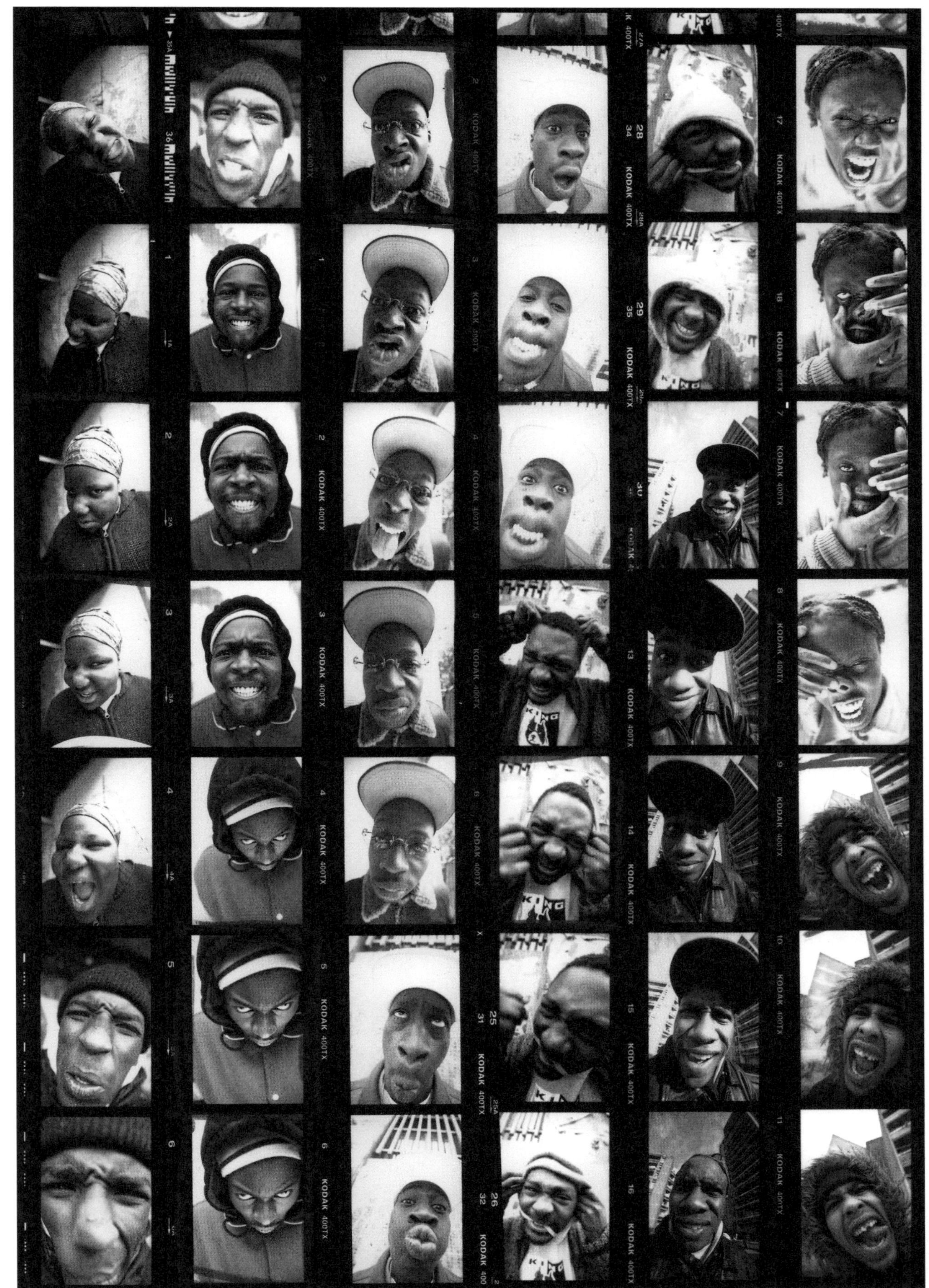

Portrait of a Generation contact sheet, 2006

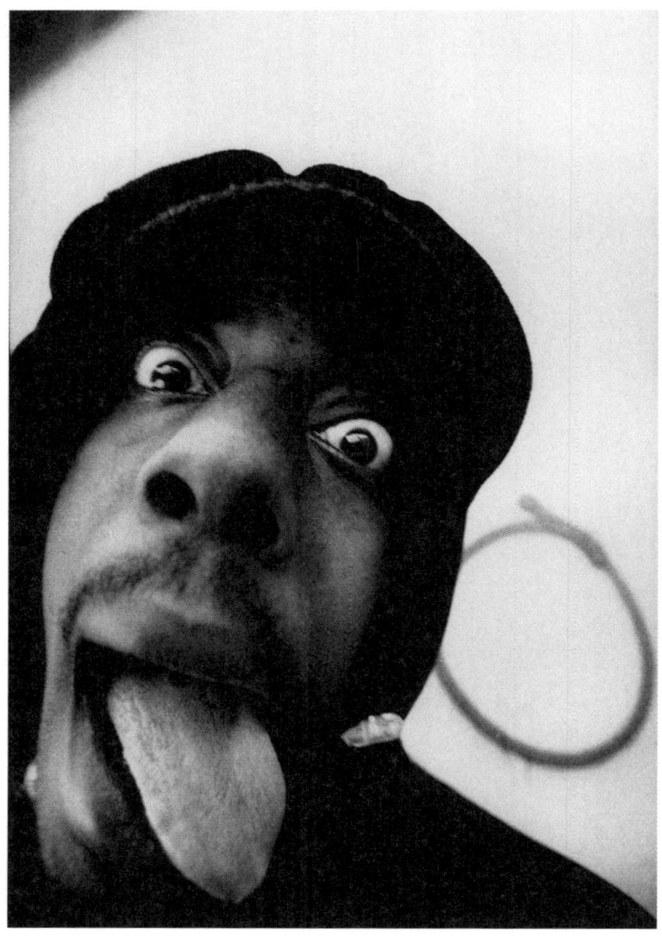

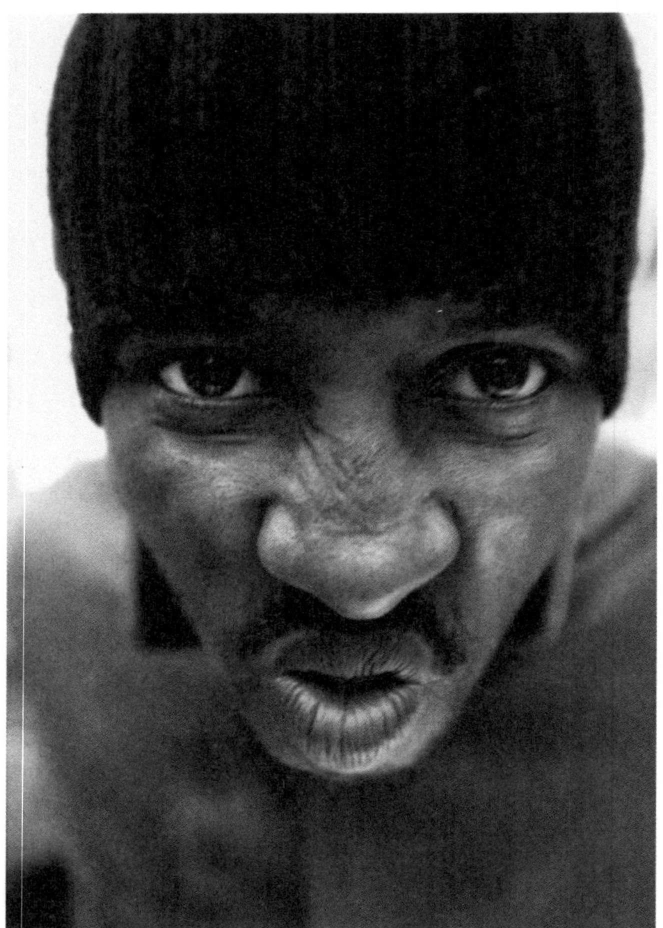

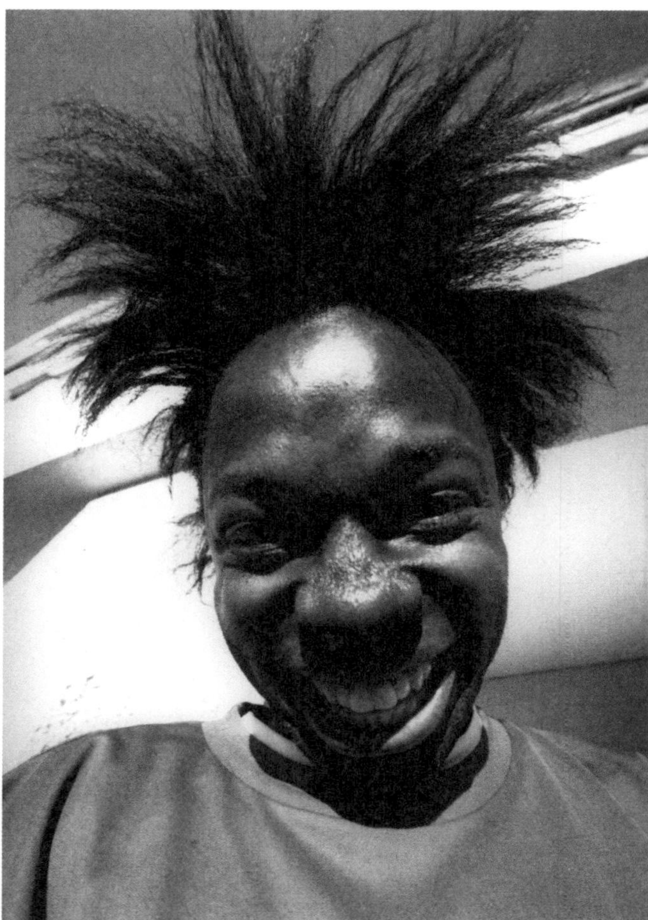

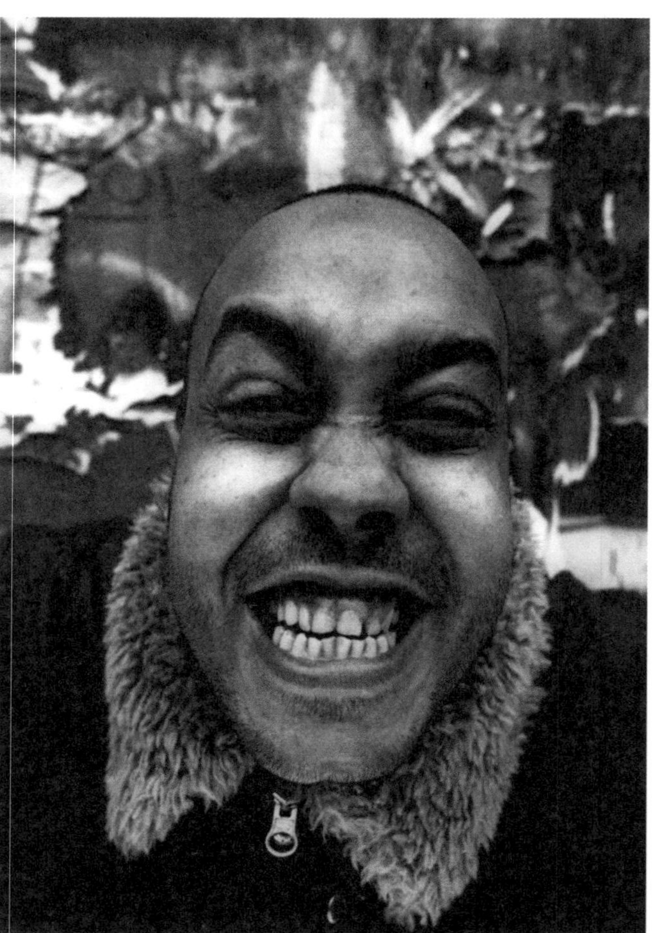

(top) Bélé, Les Bosquets, Montfermeil, 2006
(bottom) Gered, Les Bosquets, Montfermeil, 2006

(top) Ladj Ly, Les Bosquets, Montfermeil, 2006
(bottom) La Tchatch, Les Bosquets, Montfermeil, 2006
(right) Byron, La Forestière, Clichy-sous-Bois, 2006

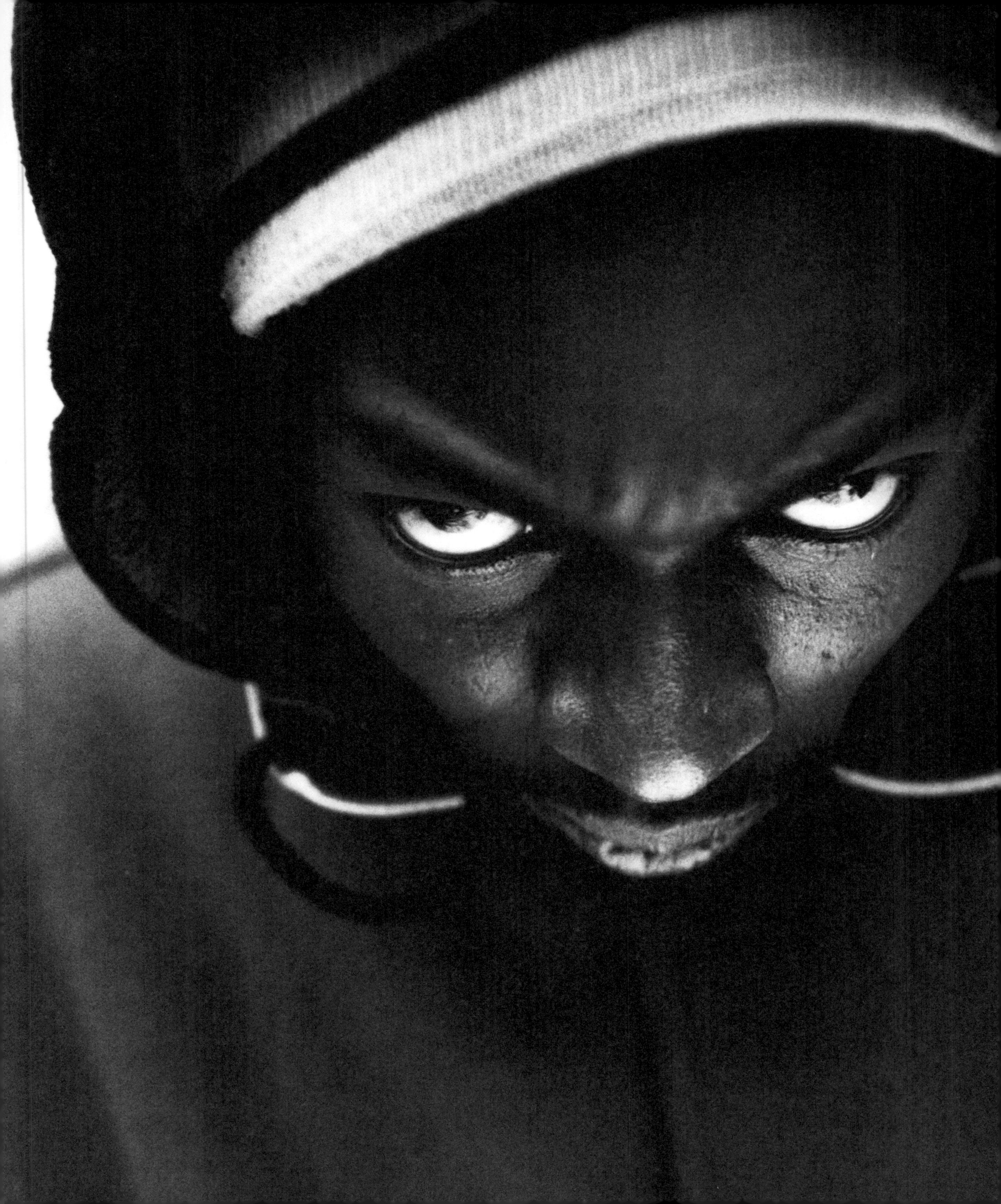

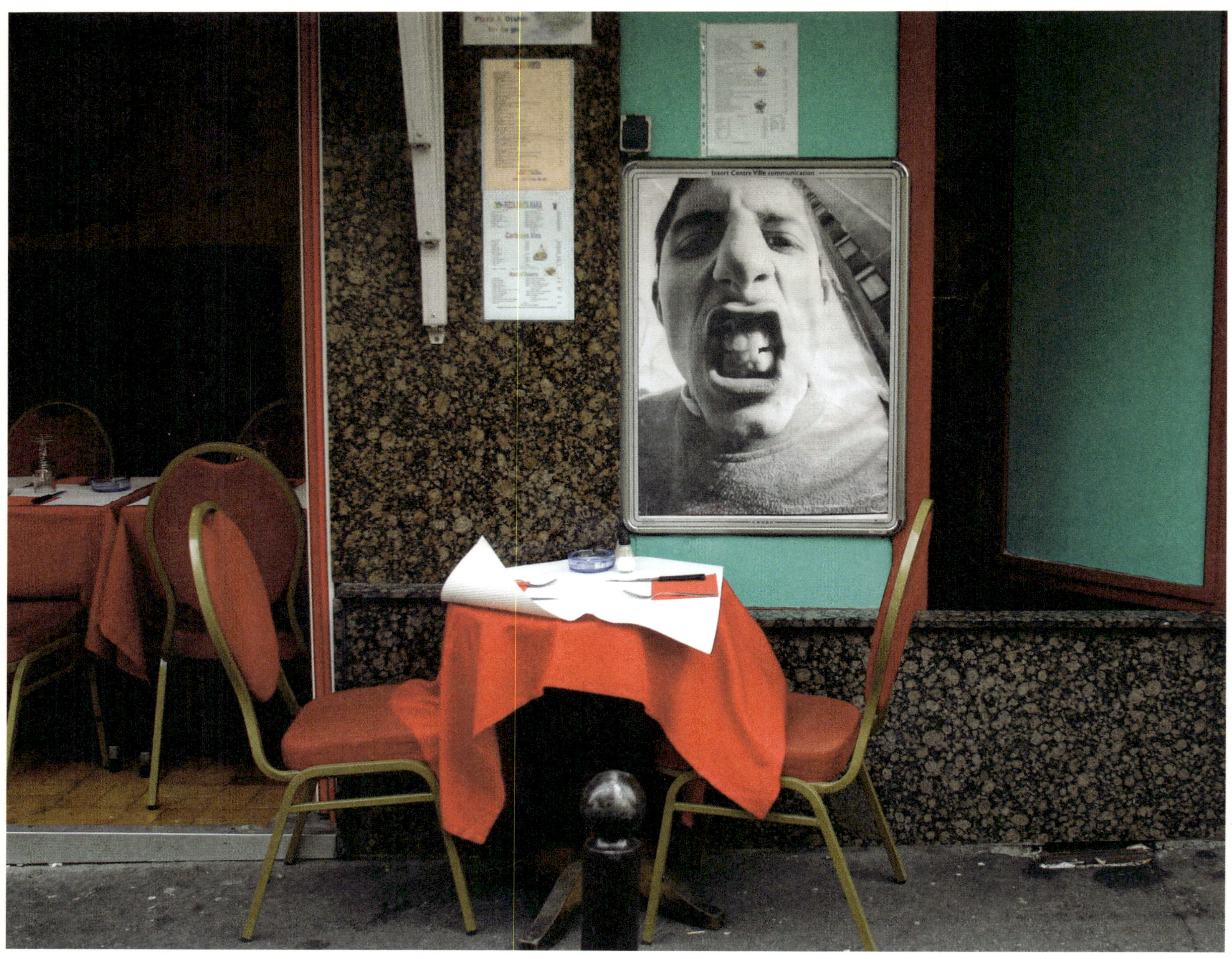

Christoph, Ex-La Forestière, Clichy-sous-Bois, 2006
Pasting in the 17th arrondissement, Paris, 2006

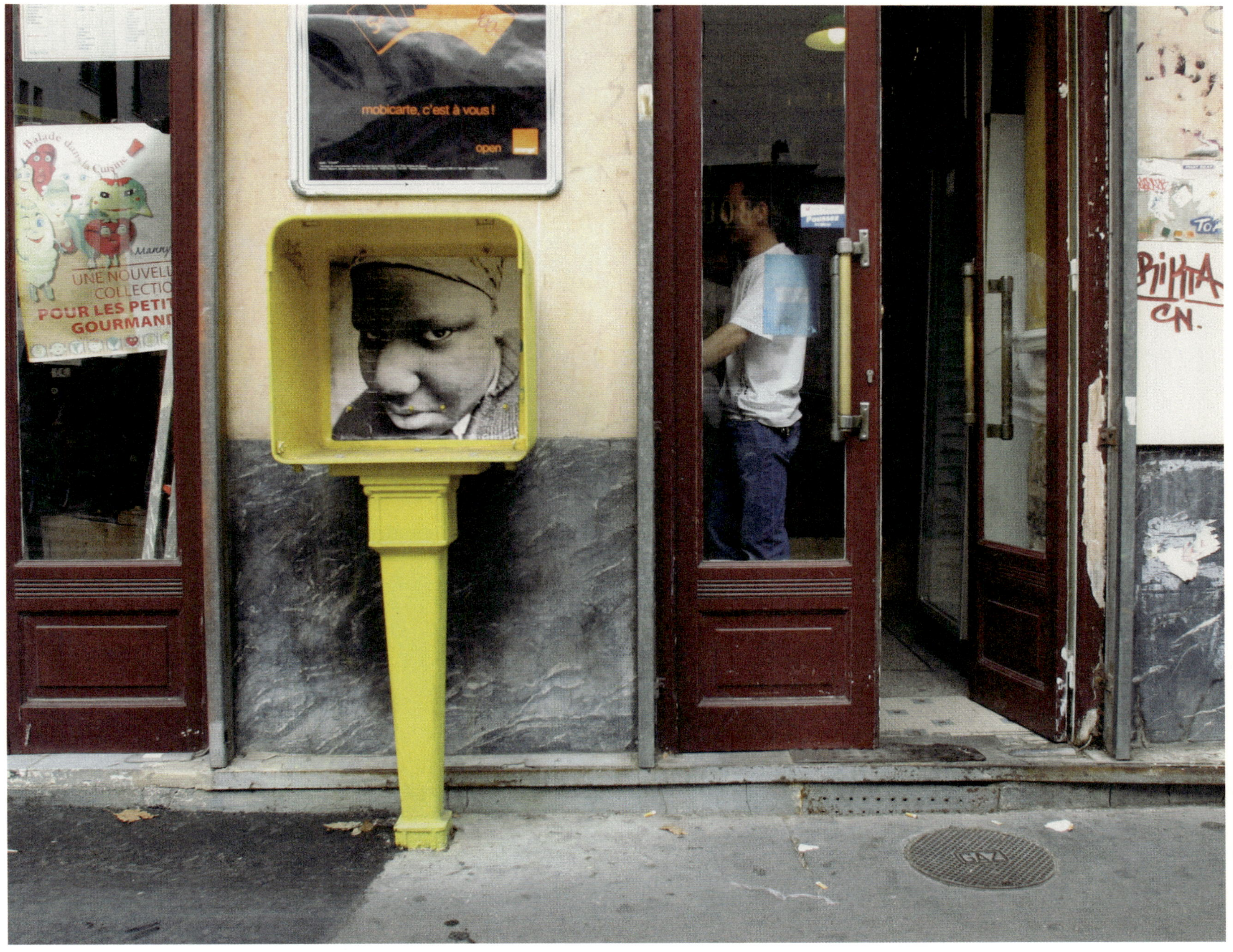

Araba, La Forestière, Clichy-sous-Bois, 2006
Pasting in the 11th arrondissement, Paris, 2006

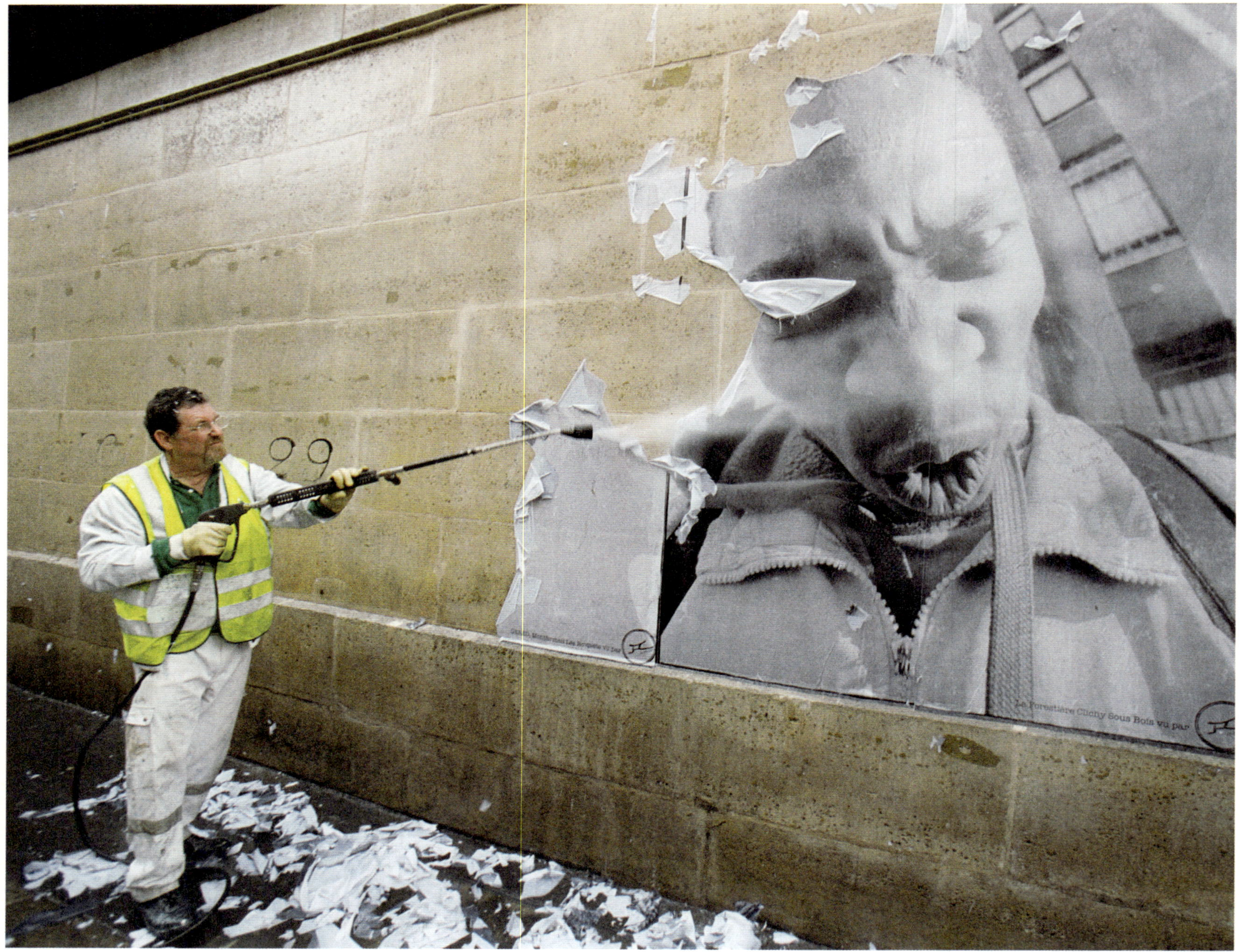

Deinstallation of JR's outdoor exhibition on the walls of the Blancs Manteaux Space, Paris, 2006

'I had to wake up very early every morning of the week to photograph the employees of the city cleaning the walls, because I didn't know which day and at what time they would come. A few months earlier, in the projects of La Courneuve, the Interior Minister had suggested cleaning out the *banlieues* with a Kärcher (a well-known brand of high-pressure water cleaner). At that time, this image took on a completely different meaning. In less than an hour all the portraits had disappeared.' – JR

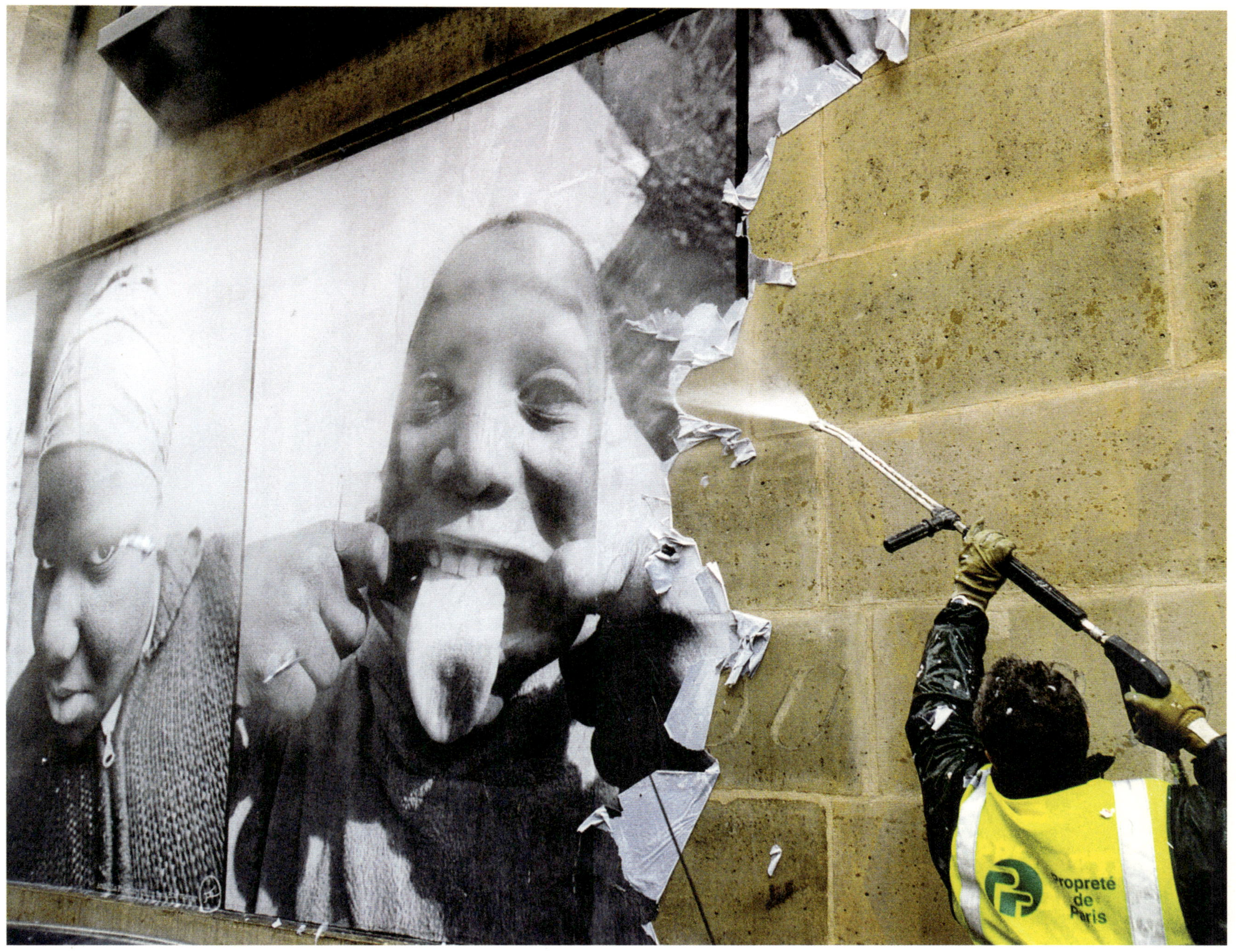

Deinstallation of JR's outdoor exhibition on the walls of the Blancs Manteaux Space, Paris, 2006

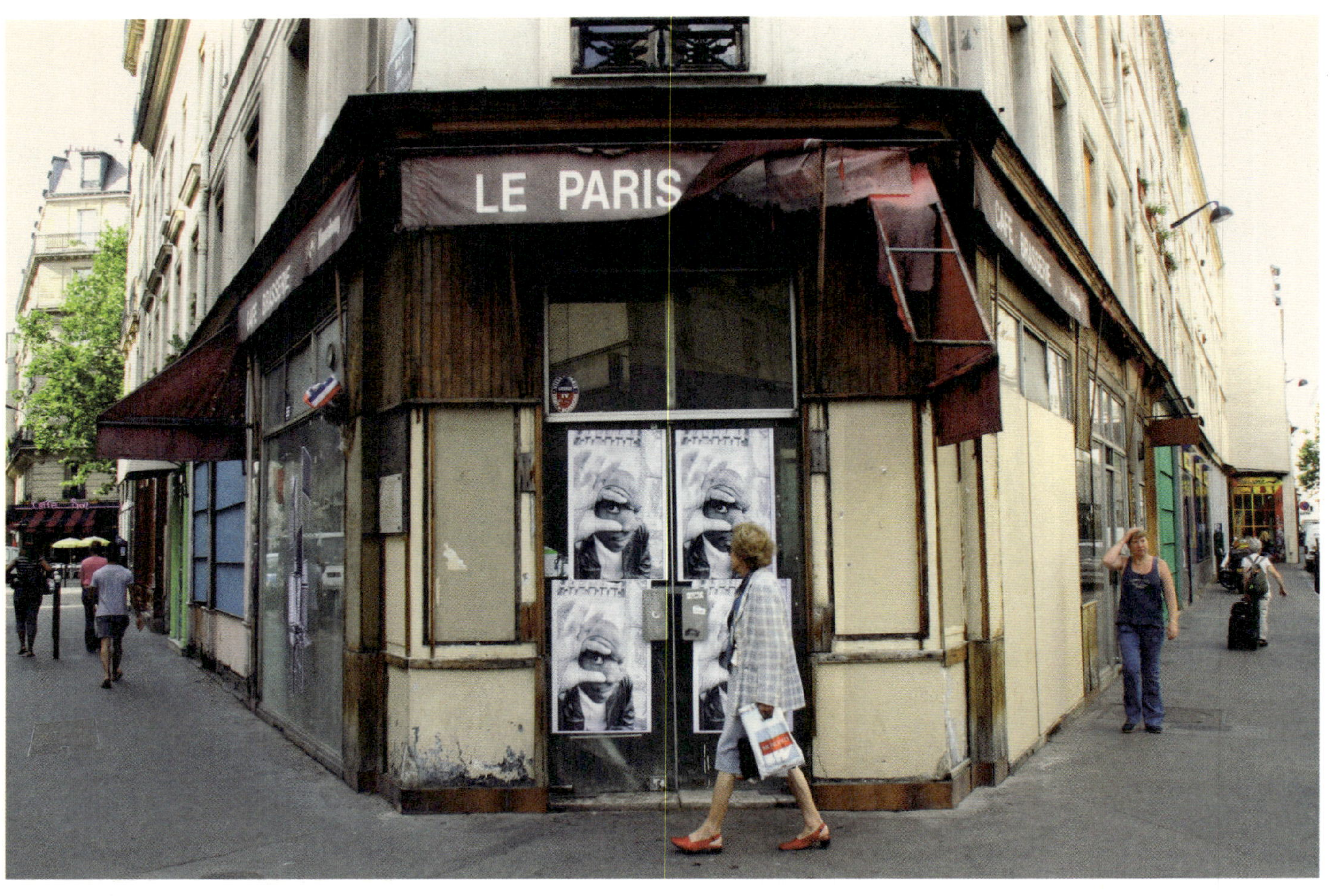

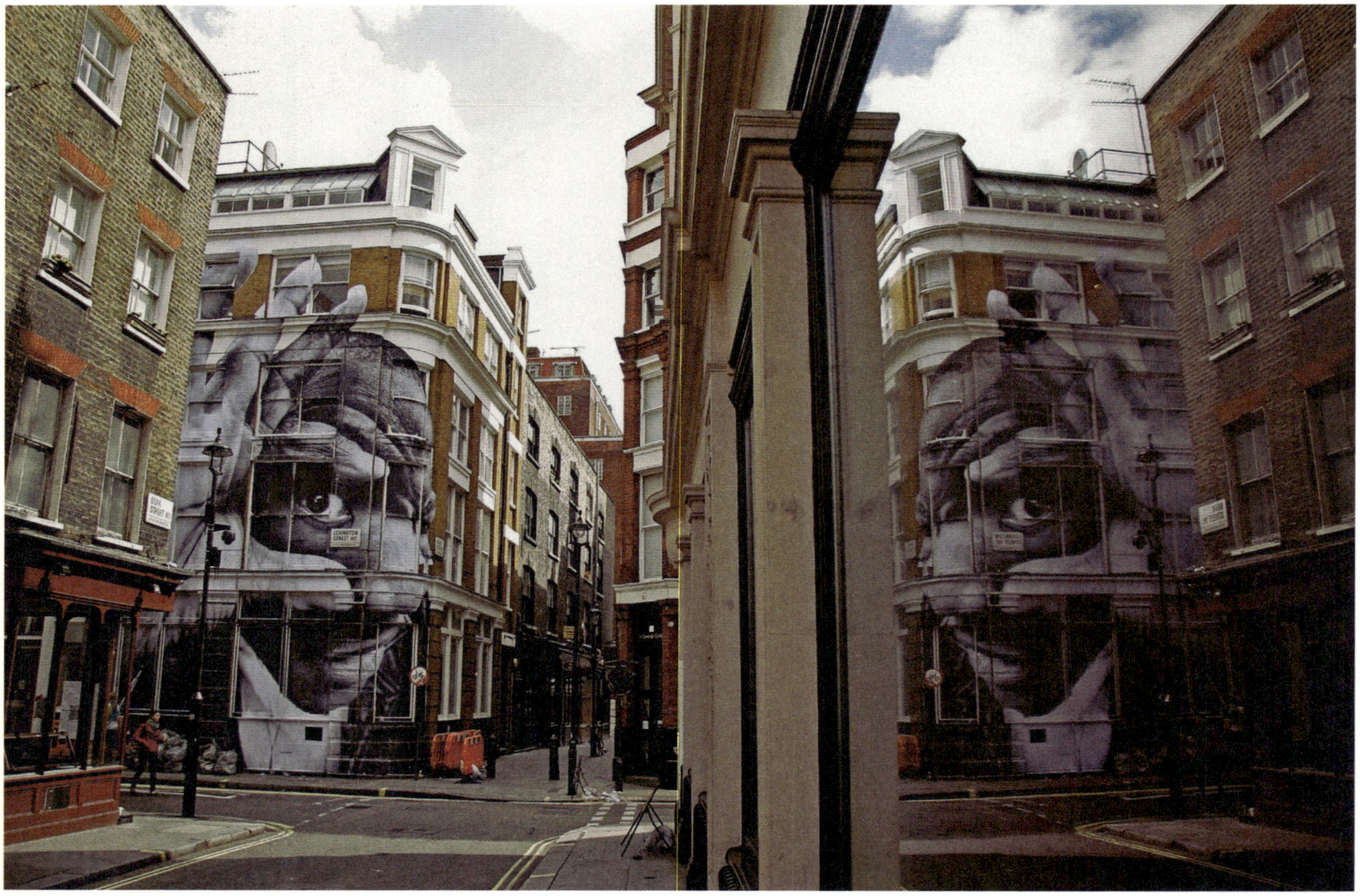

Lil Pimp, Les Bosquets, Montfermeil, 2006
(top) Pasted in the 4th arrondissement, Paris, 2006
(bottom) Lexington Street, London, 2008

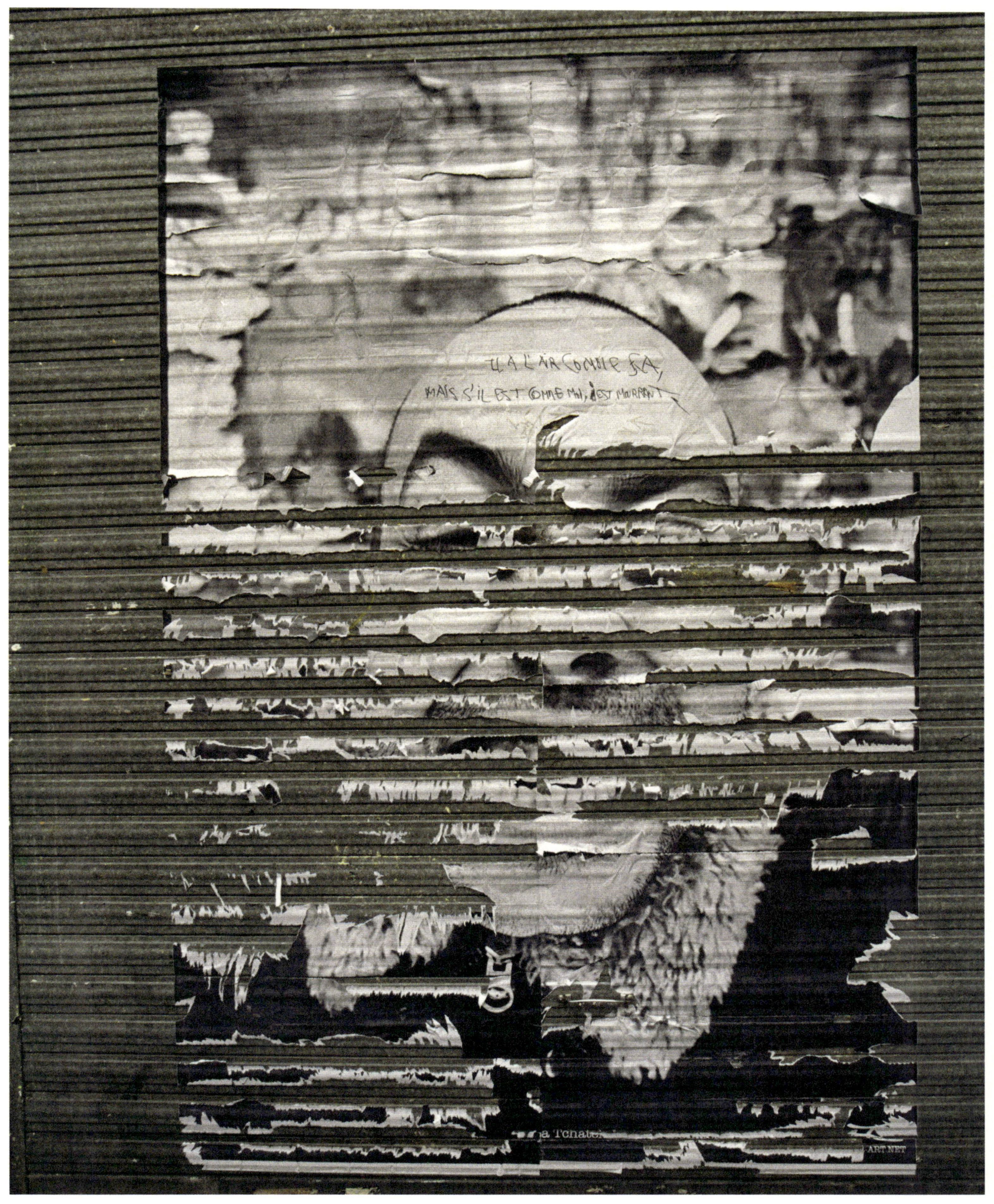

La Tchatch, Les Bosquets, Montfermeil, 2006
Pasted in the 11th arrondissement, Paris, 2006

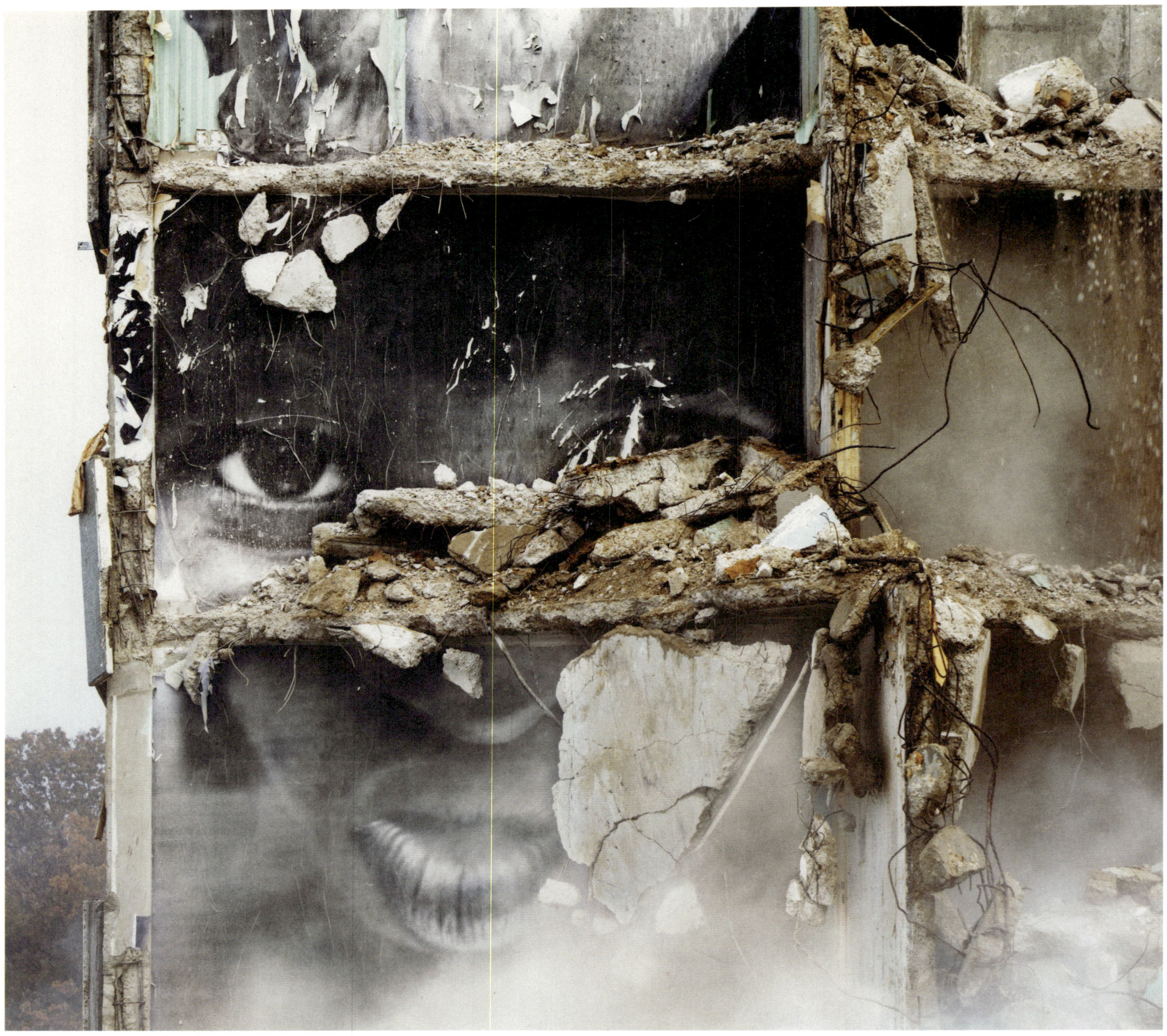

(above) *B11, Destruction #8*,
Les Bosquets, Montfermeil, 2013
(right) *B11, Destruction #2*, Les Bosquets,
Montfermeil, 2013
(overleaf) *B11, Destruction #4*, Les Bosquets,
Montfermeil, 2013

'These were the buildings in Les Bosquets where we did the first *Portrait of a Generation* actions. We heard that they were going to be demolished but we couldn't get authorization to paste inside. So we got plans from the former inhabitants, and we entered at night, twenty-five of us, and spread out over all the different floors. We pasted eyes in someone's kitchen, a nose in someone else's bathroom, and a mouth in a living room... When we came down, the police arrested us but they couldn't understand why we had just spent hours in this building that was about to be destroyed. The pastings were so big that they couldn't see what they were. The next day, when workers started the demolition, the portraits were revealed, little by little, while the cranes were "eating" the building. Only the people that were in the neighbourhood that day witnessed the gigantic spectacle unfold.' – JR

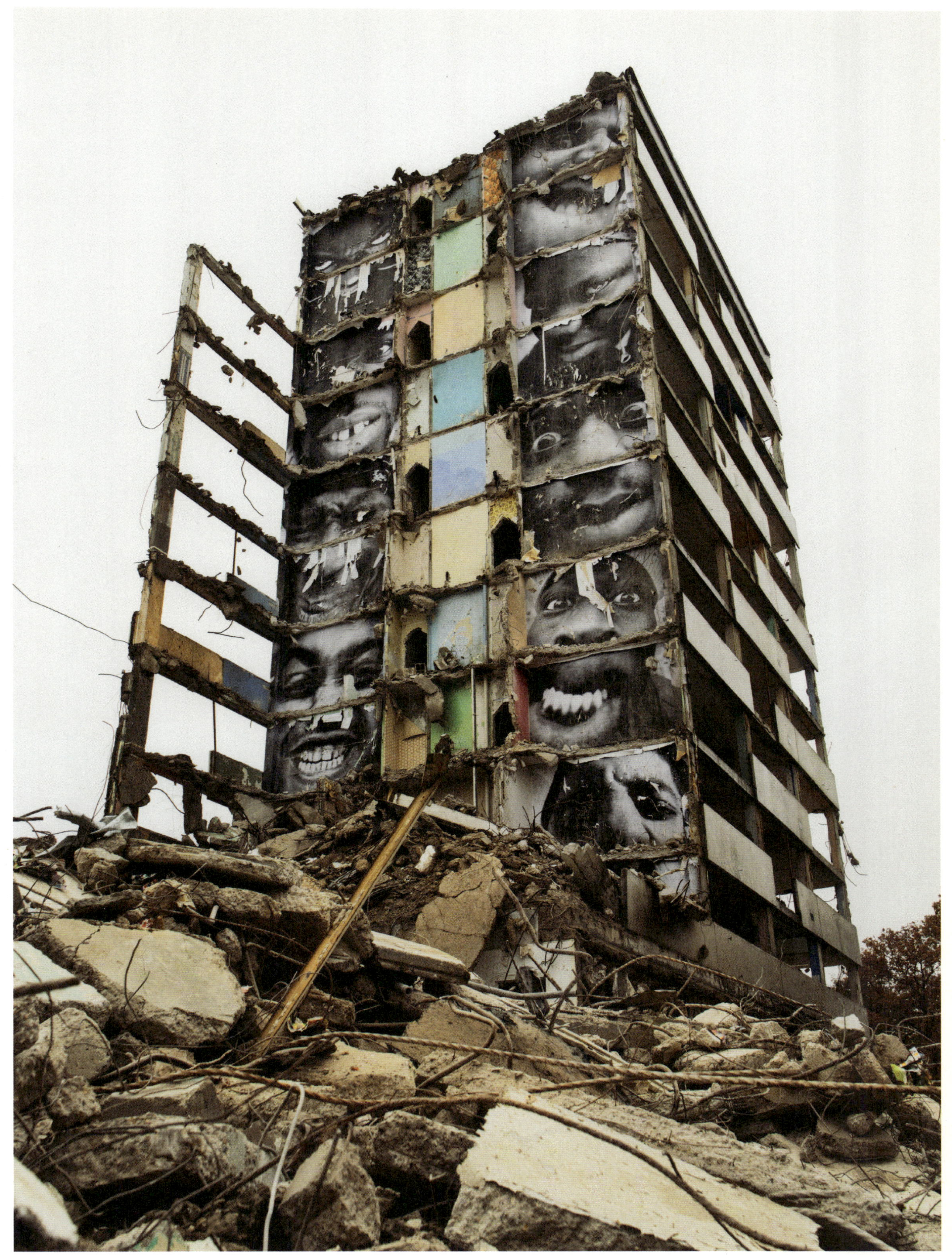

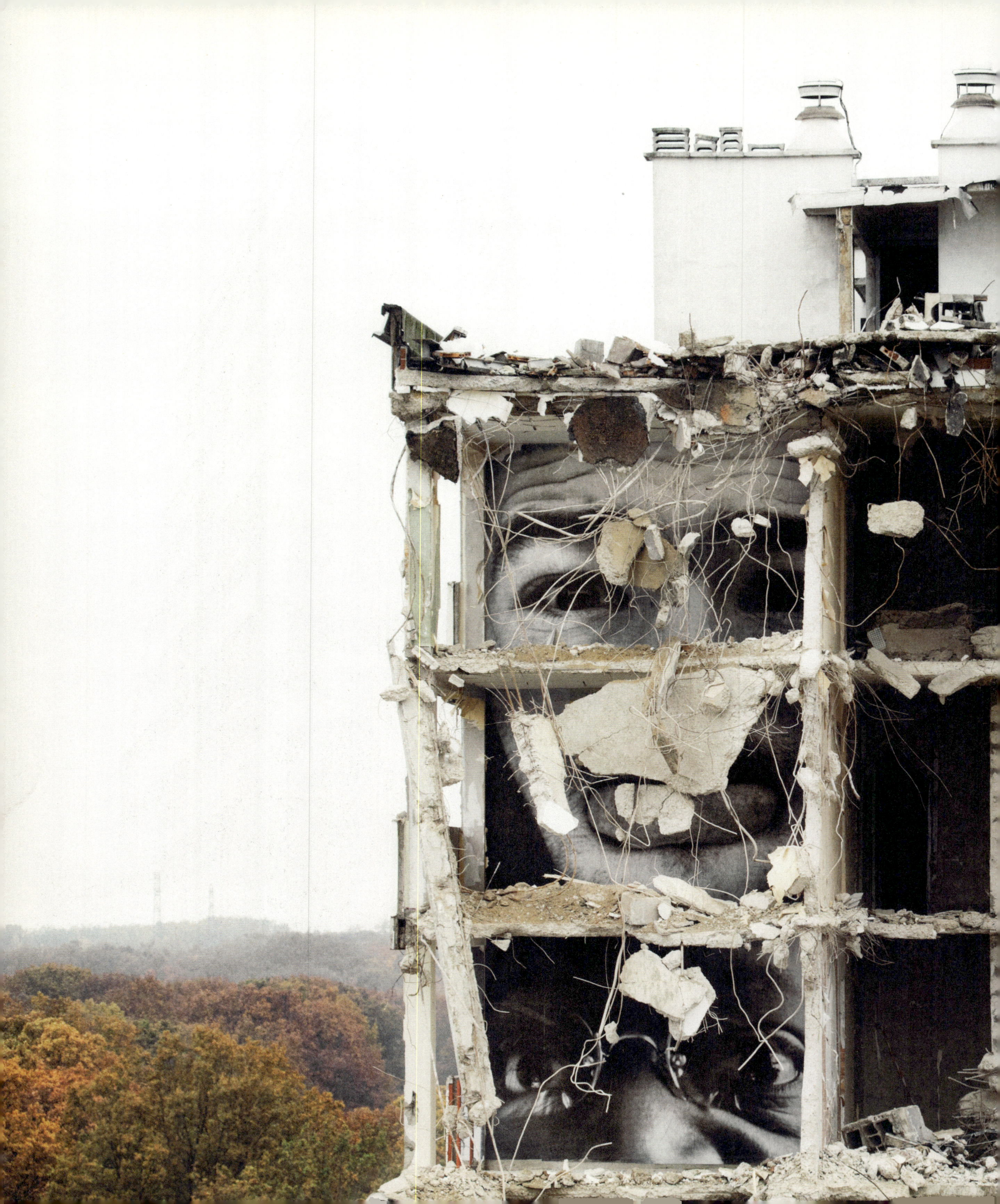

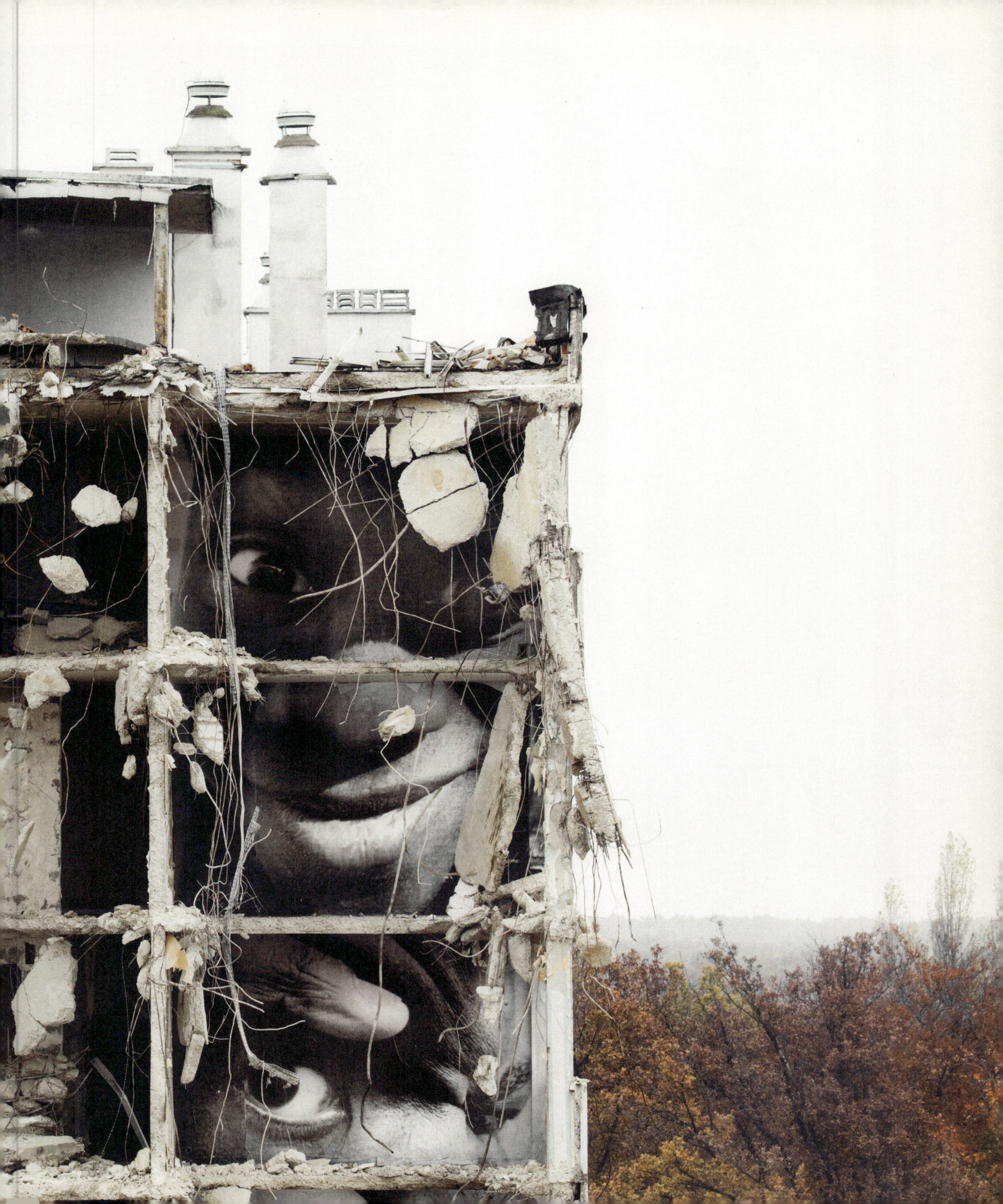

FACEF

2

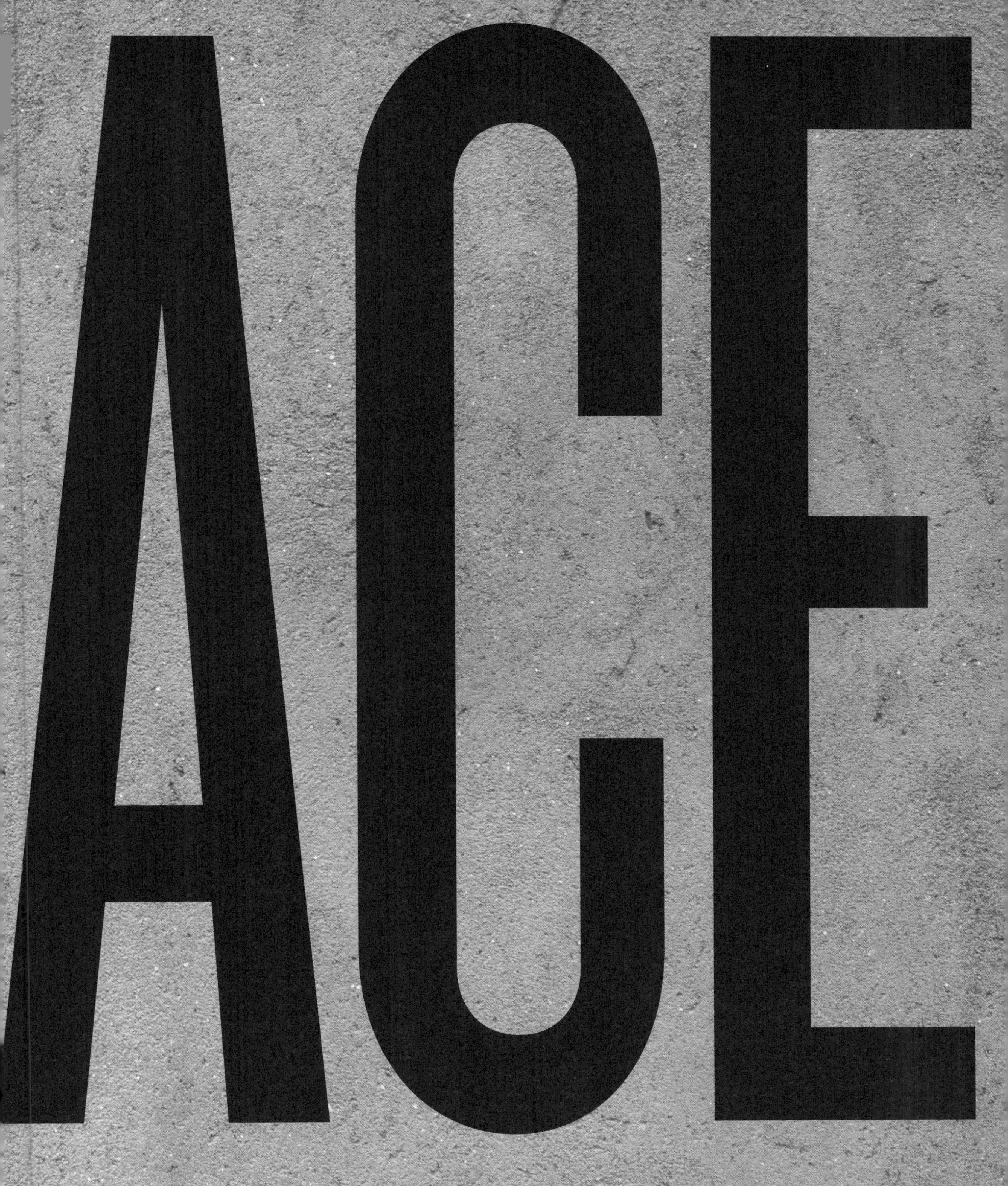
ACE

In 2005, JR and his friend Marco went to the Middle East to explore the reasons behind the Israeli–Palestinian conflict and investigate the everyday tensions between the two communities living side by side.

They travelled through both Israel and the West Bank and were fascinated by this tiny area of land where you can see mountains, sea, deserts and lakes, love and hate, hope and despair next to one another in a place that is holy for Judaism, Christianity and Islam. The two artists were struck by how difficult it was to tell the people apart; often it seemed like Israelis and Palestinians were twin brothers raised in different families. The artists decided to confront this head on by putting portraits face to face.

As a result, in 2007, JR and Marco organized the largest illegal photography exhibition ever. They took portraits of Palestinians and Israelis with the same profession, and pasted them next to each other, in monumental formats, in unavoidable locations in both Israeli and Palestinian cities and on either side of the Separation Wall. Men and women, religious and secular, soldiers and policemen, farmers and professors – all agreed to pose, to participate, or to lend their walls, although sometimes only after tense discussions.

JR and Marco wanted everyone to laugh, for once, and to invite dialogue by seeing portraits of the 'other' side by side. Passers-by were invited to guess who was the Israeli and who was the Palestinian – often they could not tell them apart. By participating, everyone was showing support to a two-state solution in which Israel and Palestine could live peacefully within safe and internationally recognized borders. The project showed that what we call 'possible' can change; this artistic action, which experts had thought impossible, proved that limits can move.

The portraits were later exhibited in huge formats all over the world, from Geneva to the Rencontres d'Arles and the Venice Biennale. A film entitled *Faces* was broadcast on Israeli and Arab television, and received several awards including, among others, from the International Muslim Film Festival and the UK Jewish Film festival.

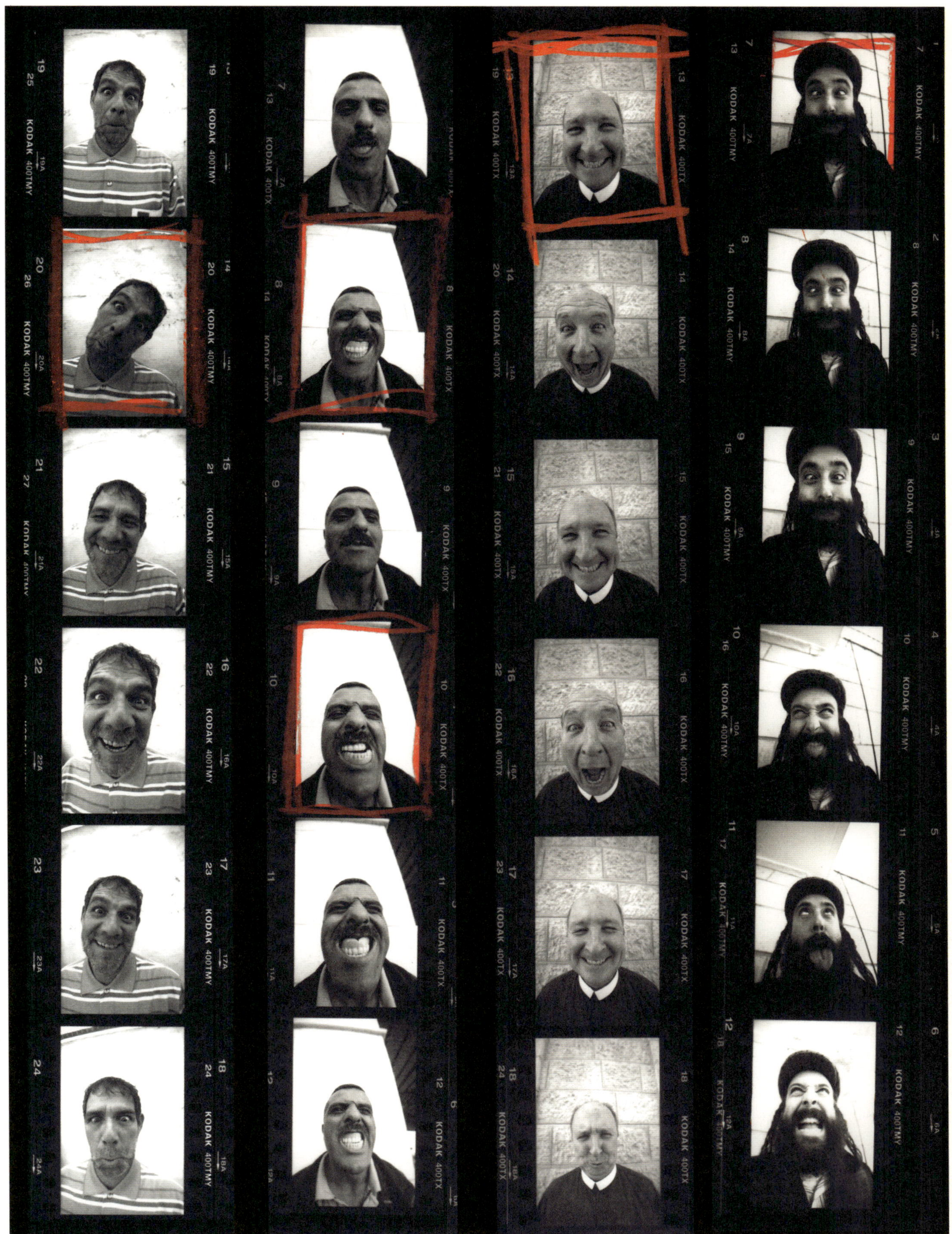

Face 2 Face contact sheet, 2007

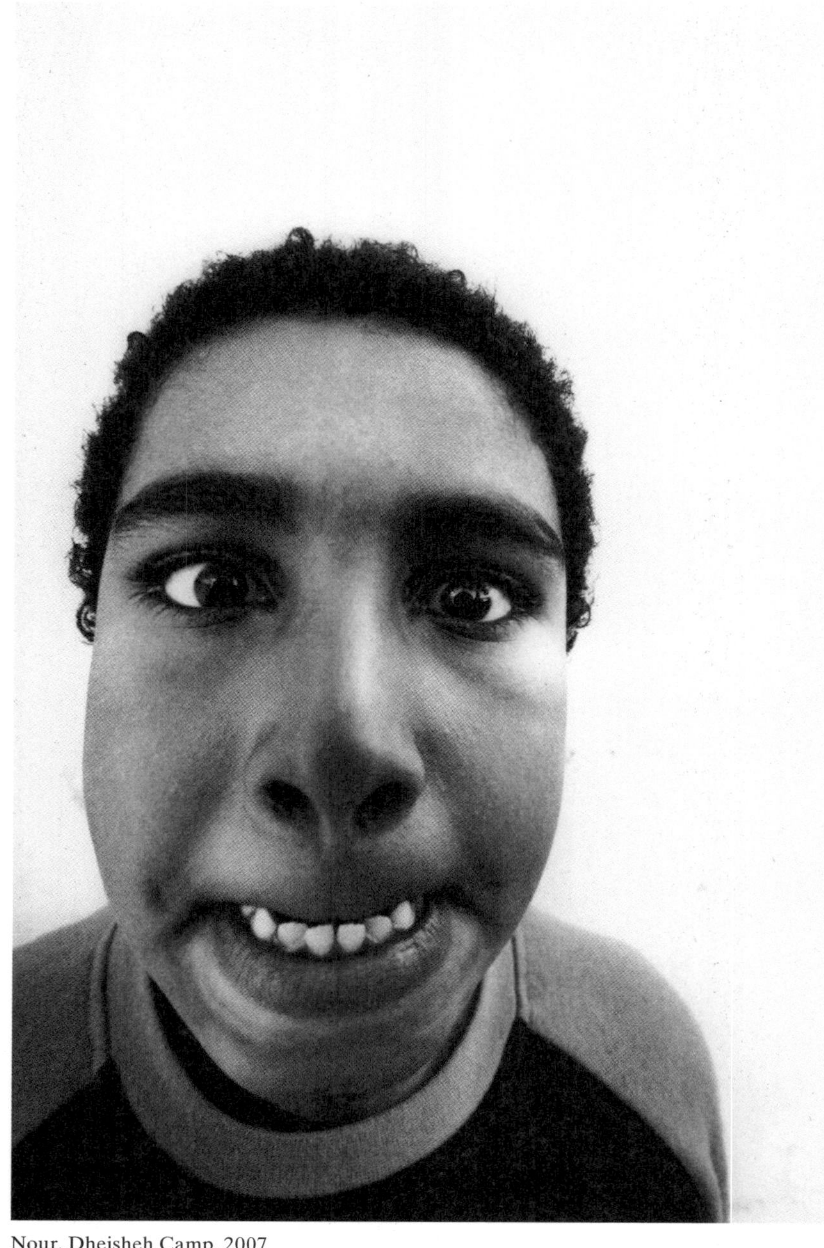

Nour, Dheisheh Camp, 2007

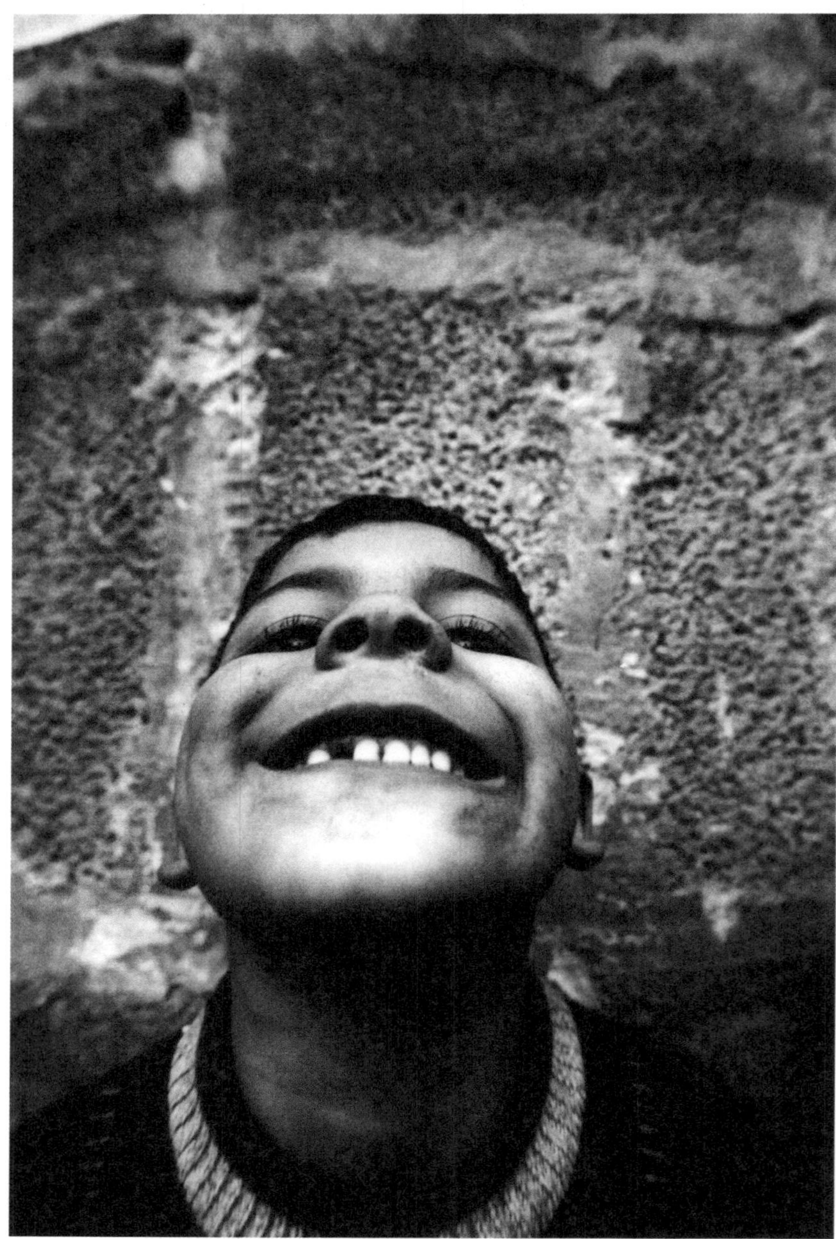

Edo, Jerusalem, 2007

SCHOOL KIDS

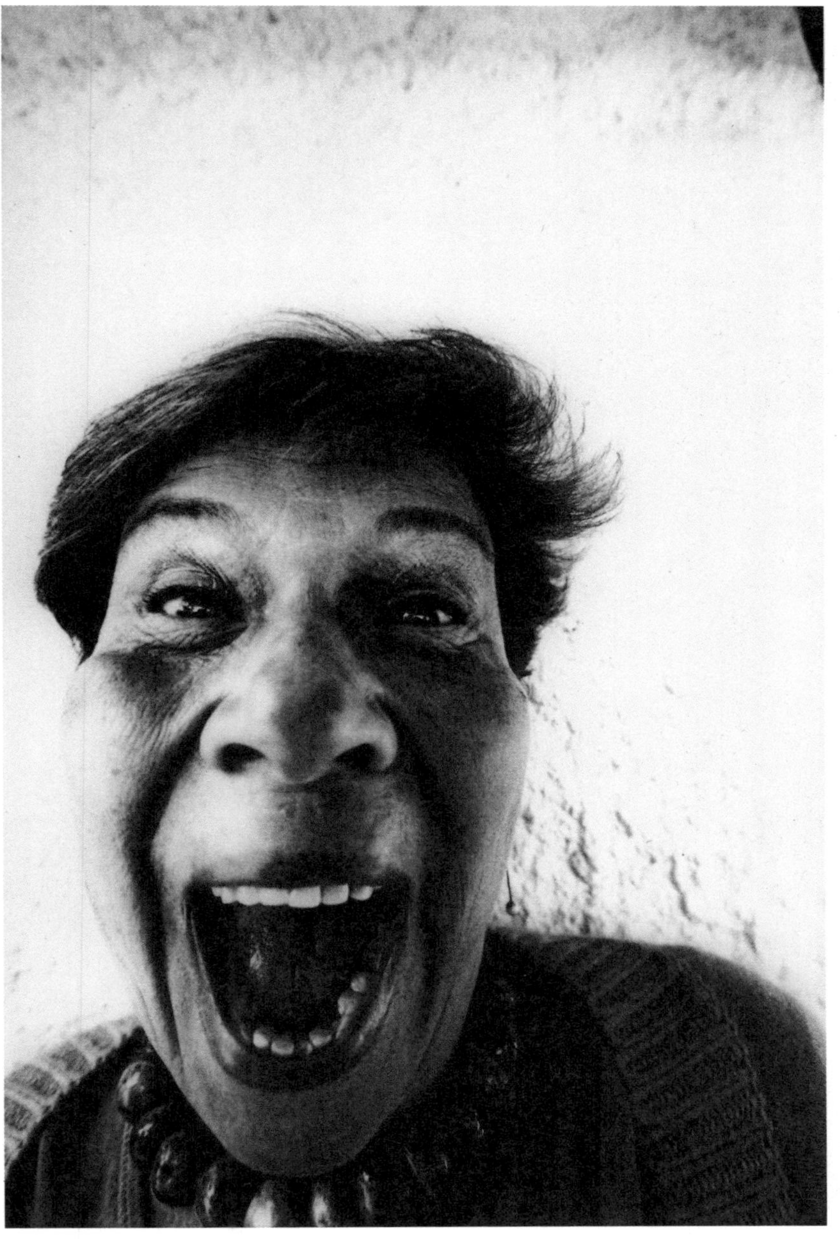

Drora, Kfar Sava, 2007

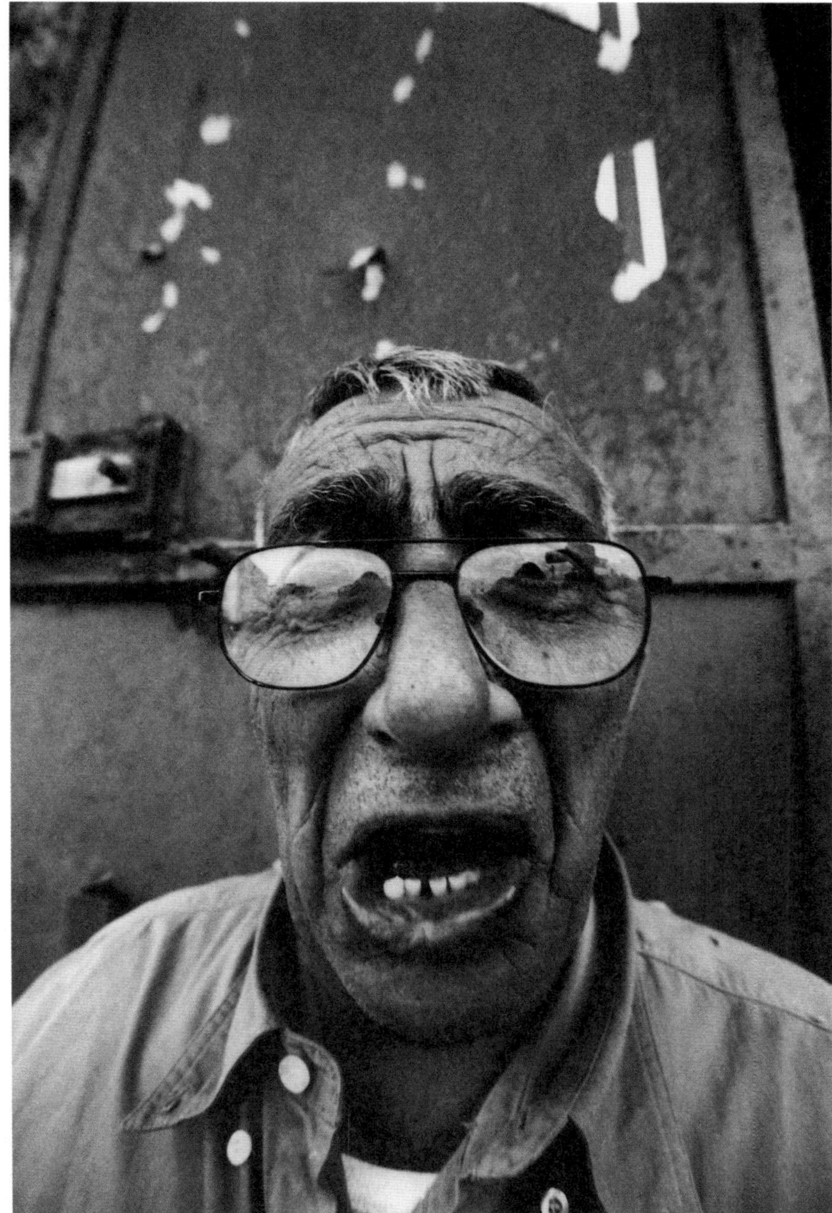

Anton, Bethlehem, 2007

SCULPTORS

Sculptors, Market in Ramallah, West Bank, 2007

'I asked this grocer in Ramallah if we could paste on his wall. Our guide had told us "here, you can do anything but paste over the face of a martyr". There were still bits of posters of martyrs and political posters on the wall so I told him I didn't want to interfere with any political message. He took my arm and told me "you asked for the wall, now you do it". The crowd was curious about the faces, and a discussion started.' – JR

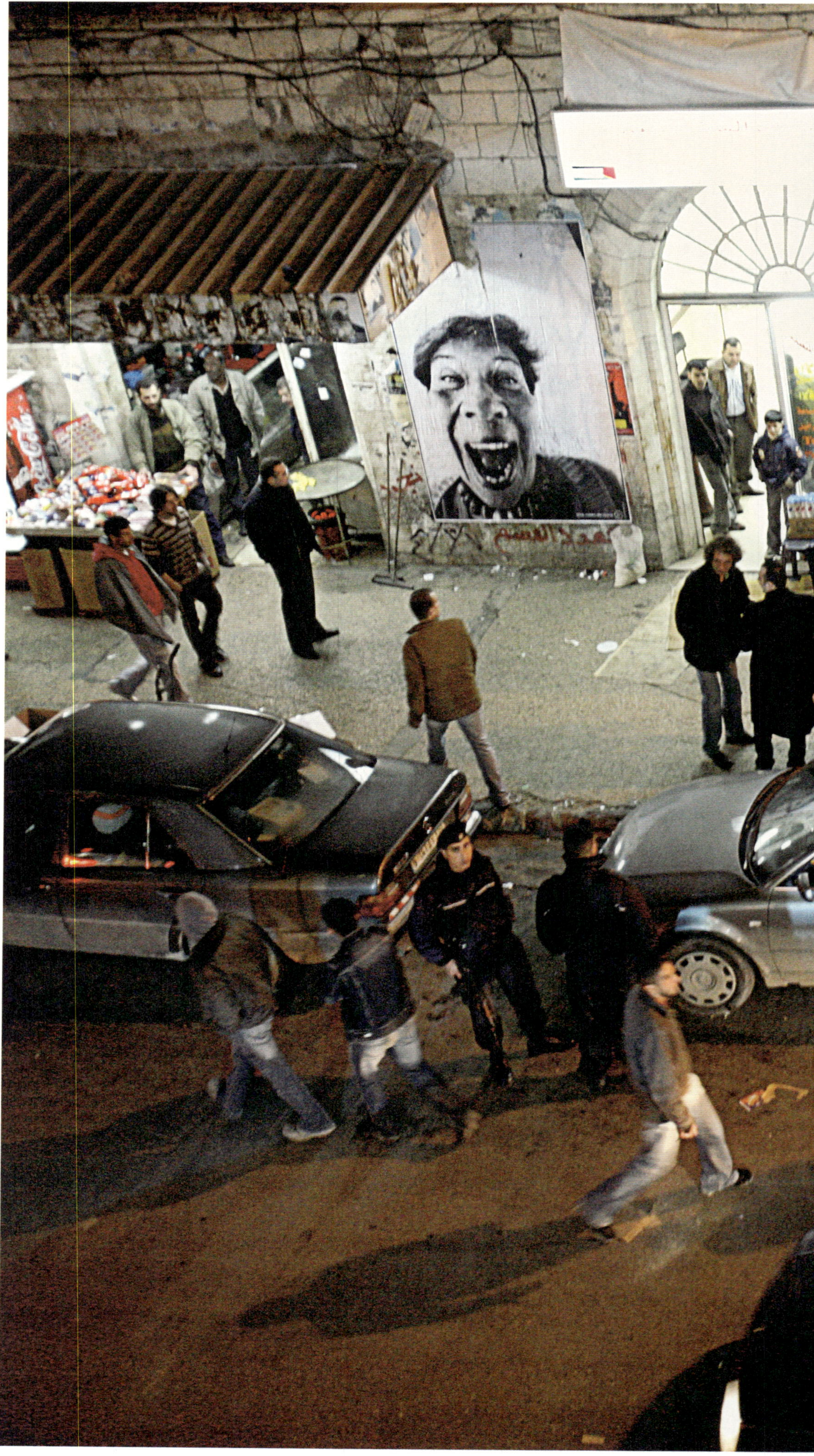

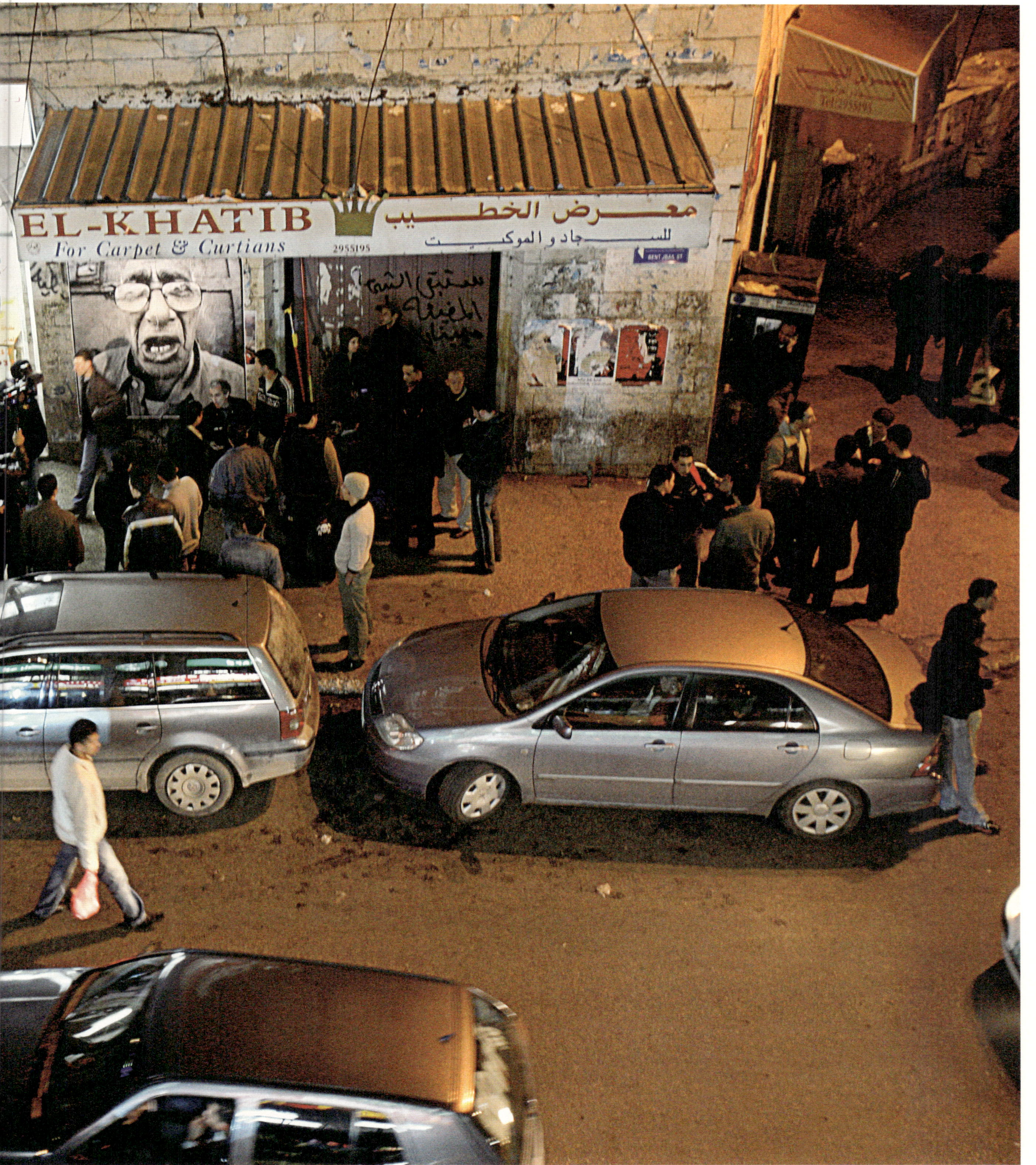
EL-KHATIB
For Carpet & Curtians
2955195
معرض الخطيب
للسجاد و الموكيت

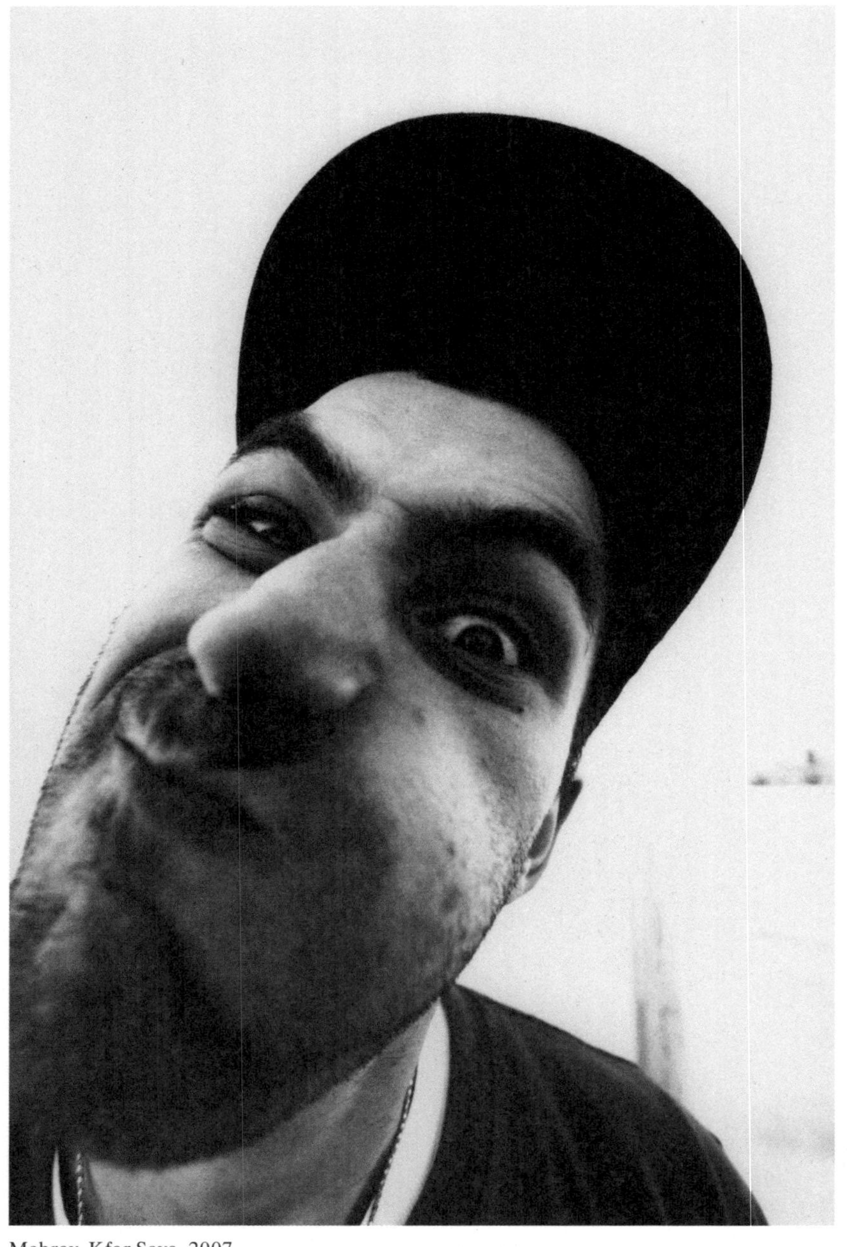

Mehrav, Kfar Sava, 2007

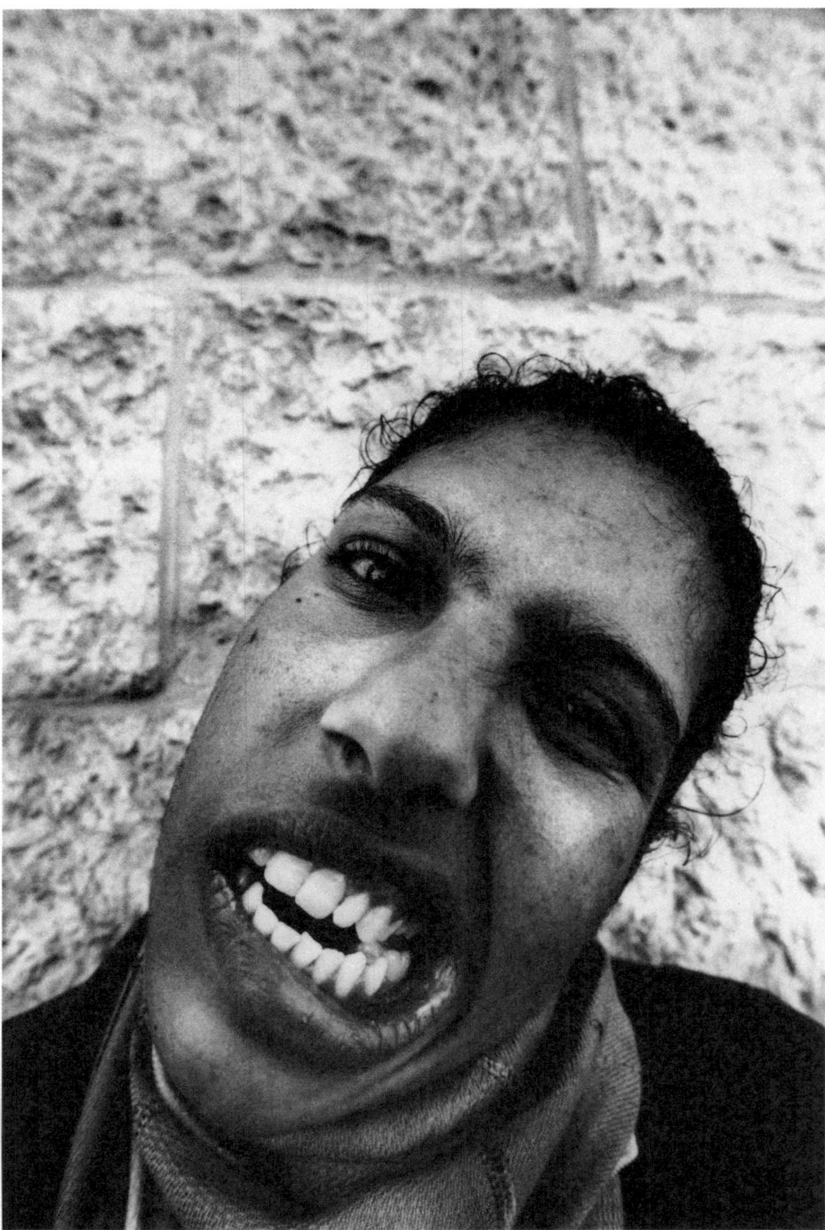

Areej, Dheisheh Camp, 2007

ATHLETES

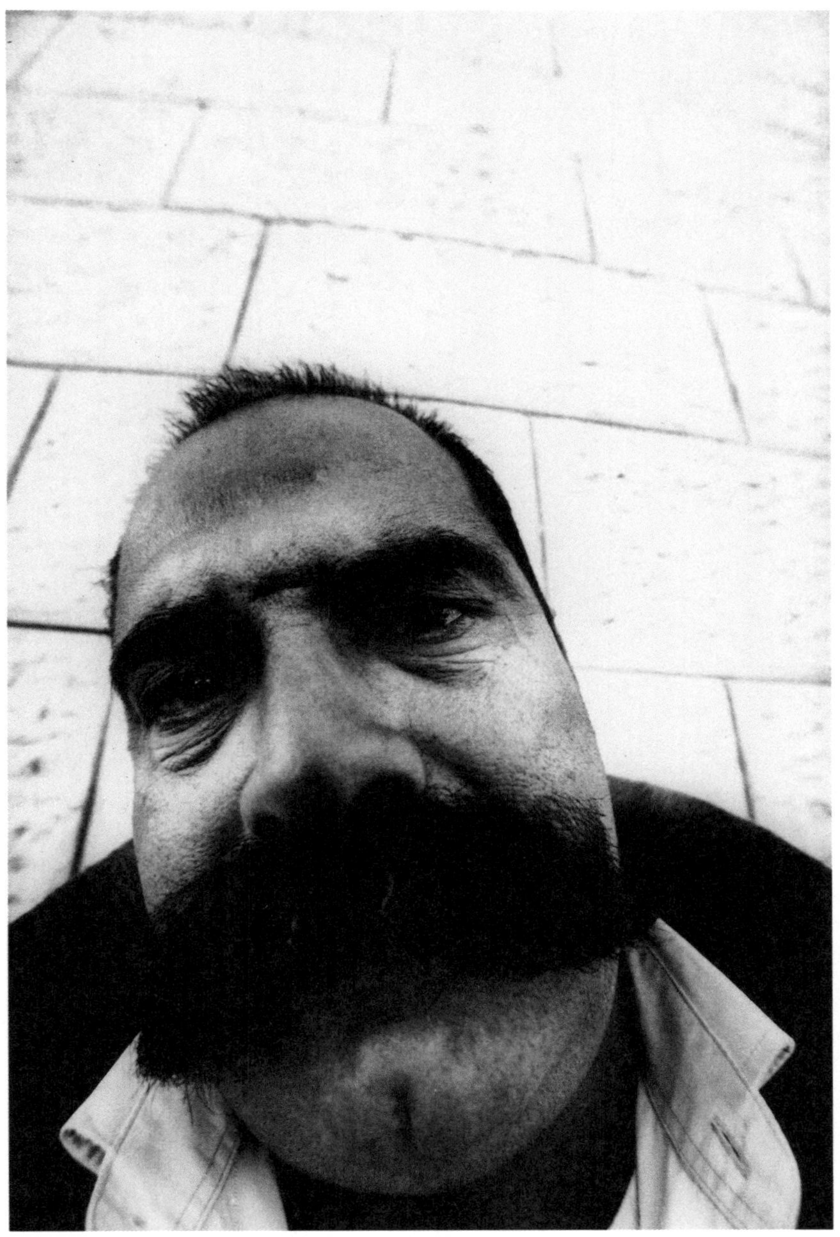
Khader, Bethlehem, 2007

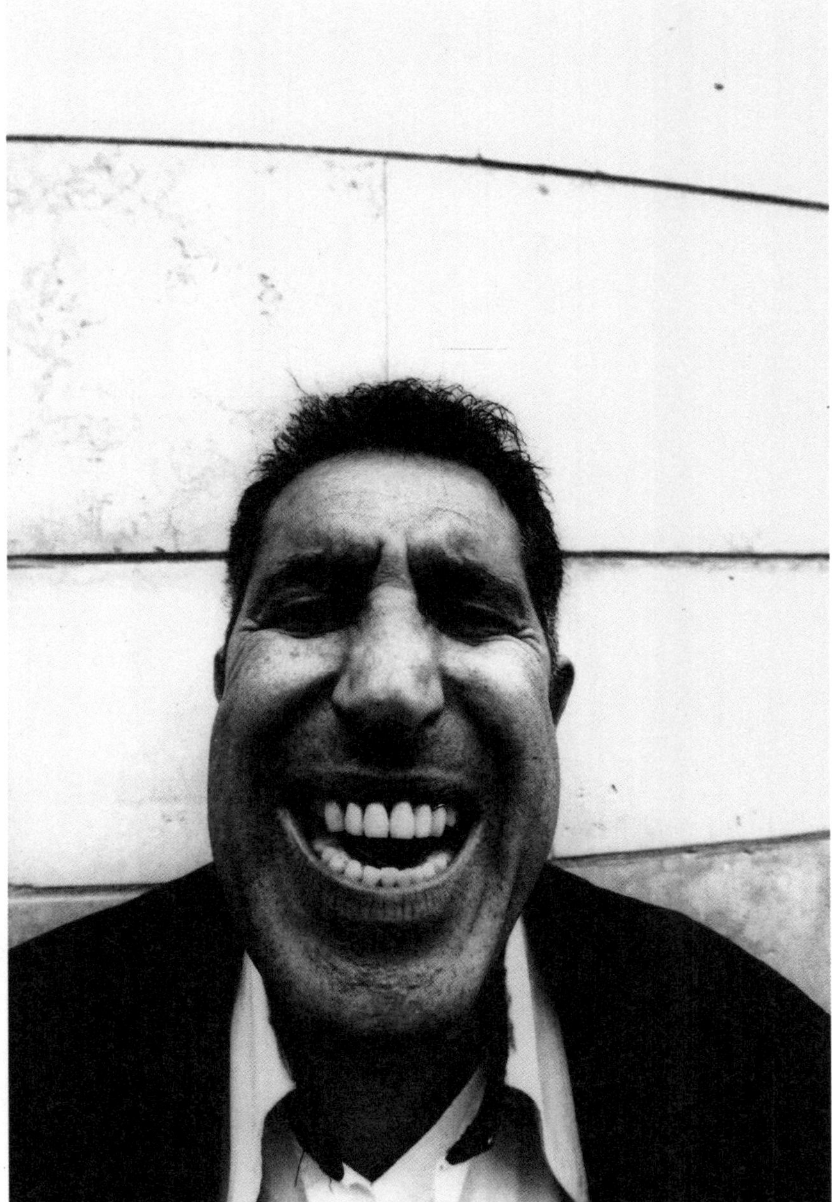
Albert, Haifa, 2007

SECURITY GUARDS

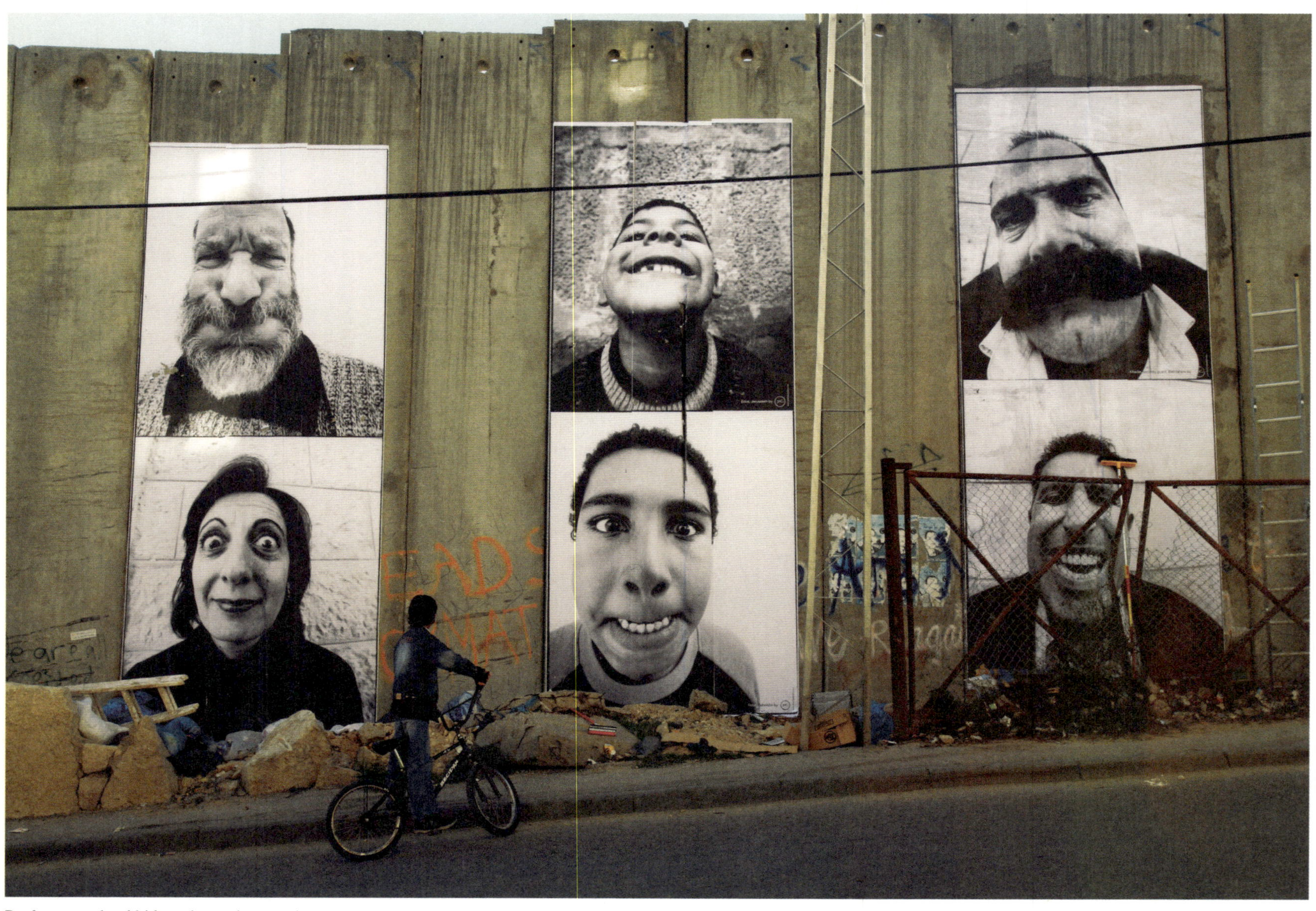

Professors, school kids and security guards,
Separation Wall, Palestinian side, 2006

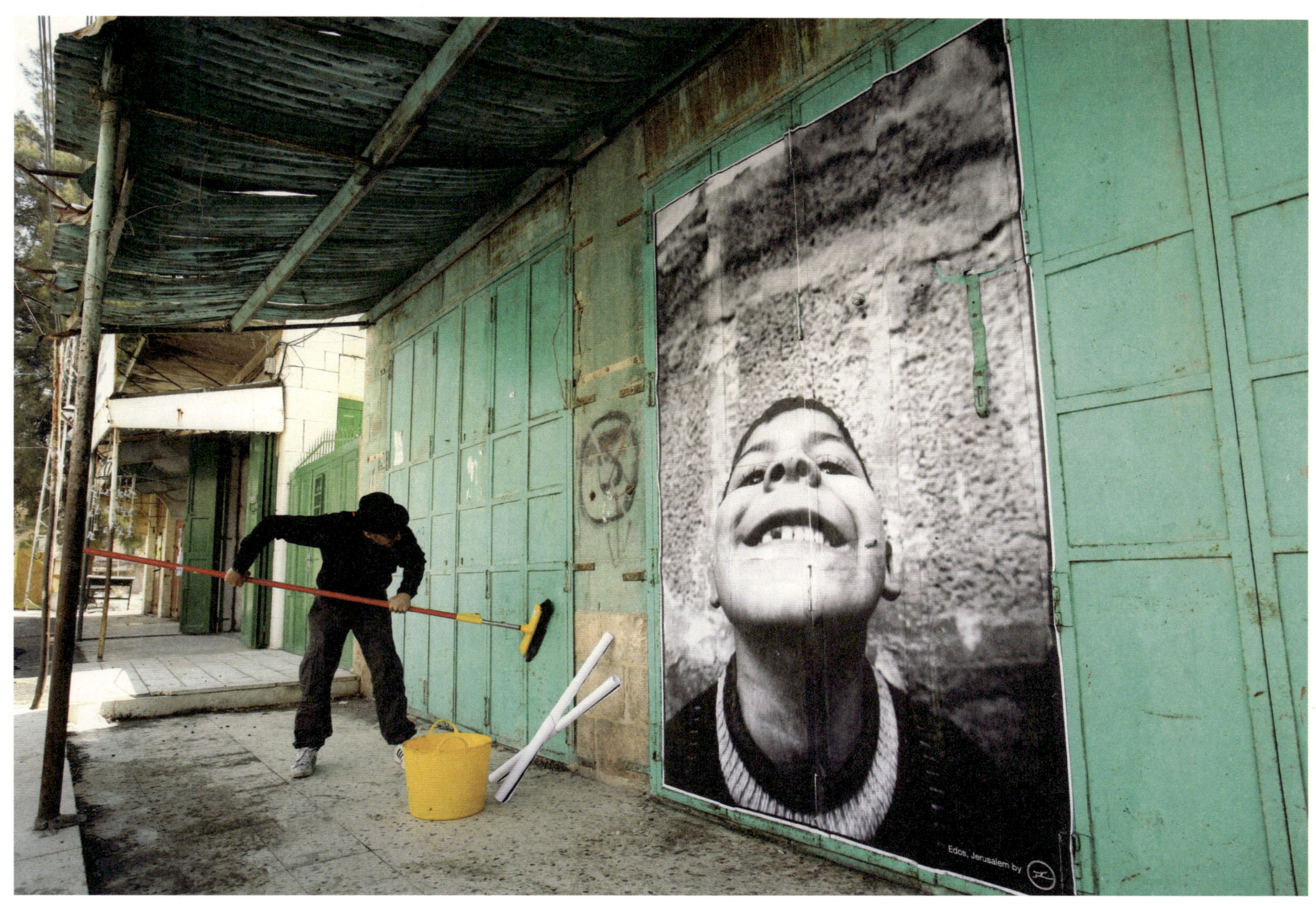

School kids, Dheisheh Camp, 2007

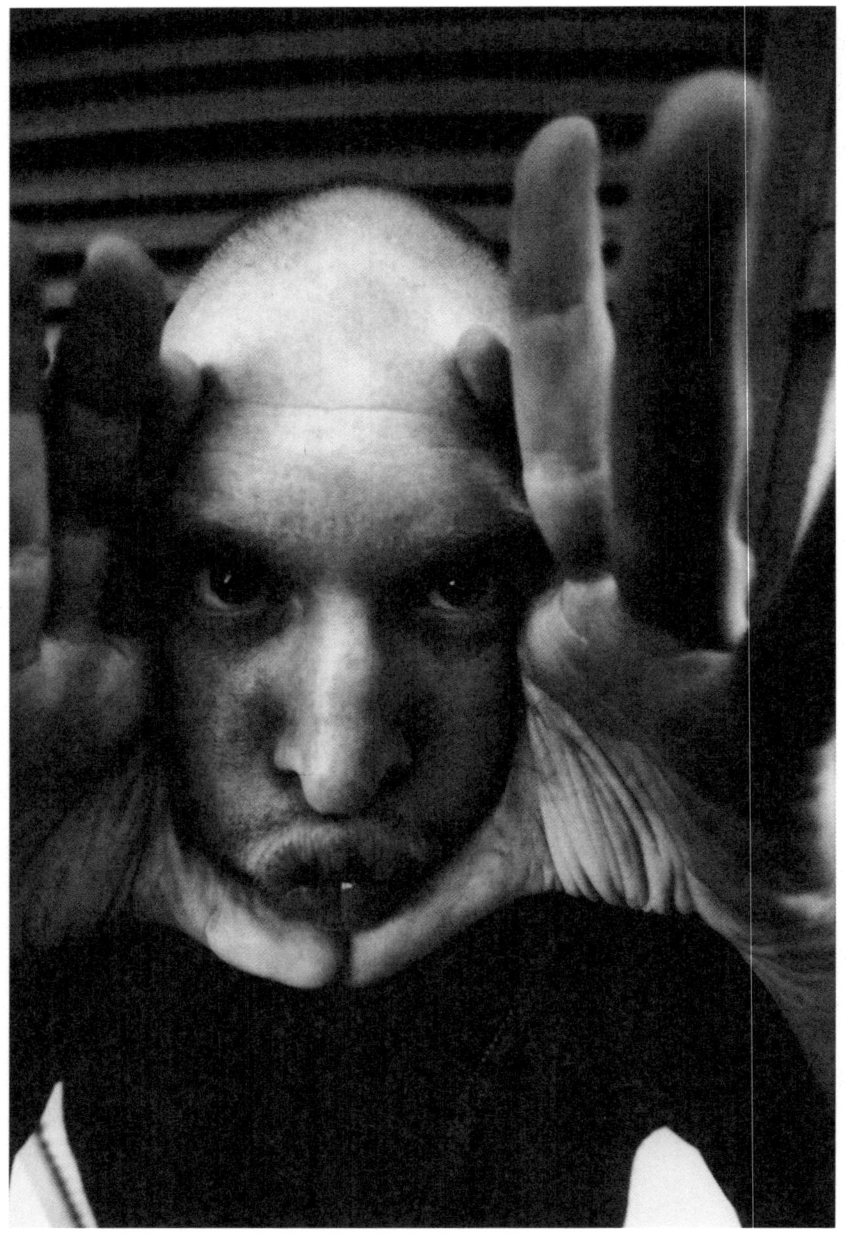
Ronen, Tel Aviv, 2007

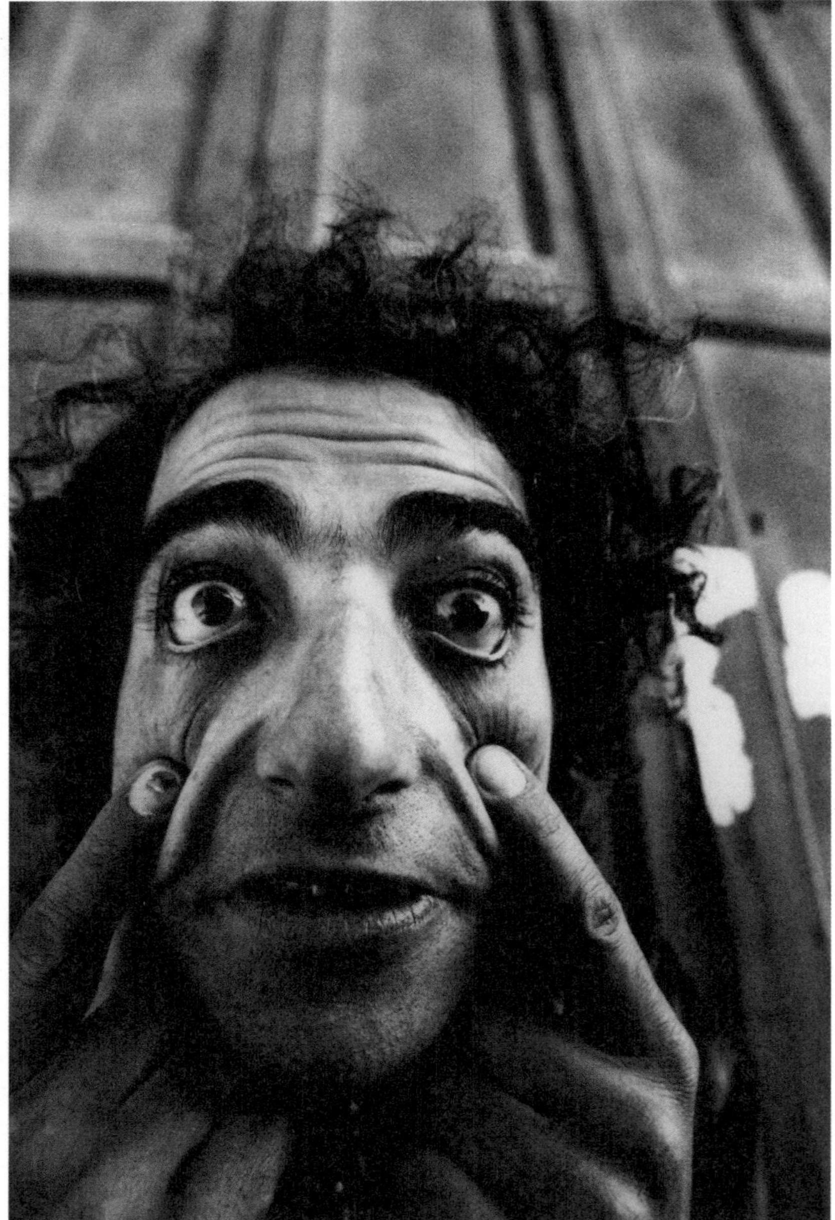
Ayman, Bethlehem, 2007

ACTORS

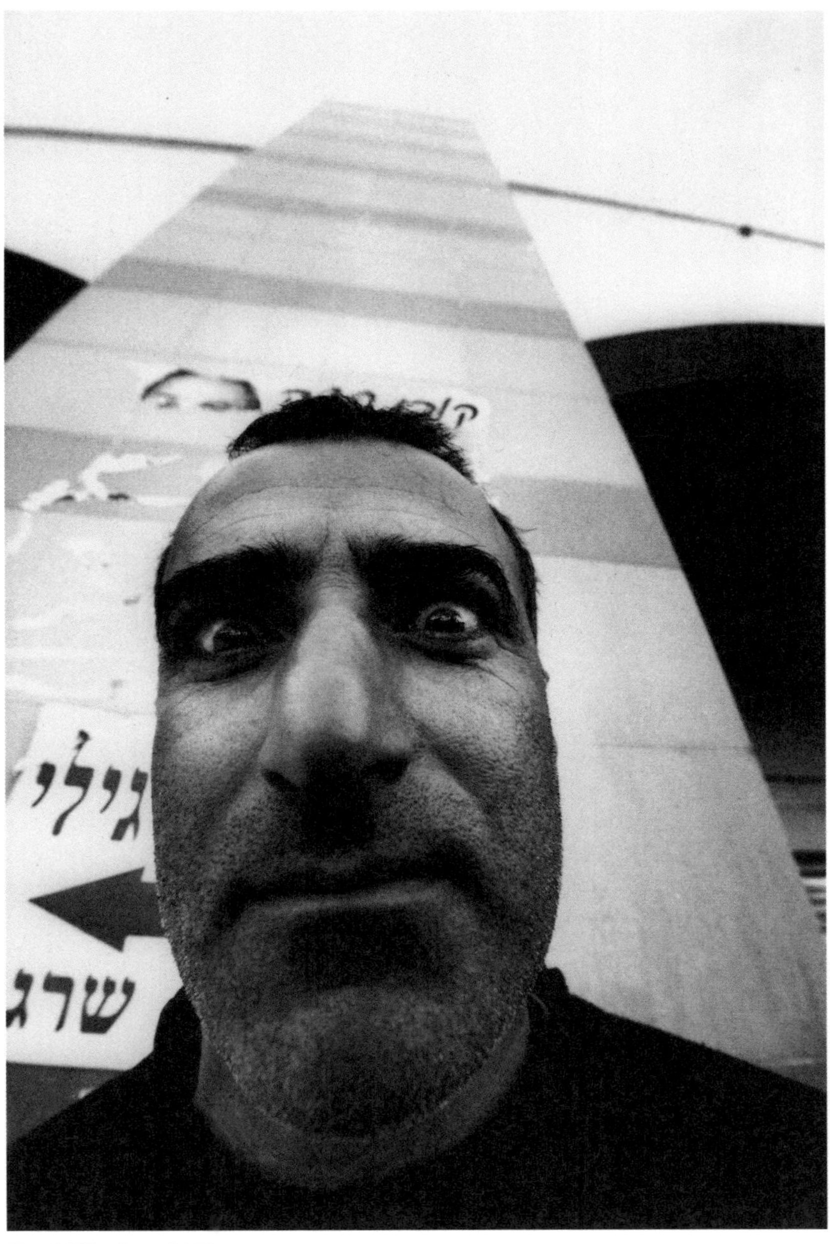

Yosef, Kfar Sava, 2007

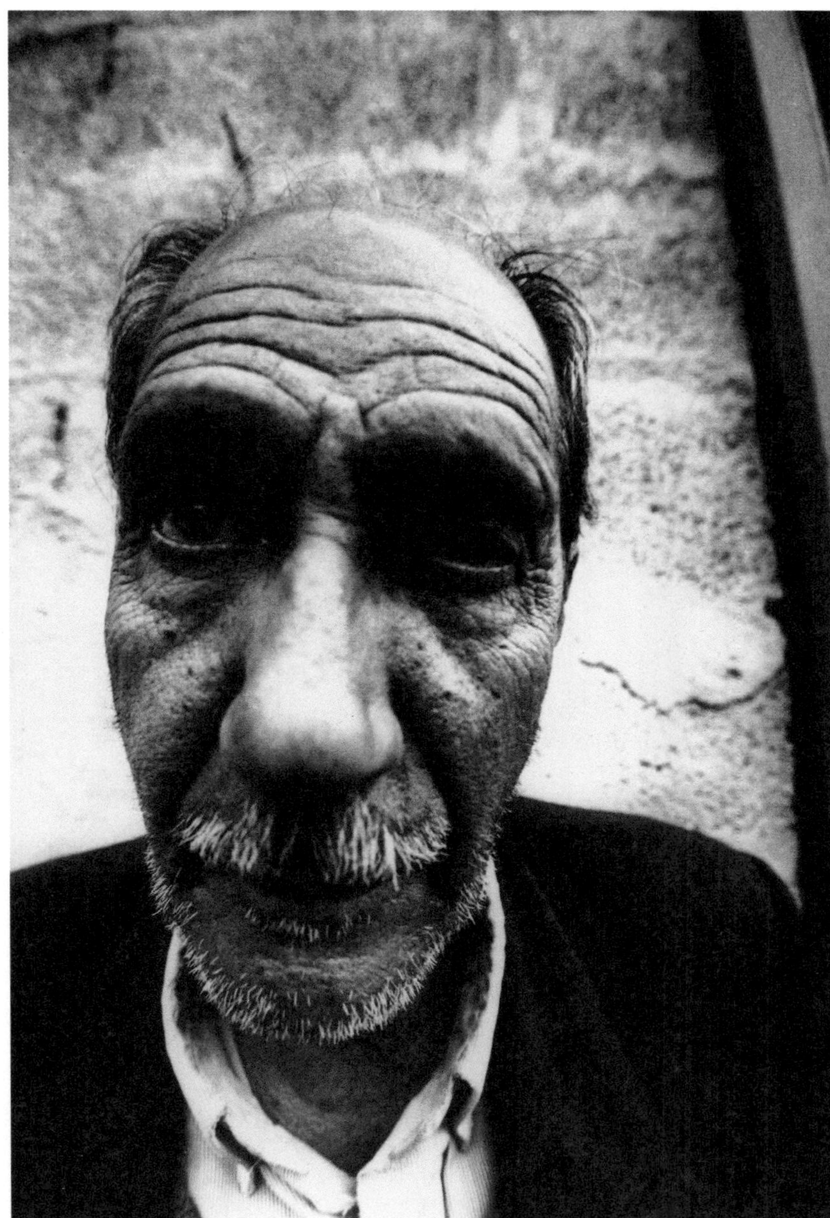

Muhammad, Dheisheh Camp, 2007

GROCERS

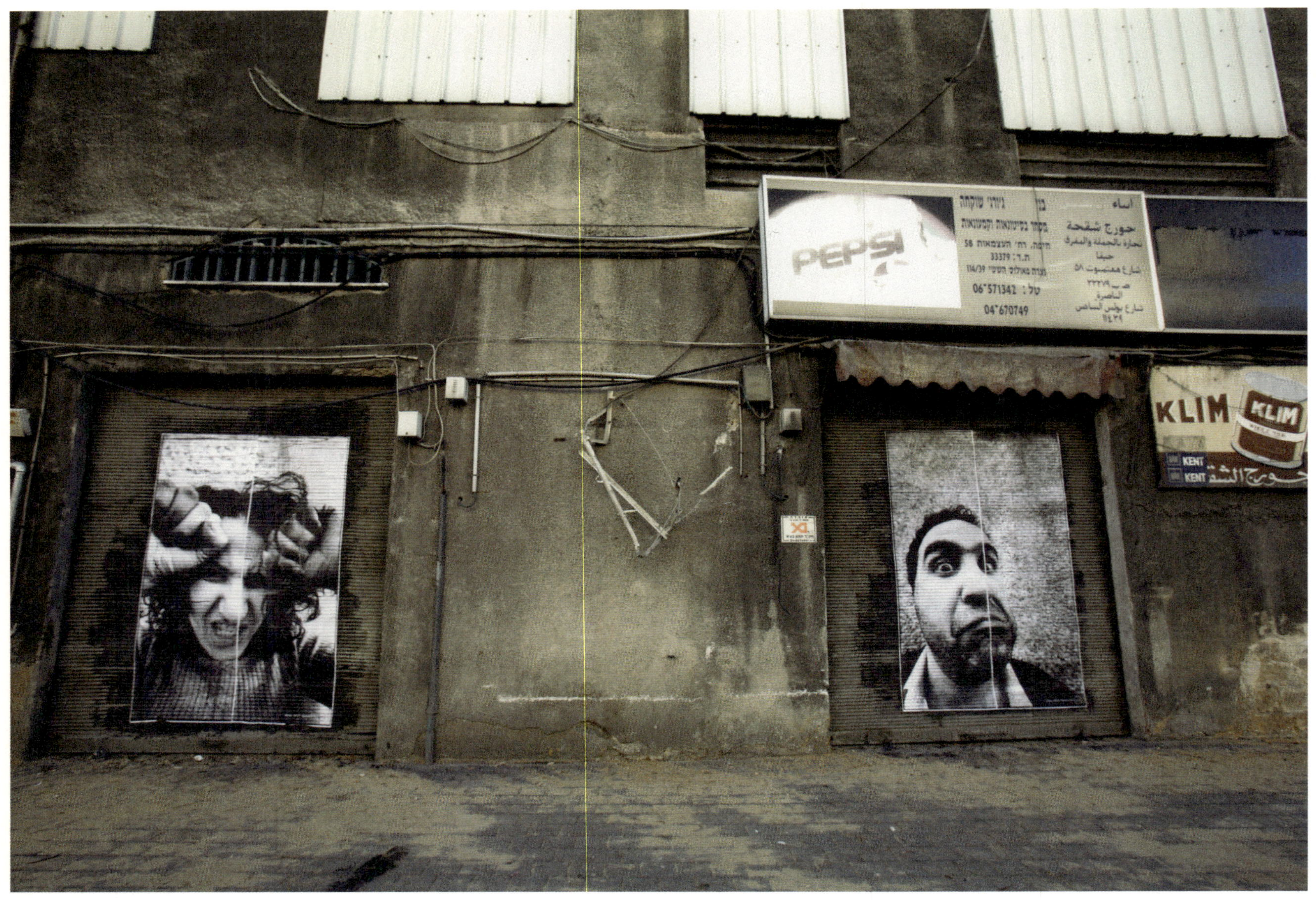

NGO workers, Haifa, 2007

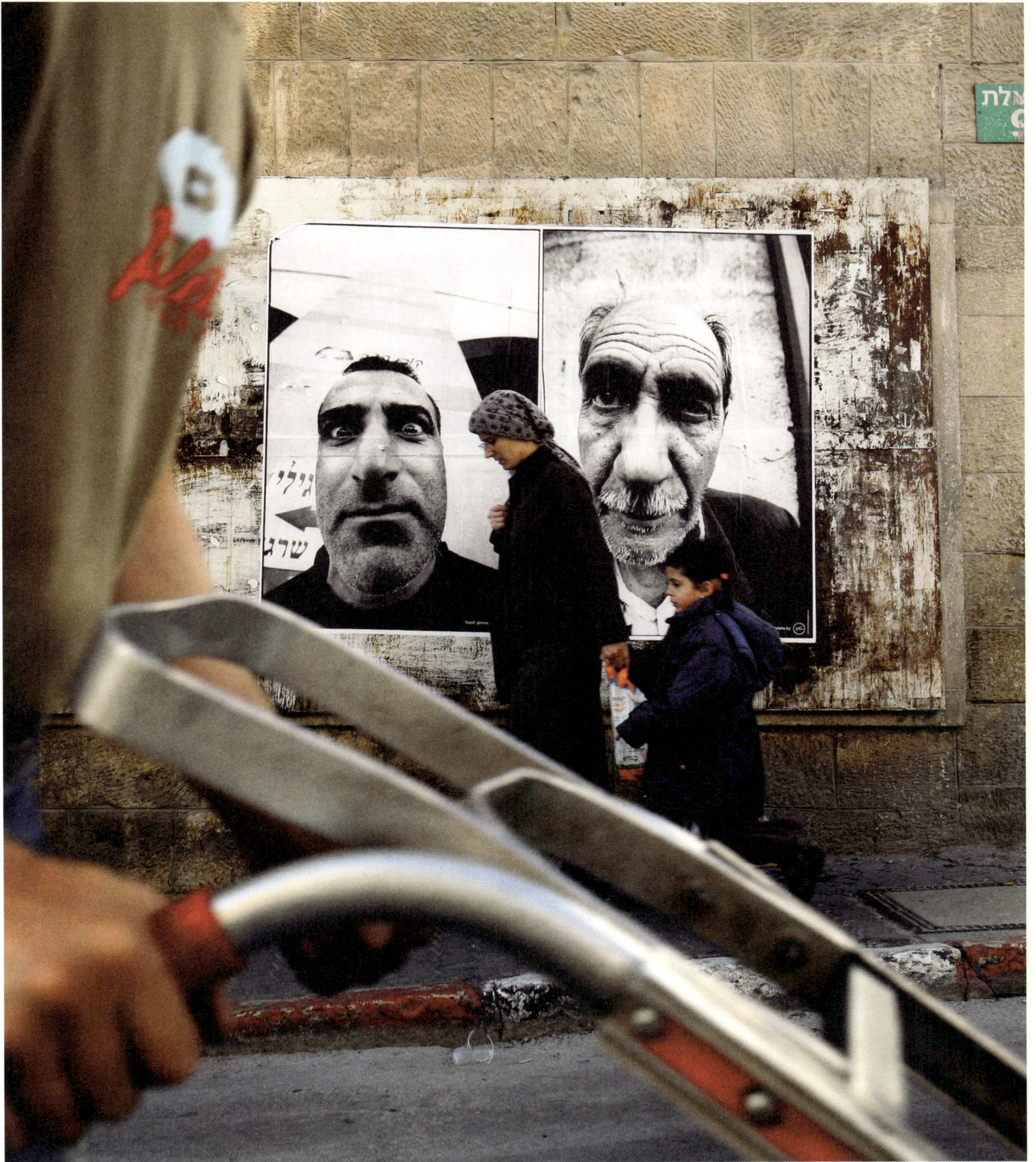

Grocers, Jerusalem, 2007

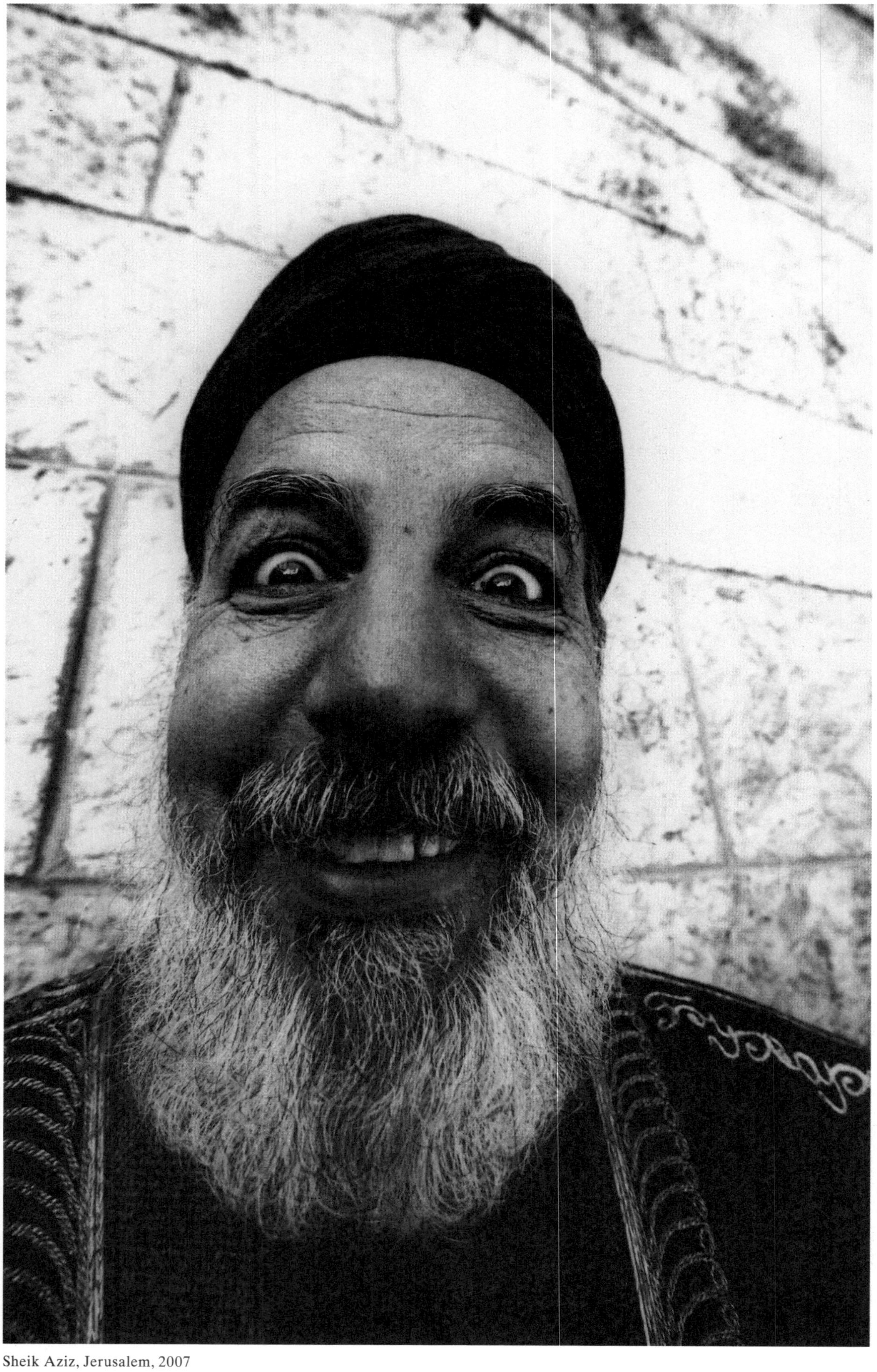

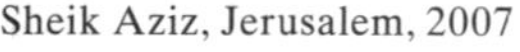
Sheik Aziz, Jerusalem, 2007

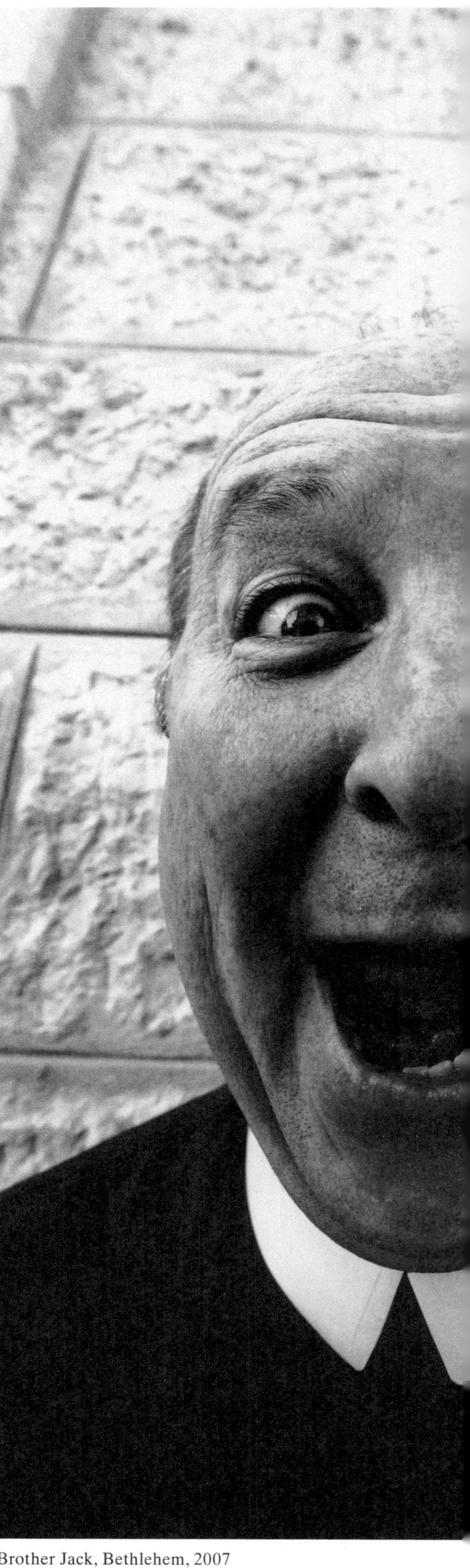
Brother Jack, Bethlehem, 2007

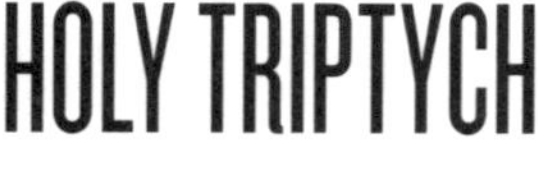
HOLY TRIPTYCH

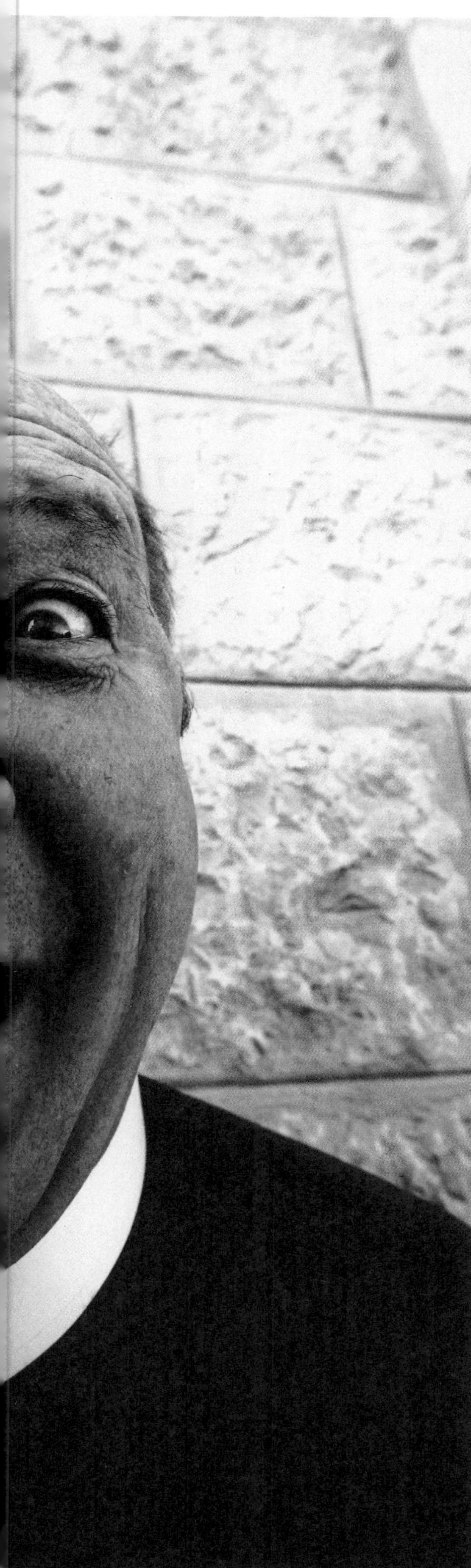

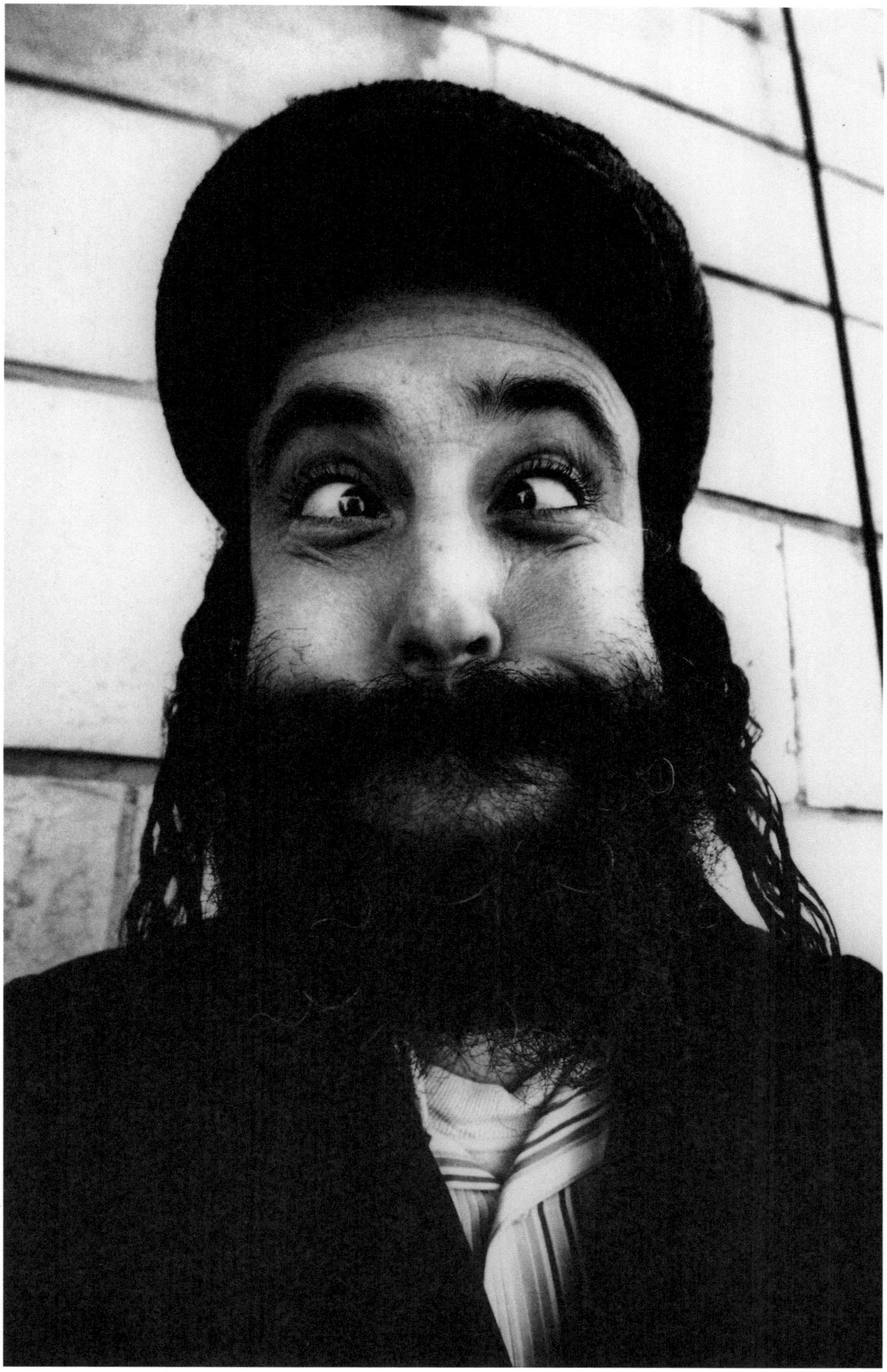

Reb Eliyahu, Jerusalem, 2007

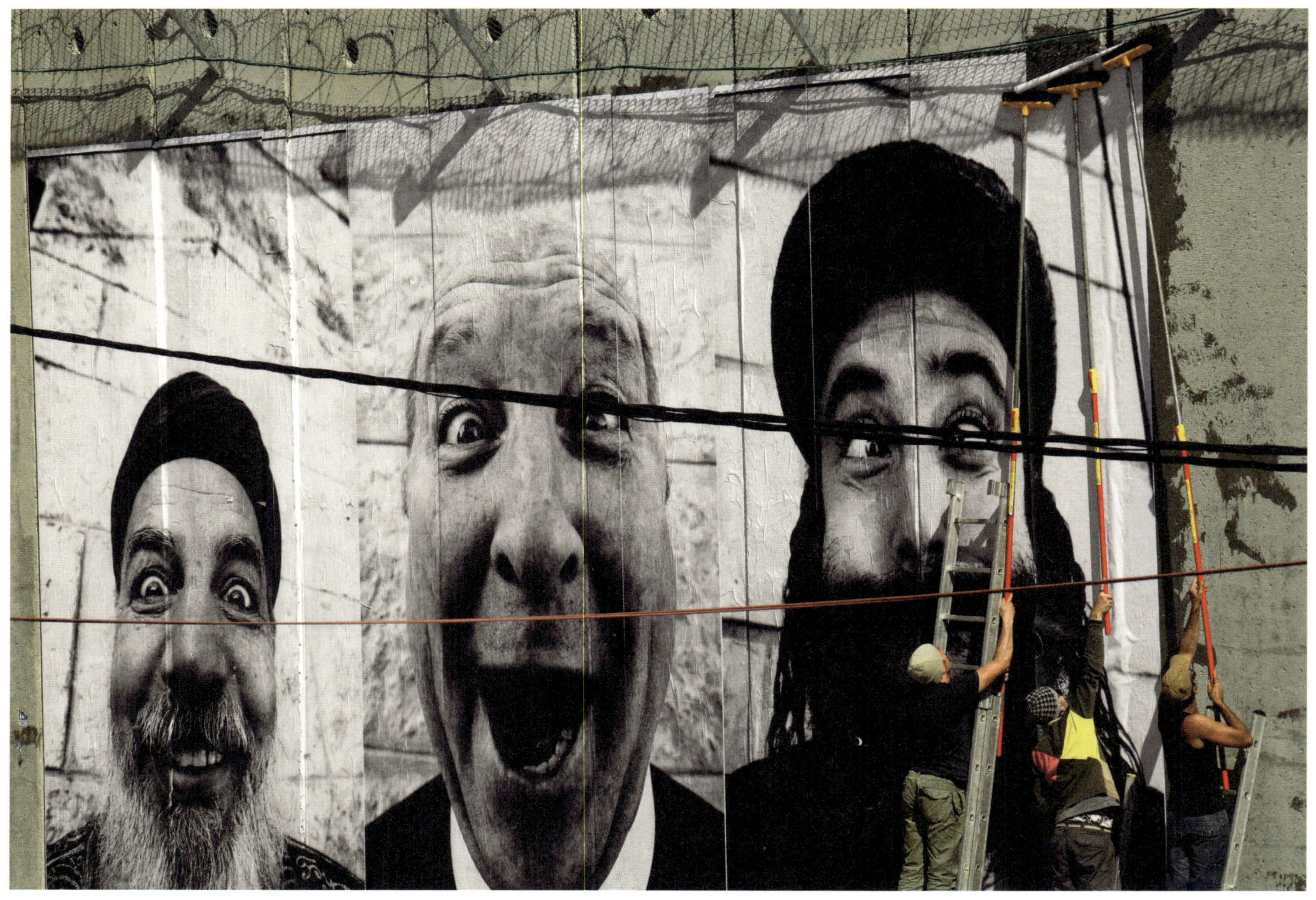

Separation Wall, Israeli side, Abu Dis, Jerusalem, 2007

Nuns in Action, Separation Wall, Palestinian side, Bethlehem, 2007

'We were pasting on the Palestinian side of the wall and these nuns walked by and recognized the priest, Brother Jack. They were from Italy, and took the extension poles to paste his nose.' – JR

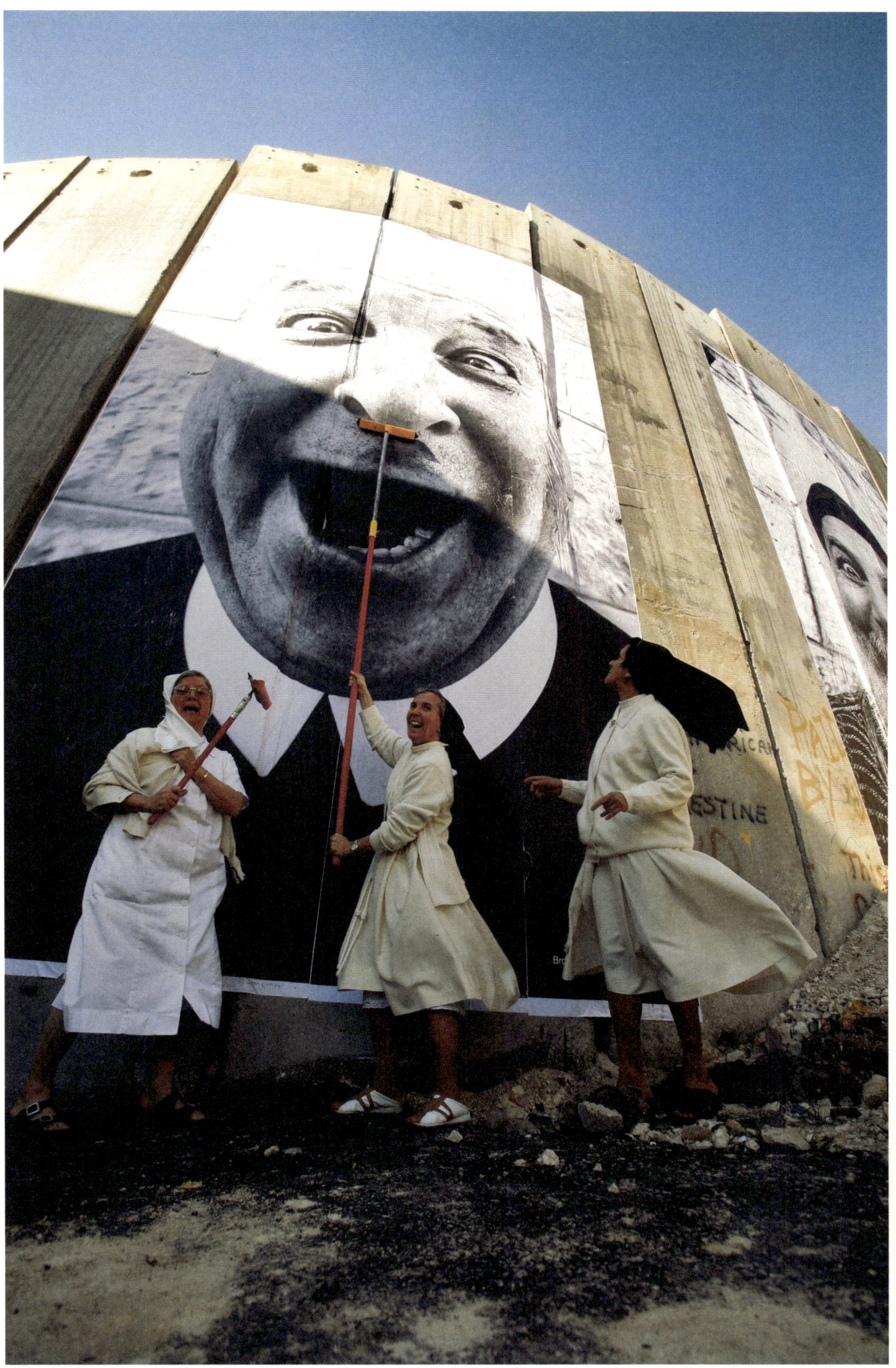

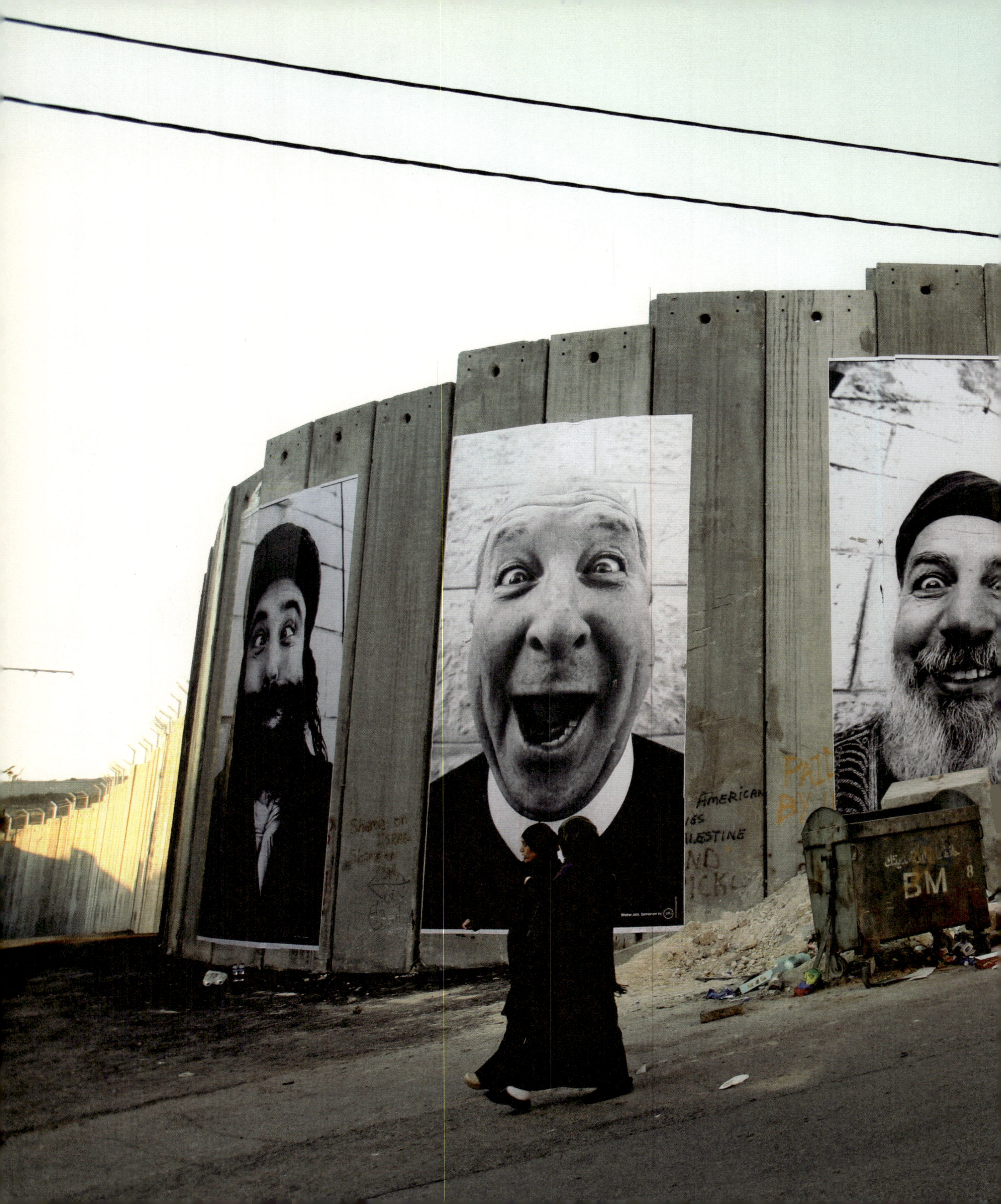

Shame on
American
BM

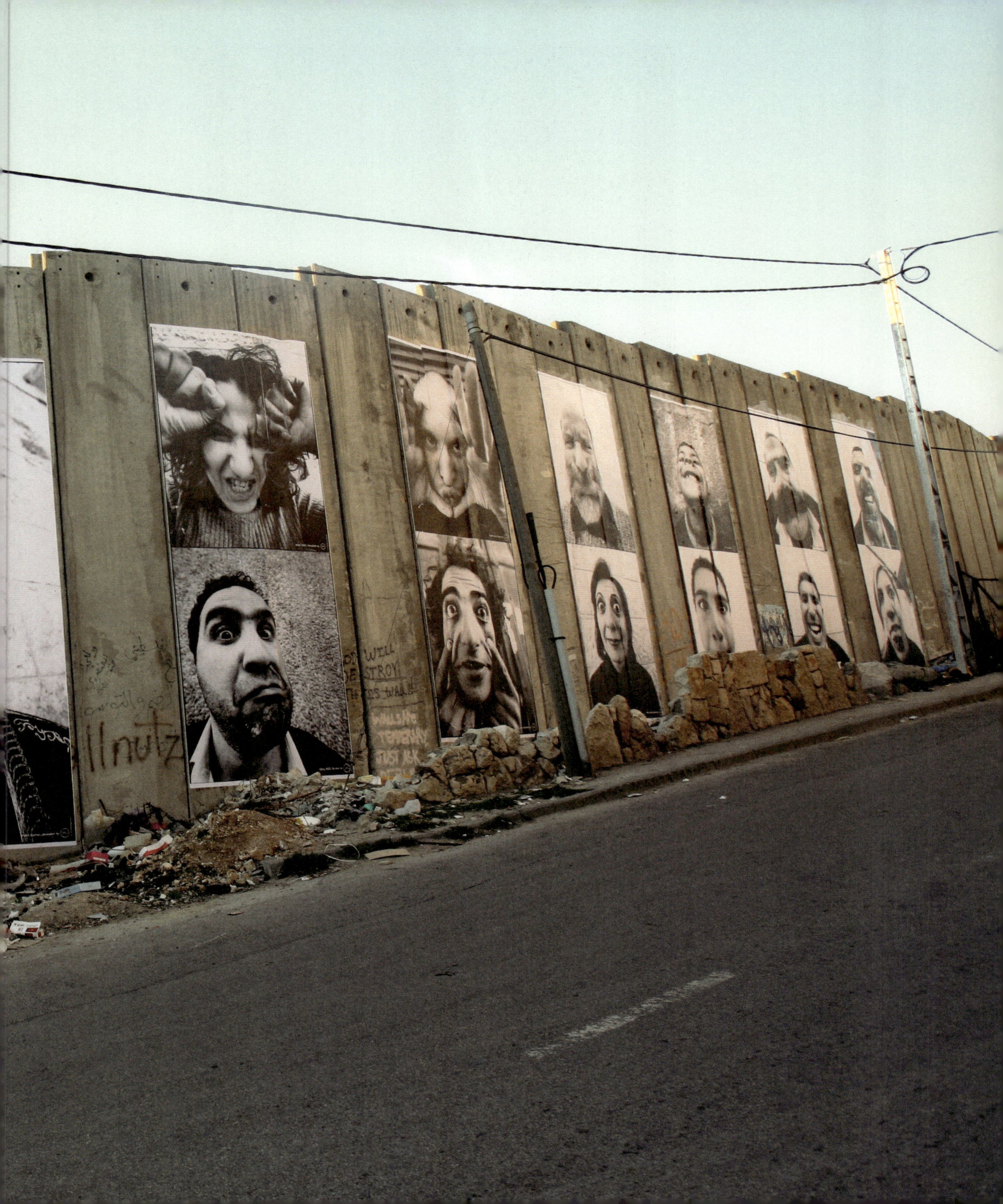
llnutz

(previous page) Separation Wall, Palestinian side, Bethlehem, 2007

(right) Exterior of the Arsenale, Venice Biennale, Venice, 2007

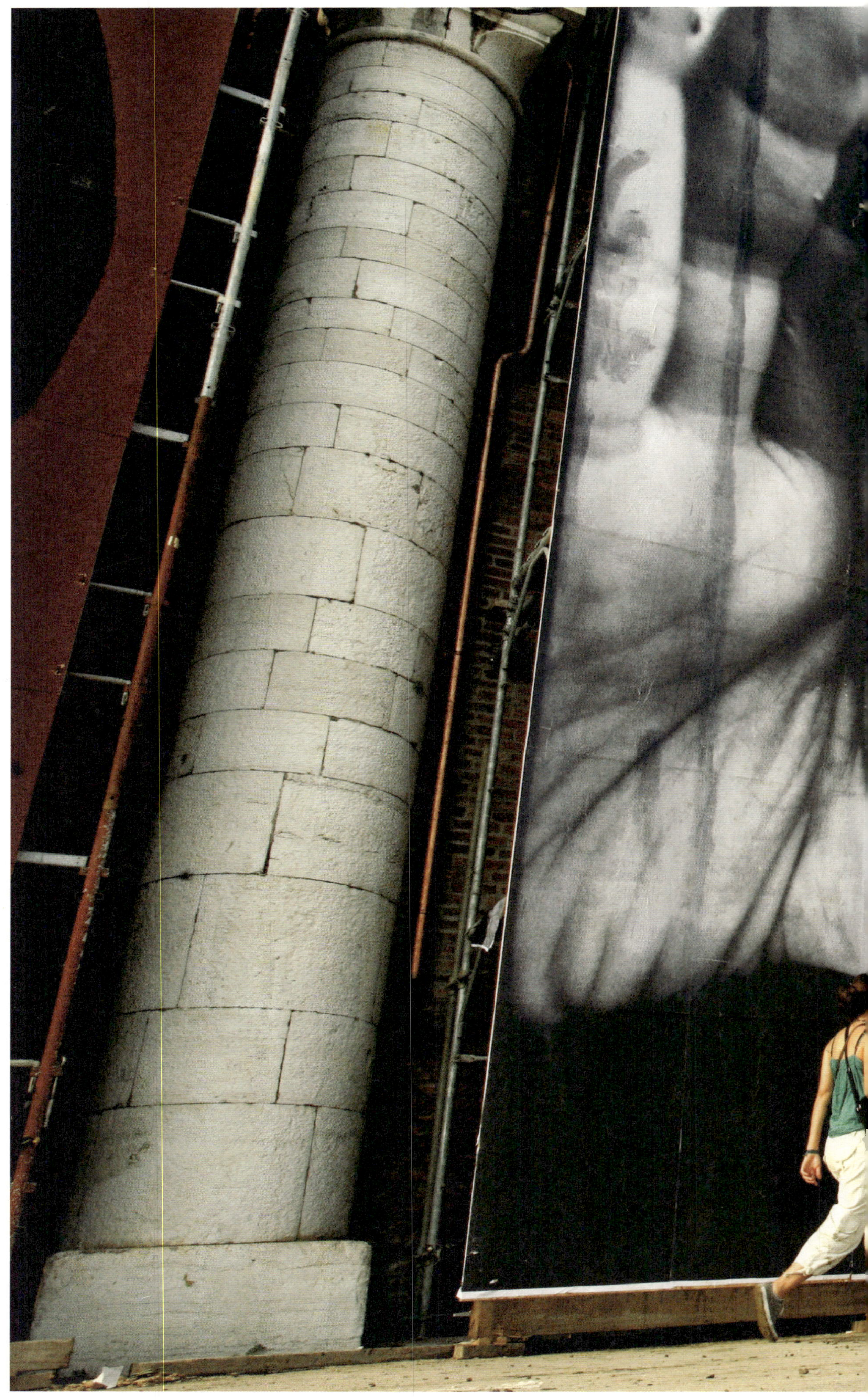

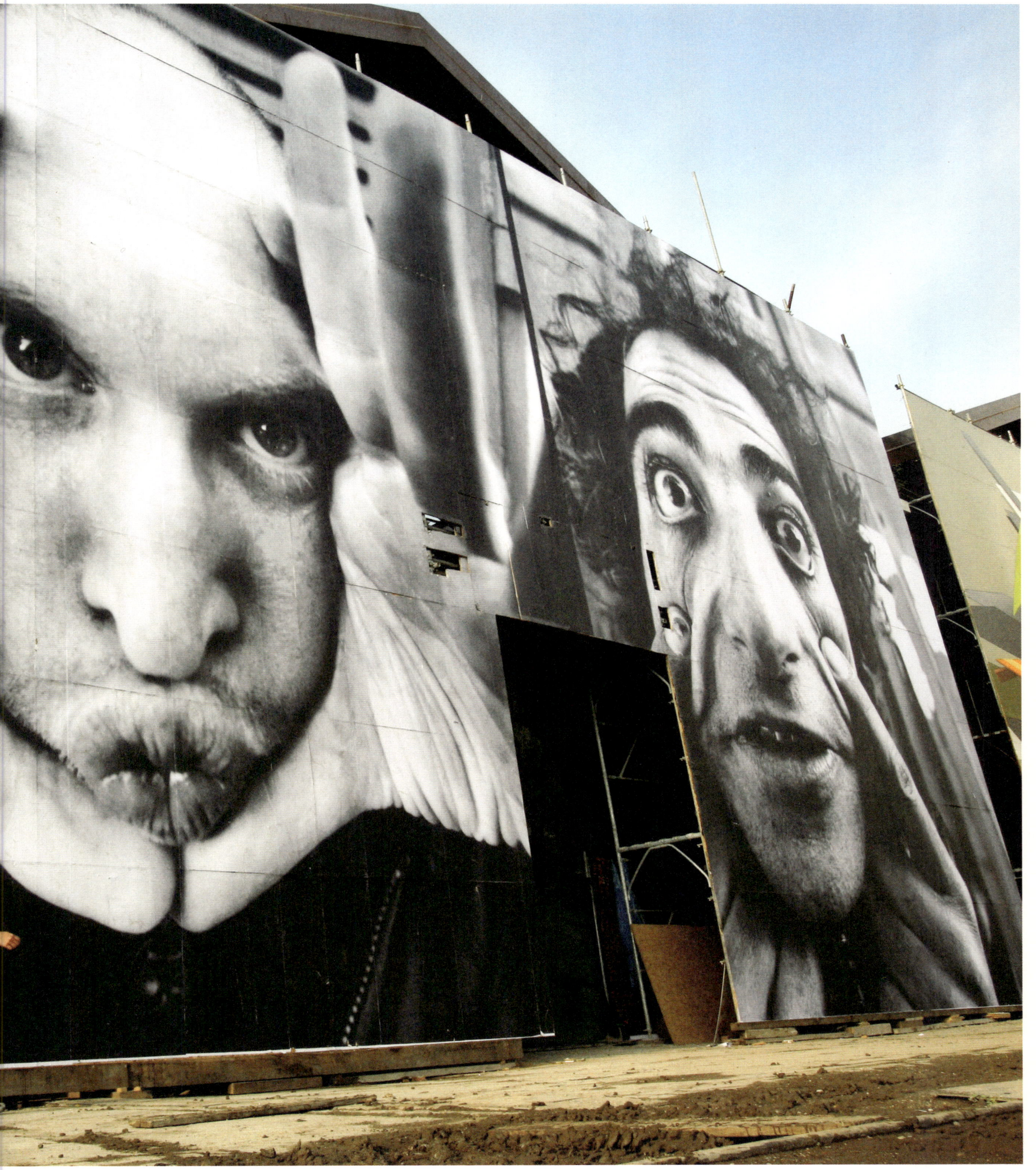

WOM

EN ARE

HEROES

Women play an essential role in society but, travelling in conflict zones, JR realized that they are often the primary victims of war, crime, rape and political or religious fanaticism. JR's intention in the *Women Are Heroes* project was to underline women's pivotal role in society and to highlight their dignity by photographing them in their daily lives and pasting their photographs in places that would make sense – in their villages, in cities nearby, or on the other side of the world.

JR asked the women if they wanted to make a face. Some preferred to pose silently in front of the camera, allowing everything they had been through to be read in their eyes. Others agreed and within seconds switched from a face of mourning to loud, uncontrollable laughter.

Working in the Morro da Providência favela in Rio de Janeiro, Brazil, JR pasted huge photos of the faces and eyes of local women on buildings covering the favela's mountainside. In Kenya, he put the eyes and faces of women from the slums of Kibera on their rooftops, using water-resistant material that provided the additional benefit of protection from the rain. He also pasted eyes on a working train. In India, he pasted huge, seemingly blank white posters to the walls. The images were hidden in a sticky material that gathered dust and colour pigments during Holi festival of colours, revealing the portraits. In Cambodia, JR worked with women who faced eviction due to encroaching gentrification, and were fighting for their right to remain in their homes. In war-torn Sierra Leone, Liberia and Sudan, JR's pastings brought a haunting human presence to harsh environments of social conflict. At the end of each project, a book was made and distributed to the participants.
In 2010, a film about the project was part of the Official Selection of the Cannes Film Festival.

The participants often asked JR to make their stories travel – as a way of voicing what they had gone through and what they had resisted, and of telling the world that they existed. They knew that the visual language of pulling faces was something universal that would be understood in Europe or the United States as much as in their own village.

Women Are Heroes ended in July 2014, when 2,600 strips of paper were pasted in 10 days on a container ship in Le Havre, France, with the help of dockers at the port. The ship then travelled across the globe to Malaysia.

(right) Haya Massaley, Intercontinental Hotel, Monrovia, Liberia, 2008

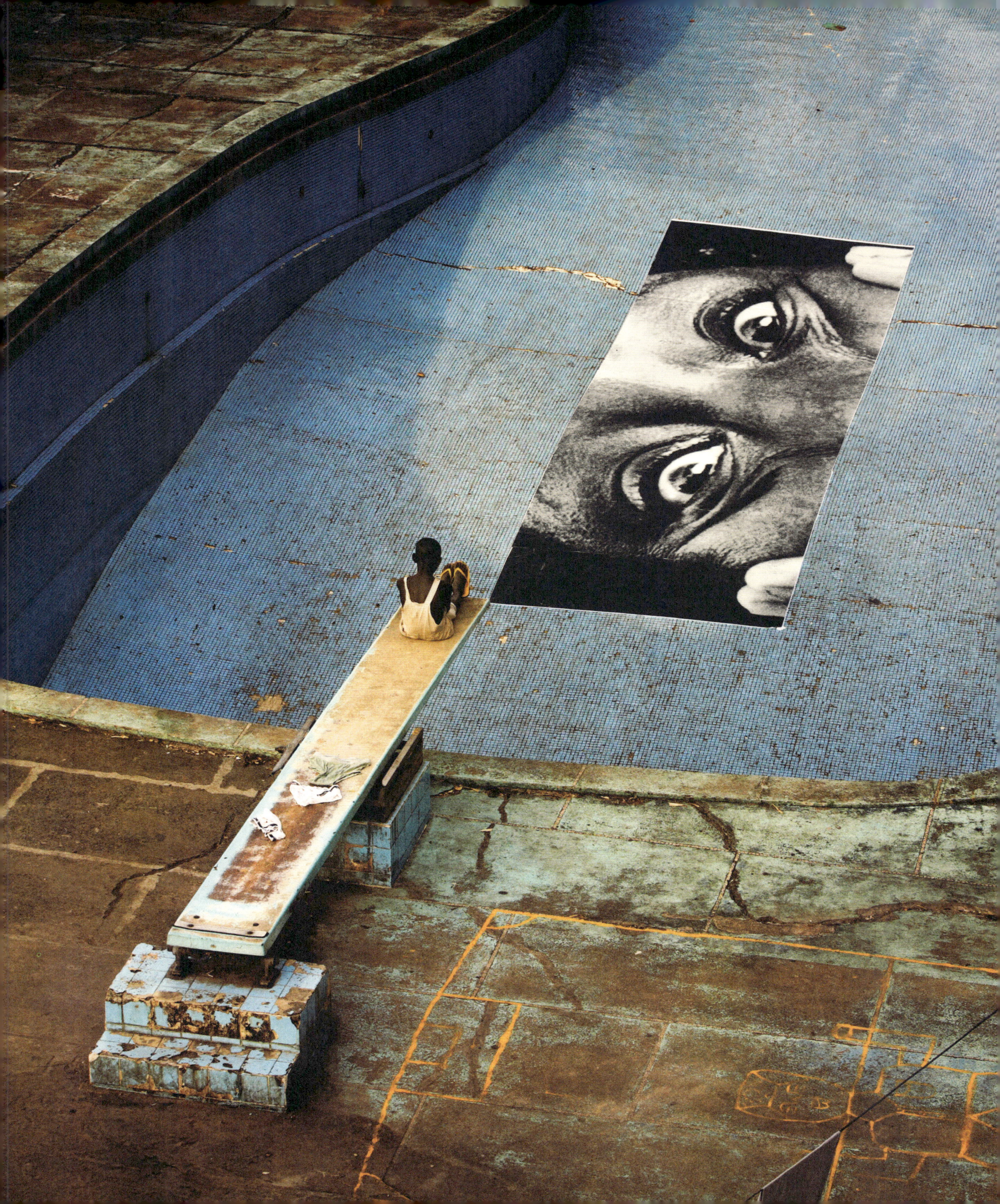

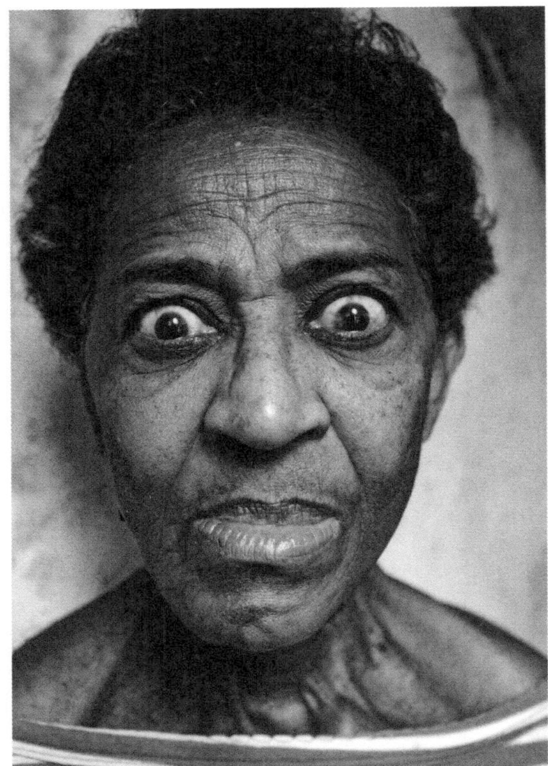

Linda Marinho De Oliveira
Brazil

'My husband died about twenty years ago. I have three kids, grandchildren and great-grandchildren. I love this favela – what I love best is when the whole community gets together for a celebration.

My deepest wish is that the police would stop shooting whenever they show up. It would protect our kids. All the kids play on the square and ride their bikes there, it's so sweet.

It wasn't always like this. It's only been like this for the past thirty years. Unfortunately the way out of this situation is blocked – by corruption. And who suffers from all this? The poor and the kids who have nowhere to play anymore.'

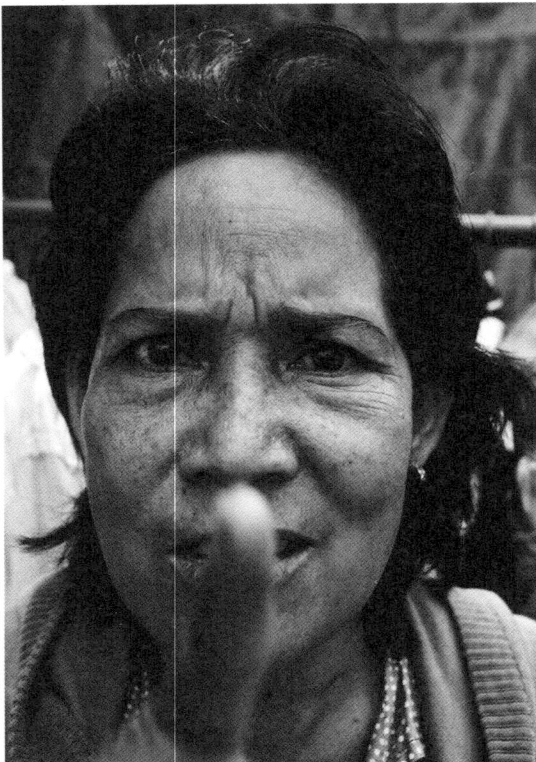

Chantha Dol
Cambodia

'I'm fifty-one years old. I was the victim of an agreement between a property developer and the local authorities, who drove us out of our homes in order to redevelop the land. Only the women continued fighting to keep our land. From one day to the next we saw the police coming in with tear gas, bulldozers and fire hoses to drive us out. They sent me to prison, then to a hospital. When I went back, everything was gone.

I agreed to have my photograph put up so that the men in power would open their eyes and take a look at our condition. Words are no longer enough. I want people to ask themselves why these photographs of women were put up on the walls.'

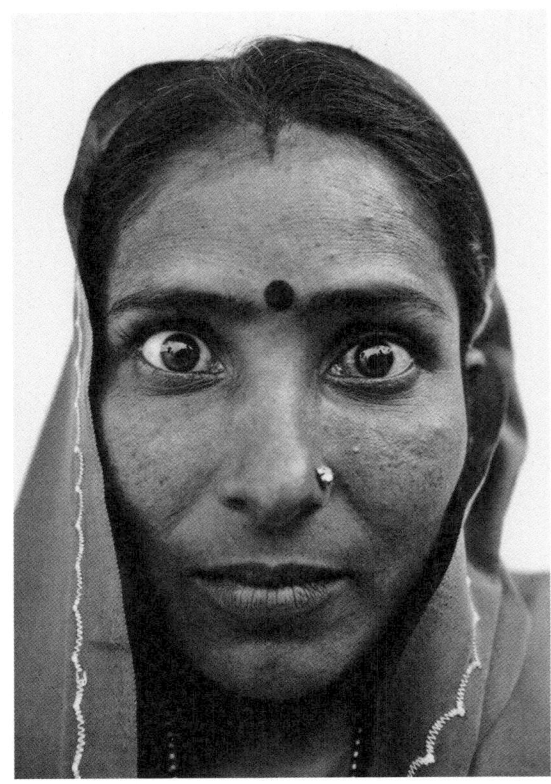

Urmila Devi
India

'My parents married me off when I was fourteen. My husband's elder brother had his eye on me. I refused to give in to him, left my husband and returned home. My brother-in-law came looking for me and beat me with bamboos, until I bled. Four or five years went past without my husband coming to look for me.

I was remarried but in Delhi my husband's earnings were no longer enough. Life was very expensive, and I got in with a bad crowd... a group of women who were prostitutes. I met rich people who had everything they wanted, and I began to earn a lot. My husband knew nothing about it. My body became the victim. I was ashamed, I am ashamed to talk about it. I slept with senior officials, judges and police officers. They promised help in return, as well. Then one day I was put in prison but was conditionally discharged.

Today, my husband transports building materials on a wheelbarrow, while I work in a large household. It's a better way of life and I have regained my self-respect.'

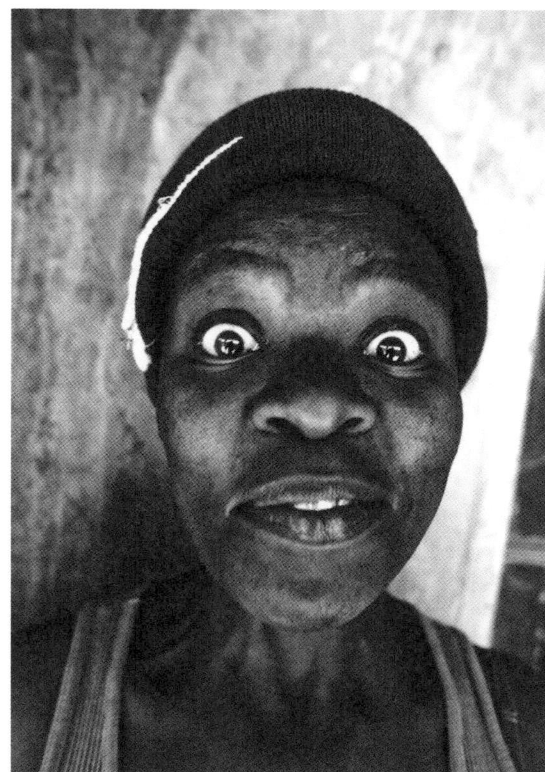

Judith Anyango
Kenya

'I need my photo to be on that train so that everyone in this world or even in our country will want to know who I am.

I am a business woman. I go to the market, pick potatoes, cut them, deep-fry them and when they are ready, sell them. That's what we call chips. I do it for my little Dennis.

I need to strengthen the message for women who just sit and wait for their husband. If you do this, when your husband dies, you find life very difficult. But when you get used to what you are doing, you realise that life is simple with or without a husband. That's why I am happy.'

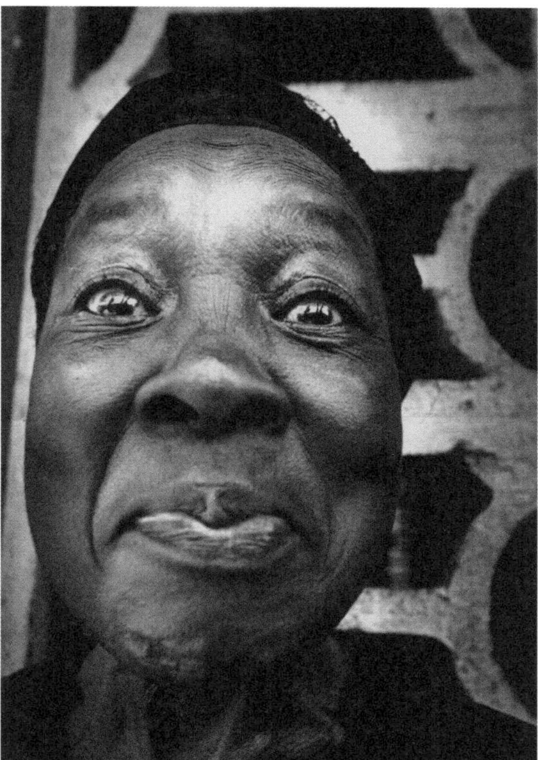

Sara Toe
Liberia

'I had six children. During the war we lived in the country. Three of my girls were taken by the rebels to the bush. All three died there. My fourth daughter was pregnant. "Is there a boy inside? Is there a girl inside?" The rebels opened her belly and took the child out. Then they ran away.

We stayed in the bush for four months and survived on cabbages. Until the ECOMOG came and we went to Ghana. When I came back, my house was broken and my son had passed away. I live with my only daughter now.

I am sad because I lost my big family. I grieve for those lost in the war.'

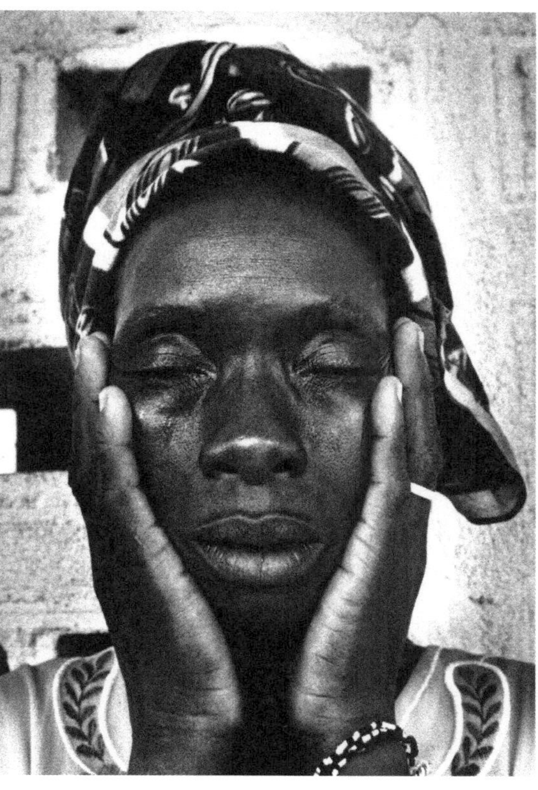

Baindu Gbembo
Sierra Leone

'During the war I was with my first husband. I was pregnant. I gave birth in the bush because of the cold. We had no food to eat. Before the war my life was so nice. Now I am really suffering. I pray to God to help my children help me before I die because I don't have the strength. My children and I sell palm oil for 400 leone per pint. When there is no palm oil, I beg to my second husband's relatives.

The best period of my life was when I was a kid, at the age of fifteen. My relatives did everything for me. But now I am alone. I do everything for myself and my children.'

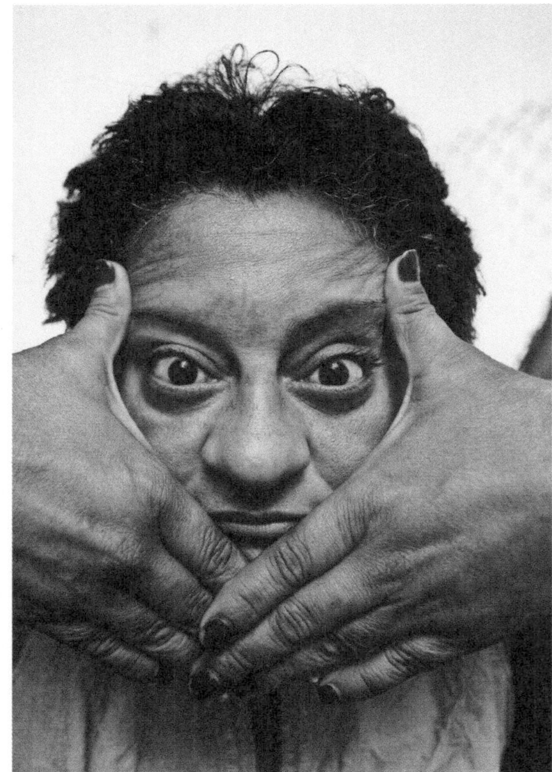

Rosiete Marinho
Brazil

'This is my home. I love this place with all my heart, and that love is what drives me to do things to make it better here.

I always try to tell stories about who we are and where we come from to the kids who live nearby – to teach them our history. We're part of this country's history too.

I'm the mother of two children and I have two granddaughters. My house is called the "Widows' house" because my mother, my aunt, my daughter and I are all widows. But life goes on. Women are the role models here.

What I'd really like is for the kids here to have the same kind of childhood I had, for them to have the respect I had for the elderly and the wisdom I had not to get into drugs. It's so easy to get into drugs nowadays that kids think it's normal. They have no chance of seeing life from the other side, from the side of society that has rejected them but where they might find a place for themselves tomorrow.

We have doctors, engineers, lawyers, professors in schools and universities and top nurses here. Most of the inhabitants here are dignified people. And that dignity is what we need for the children today.'

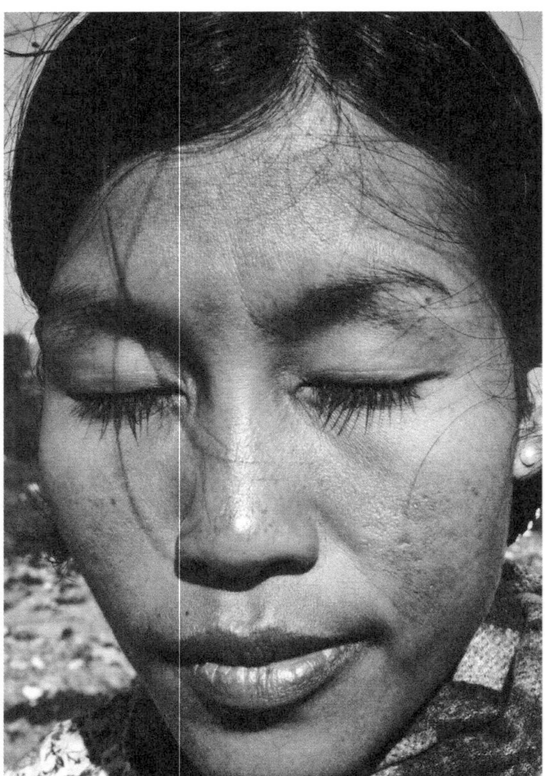

Ratana Loeung
Cambodia

'I'm twenty-eight years old. I was born in Siem Reap. Now I live in Phnom Penh.

After school I would often go to the dump and search through all the rubbish. Once a week I sold what I collected. My life was hard here. My parents also came to live in Phnom Penh. We had no house, so everyone lived at my aunt's. My father's salary wasn't enough, so I left the house and went to Beung Tompon to work.

I like cleanliness, beauty and my skin. When I was working at the dump, I had figured out everything I needed to protect my entire body. I would pick up everything that could be sold, including plastic, glass, iron, cans, etc.

I think I'm strong because I've always helped my family. Wherever I've been, I've always saved a bit of money to send to my mother. I worked overtime, day and night. I've always cried deep down in my heart, my whole life long. But no one has ever known it.

I'm really pleased to have my photograph taken. For me these pasted-up photographs are a form of living art that tells the real story of people's lives. I hope to represent all the children who have worked in this dump.'

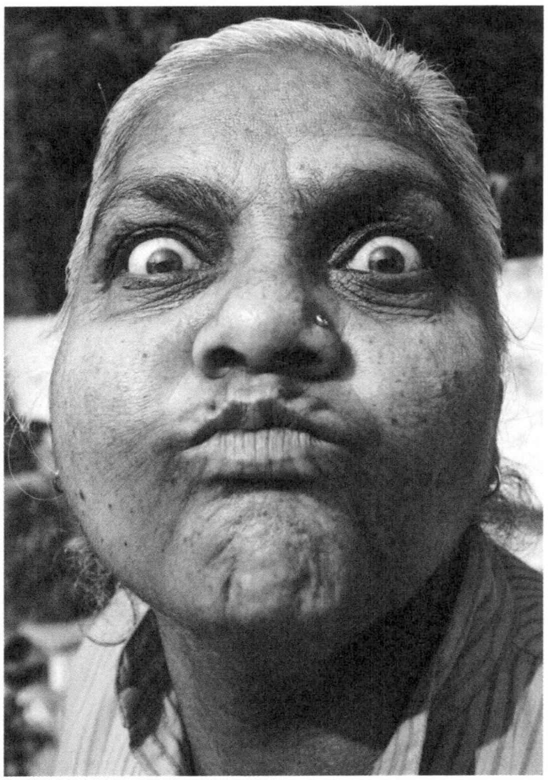

Shanti Mehrar
India

'I come from the village of Nasirabad in Rajasthan. I spent my childhood in the hills of Rajasthan, crushing wheat, breaking stones in the mines and gathering wood. Every day, I would break a crate of stones for the railways. I was paid ten paises. My family travelled between Rajasthan and Delhi to earn a living. I never went to school.

It was the same in Delhi. We mixed tar by hand, then carried it on our heads. It dripped on to our faces and bodies.

I was married off very young. I was only a child. But I left him. Then I chose a partner from a different caste, someone I loved – I wasn't even eighteen! For some years, life was good.

There is a university near the Kashmiri Gate, whose foundations I laid. At that time, I wore traditional dress, a long skirt, a blouse and veil. Today, I have come back to that same university to lecture on women's rights! So, when I think of all that, I am proud. Once I carried and laid bricks. Now I am laying the bricks of thought, of experience, to build a different society.'

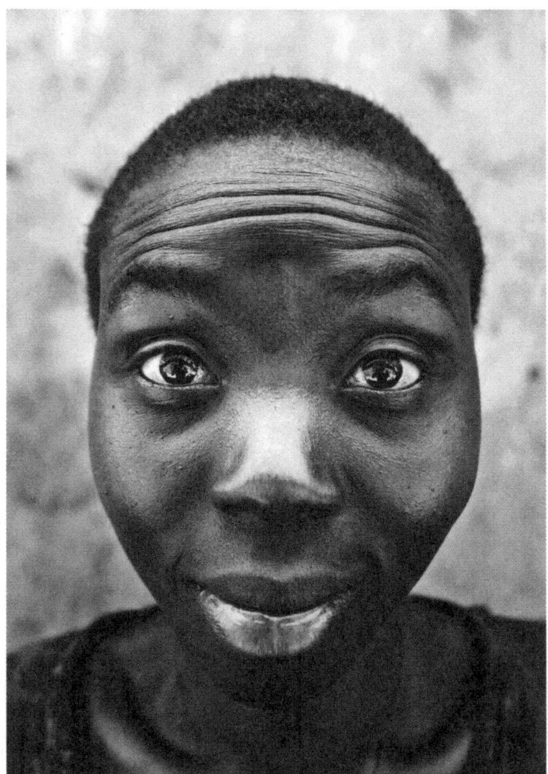

Grace Akoth
Kenya

'I am twenty-seven years old and was born in Kisumu. I have lived in Kibera ever since I was married nine years ago. I had my first child within a year, but then I had difficulty getting pregnant again and my husband started to beat me. After six years I had not given birth to another child and his mother began to encourage him to marry another woman who could give him more children. Then God blessed me and sent a baby to me last year. It was a miracle. My youngest child is now one year old.

I have had a job as a tailor for the last four years. I work every day except Sunday. I try to help in the community by taking part in a women's group. There are about fifteen of us and we each contribute ten shillings per day. The money is then given to one of the women in the group and we rotate the recipient each day.

I was very happy to be involved in this project. The canvas on my roof helps to keep the rain out. Before I had the canvas, I had a problem with leaks whenever it rained!'

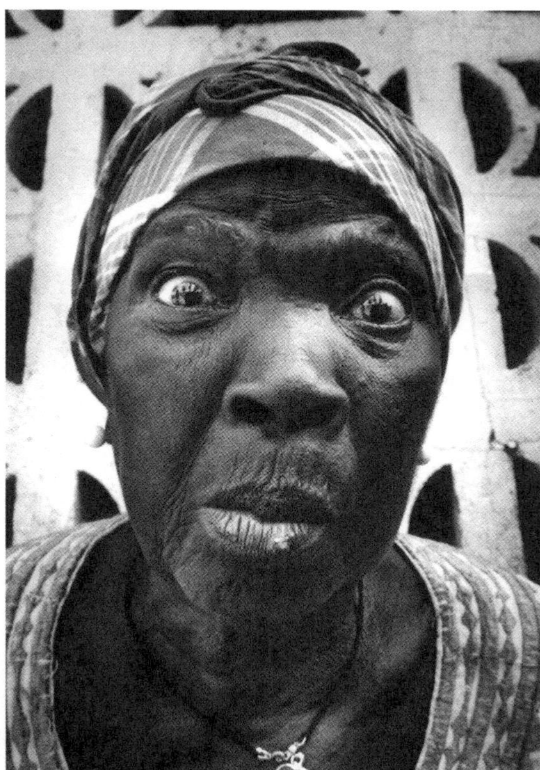

Jessie Jon
Liberia

'I am around ninety years old. When I was young, I worked hard. I enjoyed my life so much before the war. I was very happy with my husband. I tattooed his initials on my chest. Sadly, he died in 1976.

The worst day of my life is still buried deep inside my soul. Before the war I had two daughters. But then the war started. My daughter was pregnant. We started running away but my daughter's belly was very big and we had to rest. The soldiers asked: "Is it a girl? Is it a boy?" They opened her belly and took the baby out of her stomach. They threw the baby in the water and killed my daughter. Then I ran away and walked alone in the bush. The war killed my two daughters and my son. Now I have nothing.

I have a large family, 108 in total with my children, my grandchildren and my great-grandchildren. I feel that I am now living in a better country thanks to Ellen, our President. She has done a lot for health and education. Women are better leaders. They don't want to fight again and again. The day she was elected, I was so glad that I danced.'

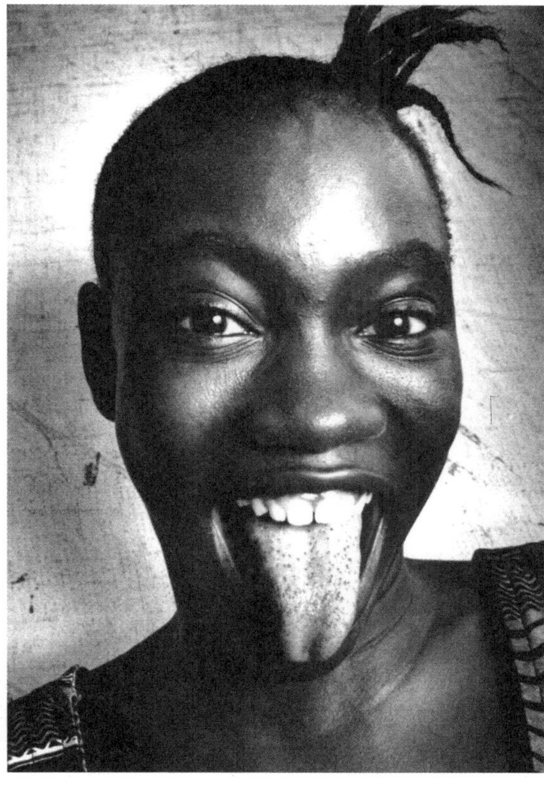

Musu Rogers
Sierra Leone

'Not long ago, I gave birth. My little girl is only six months old and weighs four kilograms. Her name is Kadiatu. She is my first child. The birth was very difficult. My uncle's wife was there to help me. When Kadiatu grows up, I'd like her to go to school, but we haven't much money. My father died when I was fifteen. I survive thanks to my mother, with whom we live. She is an example for me, I hope I will be as good a mother as she is. One day I hope to become a hairdresser.'

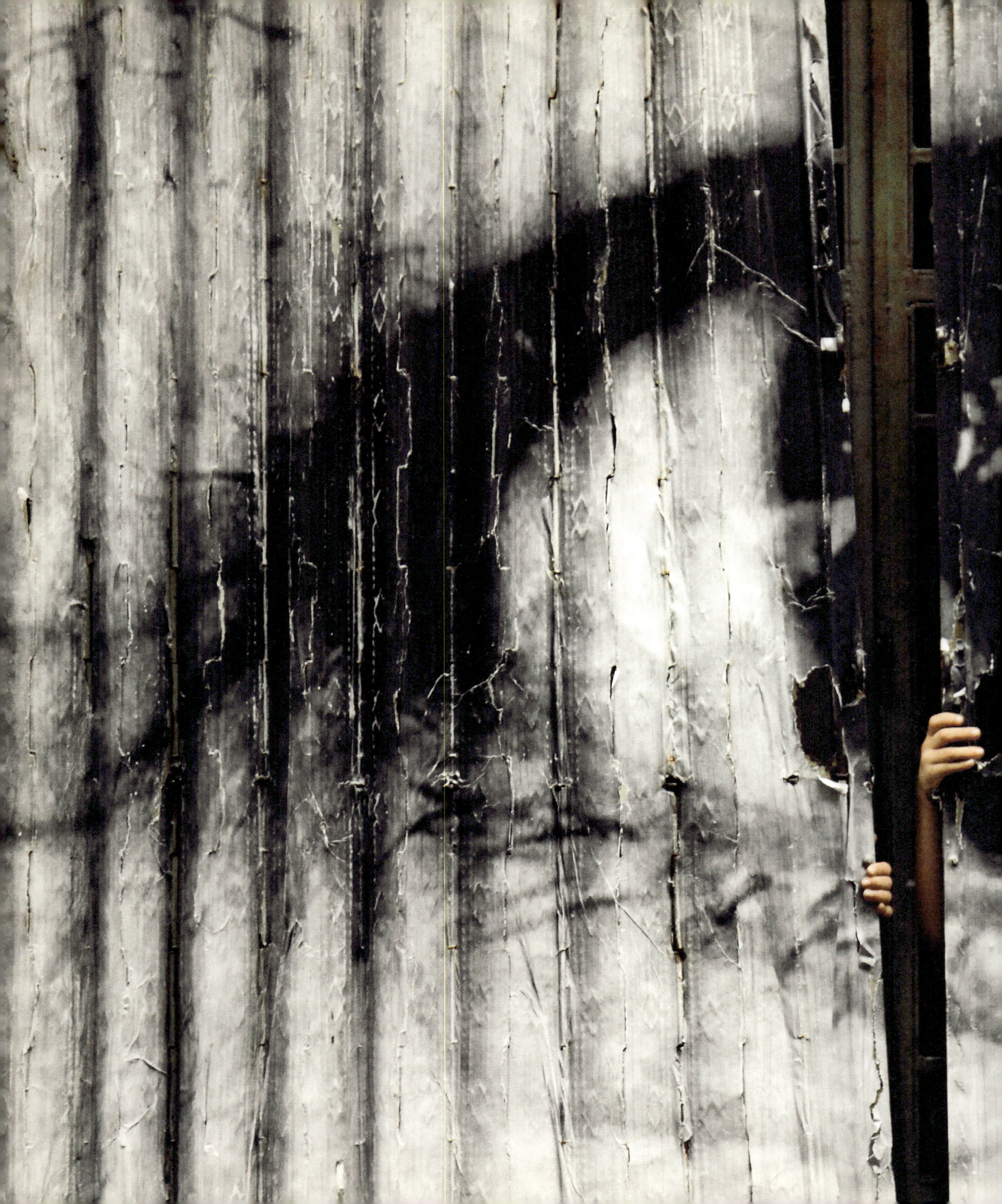

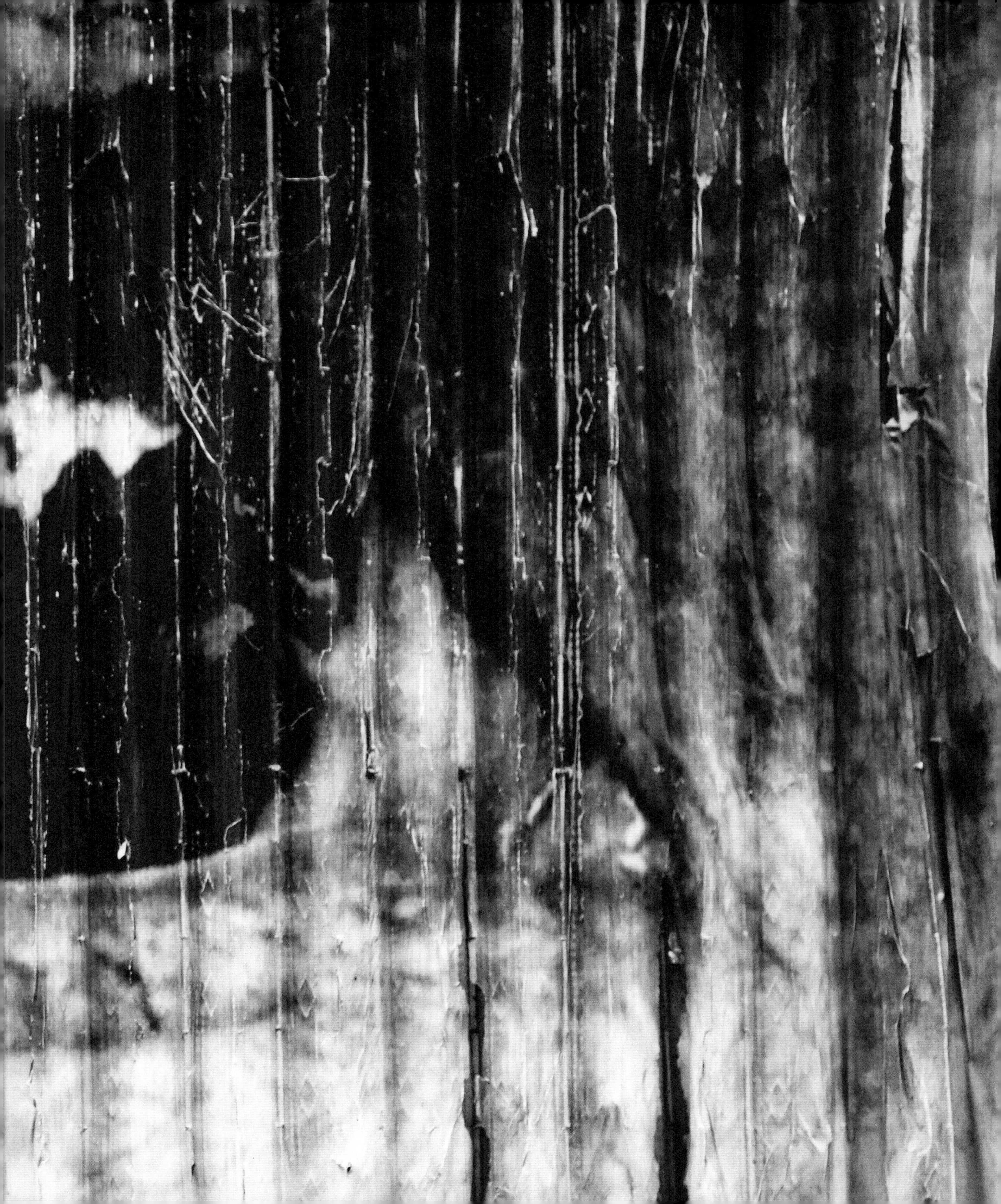

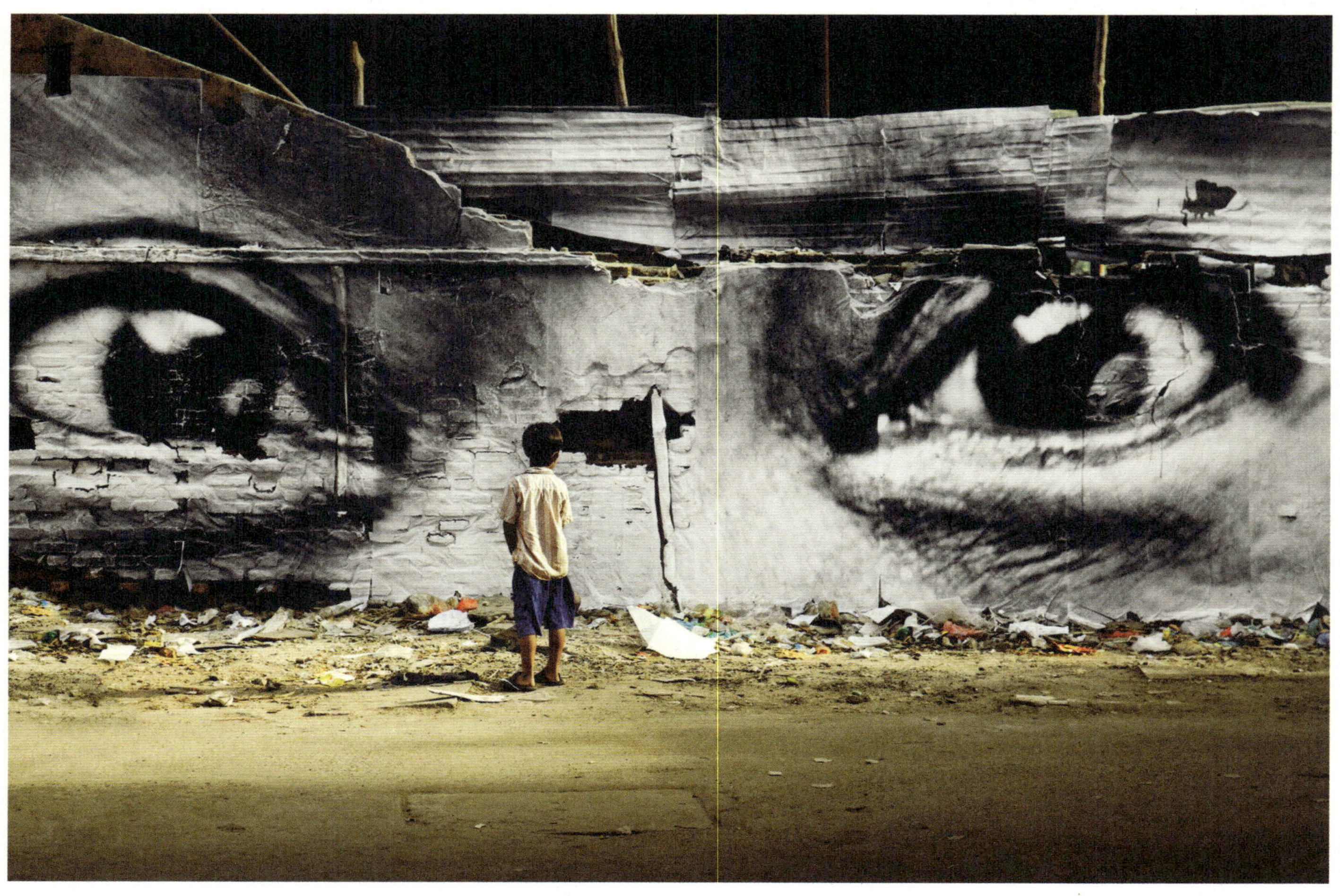

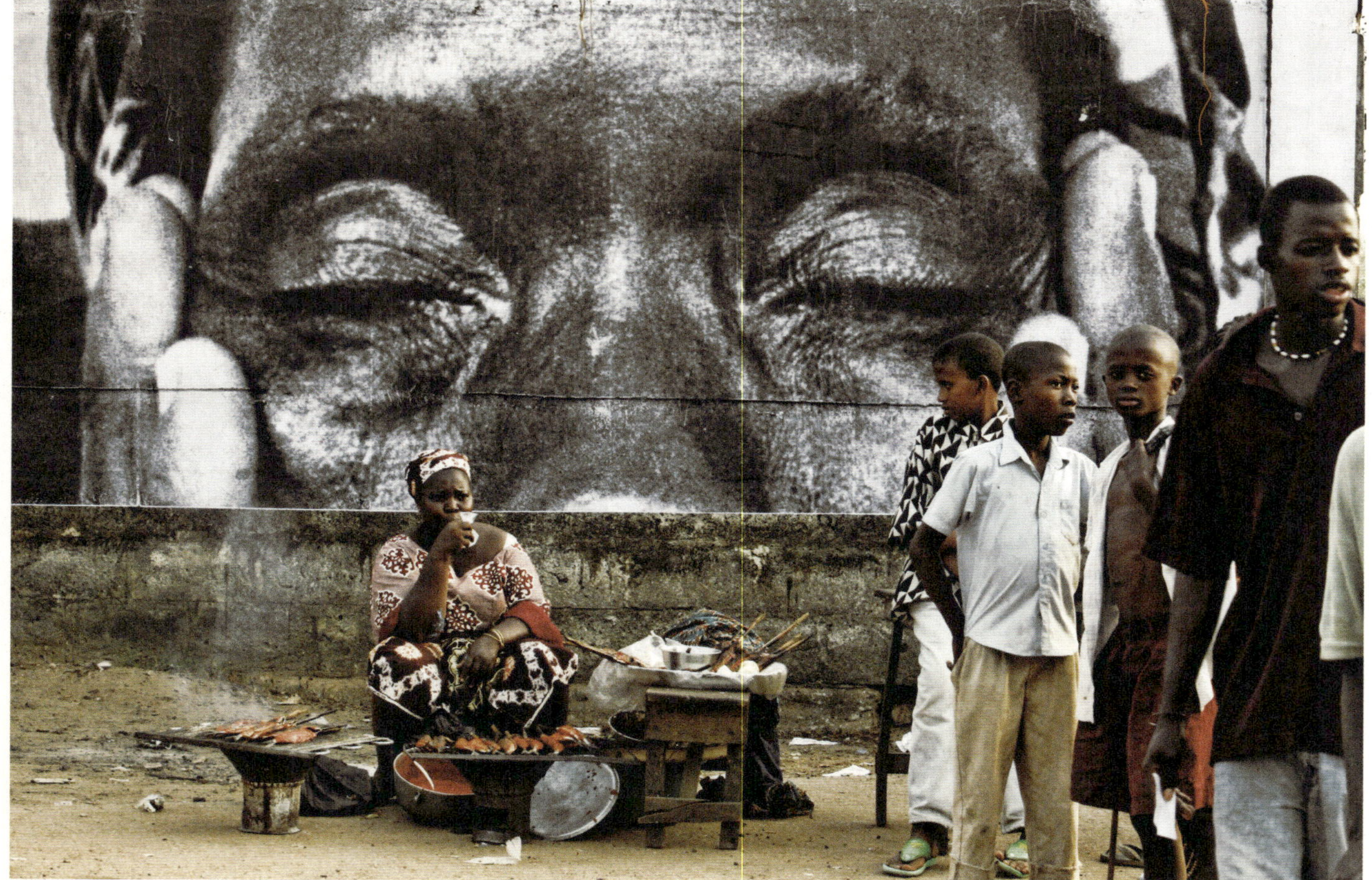

(top) Peng Panh, Phnom Penh, Cambodia, 2009
(bottom) Baindu Gbembo, Kenema, Sierra Leone, 2009
(previous page) Sinou Vissaka, Phnom Penh, Cambodia, 2009

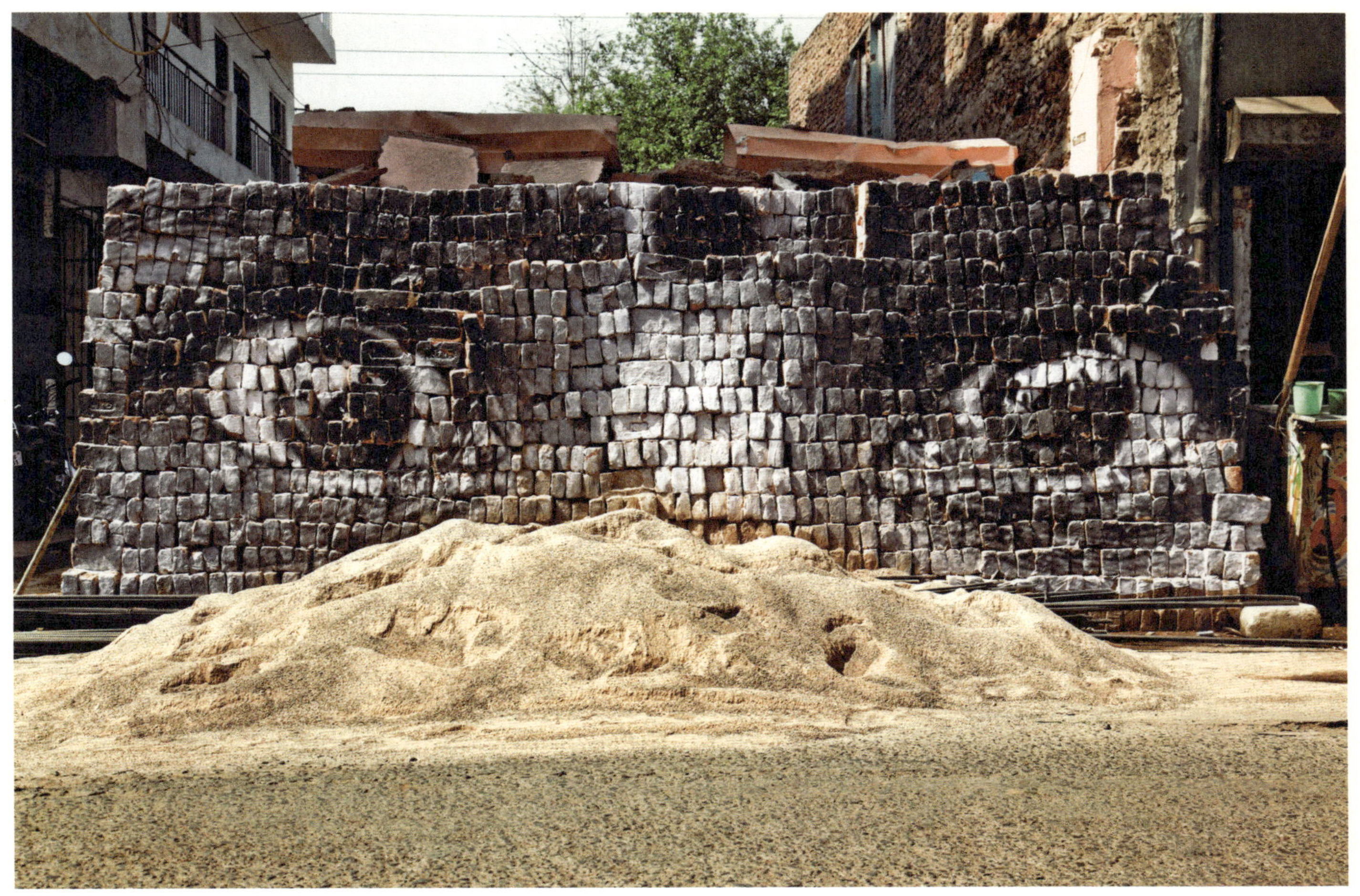

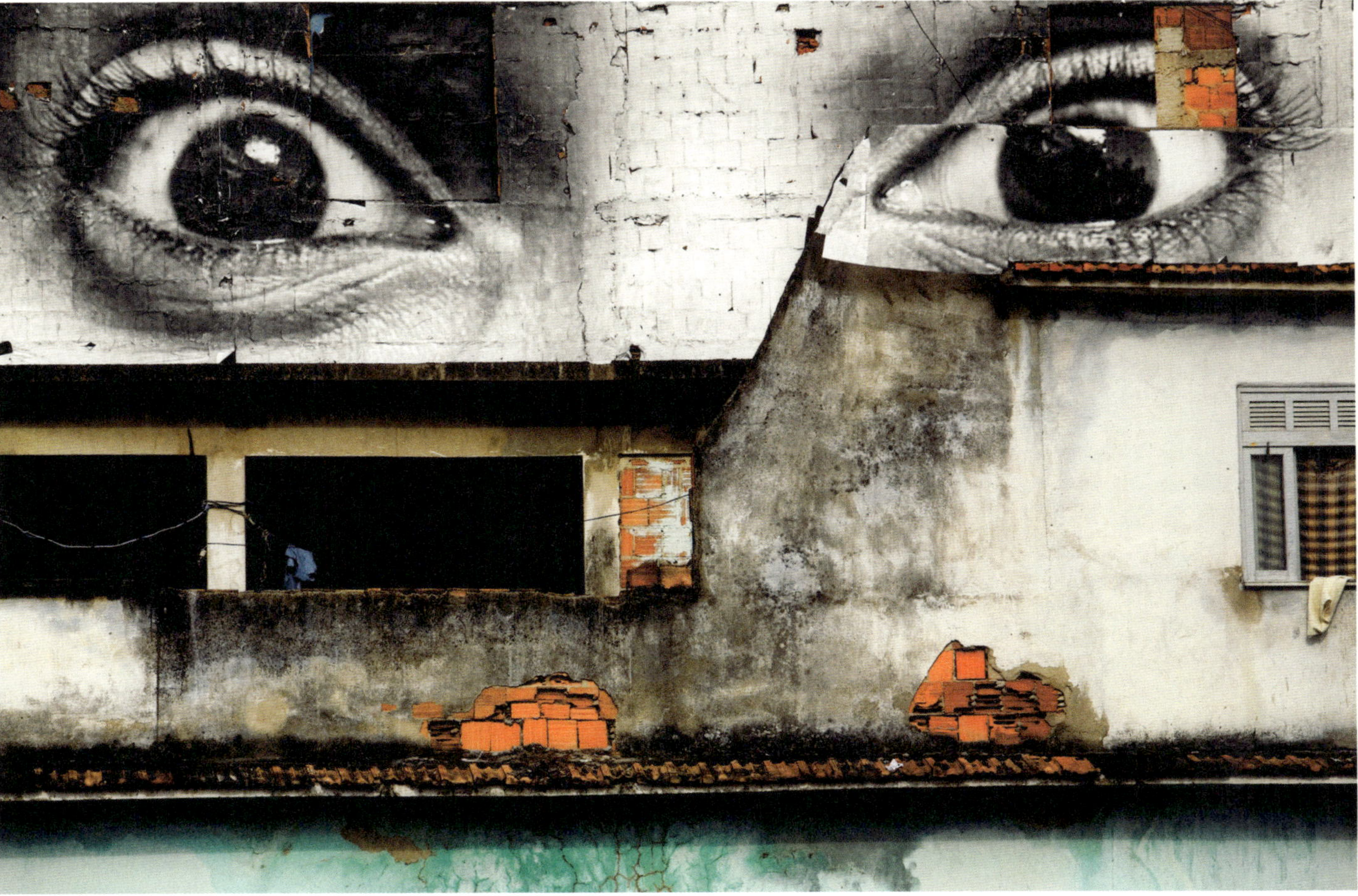

(top) Urmila Devi, New Delhi, India, 2009
(bottom) Elaine Vilela Gomez, Morro da Providência favela, Rio de Janeiro, Brazil, 2008

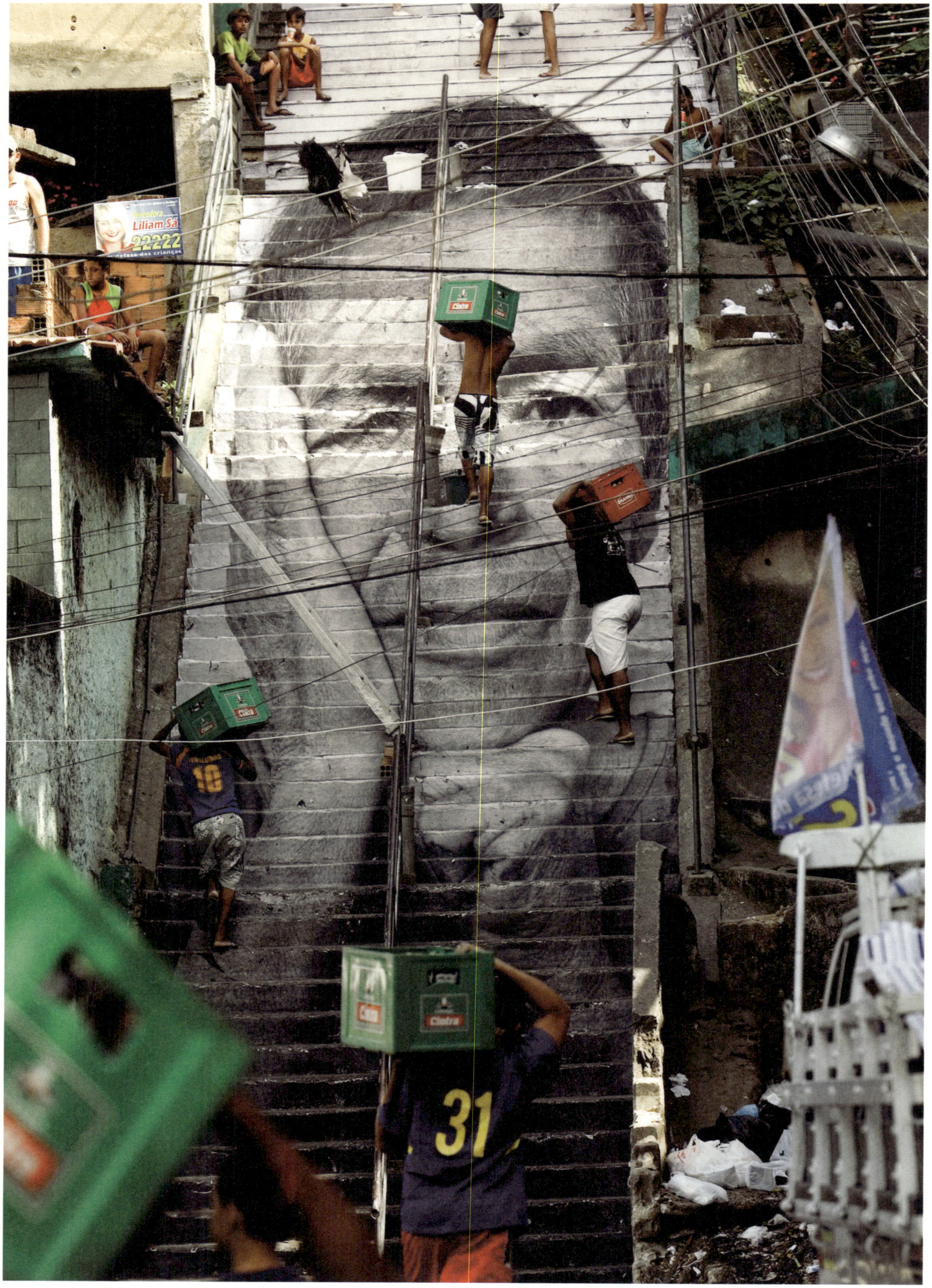

Benedita Florenio Monteiro, Morro da Providência favela, Rio de Janeiro, Brazil, 2008

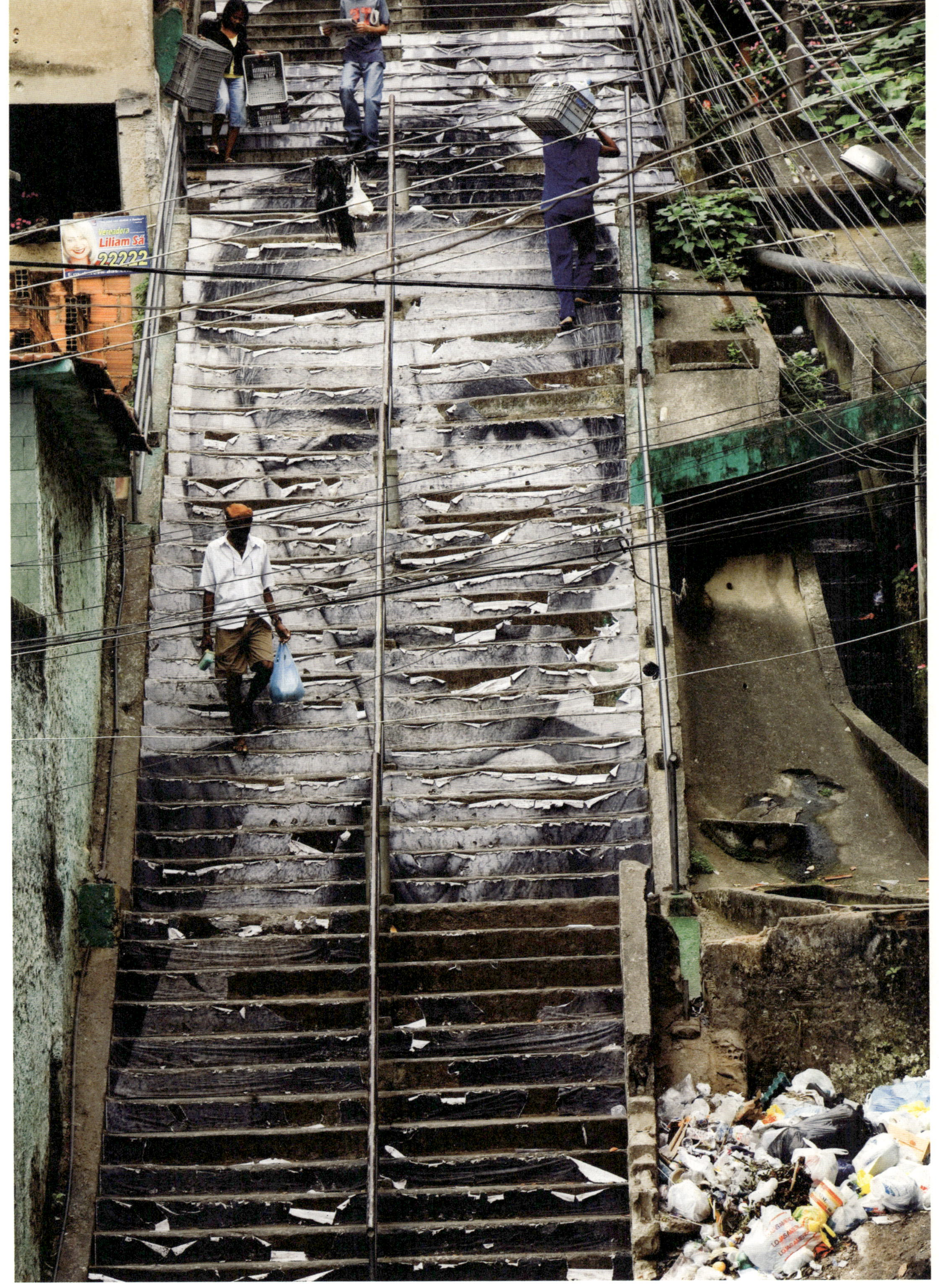

Benedita Florenio Monteiro, Morro da Providência favela, Rio de Janeiro, Brazil, 2008. A few days after the pasting.

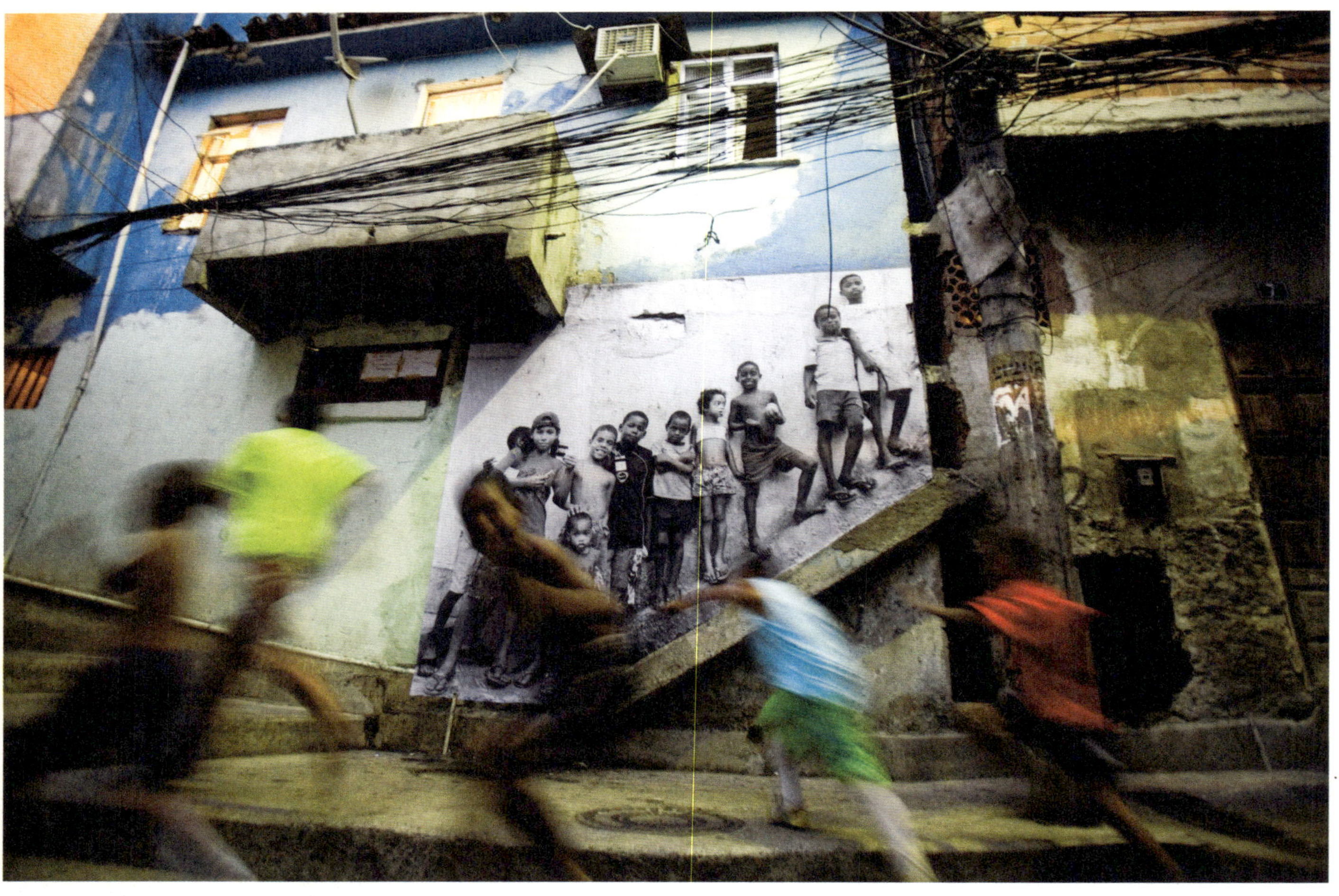

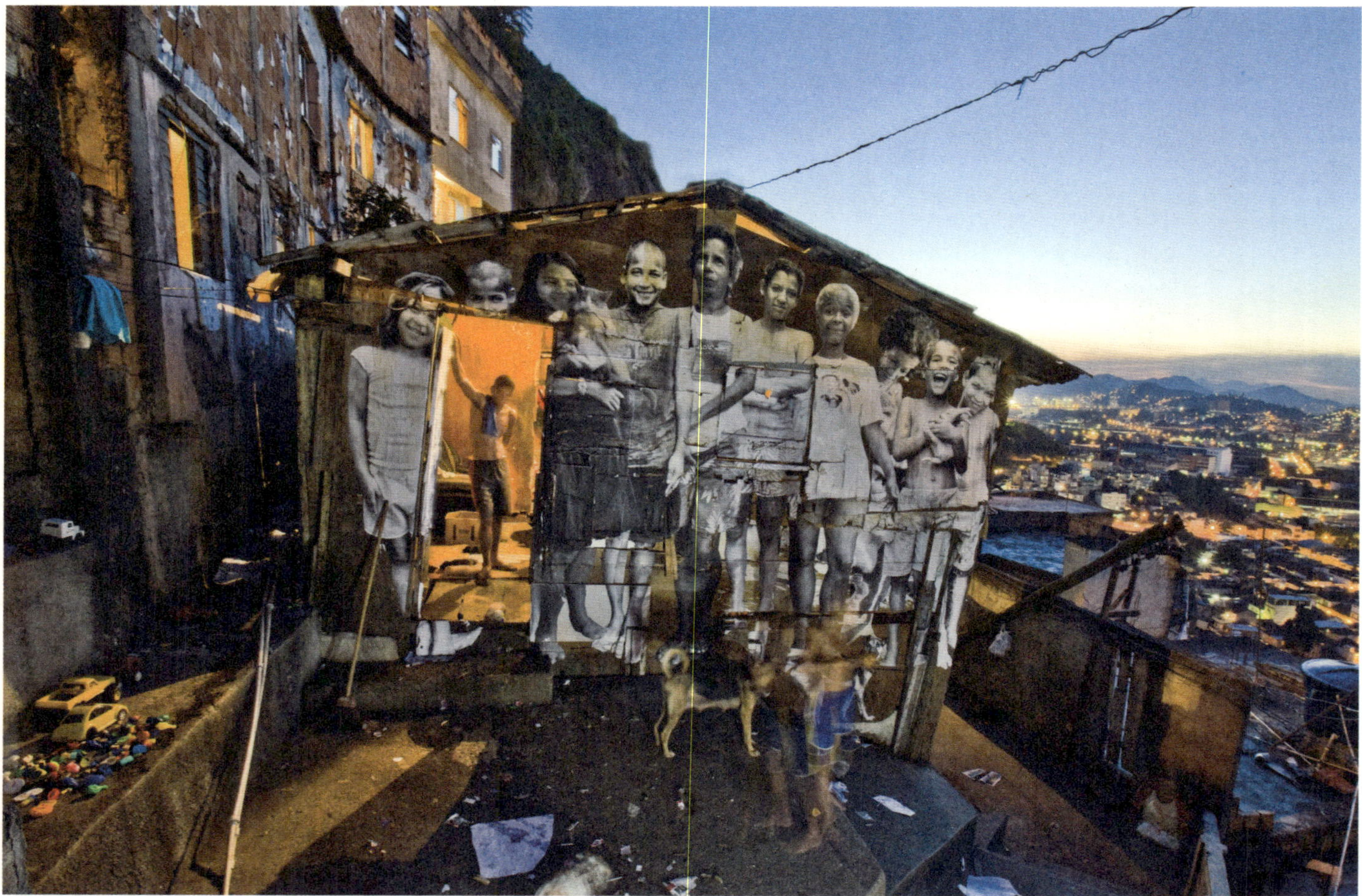

(top) Morro da Providência favela, Rio de Janeiro, Brazil, 2008
(bottom) China House, Morro da Providência favela, Rio de Janeiro, Brazil, 2008

(right) Morro da Providência favela, Rio de Janeiro, Brazil, 2008

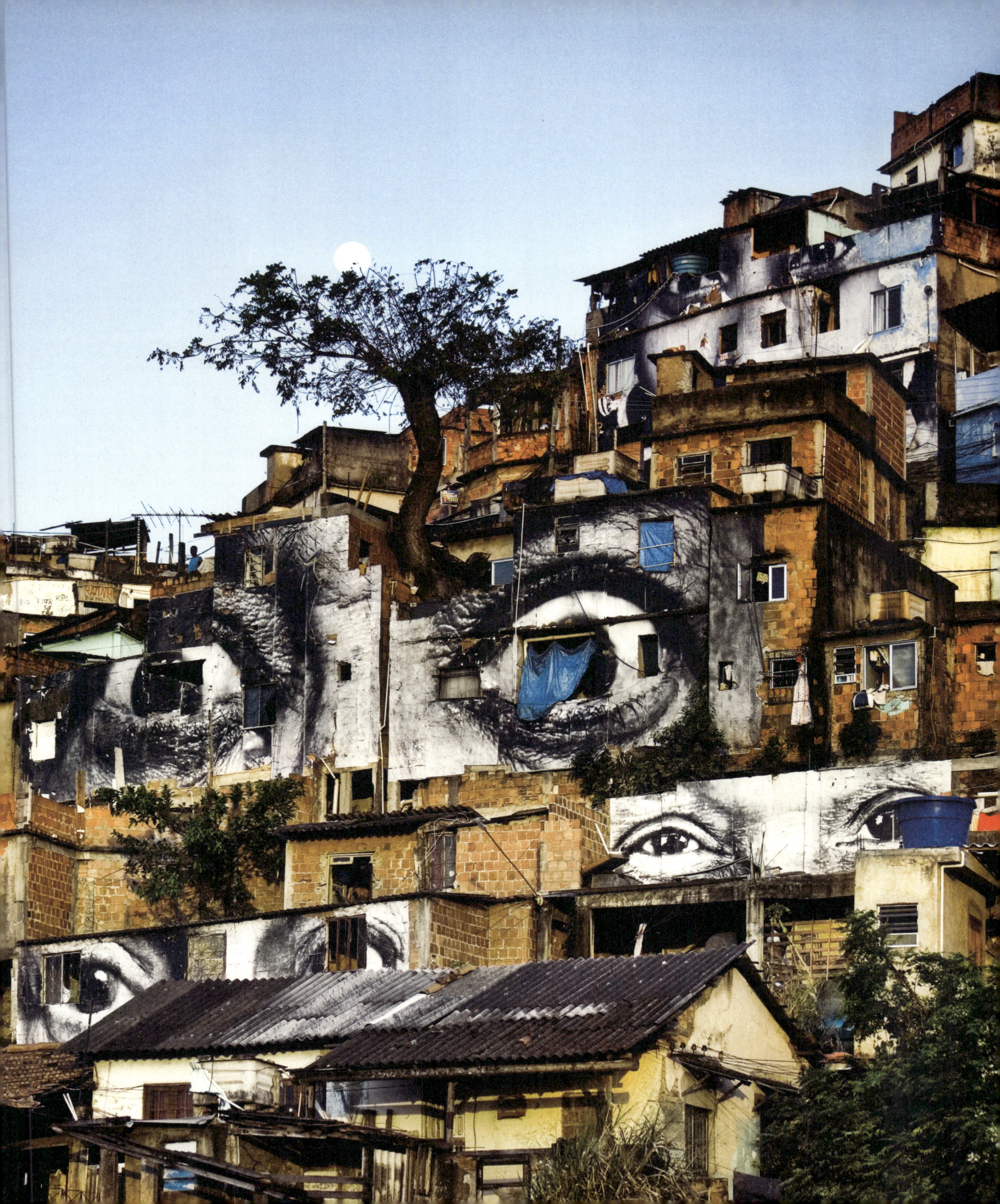

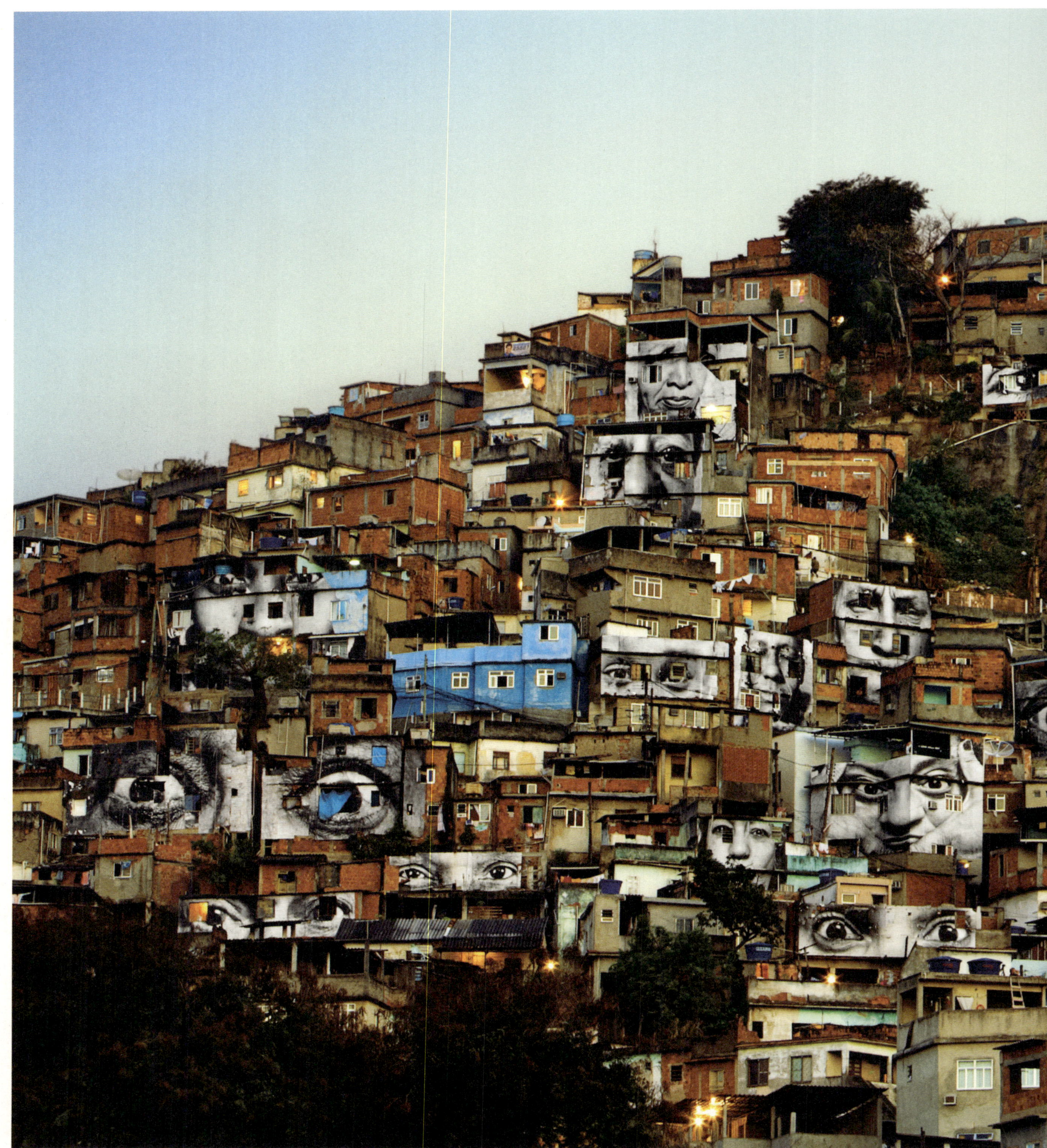

Morro da Providência favela, Rio de Janeiro, Brazil, 2008

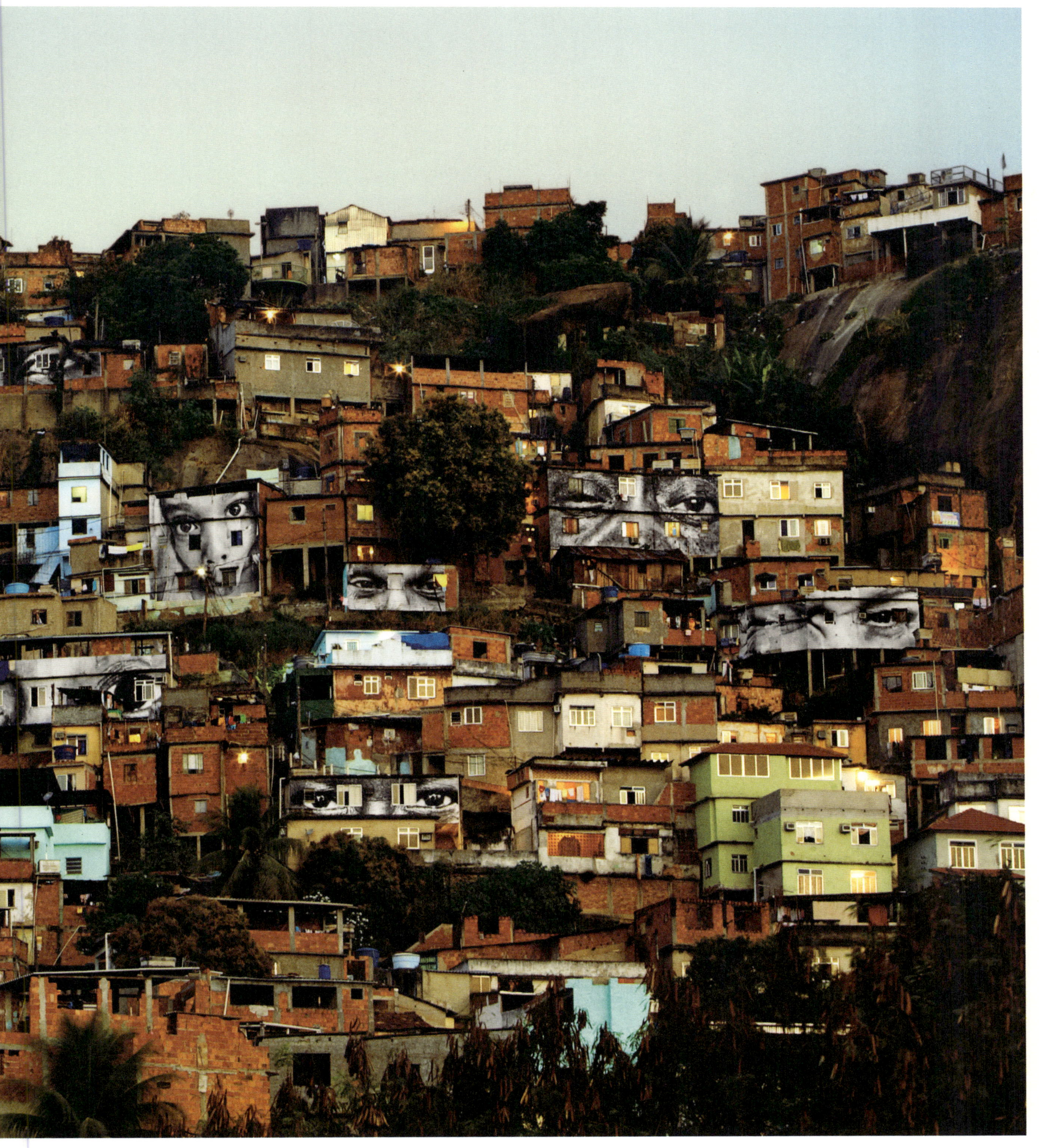

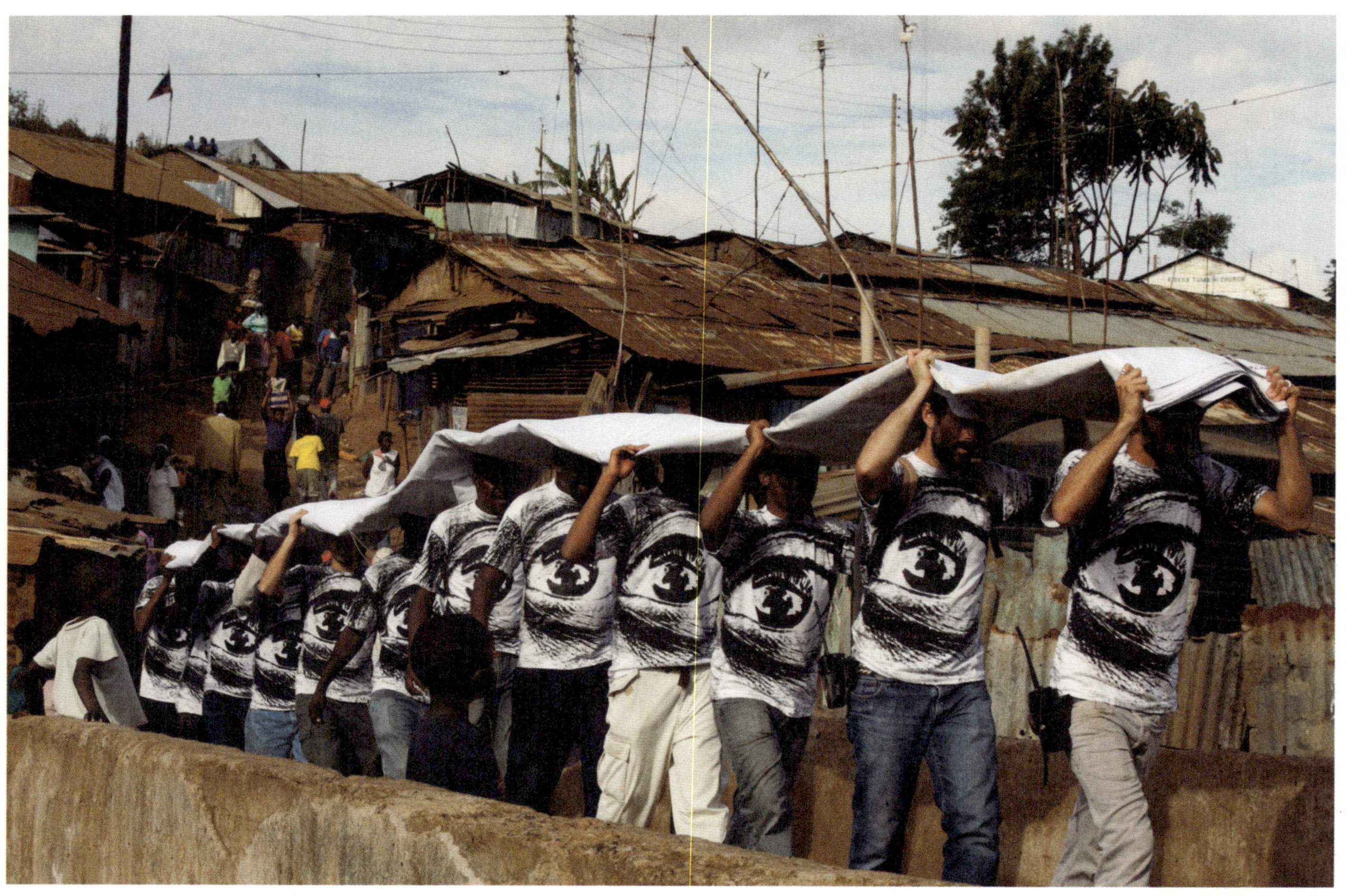

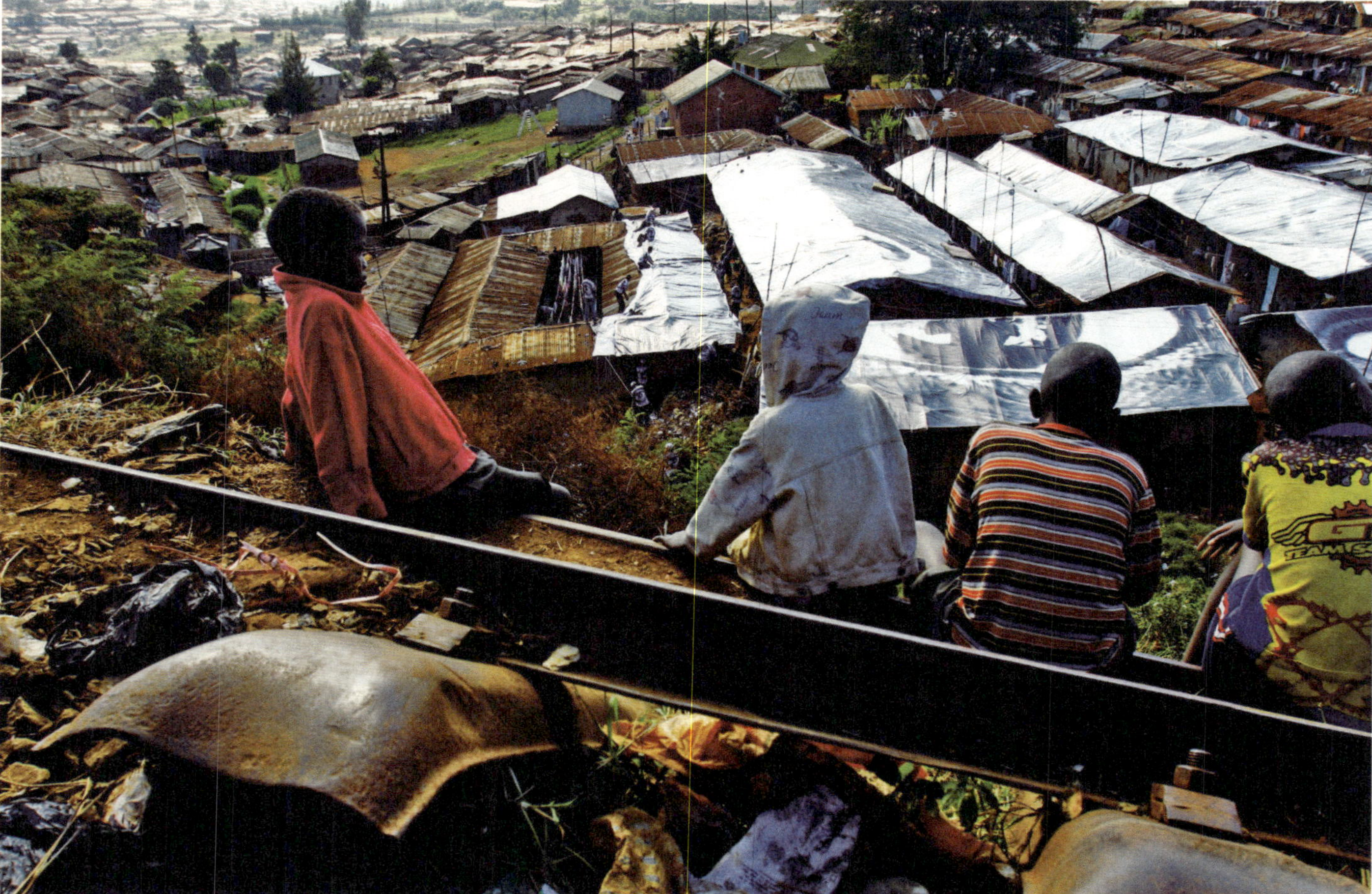

Installing on the rooftops in Kibera, Kenya, 2009

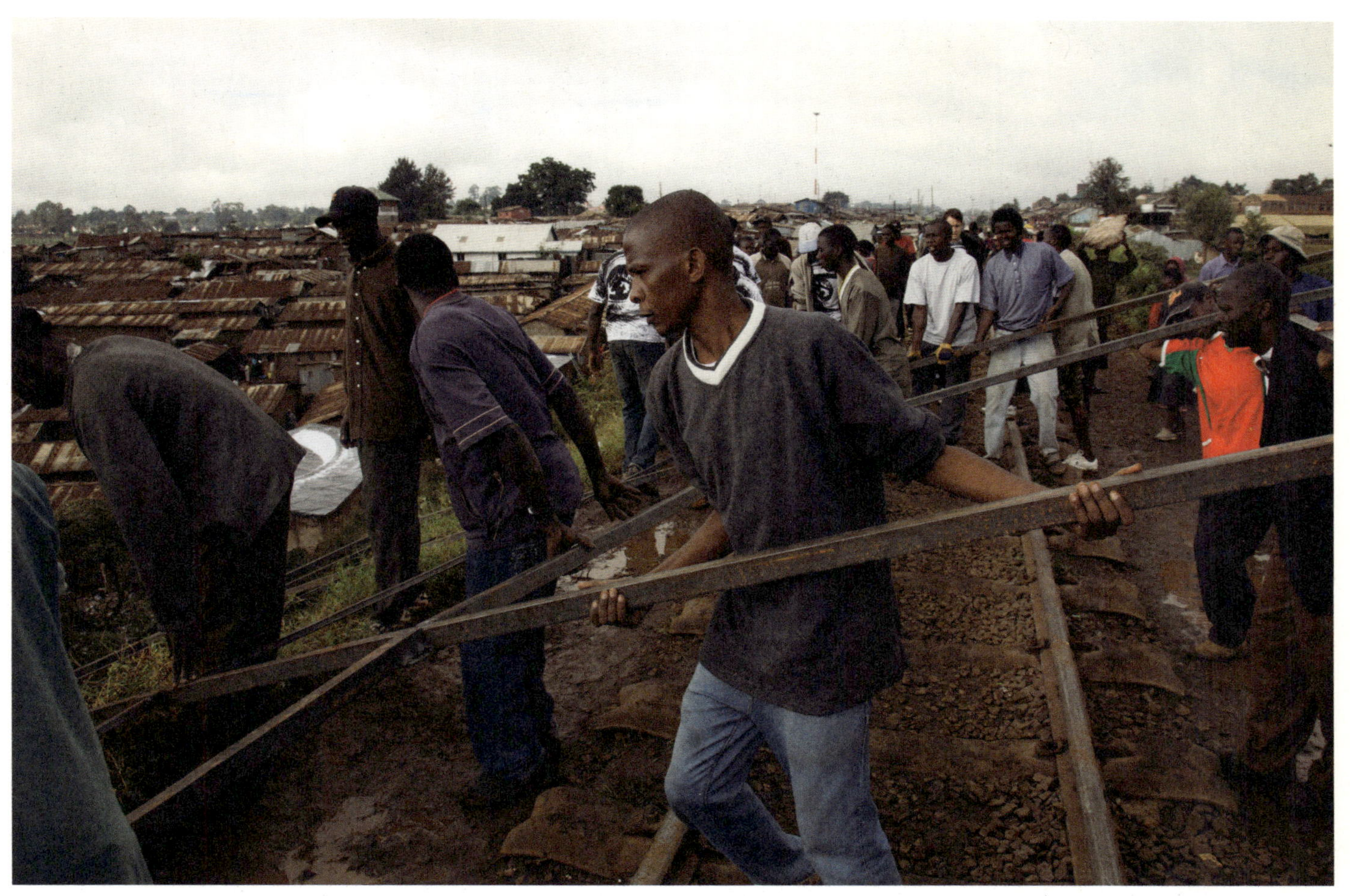

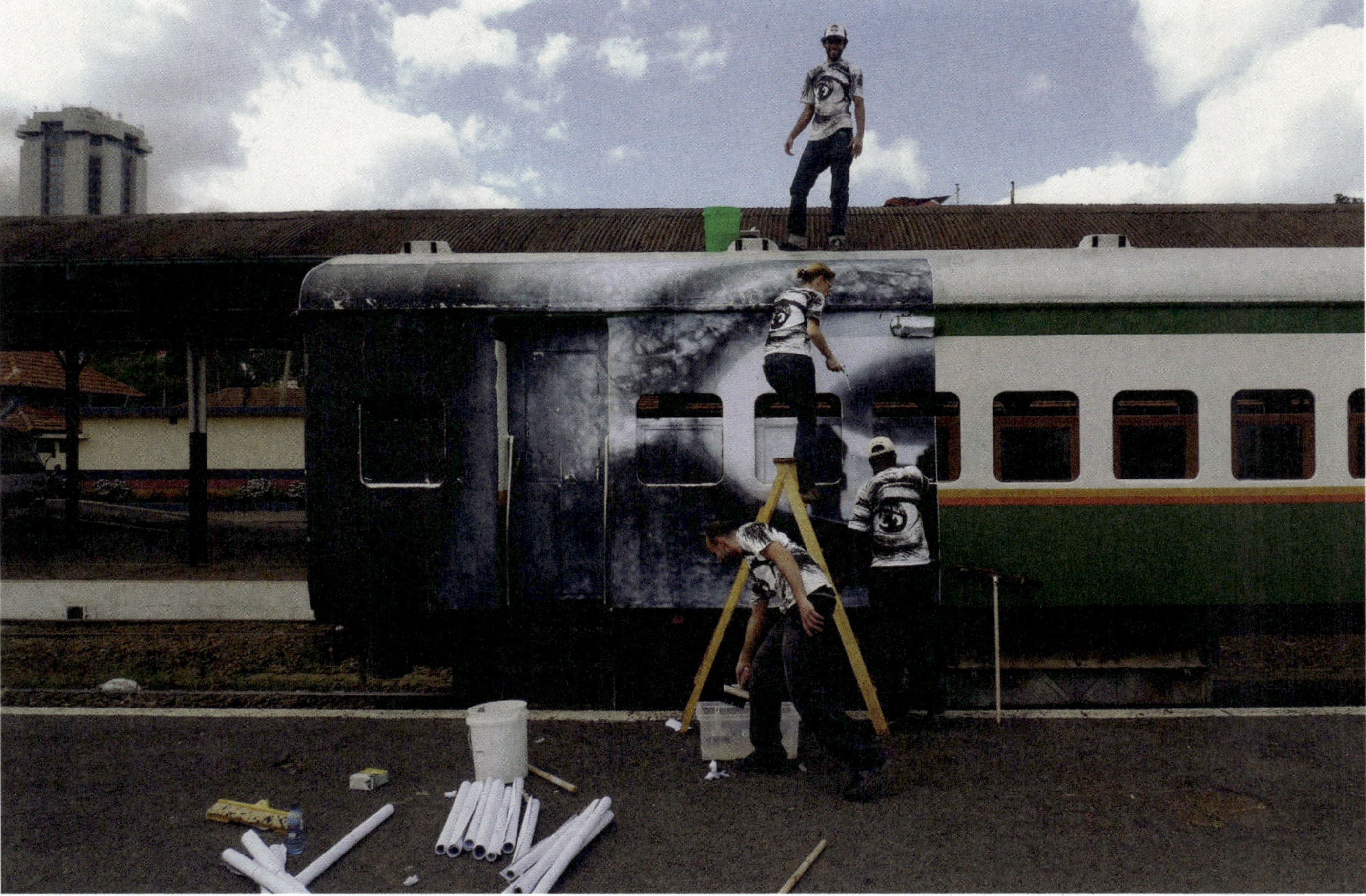

(above) Pasting on the hillside and on a train in Kibera, Kenya, 2009
(overleaf) Train passing, Kibera, Kenya, 2009

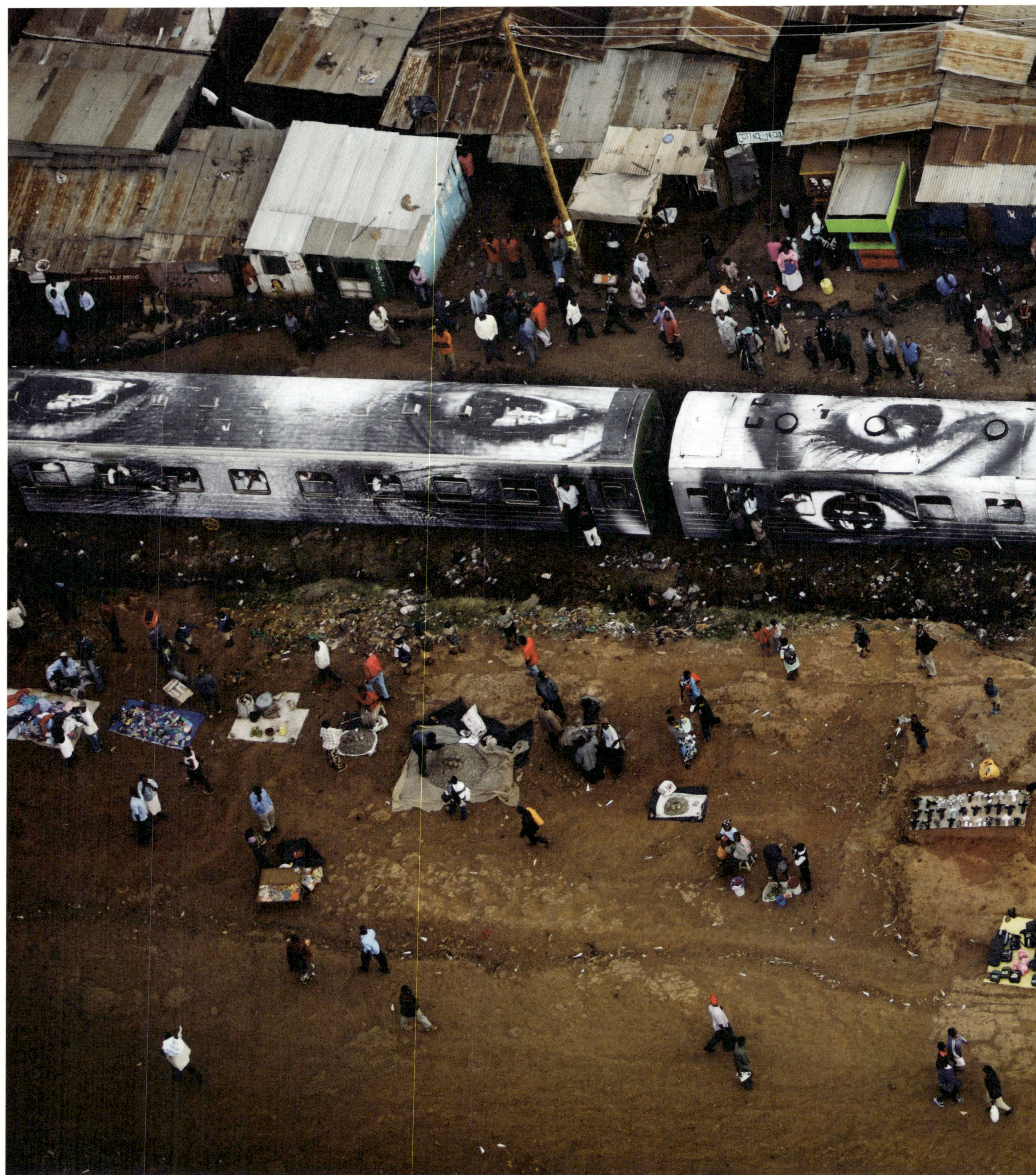

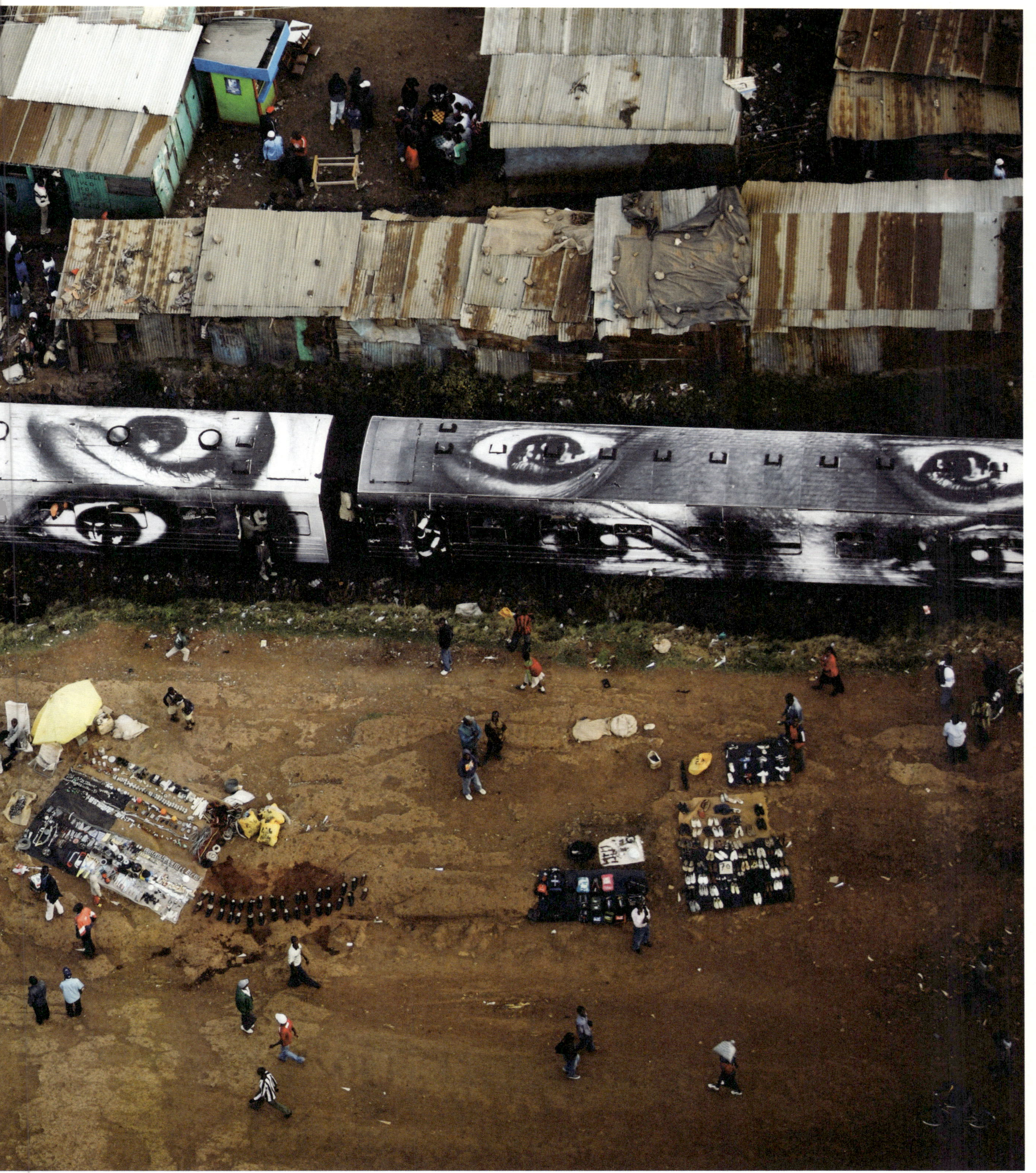

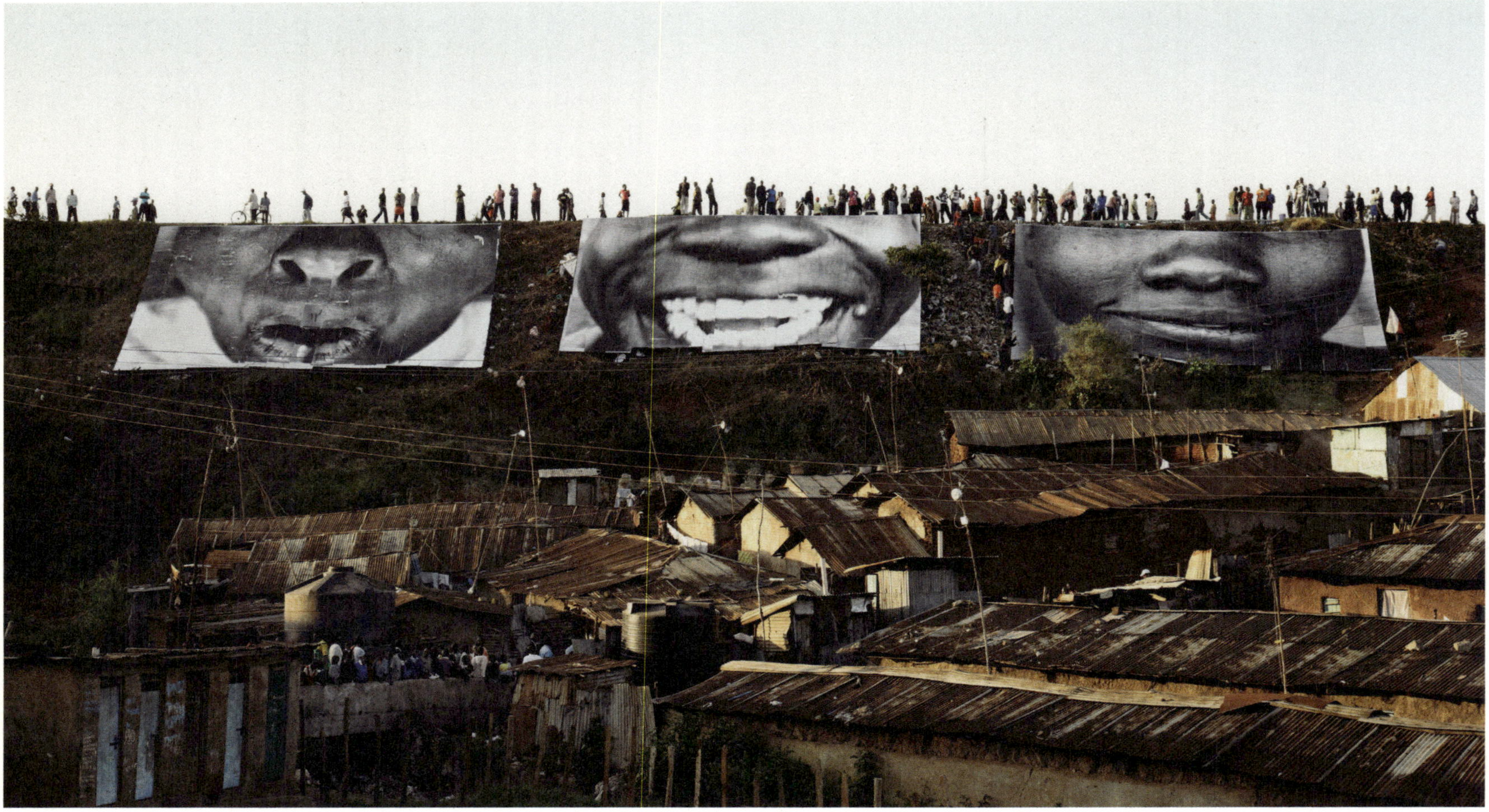

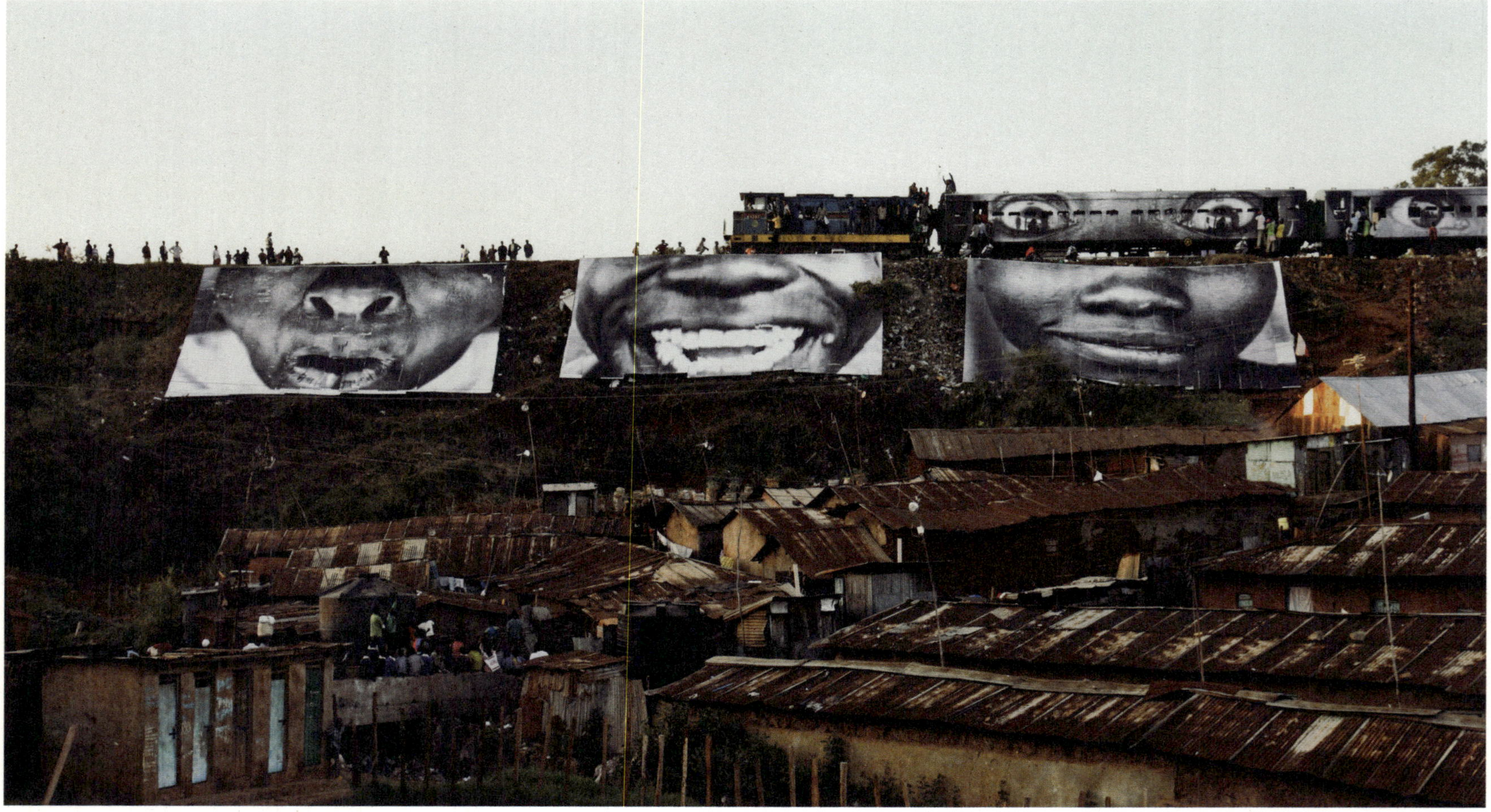

Train passing, Kibera, Kenya, 2009

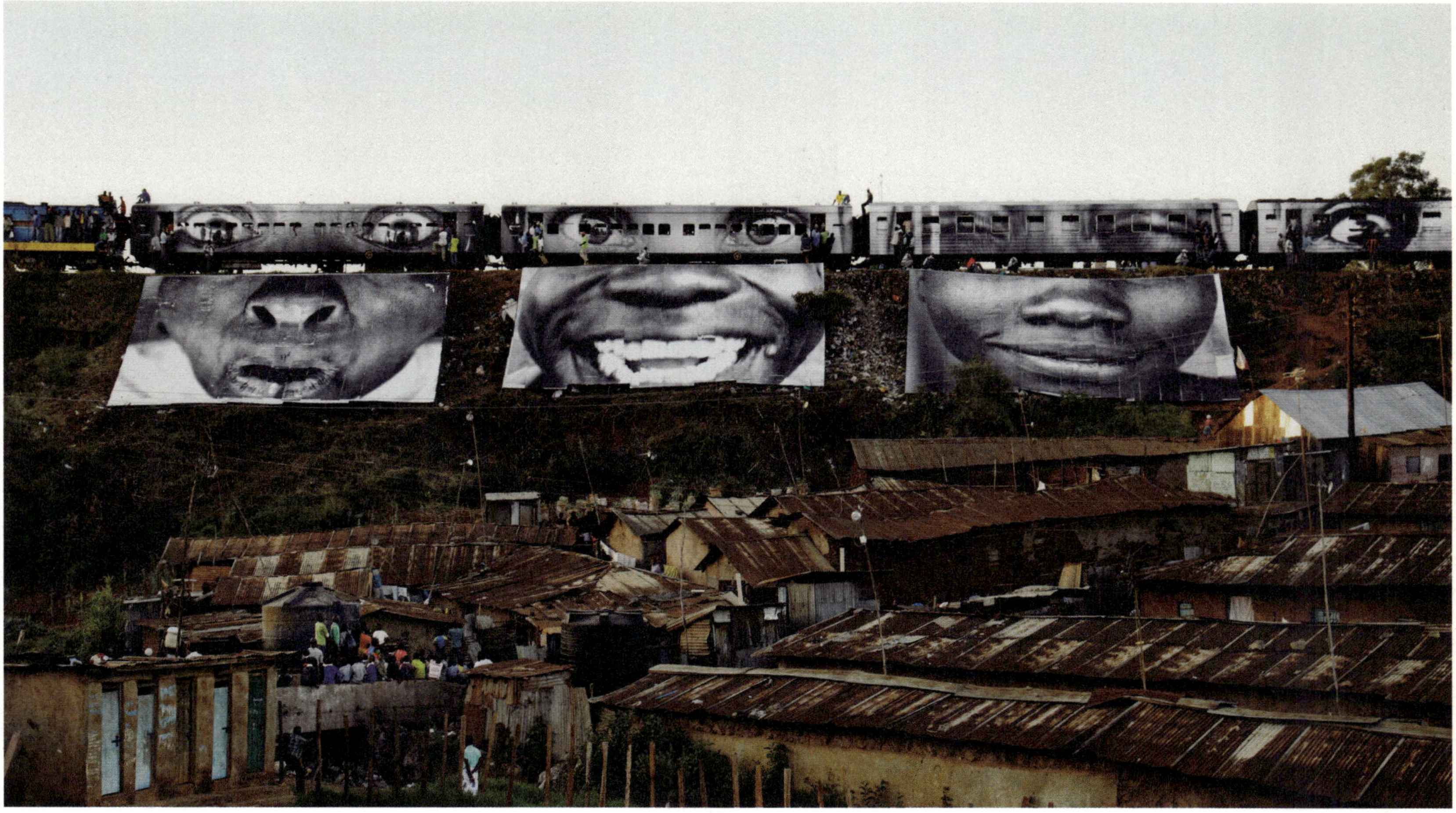

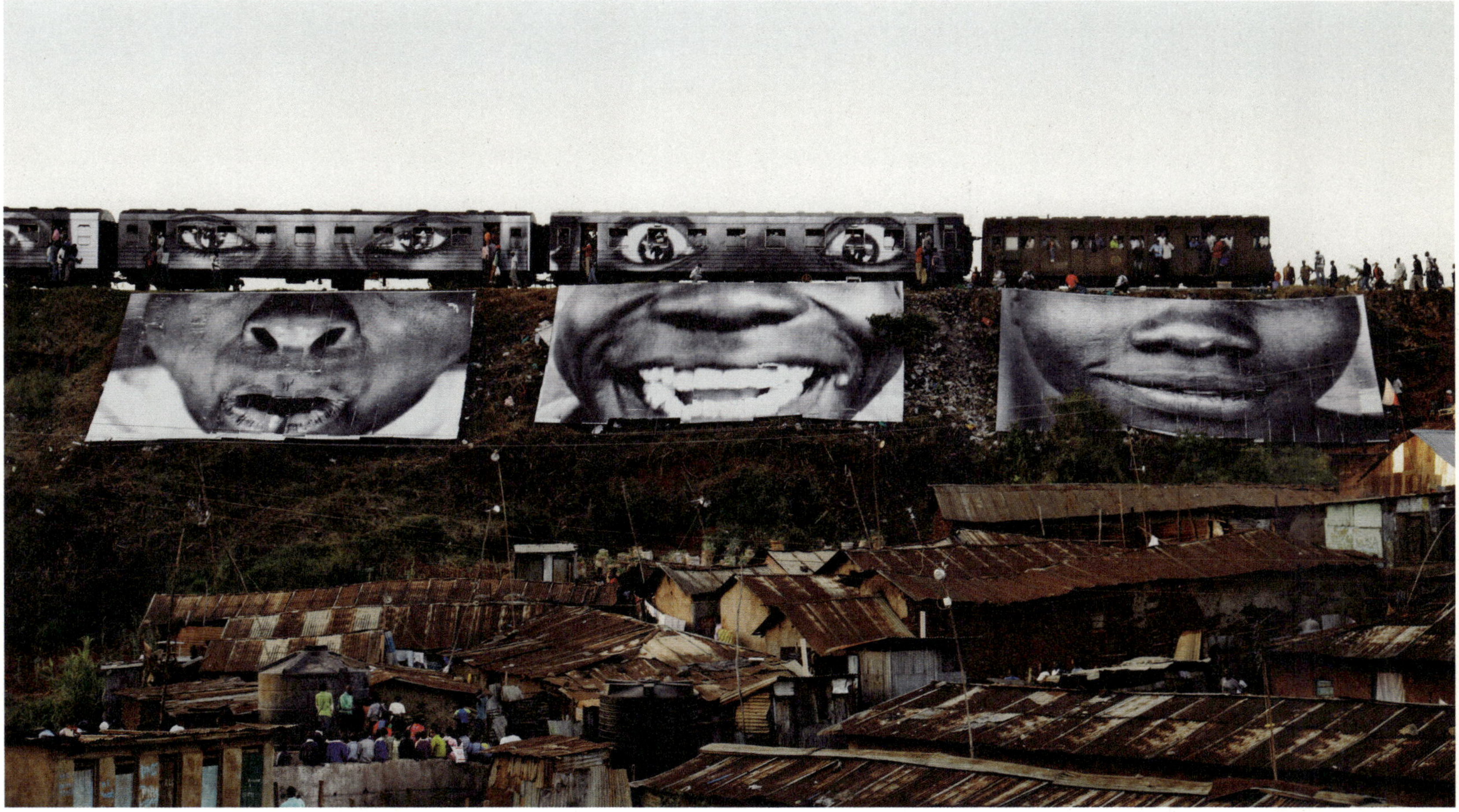

Train passing, Kibera, Kenya, 2009

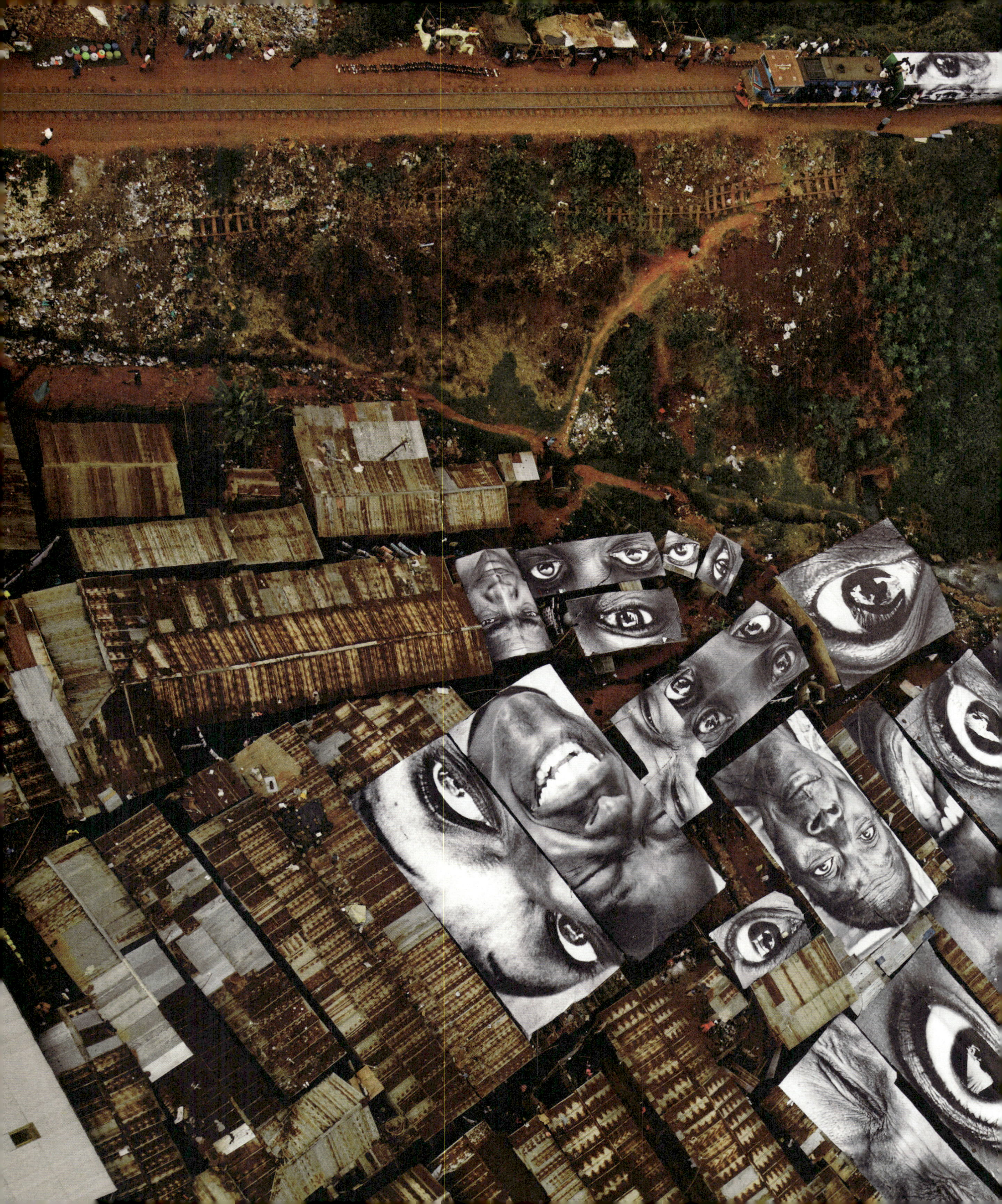

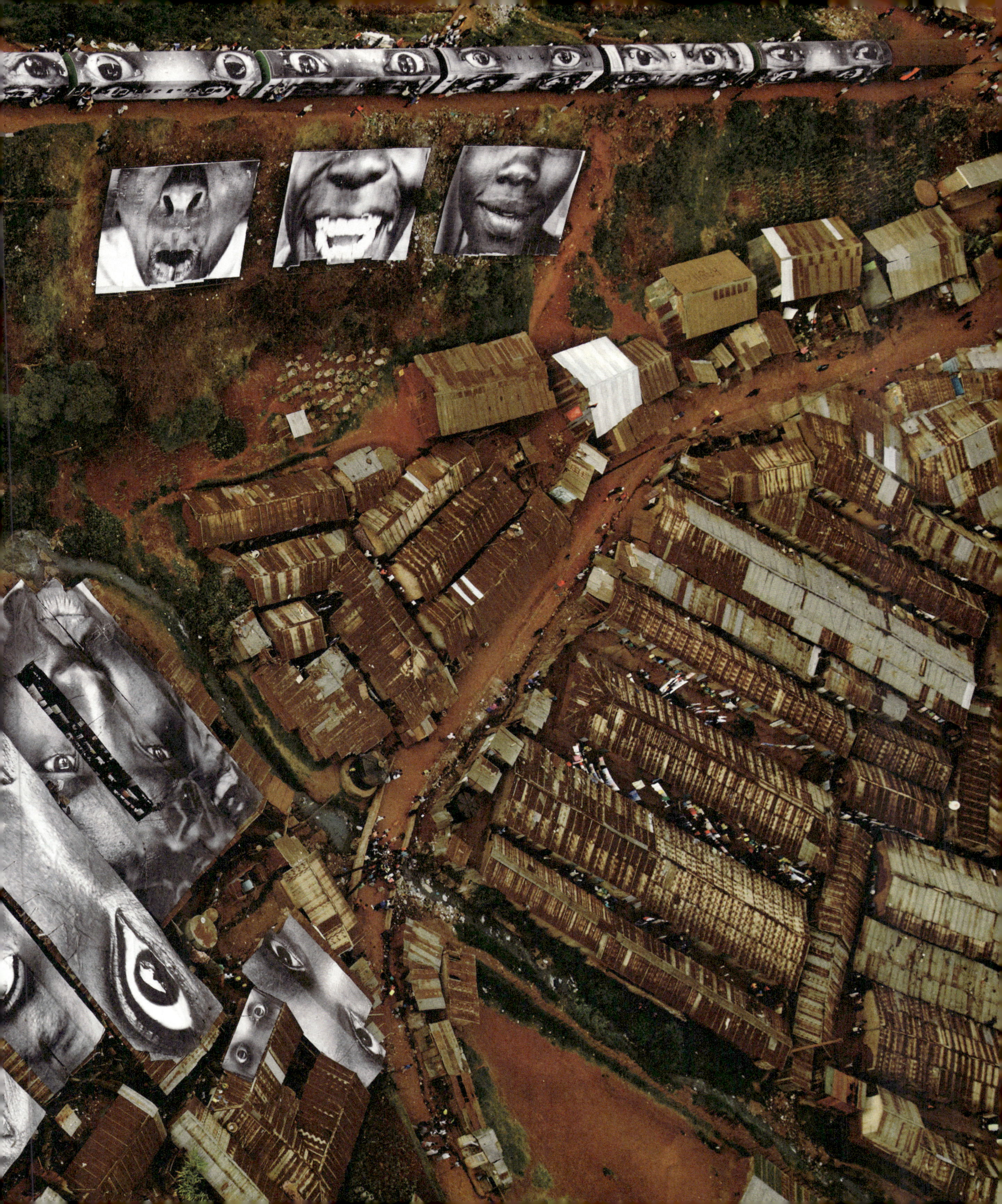

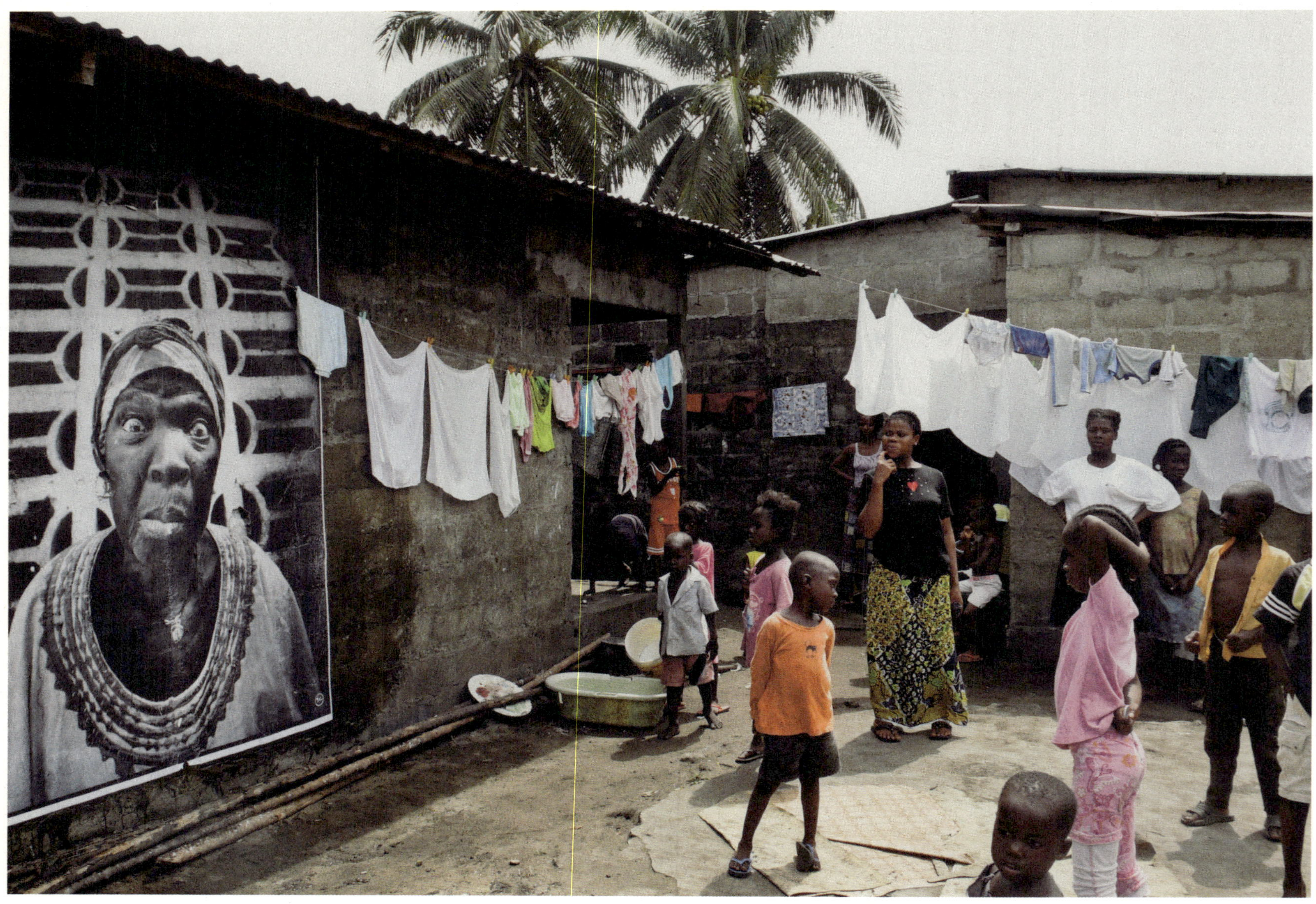

Jessie Jon, Monrovia, Liberia, 2008
(previous page) Kibera, Kenya, 2009

'When the train passed, it connected twice with the faces on the hillside. On the second time, I photographed it from a helicopter above Kibera. Most of these eyes are still on the roofs today, because they are made of vinyl so they protect the houses from the rain. Every year we go back to cover more roofs, and in 2015 all of the roofs in this picture were covered with eyes and faces.' – JR

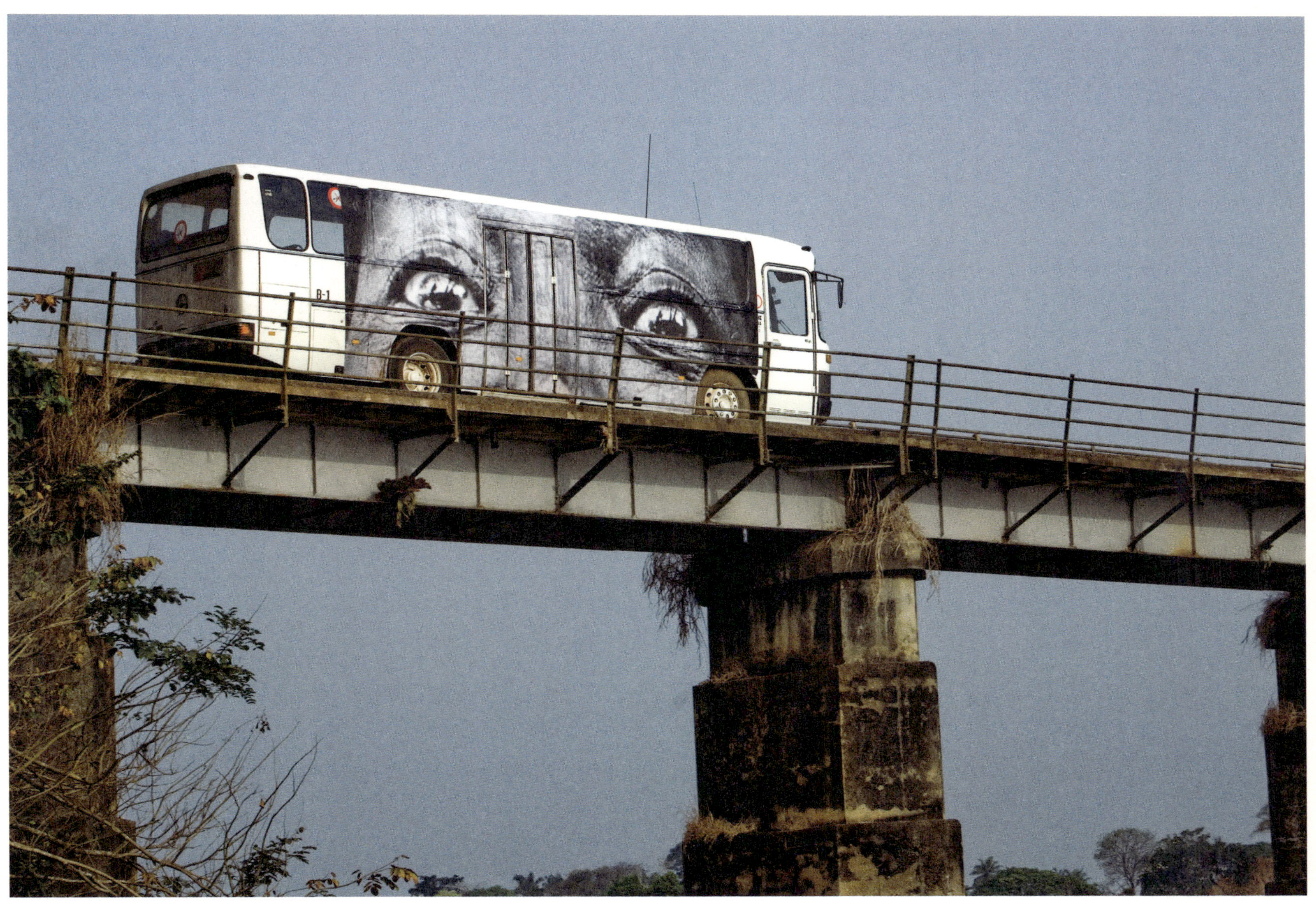

Sara Toe, Bo, Sierra Leone, 2008

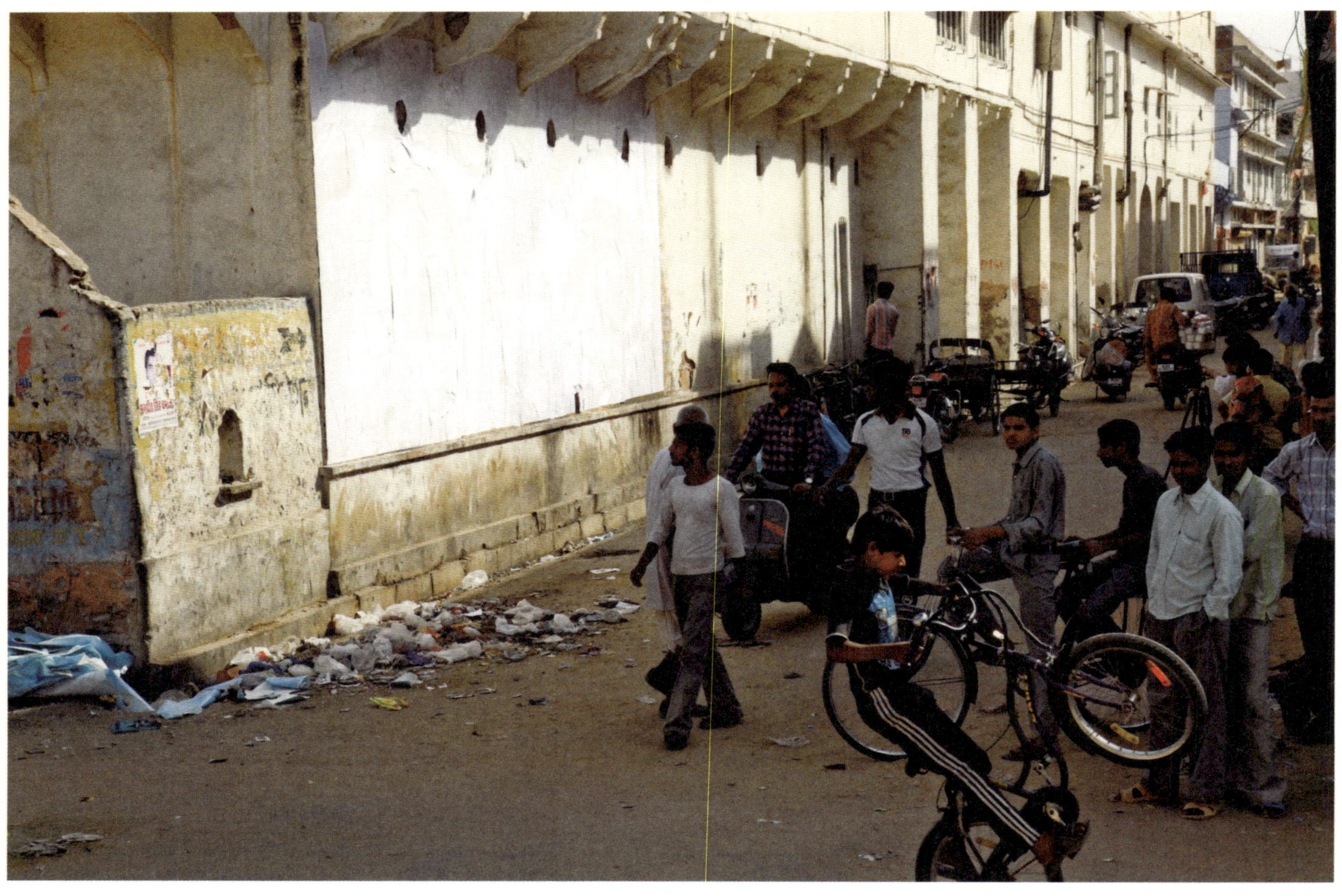

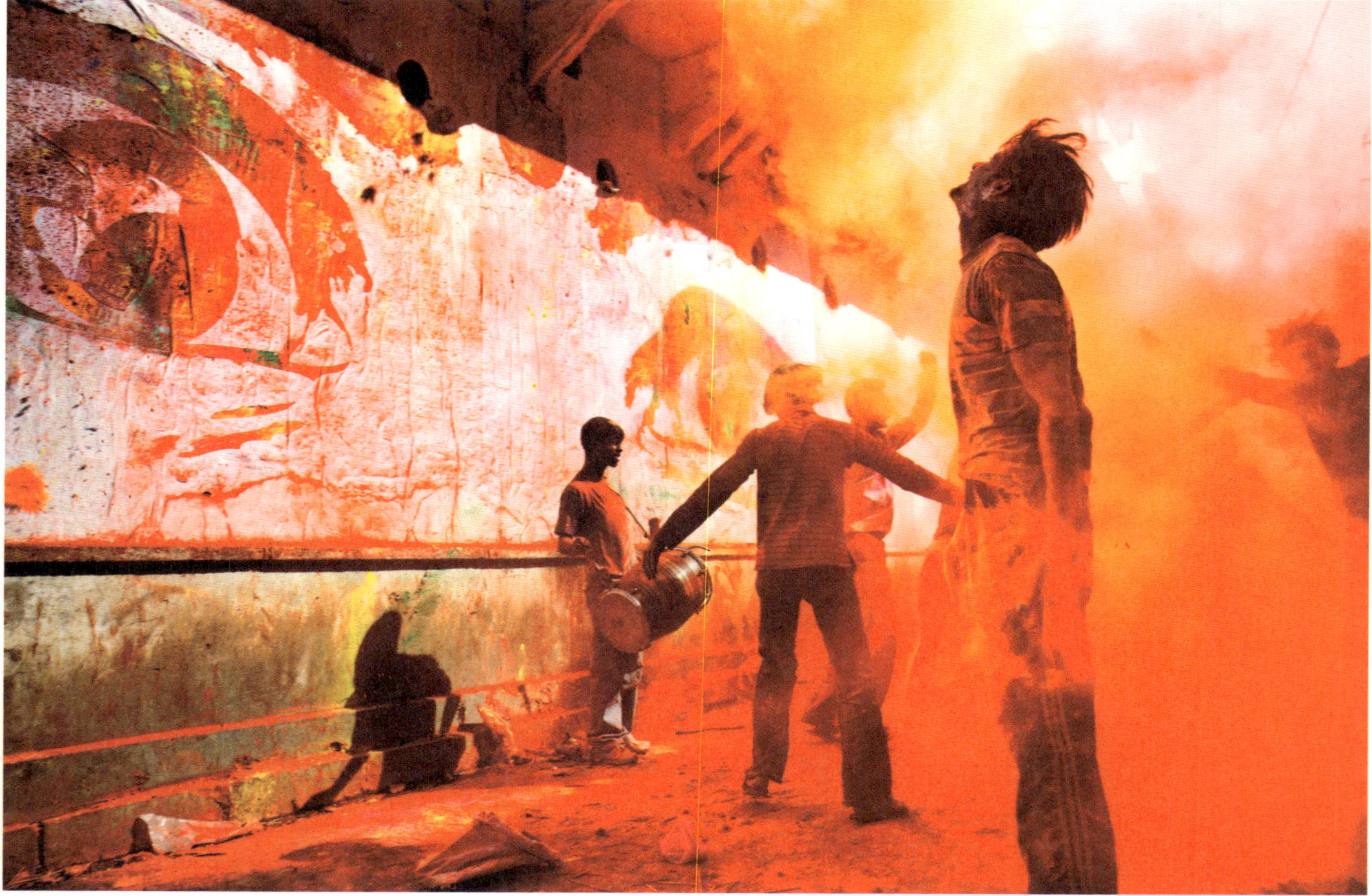

Holi Festival, Jaipur, India, 2009

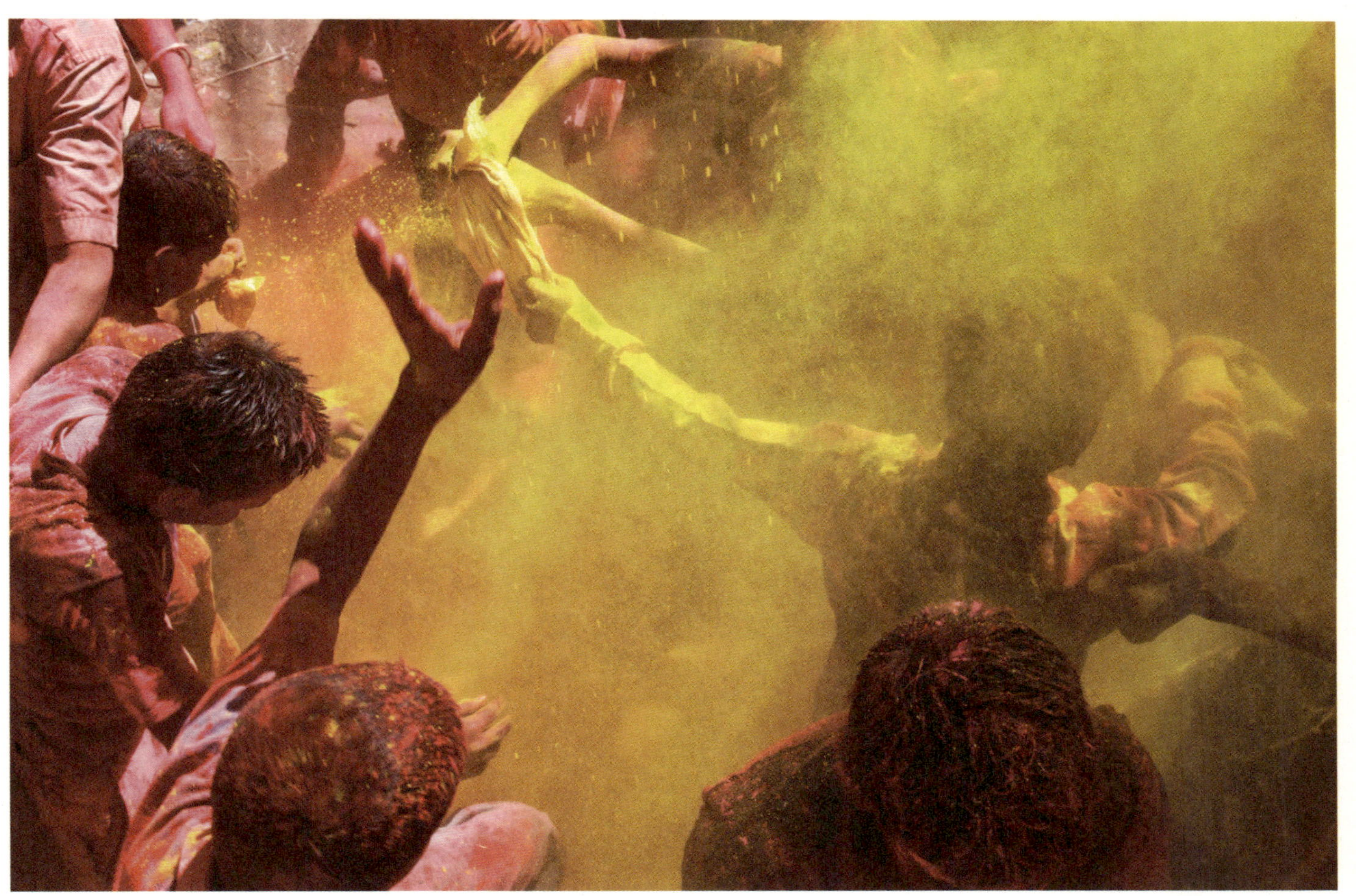

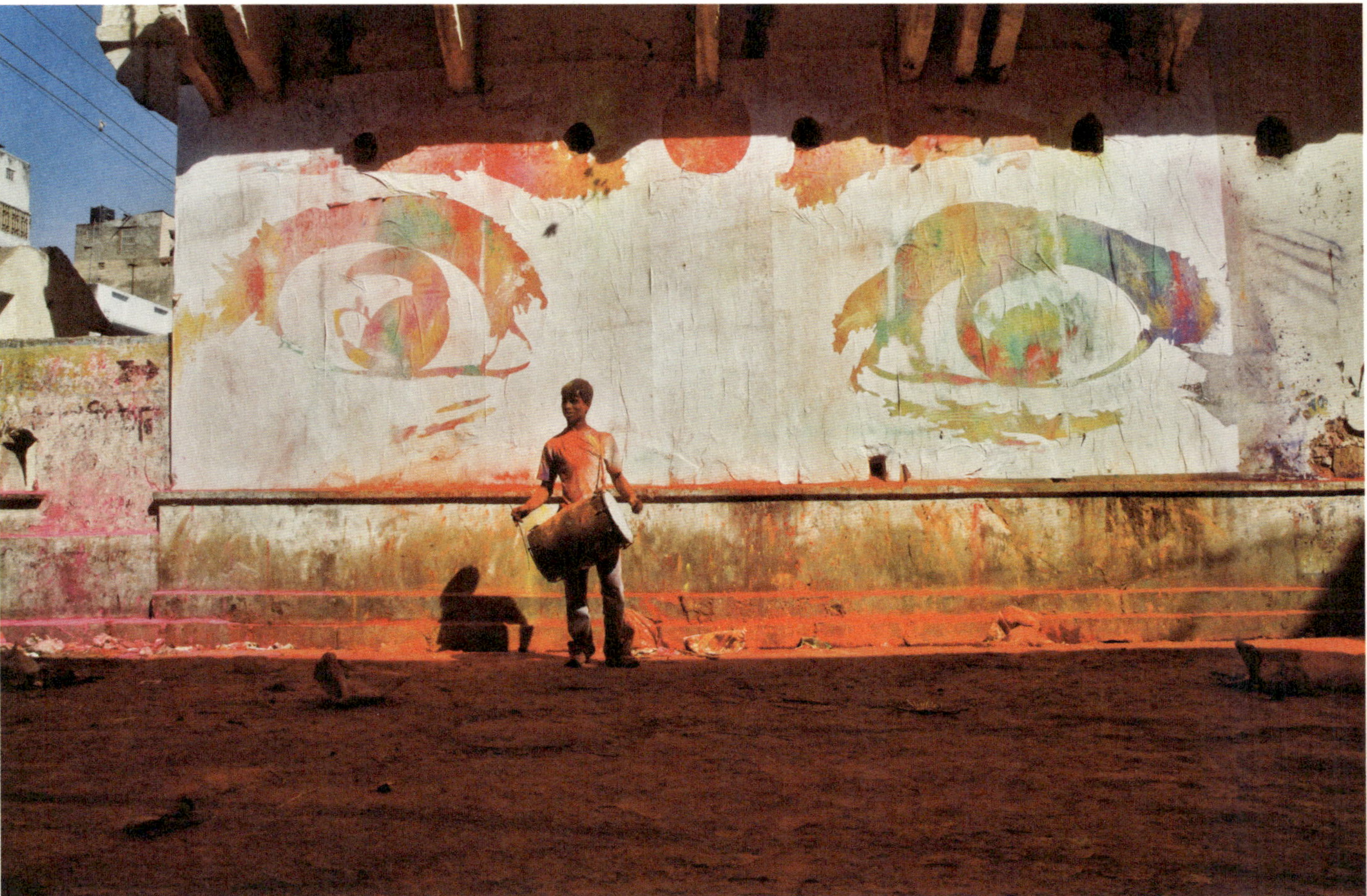

Holi Festival, Jaipur, India, 2009
(overleaf) Marché aux Herbes, Brussels, Belgium, 2008

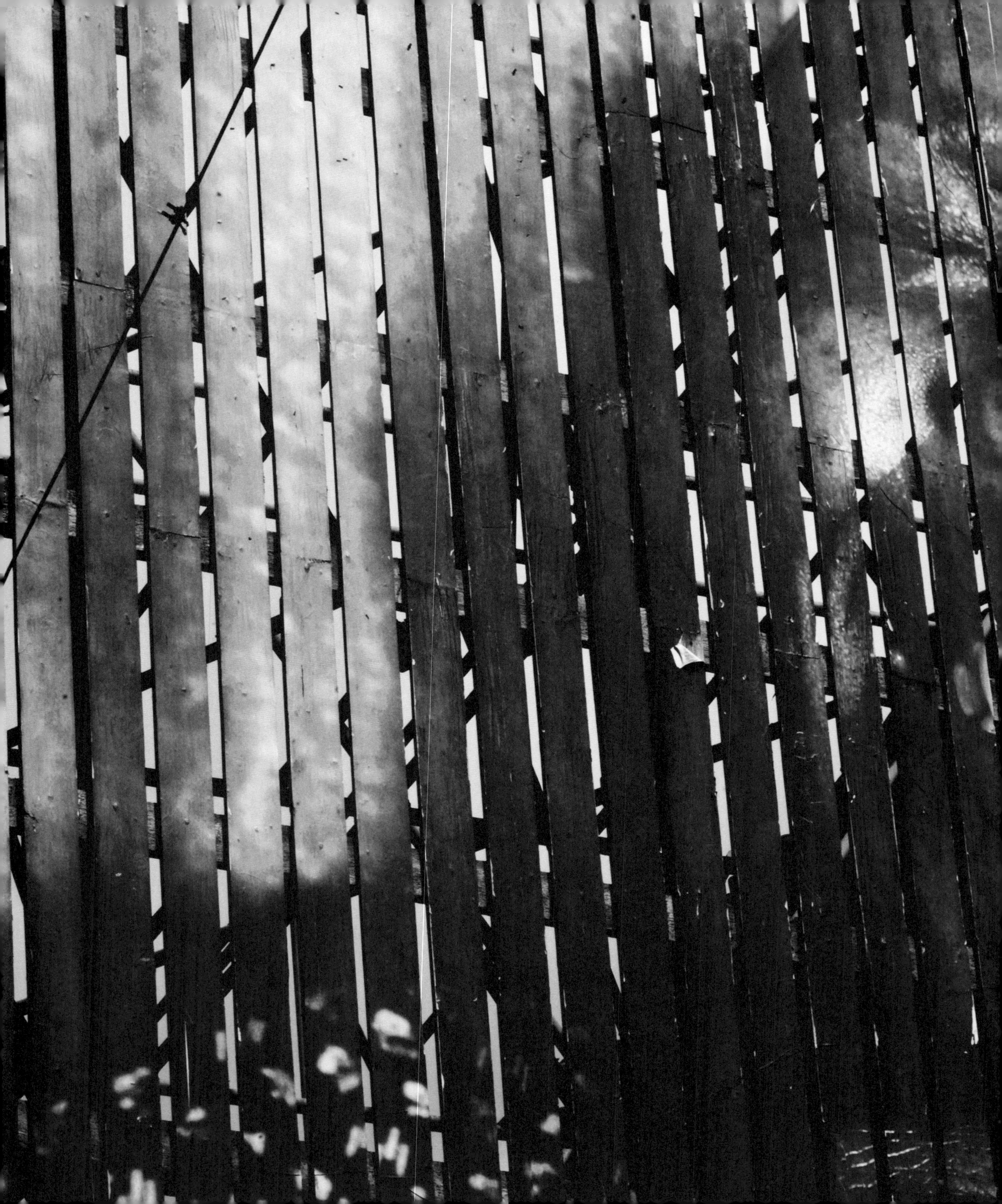

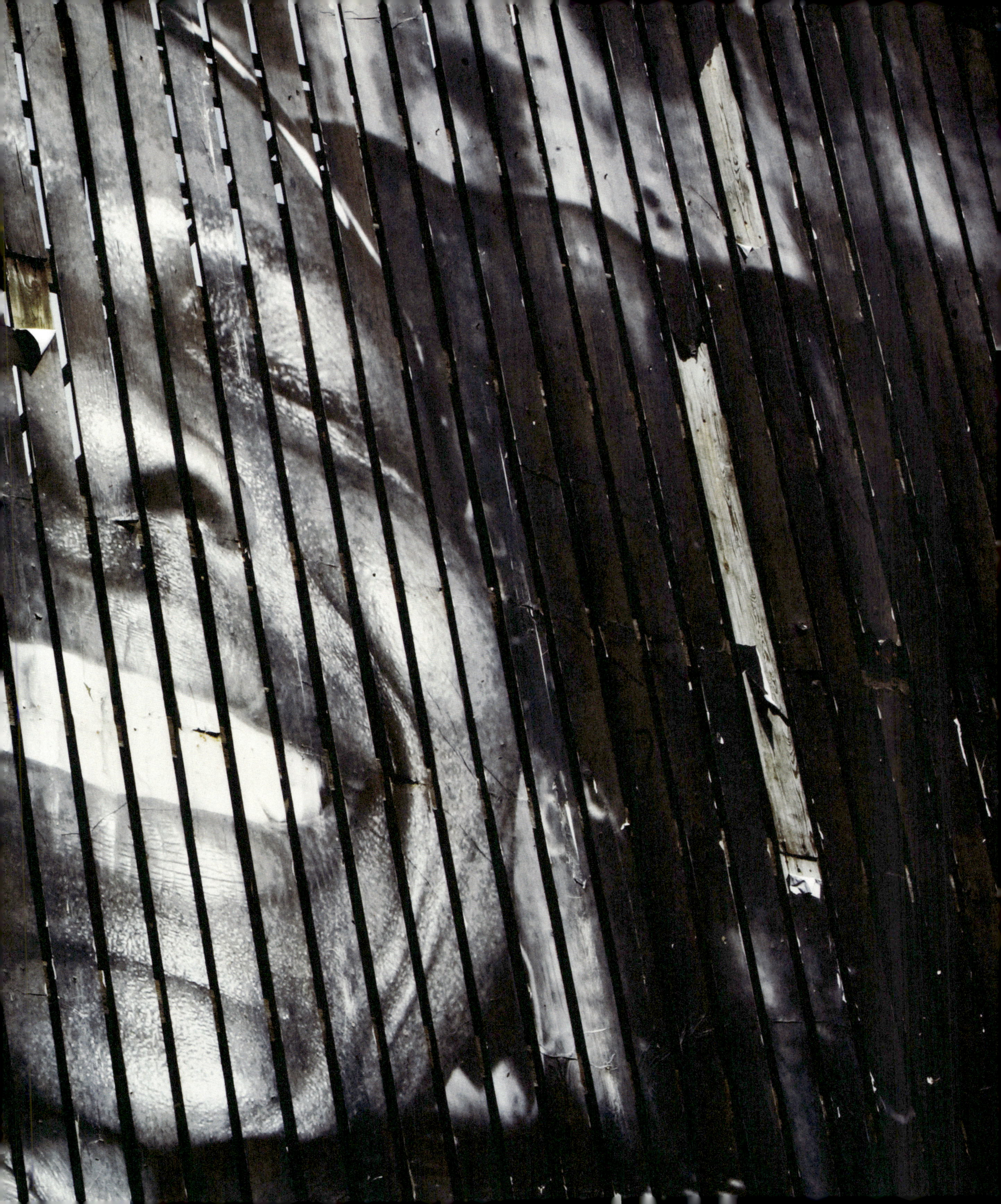

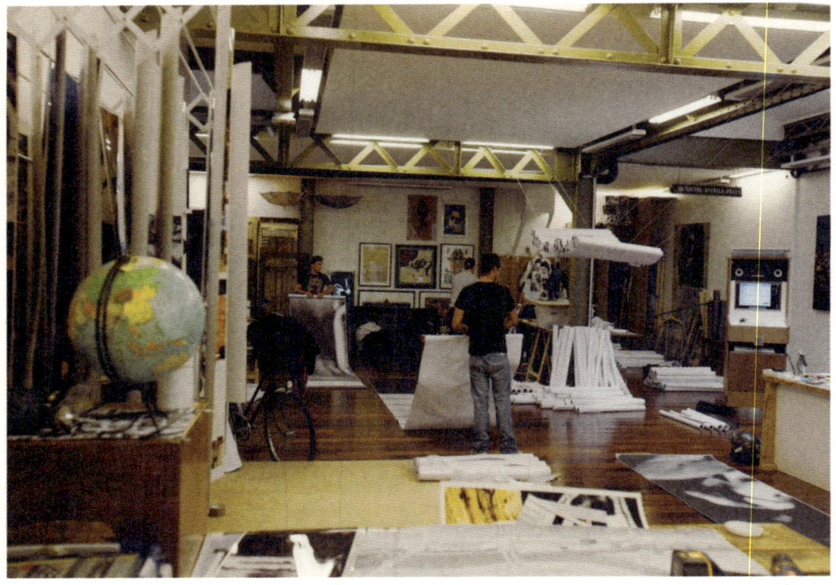

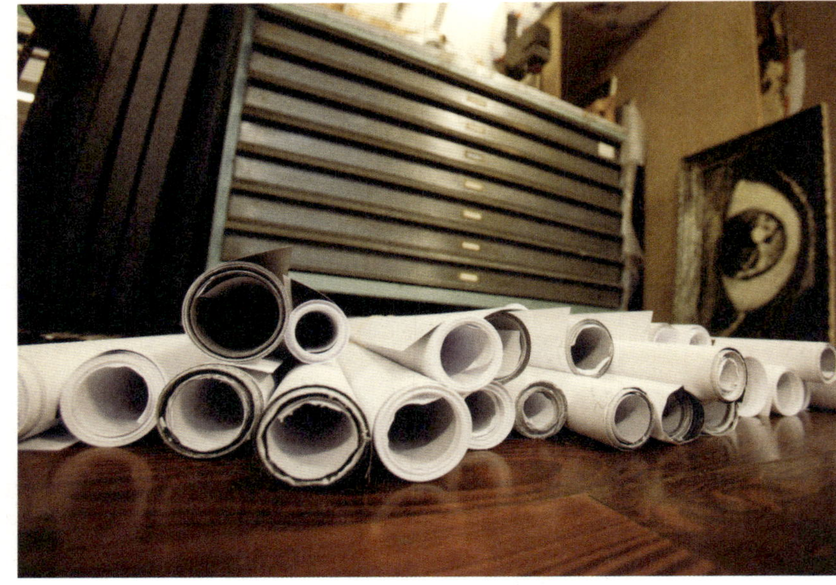

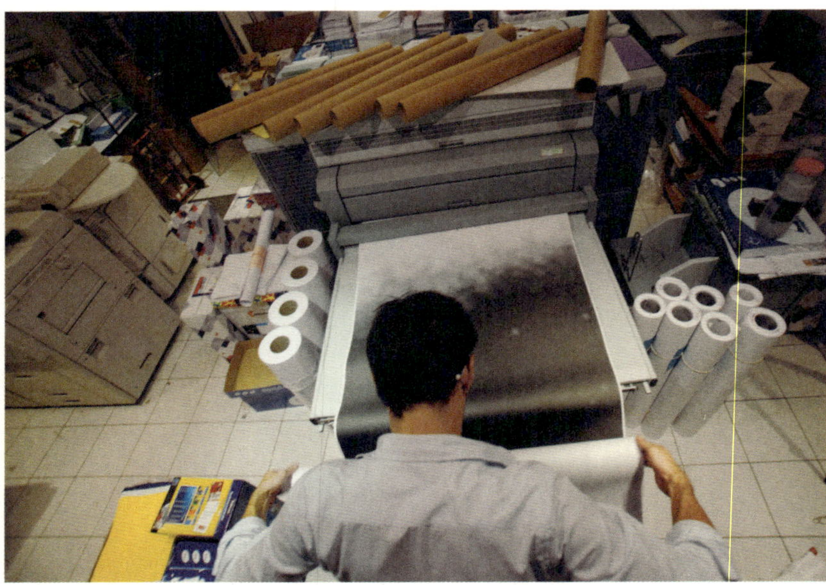

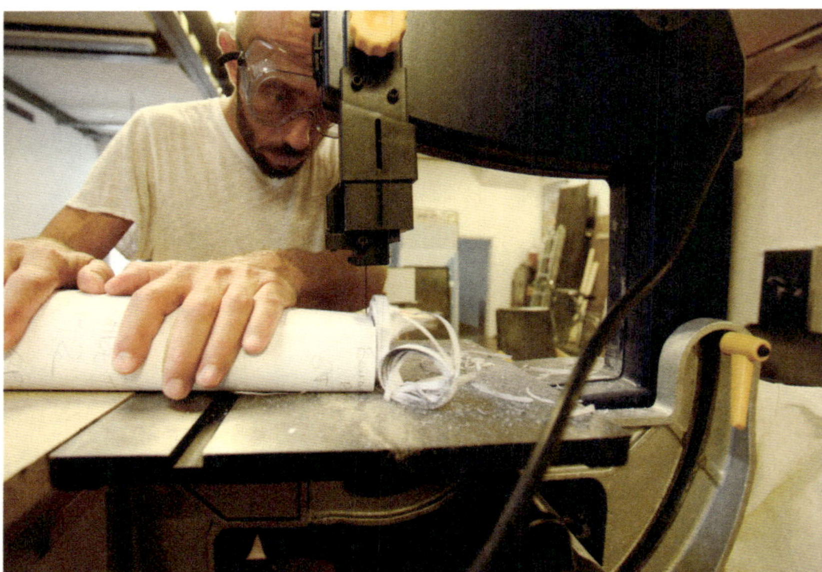

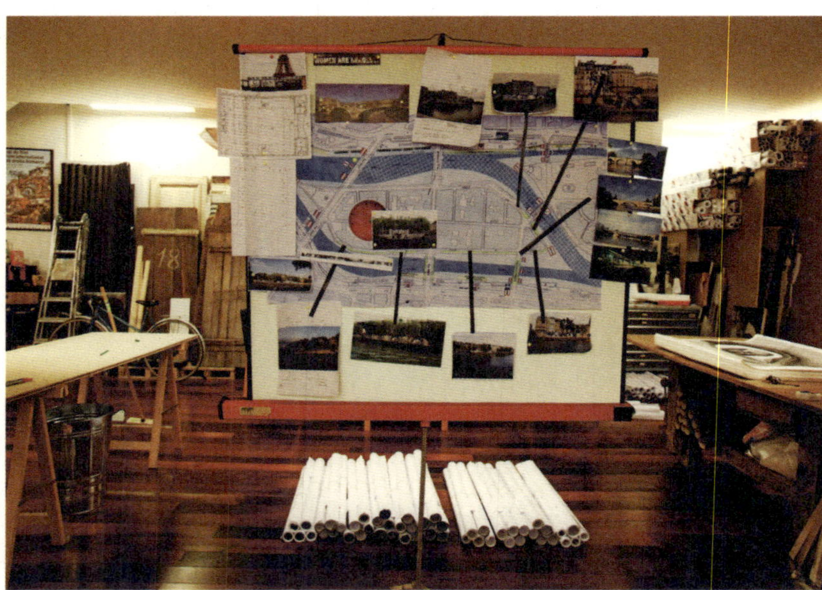

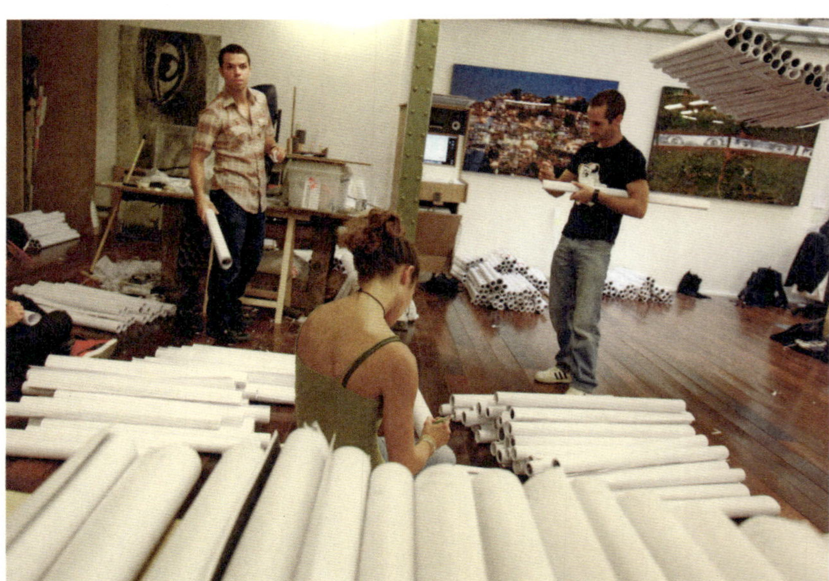

Preparing for a city-wide outdoor exhibition in Paris,
JR's Paris studio, France, 2009

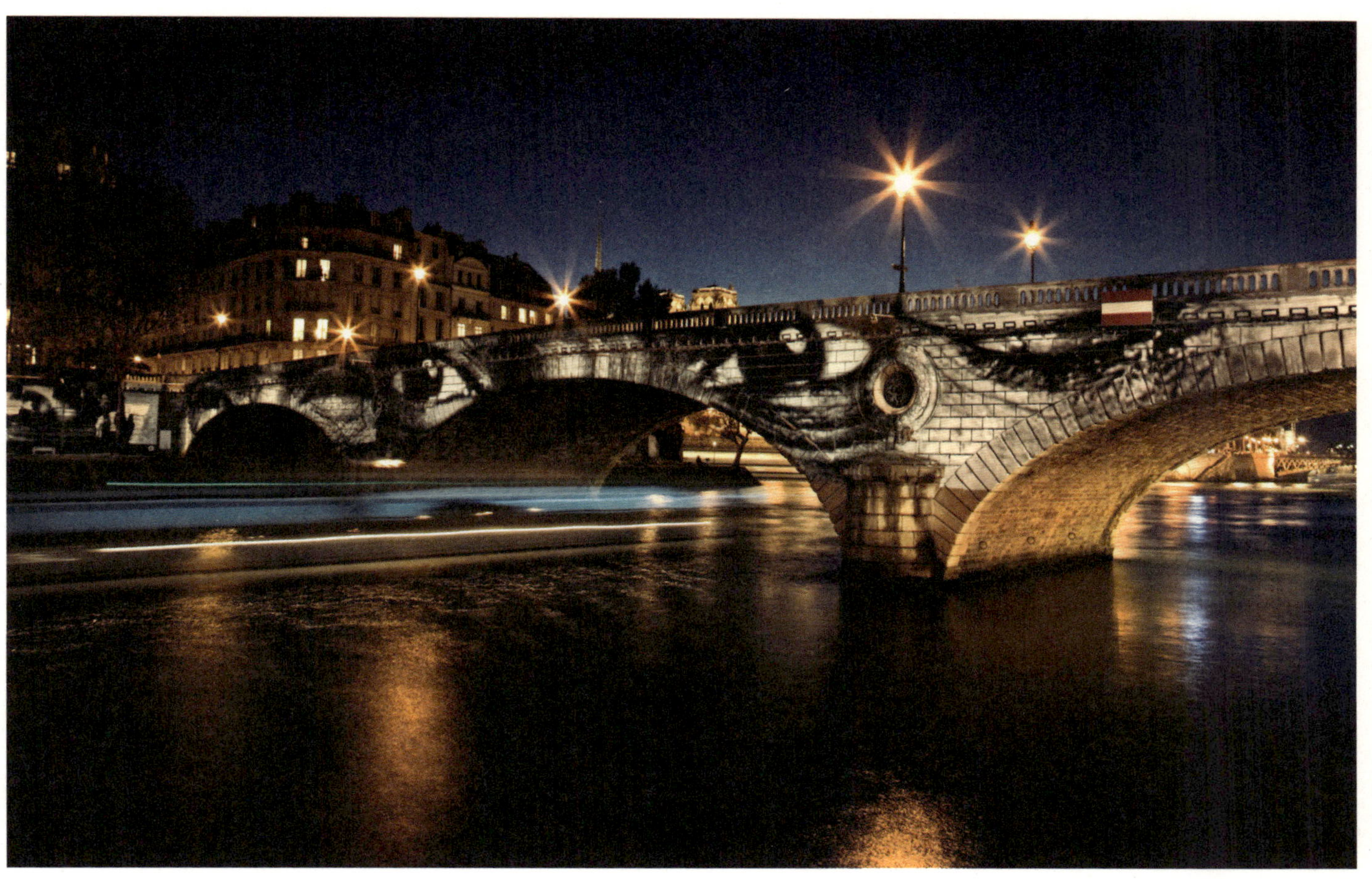

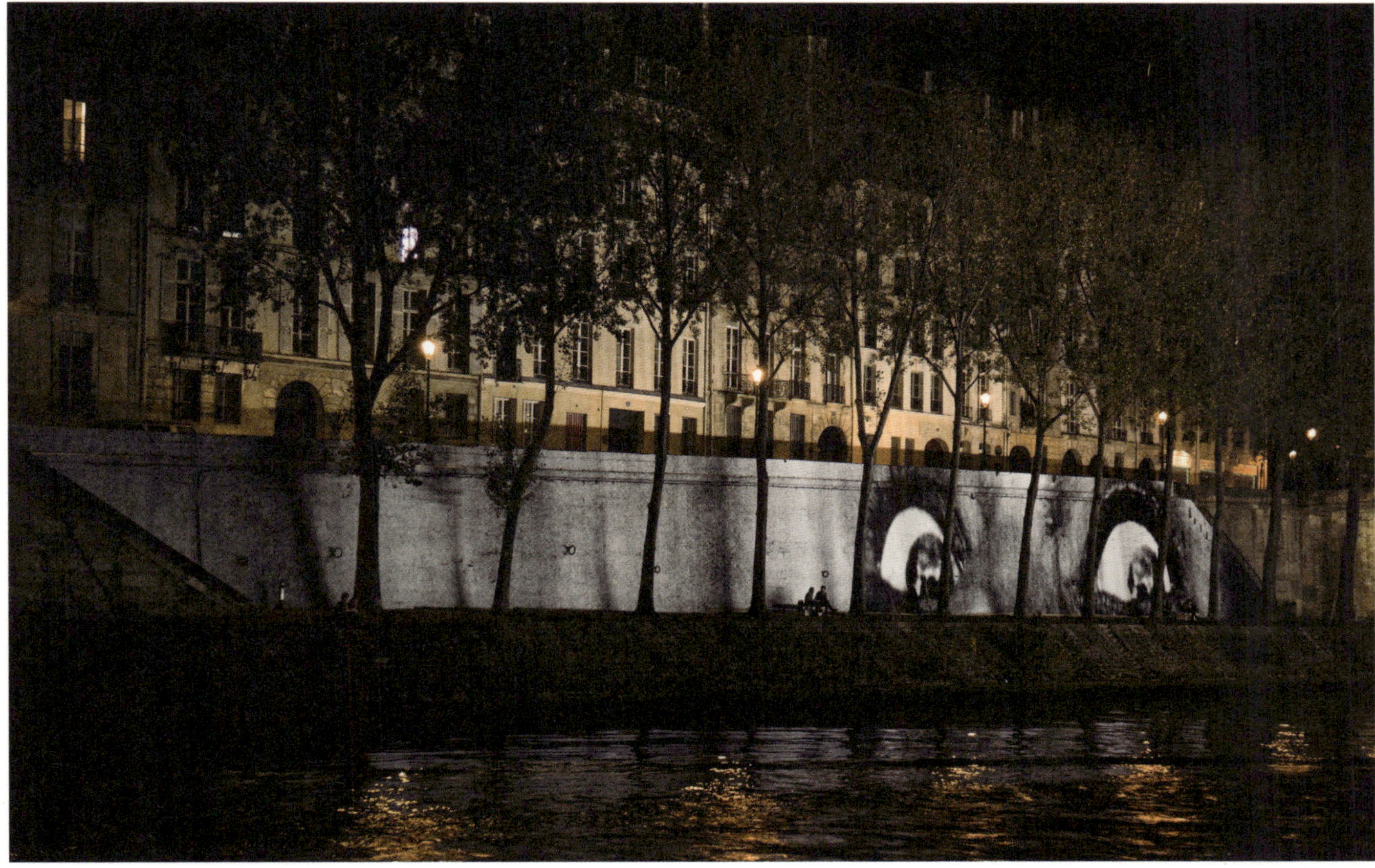

(top) Pont Louis-Philippe, Paris, France, 2009
(bottom) Bernadette, Quai d'Anjou, Paris, France, 2009
(overleaf) Île Saint-Louis, Paris, France, 2009

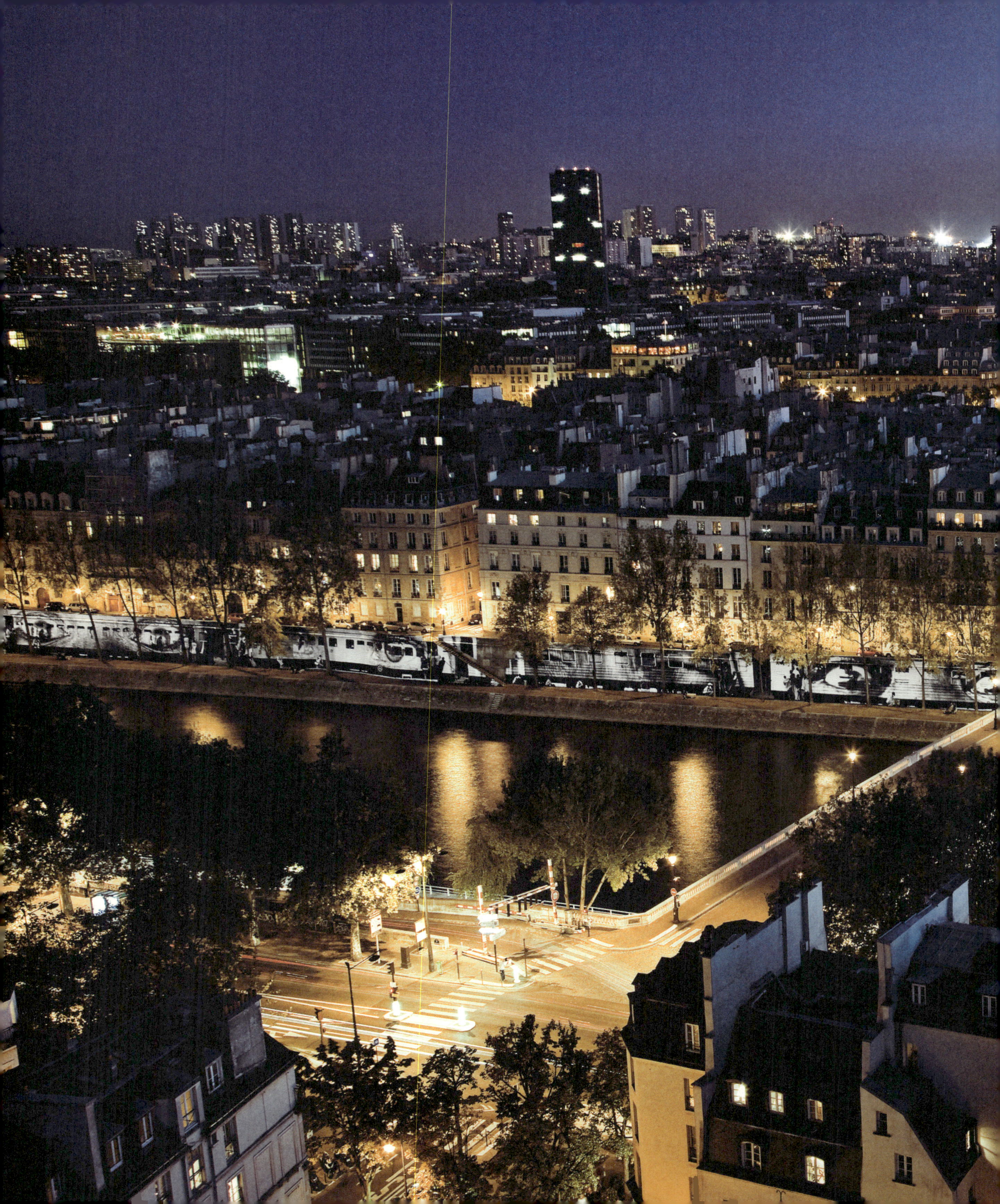

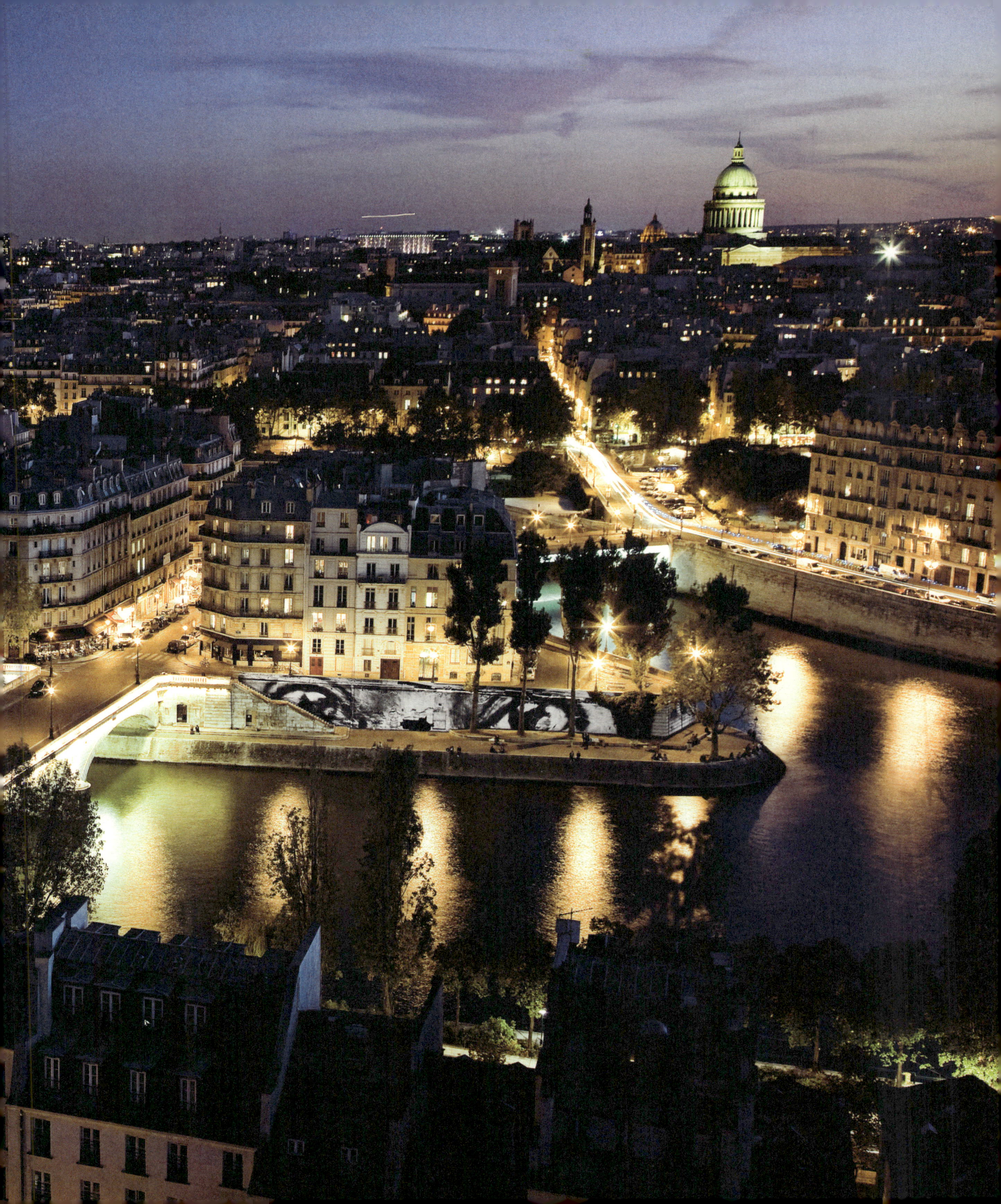

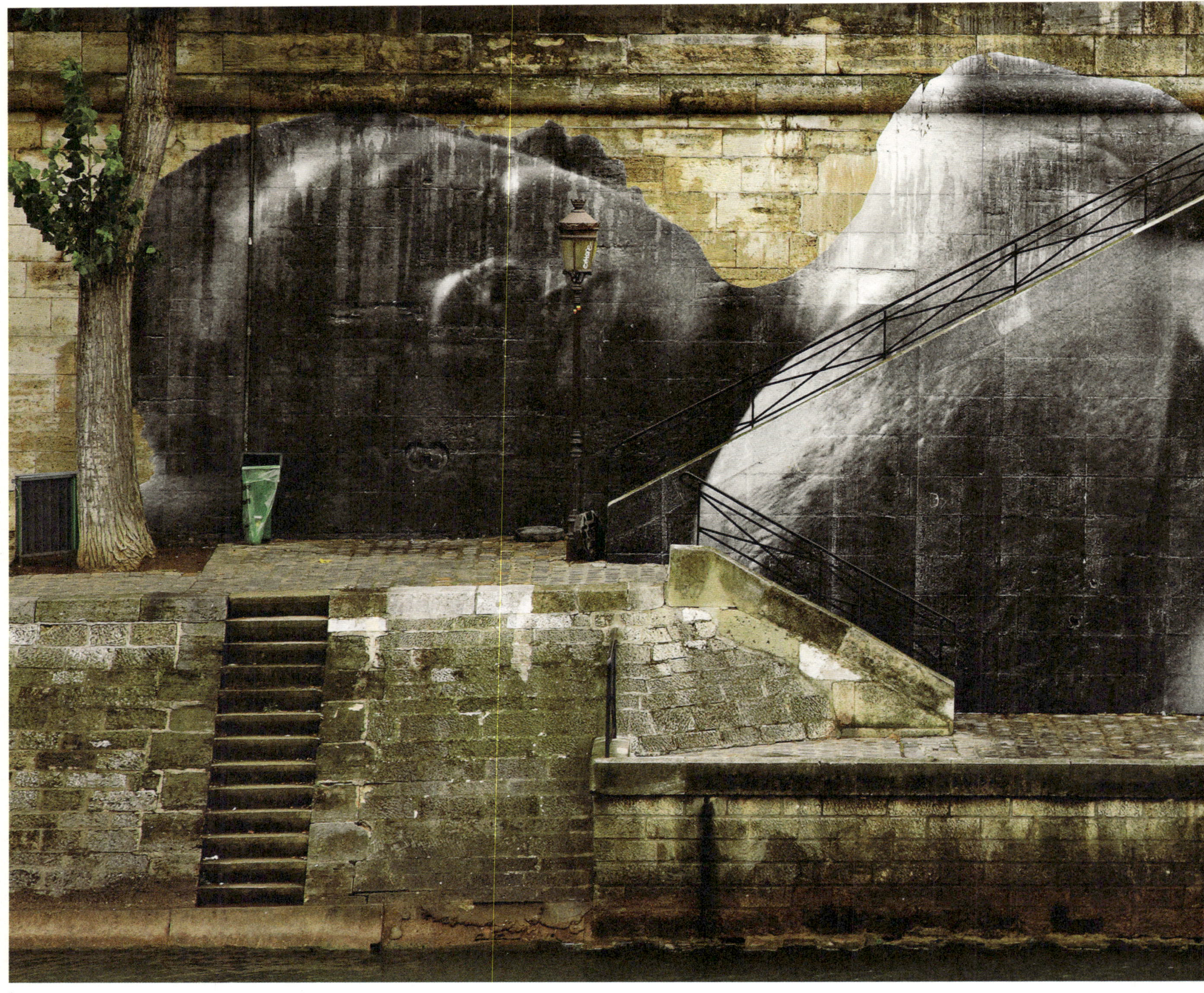

Île Saint-Louis, Paris, France, 2009

'In 2009, we put up a *Women Are Heroes* exhibition on walls all around Ile Saint-Louis in the heart of Paris. It took fifteen days to paste on walls that added up to 800 metres (2,625 feet) in length. Over 100 volunteers participated, coming to help after work, or even taking days off. We had morning, afternoon and night shifts every day. We met hundreds of people, and some became part of the team.' – JR

(overleaf) Le Havre, France, 2014

'I had dreamt of doing a pasting on a ship for years, but contacting the shipping companies directly seemed very complicated. One day a friend introduced me to some dockers from Le Havre. The head of the trade union knew my work and agreed to help. He opened the doors for us and we did an action on a 400 metre-long container ship with the help of all the dockers, who came to help during their breaks. We pasted on over 180 containers in 2 weeks, and the eyes of that woman ended up travelling all the way to Malaysia on the ship.' – JR

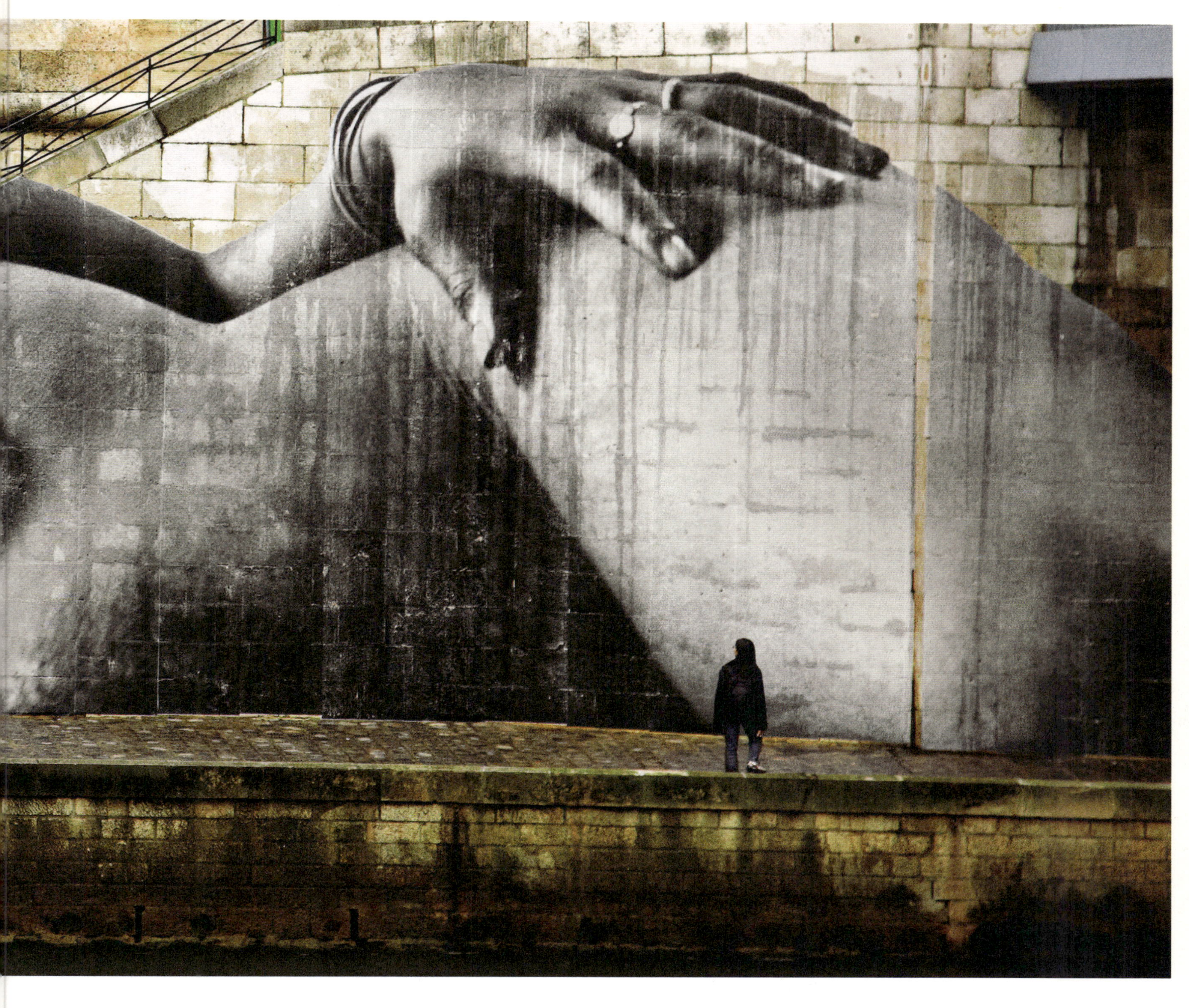

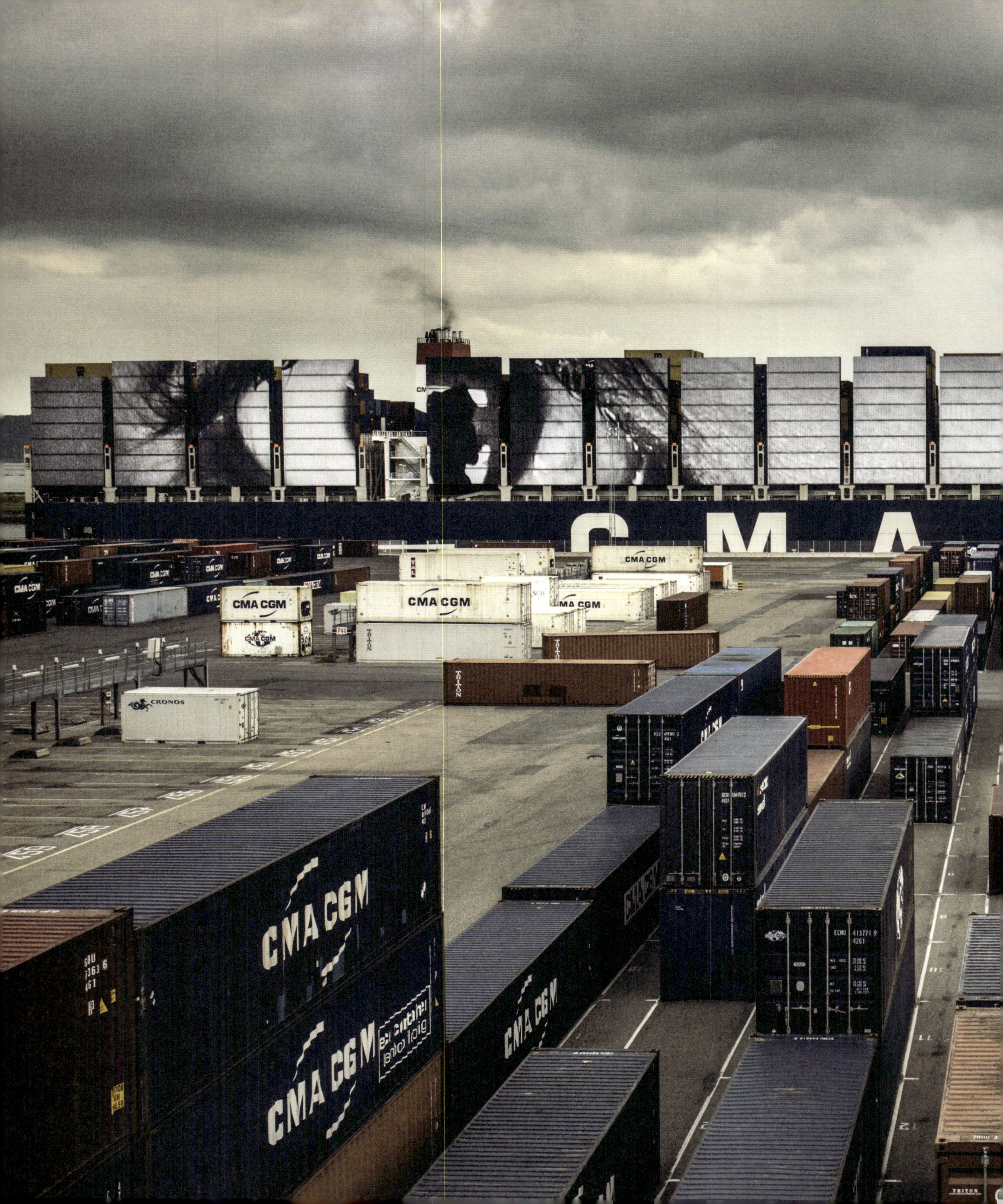
CMA CGM
CRONOS
CMA CGM
CMA CGM
CMA

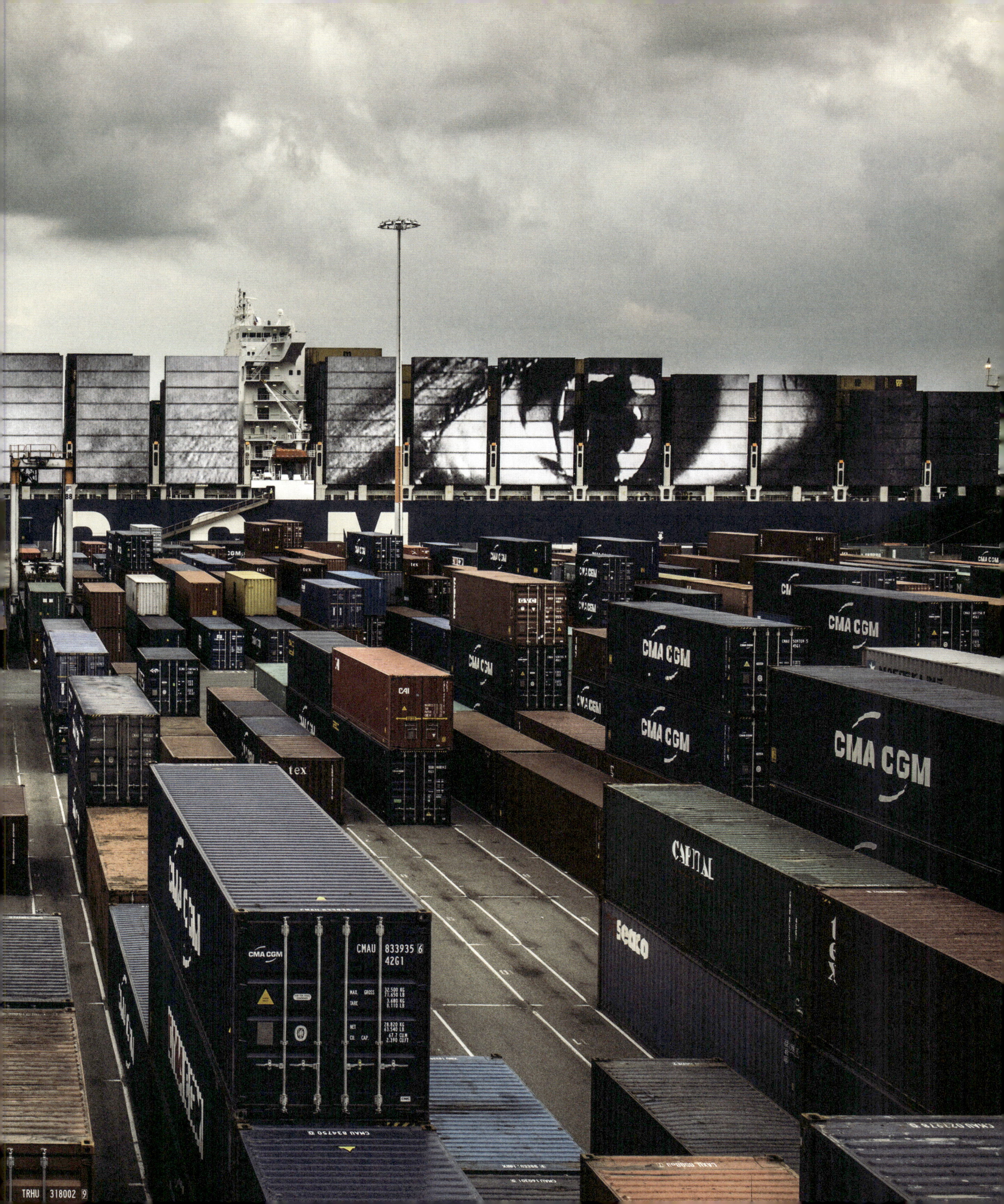
CMA CGM
CMA CGM
CMA CGM
CMA CGM
CMA CGM
CAPITAL
seaco
tex
CAI
CMAU 833935 6
42G1
TRHU 318002 9

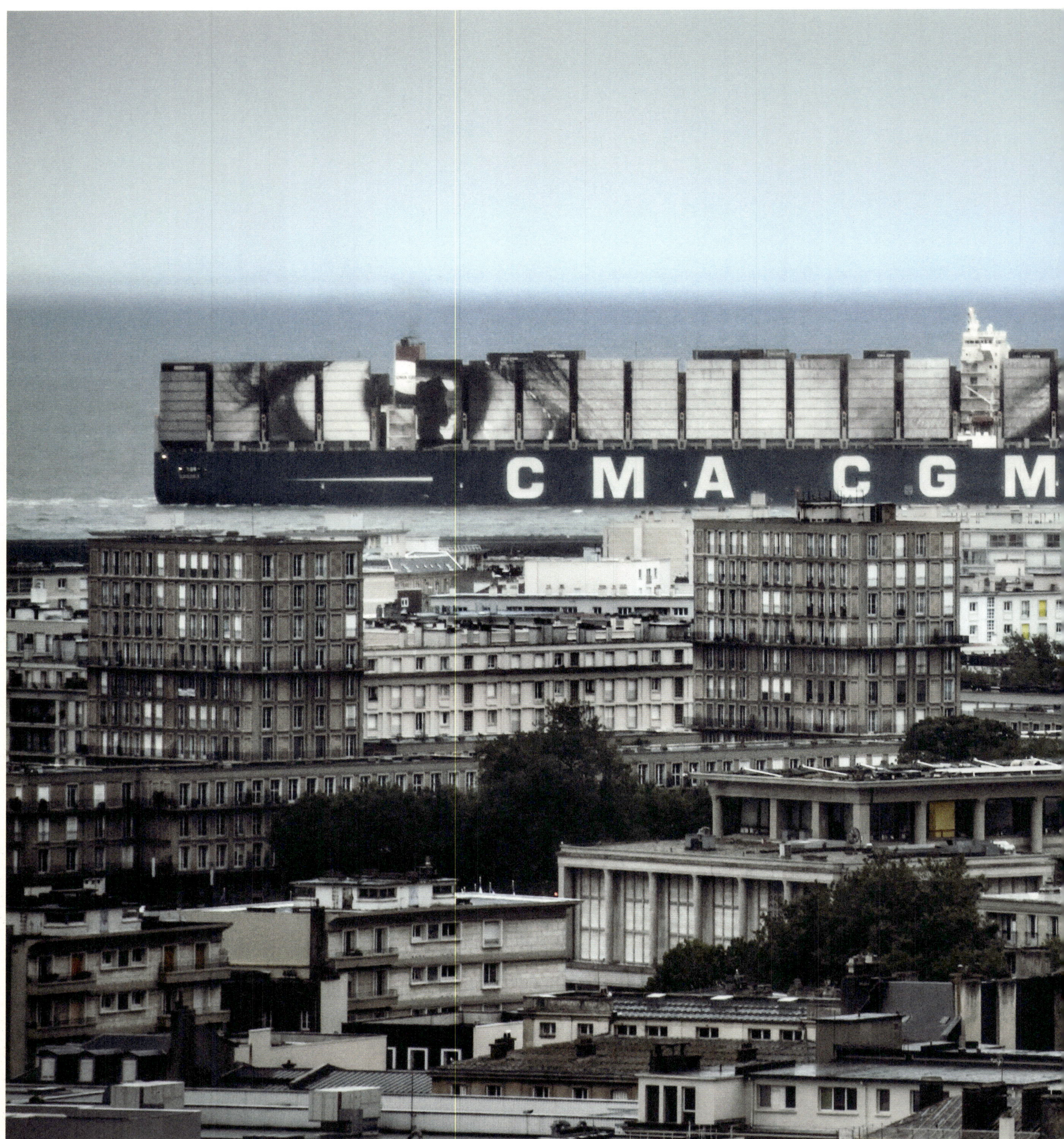

Le Havre, France, 2014

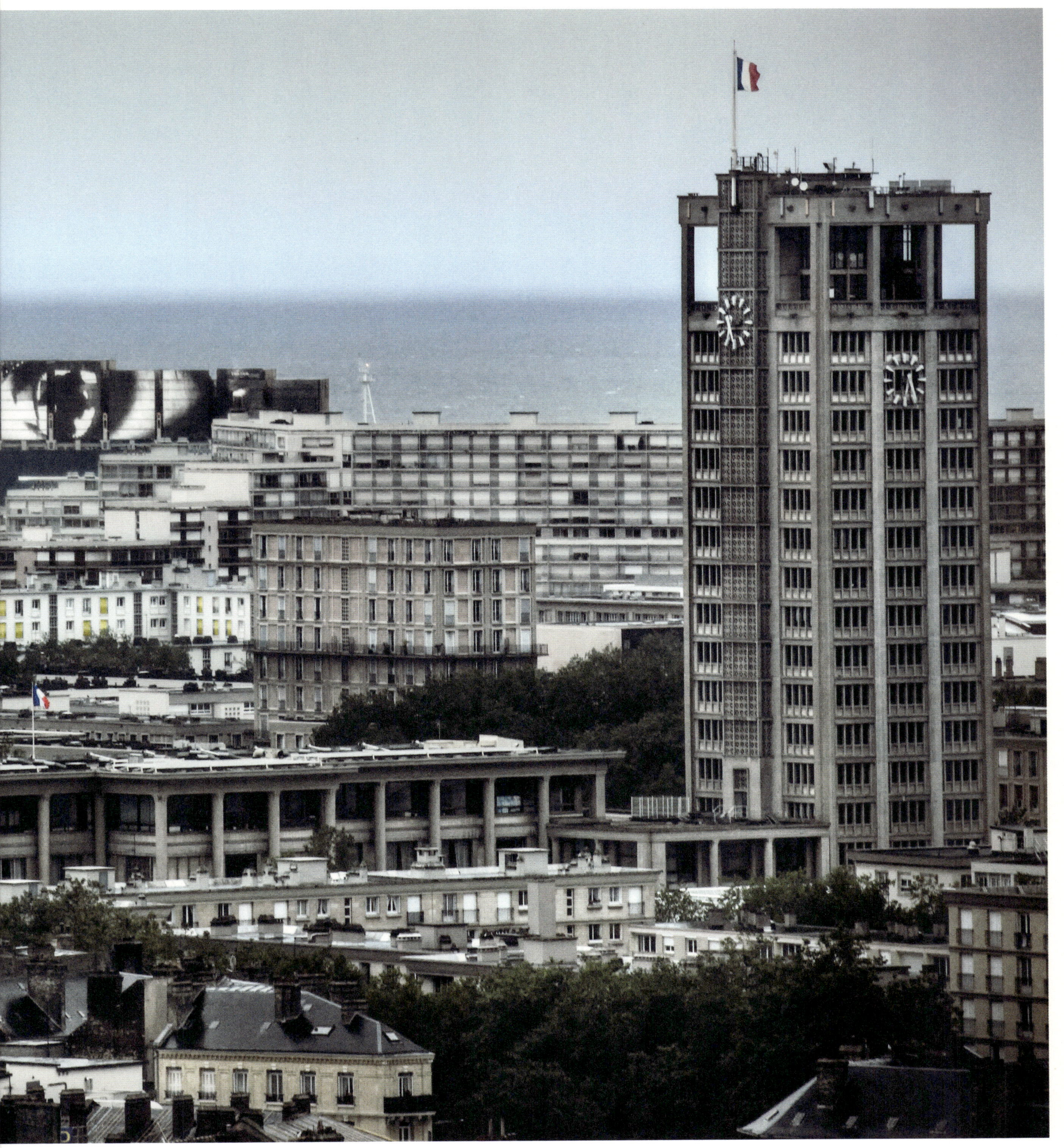

WRINKLES

OF THE

CITY

Wrinkles of the City paints a picture of the twentieth century by exploring the lives of those who witnessed their cities become scarred by the course of history, economic growth and socio-cultural changes. Its goal was for the elderly's personal stories to symbolically confront the walls of their city, and for the city and its inhabitants to confront their wrinkles and the stories of their elderly.

JR travelled to cities in Spain, Cuba (with the artist, José Parlá), China, Germany, the United States and Turkey that had all experienced some of the most significant upheavals in the twentieth century. He spoke to elderly residents about their lives and was curious to learn how a lifetime can be summarized in just a few sentences. He wanted to know about the joys and the heartaches that time cannot erase from memory. The people that JR worked with during *Wrinkles of the City* witnessed General Franco's raid on Cartagena in 1939; Fidel Castro's rise to power in Cuba in 1959; the Cultural Revolution in China from 1966 to 1976; the end of racial segregation in the United States in the 1960s; the fall of Hitler and the division of Germany in 1945; and the secularization of Istanbul after 1924.

JR's method of using huge pastings to confront the ever-evolving architecture of the city allowed the oldest generation, people who seem to have lost significance socially, to become visible once more and to share their memories of the past, which has shaped our present. The individual stories of the elderly show in their facial features, just as the history of the cities shows in the buildings where the portraits are pasted.

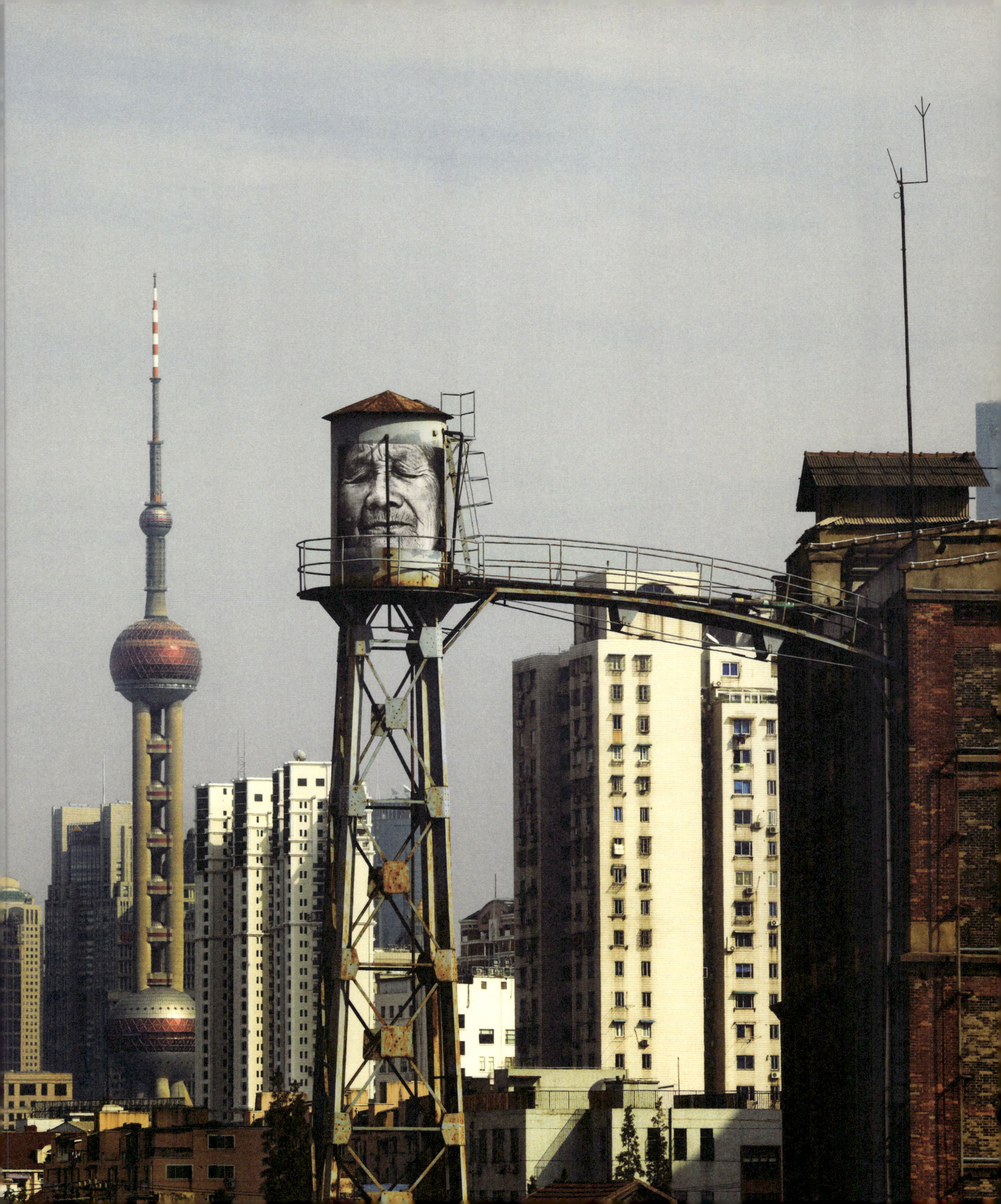

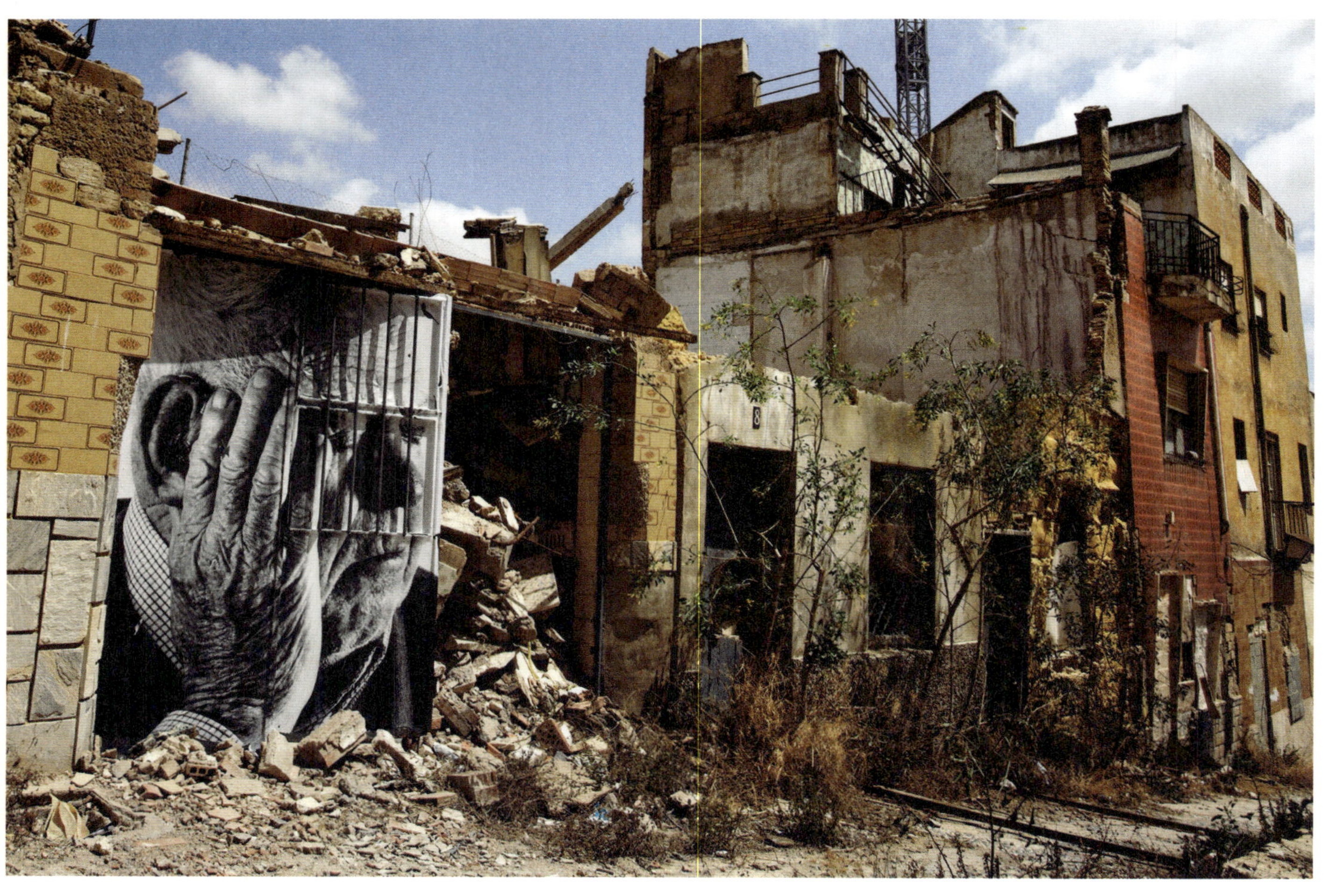

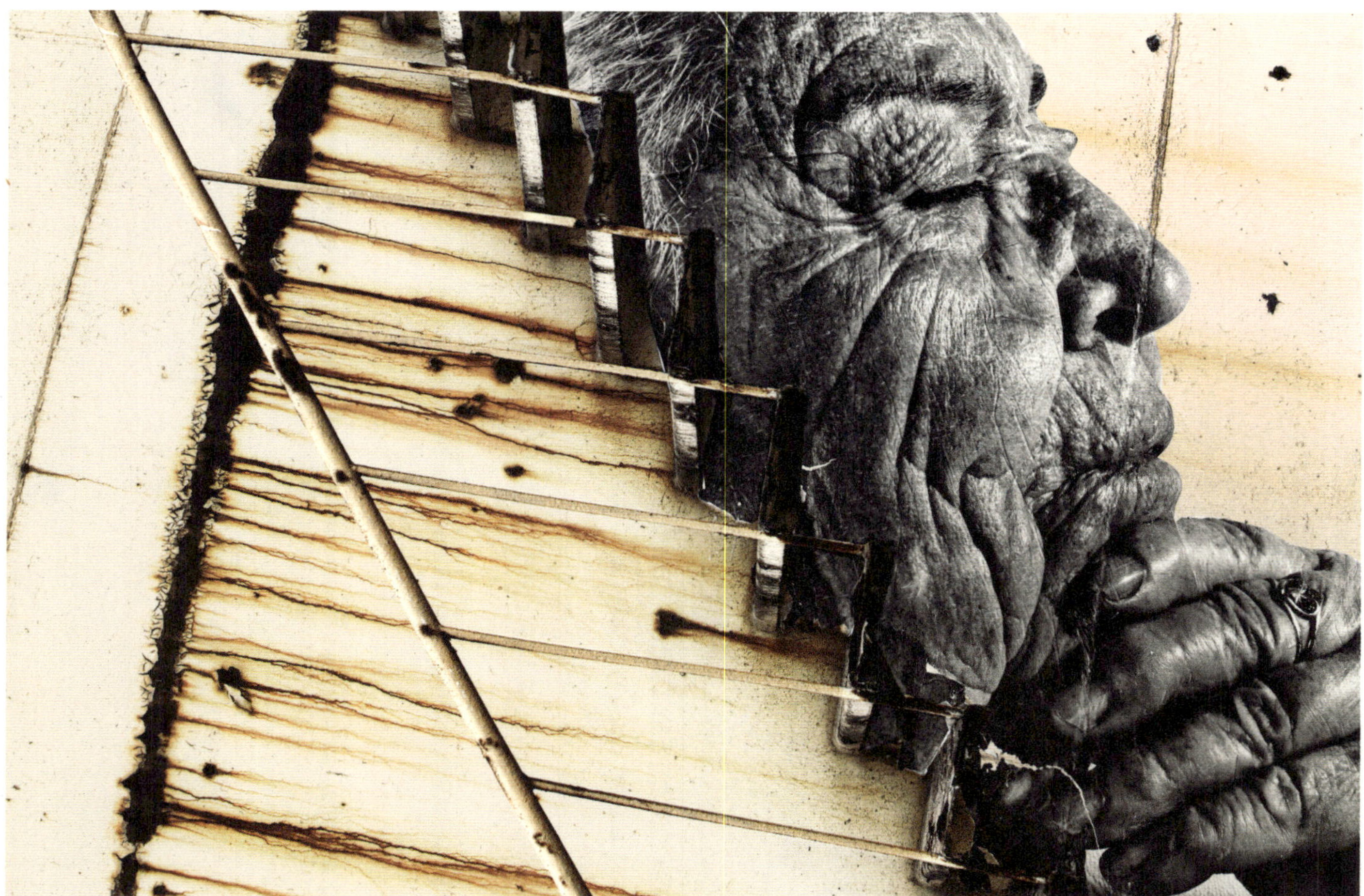

(previous page) Zhao Liying, Shanghai, China, 2010
(top) Jose Martinez Roca, Cartagena, Spain, 2008
(bottom) Maria Corbolan Ferandez, Cartagena, Spain, 2008

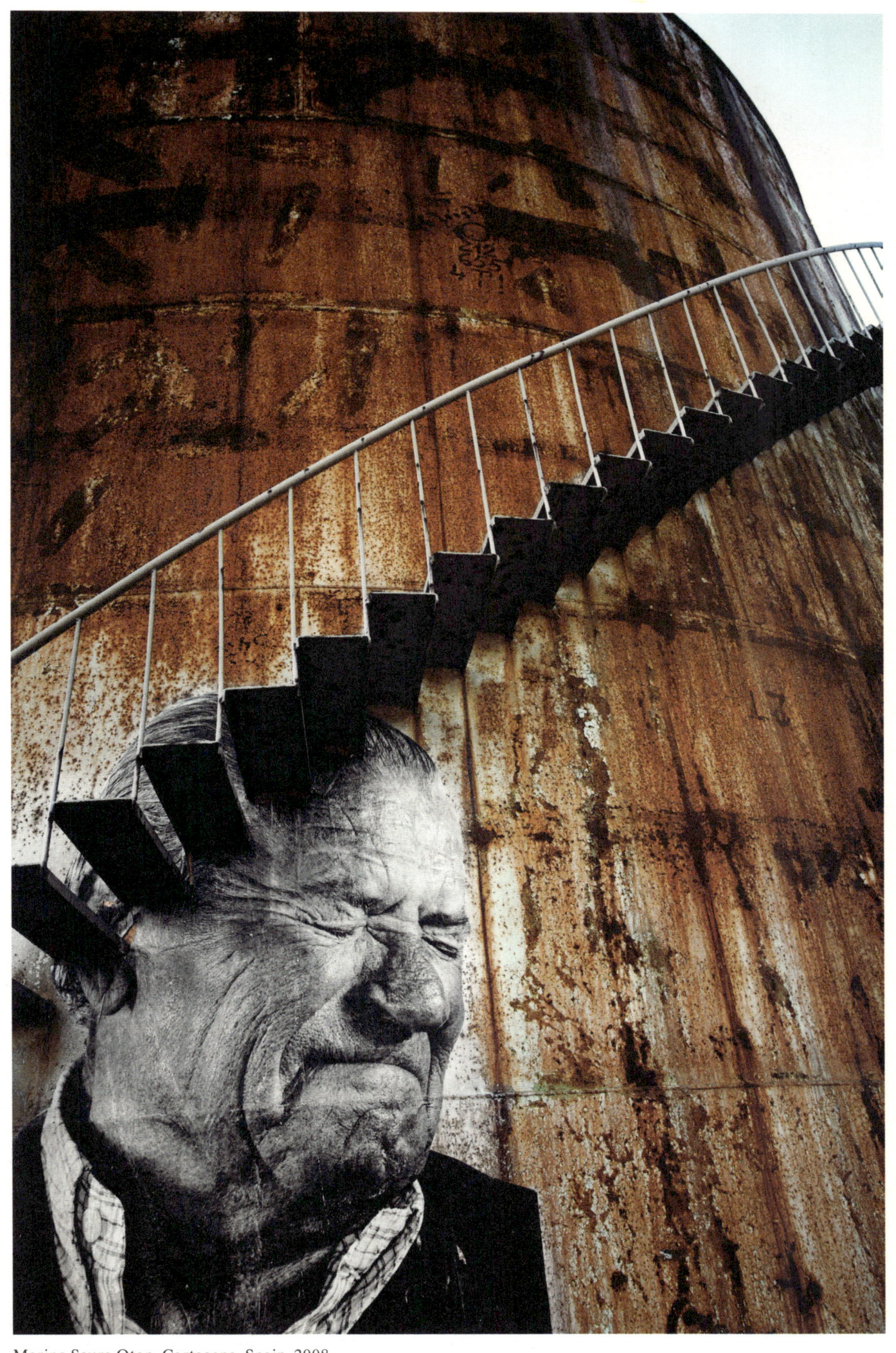

Marino Saura Oton, Cartagena, Spain, 2008

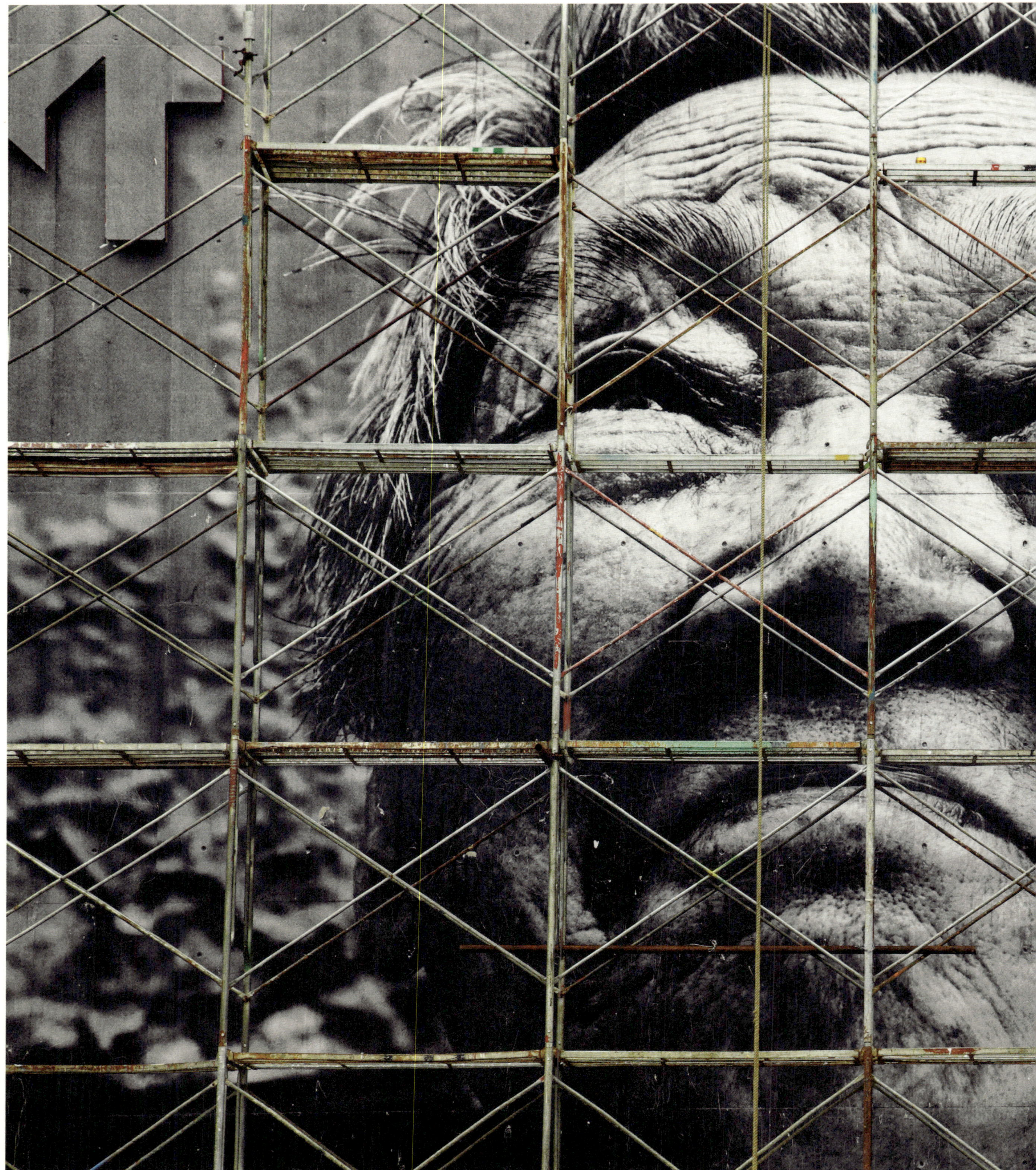

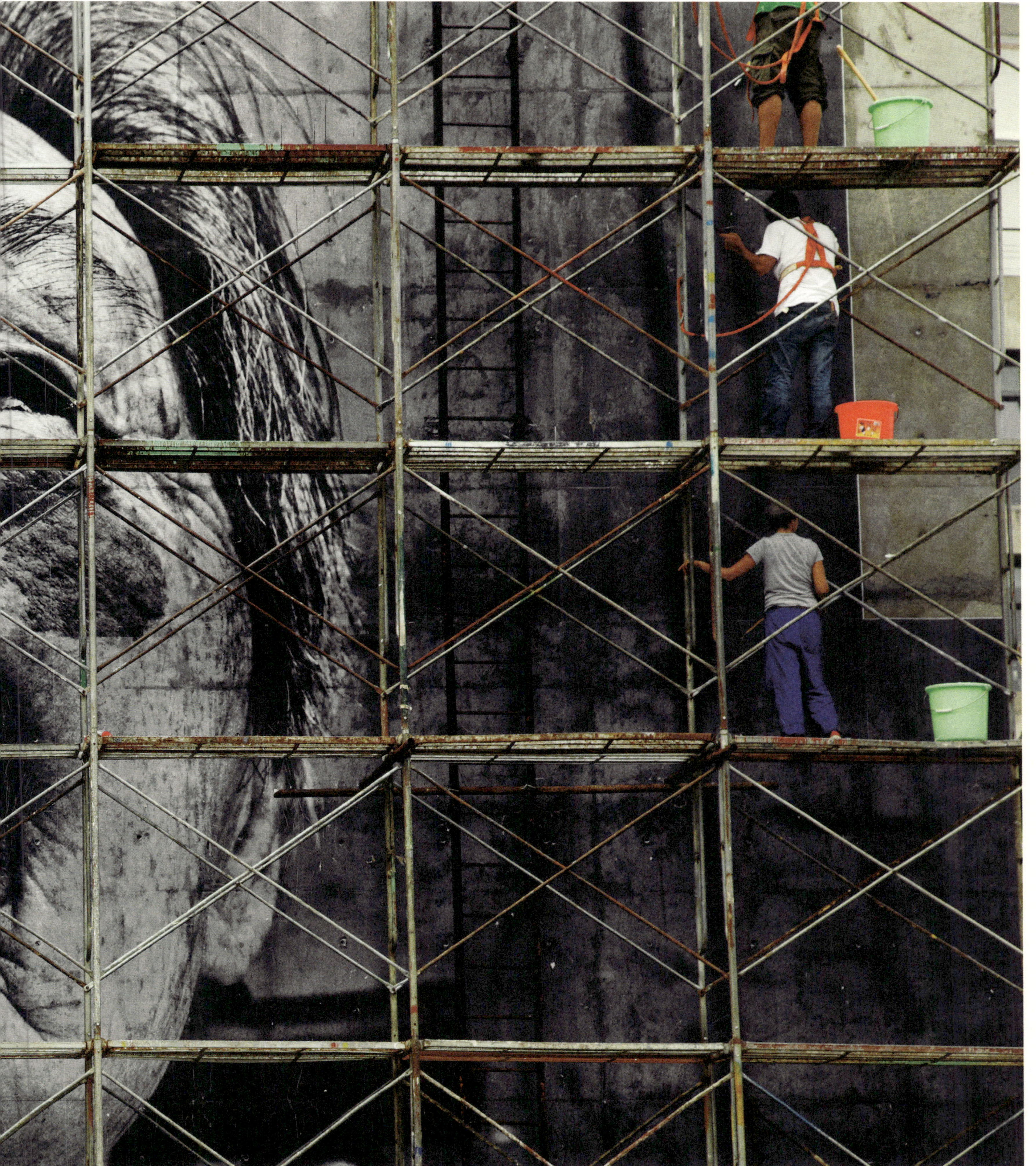

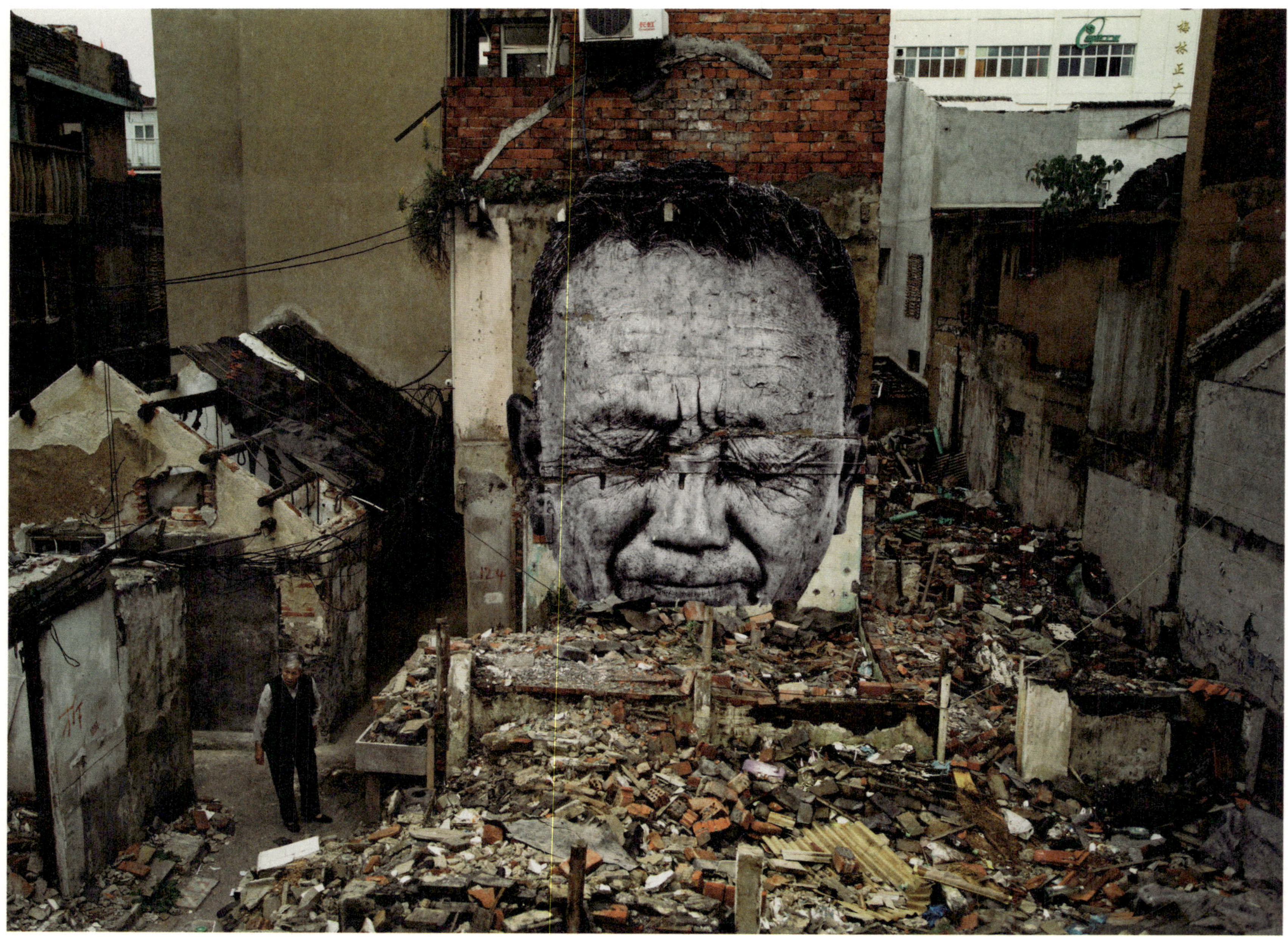

(previous page) Shi Li, in progress, Shanghai, China, 2010
(above) Zhai Zhixin, Shanghai, China, 2010

'Old neighbourhoods in Shanghai are demolished to give room for skyscrapers. Often real-estate developers have trouble evicting the last inhabitants, who don't want to leave. These people allowed us to paste on their homes. They helped us, despite the difficulty of access to the locations and the pressure from the developers. The police came to visit us on this project.' – JR

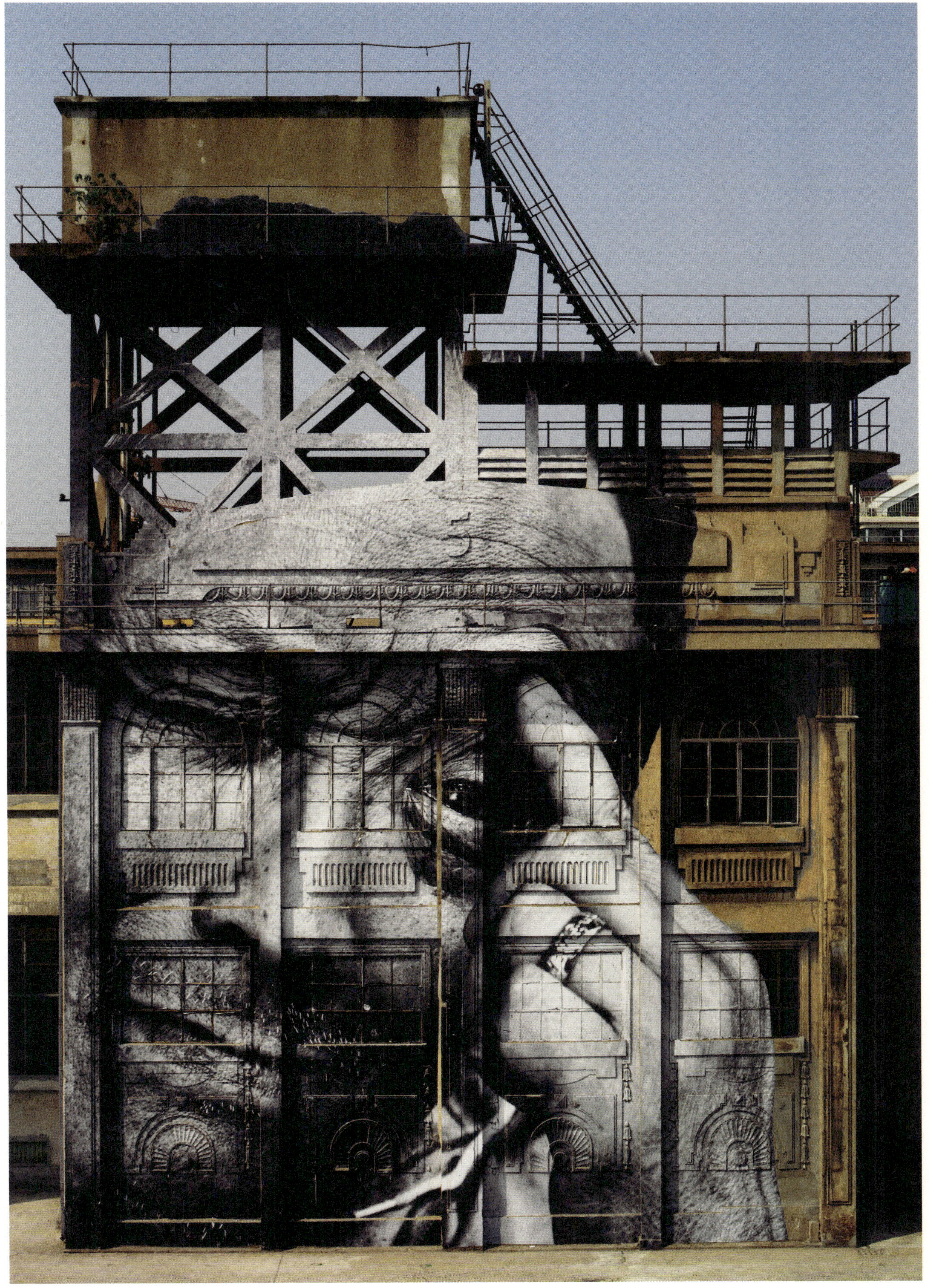

Rony Zhuang, Shanghai, China, 2010

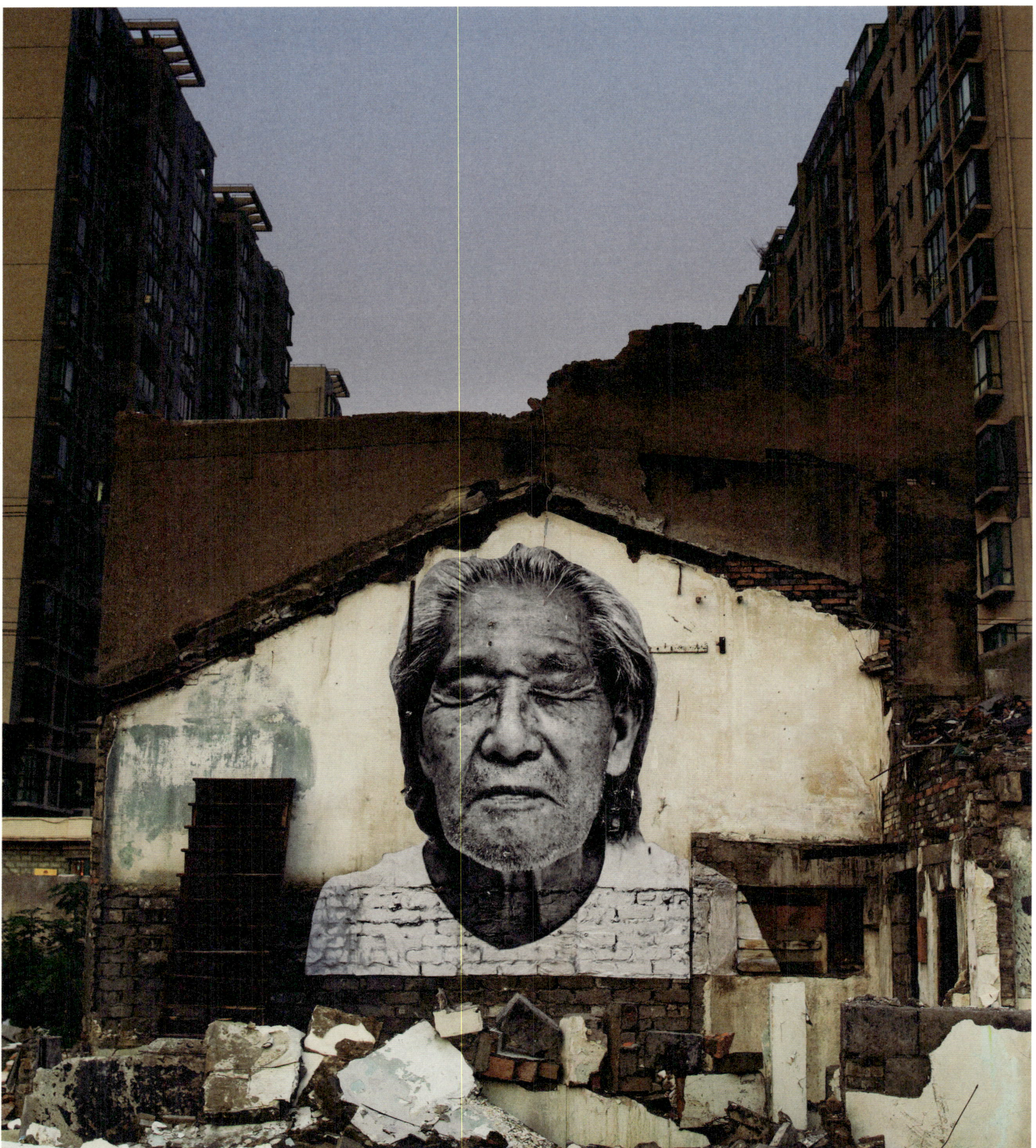
Ji Jinsui, Shanghai, China, 2010

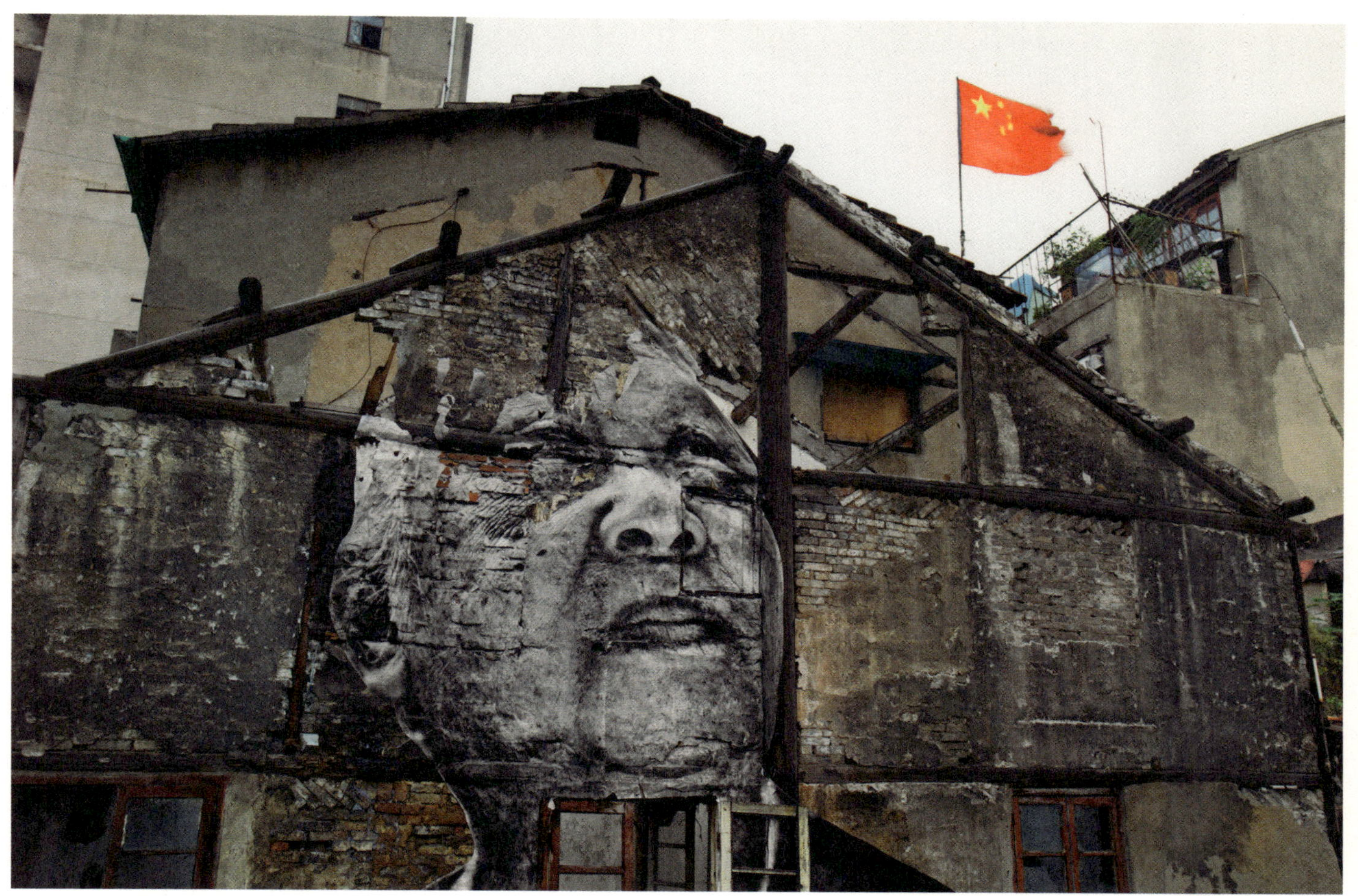

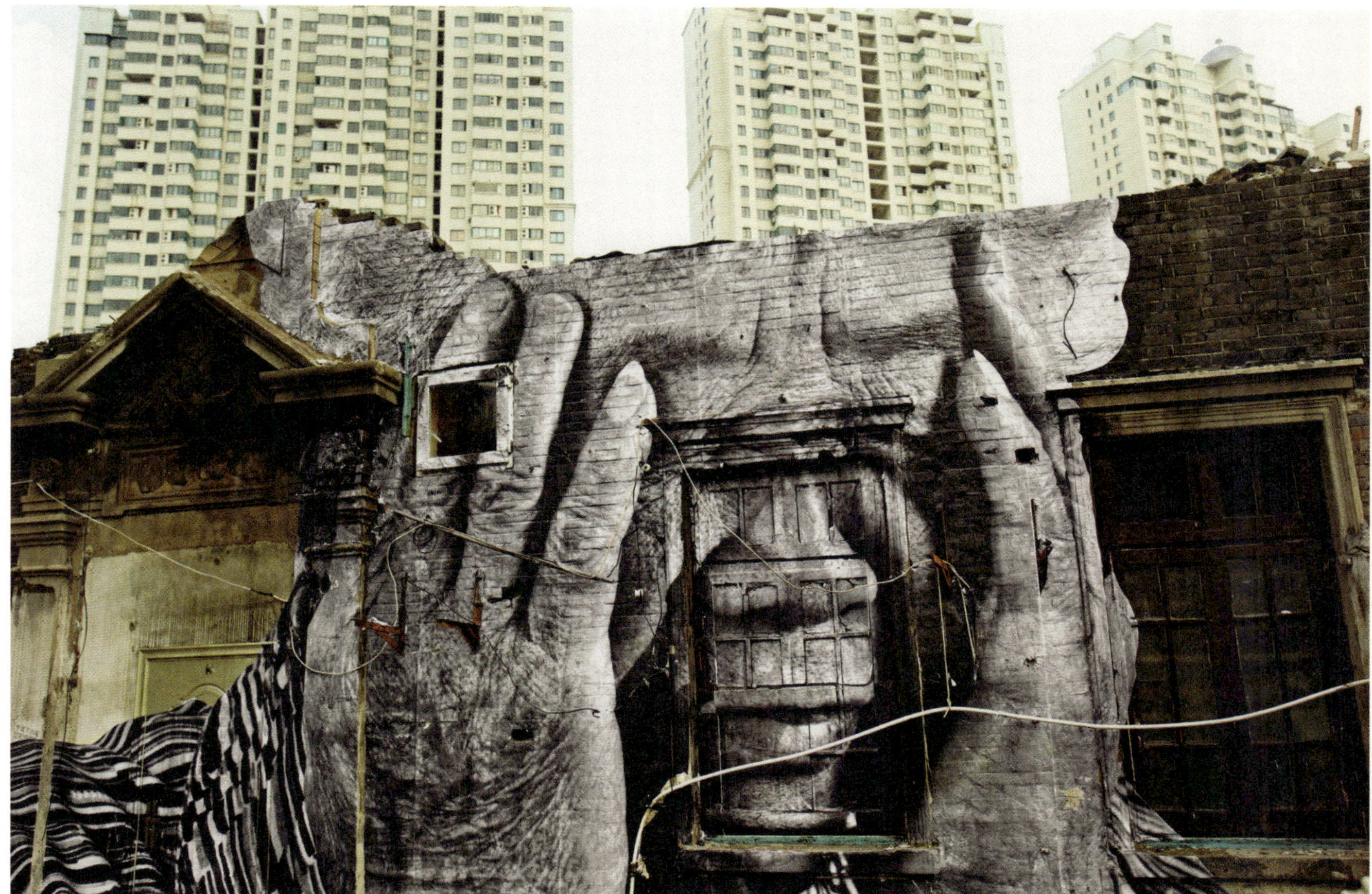

(top) Jiang Qizeng, Shanghai, China, 2010
(bottom) Wu Zhengzhu, Shanghai, China, 2010
(overleaf) Li Xuanhua, Shanghai, China, 2010

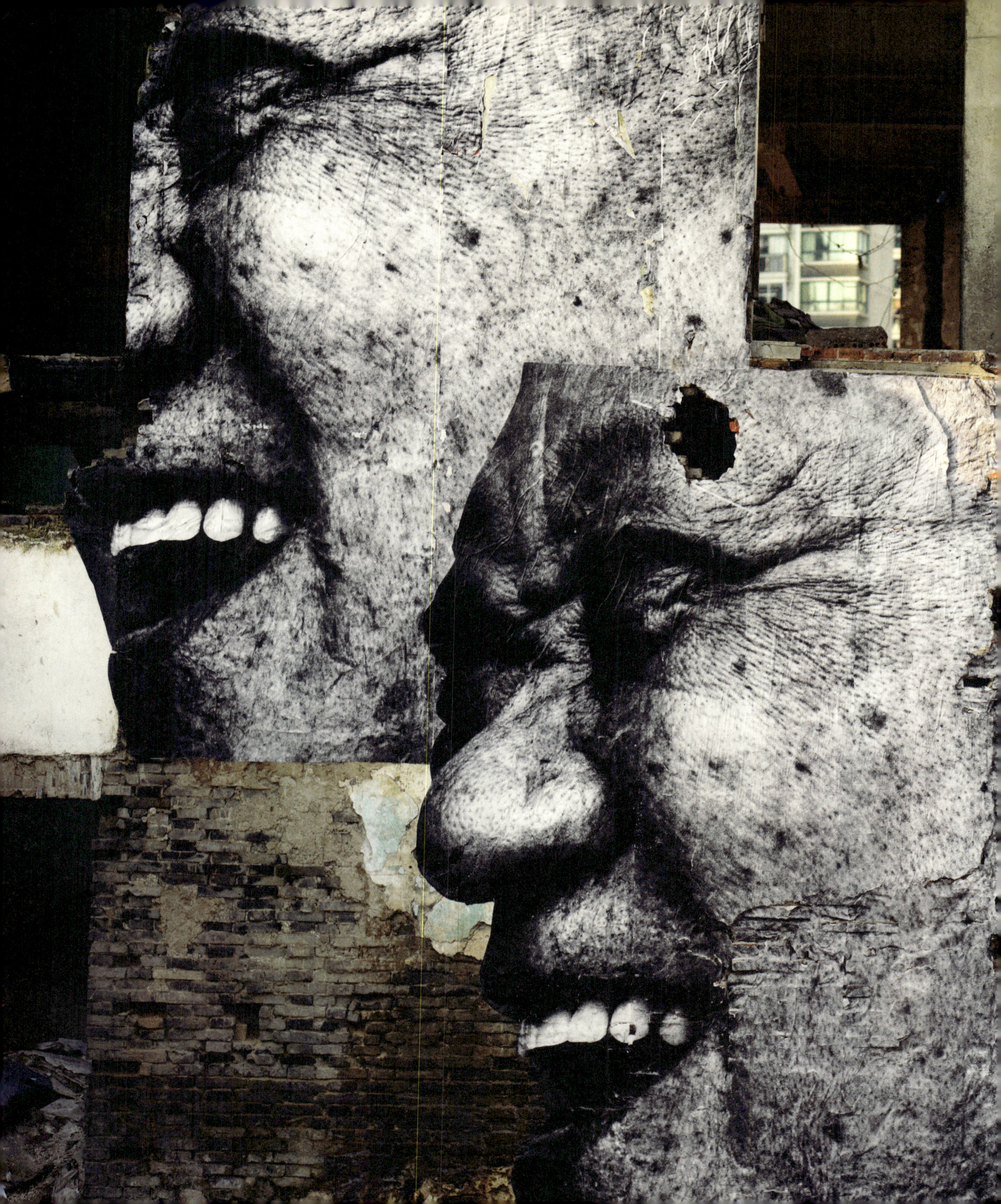

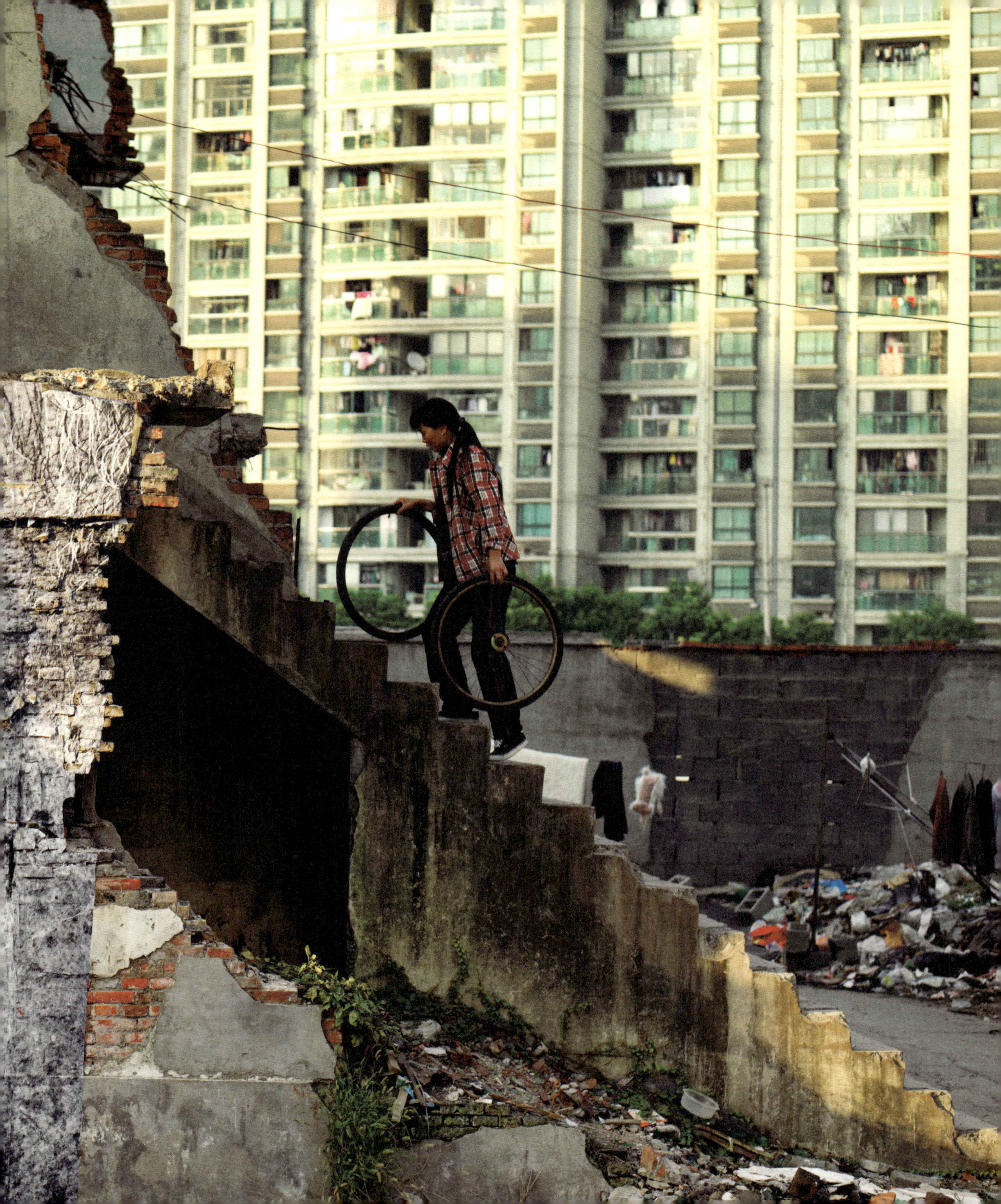

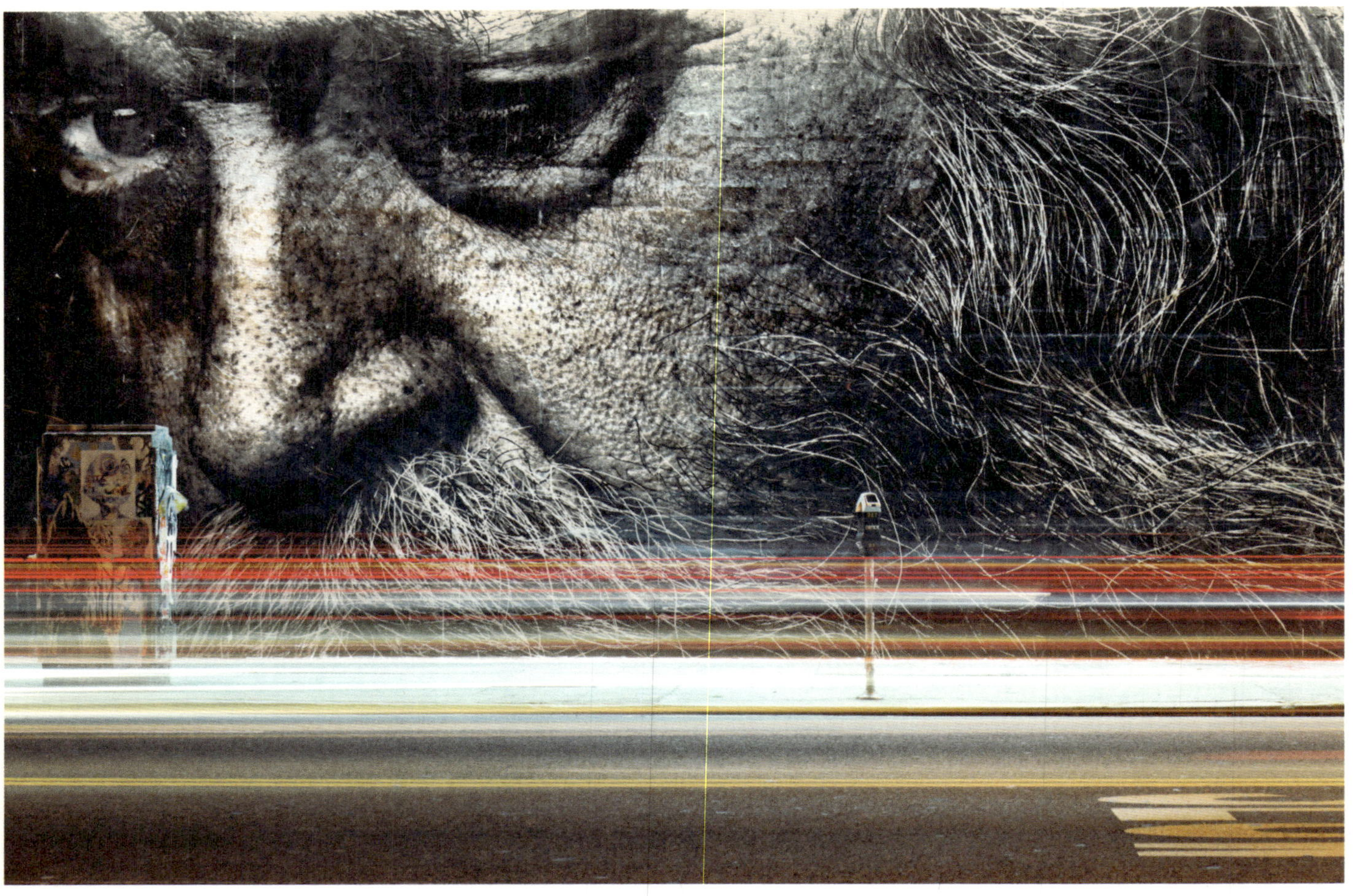

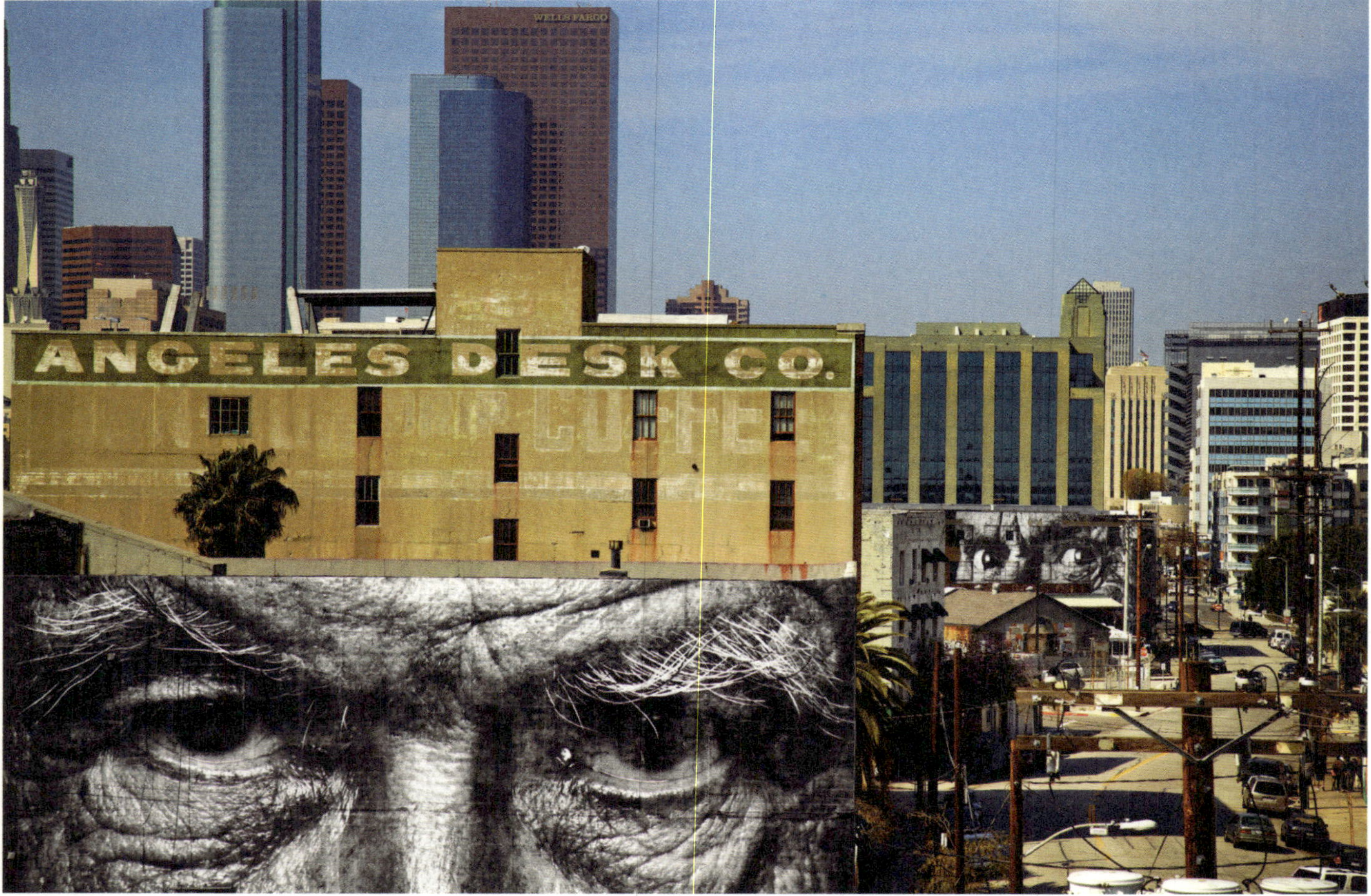

(top) John Stapp, Melrose Boulevard, Los Angeles, USA, 2011
(bottom) Michael Korhonen, Downtown, Los Angeles, USA, 2012

(right) Robert Evans, Downtown, Los Angeles, USA, 2011

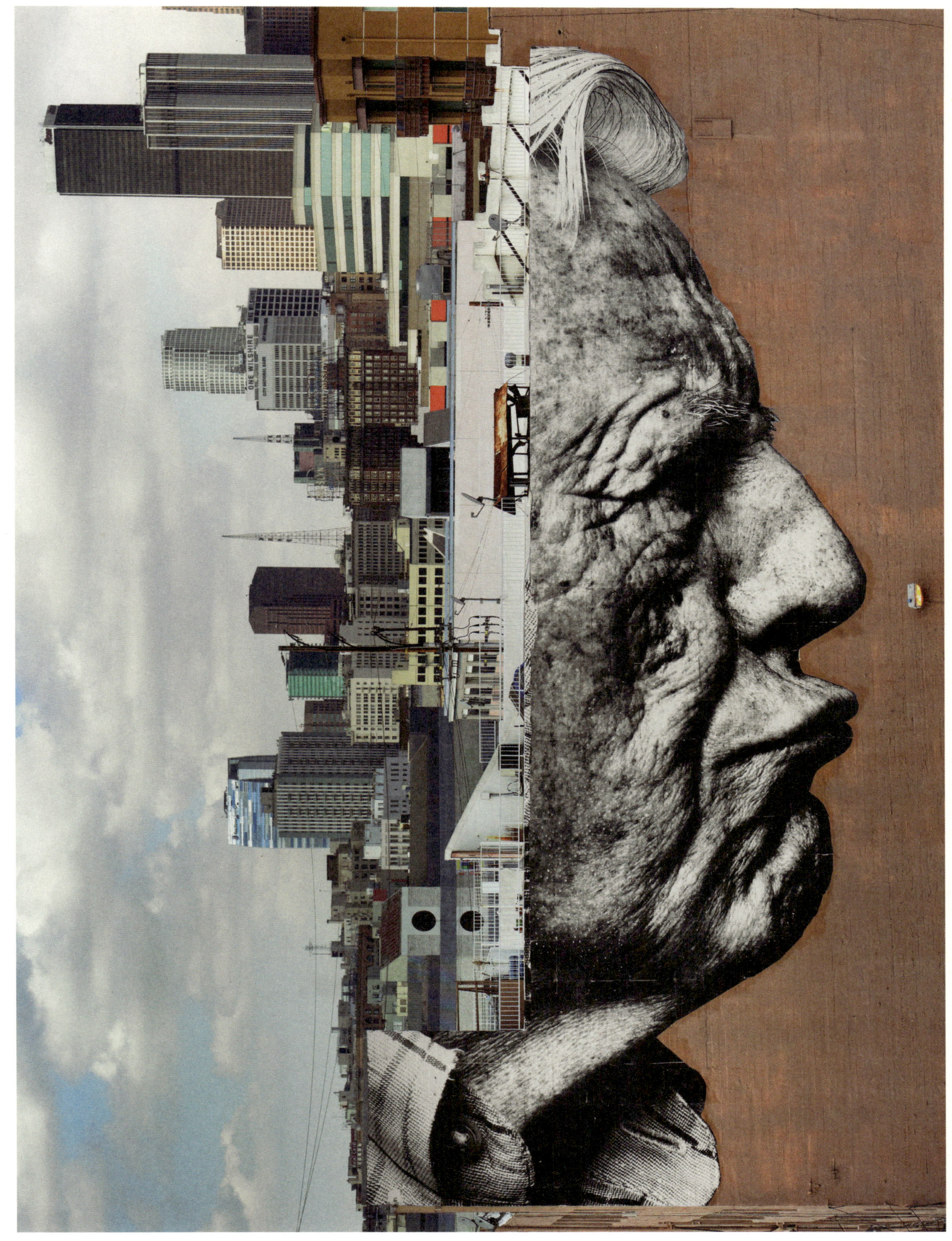
ONE WILSHIRE

Ramiro and Maria Gurrola, Downtown, Los Angeles, USA, 2012
(overleaf) Rita Guizulfo, West Hollywood, Los Angeles, USA, 2011

'It was very hard to find old people on the streets of Los Angeles – every elderly person we would talk to thought we wanted to sell them an encyclopaedia! In Havana or Shanghai, we had seen that the elderly tend to live with their family, whereas in the United States the family link seems to be more loose. We had to place ads on casting websites to find participants!' – JR

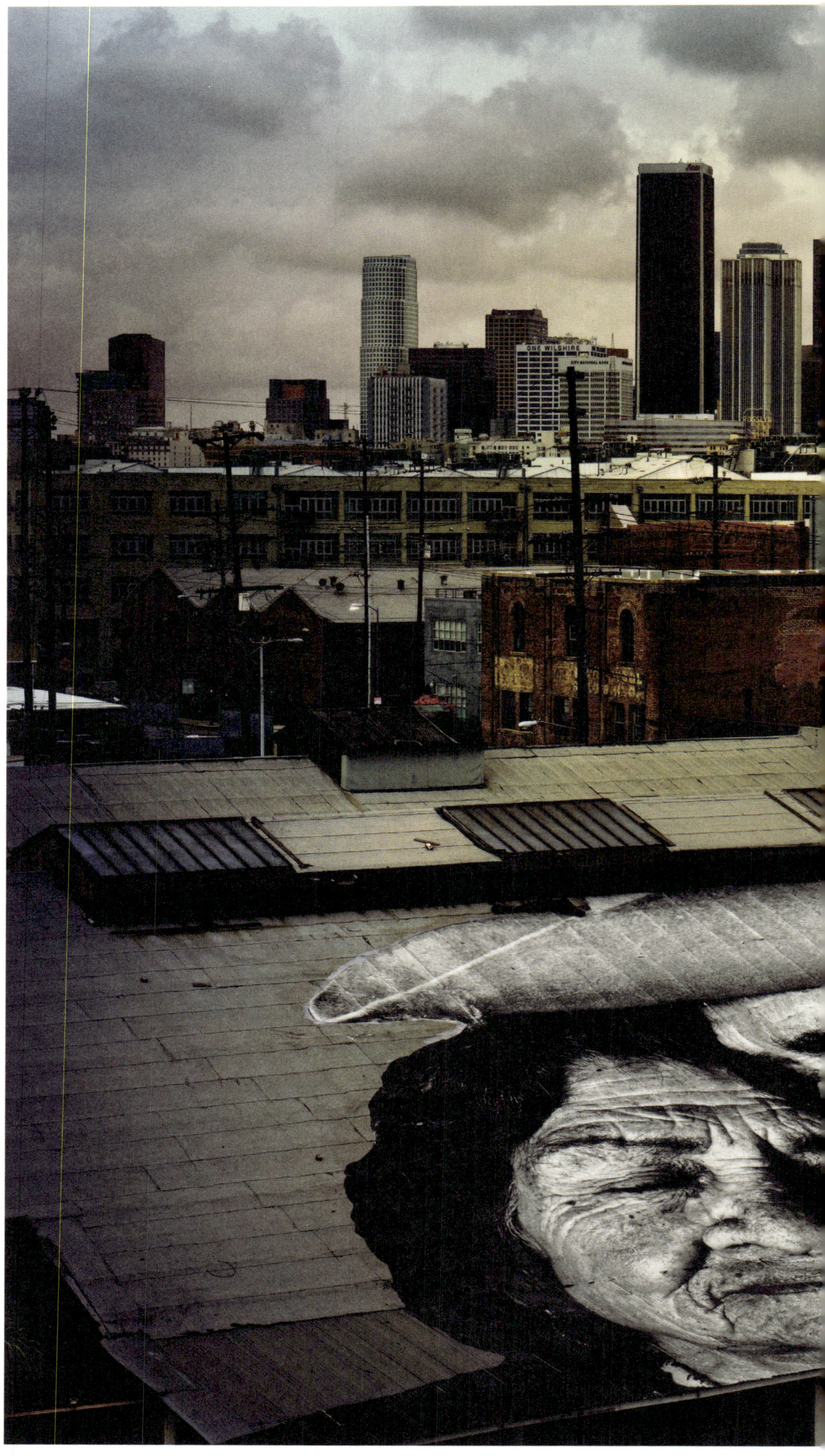

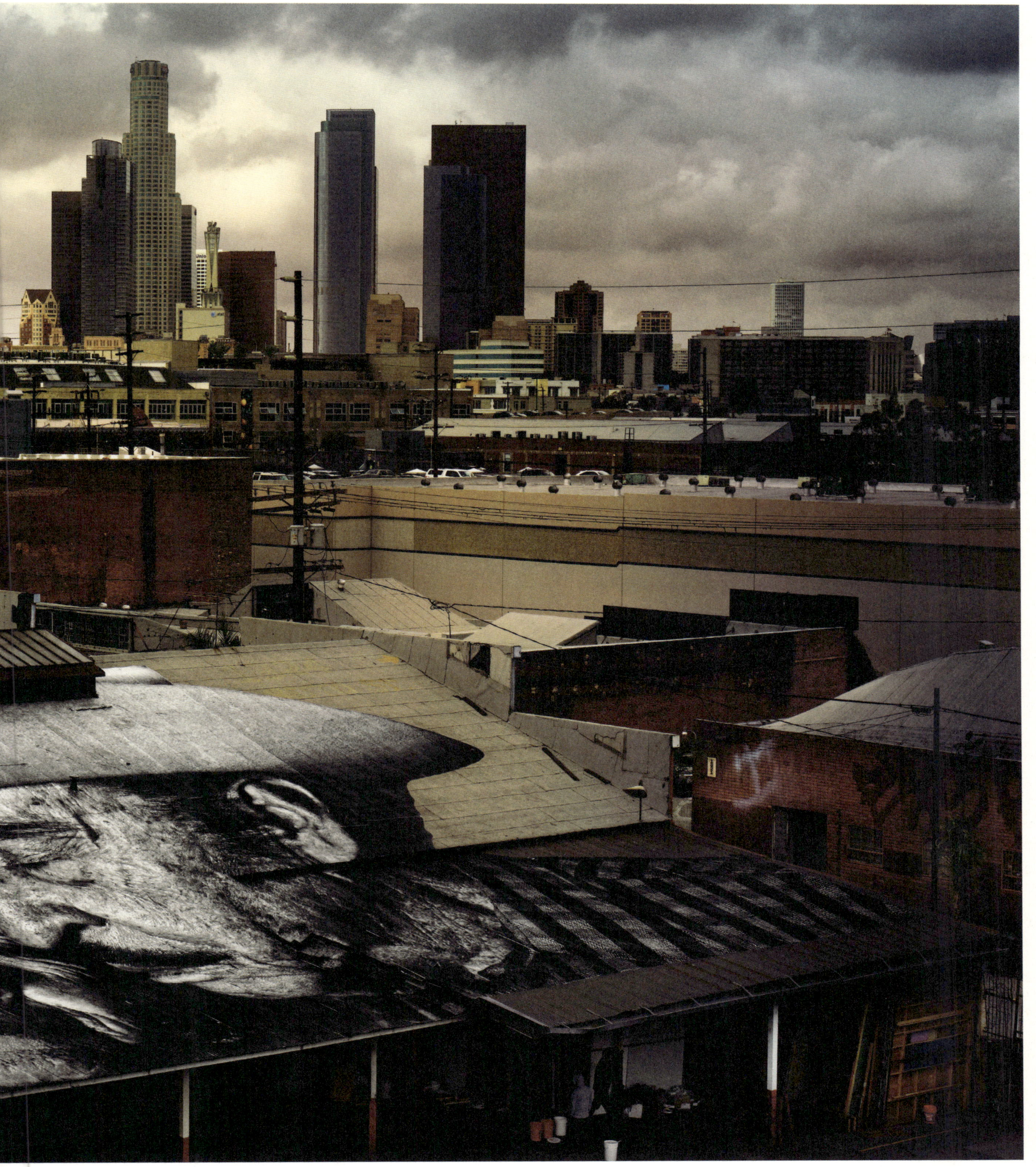

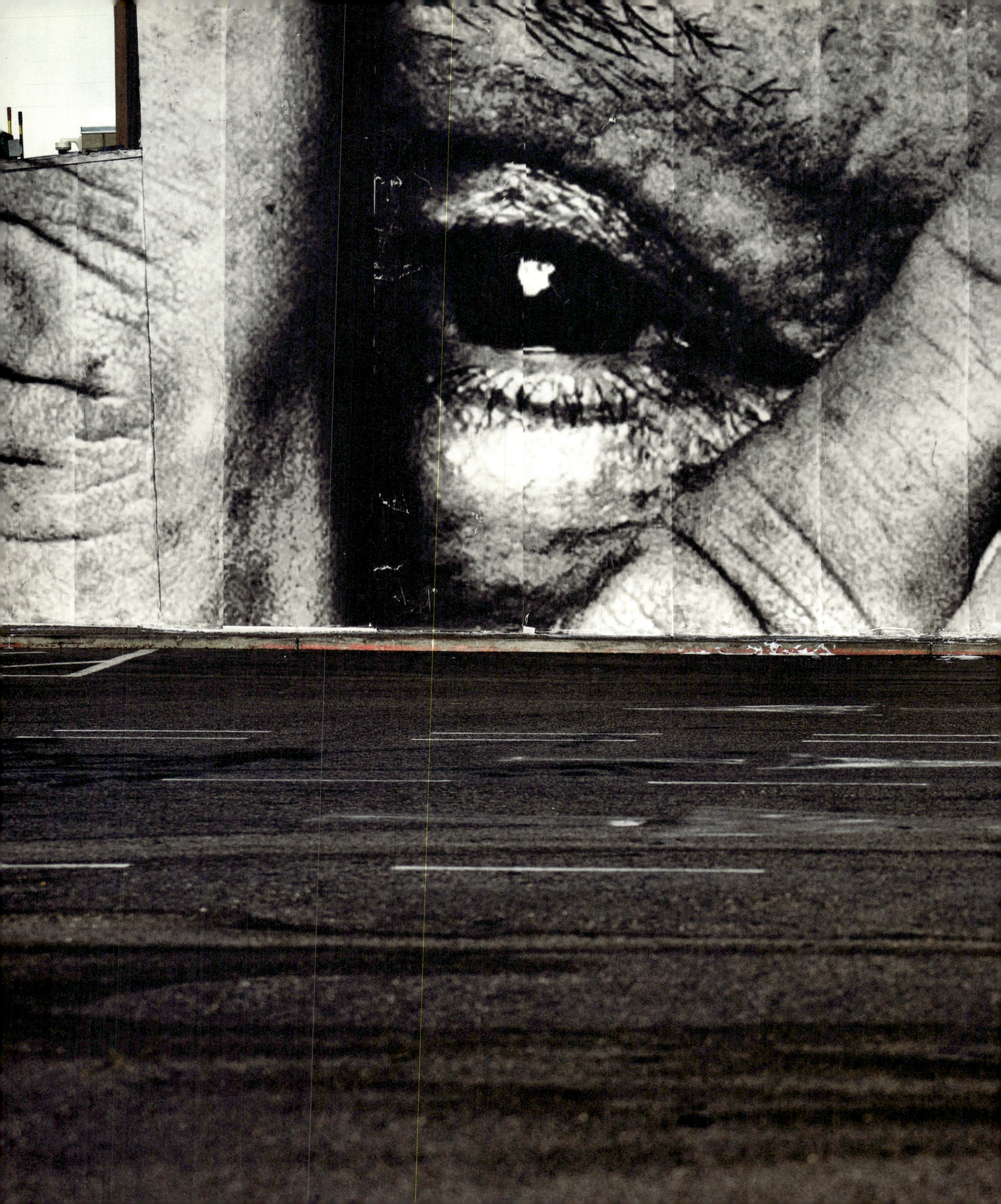

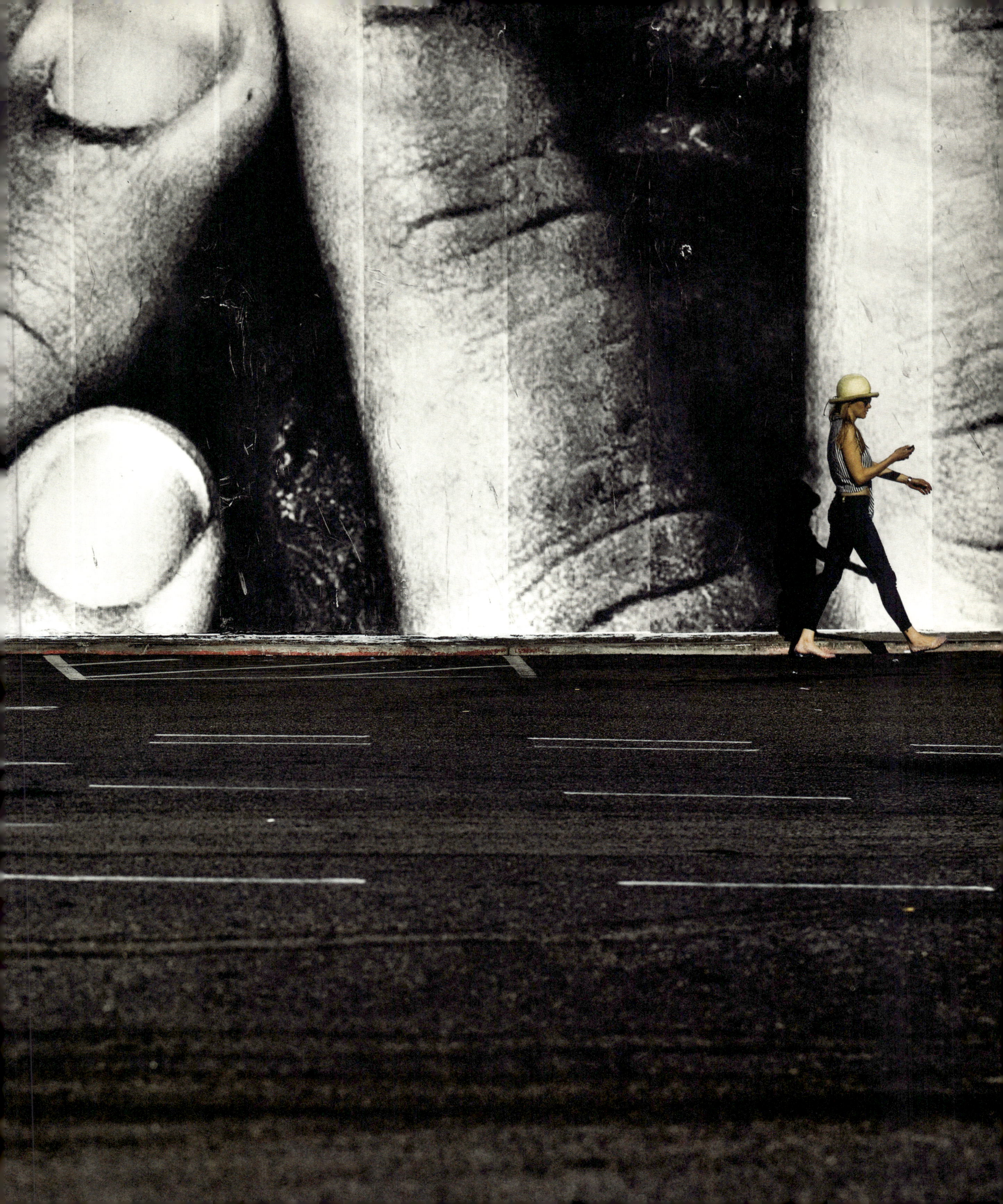

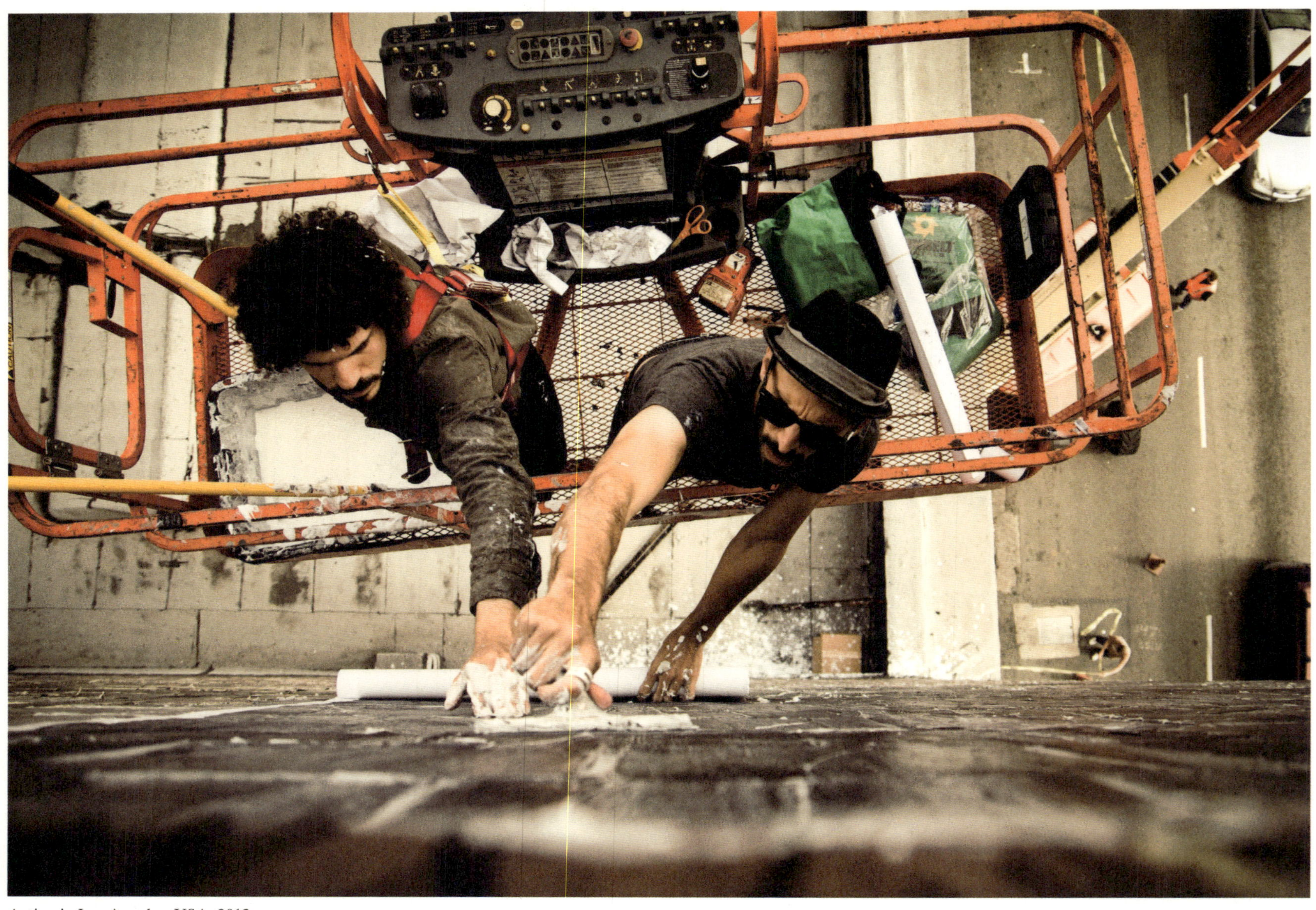

Action in Los Angeles, USA, 2012

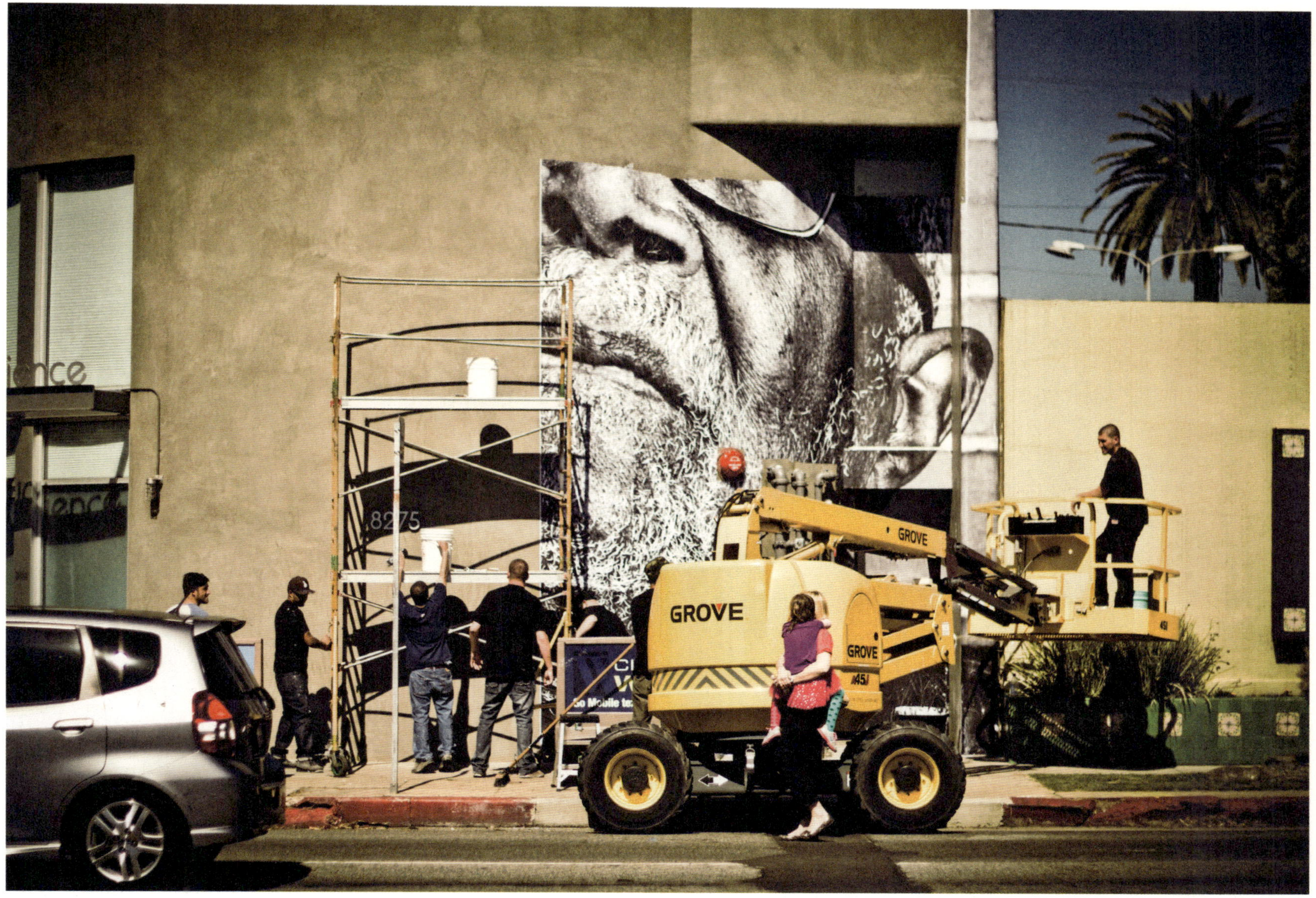

Action in Los Angeles, USA, 2012

'We pasted this image after interviewing this man, but he hadn't spoken much during the interview. A few months later, a woman entered the building in tears – the man was her father. She told us that he was a reverend who had fought for civil rights in the 1960s. We don't seek out heroic stories, but sometimes they come out by themselves.' – JR

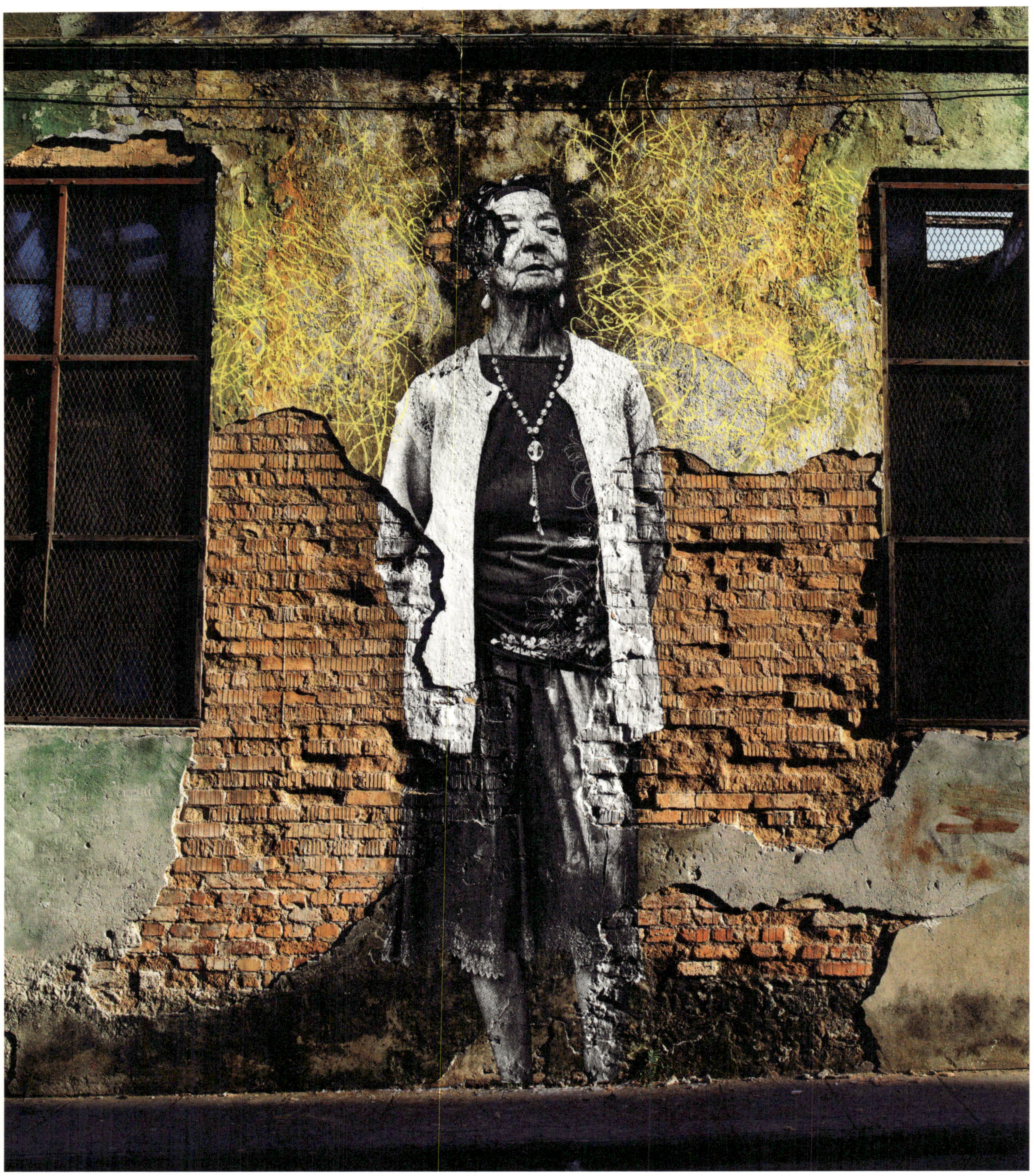

In collaboration with José Parlá, Leda Antonia Machado, Havana, Cuba, 2012 and (right) 2013

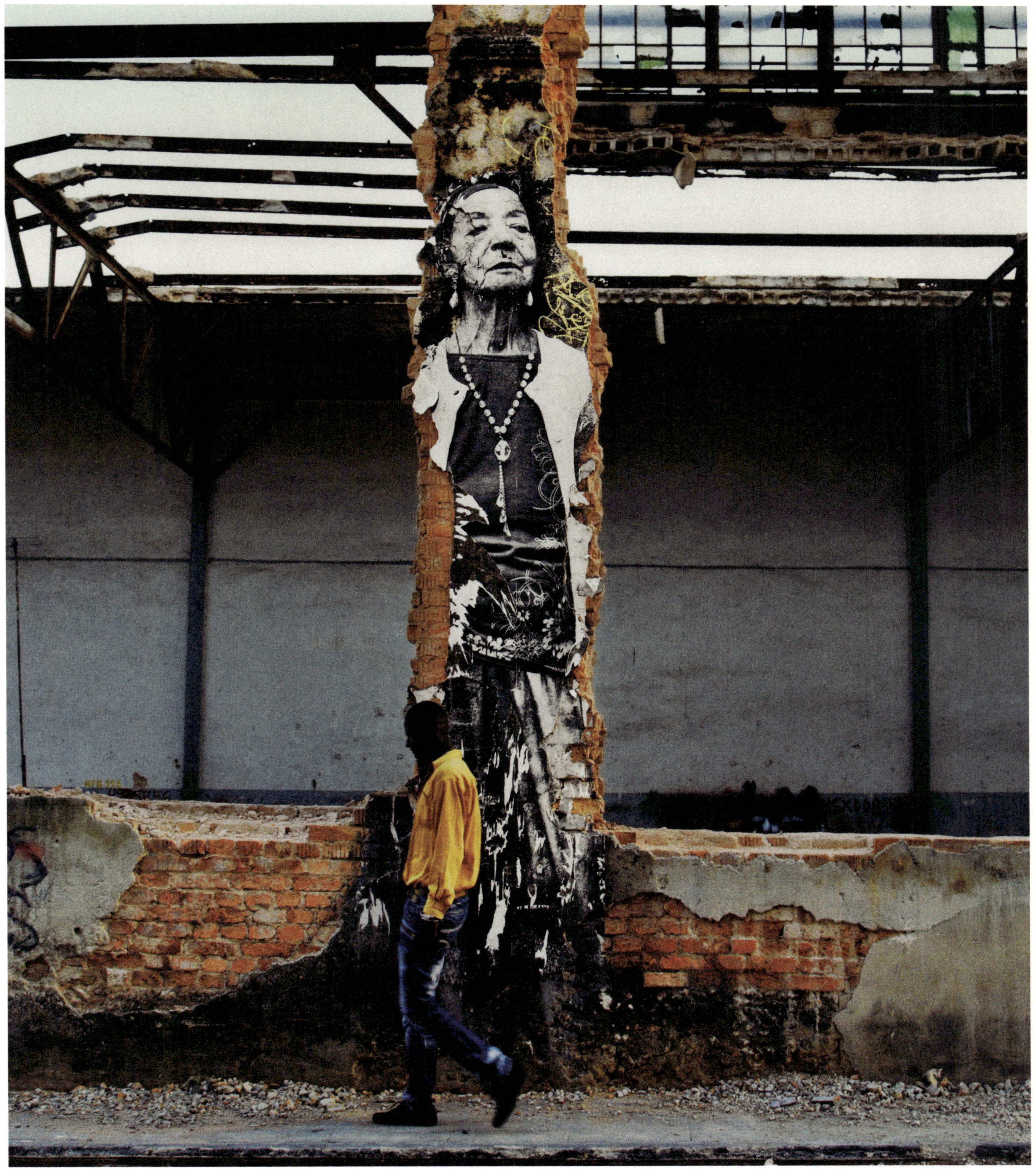

‘It was the last few days of the project and we were all exhausted. When we pasted this image, we made a mistake by pasting on the wrong wall, which created tensions within the team. A year later the building was demolished, but we realized the woman was on a pillar, which is still standing today.’ – JR

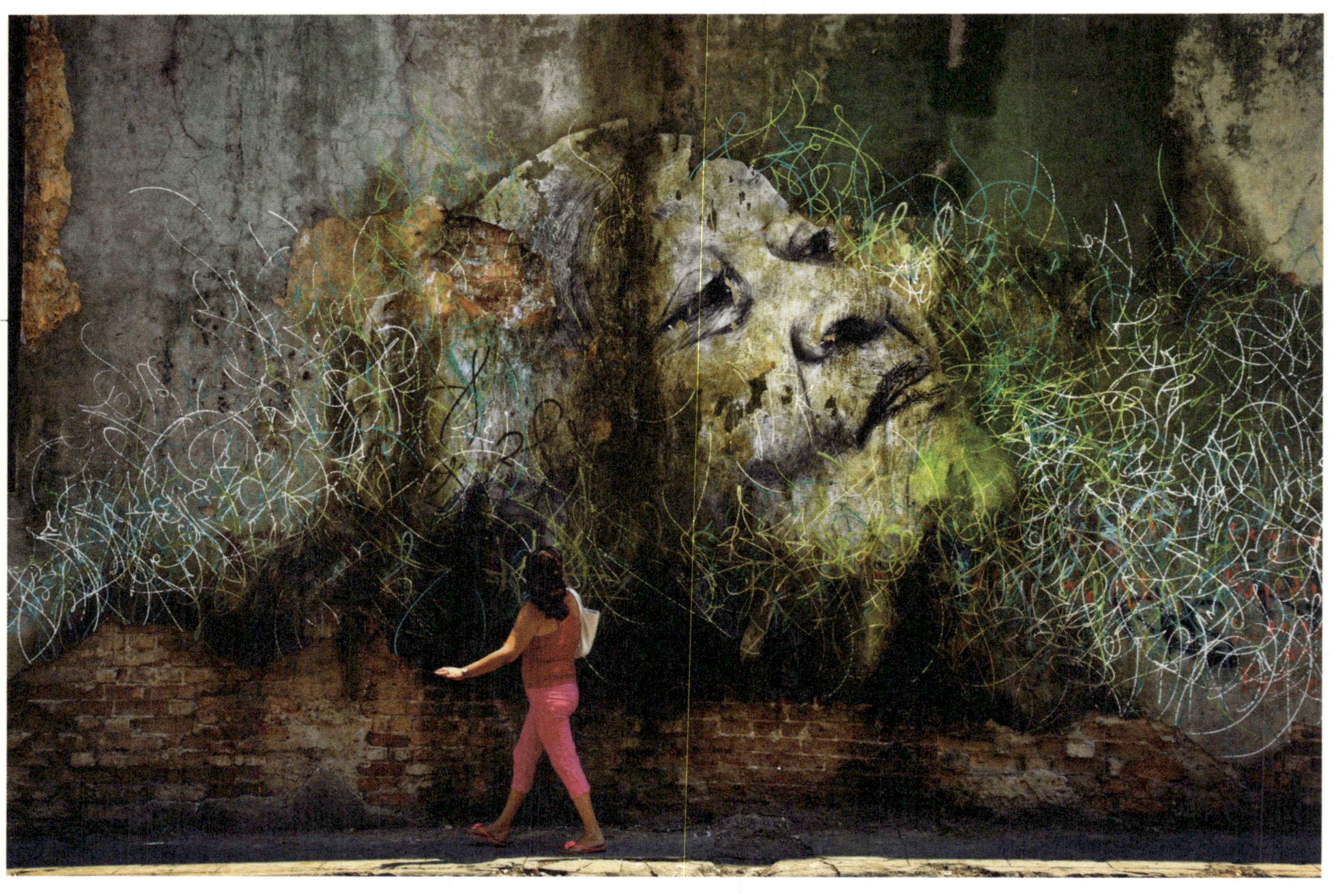

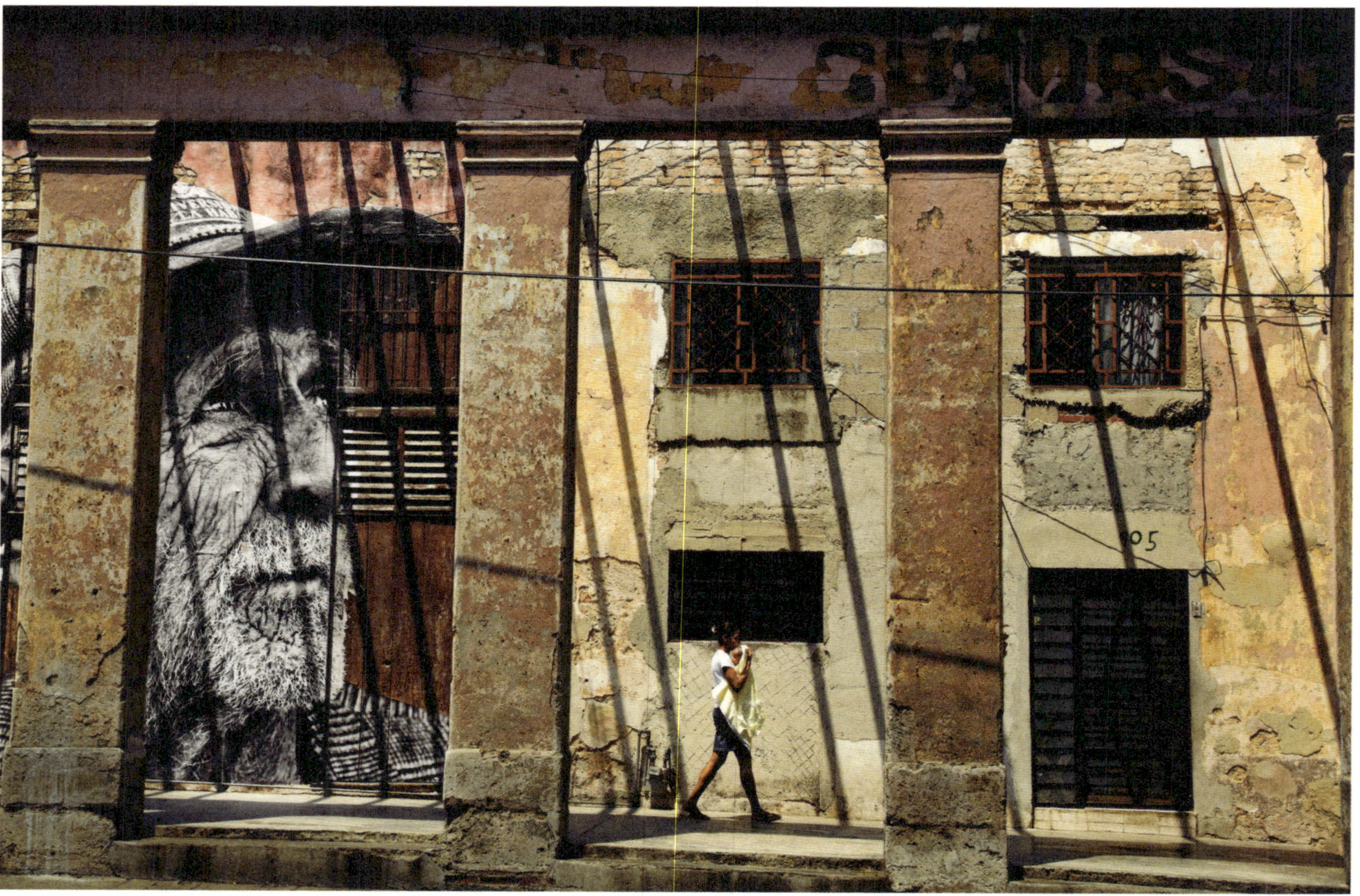

(top) In collaboration with José Parlá, Alicia Adela Hernandez Fernández, Havana, Cuba, 2012
(bottom) Miguel Pelegrino, Havana, Cuba, 2012, project in collaboration with José Parlá

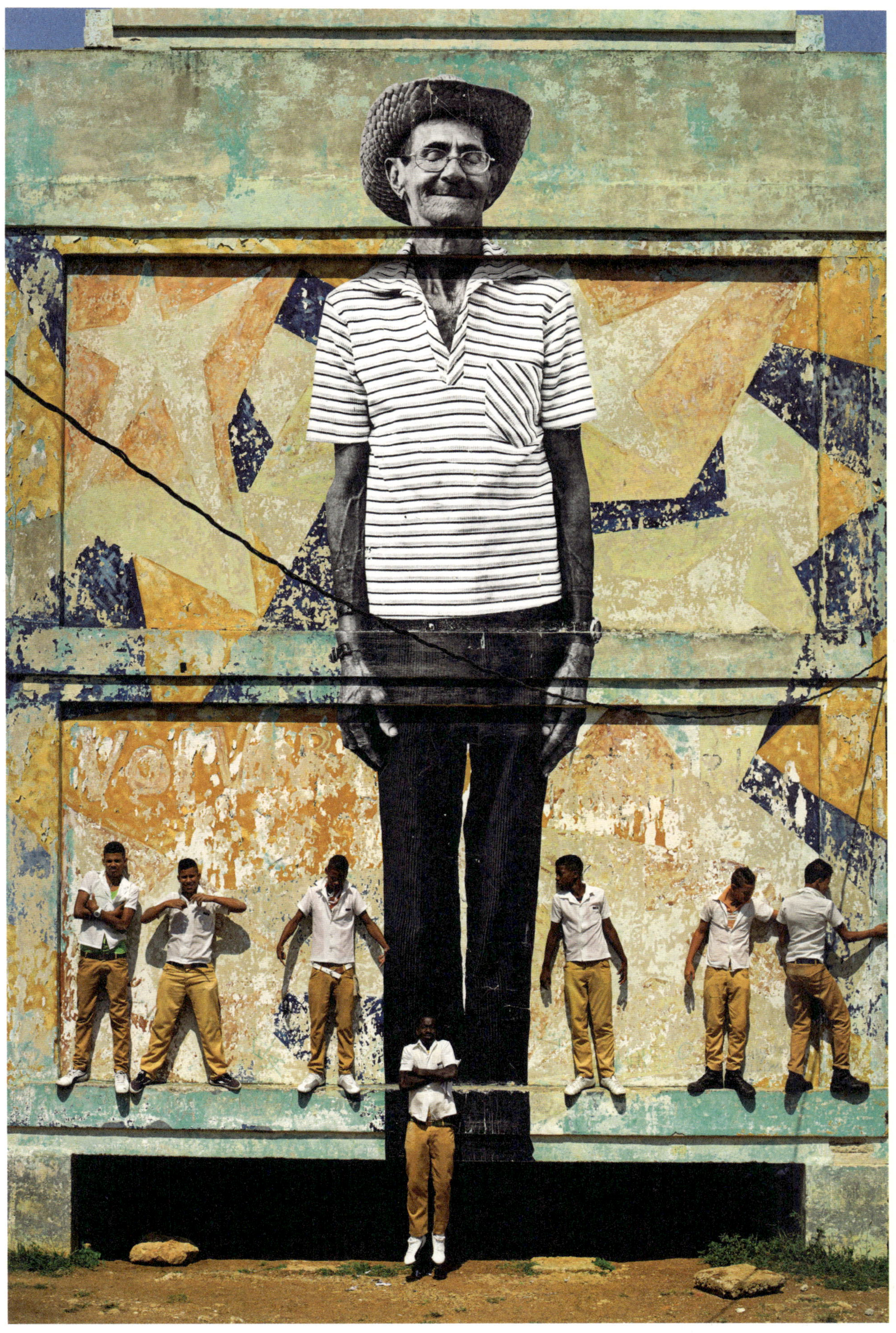

Antonio Cruz Gordillo, Havana, Cuba, 2012, project in collaboration with José Parlá
(overleaf) Rafael Lorenzo and Obdulia Manzano, Havana, Cuba, 2012, project in collaboration with José Parlá

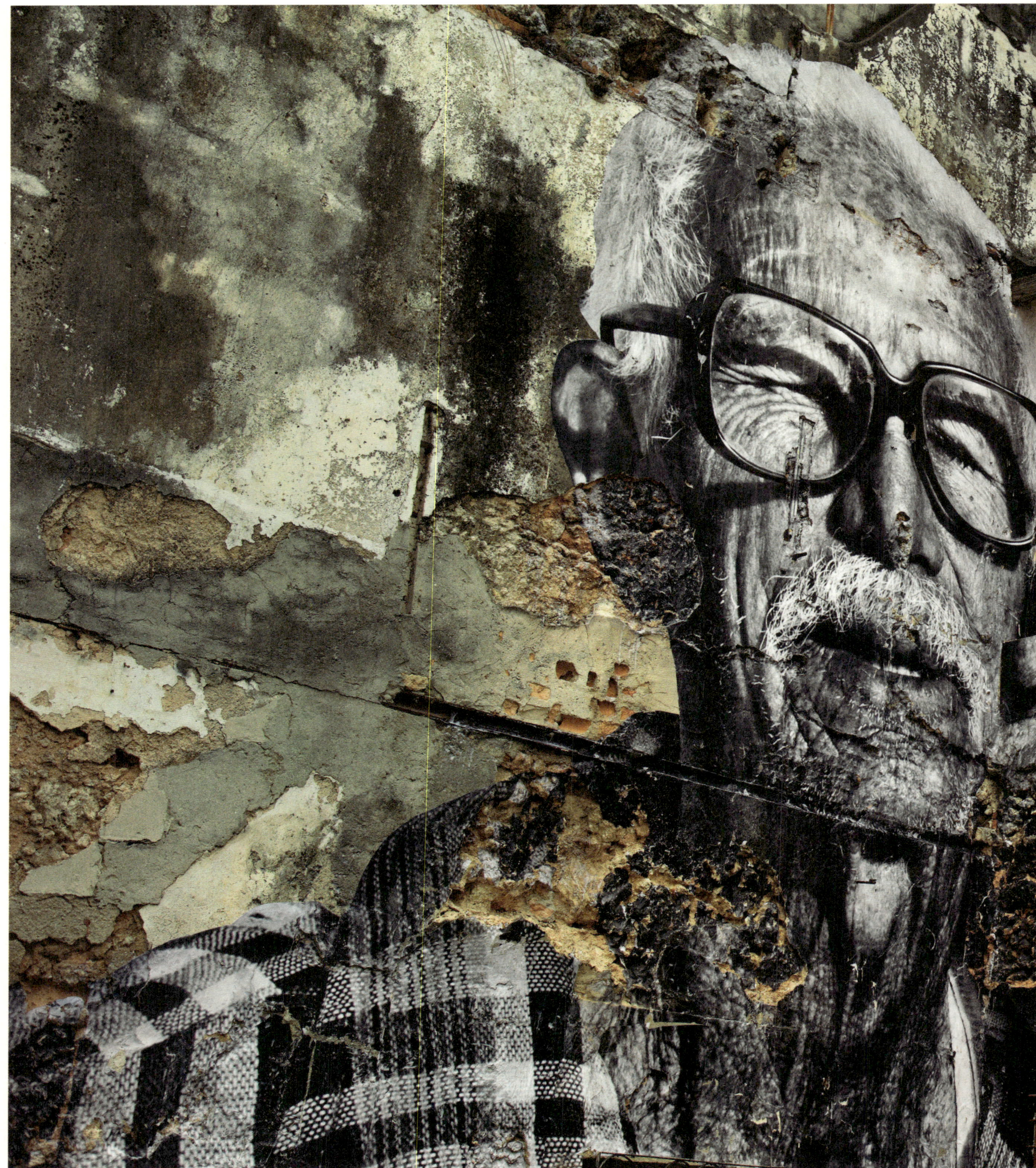

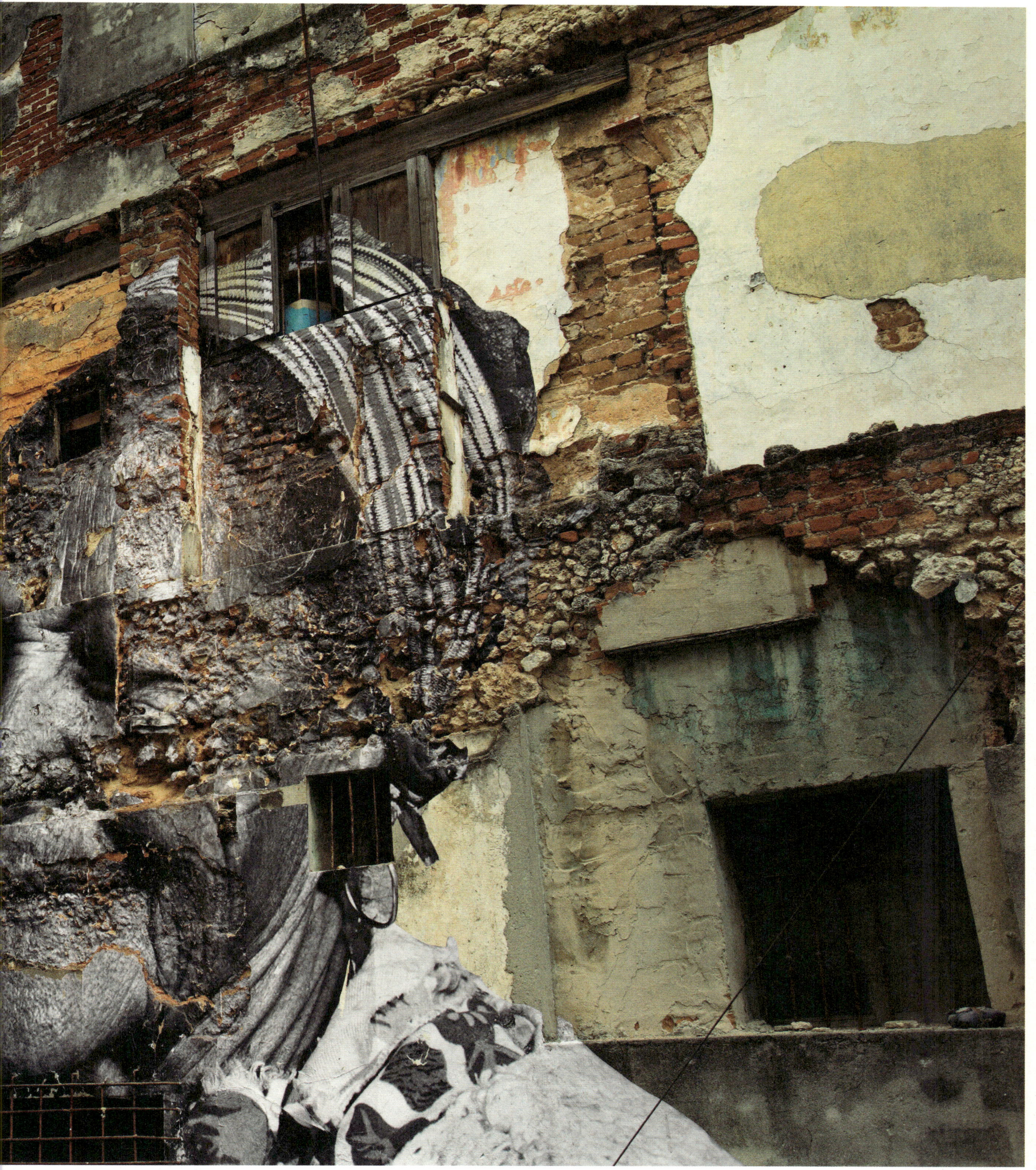

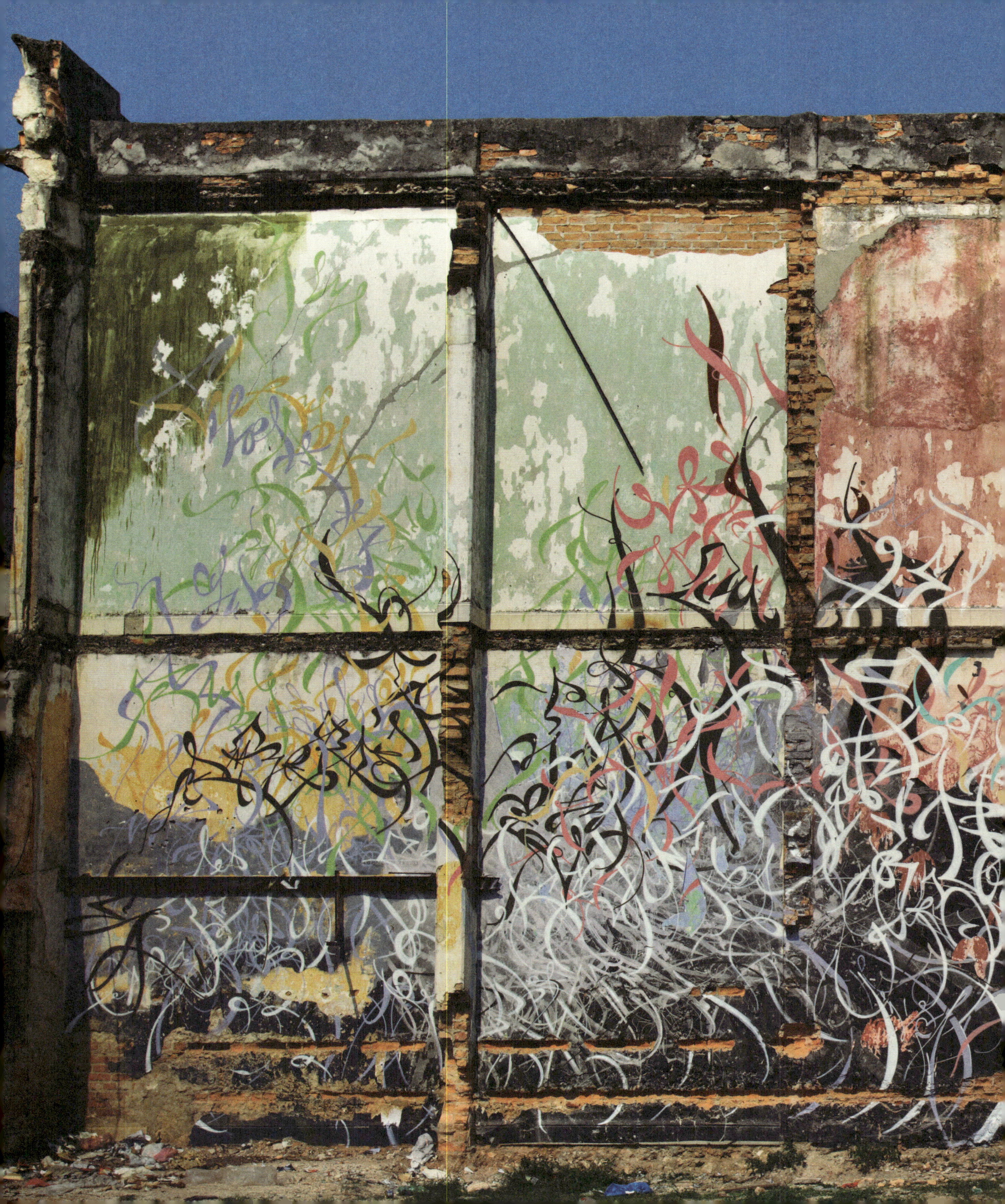

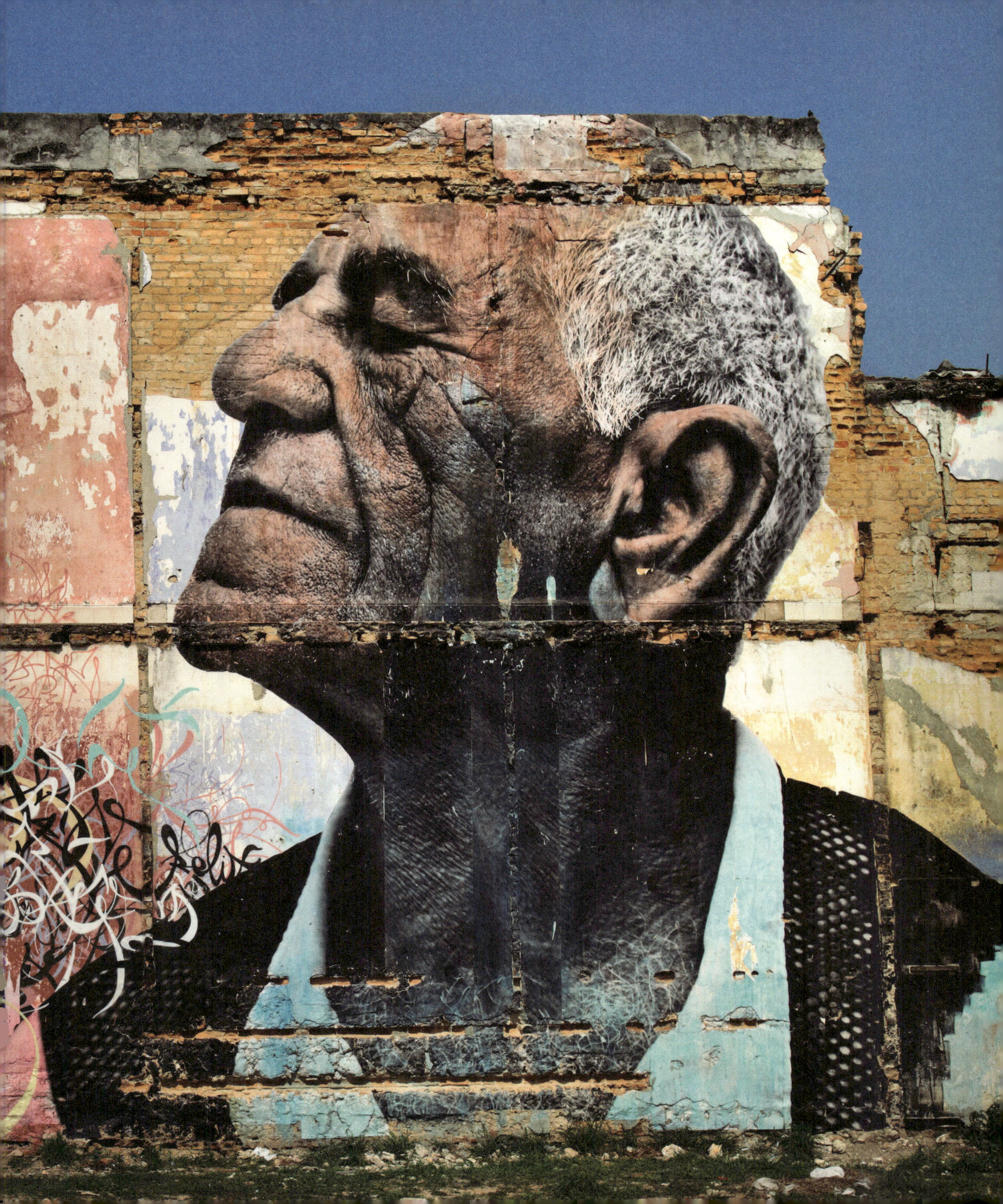

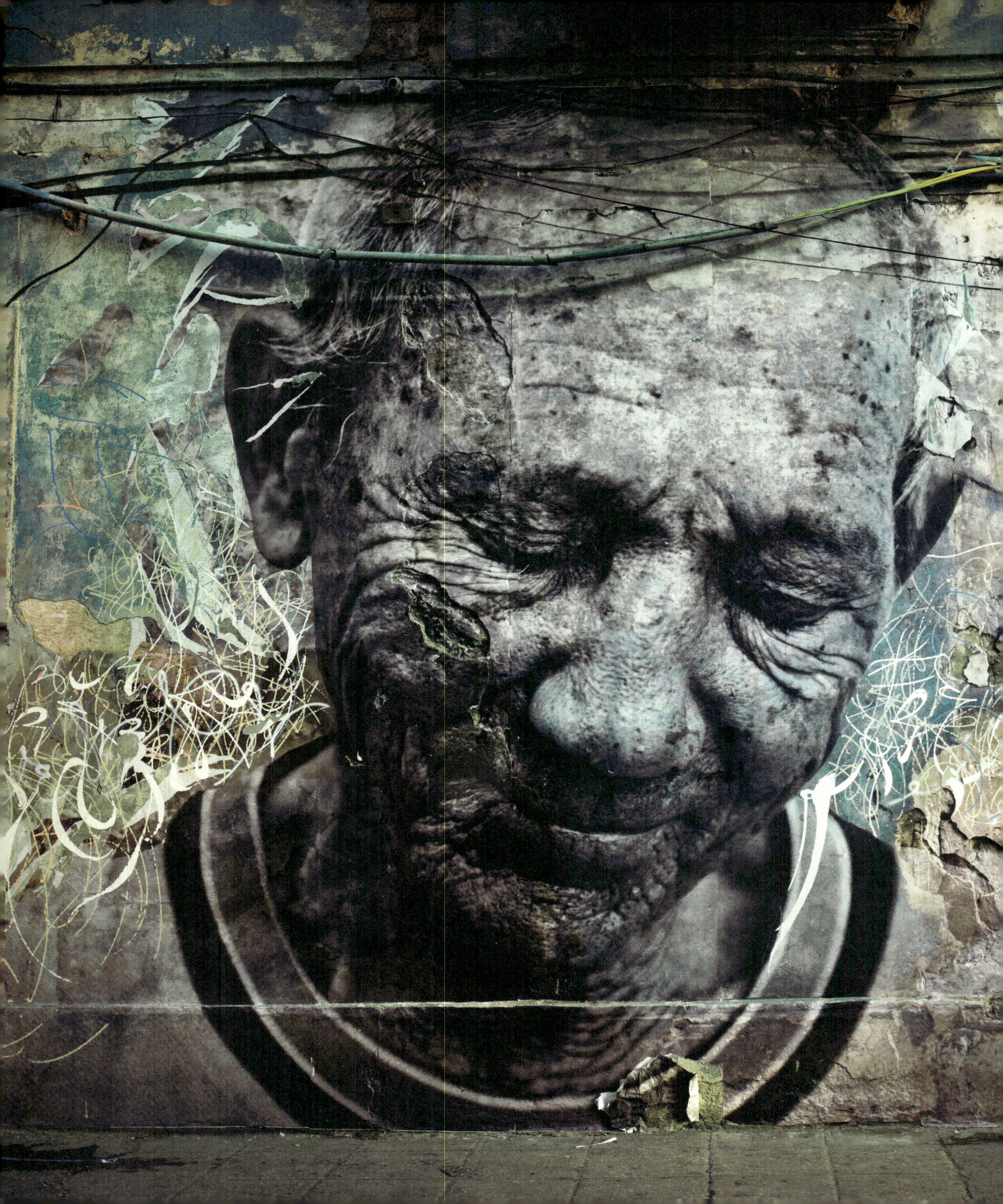

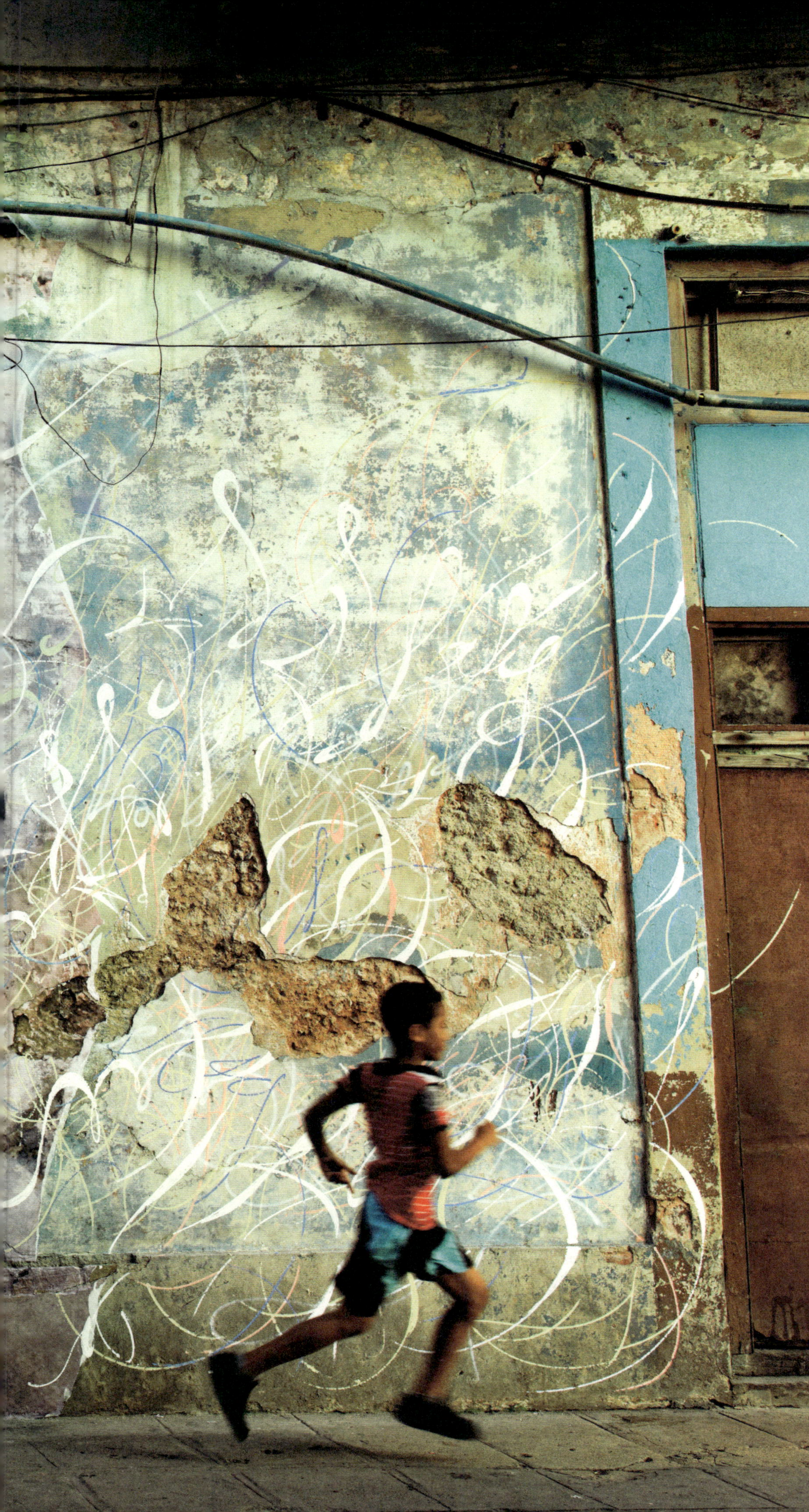

(previous page) In collaboration with José Parlá, Felix Rivera Famirez, Havana, Cuba, 2012
(left) In collaboration with José Parlá, Alfonso Ranón Fontaine Batista, Havana, Cuba, 2012

'My friend José Parlá and I pasted all over Havana. Most pastings are still there, but one year after the action, this one disappeared before our eyes. We came to visit and took pictures of it, but when we came back the next morning, it was gone. It's very special to witness the changes in a city where everything seems stuck in time.' – JR

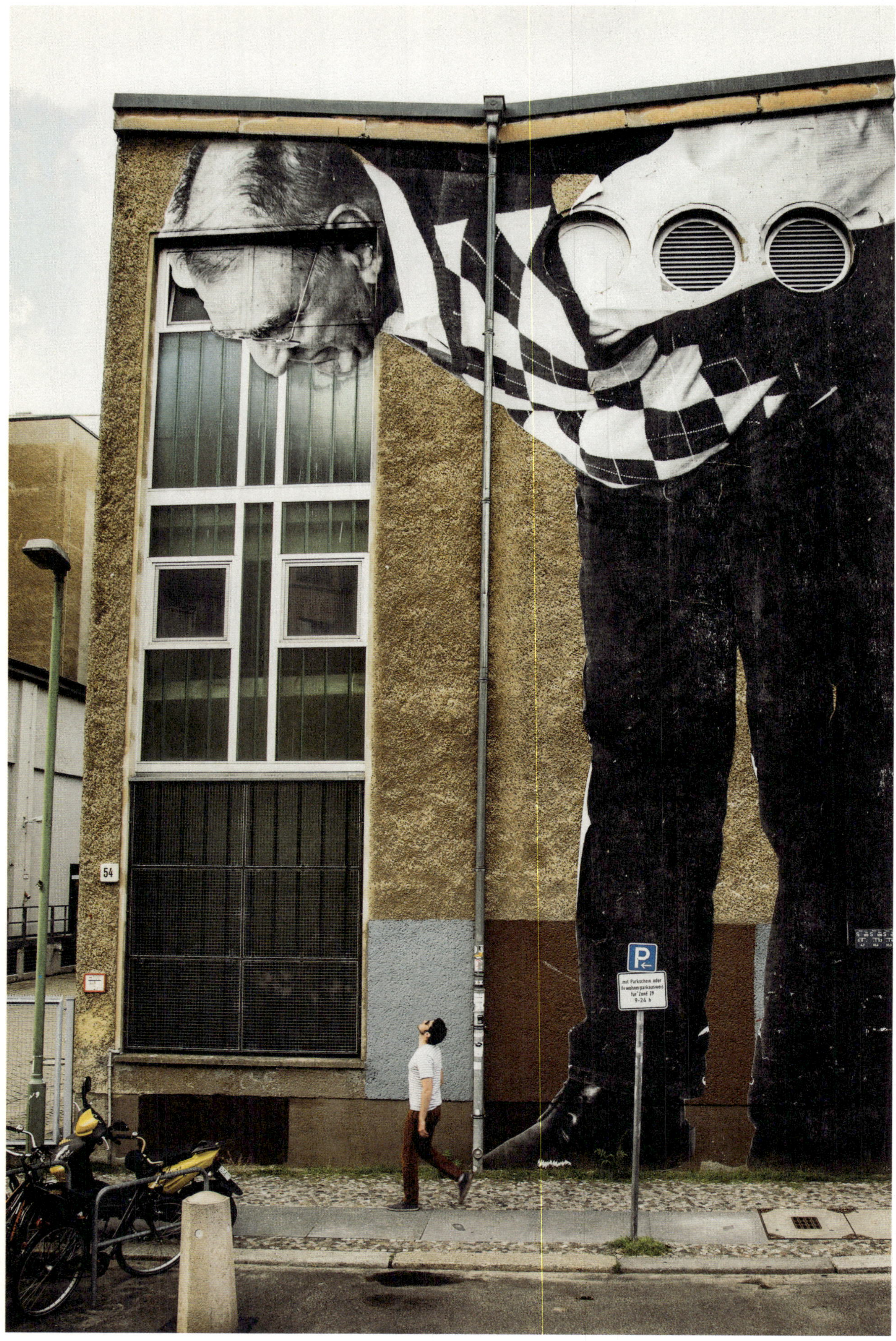

Dr Shihab Ahmed, Augustrasse, Berlin, Germany, 2013

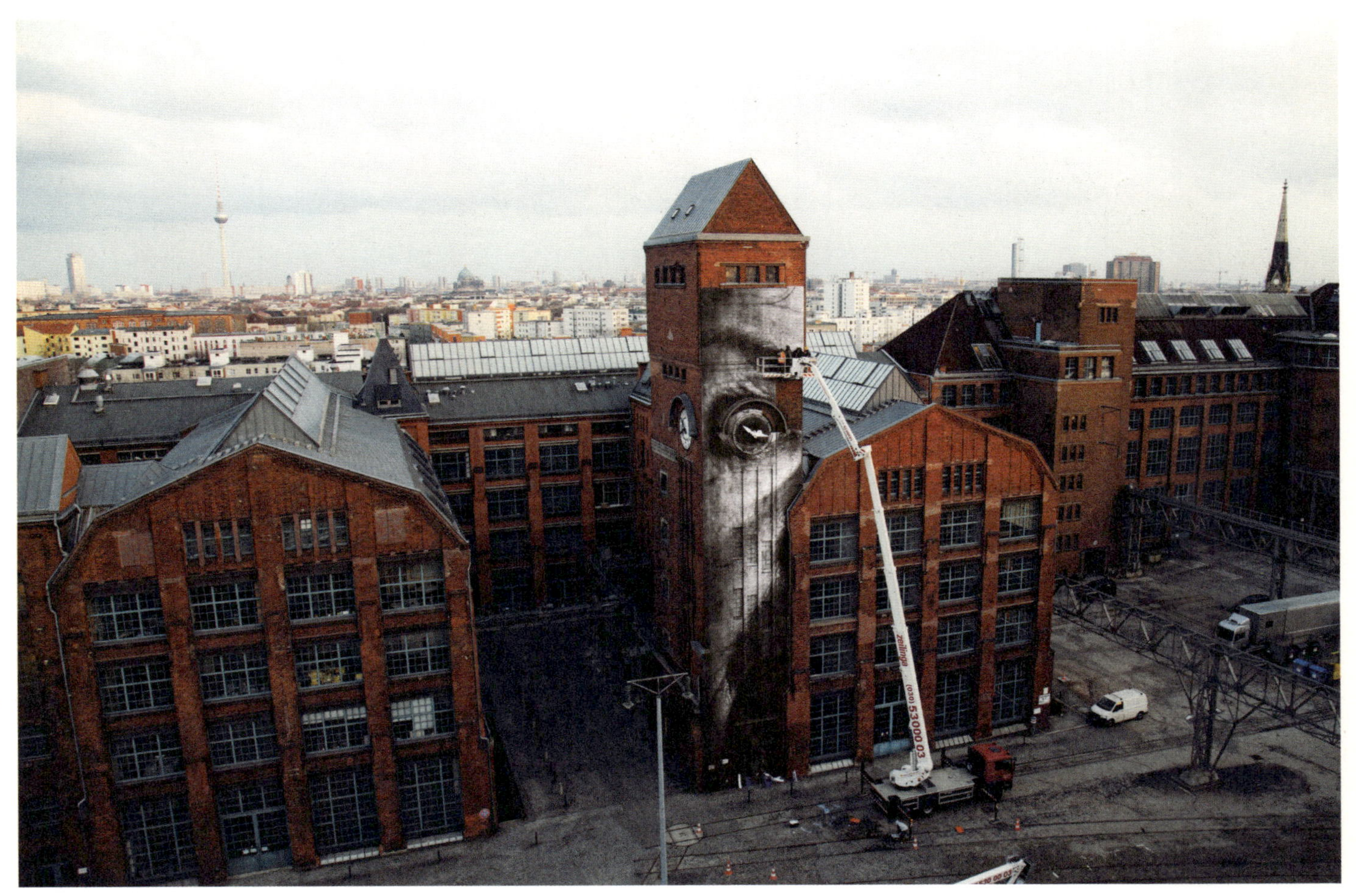

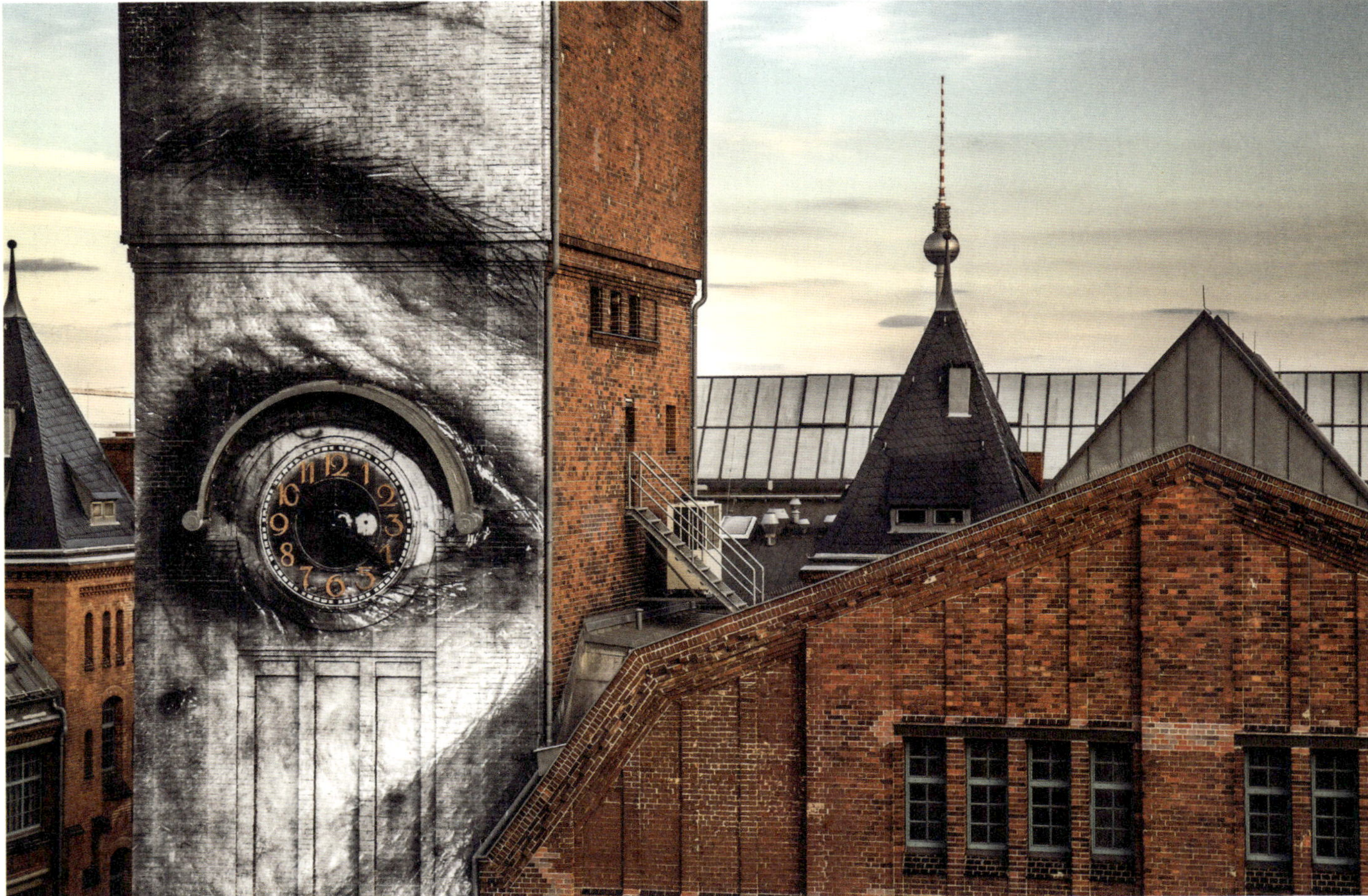

(top and bottom) Lucyna Steiner, Gustav Meyer Allee,
Berlin, Germany, 2013

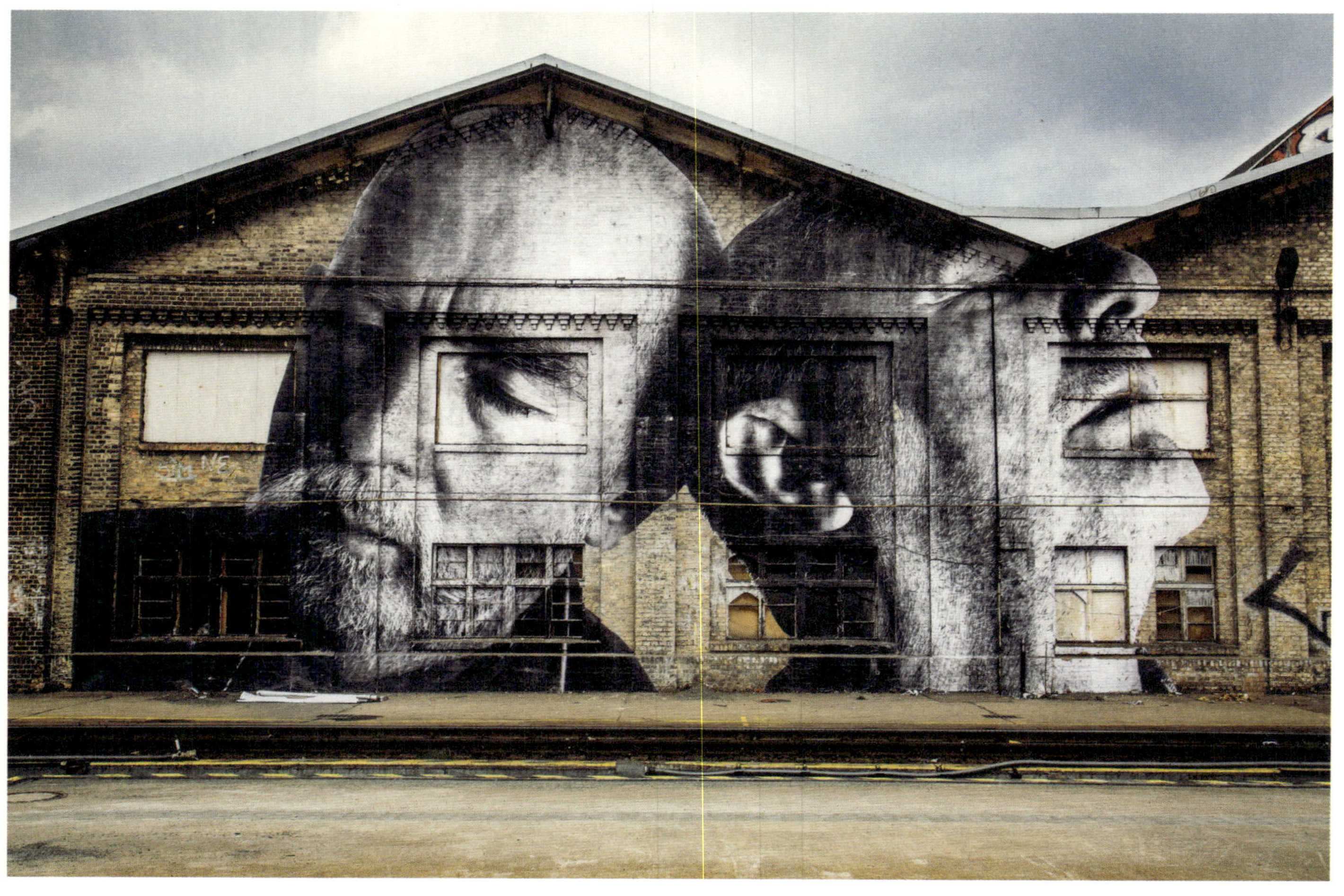

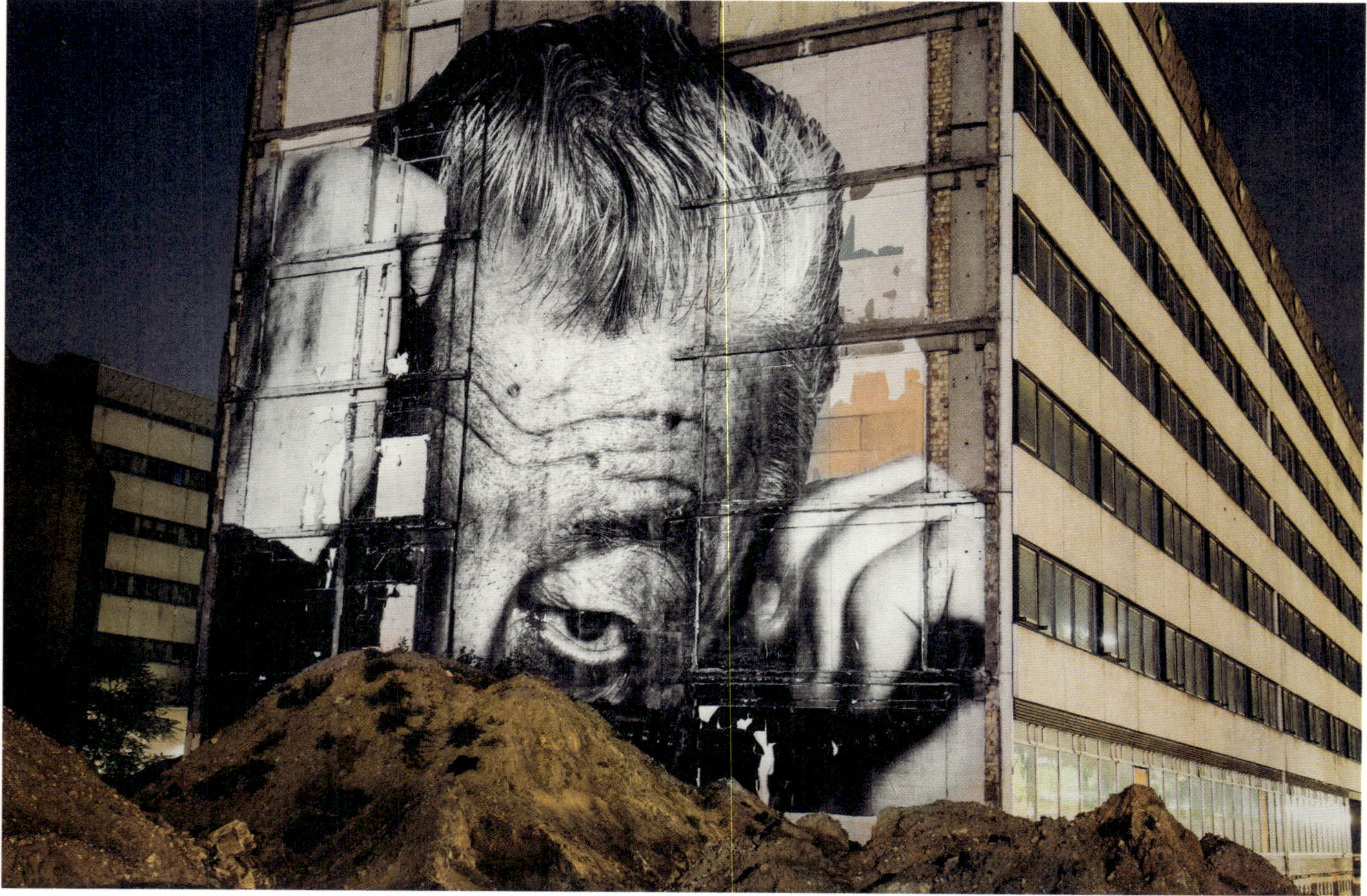

(top) Joachim Herzog and Volker Lempe, Warschauer Brücke, Berlin, Germany, 2013
(bottom) Dieter Graber, Breite Strasse, Berlin, Germany, 2013

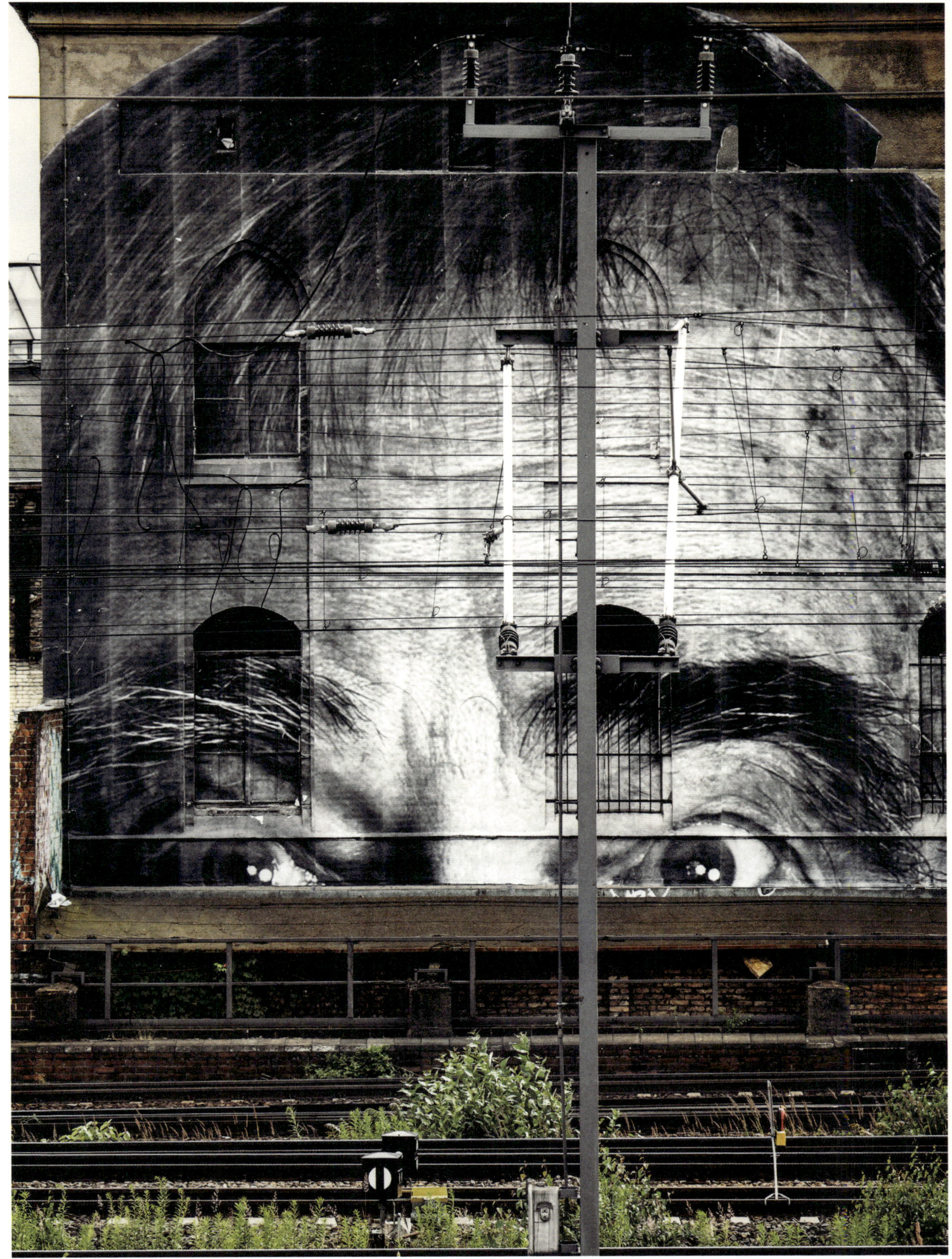

Gerhard Stoll, Postbahnhof, Berlin, Germany, 2013

UNFR

AMED

JR transforms cities into open-sky museums by pasting gigantic images onto the building façades that serve as his exhibition walls. In the *Unframed* project, however, JR stepped away from the camera. Instead of taking photographs himself, he sourced archival photographs from museums, local archives and even family photo albums.

Pasted in public urban spaces, the photographs – iconic or mundane, by both famous and unknown photographers – take on new meaning. Their architectural settings reframe the historical context within which the photographs were originally taken, and draw links to contemporary and local issues. The first *Unframed* pasting, for example, was in 2009, when JR pasted an image from the Chernobyl disaster onto a derelict house in Grottaglie, Italy, a region where the local mafia illegally buries toxic waste. He then participated in the 'Images' festival in September 2010, held in Vevey, Switzerland, where he drew on the history of photography and immersed himself into the photographic archives at the Musée de l'Elysée de Lausanne. Using the archive as a resource, he revisited works by established photographers including Robert Capa, Gilles Caron, Man Ray, Helen Levitt and Mario Giacomelli, as well as several less-known photographers. The resulting installations included an image of a minaret from a photograph by Lehnert & Landrock in 1930 from Egypt pasted onto a grain silo at a time when Switzerland passed a law against the building of mosque minarets.

In 2012, JR took the project to the United States. He used an iconic photograph by Ernest Withers from a 1968 civil rights march led by Martin Luther King in Memphis, Tennessee, and pasted it in Washington DC, covering a building next to what once was the segregated post office for African Americans. The following year, he returned to France for an action in Marseille that addressed the history of the working-class area of La Belle de Mai. Here, JR invited inhabitants to think about the memory of their streets by looking into their personal photo albums. The photographs they selected – old or recent, cropped or enlarged – were transformed into monumental artworks, which visually brought to life the collective memory of the people of the neighbourhood.

In 2014, JR took *Unframed* to Baden Baden, Germany, a town near the border with France that was the headquarters of the French occupation forces in Germany after World War II. This installment of the project addressed the history of German-French relations in the area by putting up historical photographs taken from locals' photo albums. Later that year, in New York, JR worked in an abandoned hospital complex on the south side of Ellis Island, which looks out towards the Statue of Liberty. Ellis Island was the gateway to the United States for approximately twelve million immigrants who were required to pass through in order to enter the country from 1892 to 1954. JR utilized the photographic archives of Ellis Island to create a permanent exhibition of life-size installations in the rooms of the hospital. Using the installations as film sets, he also created a short film to capture the rich history of the building, which is full of stories.

By taking historical photographs out of the archive, the museum or the album, JR revives them and challenges viewers to reflect on the importance of context – the historical context in which the photographs were taken, and where and how they are displayed – and its impact on how we read images.

(top) *Protests in Marseille for public services, 2011*, seen by JR, 11 Boulevard de la Révolution, Marseille, France, 2013
(middle) *Laurent Di Lorto during France's 1934 Cup Final*, seen by JR, 36 Rue François Barbini, Marseille, France, 2013
(bottom) *Onlookers sitting on scaffolding during a demonstration for the Popular Front in Marseille, 1936*, seen by JR, 102 Rue Loubon, Marseille, France, 2013

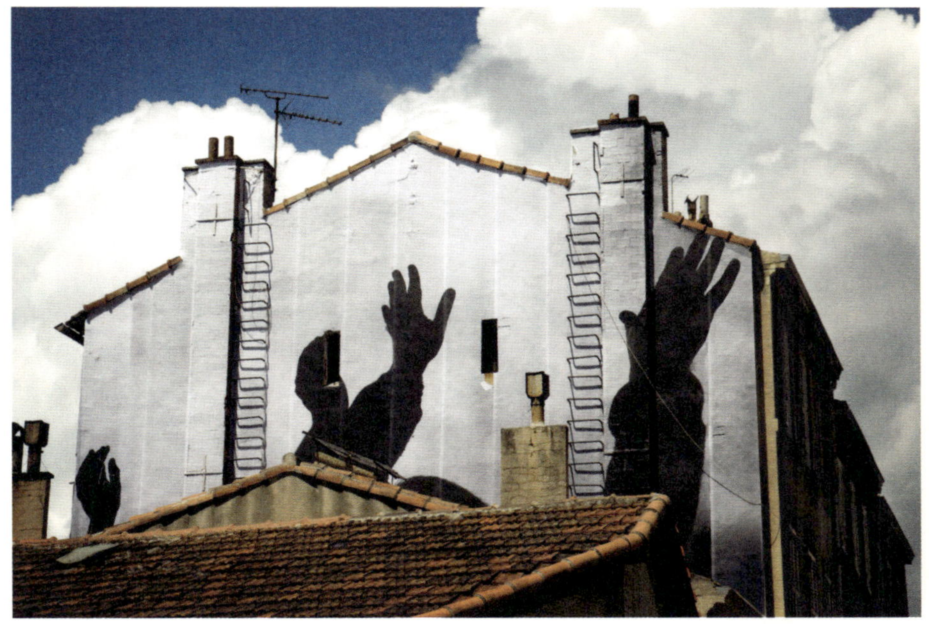

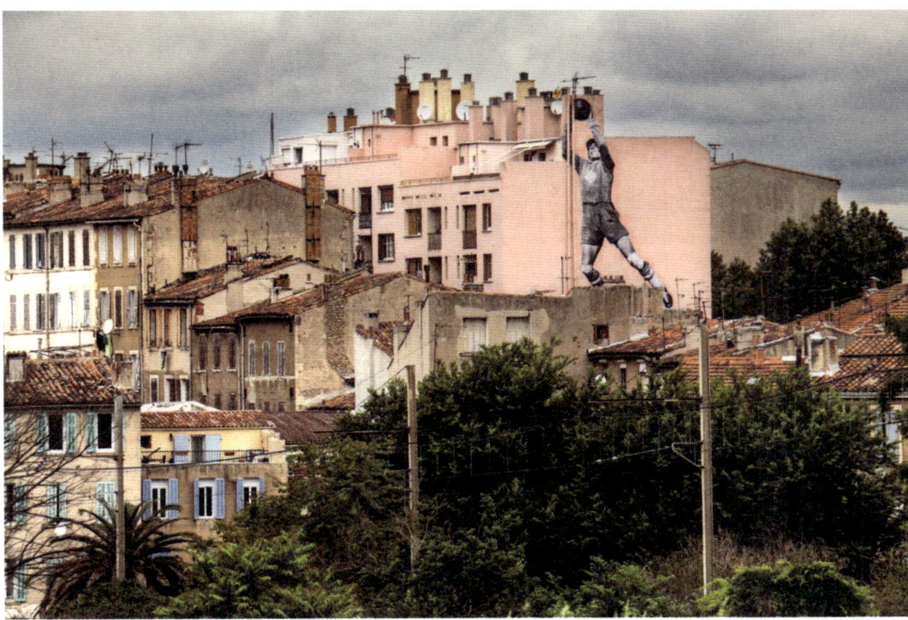

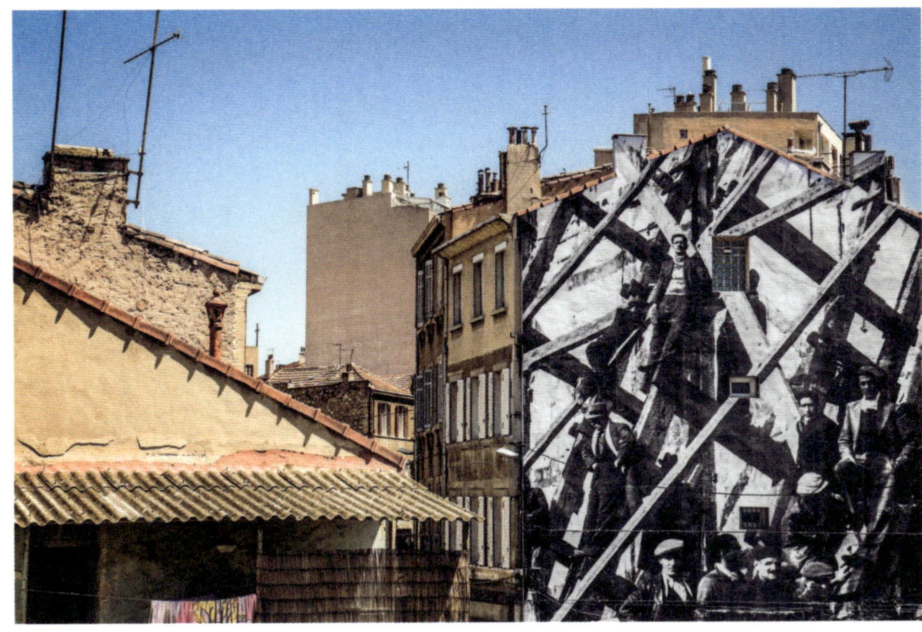

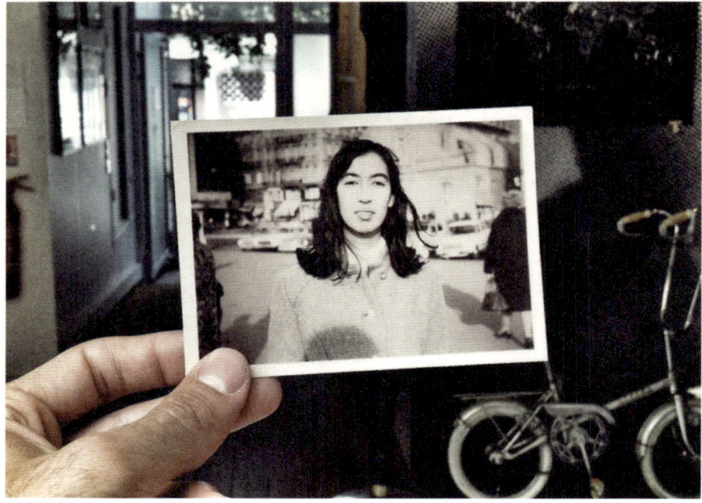

Annick Perrot-Bishop in the old port in front of La Samaritaine, 1966. Selected by Hervé Jegou

As a sideline to the project in the district of La Belle de Mai, JR had the opportunity to do an action on the iconic wall of the Cornice du President John Fitzgerald Kennedy. There was a huge portrait of Zinedine Zidane up nearby and, as a private joke, JR cropped the photo of an ordinary Marseille resident to match the Zidane one.

In the original photograph, Annick Perrot-Bishop was twenty-one years old. She was photographed by a friend on a walk in the old port in December 1966. For the pasting, JR only showed her face – a symbol of youth and vitality.

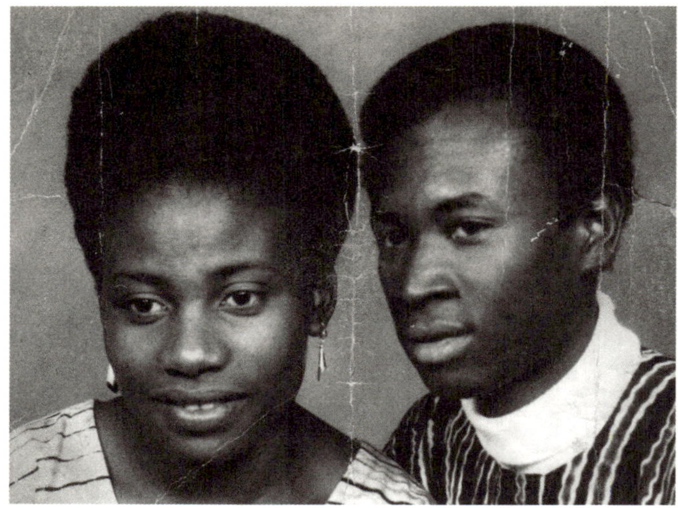

Portrait of my grandparents, Berthe and Diallo, Mali, 1973. Selected by Aramata Traoré, high school student, born 1998

'This photo has travelled extensively, to Mali, Burkina Faso, Cote d'Ivoire, Senegal and, of course, Marseille. My grandparents travelled a lot because of my grandfather's job: he was an economist. They always took this photo with them on their trips. However, it started to become damaged, so they decided to stop taking it with them.

Initially, my family didn't want me to put it forward for this project of JR's because there was a risk of it being damaged if it was taken all over the city. Eventually they came around and agreed.

We don't know where the photo was taken but we do know that my grandfather, who was returning from a trip to Europe for his studies, didn't take the time to change clothes or put away his luggage before seeing his fiancée (they were not yet married) and taking this picture with her. He was very much in love with her.

Today, they are quite old. They are retired but my grandmother opened a school in the countryside. I love my grandparents. In Mali, old people are respected. It's good for the country. And for generations, this tradition hasn't changed, we must protect it, it shouldn't disappear.

My grandparents often come to France to see their children and grandchildren. They were there when the poster was pasted. They took a picture next to the pasting, which my grandfather said they could use as evidence if people didn't believe them.'

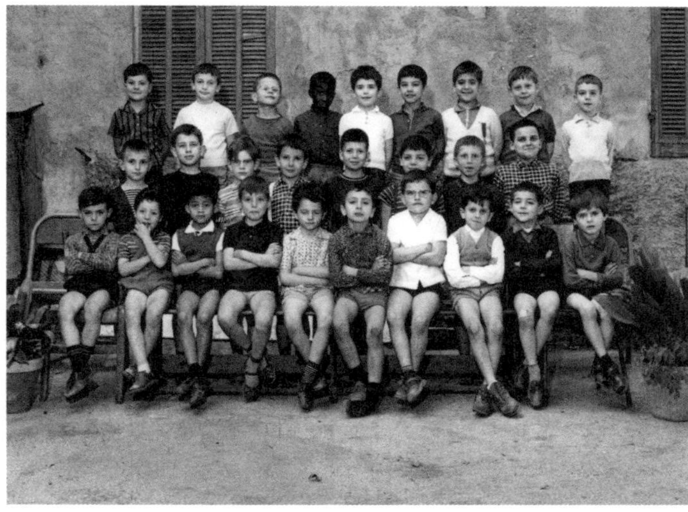

École Saint-Charles, Marseille, 1966–1967.
Selected by Thierry Mourre, marine firefighter, born 1960

'I was surprised – shocked, even – that on the opening day of the exhibition someone said, "if you took that class photo today, it would be the opposite scenario to this photo from 1967." He meant that in 1967 there was one black child, but now there might be only one white child. I replied that if you thought about the names of my classmates, they all finished with "i" or "ias" – they were all of Italian, Sicilian and Spanish. So La Belle de Mai has always been this kind of cultural melting pot. For example, the greatest cop and the greatest thug live in the same street – this isn't a cliché, it's reality.

I don't live in La Belle de Mai anymore, but my whole family are still there and I come back three times a week. When people ask me where I come from, I answer, "La Belle de Mai". I have memories everywhere here.

As an ordinary citizen, it is moving to be displayed on a wall in this way, half a century after the photo was taken.

Today, as a member of the fire brigade, I work in social centres and neighbourhoods where I inevitably come across people from all backgrounds. Is it a coincidence that I'm next to the boy called Gomis, who was the only black child in school? I was born and now work in a working-class area, which makes me wonder about why fire engines are sometimes stoned in some neighbourhoods. Most kids are excited when they see a fire engine. So what changed that made them see fire engines as enemies? All the noise in the media makes young people associate uniforms with repressive connotations. So we have set up structures and social networks to create links with young people, to avoid such incidents. Thanks to these actions, firefighters are now part of the community and we can help people. Without sounding angelic, I think the fact that I grew up in La Belle de Mai has influenced my view of working-class areas. I think there isn't a lot of space for fate in life.'

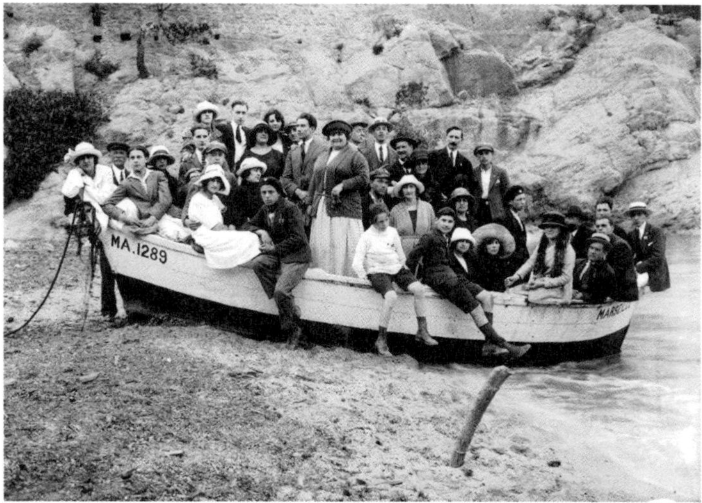

A group posing in a boat moored on the beach, c. 1930.
Selected by Ali Ahmad Ahmadi, electrician, born 1992

'The first time I saw this photo, it reminded me of my own story – of my journey here from Afghanistan between 2008 and 2010. In JR's project, every picture tells a story and anyone can see their own story in the images. This photograph told my story. I once found myself in the same situation as the people in this photo: at sea, between Turkey and Greece. There were thirty people in the boat, which was smaller than this one. It was difficult, there were women and children with us. The engine broke down and nobody knew what to do. We only had one phone to make a call. We managed to reach the Greek police, and asked them to pick us up. We called around midnight and a boat arrived at around 10 a.m. the next morning. But it wasn't the Greek police, it was the Turkish police, and we were returned to Turkey…

After that, we came to Europe by truck. I just wanted to get out of my country, it didn't matter if we ended up in France, Italy or Spain. I didn't know much about France; I had only seen pictures of Paris, and of the football team Paris Saint-Germain.

I didn't realize at first that the people in the photo were on holiday, I just noticed the shape of the boat, and the fact there were people inside, and that reminded me of my story. At first I also didn't understand why JR pasted the boat and people upside down. I know many people who lost their parents in their journey to Europe. But he explained that if the poster is upside down, then the sky becomes the sea.'

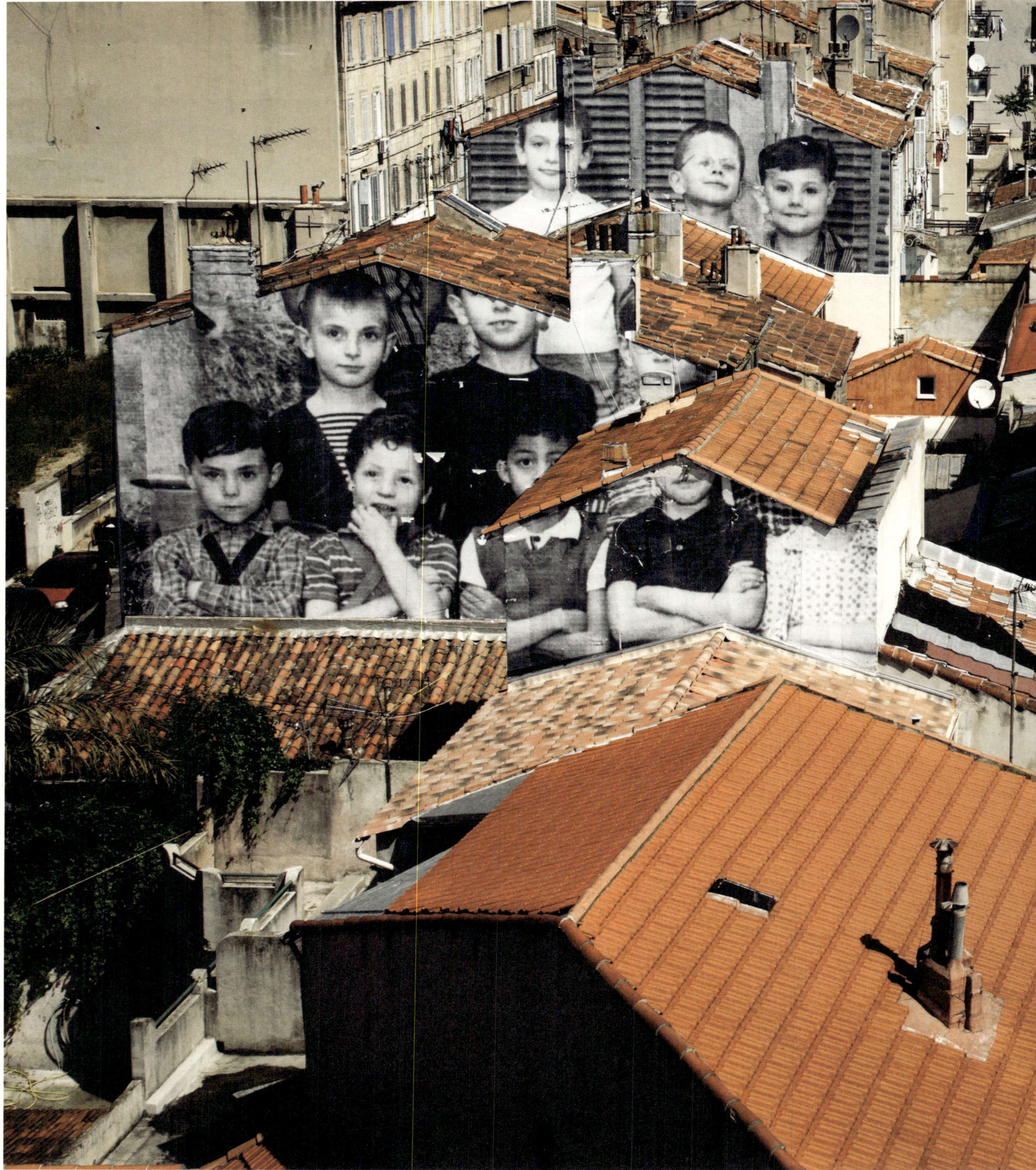

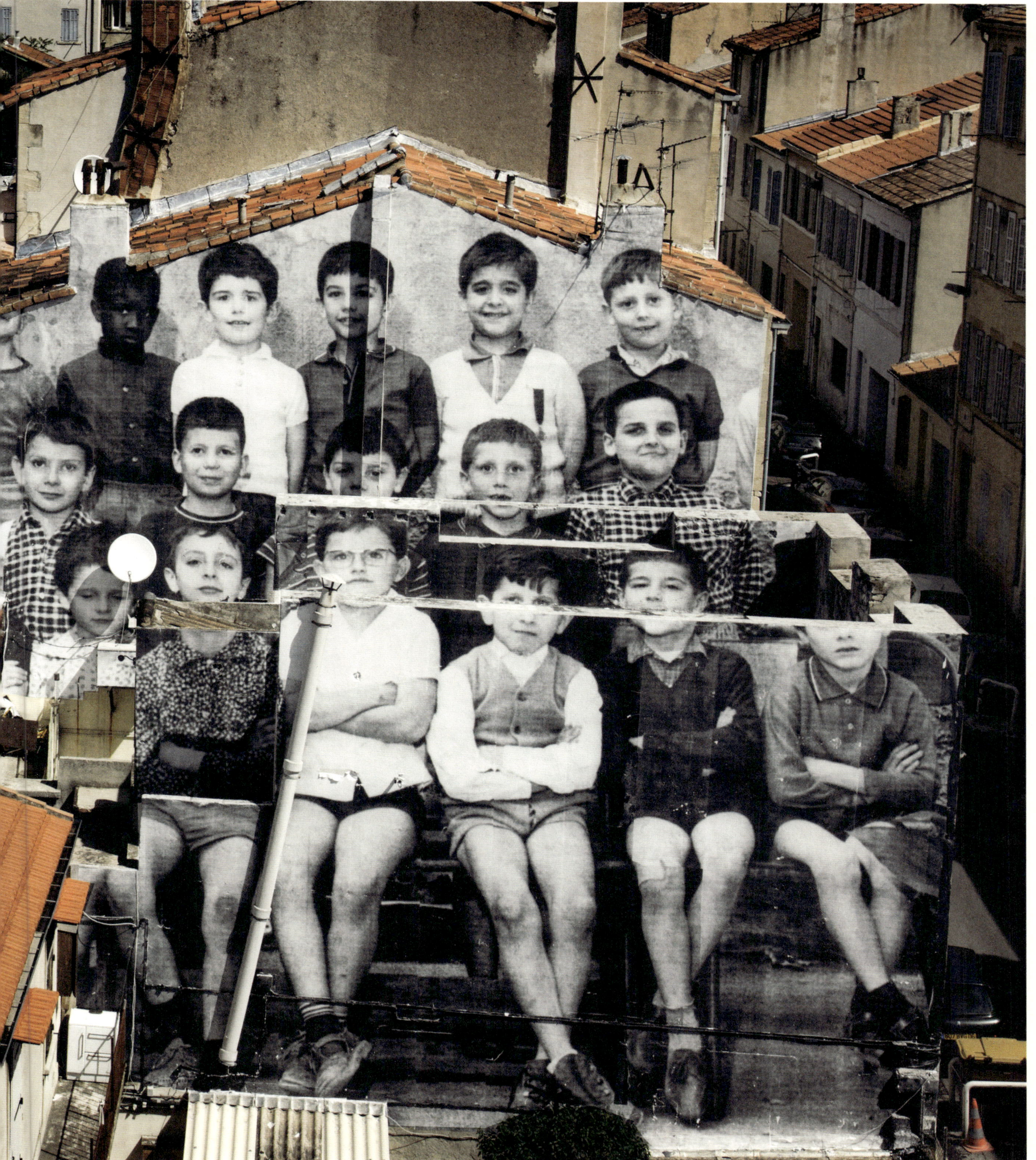

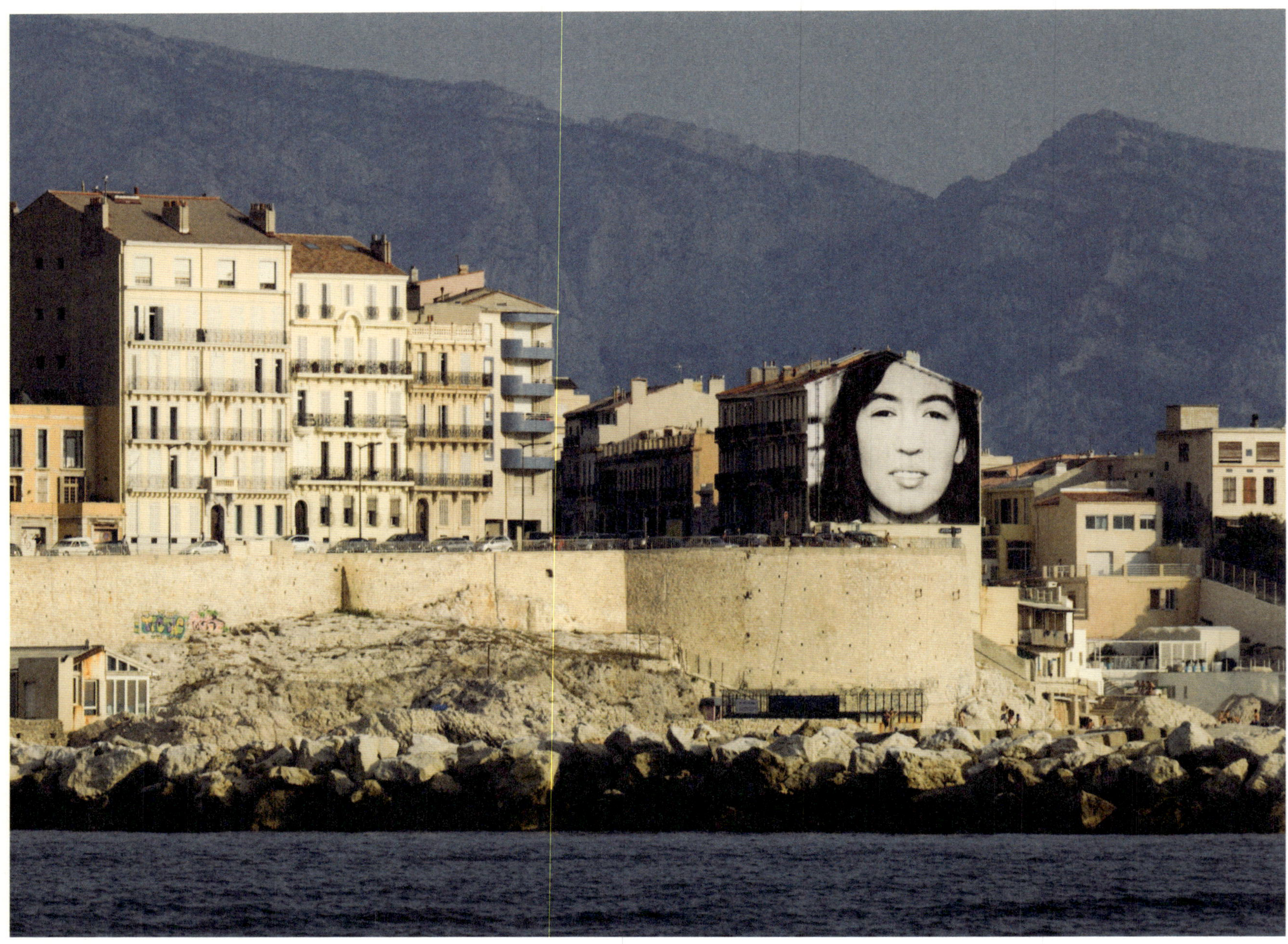

Annick Perrot-Bishop, on the old port in front of La Samaritaine, Marseille, 1966, seen by JR, Corniche du Président John Fitzgerald Kennedy, Marseille, France, 2013

(previous page) *École Saint Charles, Marseille, 1966–1967*, seen by JR, Boulevard Leccia and Boulevard Allemand, Marseille, France, 2013

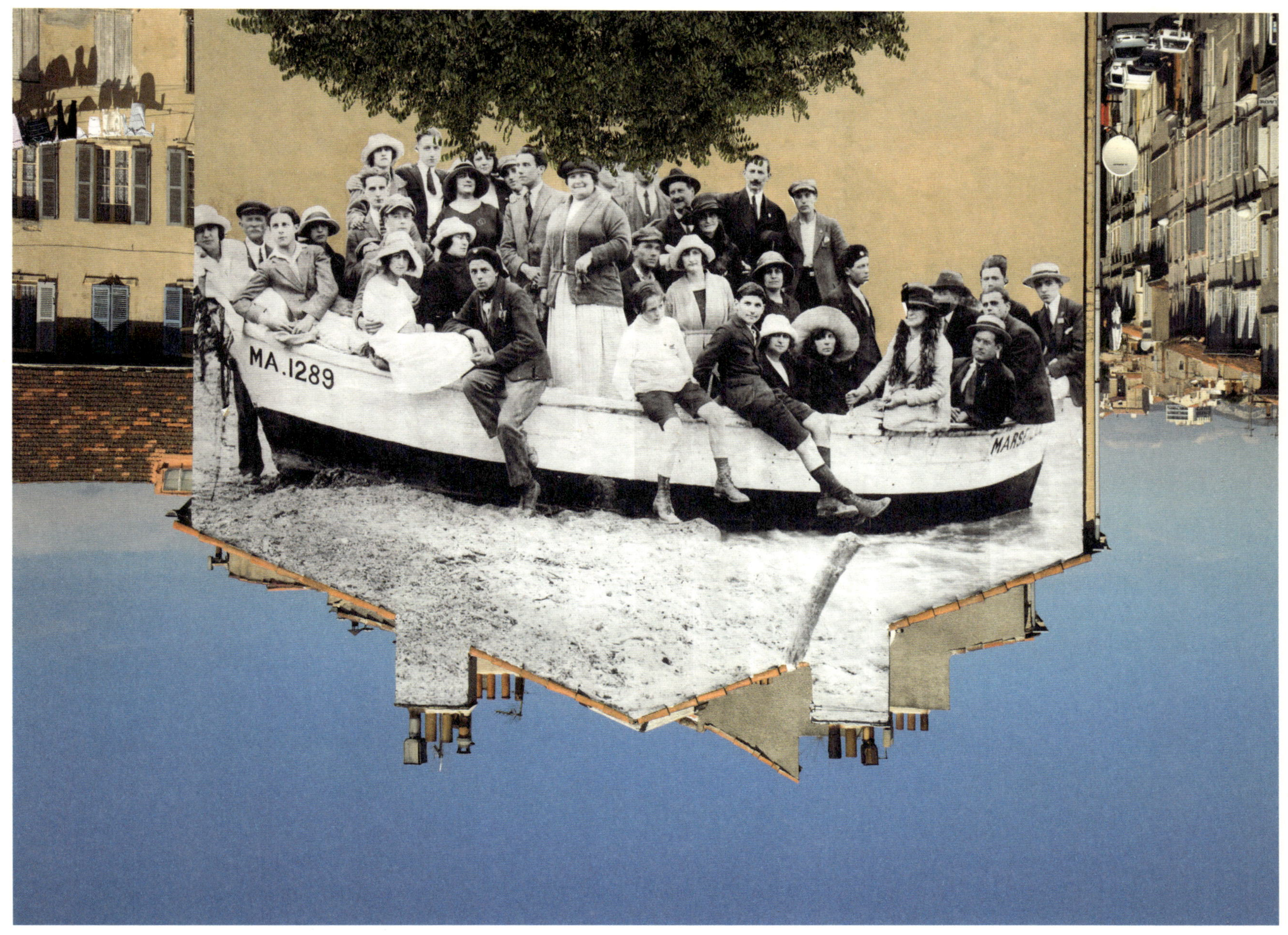

A group posing in a boat moored on a beach, Marseille, c. 1930, seen by JR, 54 Rue Clovis Hugues, Marseille, France, 2013

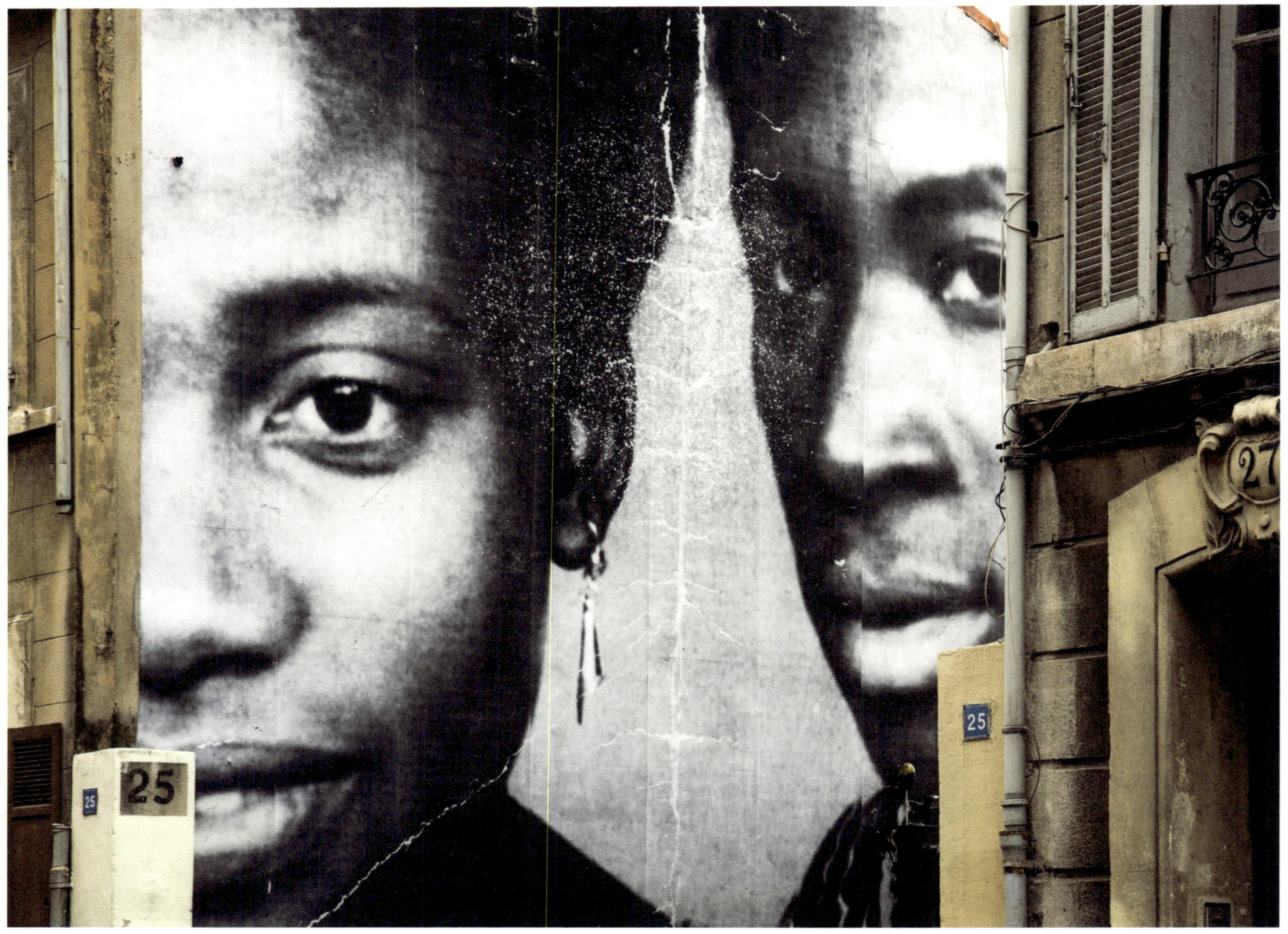

Portrait of my grandparents Berthe and Diallo, Mali, 1973,
seen by JR, 25 Boulevard Bouès, Marseille, France, 2013

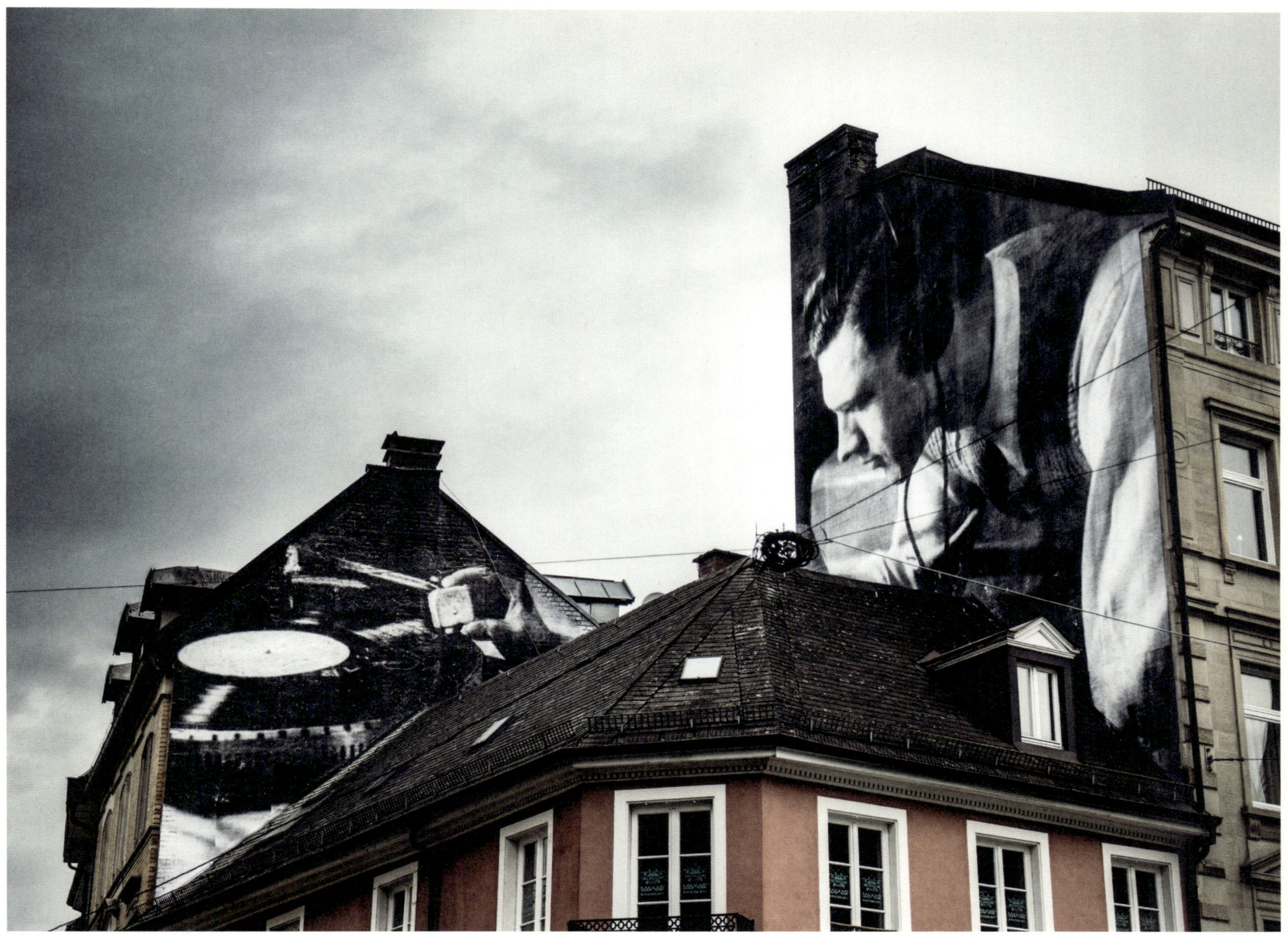

Sound engineer Heinz Stark recording on 78 rpm vinyl, 1947, seen by JR, Baden-Baden, Germany, 2014

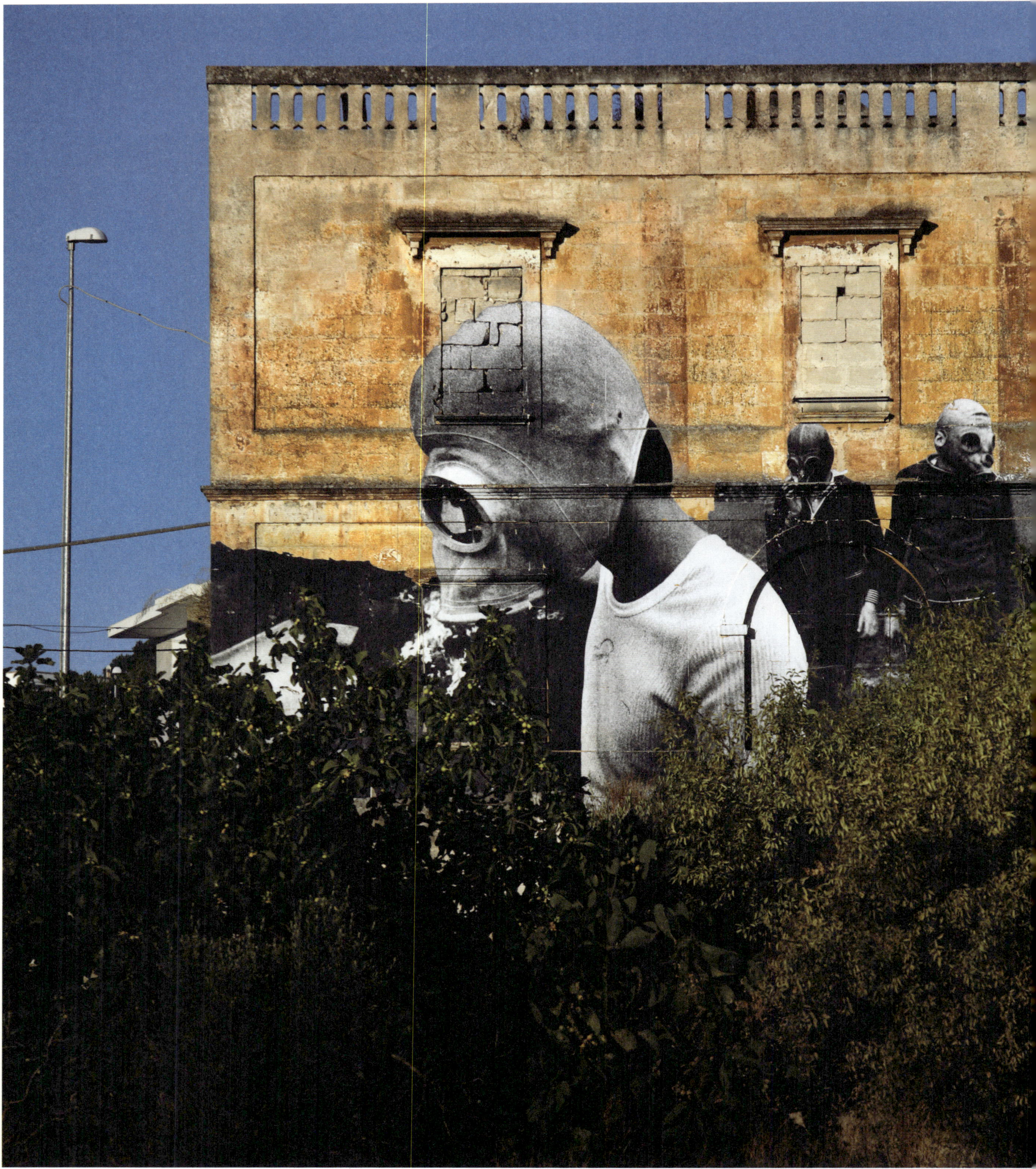

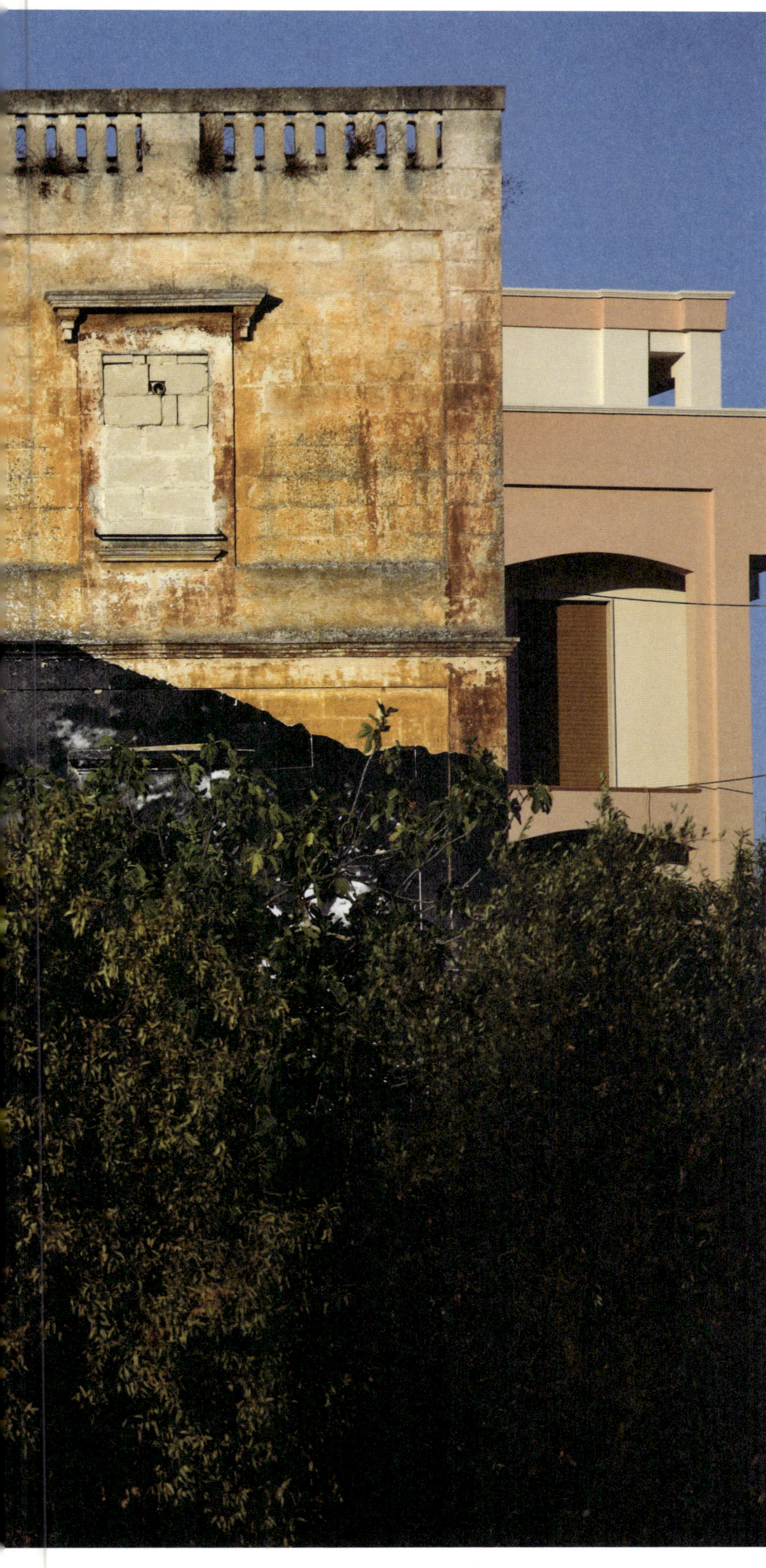

Photograph by Sergei Podlesnov, seen by JR, Grottaglie, Italy, 2009

'In the *Unframed* project, the power of the image comes from the location where it's pasted. This photograph originally taken in Chernobyl took on a whole other sense when it was pasted in Puglia, Italy, where the mafia illegally buries toxic waste in the land around the city, and the inhabitants suffer slowly.' – JR

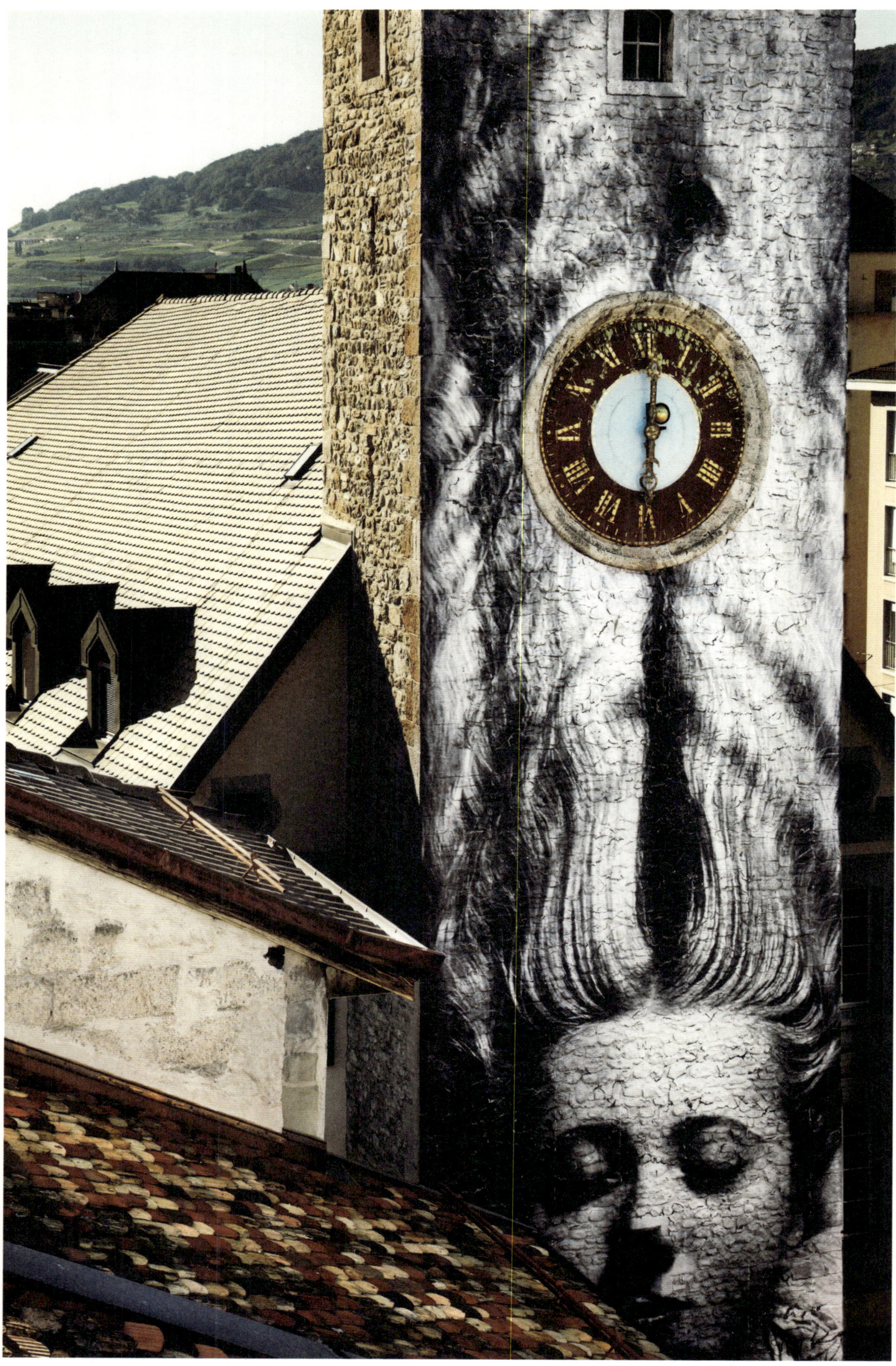

Man Ray, Femme aux cheveux longs, 1929, seen by JR,
Vevey, Switzerland, 2010

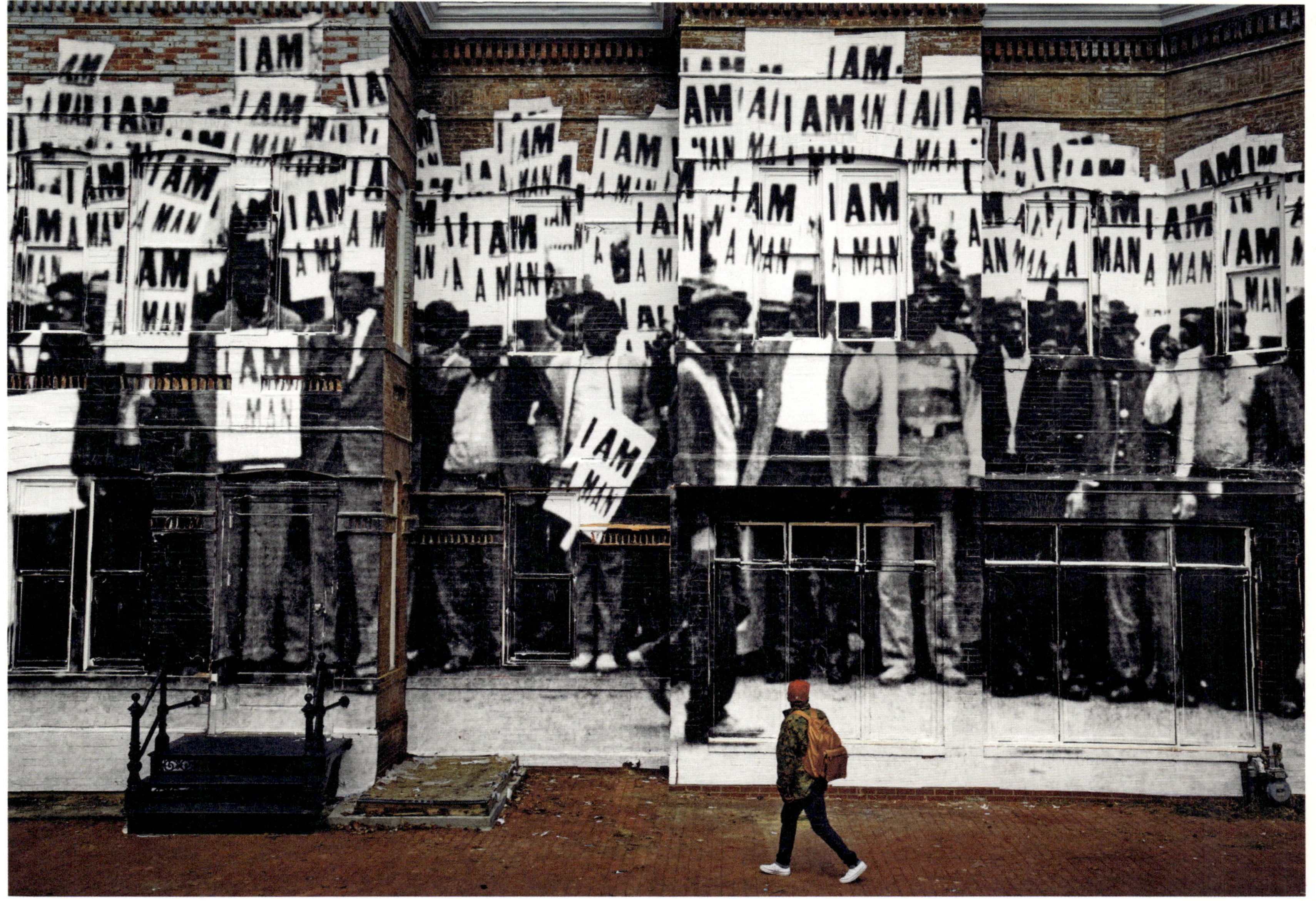

Ernest Withers, Sanitation workers assemble in front of Clayborn Temple for a solidarity march, Memphis Tennessee, 1968, seen by JR, 1401 T Street, NW, Washington DC, USA, 2012

'This pasting of the sanitation workers' protest in Memphis, 1968, was done next to a post office that used to be reserved for African Americans.' – JR

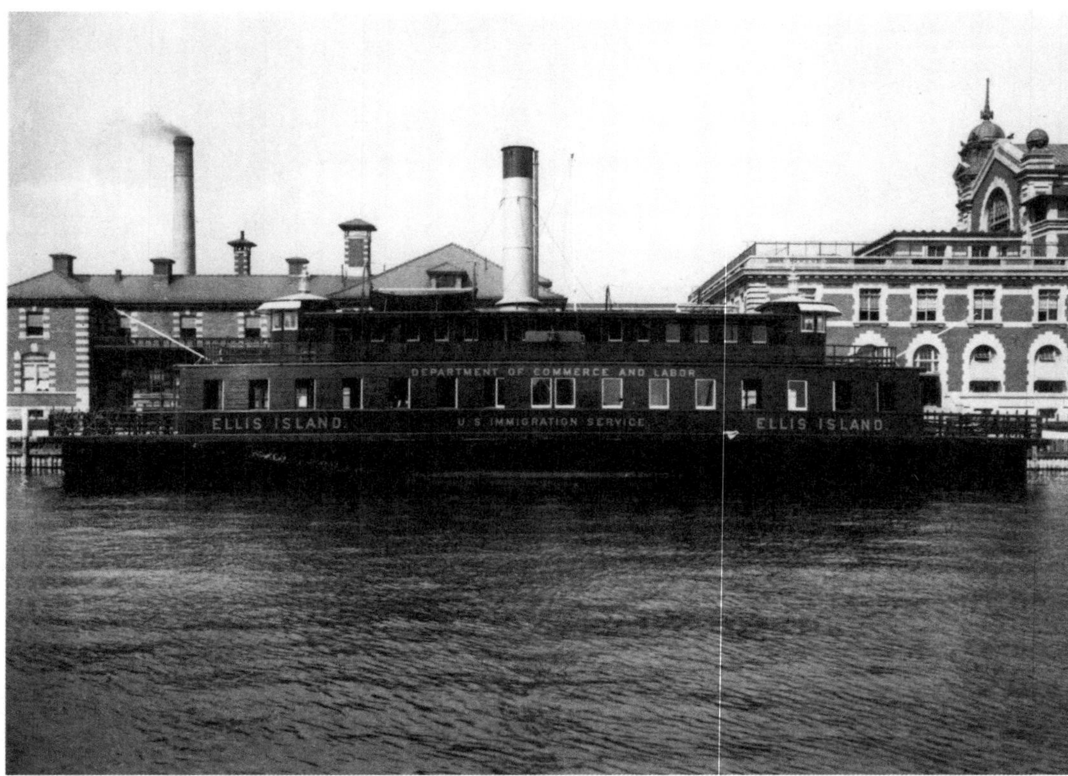

Immigration Service ferry in front of the Ellis Island Main Immigration Building, c. 1892–1930

'I saw pictures of the abandoned hospital on Ellis Island, and I really wanted to bring *Unframed* there. But it was very derelict and it took me three years to gain access to it. In 2014, when the project was given the go ahead, archival images taken from the museum could live again in the very place they were taken, on the walls of buildings that had been closed since 1954. It is crazy to think that the Statue of Liberty was so near, and yet many immigrants died in this hospital or were sent back to where they came from. Today, the project is a permanent exhibition that anyone can visit, with a hard hat tour.' – JR

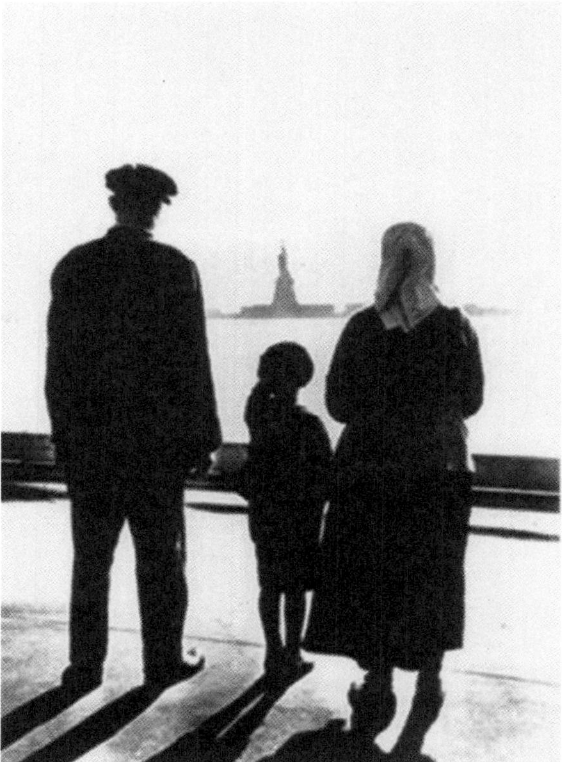

(above) *An immigrant family viewing the Statue of Liberty from the Ellis Island Immigration Station dock, c. 1892–1930*
(right) Pasting in Ellis Island, New York, USA, 2014

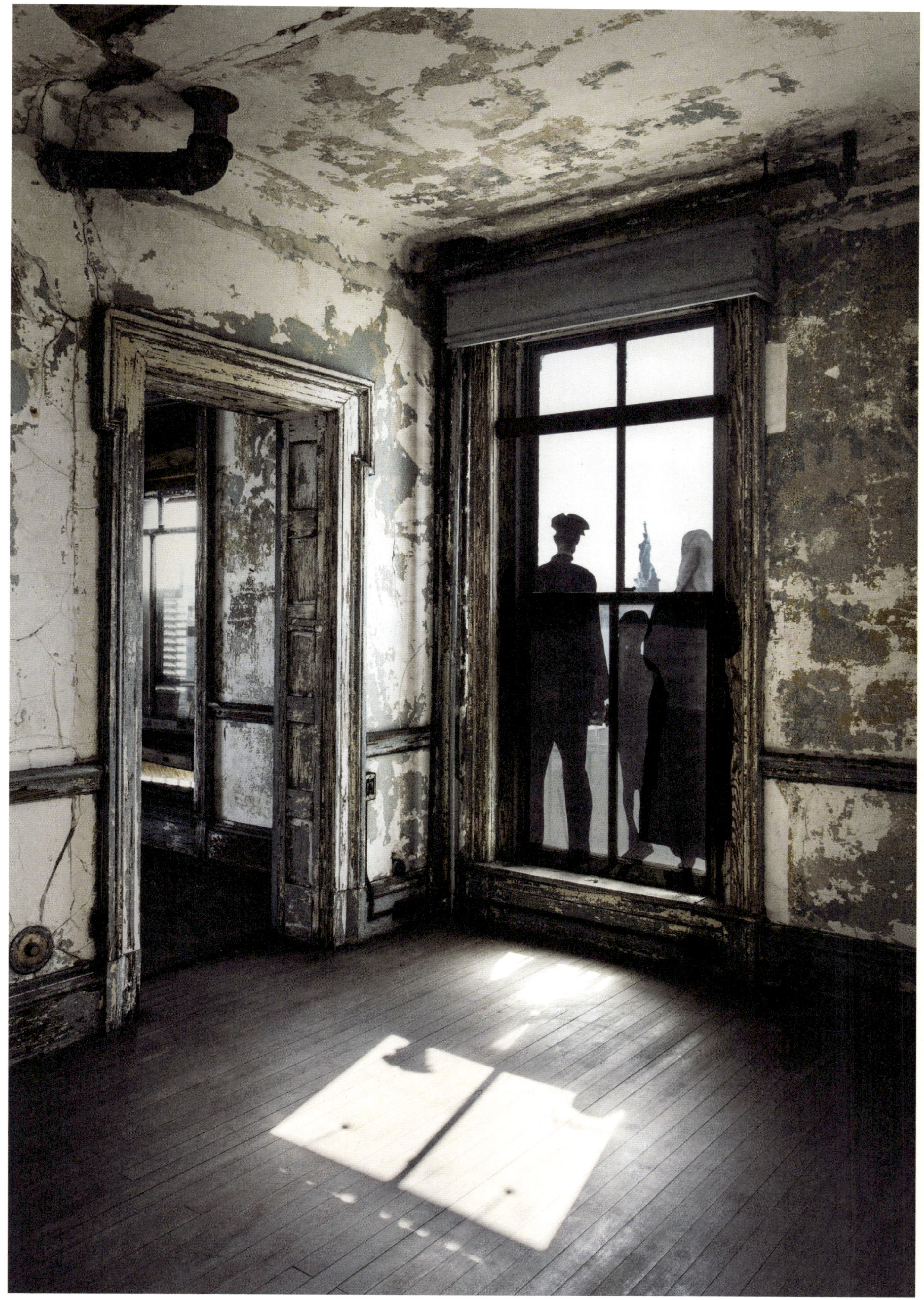

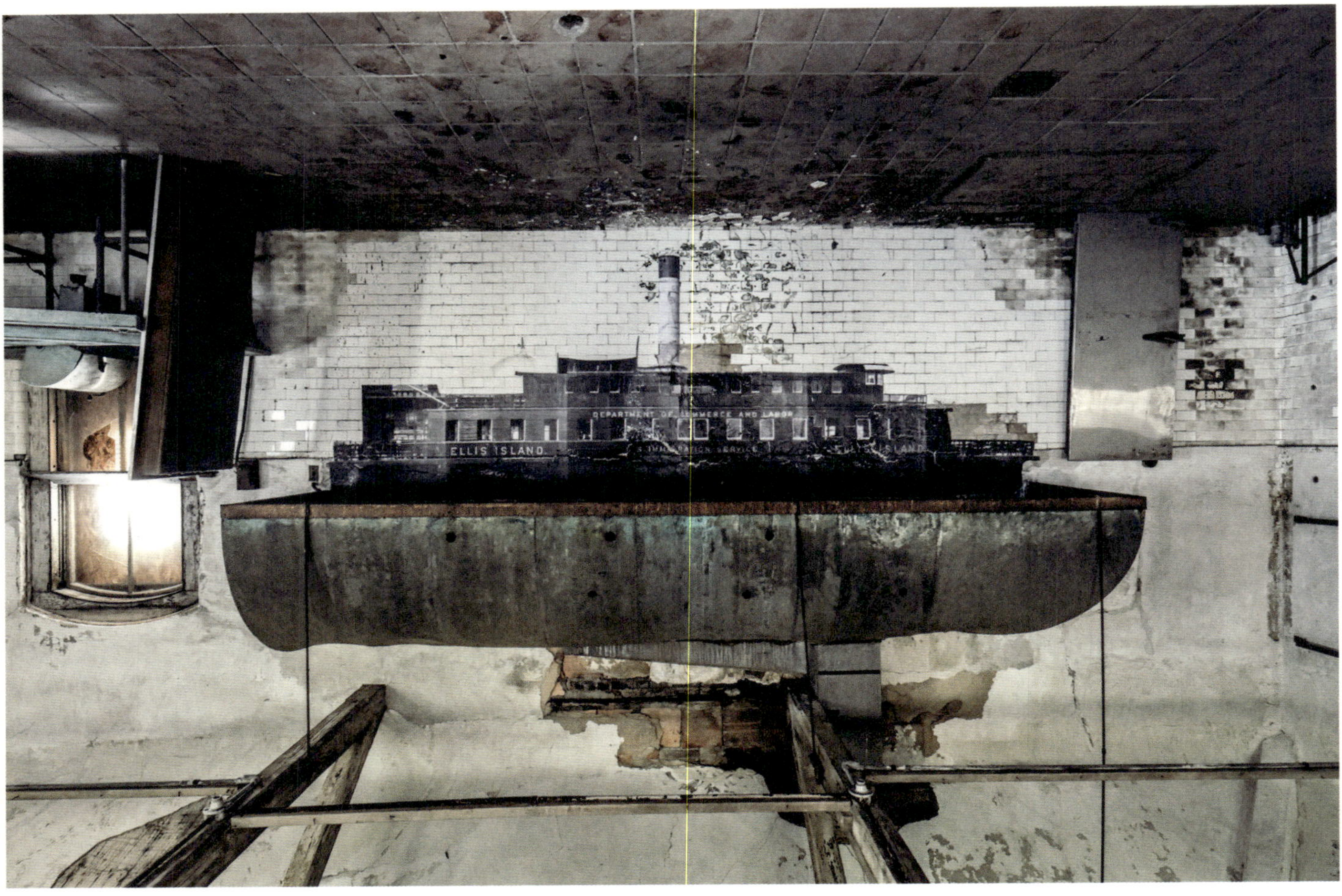

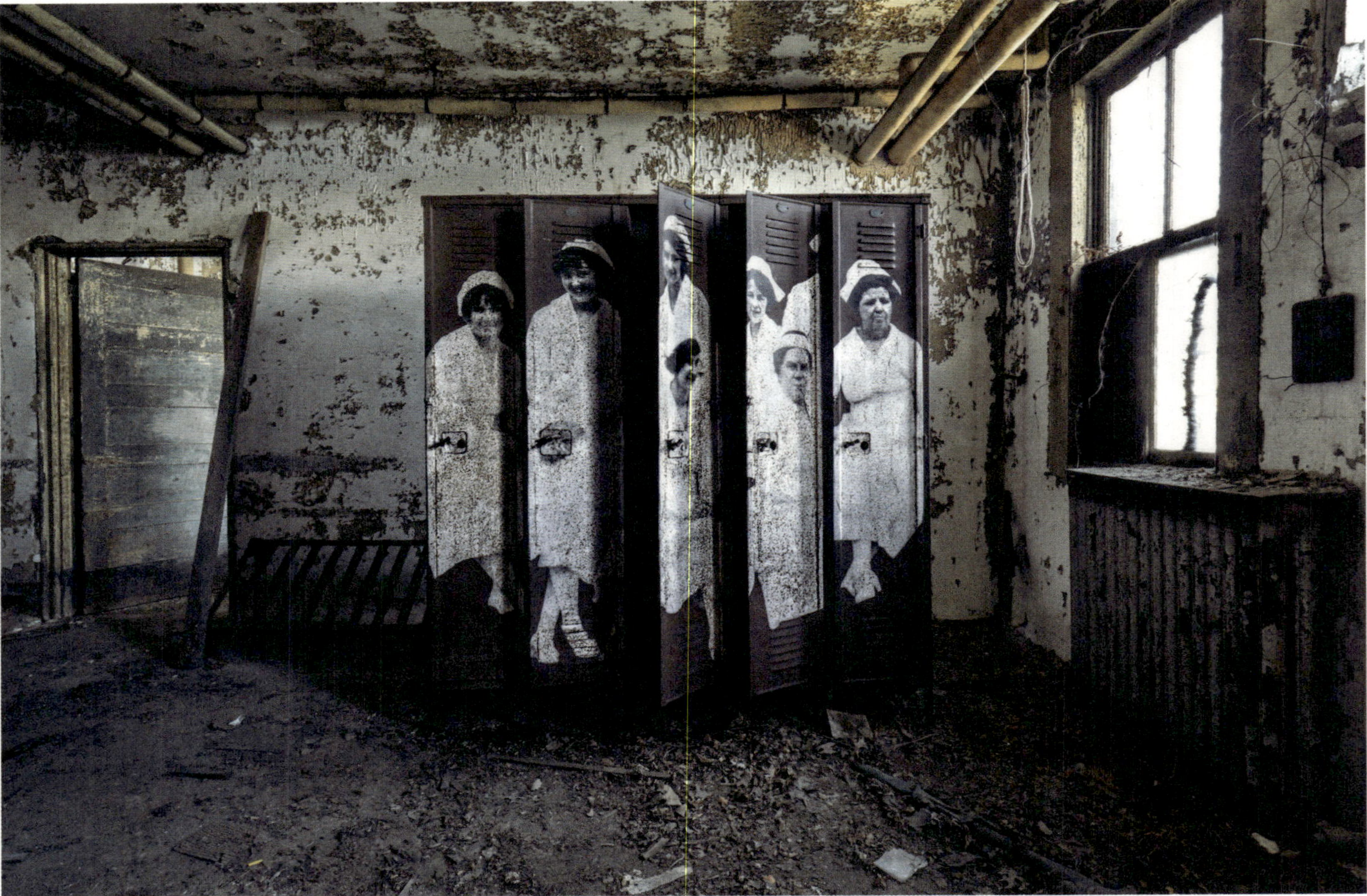

(top) *Immigration Service ferry in front of the Ellis Island Main Immigration Building, c. 1892–1930*, seen by JR, Ellis Island, New York, USA, 2014

(bottom) *Nurses at Ellis Island Hospital, c. 1892–1930*, seen by JR, Ellis Island, New York, USA, 2014

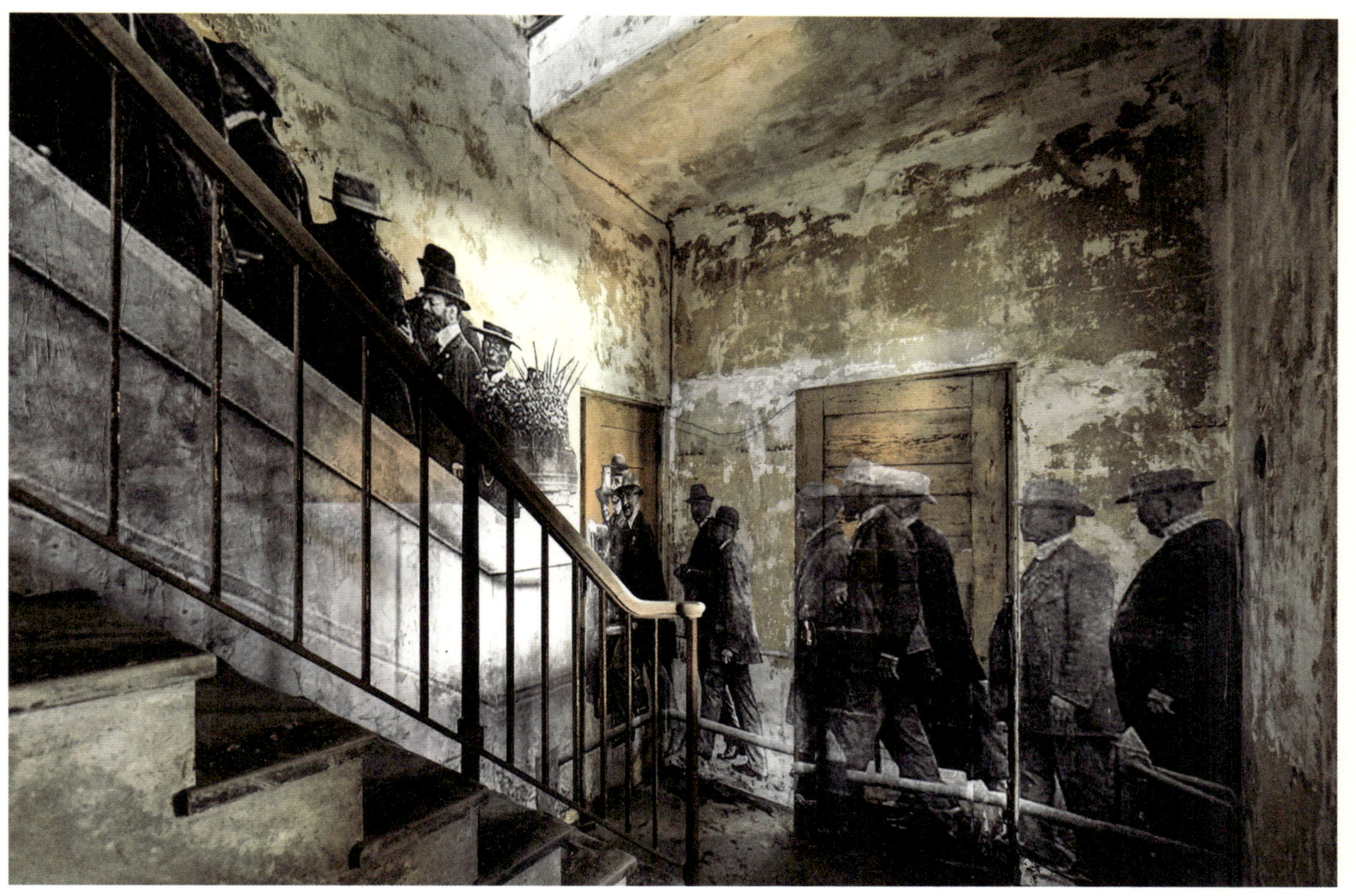

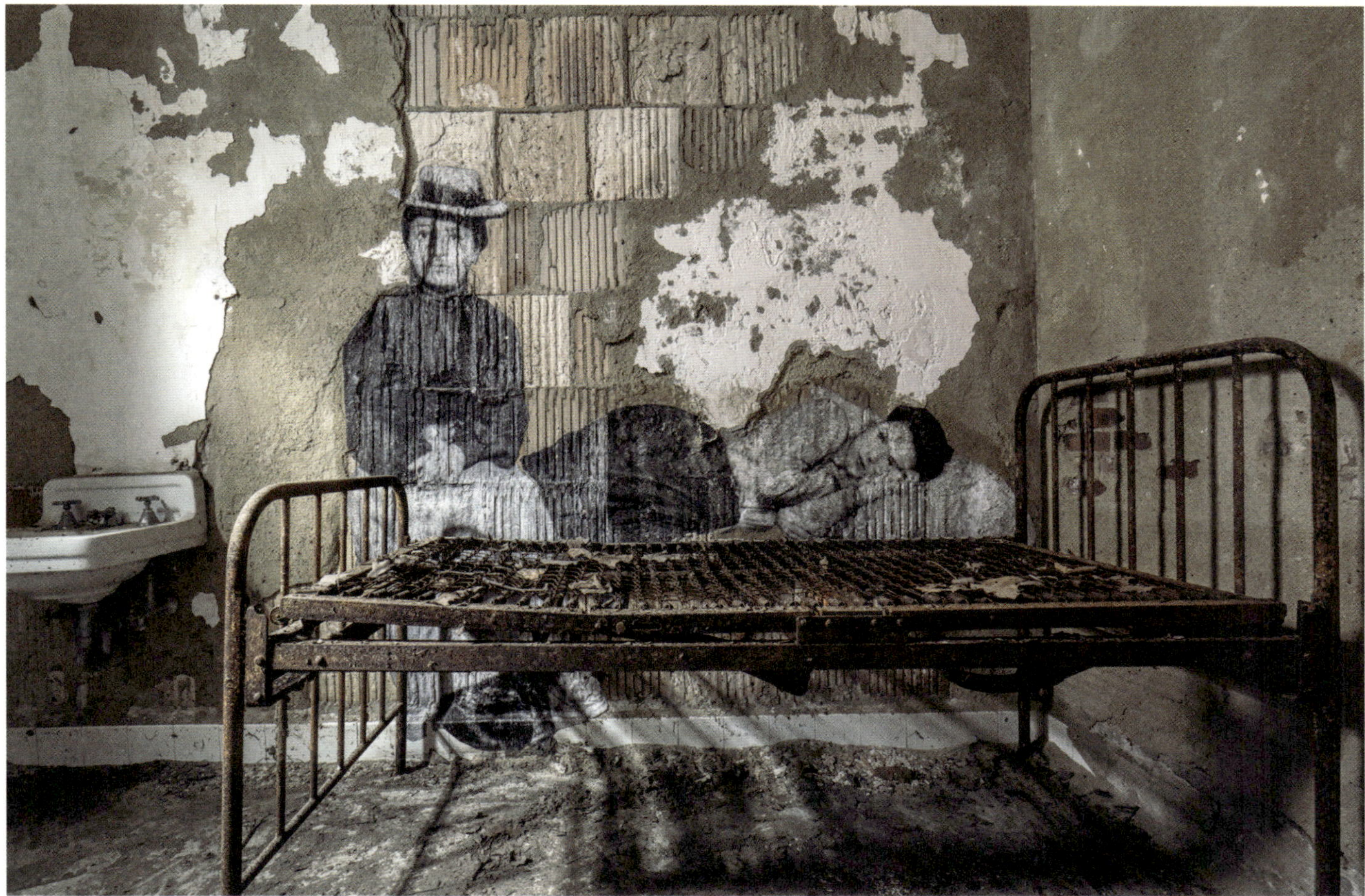

(top) *Hygiene Congress delegates, c. 1892–1930,* seen by JR, Ellis Island, New York, USA, 2014

(bottom) *Immigrants about to head back to their starting point, c. 1892–1930*, seen by JR, Ellis Island, New York, USA, 2014

INSIDE

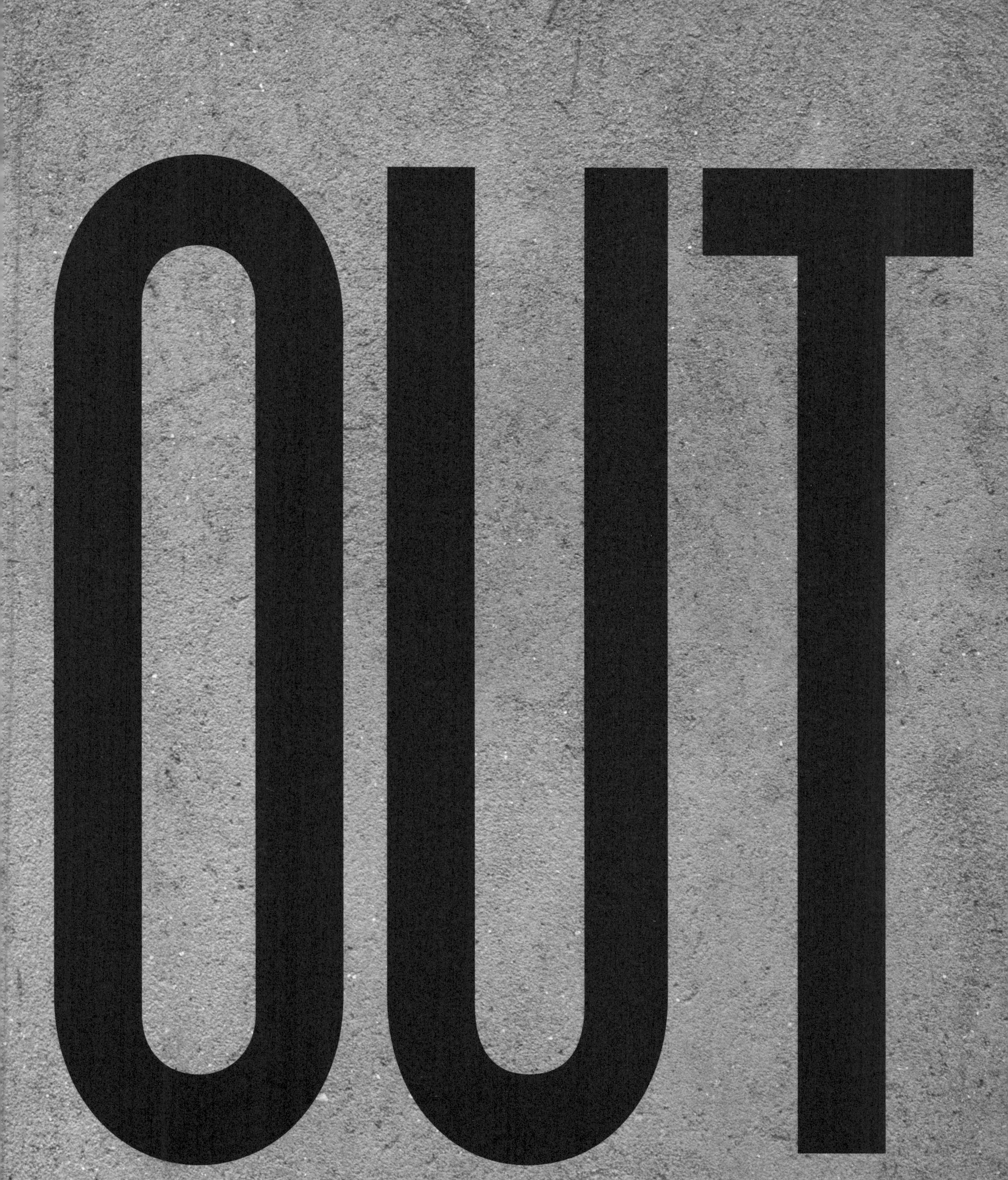
OUT

JR received the TED Prize in 2011, awarded to an individual for their creative vision for global change. He launched *Inside Out* – a global art project inspired by his large format pastings – funded by the sale of some of his artworks, as well as by donations from participants. Stepping away from the making process entirely, JR created the vision and facility for a participatory art project of unprecedented ambition and scale. He no longer took the photographs nor pasted them onto buildings. Instead he inspired others to use his medium and provided the means for anyone to do so.

Inside Out gives individuals and groups from all corners of the globe the opportunity to use their own portraits to voice a statement of what they stand for. Using the *Inside Out* website, anyone can participate by gathering in a group of five or more and submitting their portraits to the website. These are then printed in the *Inside Out* studio in New York and sent back to the participants for pasting. The actions are documented, archived and exhibited online. People all over the world have used *Inside Out* to make political, social, environmental or artistic statements, mostly through group actions, ranging from five people to thousands, from Malawi to Pakistan, from the United States to Tunisia.

Another approach to taking part in the project is through the *Inside Out* photobooths. Either freestanding or contained within travelling trucks, the photobooth printers are brought to the street by JR's team, enabling the public to participate instantly and free of charge. People receive their poster immediately and can paste it on a wall nearby. Tens of thousands of portraits have been printed at photobooths located around the world in museums and galleries: in Paris, Arles, Vevey, Tel Aviv, Ramallah, Bethlehem, Tokyo, Abu Dhabi, Hong Kong and Baden Baden.

Photobooth trucks have been installed in Paris, London, Amsterdam, Israel, Japan, Cincinnati, Dallas, Shanghai, New York, and in twenty more cities across the United States. In 2014, more than 4,000 portraits were collected through a photobooth truck that travelled through France. They were used to create a monumental installation that surrounded the exterior drum of the Pantheon's dome in Paris and covered the floor inside the monument.

In the first 4 years of the project, more than 250,000 people participated in *Inside Out* in more than 120 countries, and in 2013 a documentary film, *Inside Out*, premiered at the Tribeca Film Festival, revealing the working process behind the project and the remarkable levels of participation in the project around the world.

(right) *Inside Out* photobooth, Galerie Perrotin, Paris, 2011
(overleaf) Port Au Prince, Haiti, 2012
389 portraits
Statement: Rising Souls, Haiti, standing for the resilience of Haitians

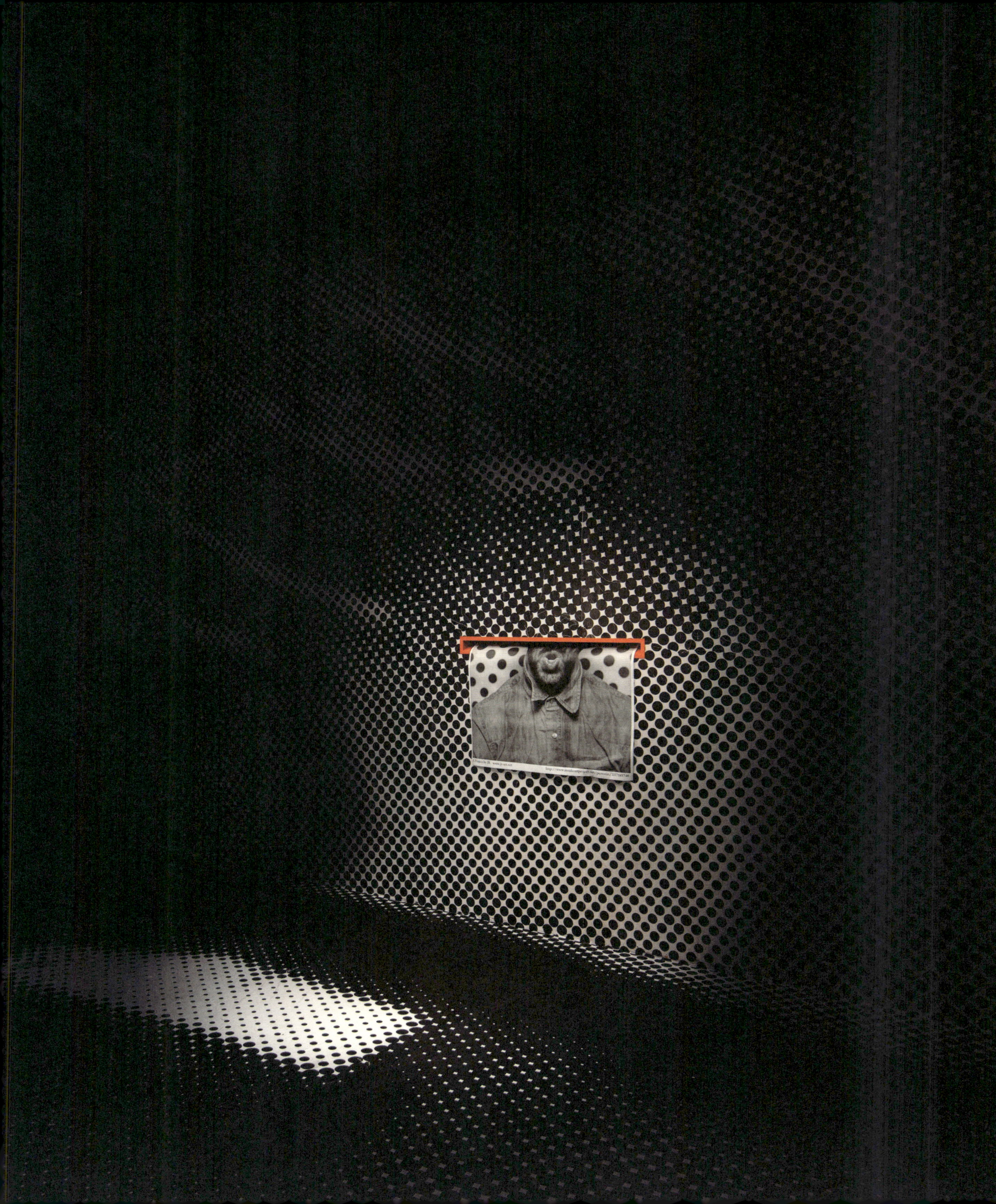

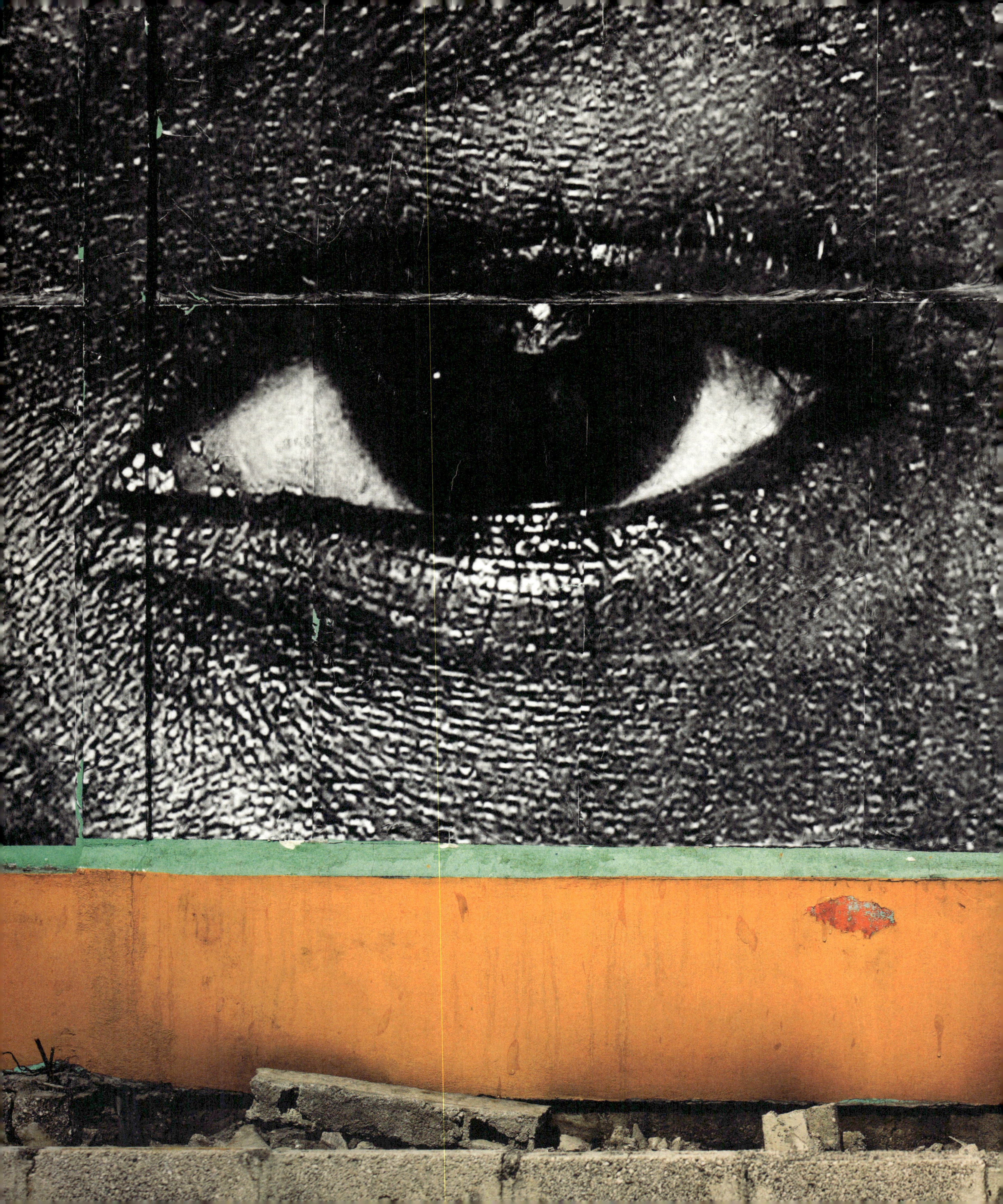

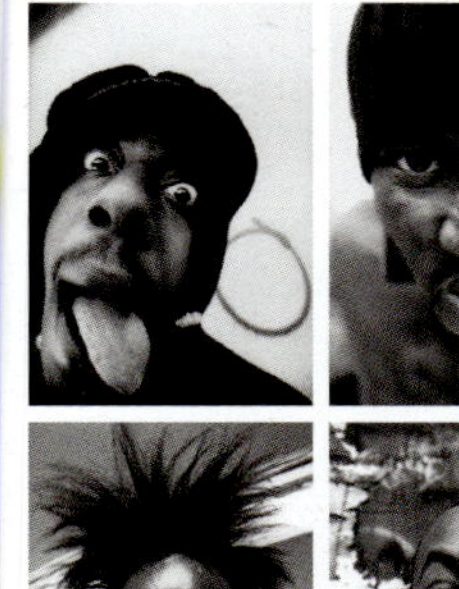
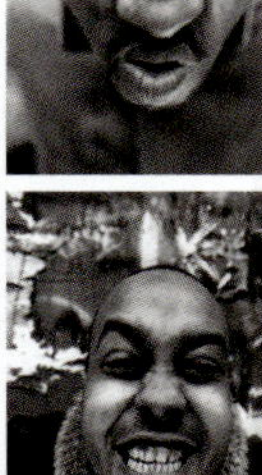
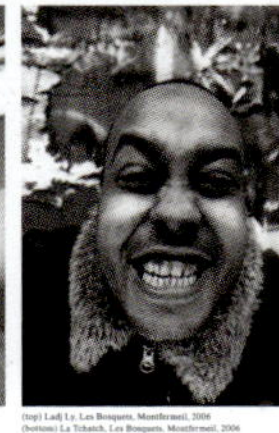
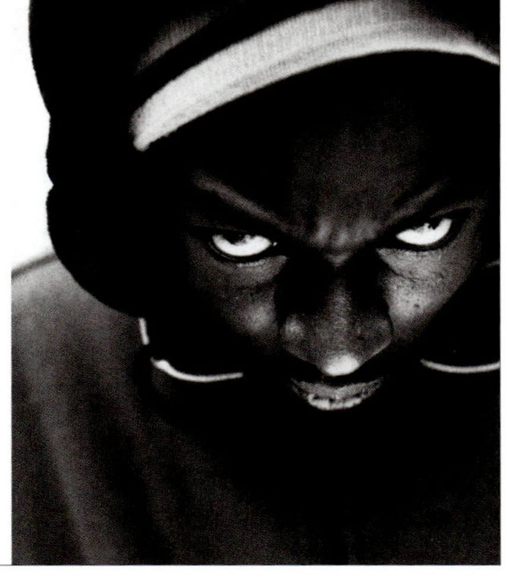

'ART IS NOT SUPPOSED TO CHANGE THE WORLD, BUT TO CHANGE PERCEPTIONS. ART CAN CHANGE THE WAY WE SEE THE WORLD.' – JR

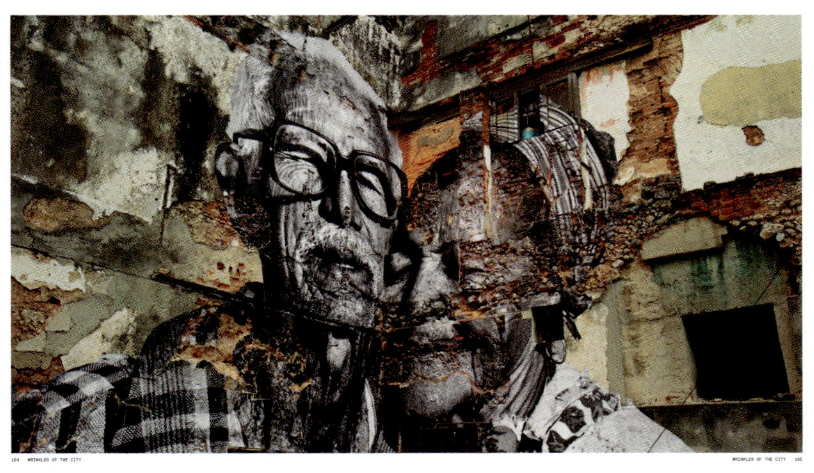

- JR exhibits in the streets of the world, mixing art and activism, and addressing themes of commitment, freedom, identity and limit. In today's climate of globalization, his site-specific, public interventions across the globe are urgent acts that give voice and presence to both subject and viewer through the language of photography.

- Made in close collaboration with JR, this is the first retrospective book to cover all bodies of his work to date and features work-in-progress photographs and behind-the-scenes documentation of his studios in Paris and New York.

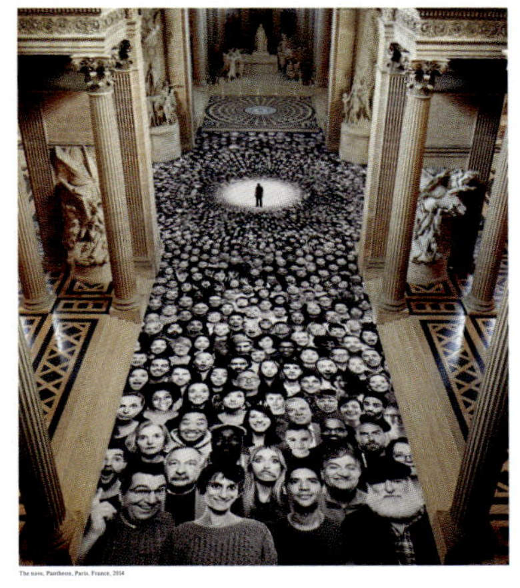
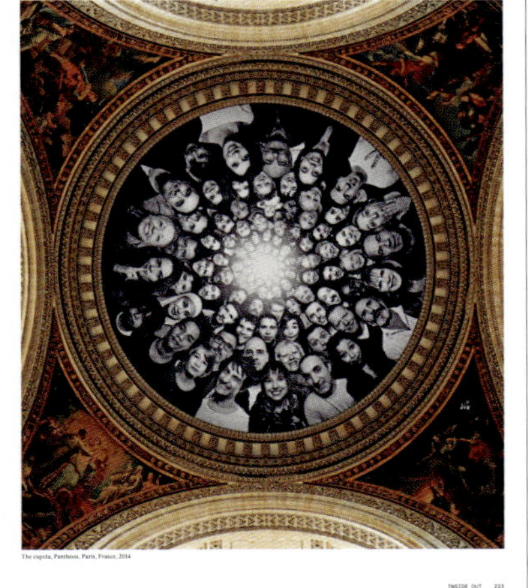

- With 500 images, this book also includes his collaborations with artists and institutions such as the New York City Ballet, a section devoted to artworks and exhibitions, a chronology and an illustrated bibliography and filmography.

- This book features a specially commissioned graphic biography by comic artist Joseph Remnant and a survey essay by Nato Thompson, Chief Curator of Creative Time, New York.

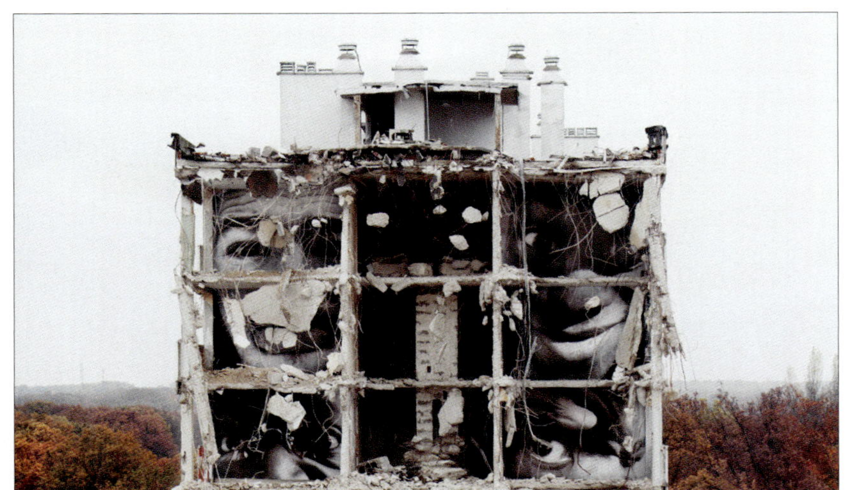

JR first garnered major international attention at the age of 27 when he won the TED Prize, after which he launched his *Inside Out* project, which has since drawn over 250,000 participants internationally. His giant black-and-white close-up portraits – pasted on buildings and streets, trains, buildings and monuments – allow locals to have presence and show ownership of their surroundings.

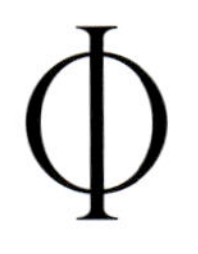

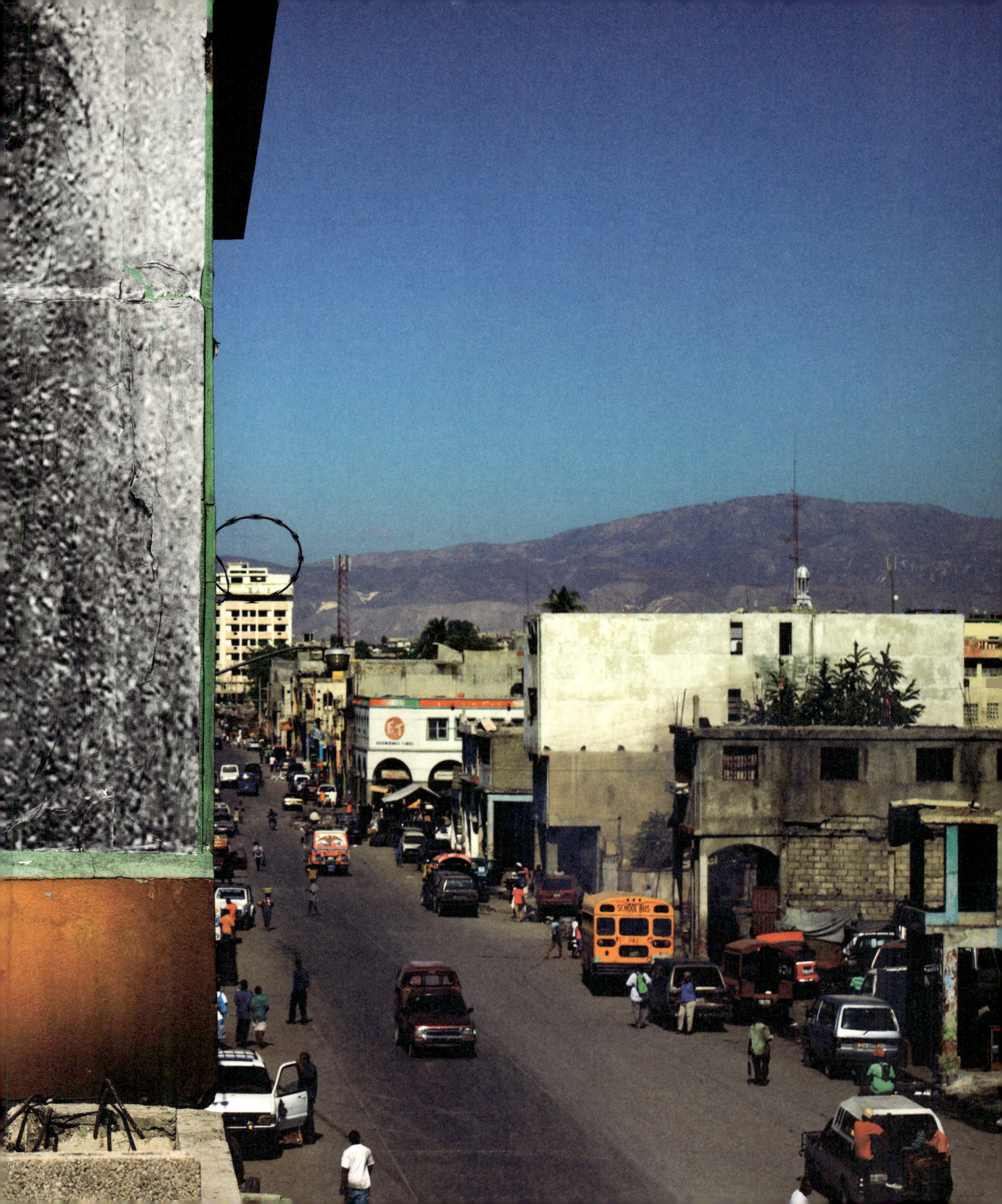
SCHOOL BUS

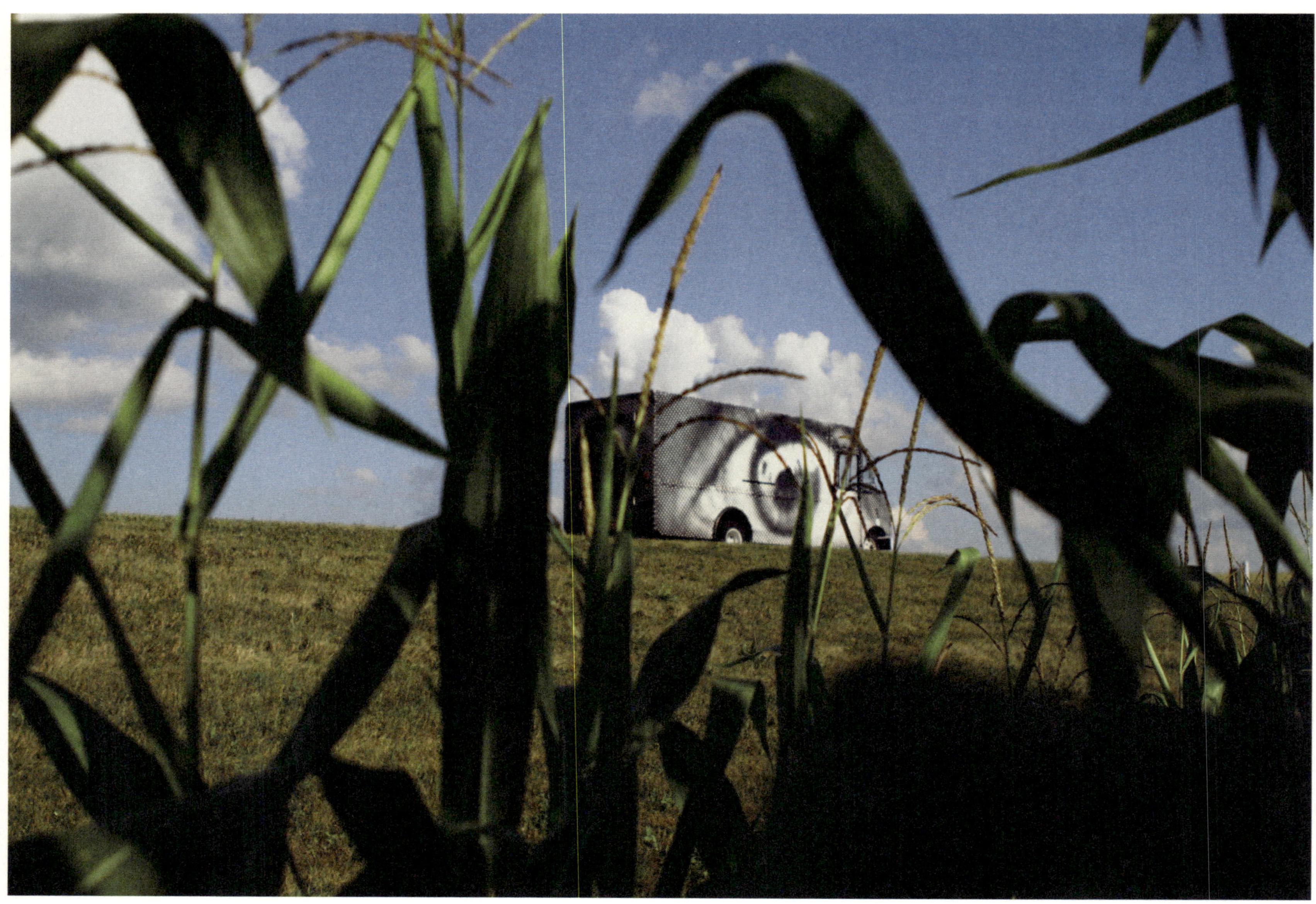

Photobooth truck on the road as part of the *Inside Out* '11M' project in twenty cities across the USA, Illinois, USA, 2012
10,000 portraits
Statement: A nationwide participatory art initiative aimed at creating a portrait of America that includes immigrants and the descendants of immigrants alike.

Going beyond political debate about the 11 million undocumented immigrants living in the USA, these portraits remind us that behind the numbers are real human stories. *Inside Out* '11M' aimed to start a conversation about immigration.

Photobooth trucks travelled to cities across the country, and people in any city could add their faces to this portrait of the United States and create their own installations.

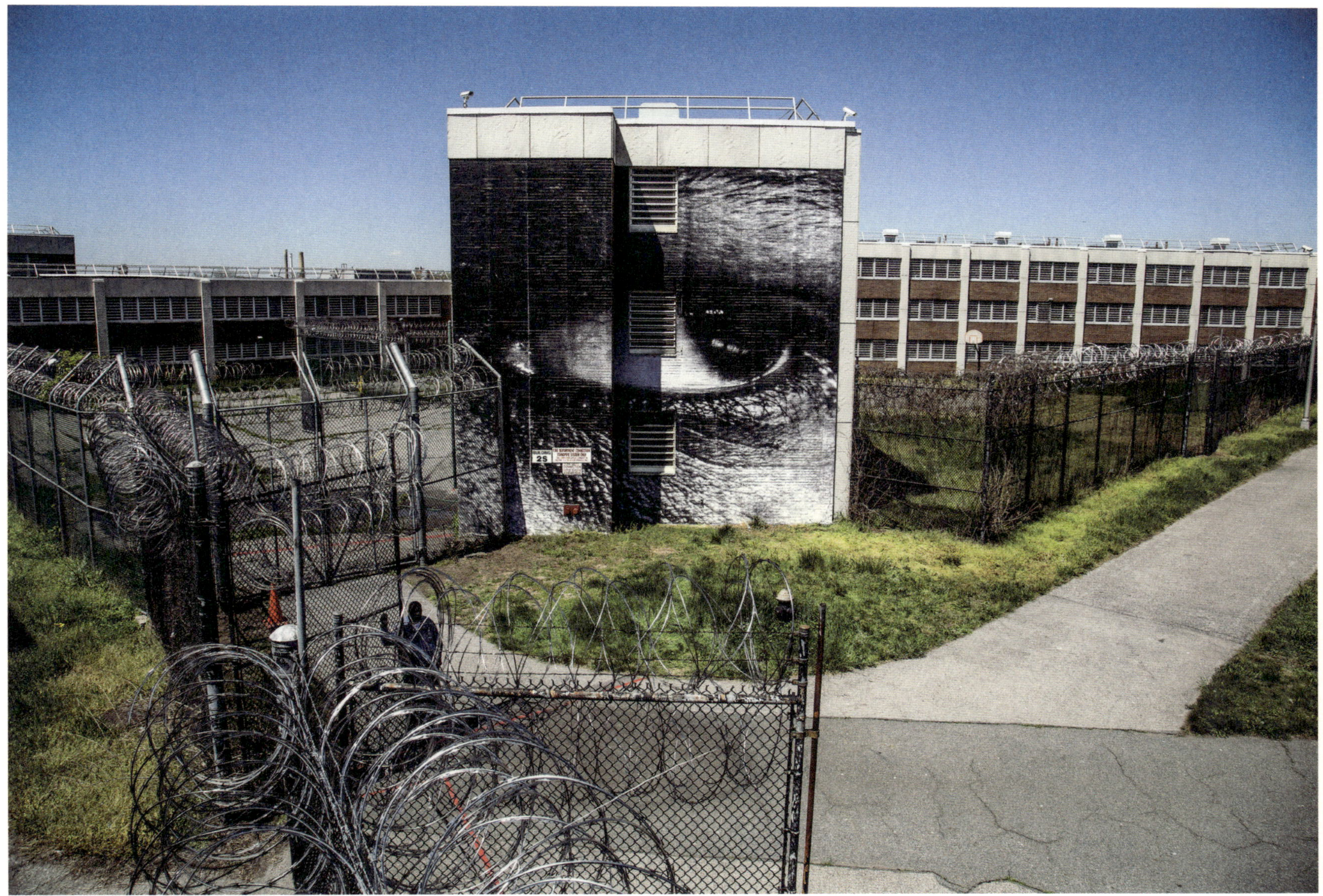

Rikers Island prison, New York, USA, 2013

'In May 2013, I was invited to screen *Inside Out*, the movie, in the juvenile section of Rikers Island prison. After the screening, a few inmates agreed to participate in an action, and their eyes were pasted inside and outside the prison, thanks to the help of the warden, a former graffiti artist, who believed in the power of art.' – JR

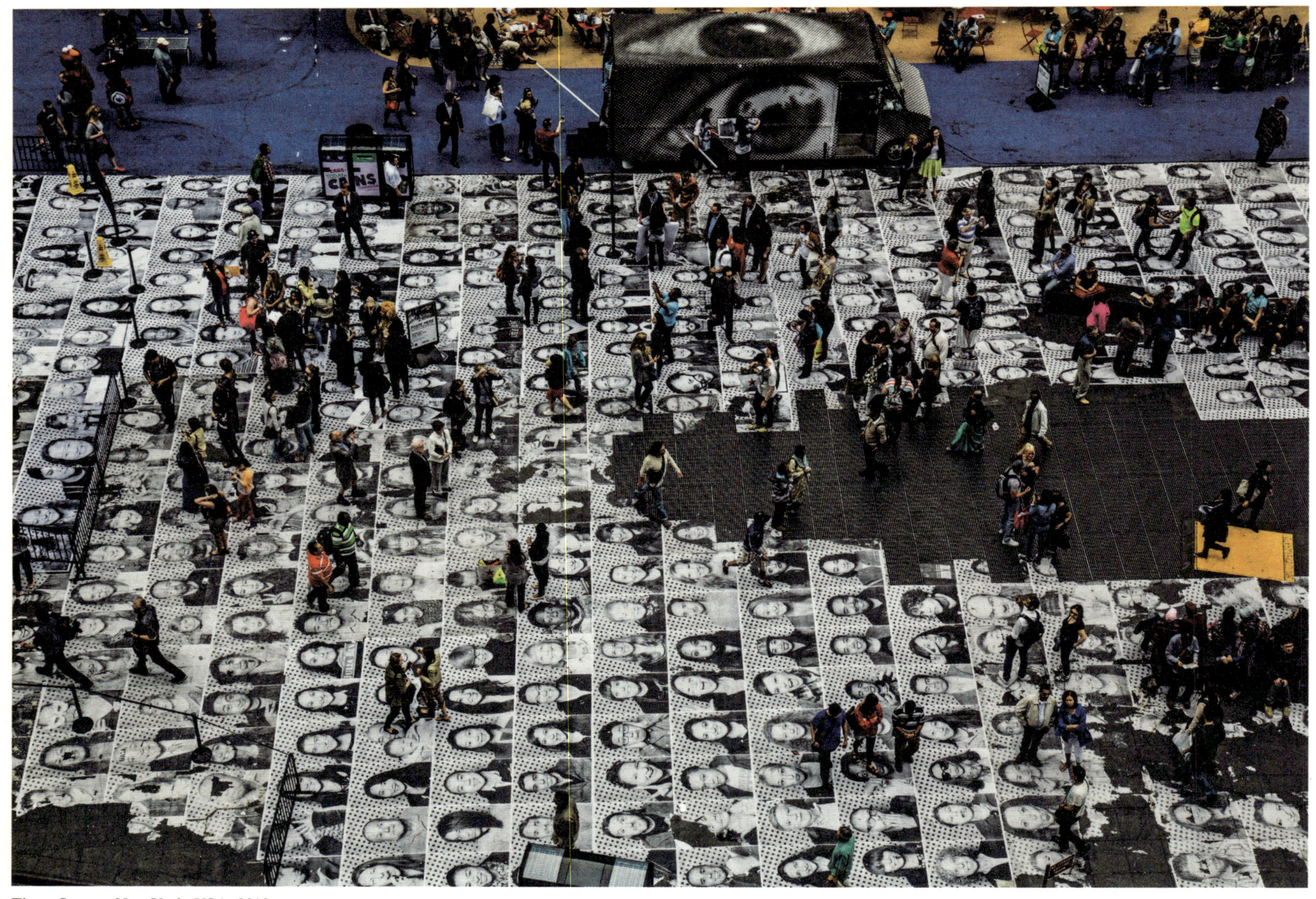

Times Square, New York, USA, 2013
5,907 portraits
Statement: From 22 April to 10 May 2013, for *Inside Out* in New York City, JR and his team invited New Yorkers and visitors to take self-portraits in a photobooth truck stationed in Times Square, the site of the world's first ever photobooth almost 100 years ago. The posters were pasted on Duffy Square in Times Square, or in the home community of the portrait's subject.

Almost 6,000 participants covered the floor with their faces. A gigantic billboard at the corner of 47th Street and 7th Avenue was also taken over by *Inside Out* portraits, and a very large eye was installed on top of it.

The project activated Times Square as a creative hub – engaging the boroughs of New York as the photobooth truck made early visits to the Bronx, Staten Island, Queens and Brooklyn. The initial portraits featured community members from New York City neighbourhoods affected by Hurricane Sandy – the Staten Island waterfront, the Rockaways, Red Hook and Coney Island.

Moreover, every night in May 2013, from 11.57 p.m. to midnight, for the 'Midnight Moment', a video art project on *Inside Out* was presented on Times Square, on most of the screens usually reserved for advertising.

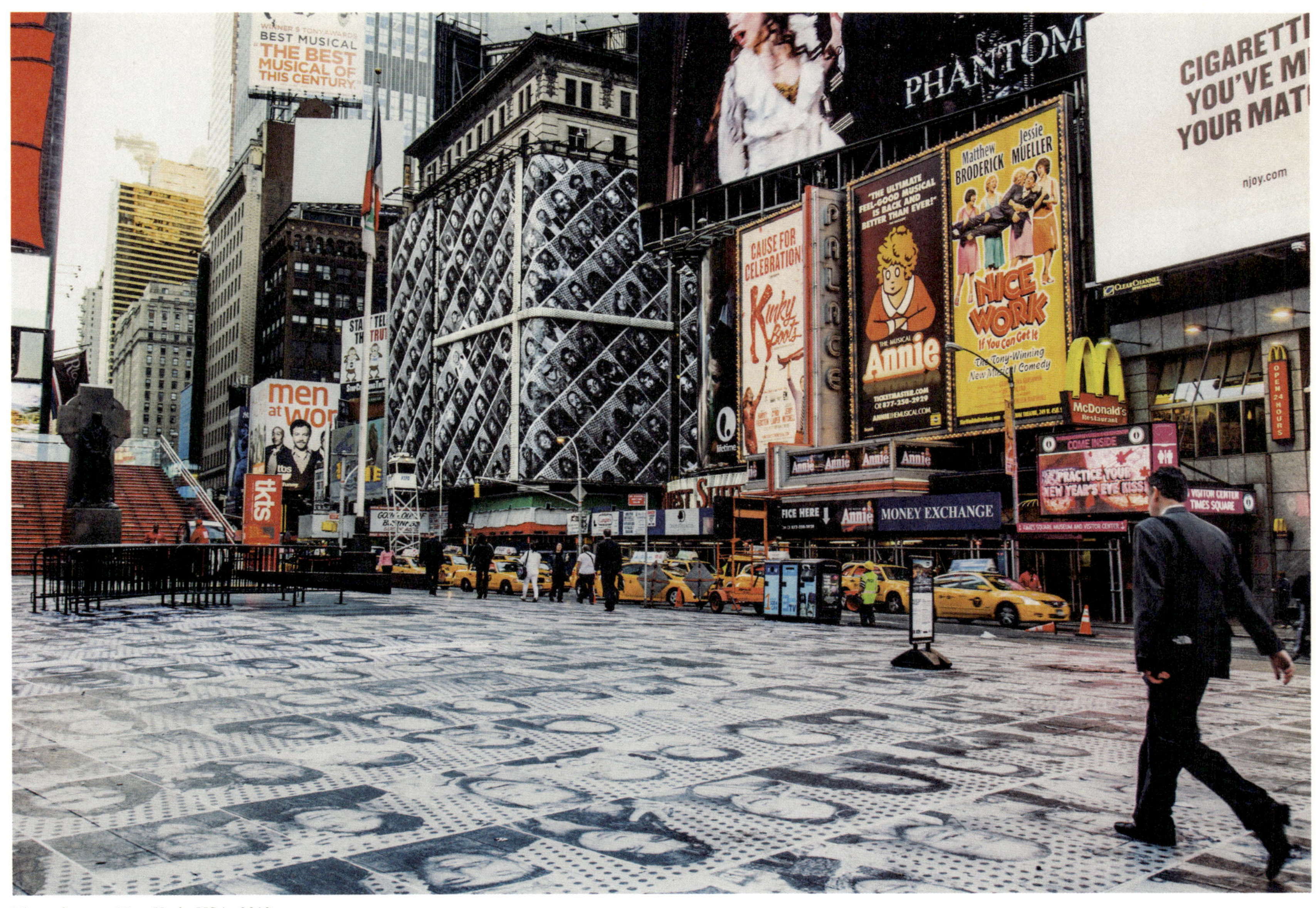

Times Square, New York, USA, 2013

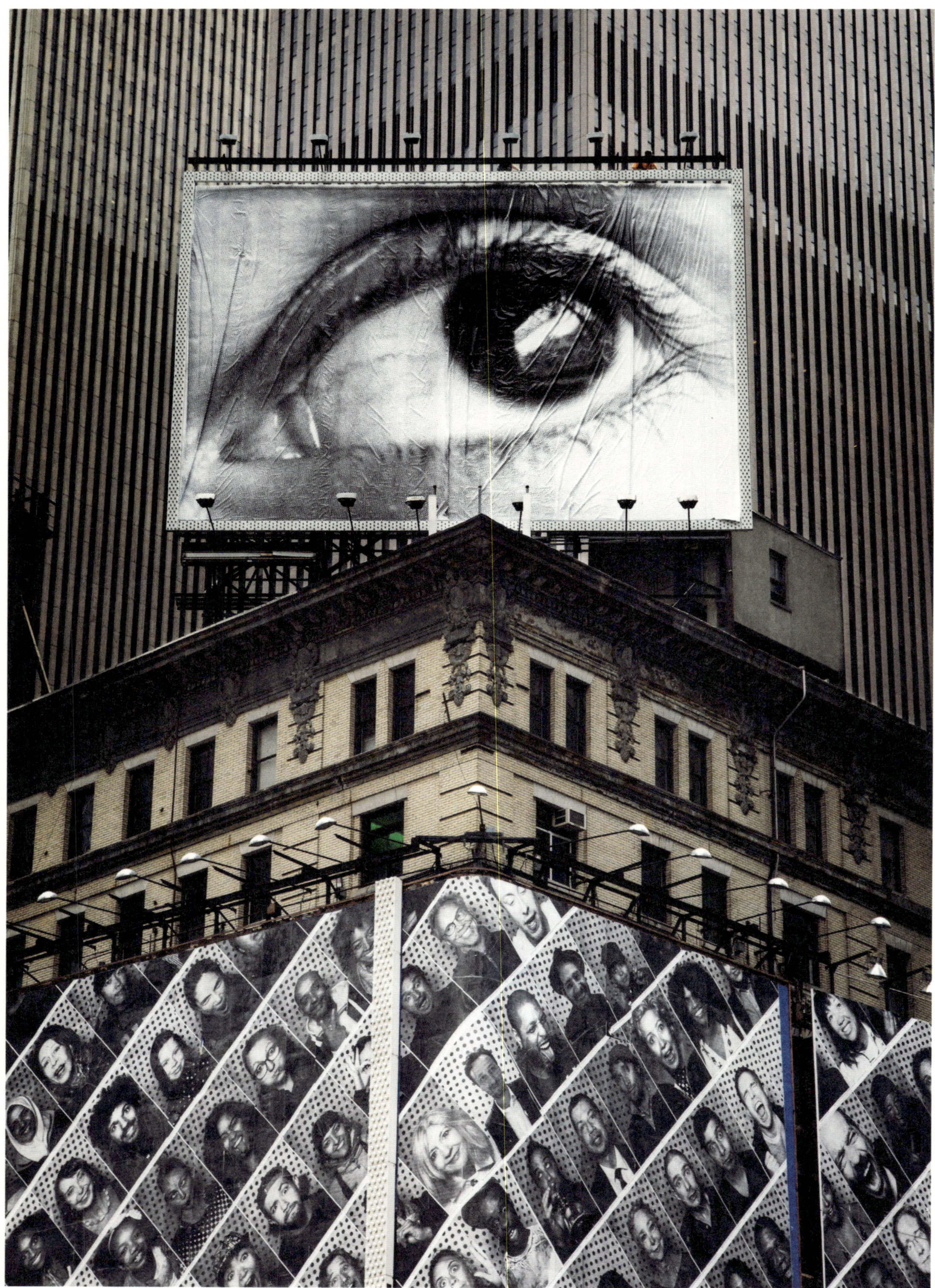

Times Square, close up, New York, USA, 2013

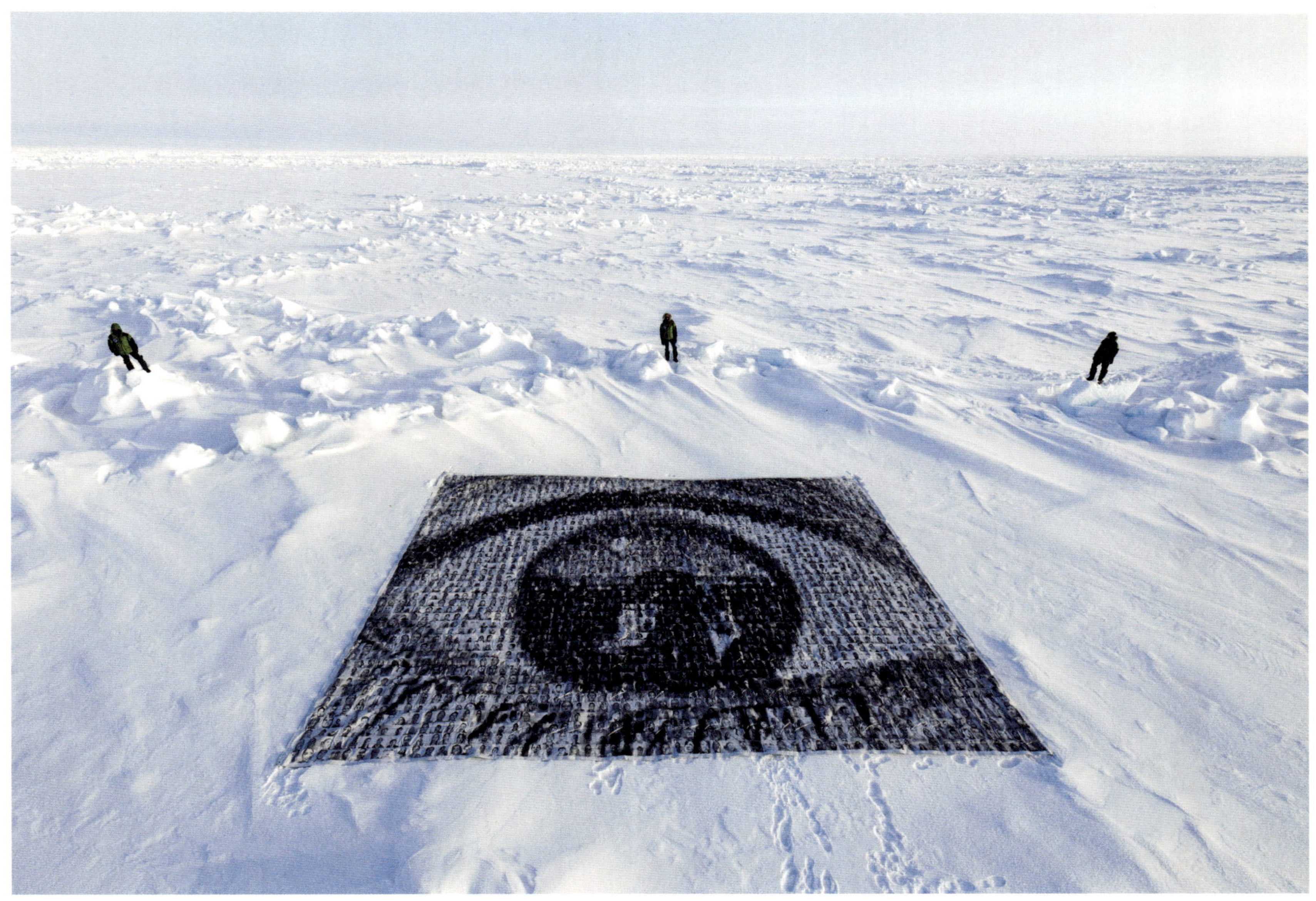

North Pole, the Arctic, 2013
4,000 portraits
Statement: The eyes of the world, at the top of the world, watching over the world: over four thousand portraits of members of the #savethearctic movement make up a giant eye on the North Pole, in a statement of defiance against destructive industry in the Arctic.

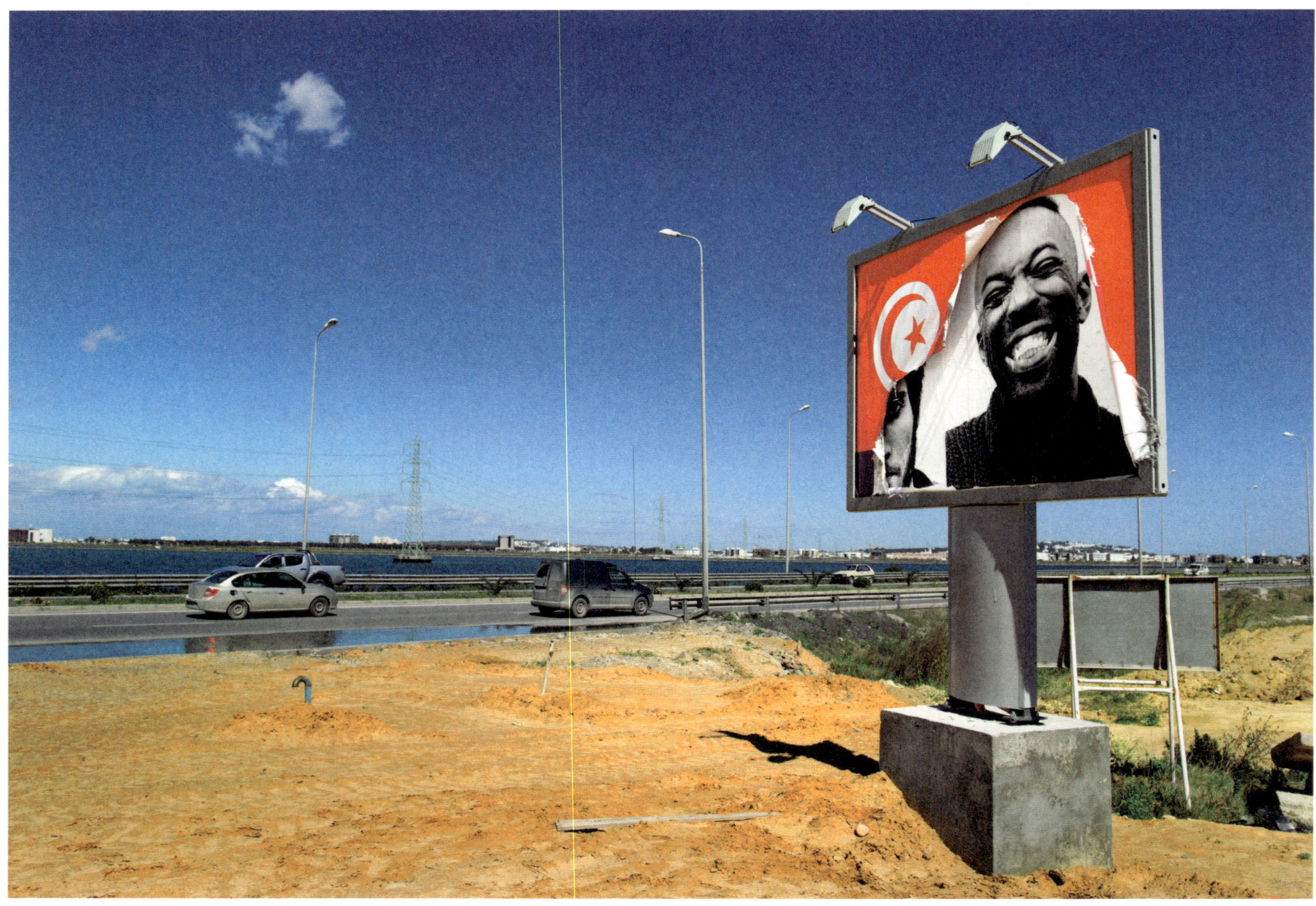

Ex-Ben Ali billboard on La Goulette Road, Tunisia, 2011
600 portraits
Statement: These people represent the different faces of the Tunisian society, people that agree to live with mutual respect for others.

Straight after the revolution, portraits of everyday Tunisians replaced the portraits of the former dictator Ben Ali in the streets of various cities.

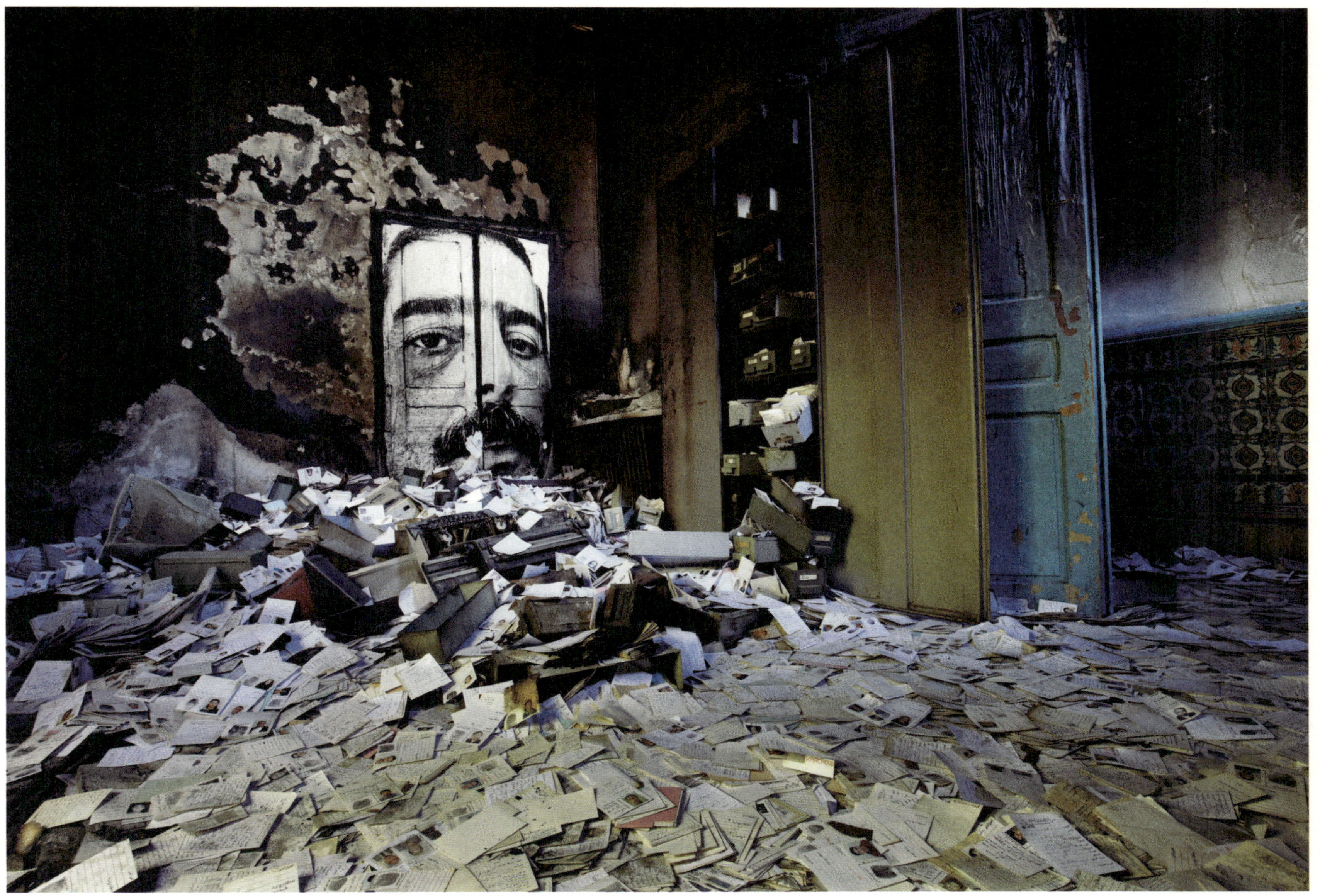

La Goulette police station, Tunisia, 2011

'On the floor lay the information cards which the police used to track the population.' – JR

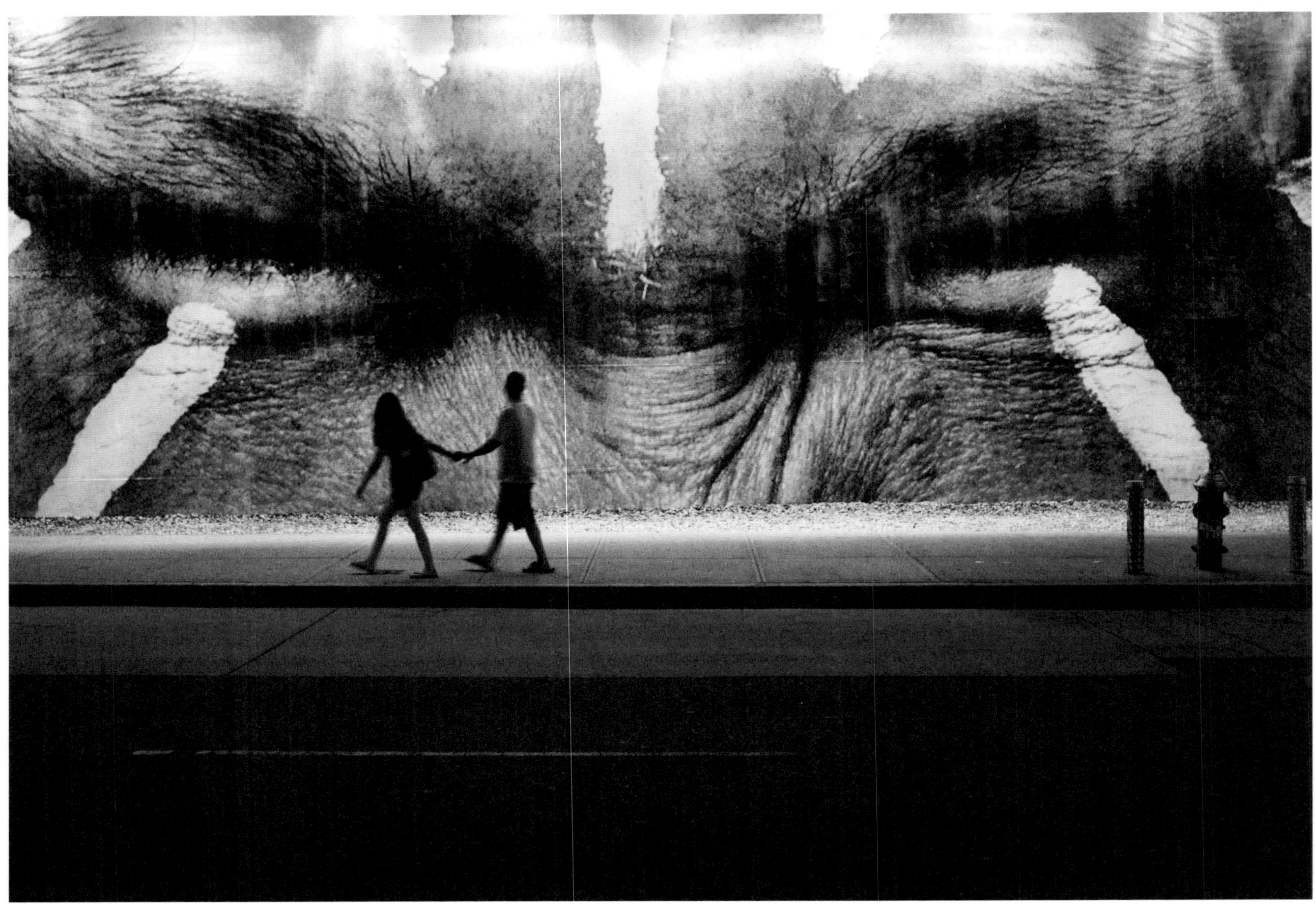

Houston and Bowery, New York, USA, 2011

'In May 2011, portraits of Native Americans from the Lakota tribe were pasted on their reservation of Standing Rock in North Dakota to say that they exist. I decided to bring this project to New York and enlarged some of the portraits to even larger sizes and pasted on different wall all over the city in 2011 and 2012.' – JR

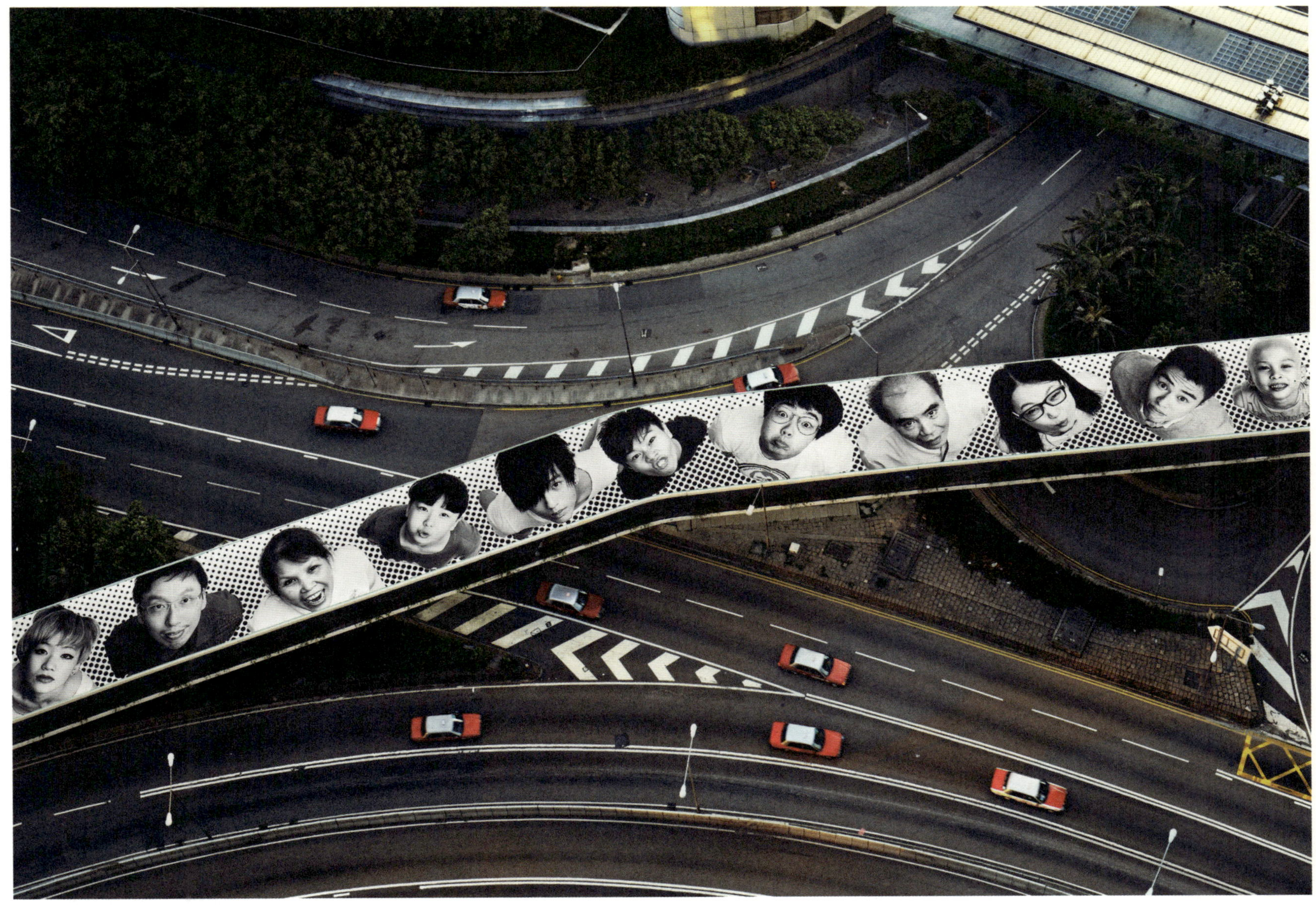

Portraits from a photobooth in Galerie Perrotin,
Hong Kong, 2012

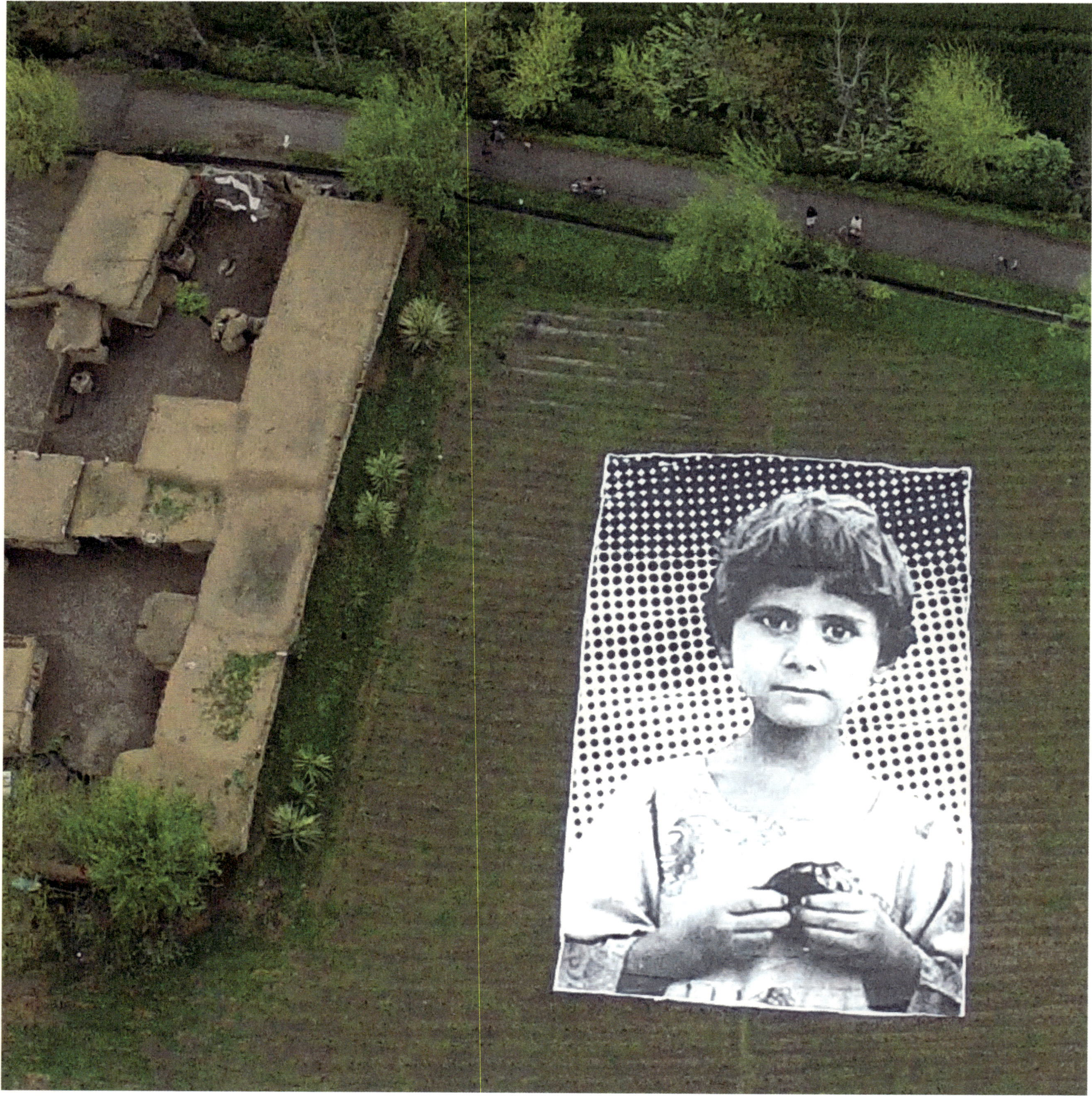

Khyber Pakhtunkhwa region, Pakistan, 2014
1 portrait
Statement: Since 2004, drone strikes in Pakistan have killed over an estimated 3,000 people. While some of these were high-profile targets, a large number were civilians including 160 children. The people who operate the drones describe their casualties as 'bug splats', since viewing the body through a grainy-green video image gives the sense of an insect being crushed.

'The organizers of this group action printed an extremely large-scale portrait of a child living in the area where the drones operated. This portrait was laid on the ground facing up, so that it would be captured by the drone cameras and transmitted to the drone operator's screen. The media response to this image was tremendous.' – JR

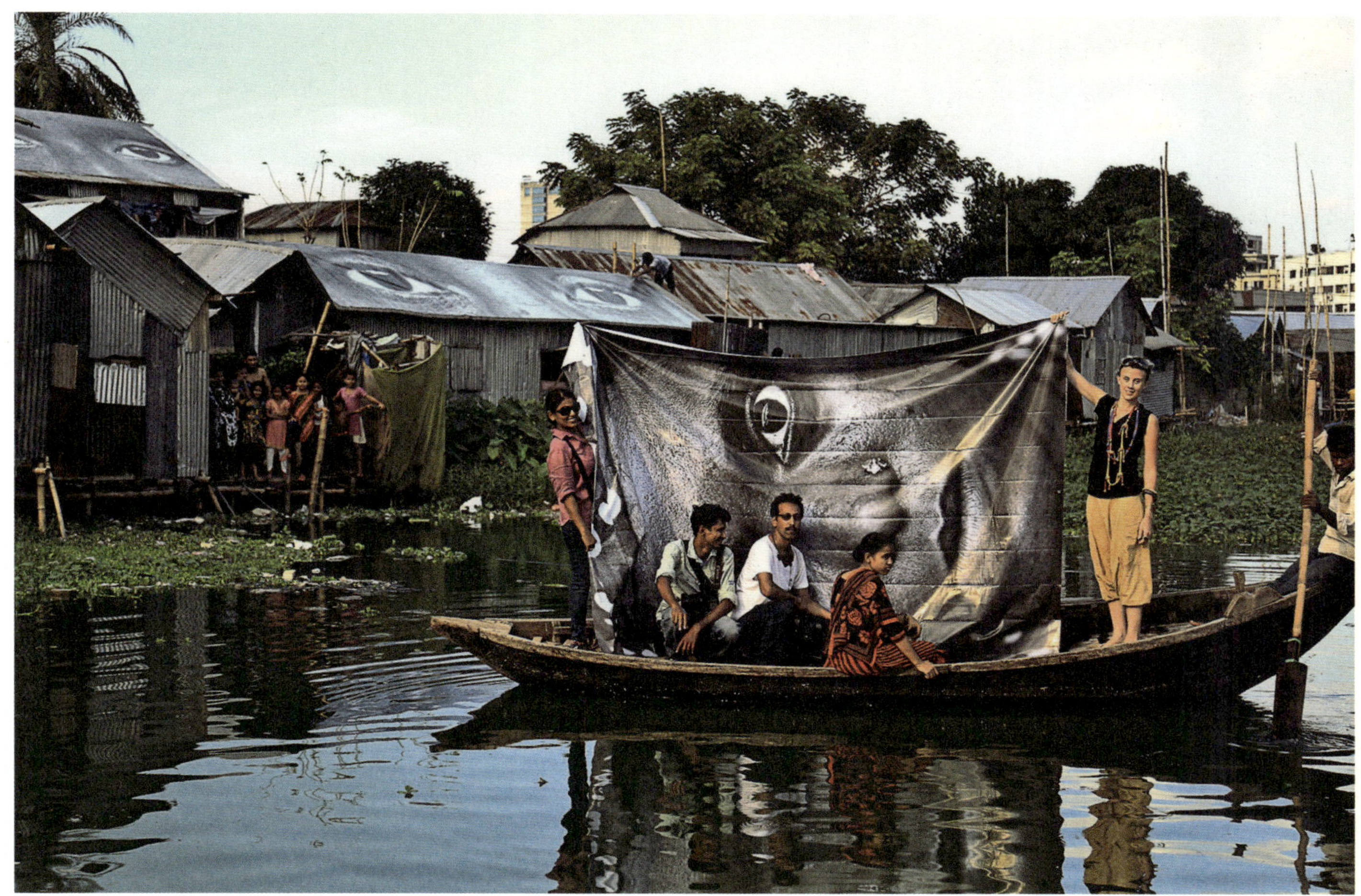

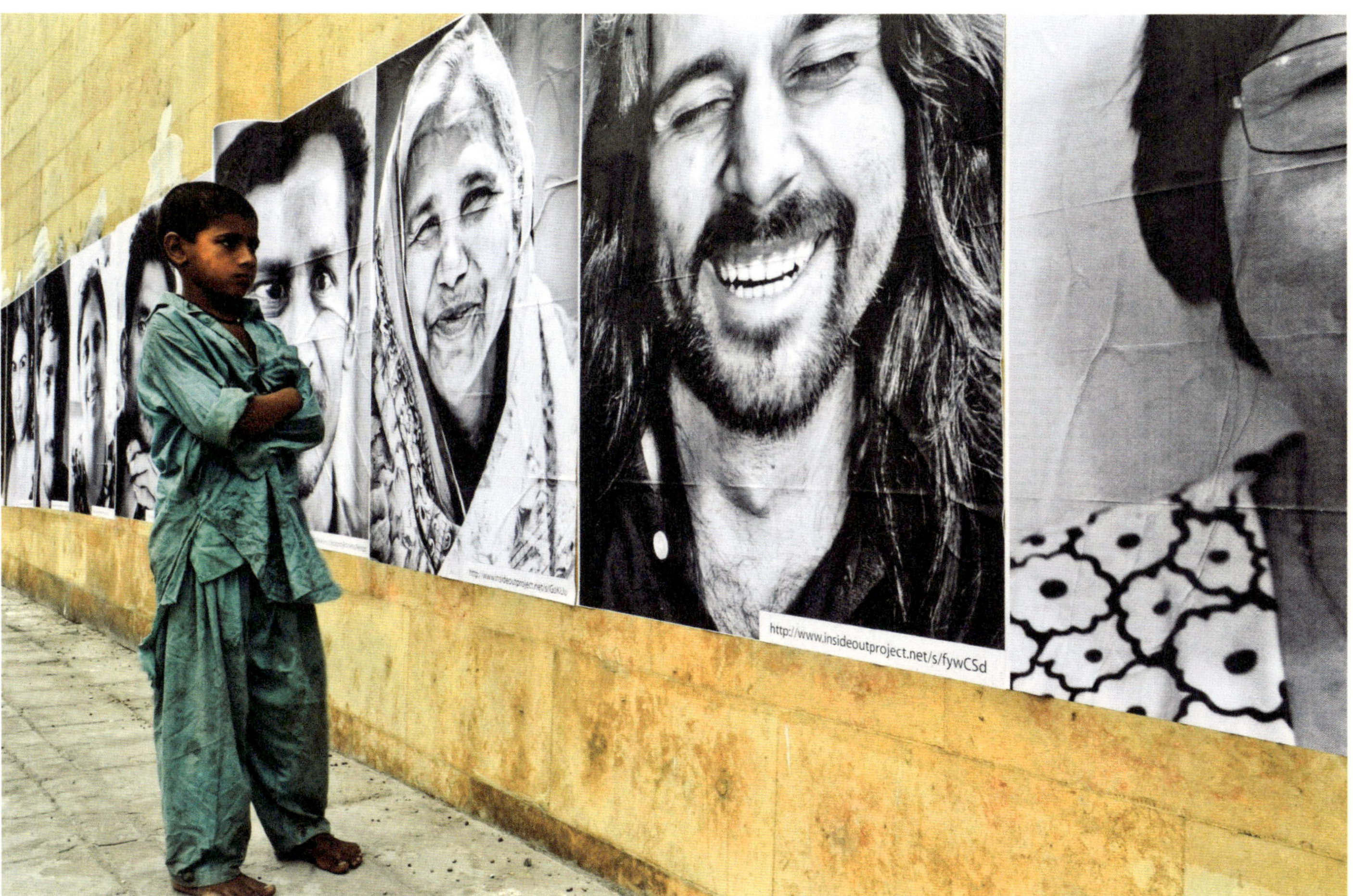

(top) Korail slum, Dhaka, Bangladesh, 2013
22 portraits
Statement: In honour of the millions of women working in the Bengali garment industry.

(bottom) TED X, Karachi, Pakistan, 2011
25 portraits
Statement: To expose the persecution of minorities in Pakistan.

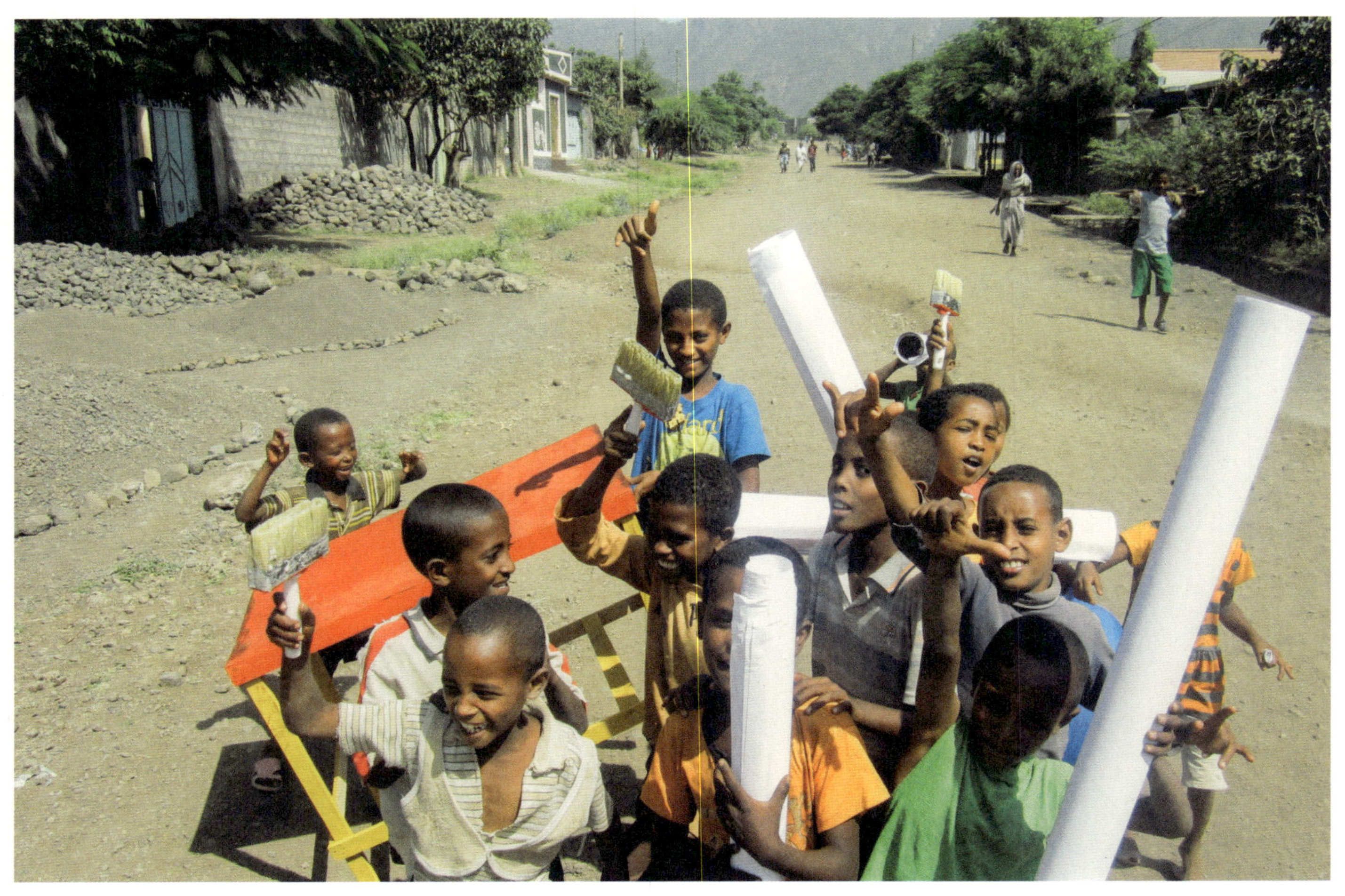

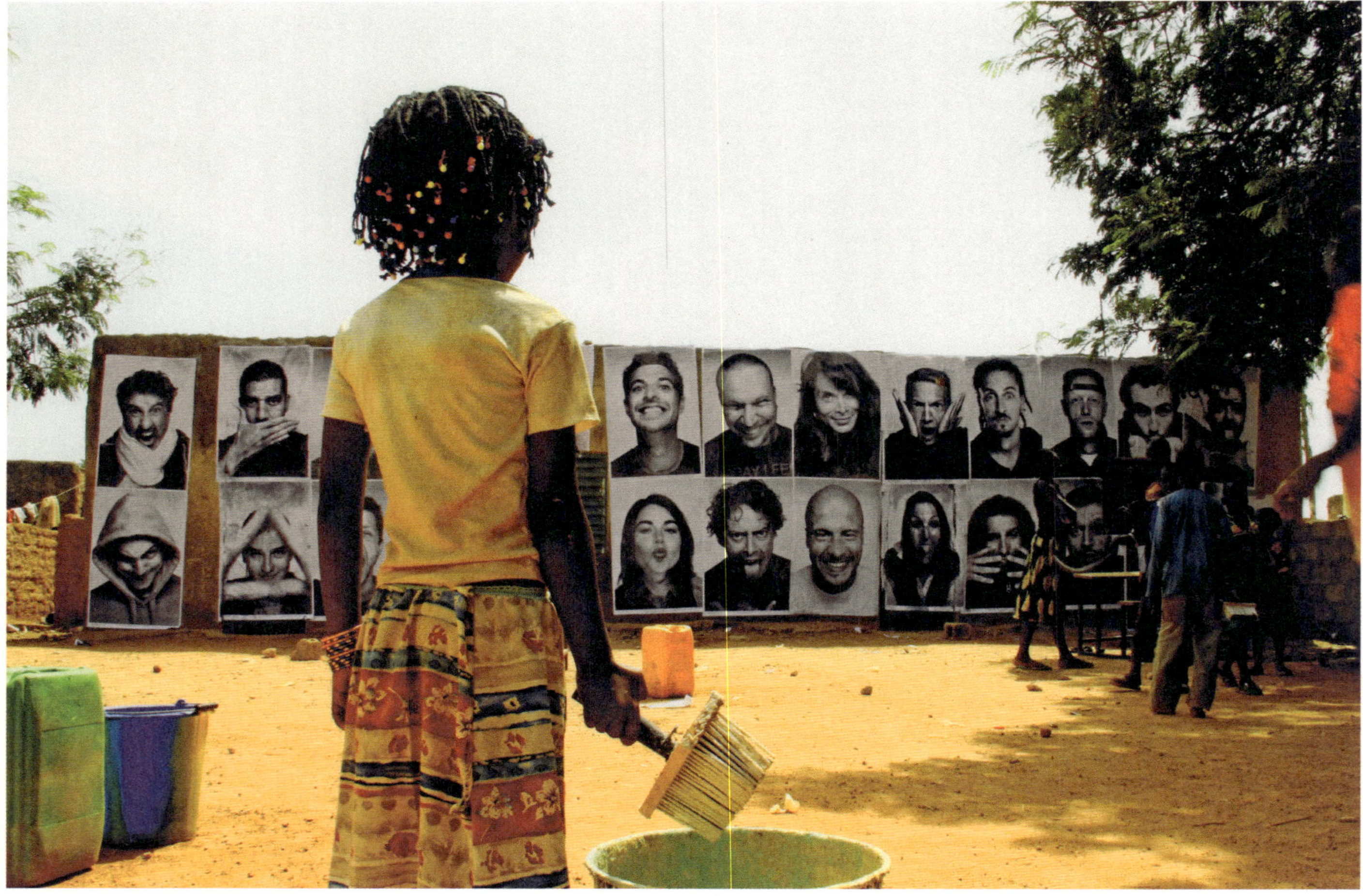

(top) Alamata, Ethiopia, 2012
500 portraits
Statement: This project was part of the global action around climate change, 'Be The Change', which took place in twenty cities in seventeen countries with 10,000 portraits.

(bottom) Ouagadougou, Burkina Faso, 2014
26 portraits
Statement: We want to show the cooperation and solidarity between France and Burkina Faso to show that we are all the same, black or white, children or adults. We are all humans.

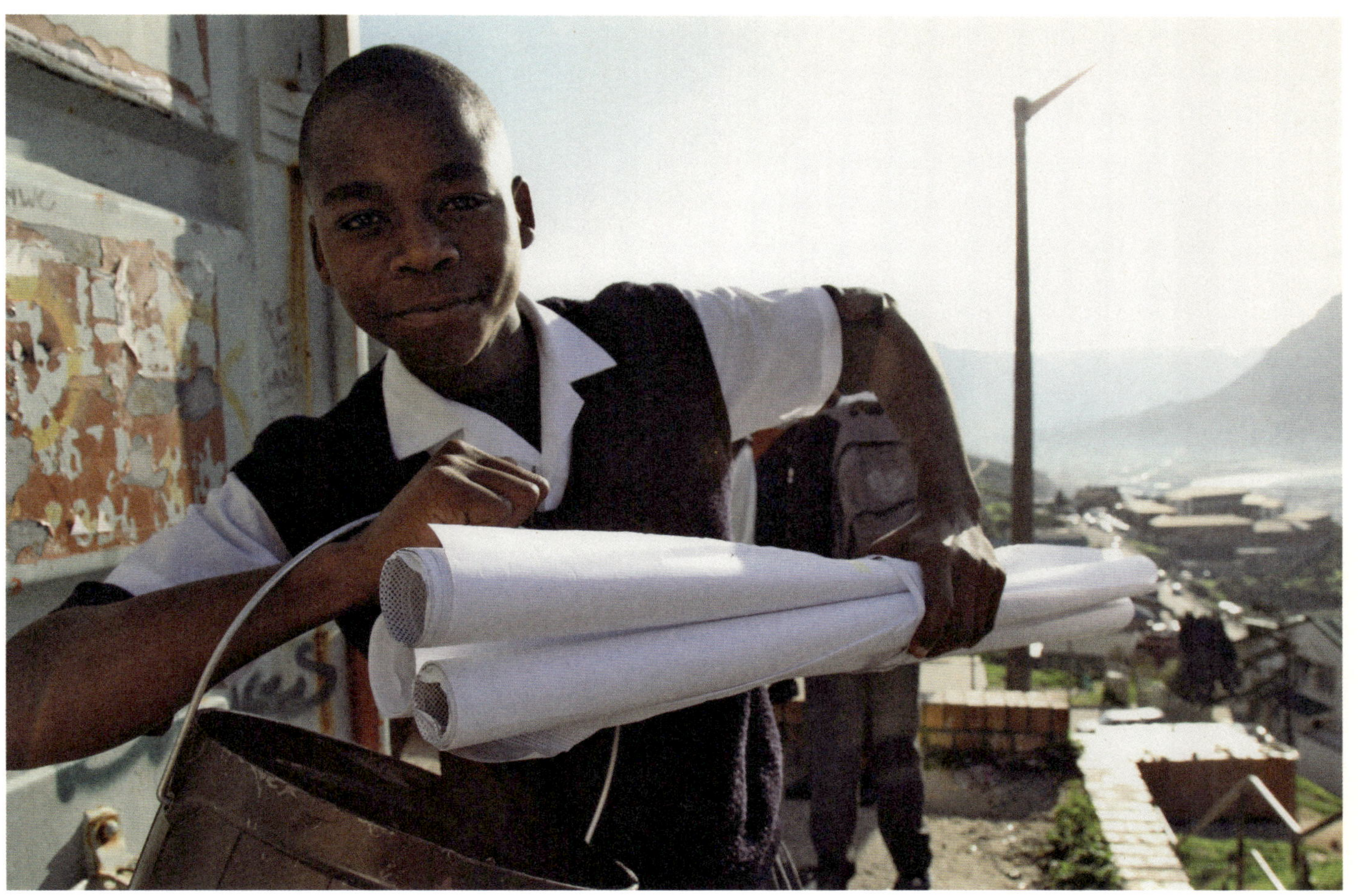

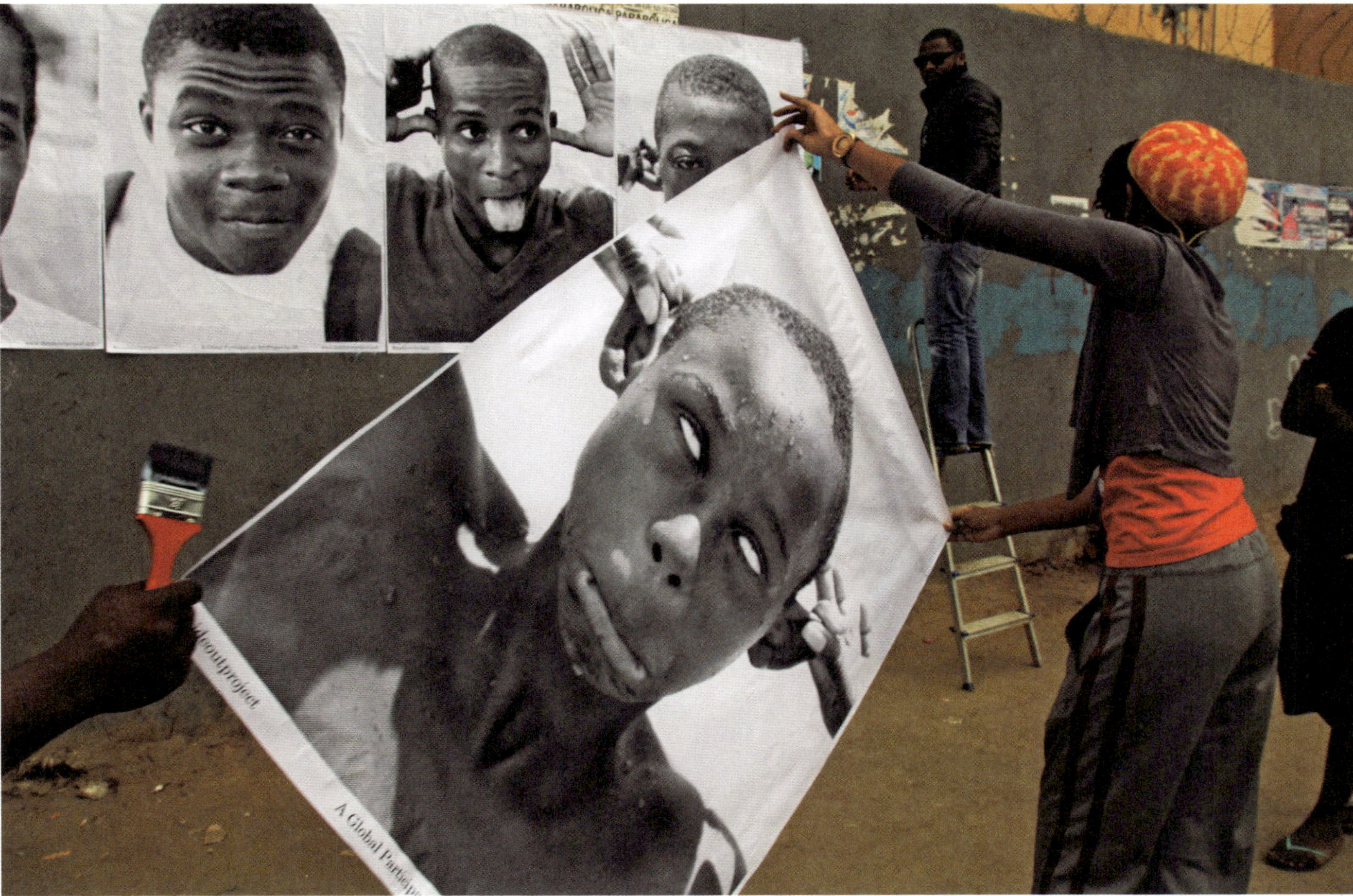

(top) Cape Town, South Africa, 2011
30 portraits
Statement: High-school students exploring and fostering dialogue around racism.

(bottom) Luanda, Angola, 2013
30 portraits
Statement: Kick out the violence!

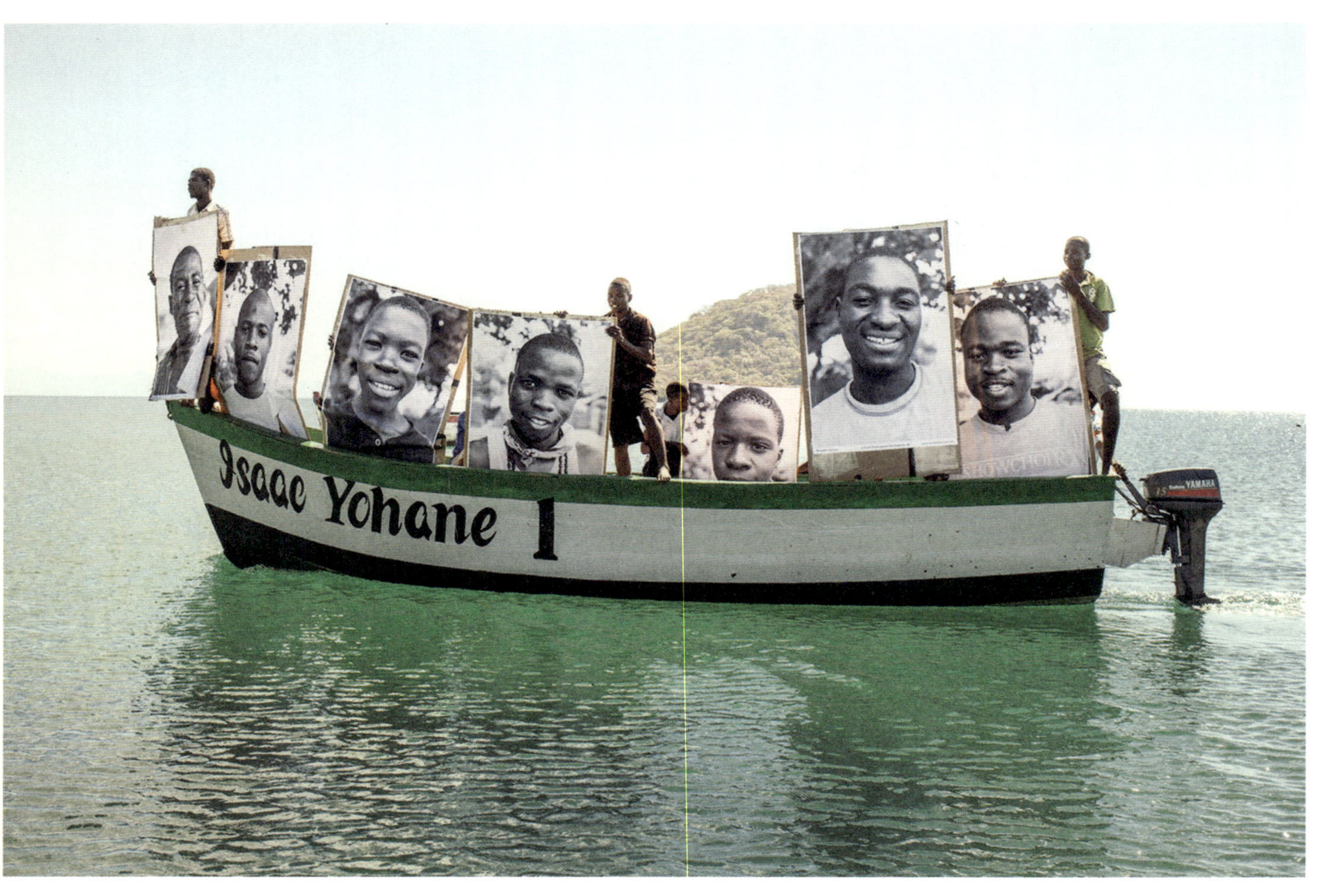

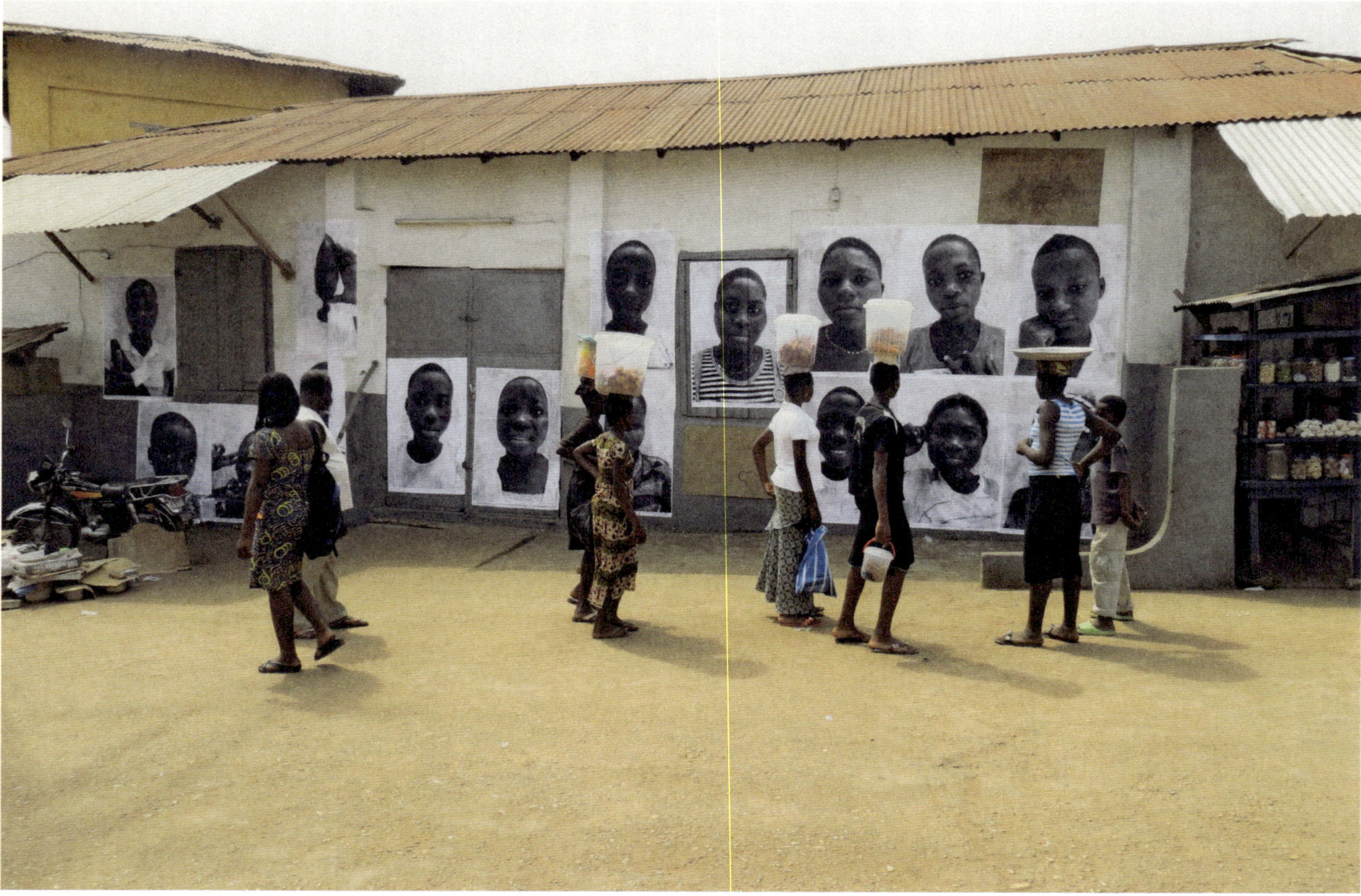

(top) Mangochi, Malawi, 2013
22 portraits
Statement: To highlight some of the challenges faced by the people working on the frontline in Malawi's food and fishing economies at a time of change in the country.

(bottom) Atakpame, Togo, 2014
34 portraits
Statement: Young woman! Leave behind your ignorance; have confidence in yourself and put yourself to work.

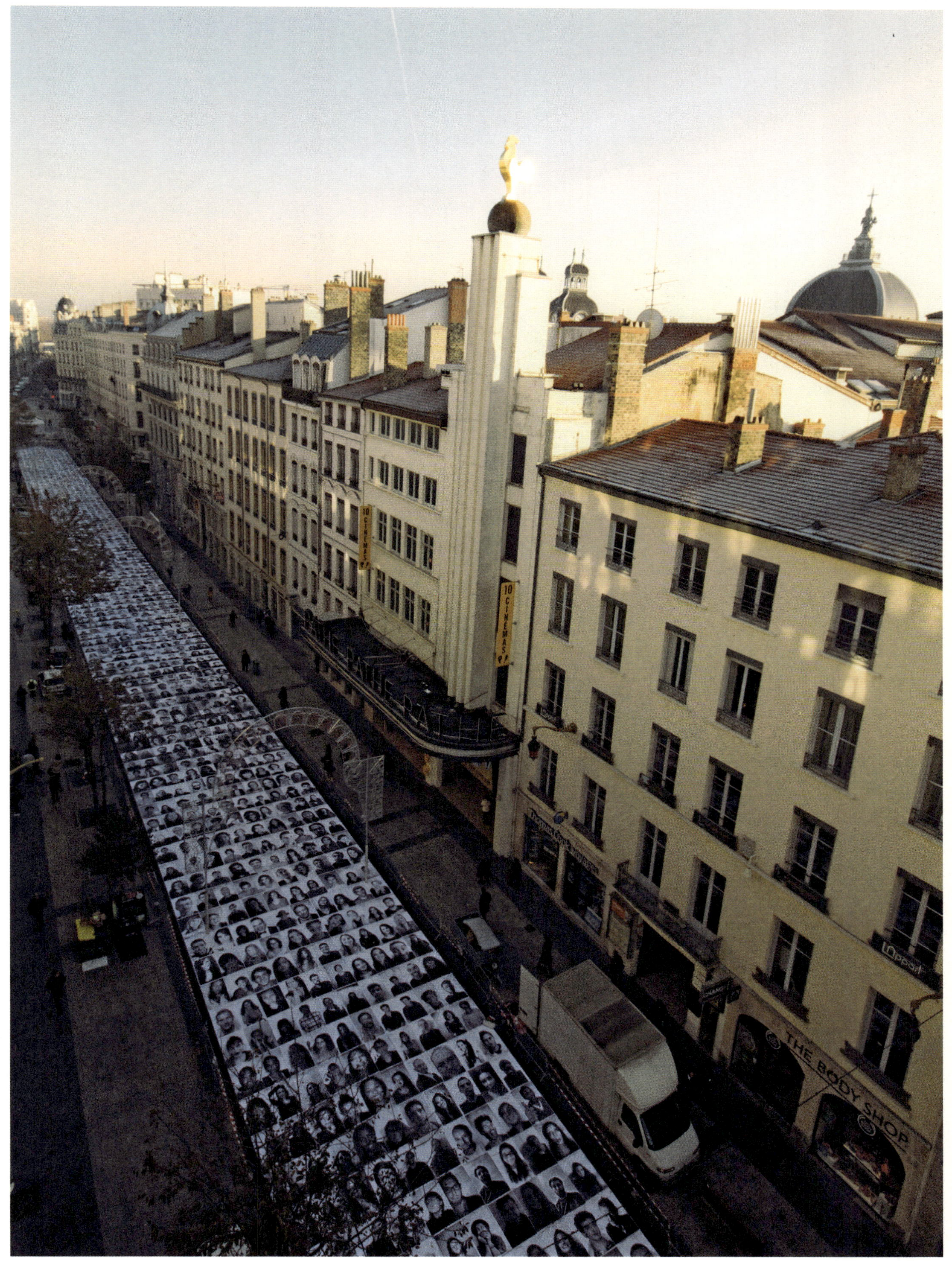

Lyon, France, 2013
2,000 portraits
Statement: To commemorate the 30th anniversary of the Walk for Equality and Against Racism that began in 1983 in Lyon.

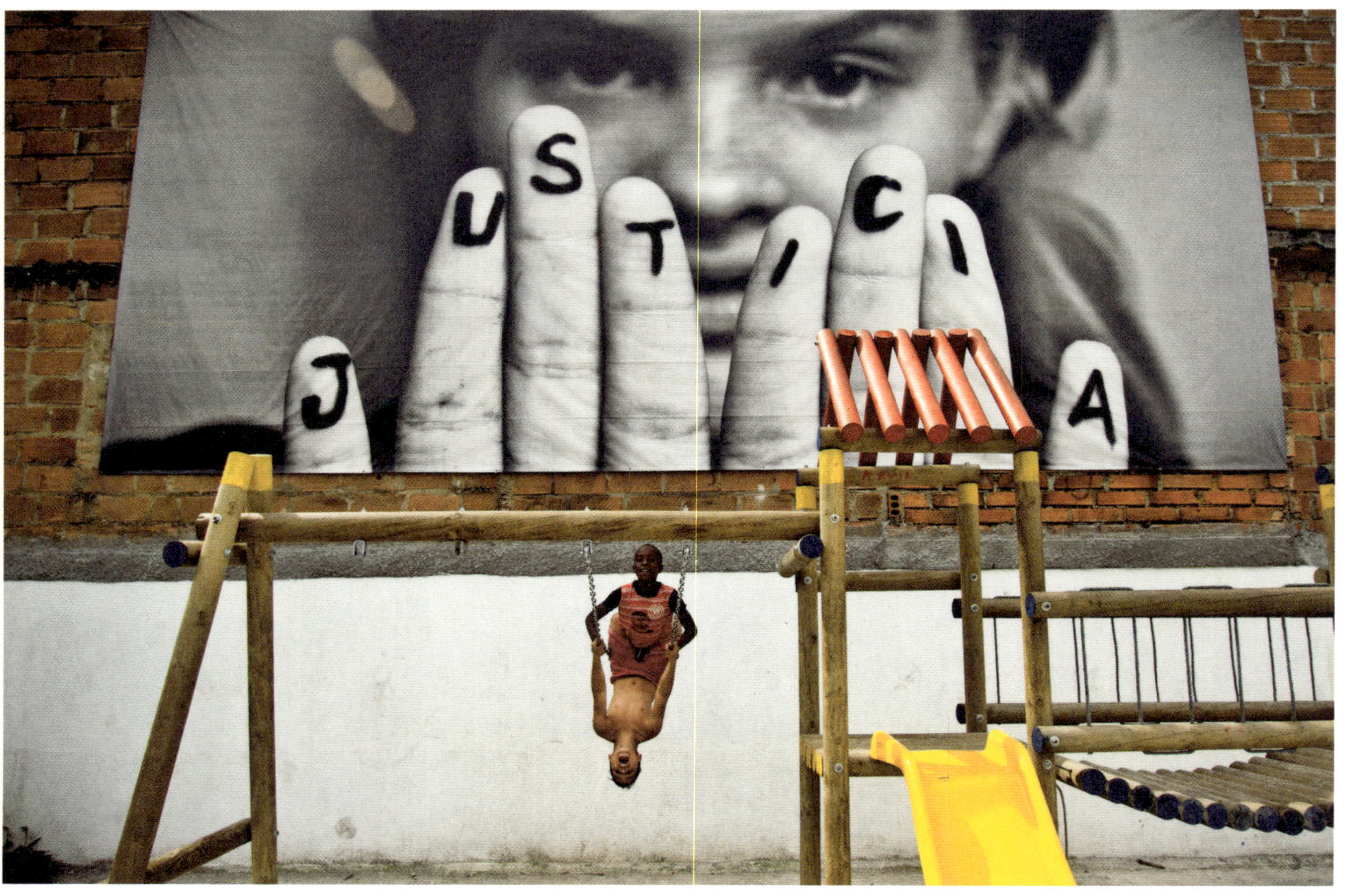

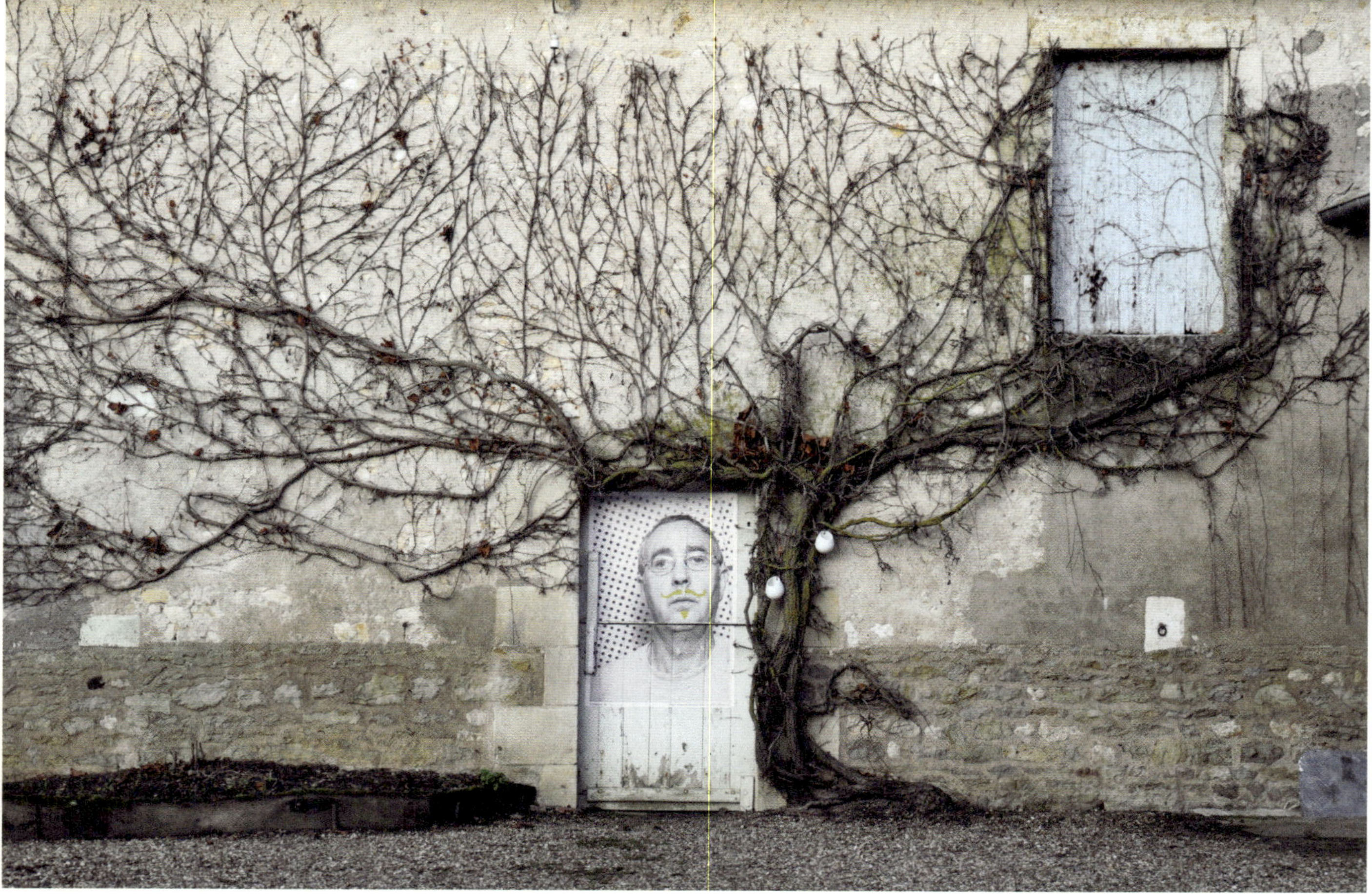

(top) Medellin, Colombia, 2011
200 portraits
Statement: Encouraging children to dream big and removing imagined boundaries.

(bottom) Arles, France, 2011
5,660 portraits
An action created from a photobooth at the Rencontres d'Arles photography festival.

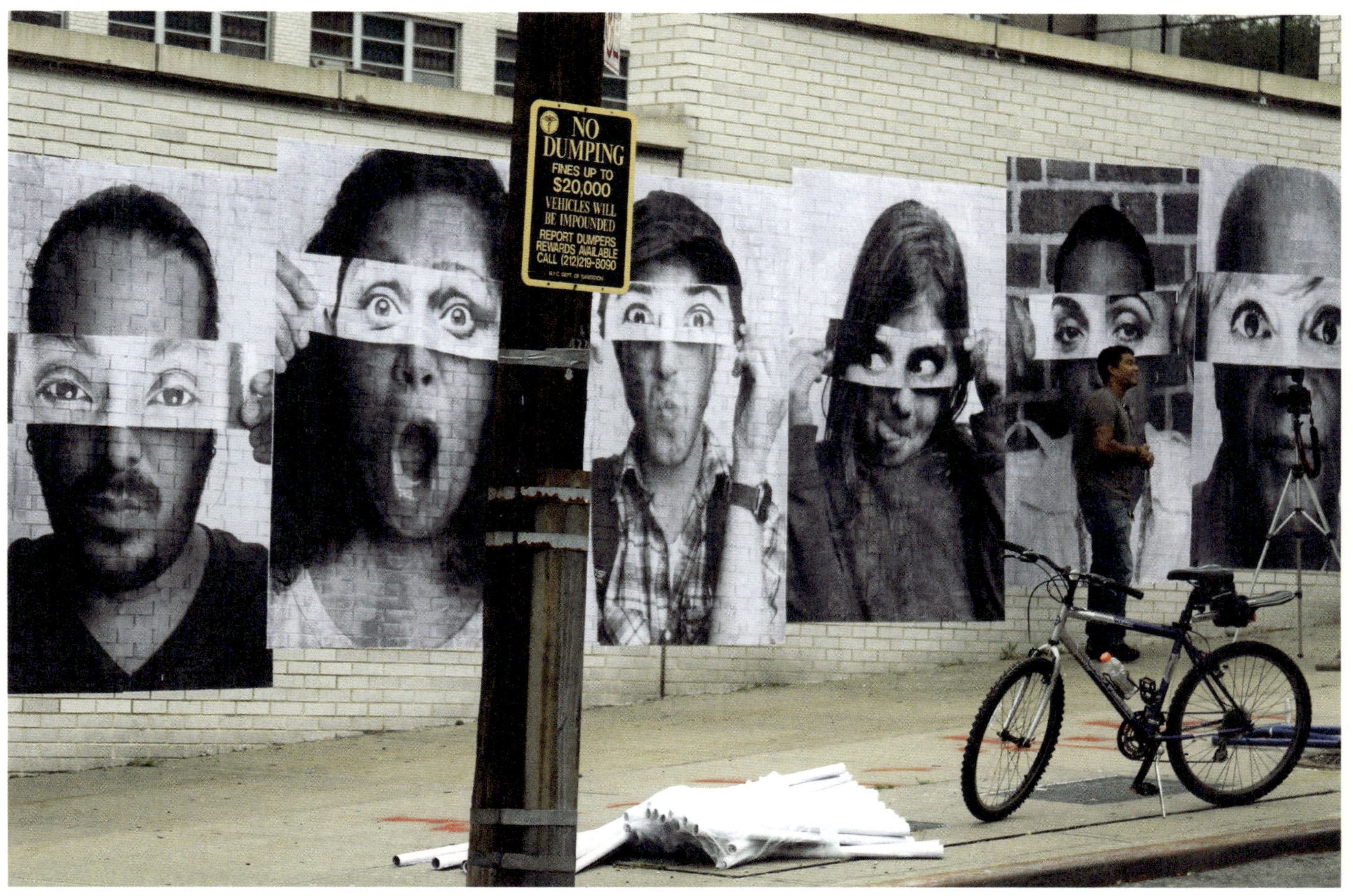

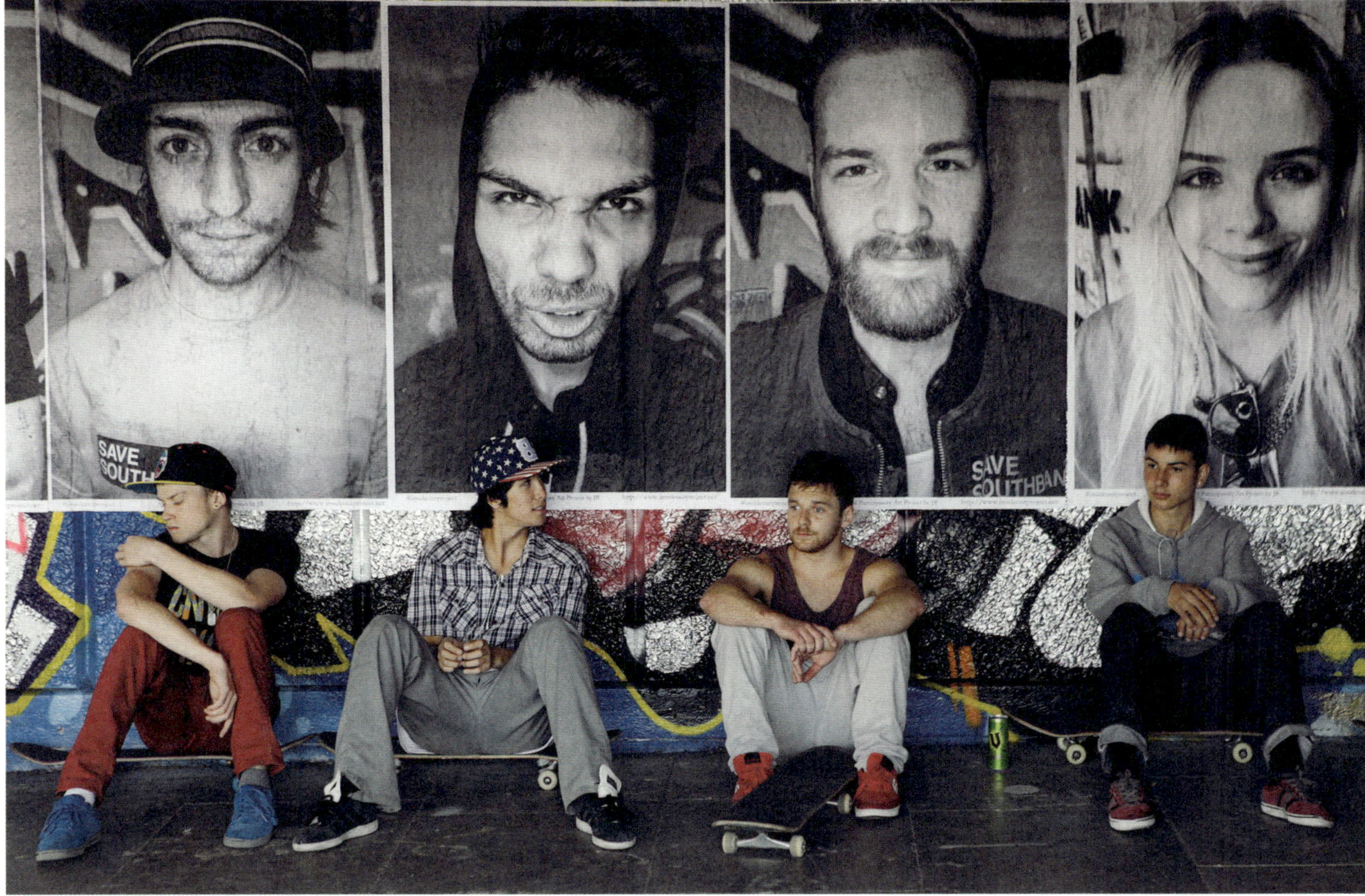

(top) South Bronx, New York, USA, 2011
142 portraits
Statement: South Bronx (S)Heroes celebrates Bronx mothers and community members by depicting Bronxites looking through mothers' eyes.

(bottom) South Bank, London, UK, 2013
25 portraits
Statement: This is our creative space where we learn and practice. We love our space. We love our place. This is our identity. This is where we ride!

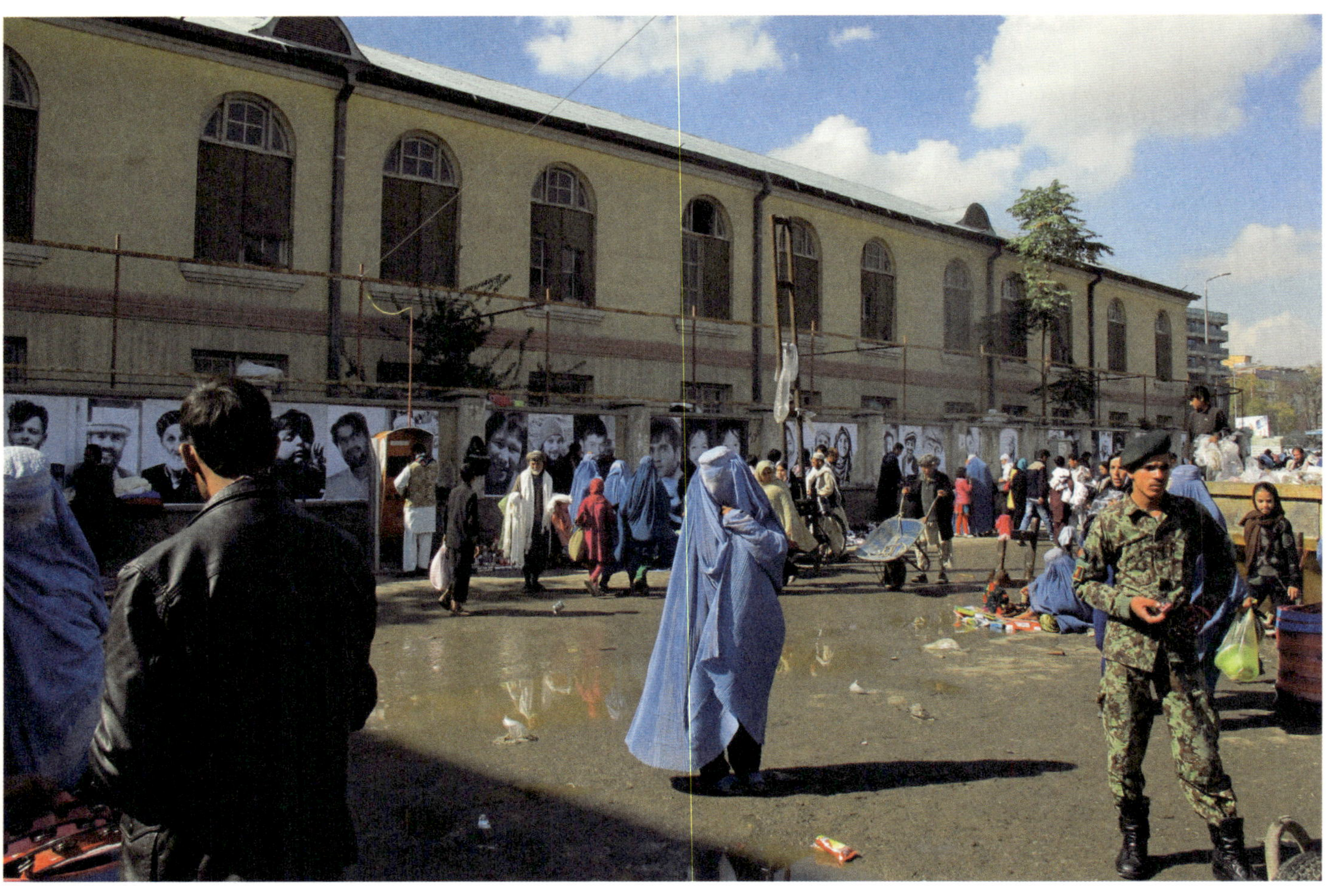

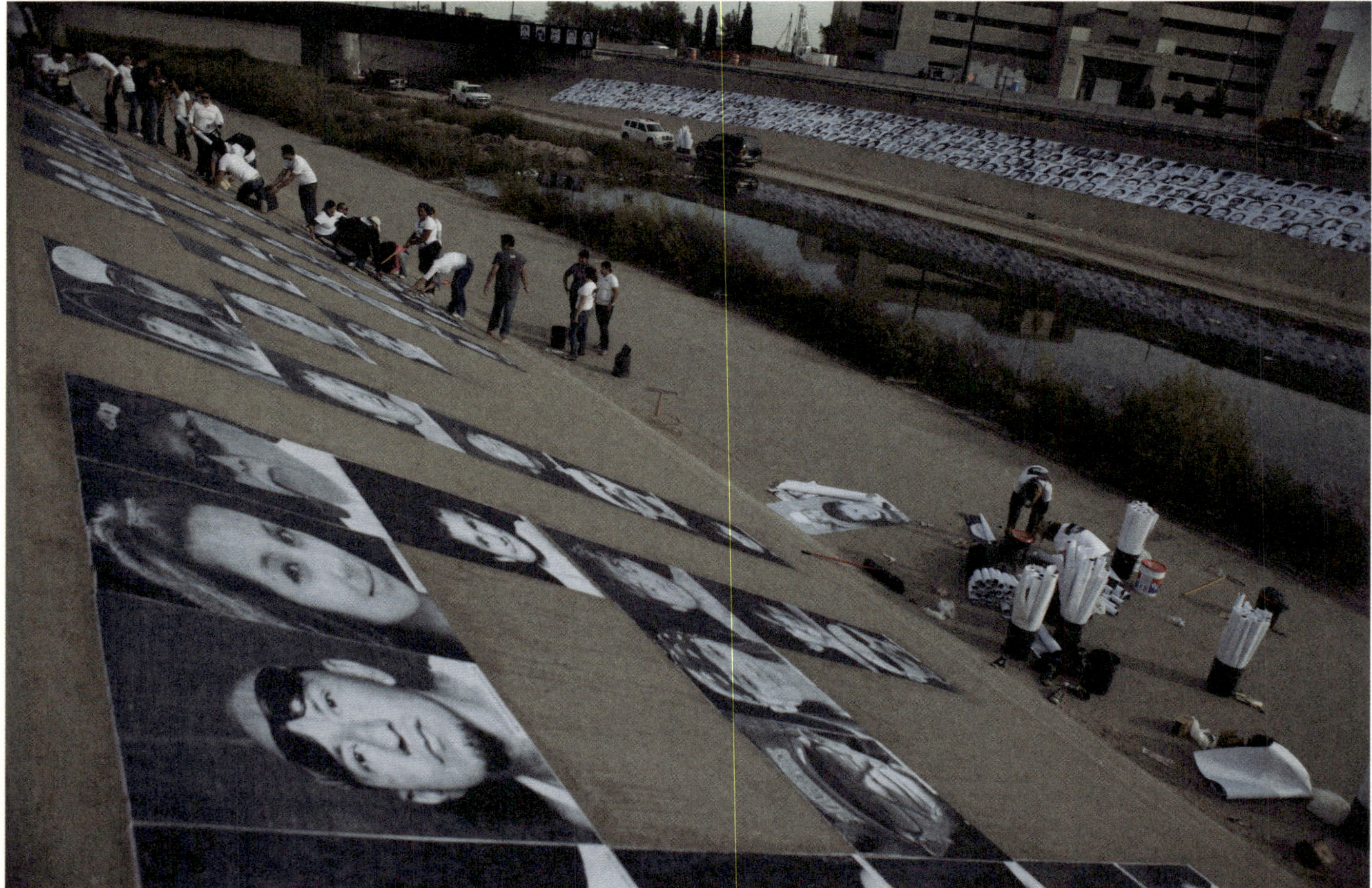

(top) ISAF HQ barricade, Kabul, Afghanistan, 2012
200 portraits
Statement: Afghanistan is not the story Khaled Hosseini and the media would have you believe. There is hope and laughter in Afghanistan and that should be celebrated.

(bottom) Rio Grande Canal, Juarez, Mexico, 2011
1,161 portraits
Statement: We stand for peace in our city, our country and the world!

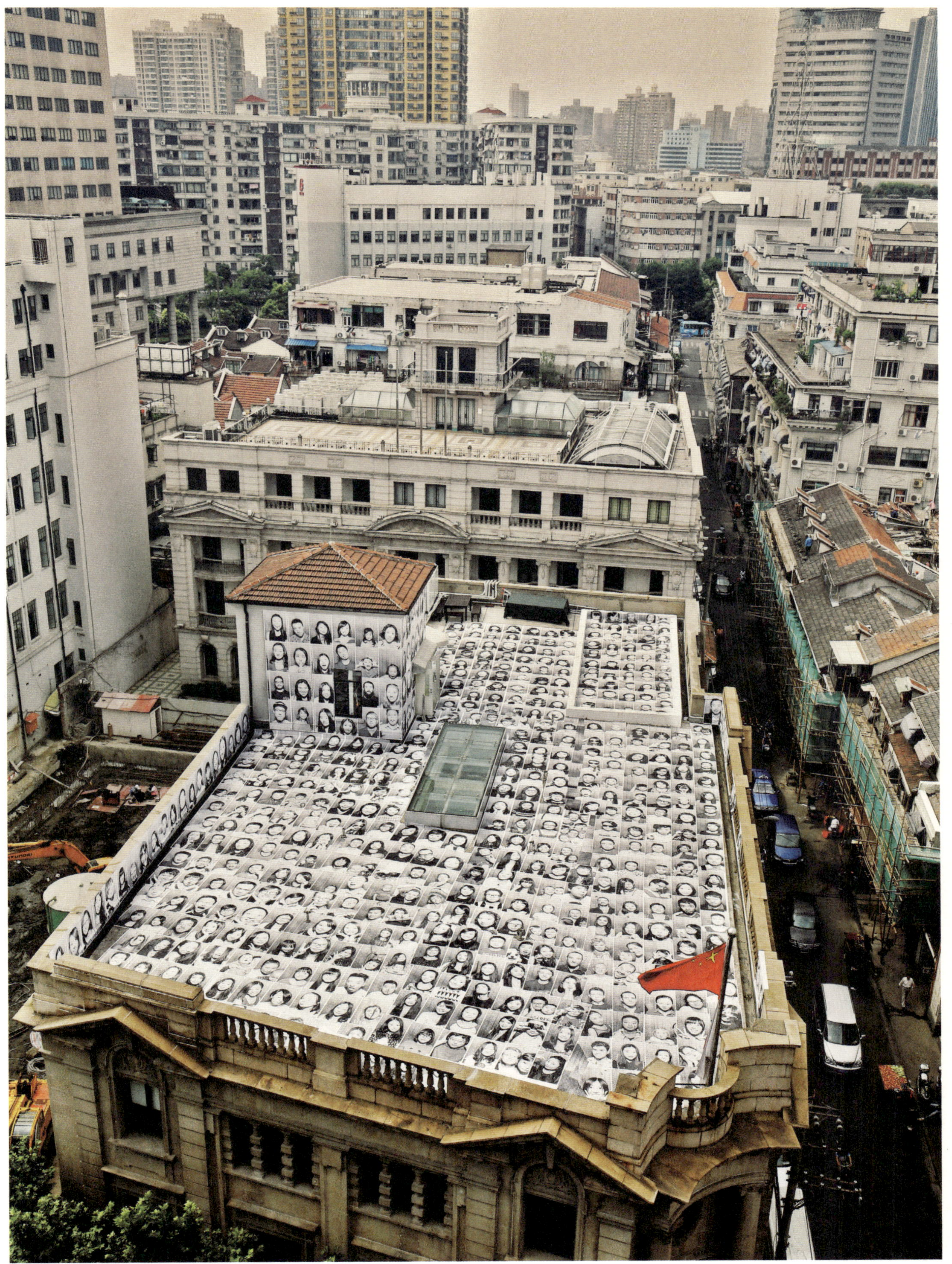

Shanghai, China, 2014
9,078 portraits
An action created from a photobooth that travelled through Shanghai for two months.

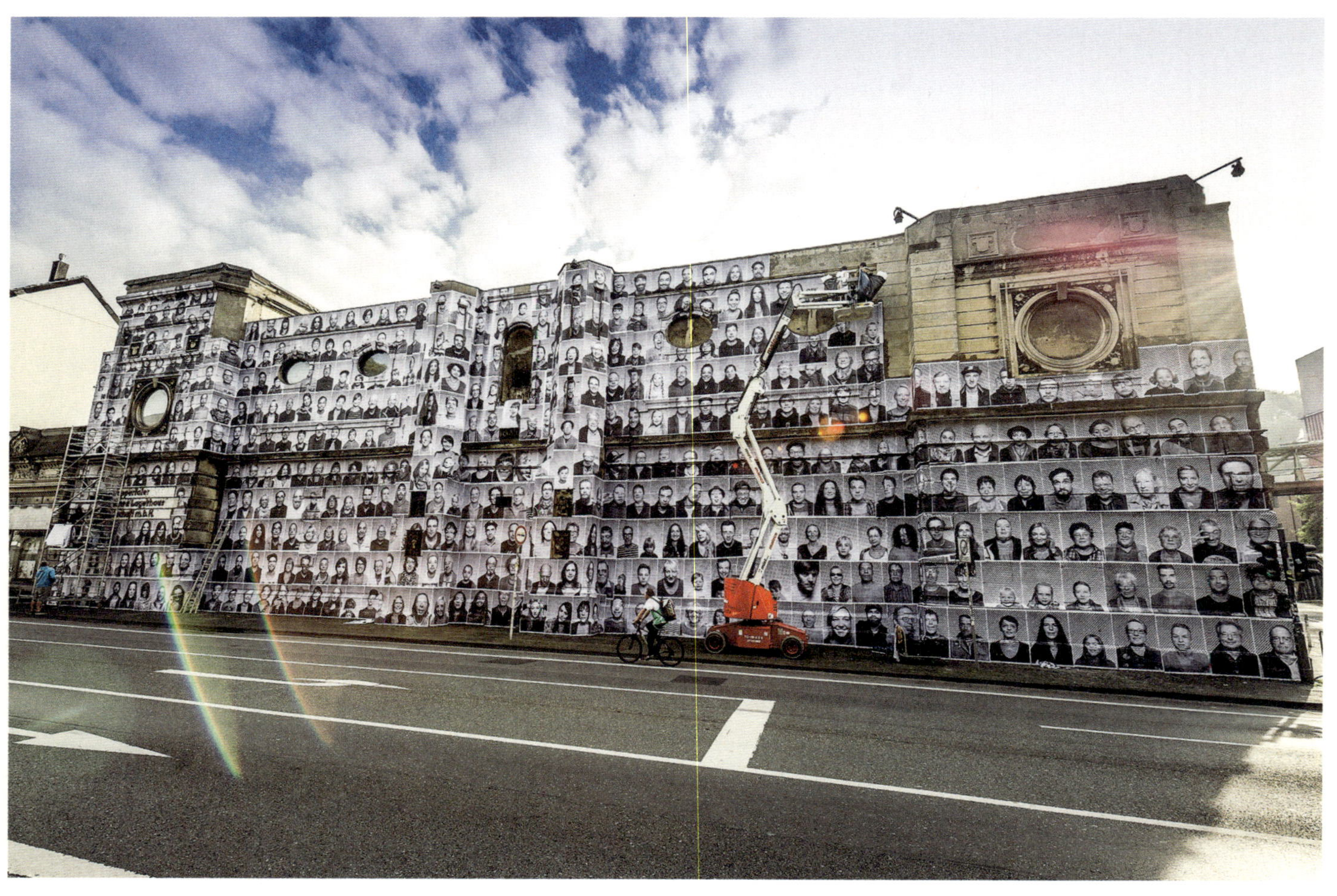

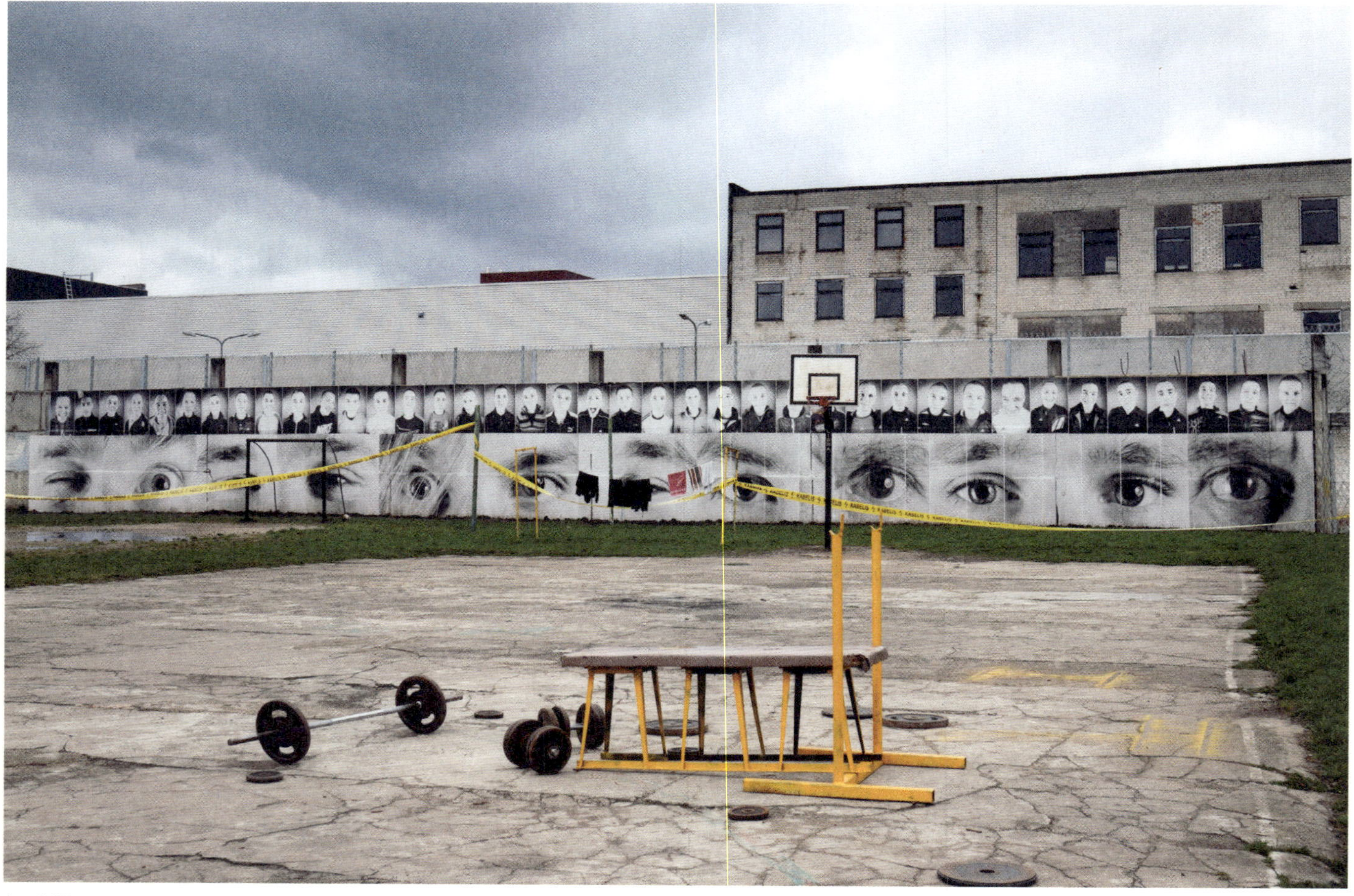

(top) Wuppertal, Germany, 2014
700 portraits
Statement: Different faces – different views.
Action from a photobooth.

(bottom) Kaunas, Lithuania, 2014
39 portraits
A group of artists was invited to the Kaunas Youth Correctional and Interrogation Facility in help gauge the impact, if any, art has had on youth offenders.

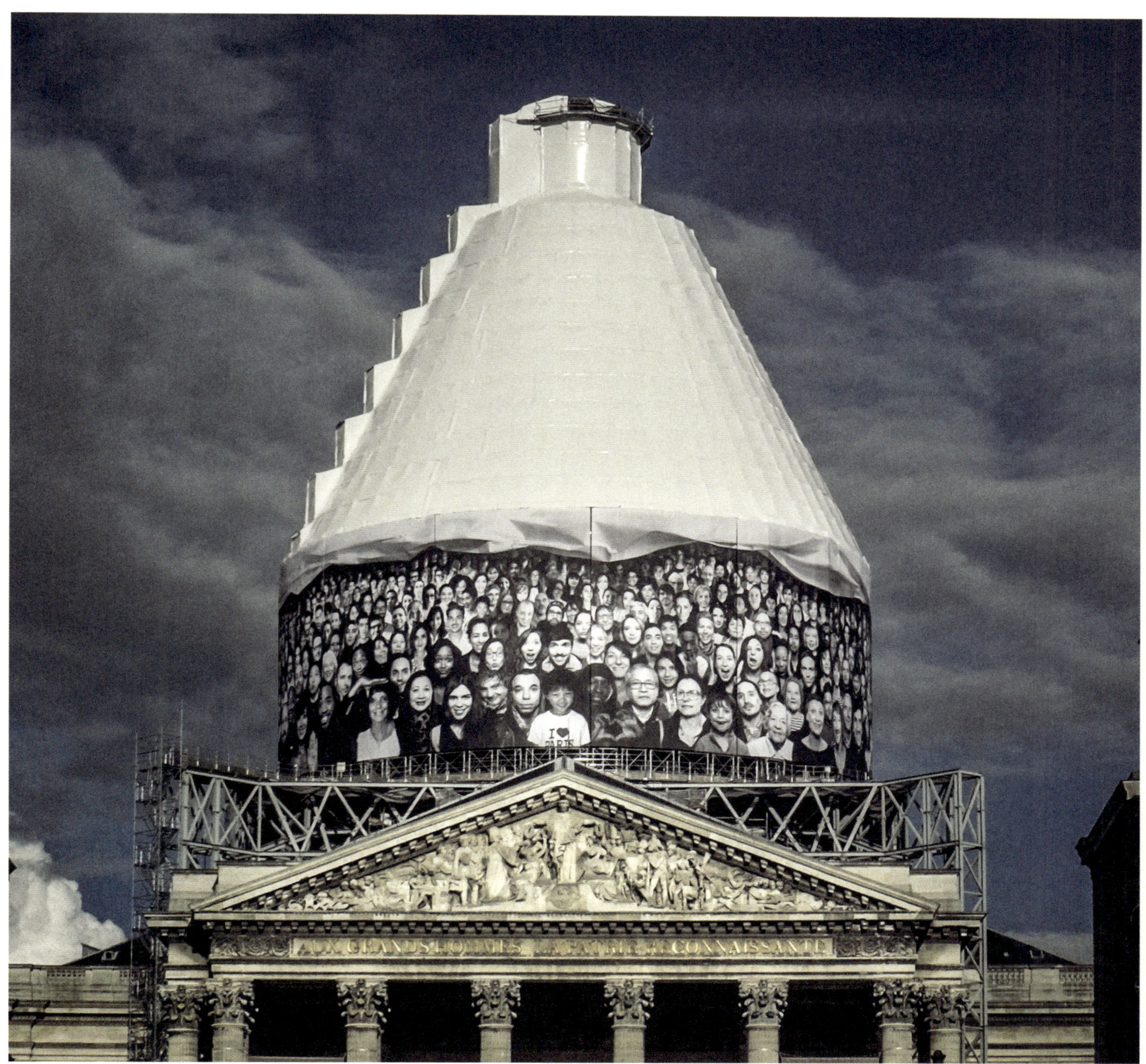

The dome, Pantheon, Paris, France, 2014
4,160 portraits
The restoration of the Pantheon is one of the largest of such projects in Europe and the monumental self-supporting scaffolding system is a great technical feat. Thousands of faces were collected in March 2014 from photos that were uploaded to the project website and at photobooths at nine national monuments in France to encapsulate the humanistic and universal values embodied by the Pantheon.

The installation covered the dome, the cupola and the floor inside the building. The exterior artwork was on view throughout the restoration phase of the dome and upper parts.

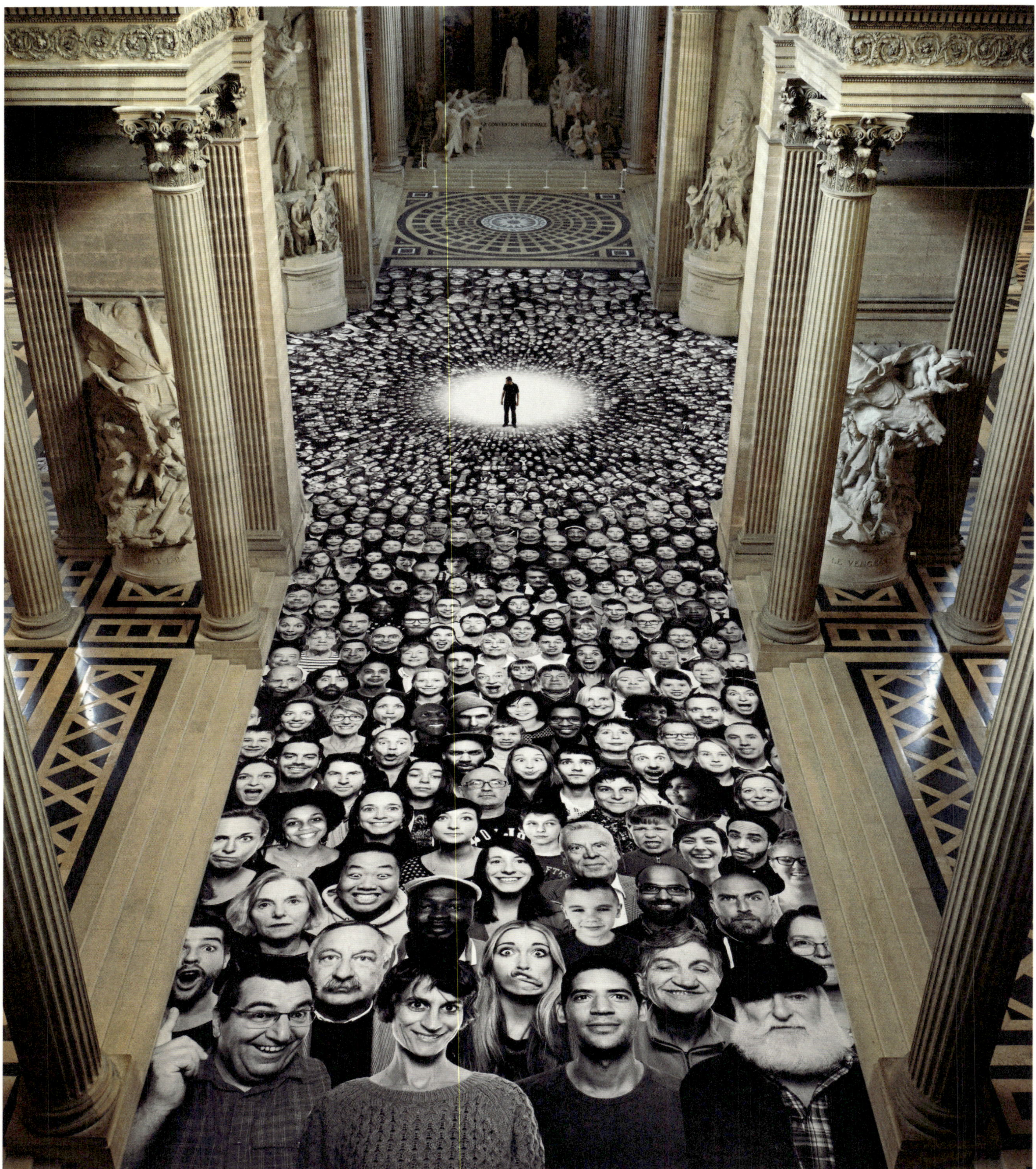

The nave, Pantheon, Paris, France, 2014

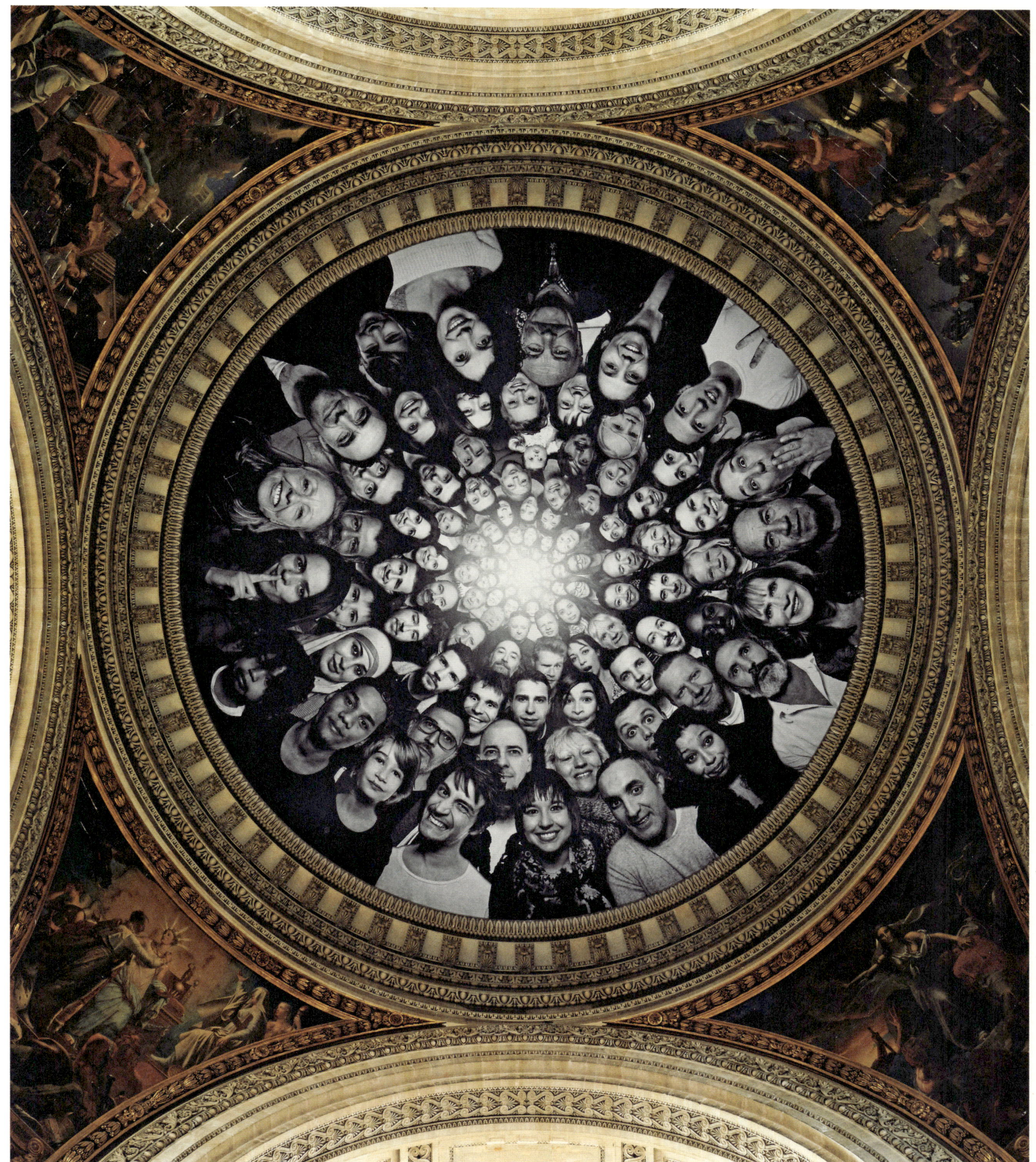

The cupola, Pantheon, Paris, France, 2014

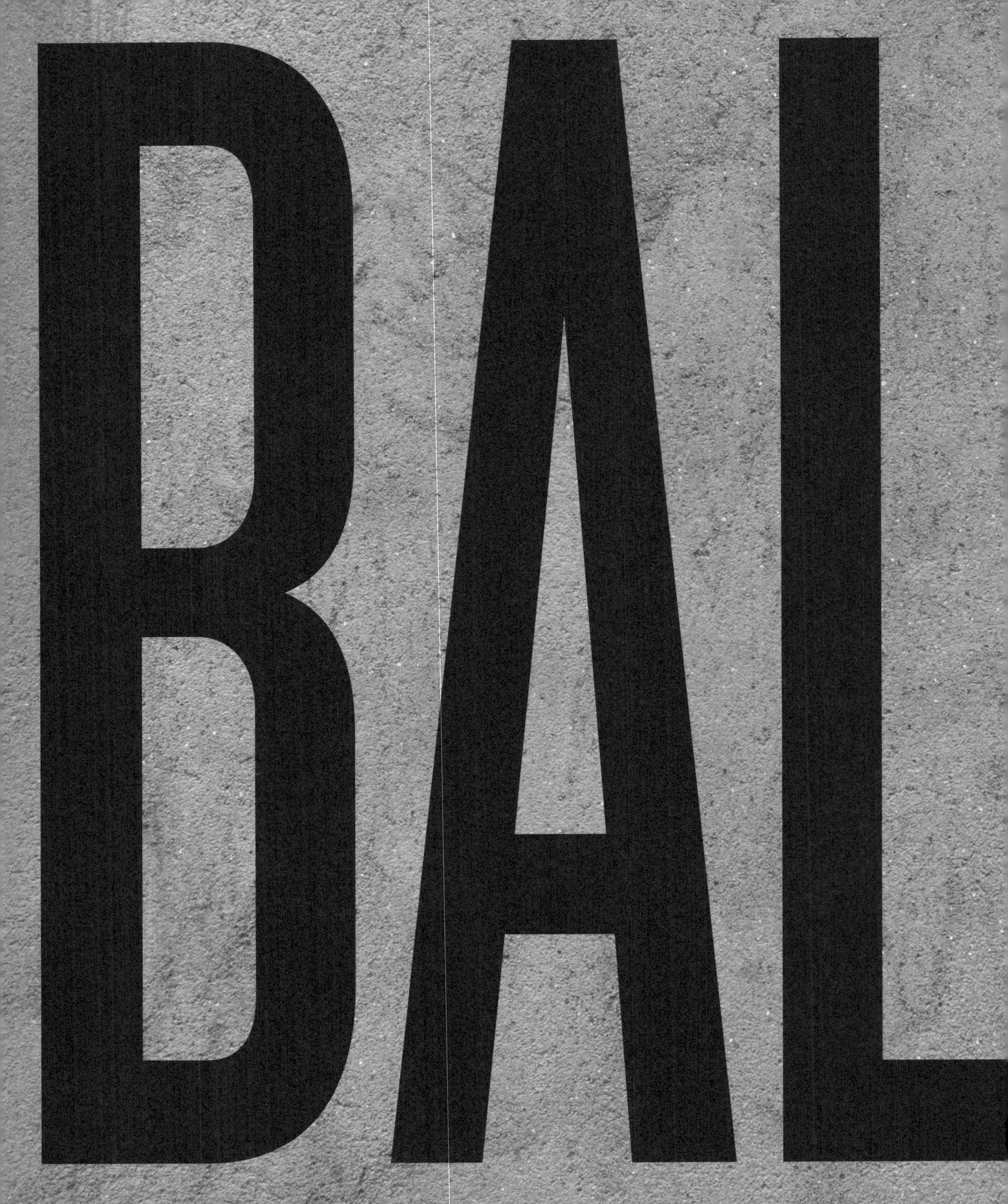
BAL

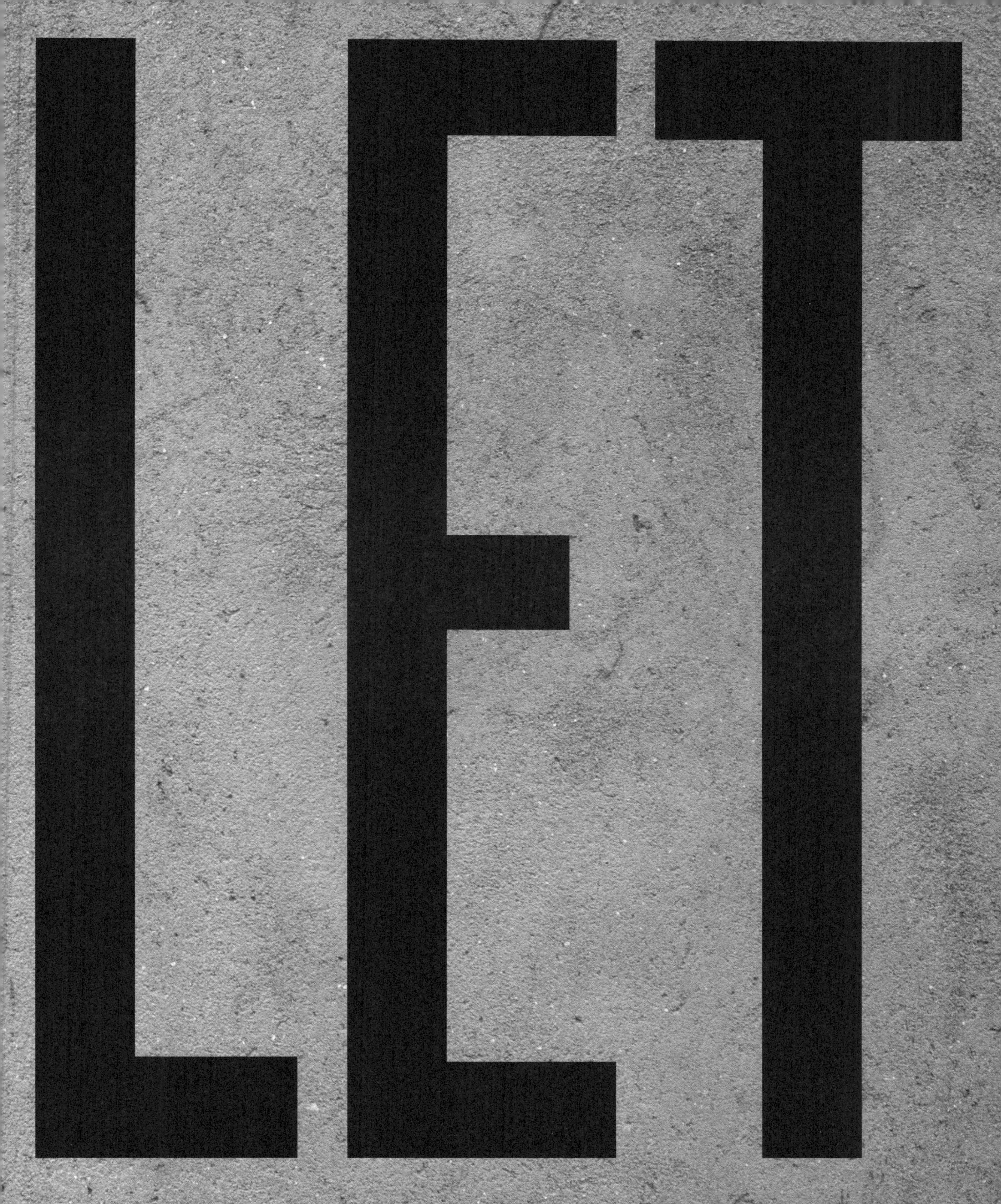
LET

JR's artistic stream is about continuity in action and creation: new projects arise from existing ones and from his interaction and collaboration with artists in other creative fields.

His creative migration to *Ballet* unfolded in various stages, each a development from the previous and all connected in one way or another to his previous projects – *Portrait of a Generation*, *Inside Out* and *Women Are Heroes*. Like his pasting projects, JR's ballet works are a celebration of art and life, with an awareness of society's front lines.

The project was initiated in 2014, when JR was invited by the New York City Ballet to create a large-scale installation in the hall of the theatre as part of its Art Series. JR photographed the ballet dancers interacting with paper, his medium of choice, and used the life-size photographs to create a giant *trompe l'oeil* rendering of an eye formed of dancers seemingly lying on the floor of the David H Koch Theater promenade. A large pasting of the ballerinas was also assembled on the windowed frontage of the theatre.

Peter Martins, the Ballet Master-in-Chief at the New York City Ballet, proposed that JR create a choreographic piece for the company. JR responded to this artistic challenge by translating the story of his friend, Ladj Ly, during the 2005 French ghetto riots, into a ballet. The piece was entitled 'Les Bosquets', after the original location of *Portrait of a Generation*. Contemporary musician Woodkid created an original symphonic score and Peter Martins transposed JR's vision and movement into formal ballet steps.
On 29 April 2014, 'Les Bosquets' premiered at the Lincoln Center, with forty-two dancers from the New York City Ballet and guest dancer Lil Buck.

A short film entitled *Les Bosquets* brought the project back to its birthplace, Les Bosquets in Montfermeil. The film blends footage from the riots in 2005 and the original *Portrait of a Generation* project with choreography performed on location by Paris Opera Ballet dancers. With music composed by Pharrell Williams, Hans Zimmer and Woodkid, JR created a space where art, social uproar and the power of images collided, creating beauty where one would not expect it. *Les Bosquets* premiered in New York at the Tribeca Film Festival in 2015. After JR's encounter with the Paris Opera Ballet dancers for the film, he created a photo series with them on the roof of the Palais Garnier, Paris.

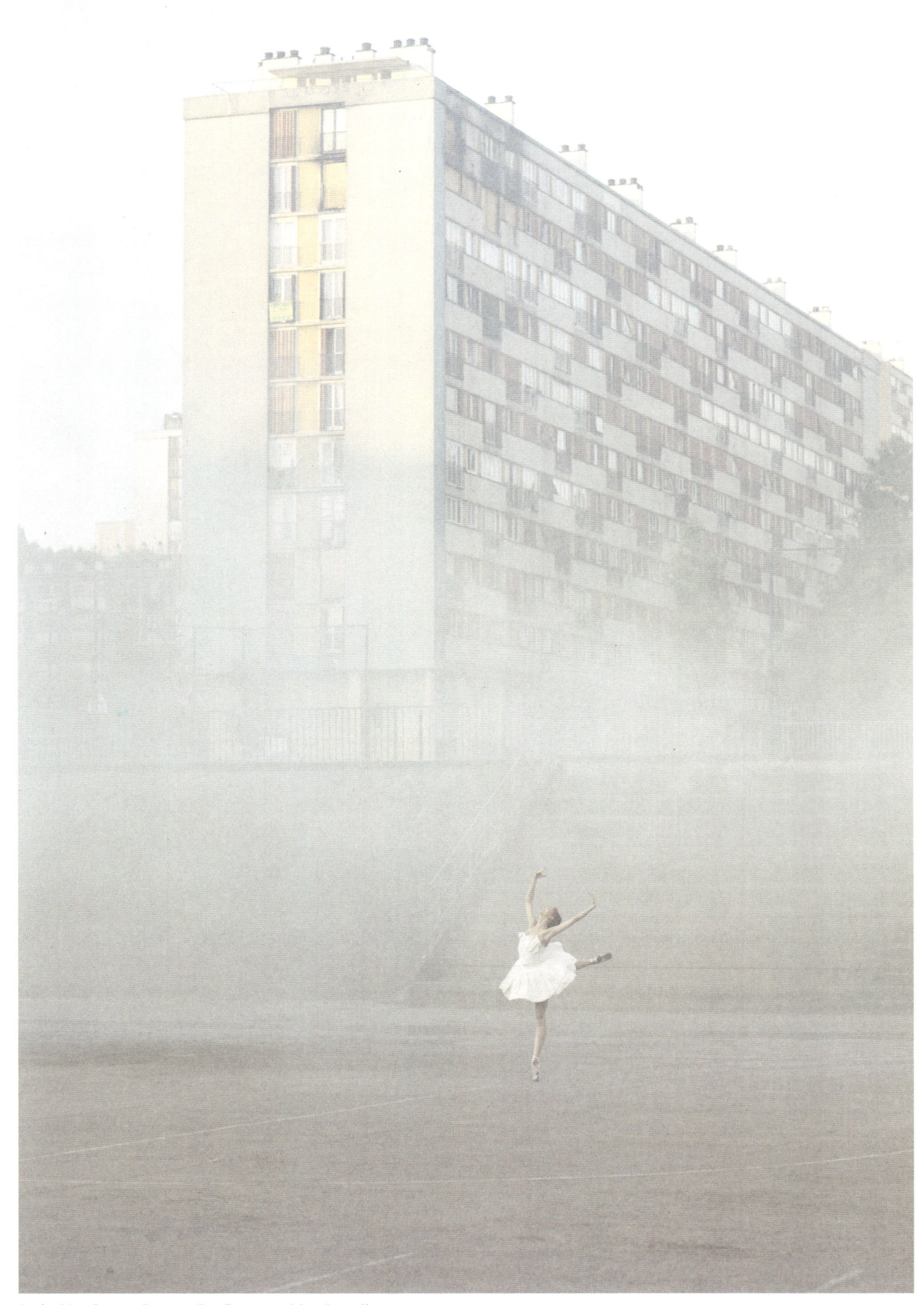

In the Mist, Lauren Lovette, Les Bosquets, Montfermeil, France, 2014

The Eye of New York City Ballet, *trompe l'oeil* photograph of eighty-one dancers from the New York City Ballet interacting with paper, 2014

'When the New York City Ballet invited me to create an installation, I decided to bring together all the dancers in the company – from the *corps de ballet* to the principals – in one image. I created this gigantic eye in paper, where each of the dance movements sculpts a little bit of the eye, and in which it's impossible to recognize the hierarchy. This image was pasted on the promenade of the Lincoln Center, and in order to see it, people from the orchestra stalls had to go up to balcony – once again reversing the hierarchy!' – JR

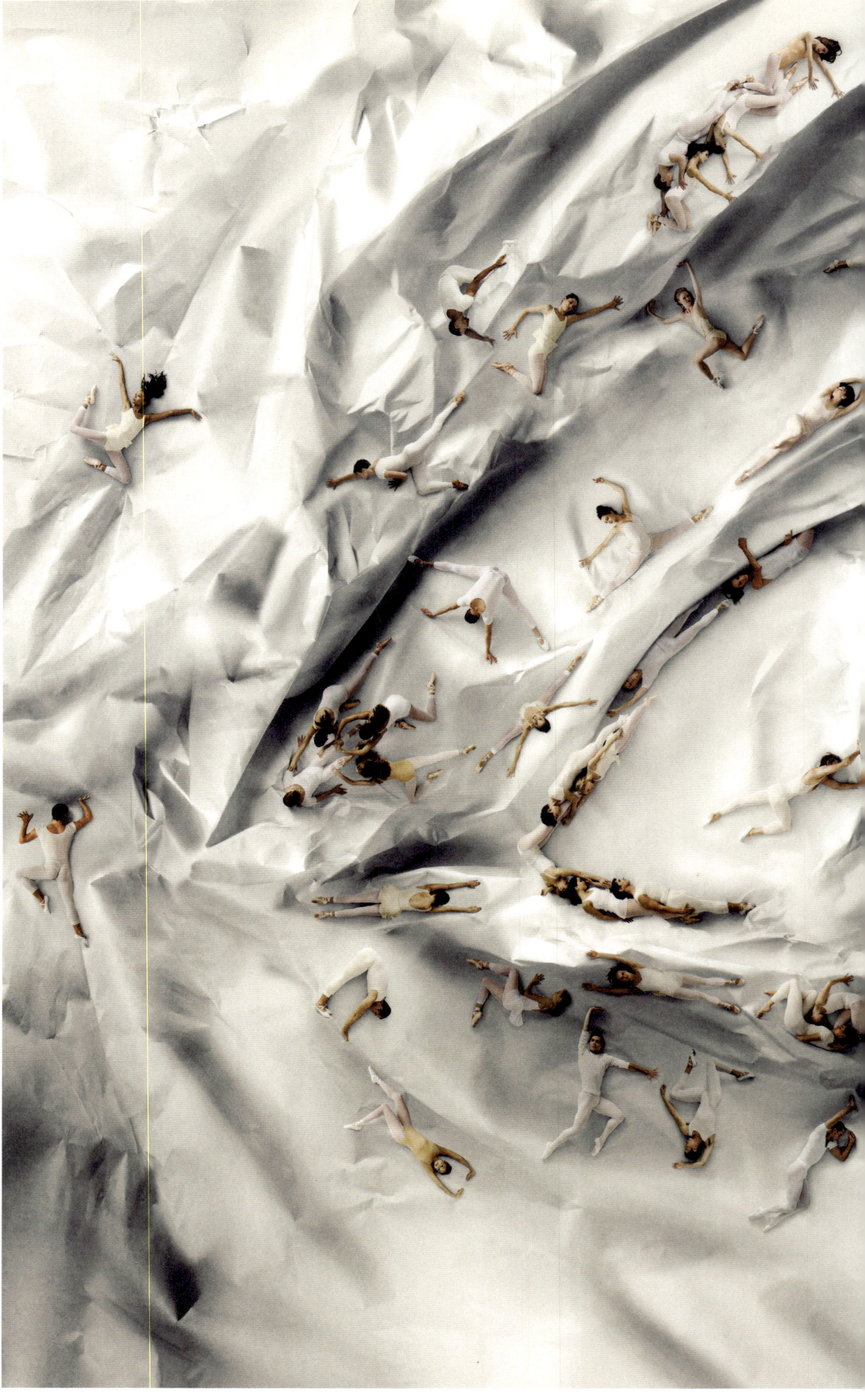

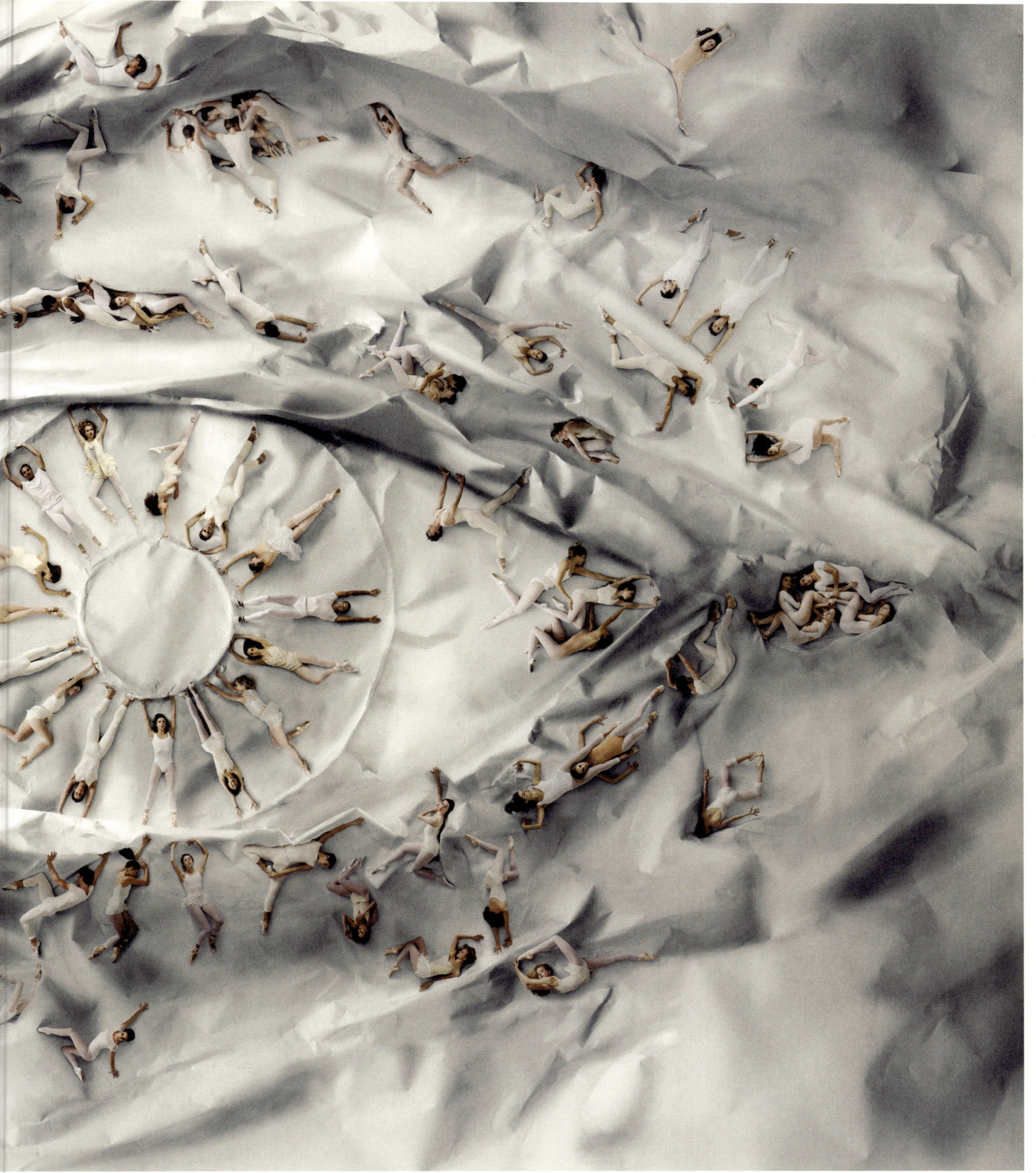

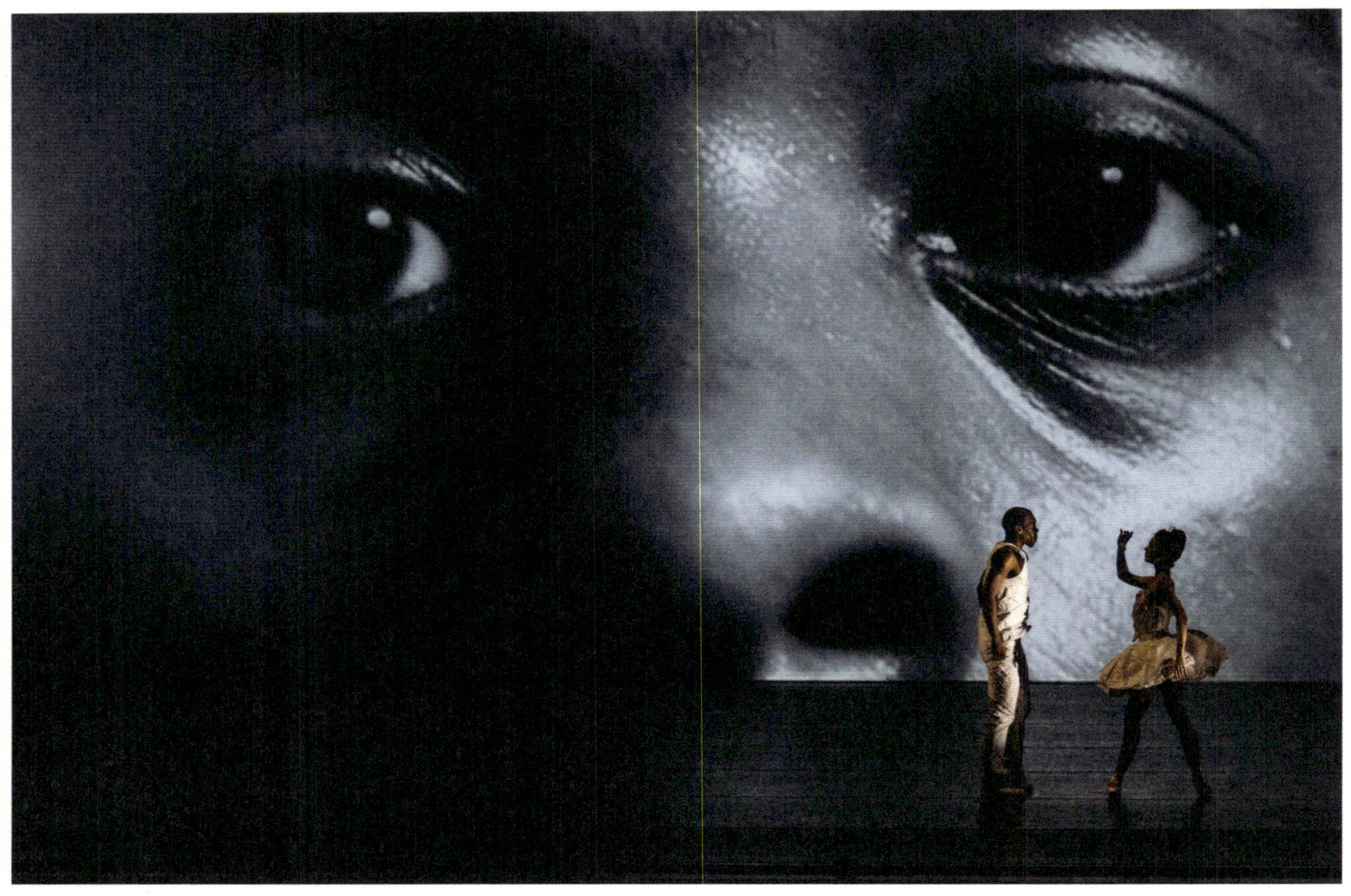

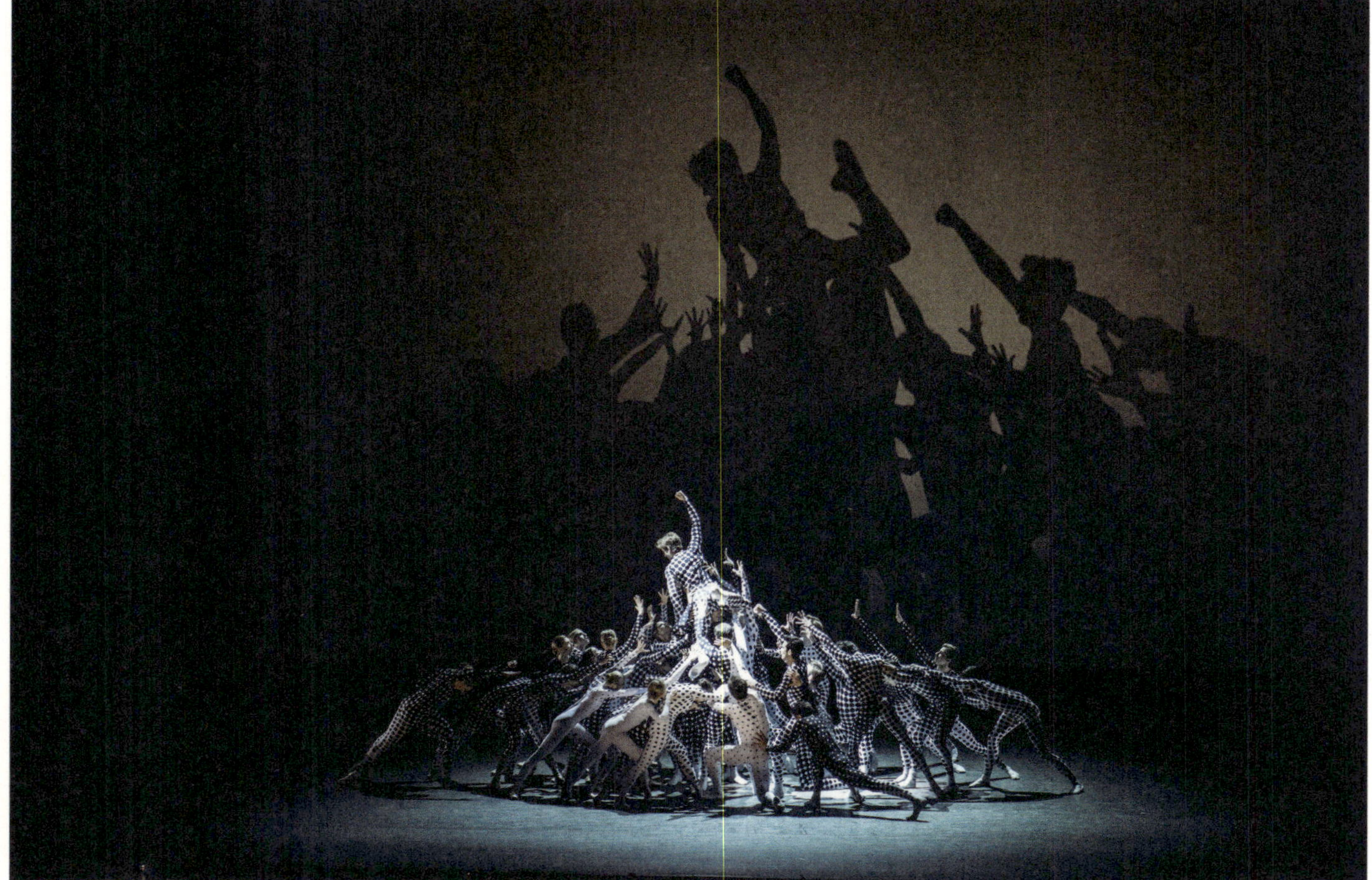

Scenes from 'Les Bosquets' ballet, created in collaboration with the New York City Ballet, with original music by Woodkid, on stage at the Lincoln Center, New York, 2014

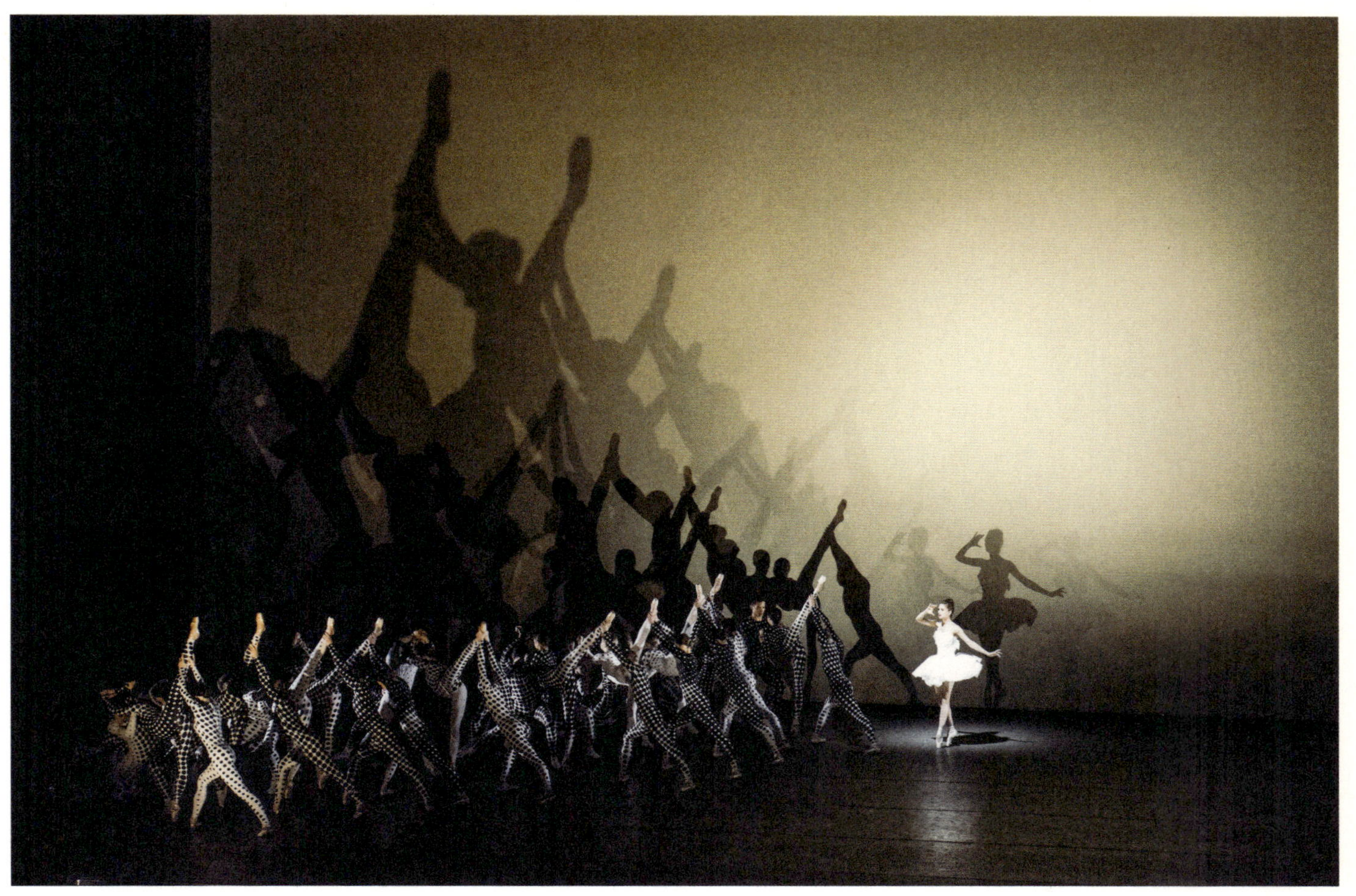

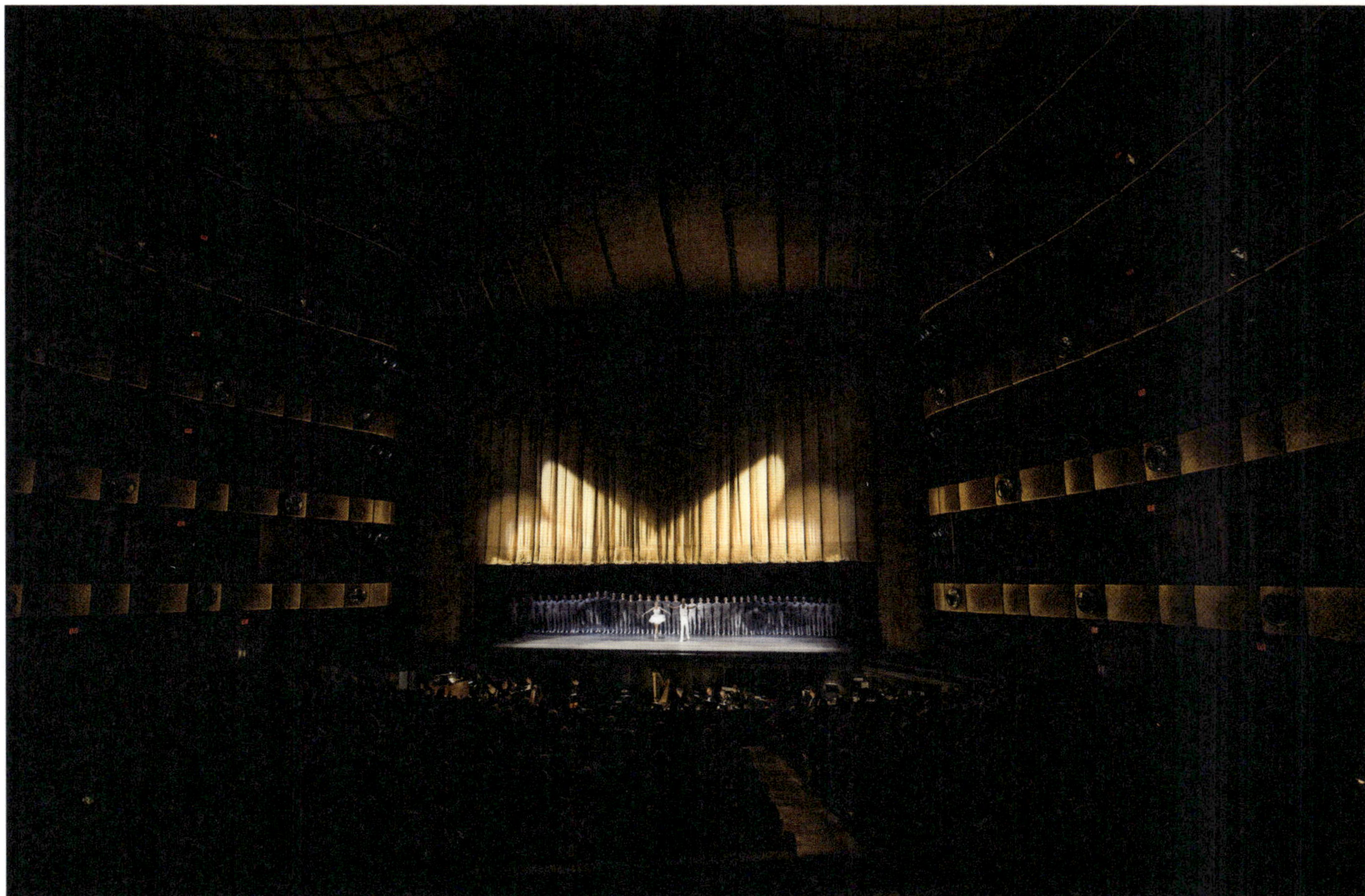

Scenes from 'Les Bosquets' ballet, created in collaboration with the New York City Ballet, with original music by Woodkid, on stage at the Lincoln Center, New York, 2014

(overleaf) Dancers from the Paris Opera Ballet, on the roof of the Palais Garnier, Paris, 2014

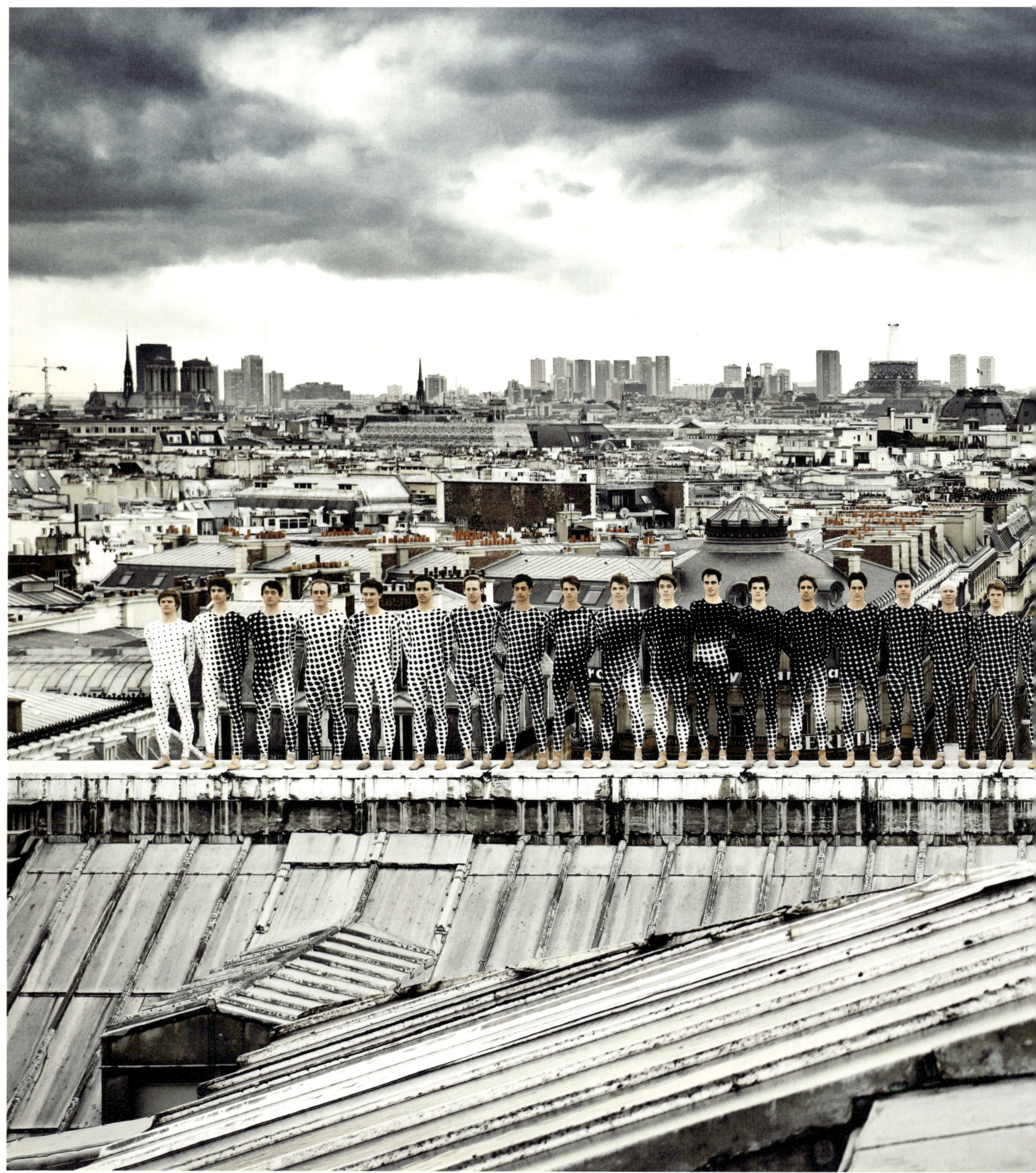

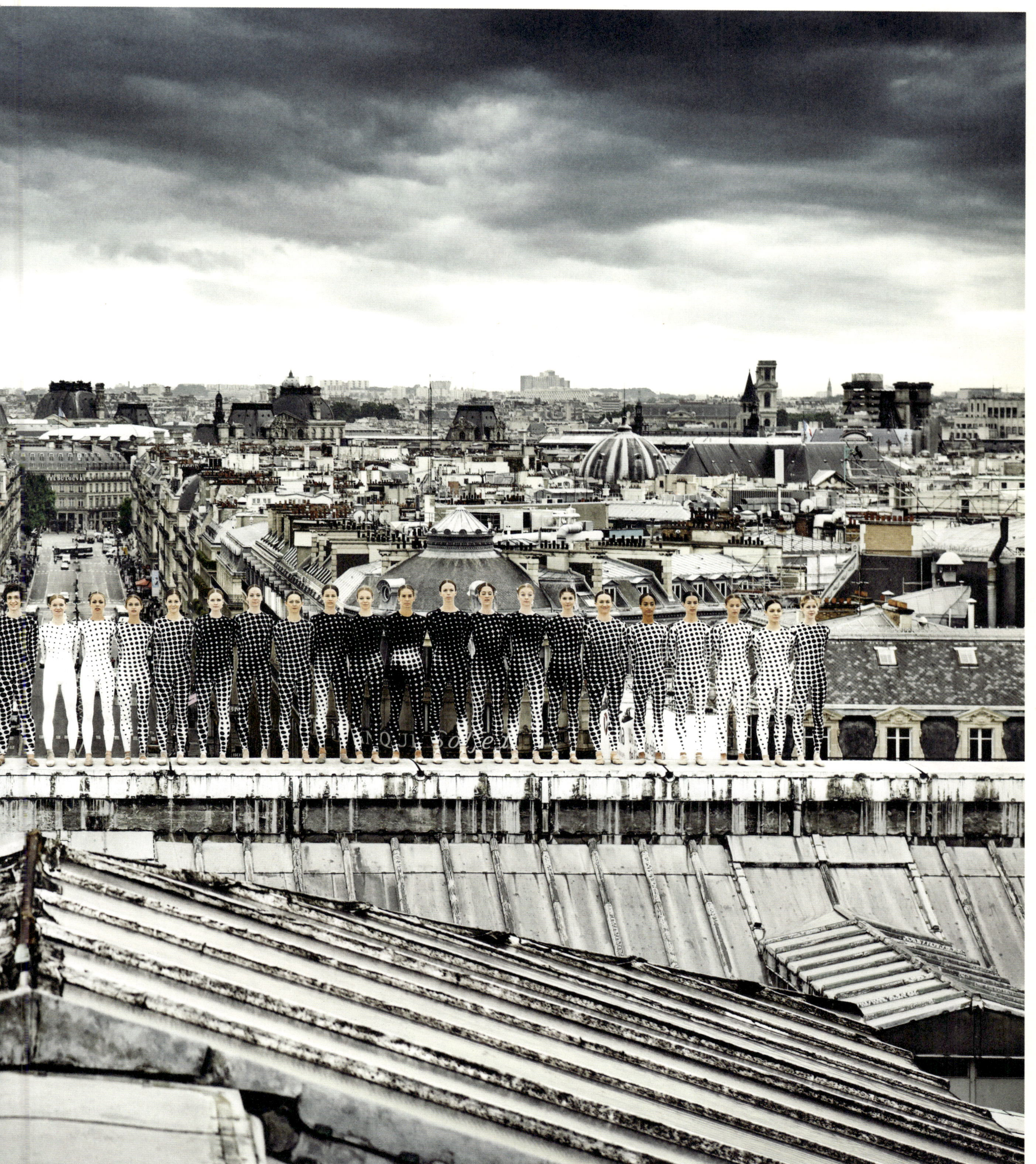

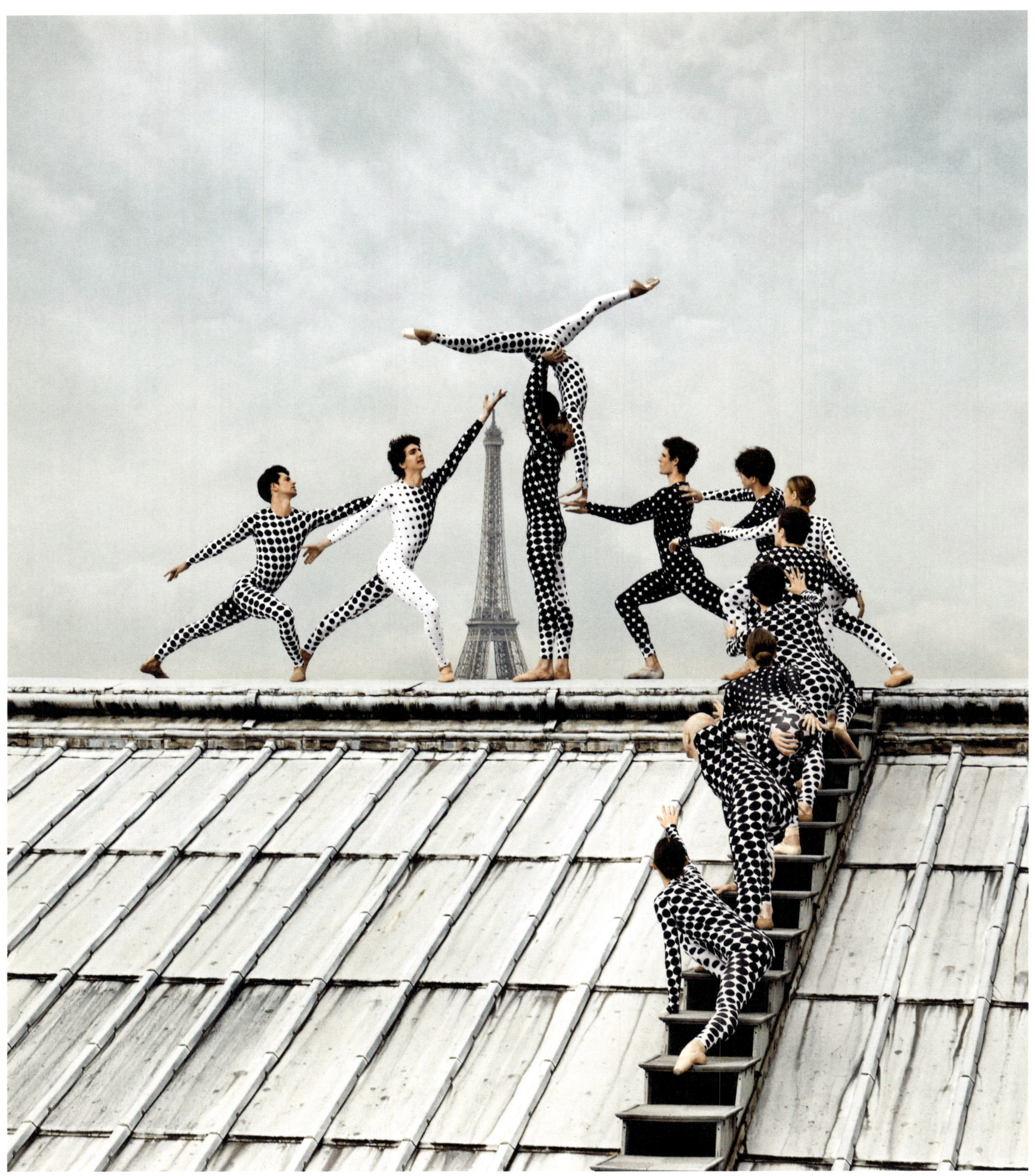

Dancers from the Paris Opera Ballet, on the roof of the Palais Garnier, Paris, 2014

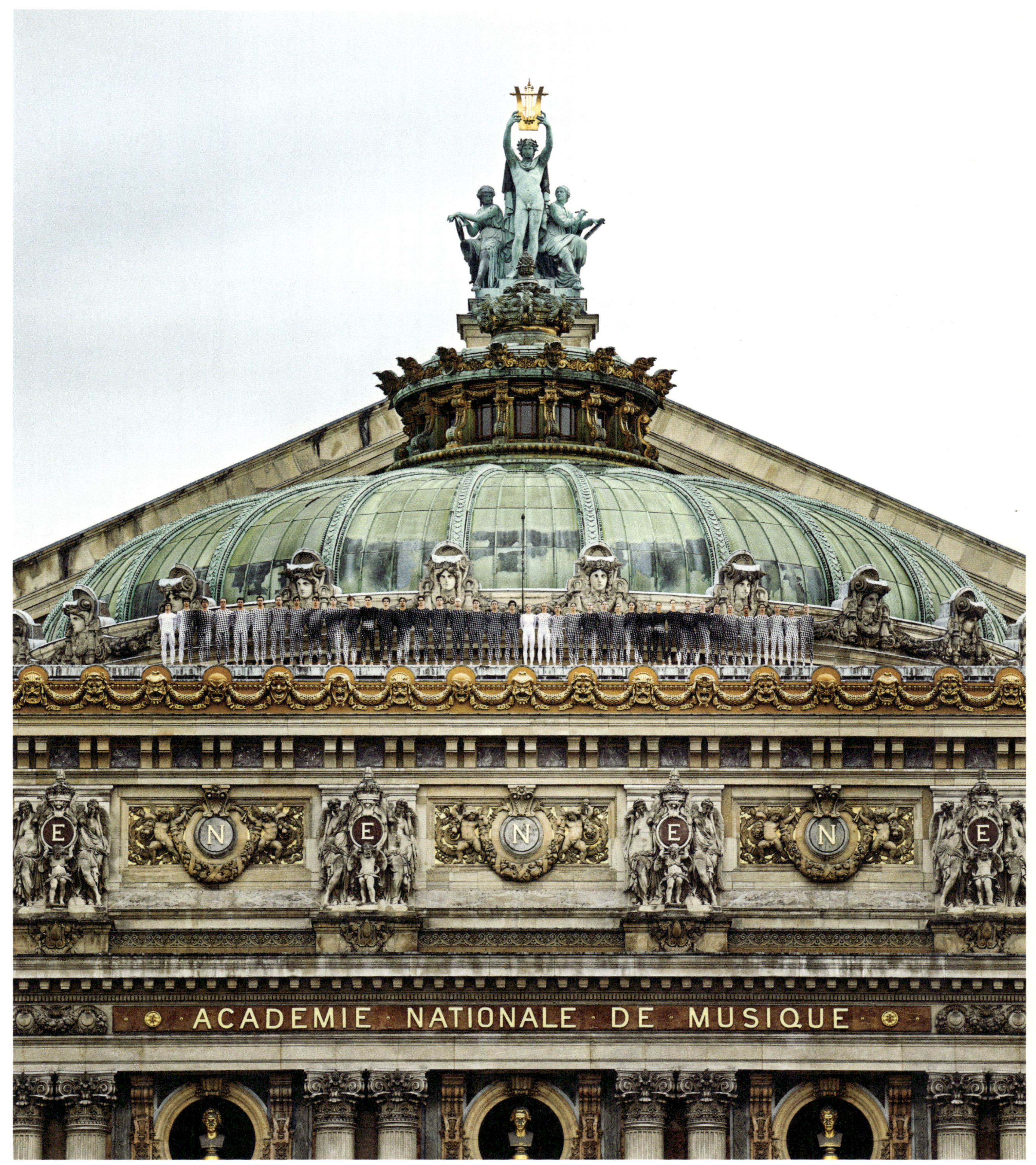

Dancers from the Paris Opera Ballet, on the roof of the Palais Garnier, Paris, 2014

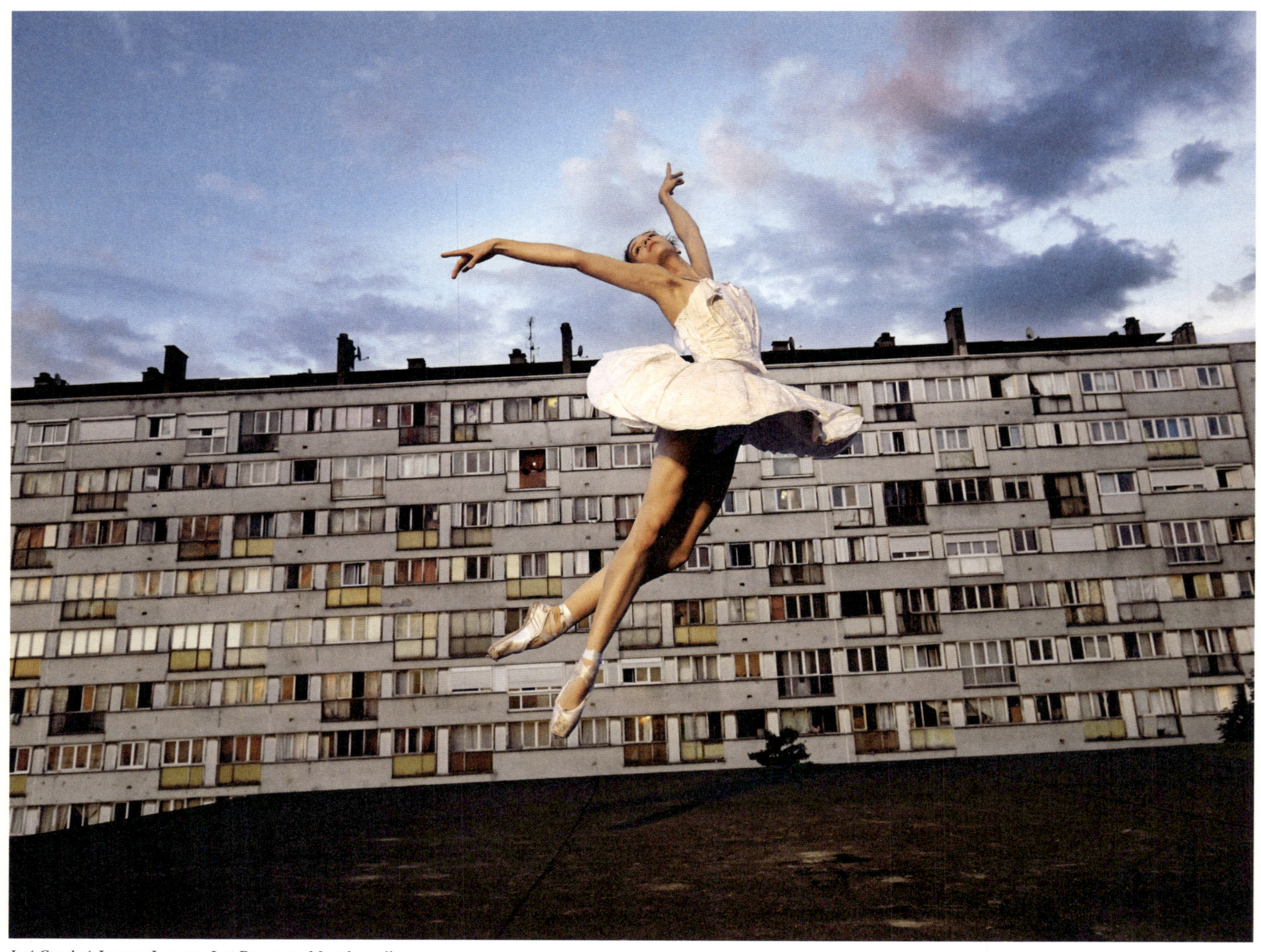

Jeté Cambré, Lauren Lovette, Les Bosquets, Montfermeil, France, 2014

'After choreographing a short ballet with the New York City Ballet based on the story of the riots in the French suburbs in 2005 and on the story of Ladj Ly who used his camera as a weapon during the riots, I decided to bring dancers from the New York City Ballet and the Paris Opera Ballet to dance in Les Bosquets, the very place the riots happened. After ten years of work here, it was a gift from the inhabitants to be able to shoot the ballet in the streets, because it has always been very complicated to shoot films in this neighbourhood.' – JR

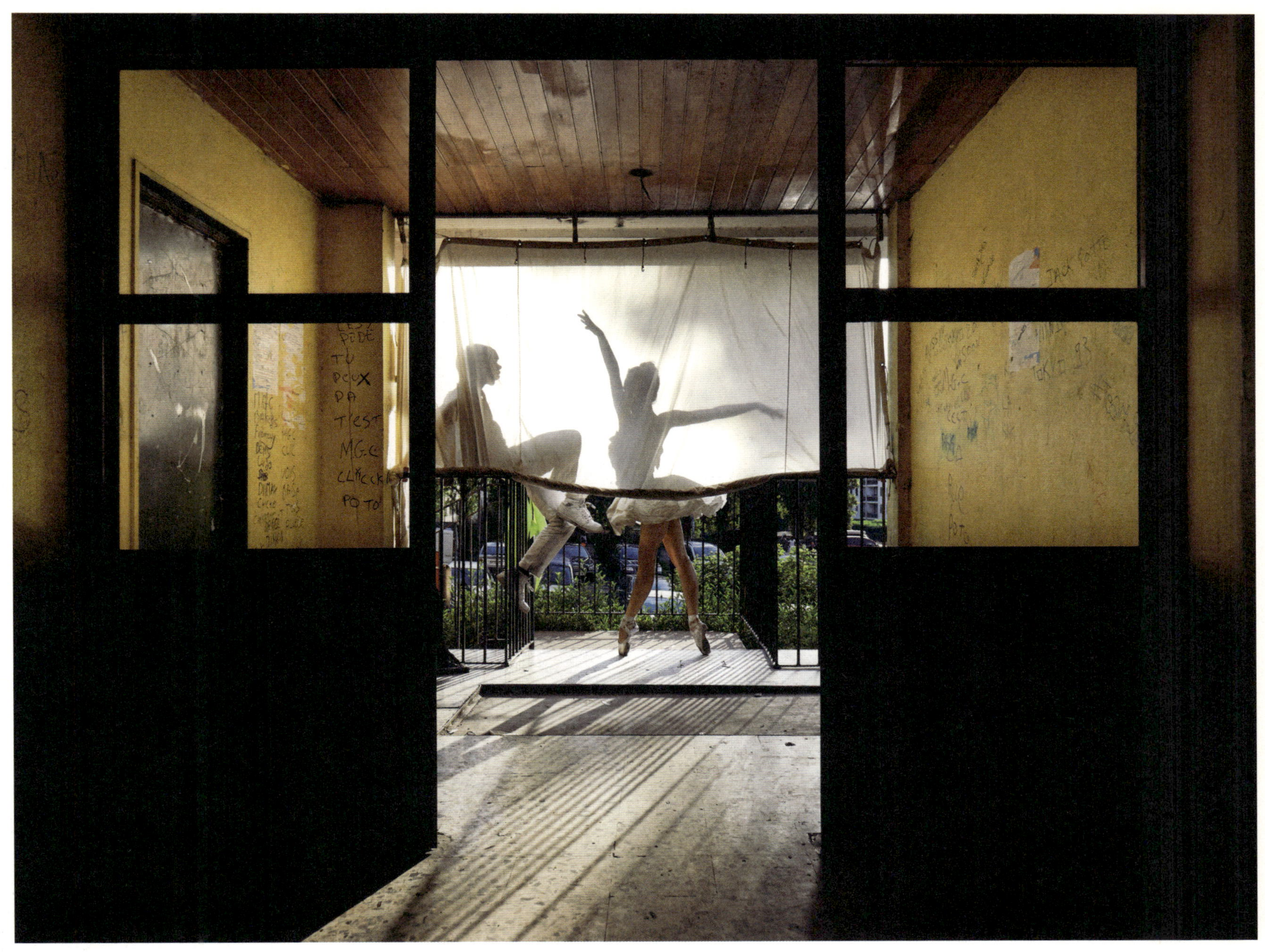

Lauren Lovette and Lil Buck's Silhouettes,
Les Bosquets, Montfermeil, France, 2014

The Ballerina in Containers, Le Havre, France, 2014

'When we were in Le Havre pasting the container ship for *Women Are Heroes* in 2014, the dockers helped us in an incredible way. During that action, one day, dancers from the Paris Opera Ballet came to help us paste. The dockers built this wall of containers, and we put this ballerina in the middle of all the steel.' – JR

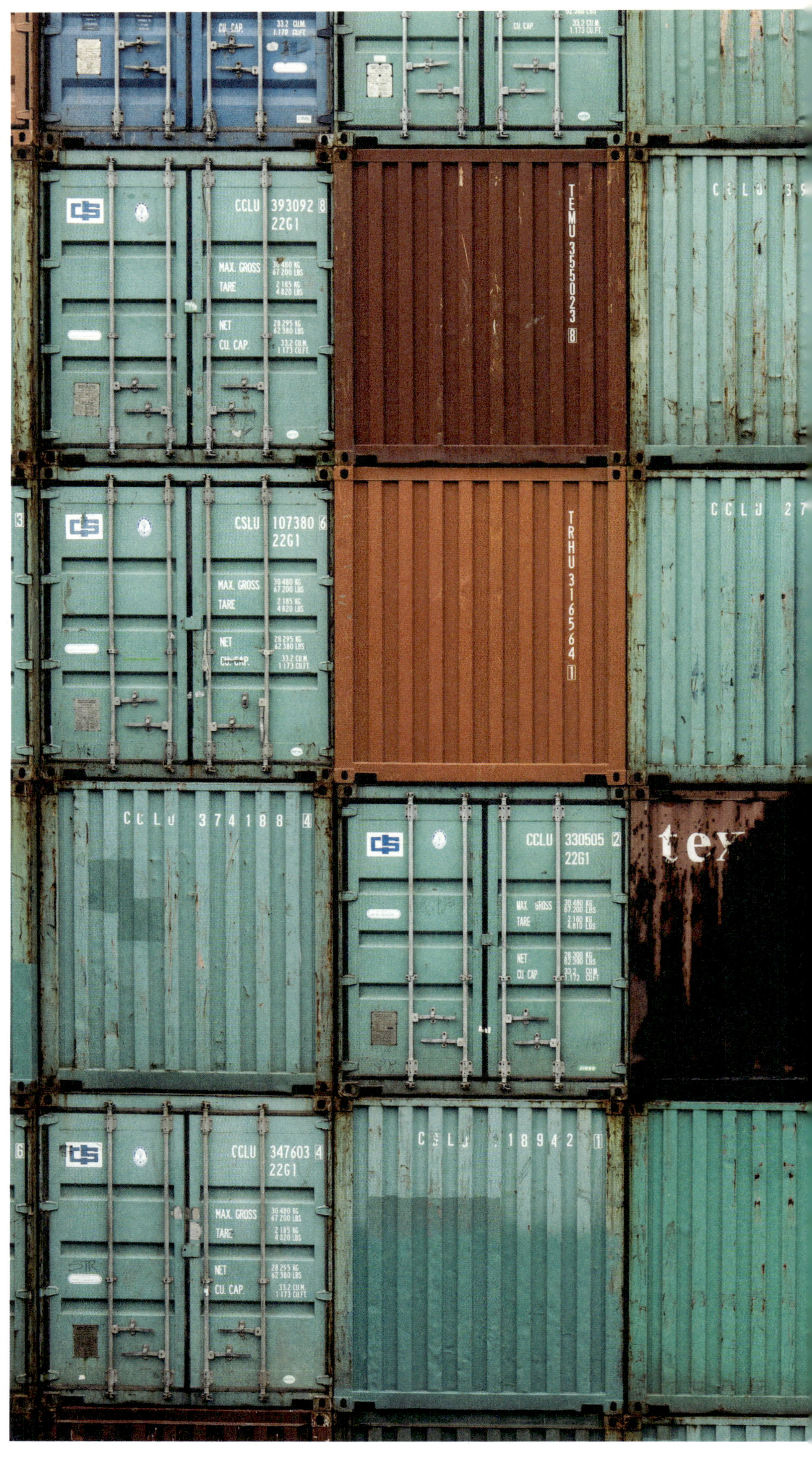

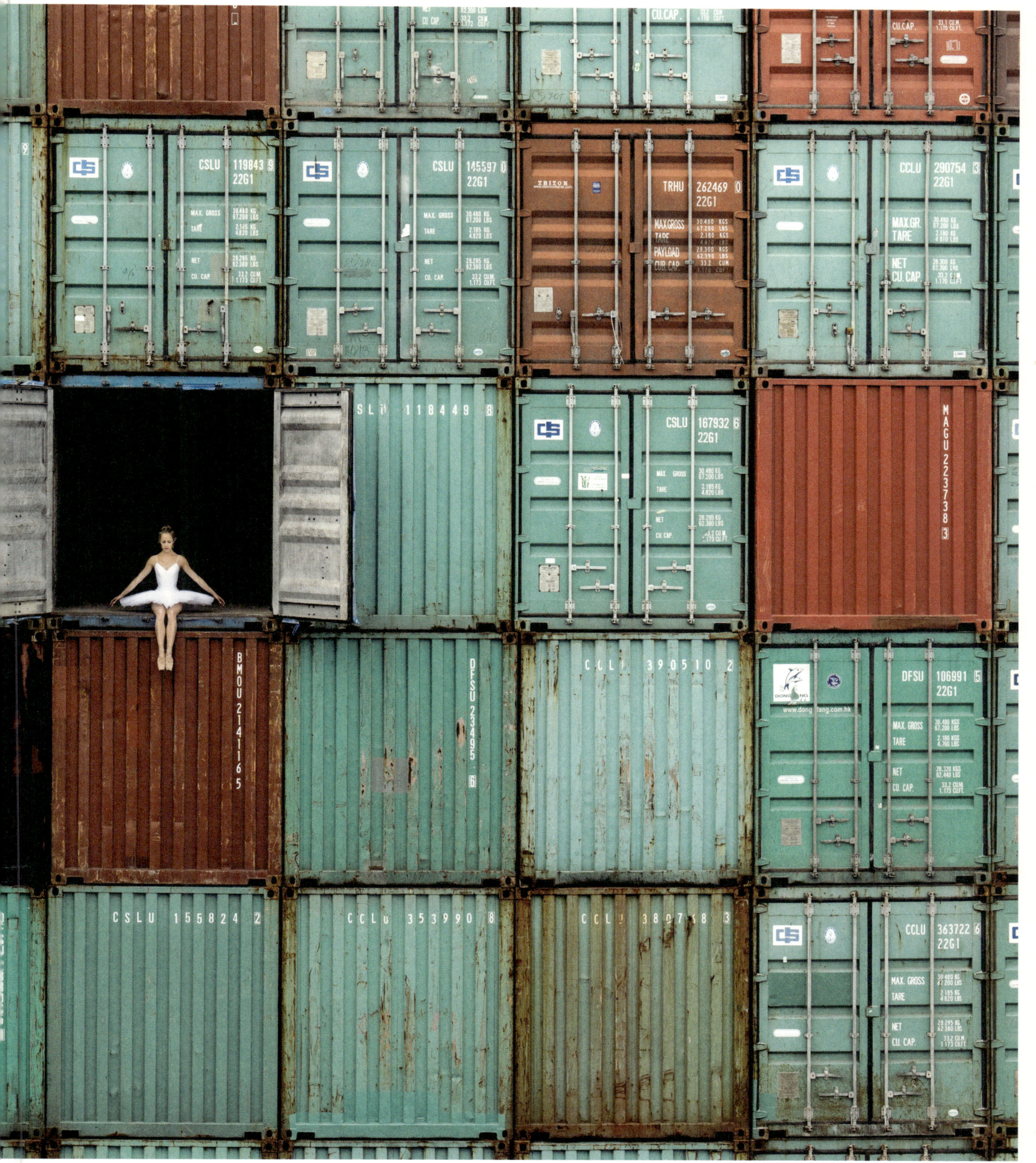
CSLU 119843 9
22G1
CSLU 145597 0
22G1
TRHU 262469 0
22G1
CCLU 290754 3
22G1
CSLU 167932 6
22G1
MAGU 223738 3
BMOU 214116 5
DFSU 106991 5
22G1
CSLU 155824 2
CCLU 363722 6
22G1

JR &

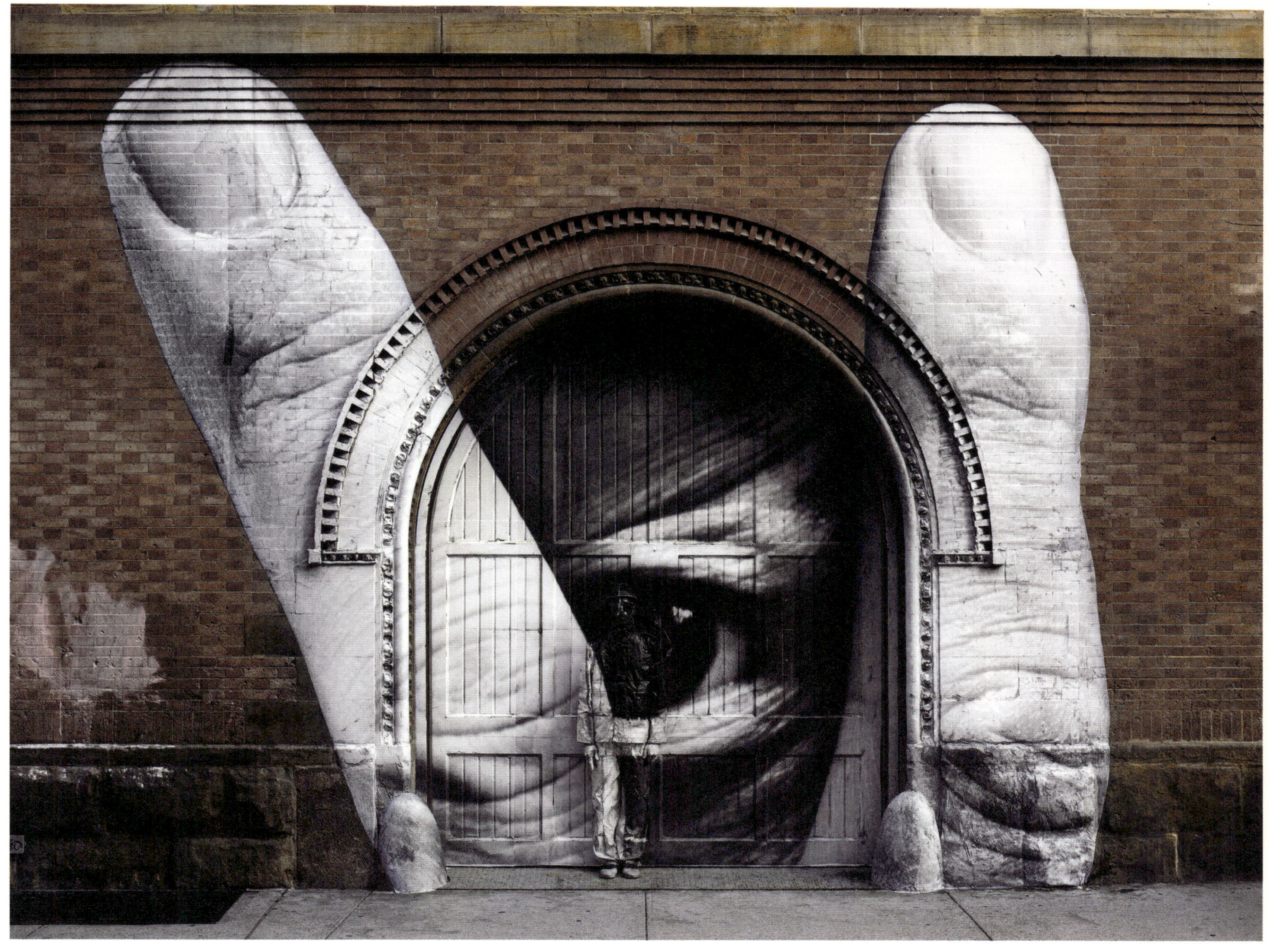

LIU BOLIN

In March 2012, Chinese artist Liu Bolin, also known as 'The Invisible Man', visited JR's studio in New York. A spontaneous collaboration ensued and JR became invisible in front of a pasting of a photograph of Liu Bolin's eye.

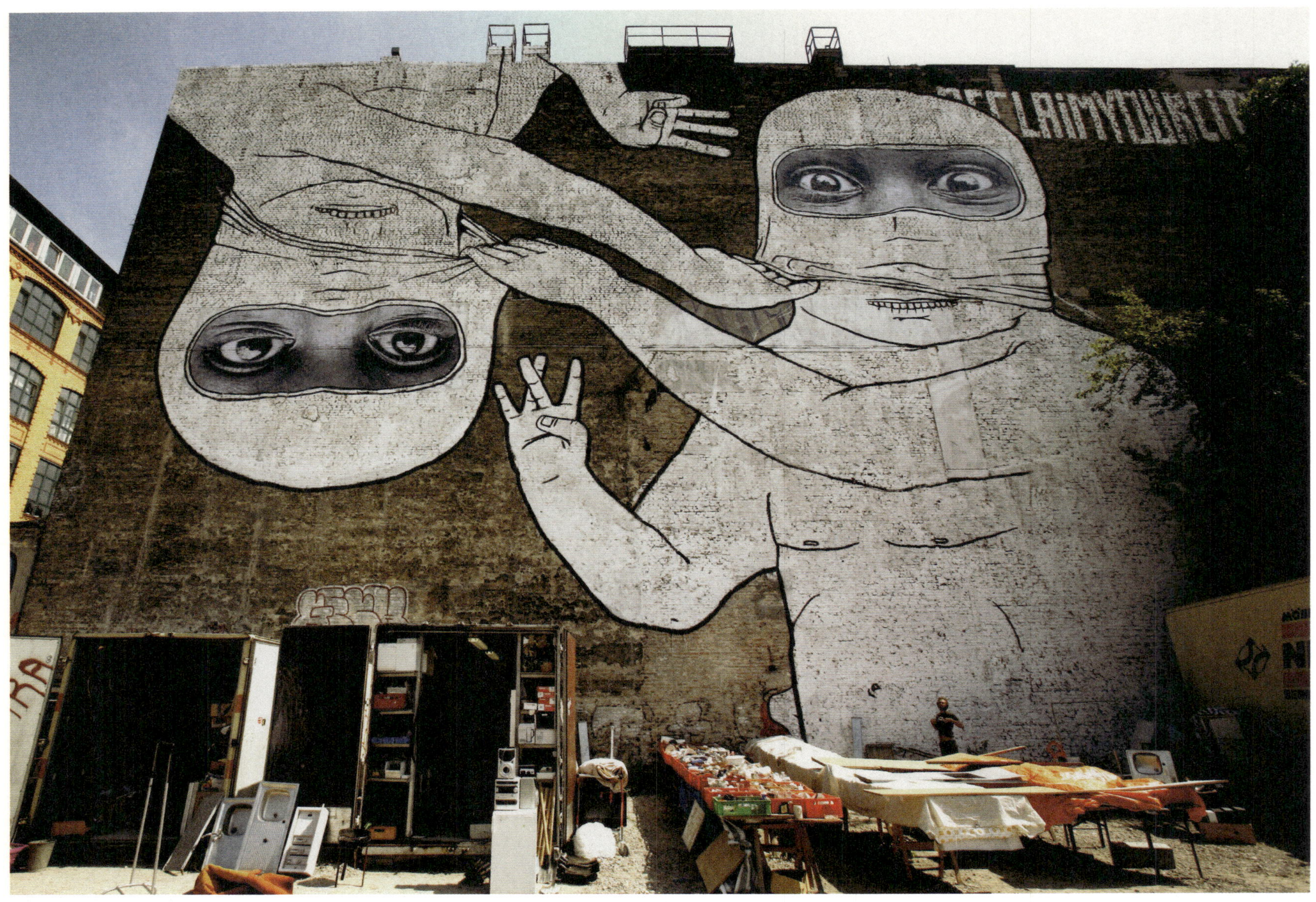

BLU

Blu is an Italian artist best known for his stop-motion videos of his graffiti. This collaboration in Berlin in 2008 was a reference to the division between East and West.

OS GÊMEOS

Os Gêmeos are Brazilian graffiti artists and identical twin brothers. During a visit to JR's studio in 2012 they painted their iconic faces on the nails of on a 3-metre-long (10-foot-long) portrait pasted on Plexiglas from *Wrinkles of the City*.

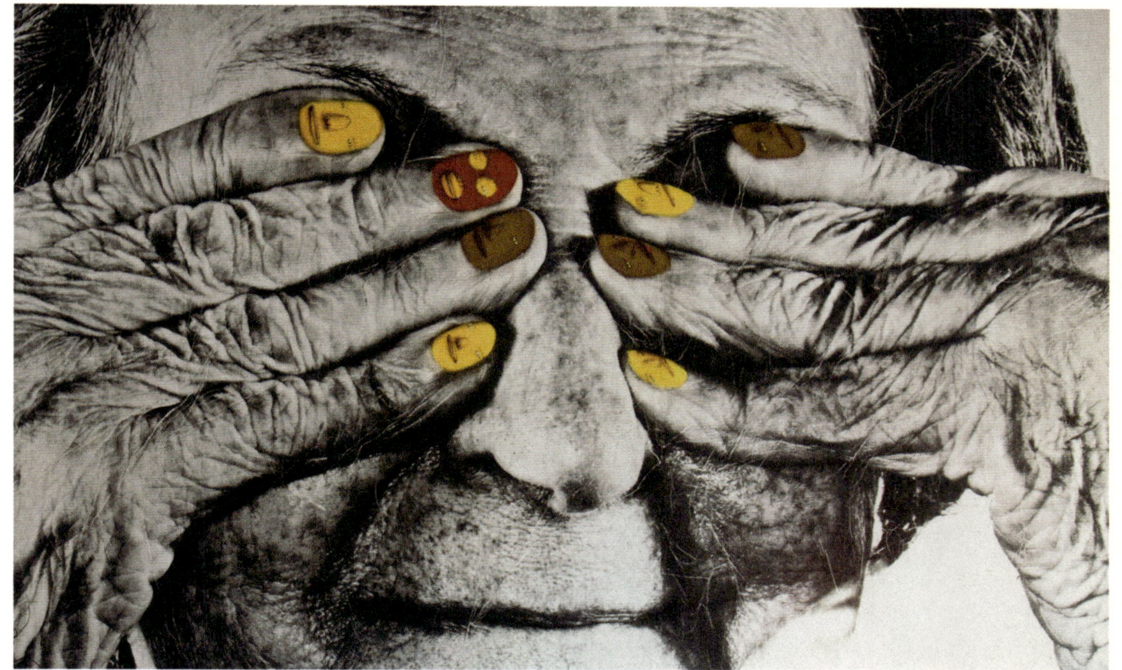

ANDRÉ

André (aka Monsieur André aka Monsieur A) is a graffiti artist from Paris. He paints a distinctive stick-figure character. JR and André were both in Miami for Art Basel, and created this collaboration.

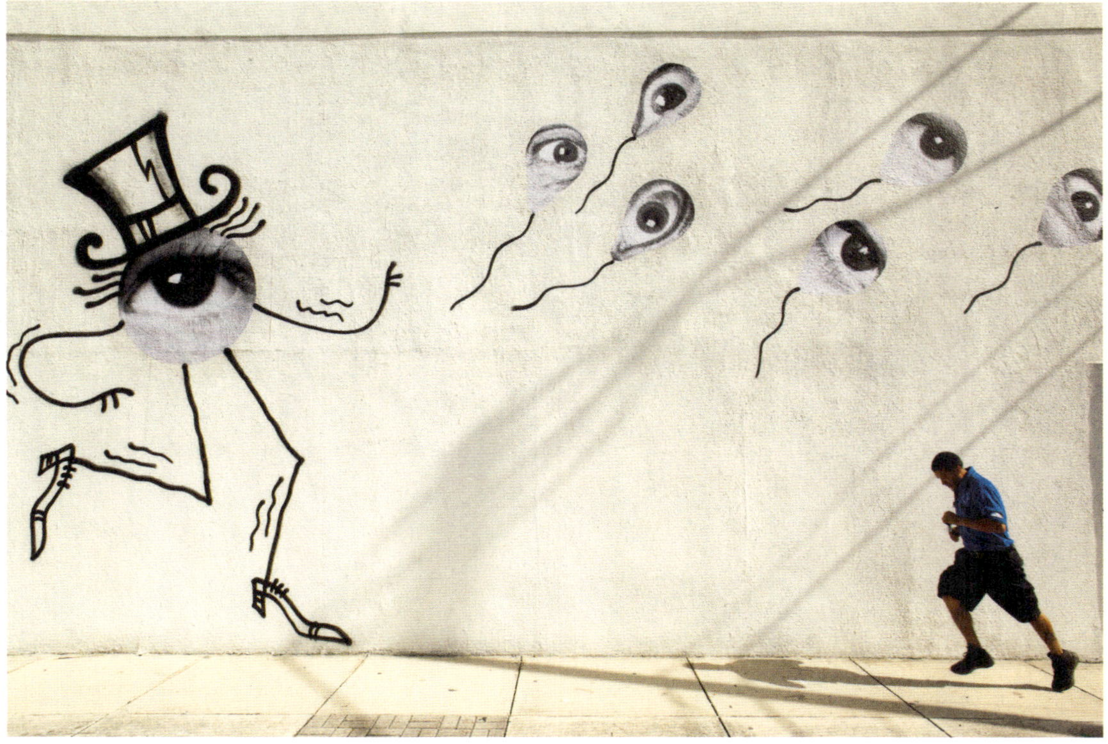

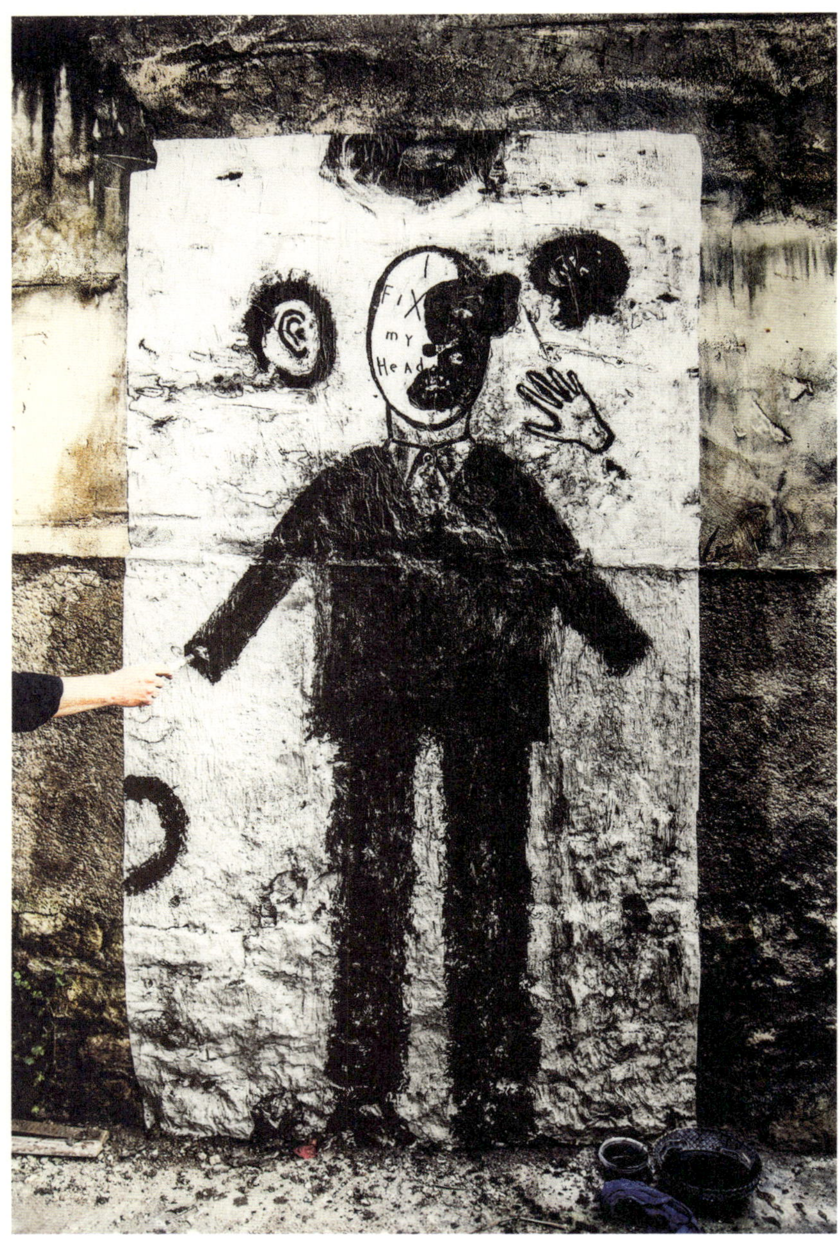

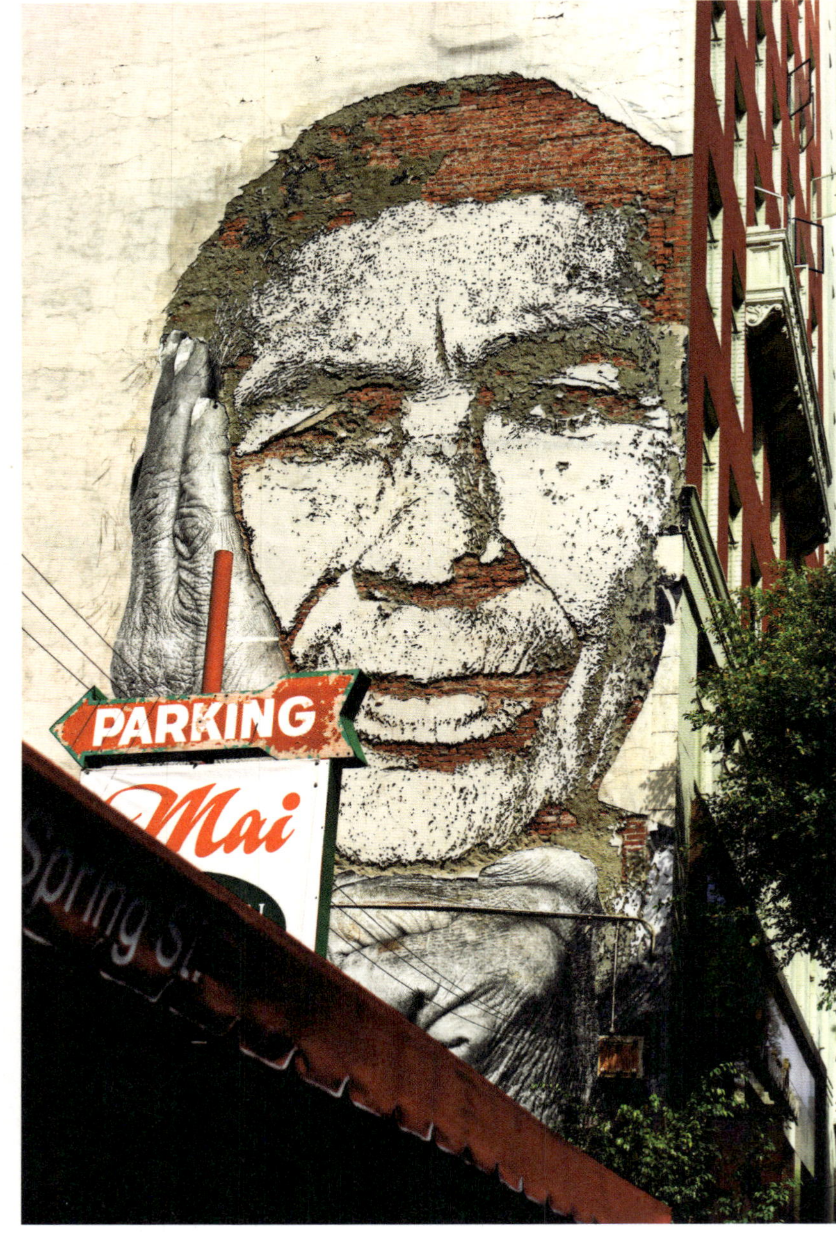

DAVID LYNCH

In 2014, JR pasted a David Lynch drawing on a wall. Lynch then continued to paint on it in situ. A lithograph was made of the photograph of the collaboration.

VHILS

Portuguese artist Alexandre Farto, aka Vhils, has developed a carving technique to interact with urban environments. In Los Angeles in 2010, he carved this portrait from *Women Are Heroes* directly into the walls, while JR pasted the hands.

ART SPIEGELMAN

(top) Art Spiegelman, *The Old Colossus*, 2015, drawing over a photograph by JR, 61 x 81 cm (24 x 32 in)
(bottom) Art Spiegelman, *A Warm Welcome*, 2015, drawing over a photograph by JR, 61 x 81 cm (24 x 32 in)

Art Spiegelman is an American cartoonist, editor and comics advocate based in New York, best known for his graphic novel *Maus* (1991). He used original immigration stories from Ellis Island to draw over JR's photographs of the abandoned hospital, for the book *The Ghosts of Ellis Island* in 2015.

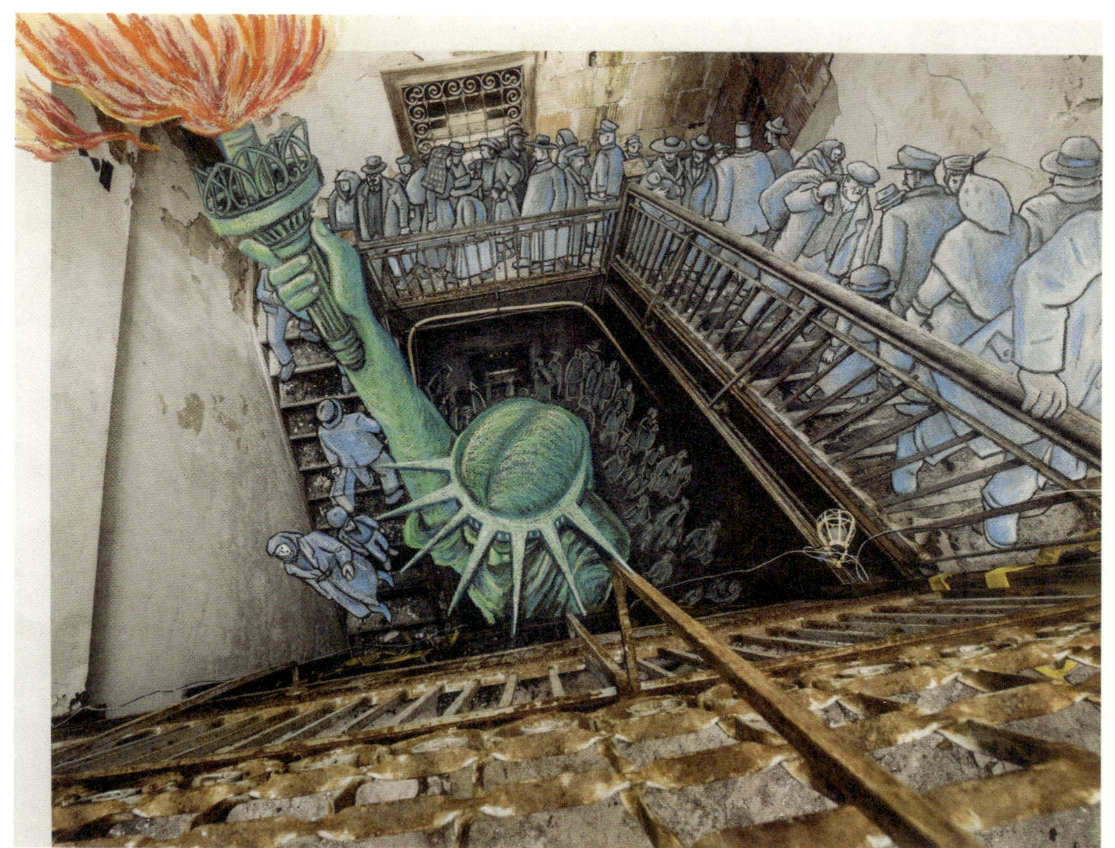

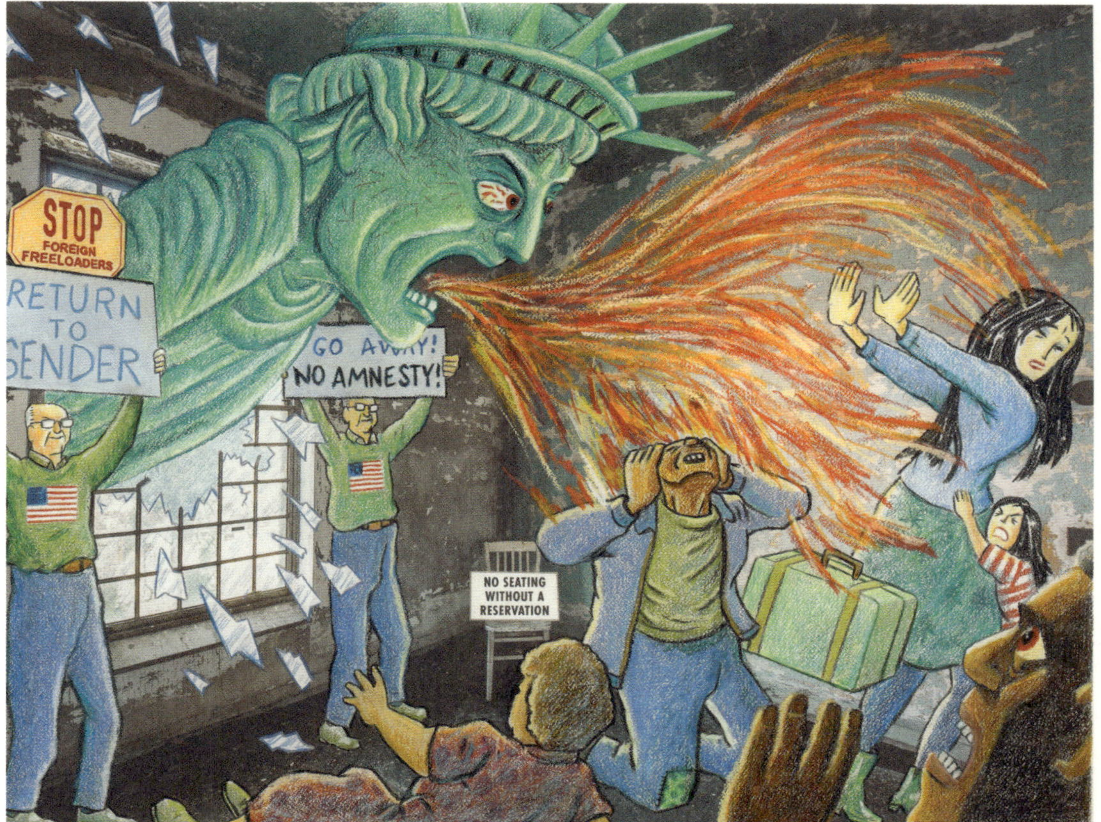

ARTWORKS AND EXHIBITIONS

JR's art mixes performance, installation, photography, sculpture, video and ballet. It is displayed in the open air and on the street for all to see, and is also shown in galleries and museums – both inside exhibition walls and outside on museum façades.

As opposed to the project pastings, JR's gallery artworks – as well as providing an encounter with his work on a different level – play an important role in the financing of his projects. The scale and ambition of his international pasting projects is determined by rigorous limits he imposes on himself. In order to remain free from specific agendas imposed by financiers, they have to be self-financed through the sale of physical artworks – photographs of the ephemeral installations, pastings on old wooden doors or inks on reclaimed barn wood. JR rejects branding, advertising and corporate sponsorship.

Paper remains JR's main medium, in galleries as well as in the streets. Pasted, transferred, crumpled or folded, paper can be mixed with many surfaces, giving the artist the ability to play with texture. JR prints on it, makes sculptures from it and photographs people interacting with it.

Seeing JR's work in the streets does not provide the viewer with any background information or the chance to see his work in light of his other projects. In addition to raising funding, gallery and museum exhibitions also open a door on JR's process to the public. JR held his first indoor exhibition in 2004 in a *loge de gardien* in Paris (the concierge lives in this room in Paris apartment blocks). Afterwards, his work was regularly shown in galleries in Paris, London and Shanghai, and in museum exhibitions – from a gigantic photobooth in the middle of Centre Pompidou, Paris, to a monumental pasting on the façade of the Tate Modern, London. Within a decade, JR had held his first museum solo exhibition at the Watari Museum for Contemporary Art in Tokyo, quickly followed by another at the Contemporary Arts Center in Cincinnati and at the Frieder Burda museum in Baden Baden.

(overleaf) *Inside Out, Eyes from Shanghai, China*, 2014,
Paper on reclaimed wood planks, dimensions variable

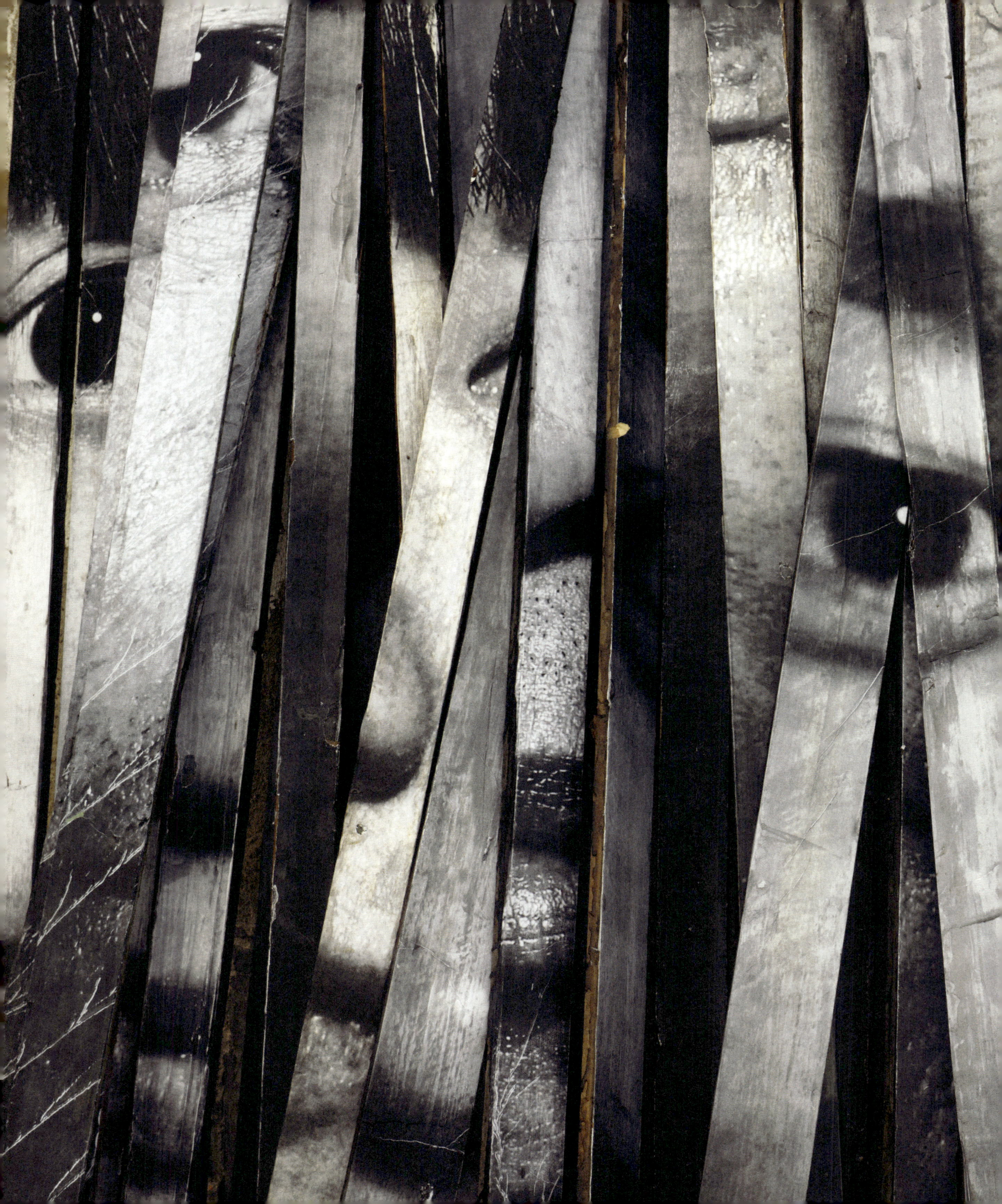

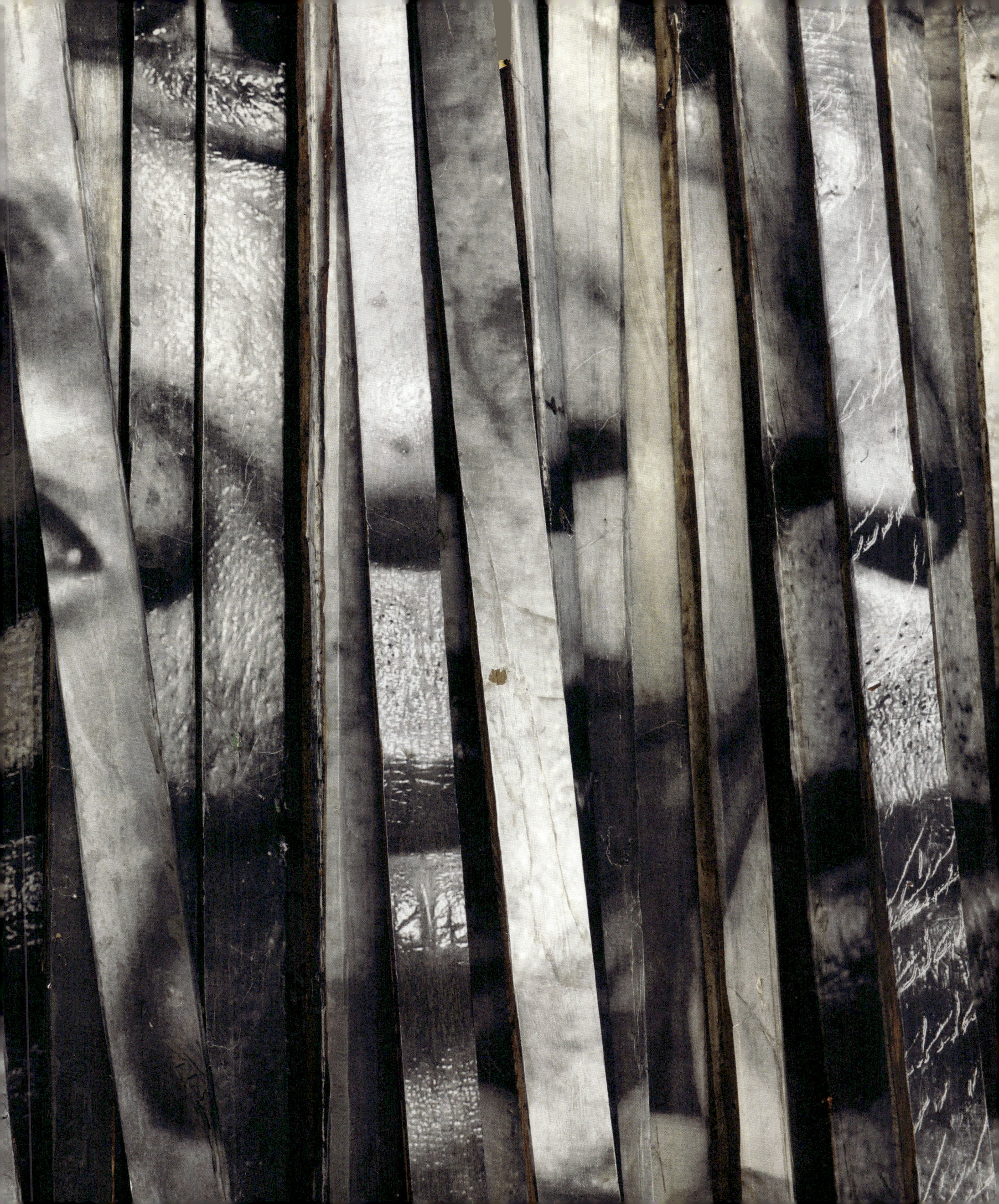

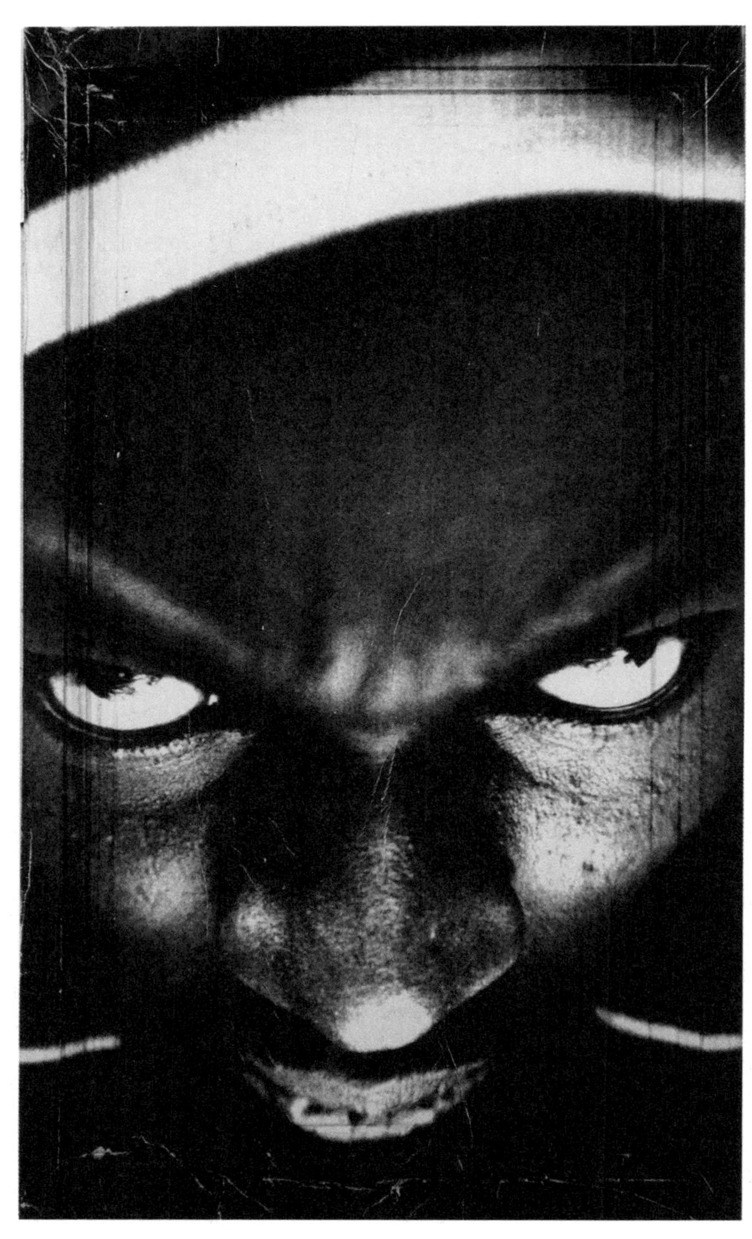

28 Millimètres, Portrait d'une Génération, Byron, 2005
Paper on wood panel, varnish, 100 x 50 cm (39½ x 19¾ in)

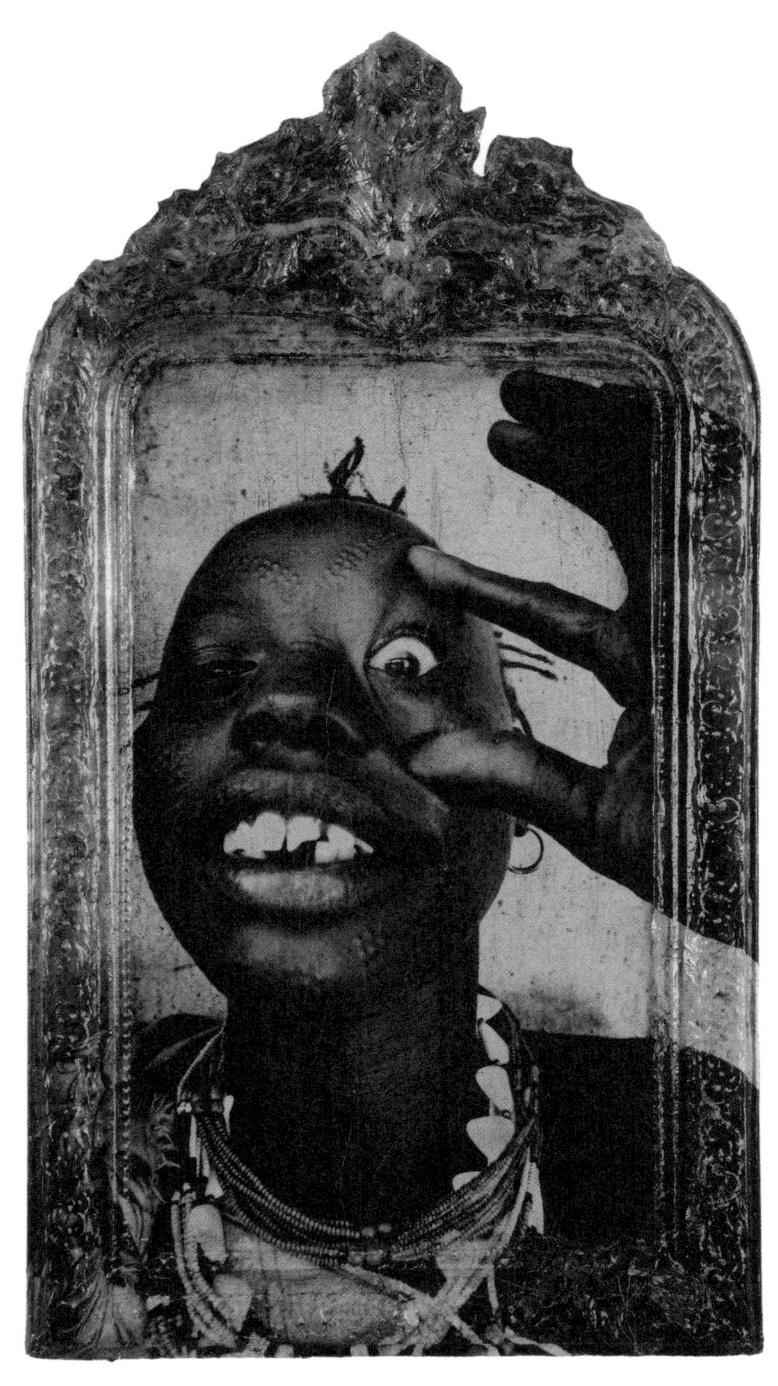

28 Millimètres, Women Are Heroes, Jane, Pibor, Sudan, 2007
Paper on mirror, varnish, 106 x 61 cm (41 ¾ x 24 in)

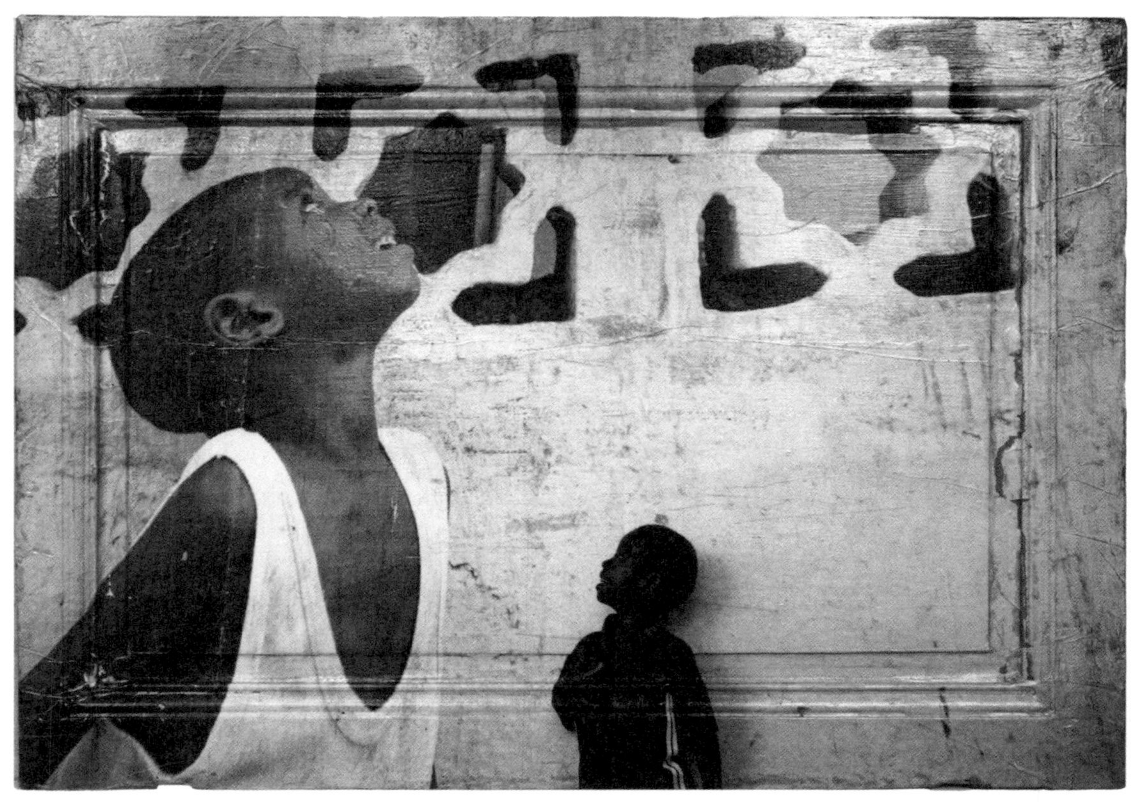

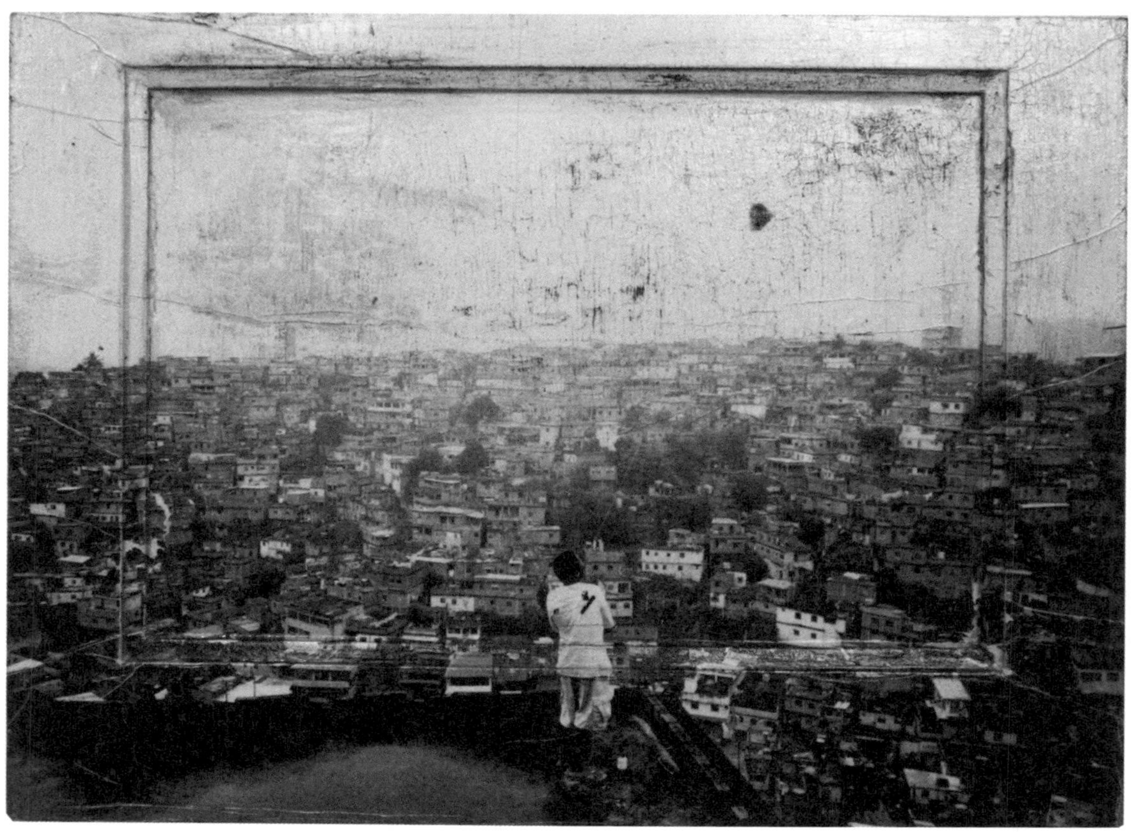

(top) *Ottis*, 2008
Paper on wood panel, varnish, 50 x 80 cm (19¾ x 31½ in)
(bottom) *Favela, Complexo do Alemão, Rio de Janeiro*, 2006
Paper on wood panel, varnish, 57 x 78 cm (22½ x 30¾ in)

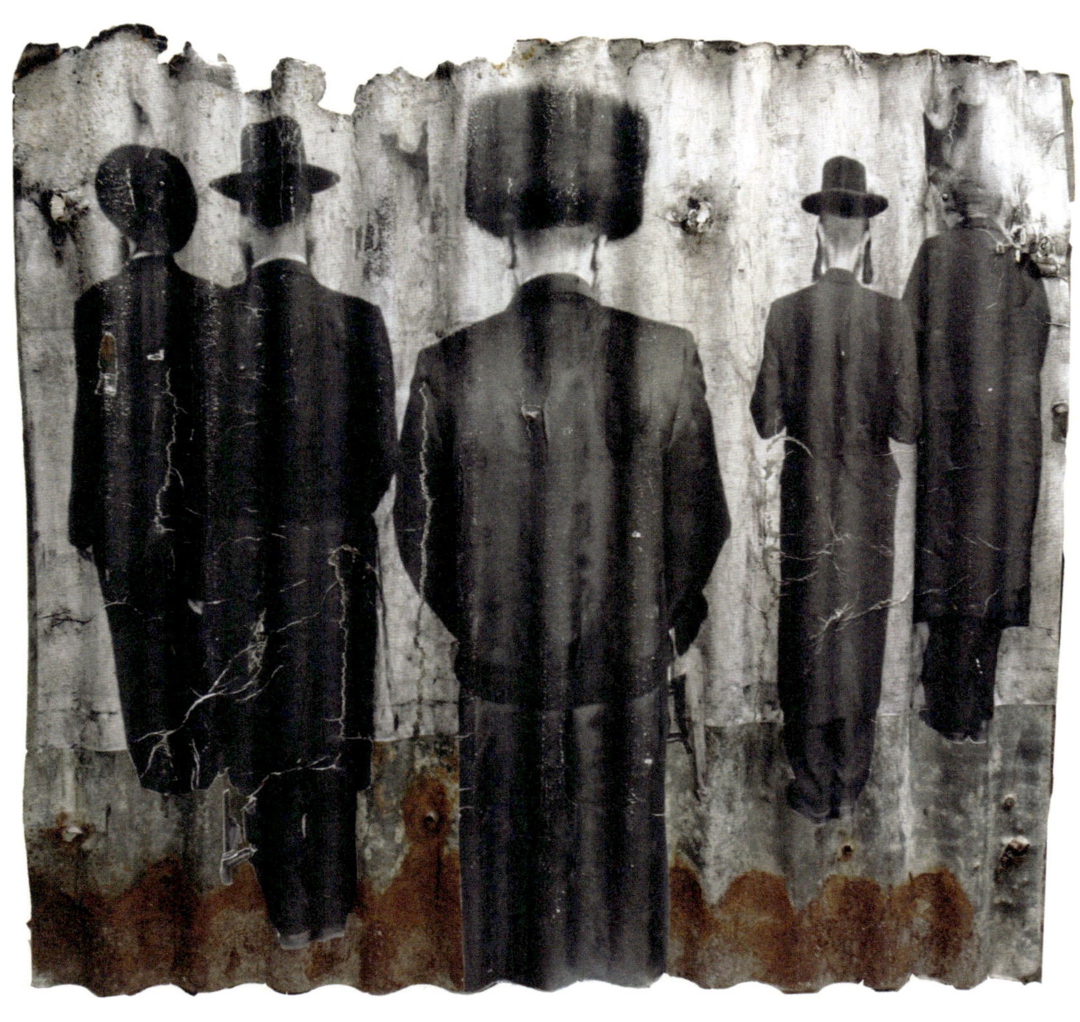

28 Millimètres, Face 2 Face, Kotel, Jerusalem, 2006/2007
Black-and-white print on paper, pasted on corrugated sheet, matt varnish, 91 x 82 cm (35 ¼ x 32 ¼ in)

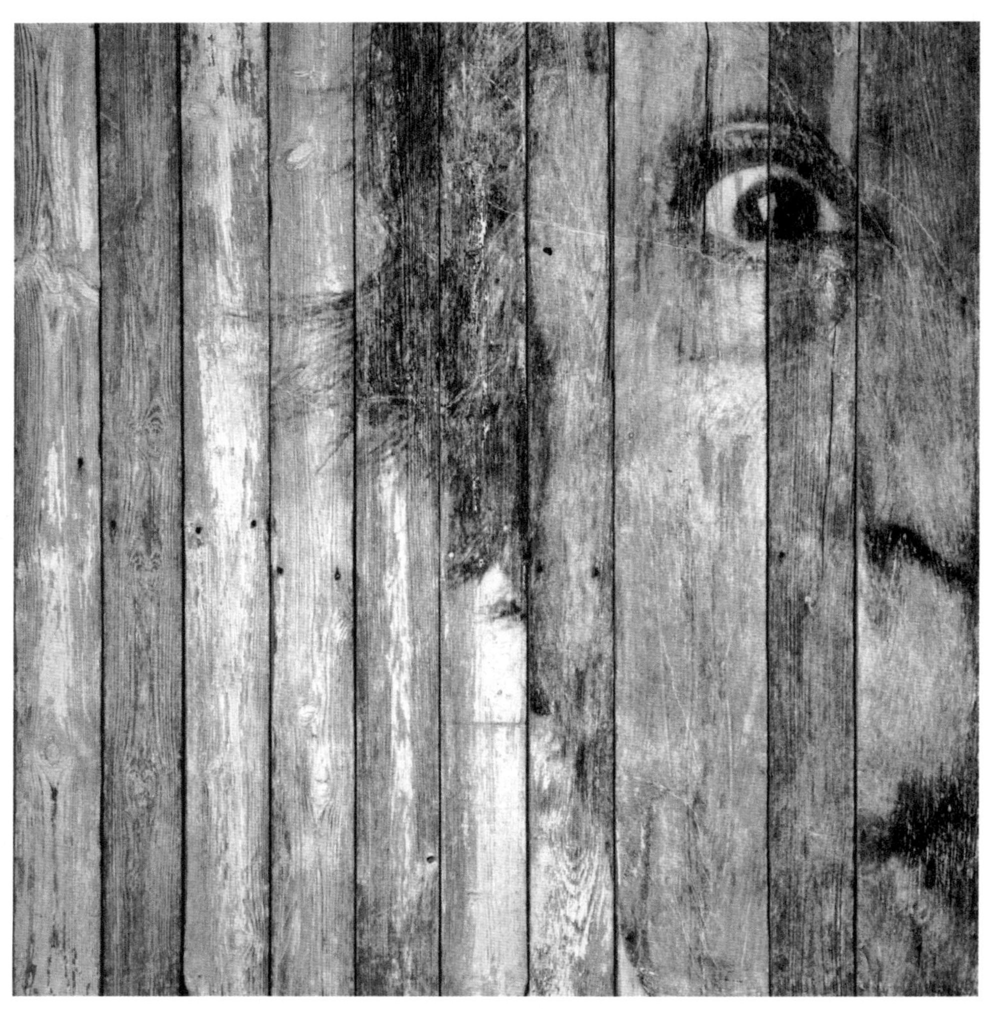

Wrinkles of the City, Los Angeles, Rita Guizulfo, USA, 2011
Ink on wood, 153 x 153 cm (60 ¼ x 60 ¼ in)

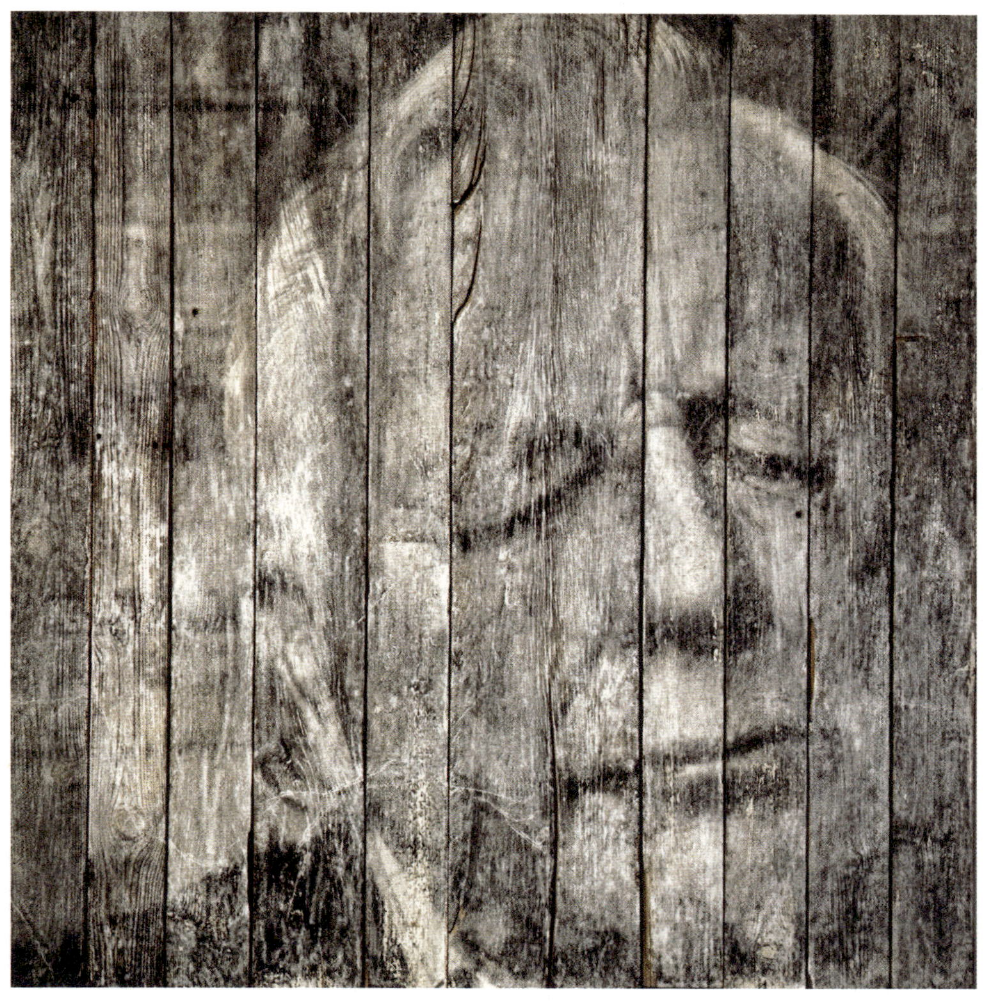

Wrinkles of the City, Los Angeles, Robert Evans eyes closed, USA, 2011
Ink on wood, 153 x 153 cm (60¼ x 60¼ in)

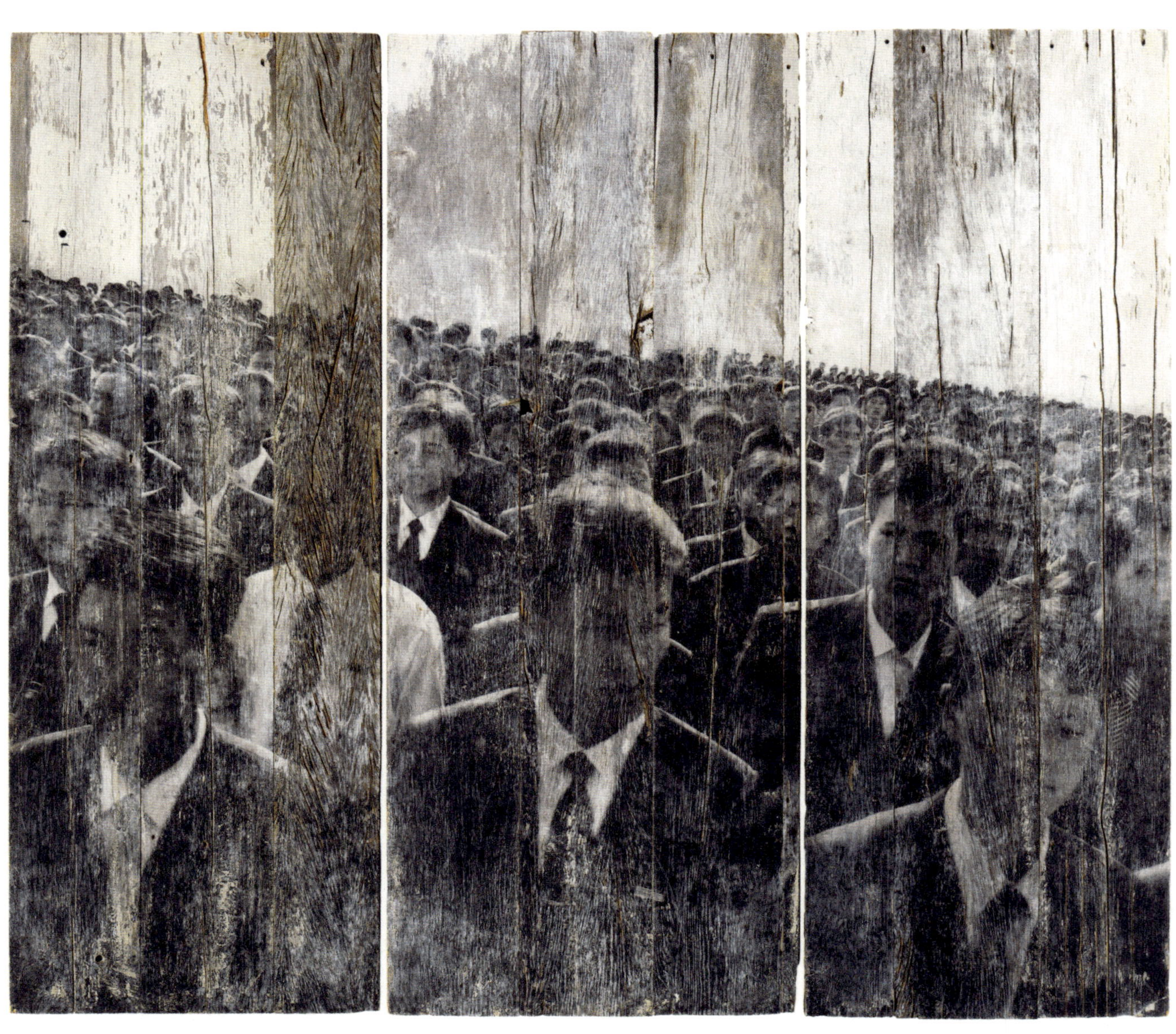

North Korea, Crowd, 2012, triptych
Ink on wood, each panel 217 x 81 cm (85 ½ x 32 in)

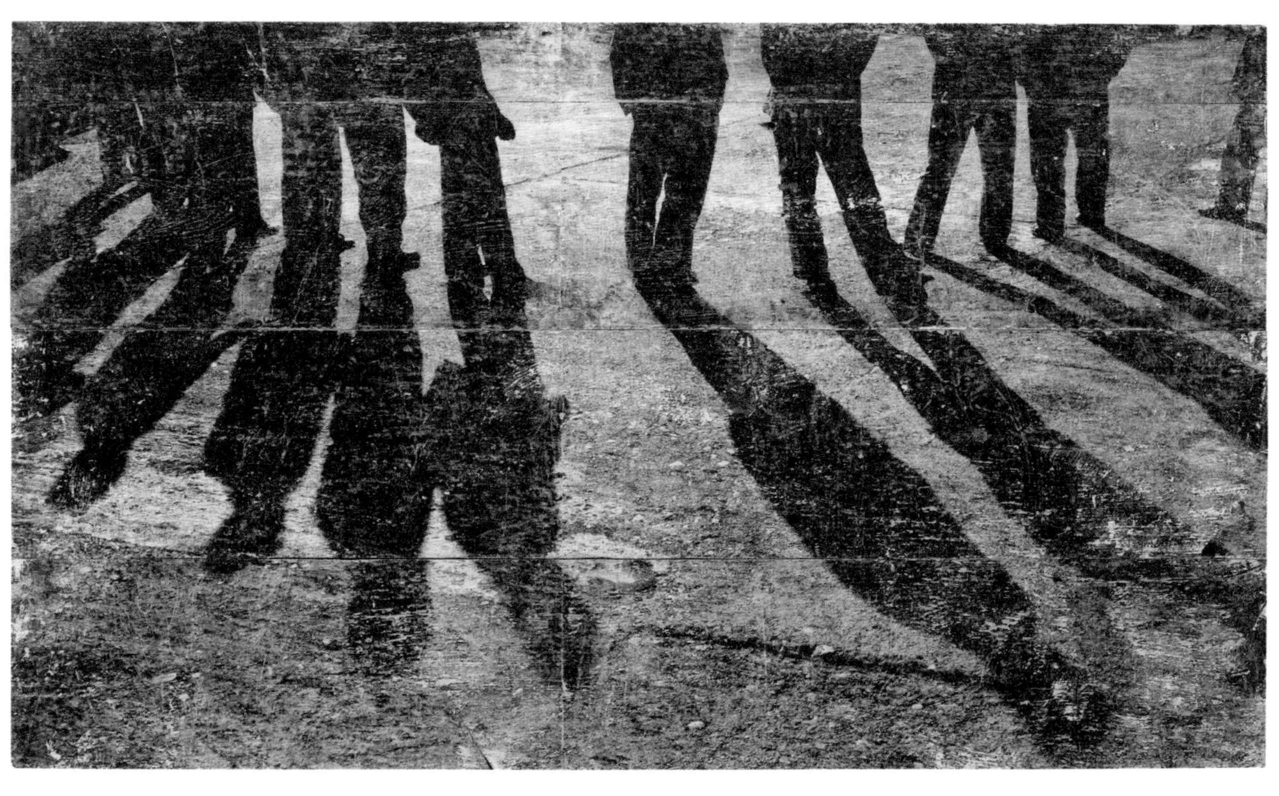

North Korea, Pyongyang, Shadows, 2012
Ink on wood, 97 x 155.5 cm (38 ¼ x 61 ¼ in)

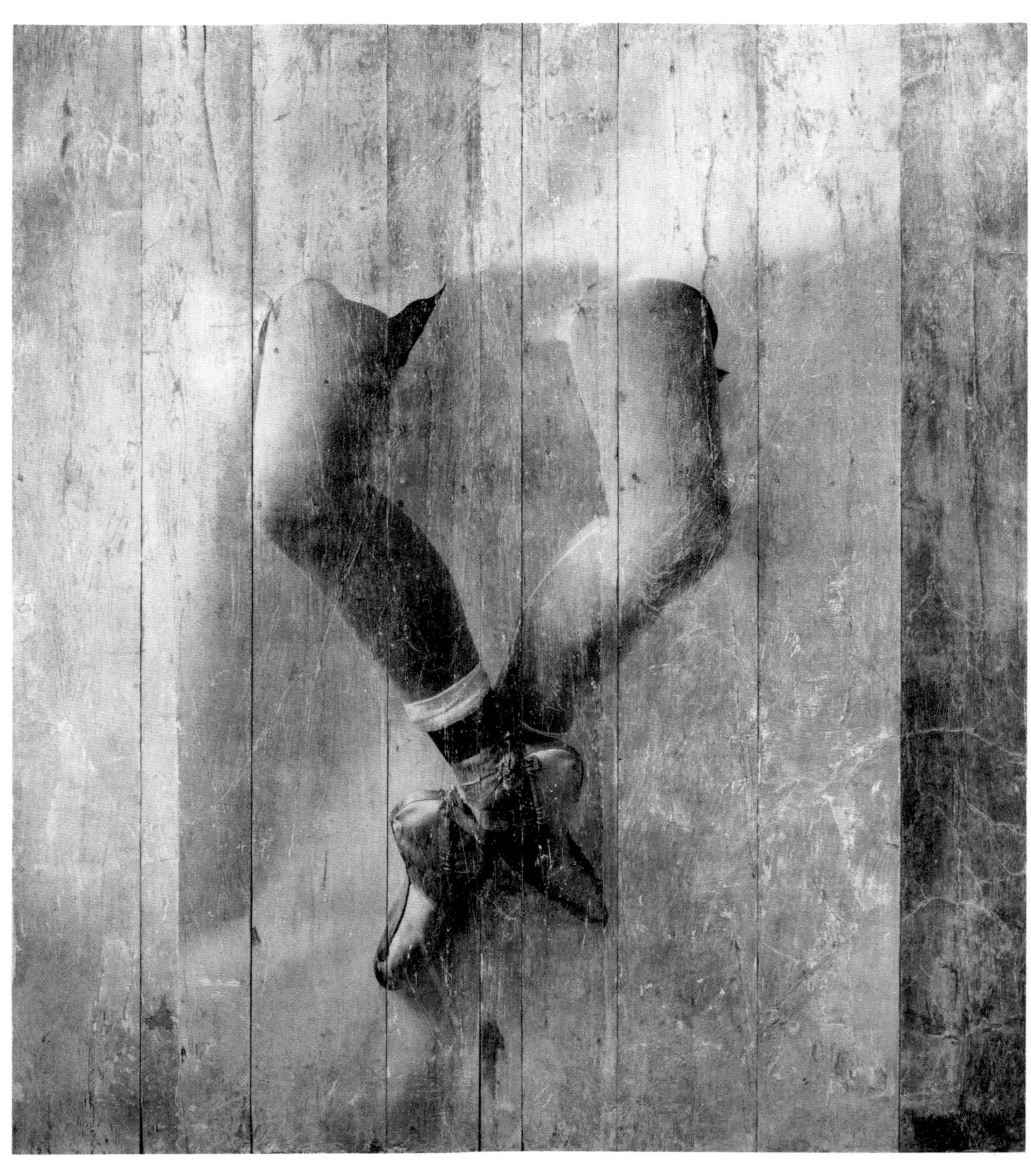

New York City Ballet Art Series, Paper Interactions #13, 2014
Ink on wood, 235 x 215 cm (92 ½ x 84 ½ in)

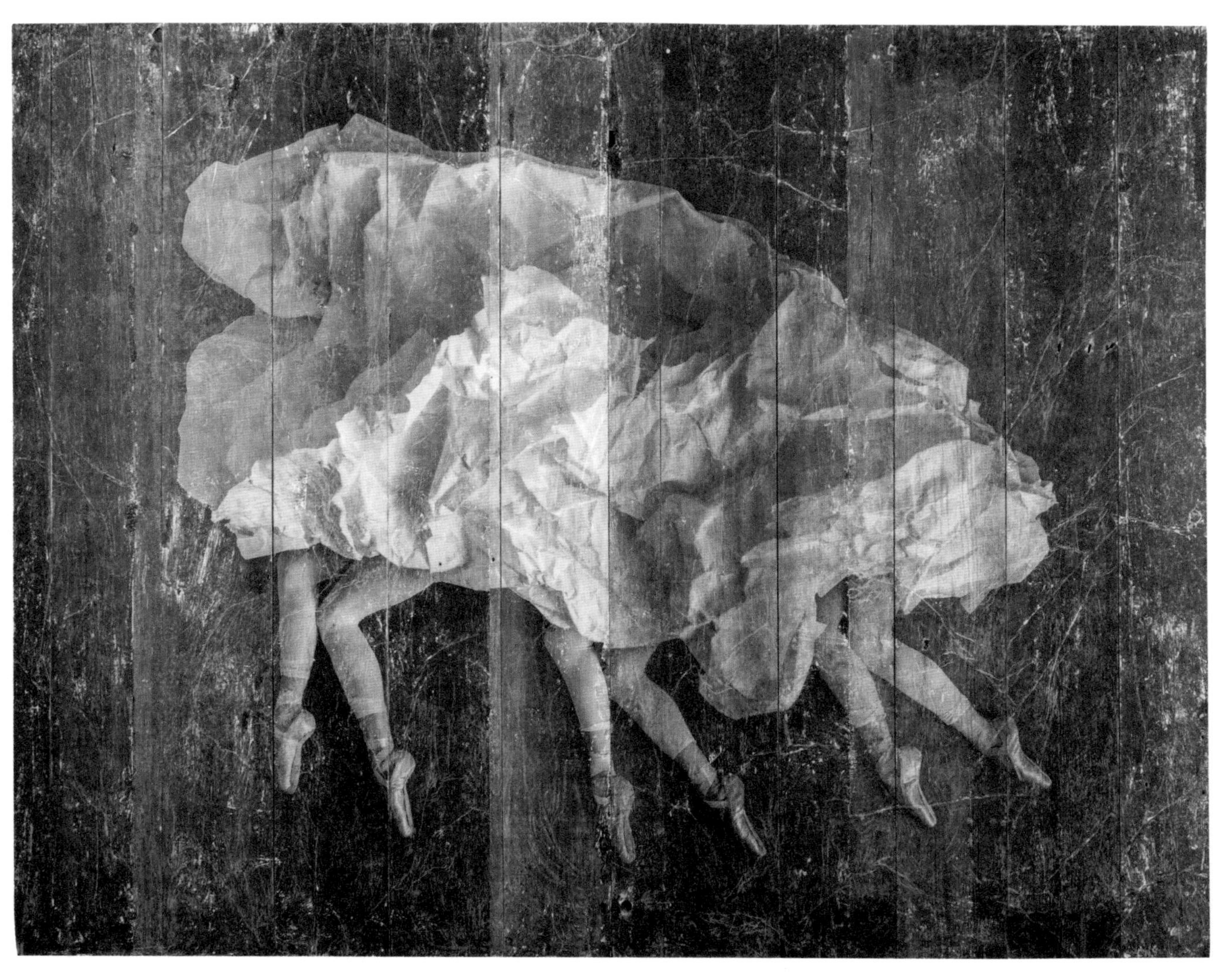

New York City Ballet Art Series, Paper Interactions #16, 2014
Ink on wood, 234.5 x 303.5 cm (92 ¼ x 119 ½ in)

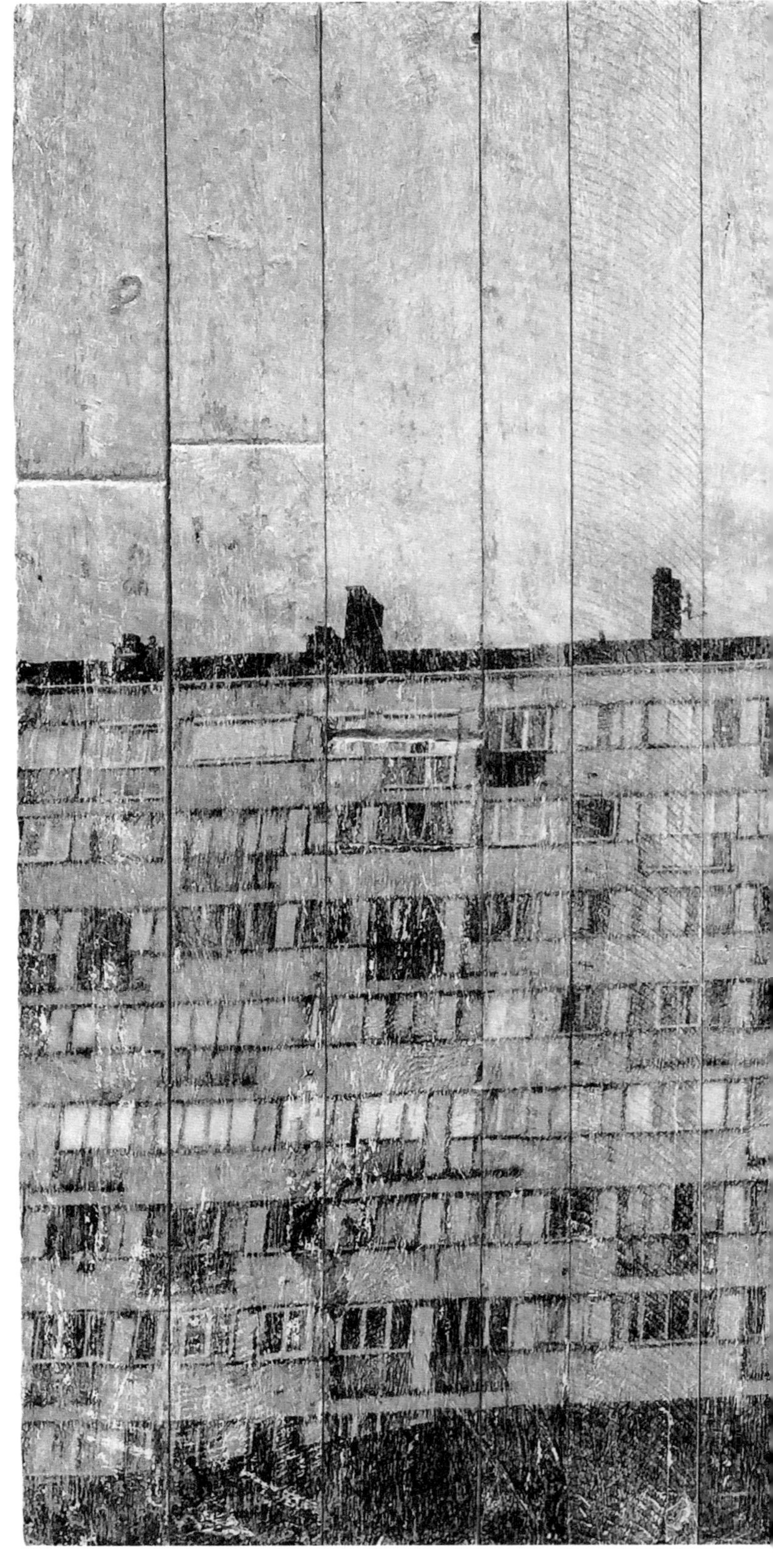

28 Millimètres, Portrait d'une Génération,
Les Bosquets, Montfermeil, France, Lauren, Jeté Cambré, 2014
Ink on wood, 228 x 366 cm (89¼ x 144 in)

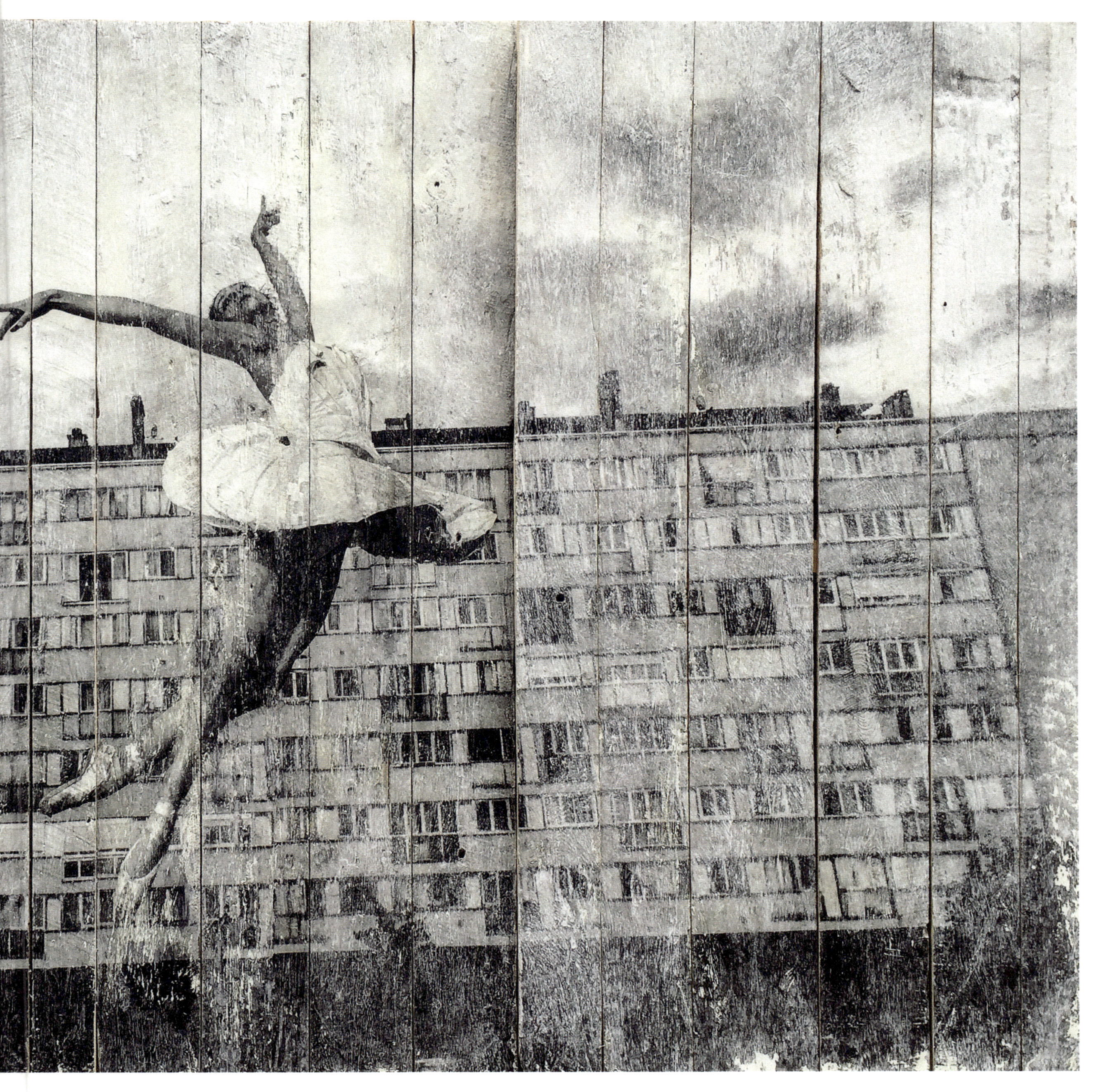

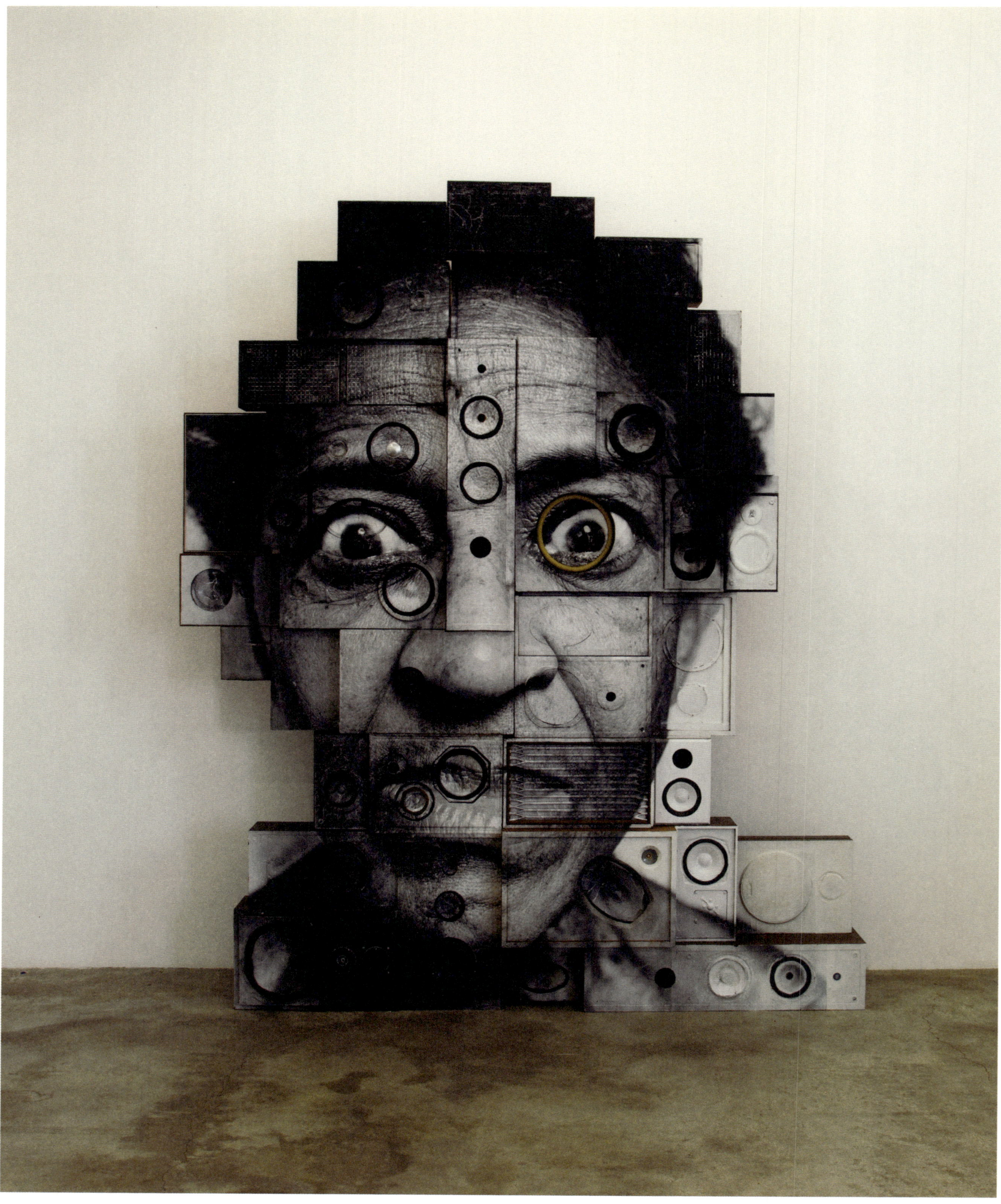

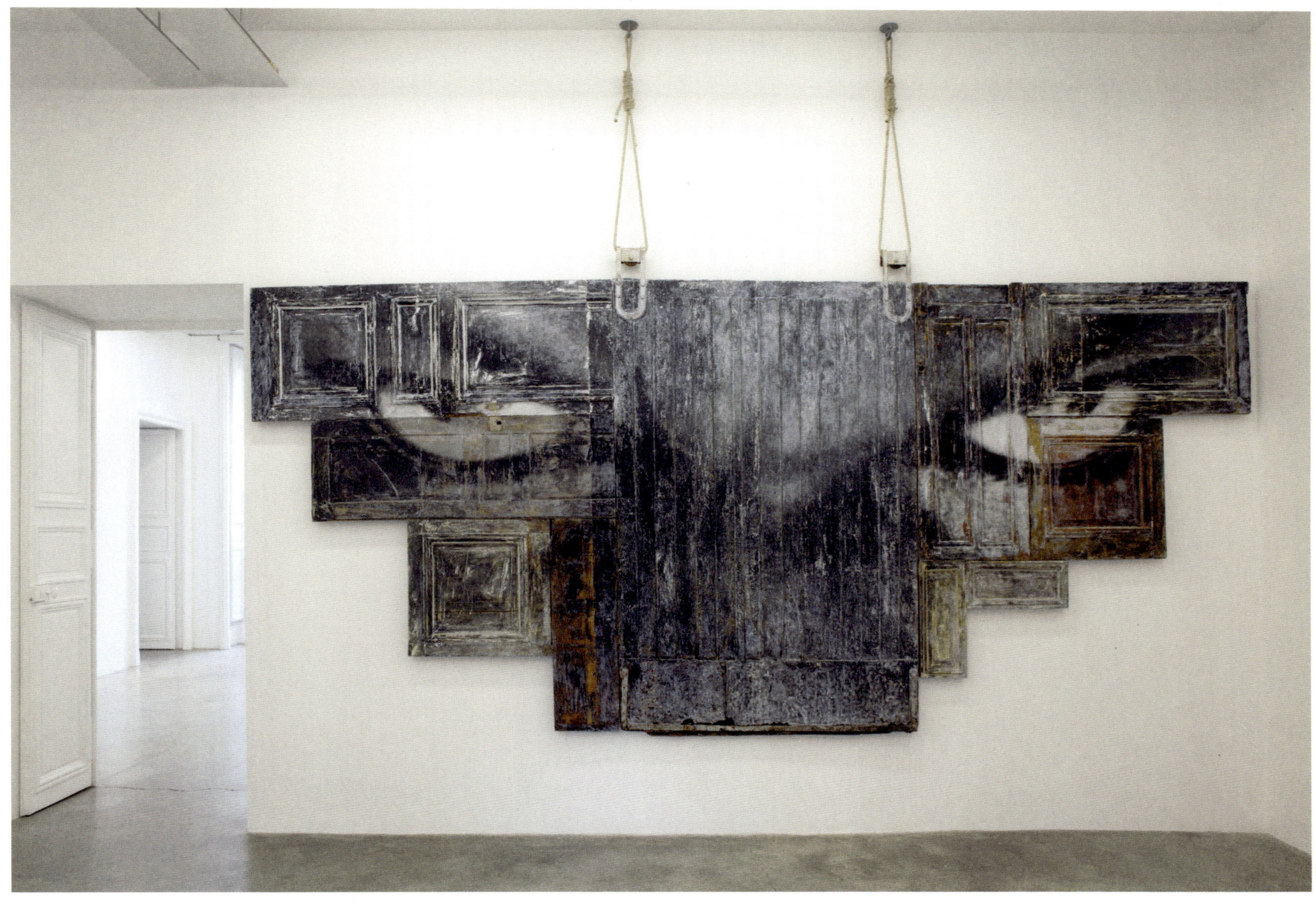

Installation view, 'Encrages', Galerie Perrotin, Paris, 2011
28 Millimètres, Portrait d'une Génération, Byron, La Forestière, Clichy-sous-Bois, France, 2005, 2011
Ink on wood, 247x544cm (97¼x214¼in)

(left) *28 Millimètres, Women Are Heroes, Action dans la Favela Morro Da Providência, Linda Marinho De Oliveira, Rio de Janeiro, Brésil,* 2008
Paper on speakers, 292x250cm (115x98½in)

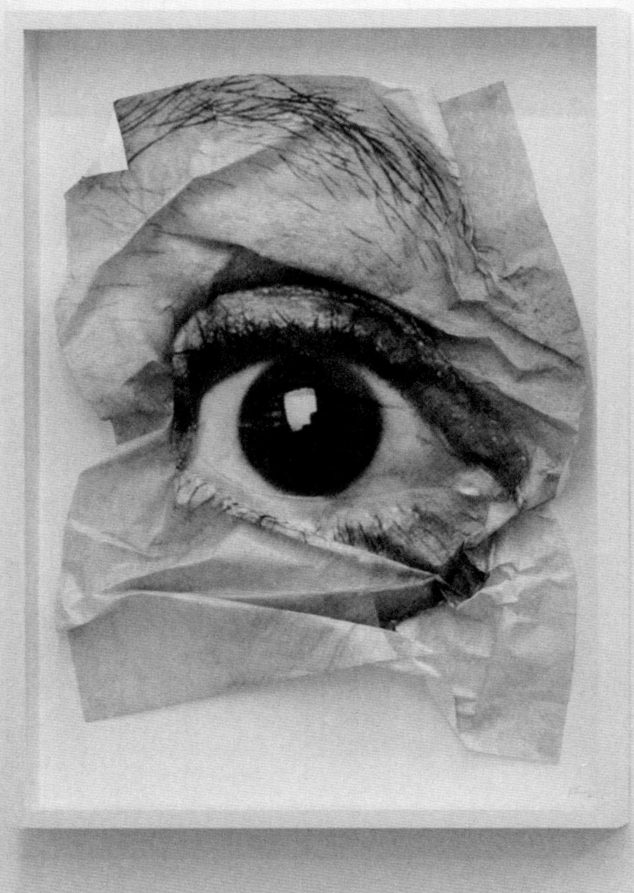

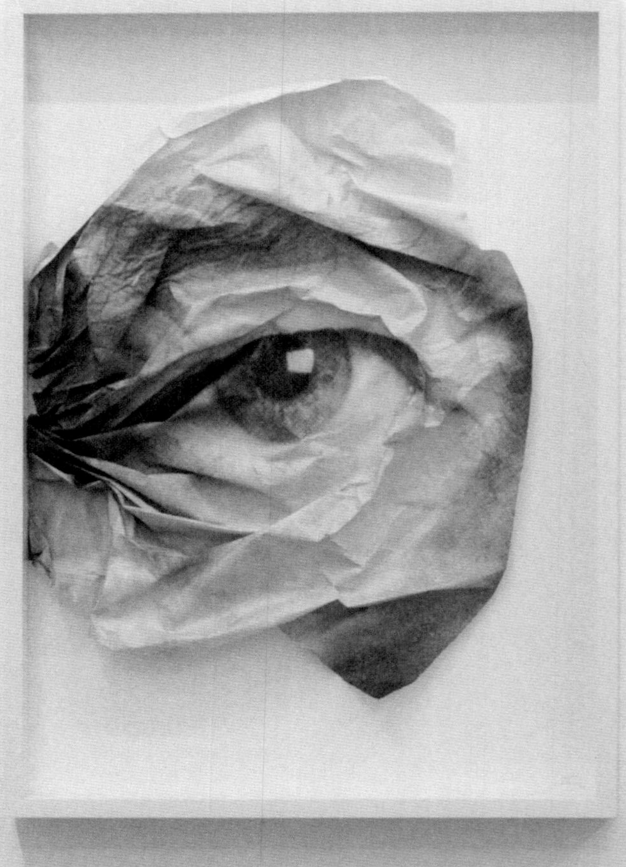

Installation view, 'Encrages', Galerie Perrotin, Paris, 2011
showing paper sculptures (from left to right)
Wrinkles of the City, Los Angeles, Oeil froissé encadré #6,
Wrinkles of the City, Los Angeles, Oeil froissé encadré #2,
Wrinkles of the City, Los Angeles, Oeil froissé encadré #4,
Wrinkles of the City, Los Angeles, Oeil froissé encadré #5,
all ink on paper, 86 x 64.5 x 8 cm (33¾ x 25½ x 3 in)

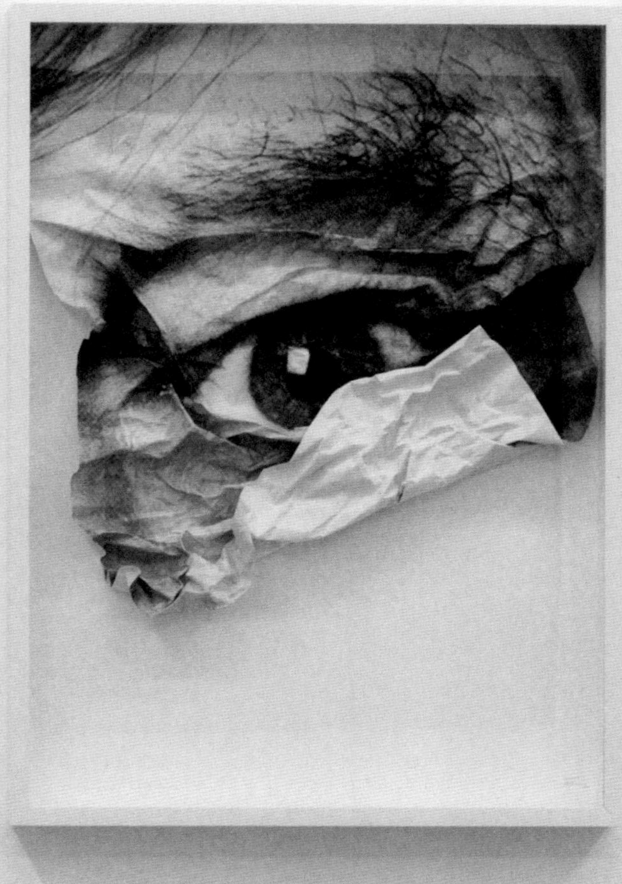

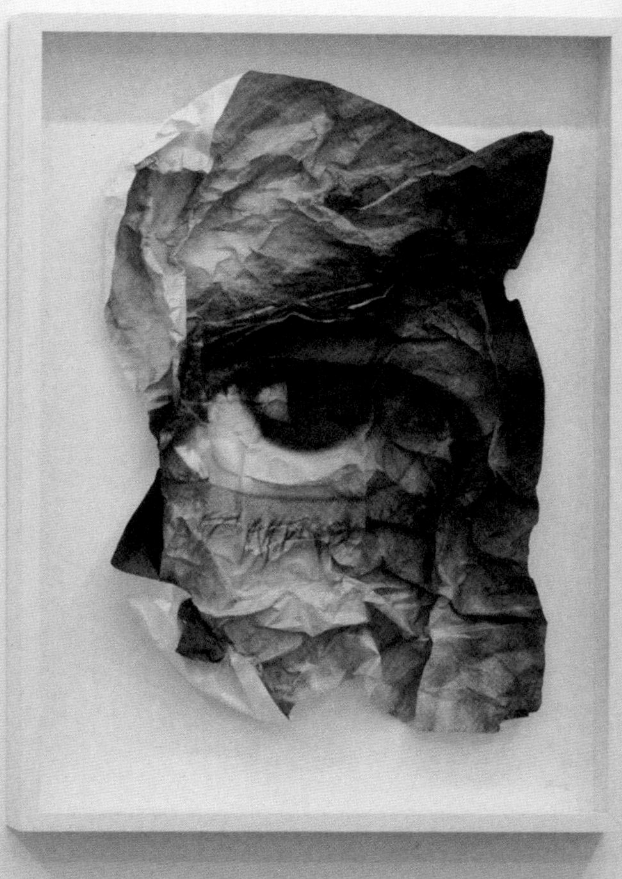

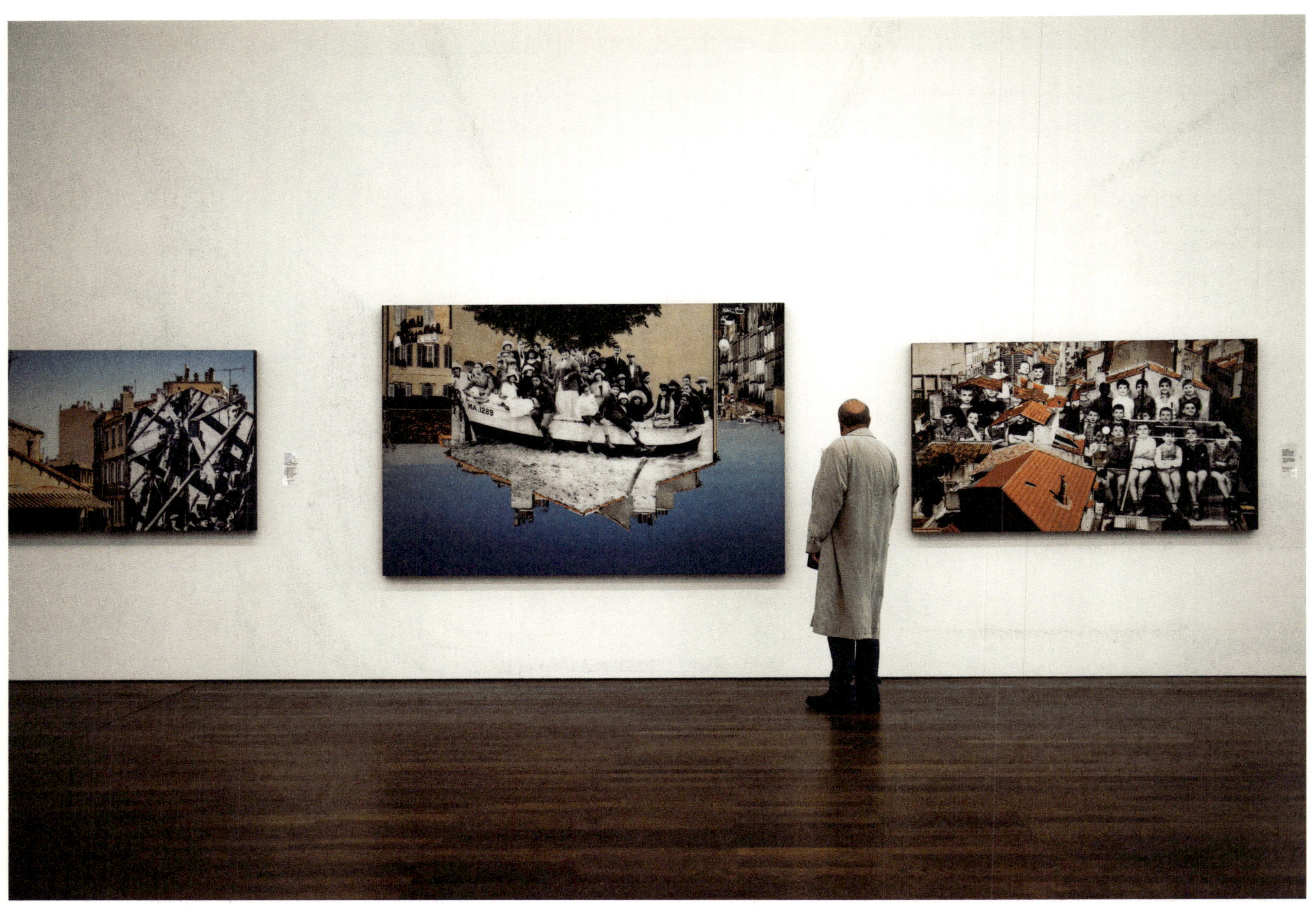

Installation view at Frieder Burda Museum, Baden Baden, 2014, showing photographs (from left to right) *Unframed, Badauds juchés sur des échafaudages derrière la Bourse, lors d'une manifestation du Front Populaire en 1936, Marseille, Photo BAUDELAIRE, Fonds Gérard DETAILLE, France, revu par JR, Marseille, France*, 2013 colour print mounted on aluminium, plexiglas and wood, 125 x 187.5 cm (49¼ x 73¾ in);
Unframed, un groupe posant dans une barque amarrée sur la plage revu par JR, Marseille vers 1930, Marseille, France, 2013, colour print mounted on aluminium, plexiglas and wood, 180 x 270.8 cm (71 x 106½ in)
Unframed, école Saint Charles revue par JR, Marseille, 1966-1967, Marseille, France, 2013, colour print mounted on aluminium, plexiglas and wood, 125 x 227 cm (49¼ x 90 in)

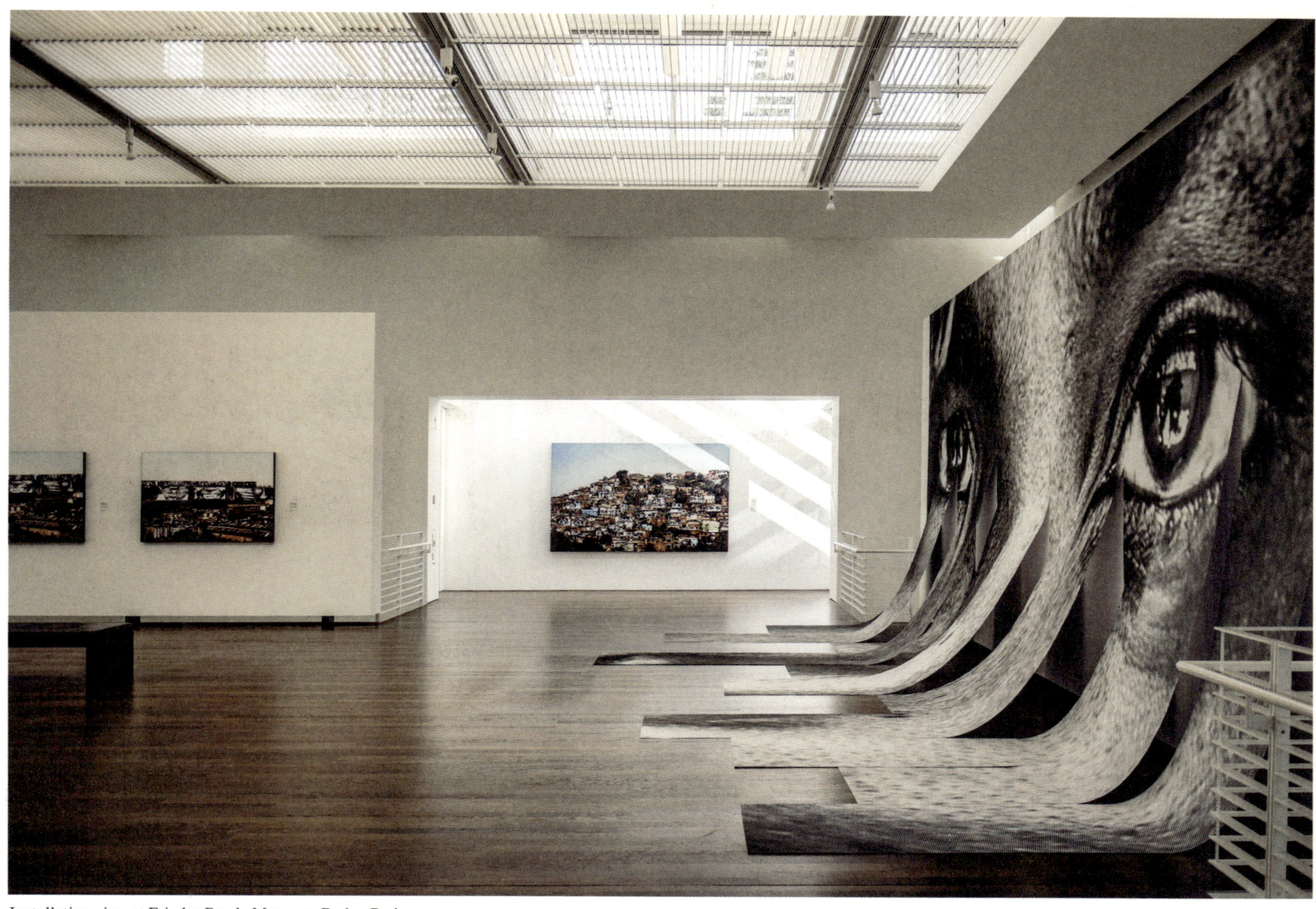

Installation view at Frieder Burda Museum, Baden Baden, 2014, showing photographs (from left to right)
28 Millimètres, Women Are Heroes, Action in Kibera Slum, Train Passage 5, Kenya, 2009, colour print mounted on aluminium, plexiglas and wood, 106 x 160 cm (42 x 63 in);
28 Millimètres, Women Are Heroes, Action in Kibera Slum, Train Passage 6, Kenya, 2009, colour print mounted on aluminium, plexiglas and wood, 106 x 160 cm (42 x 63 in);
28 Millimètres, Women Are Heroes, Action dans la Favela Morro da Providência, Favela de Jour, Rio de Janeiro, Brésil, 2008, colour print mounted on aluminium, plexiglas and wood, 180 x 301 cm (71 x 118½ in)

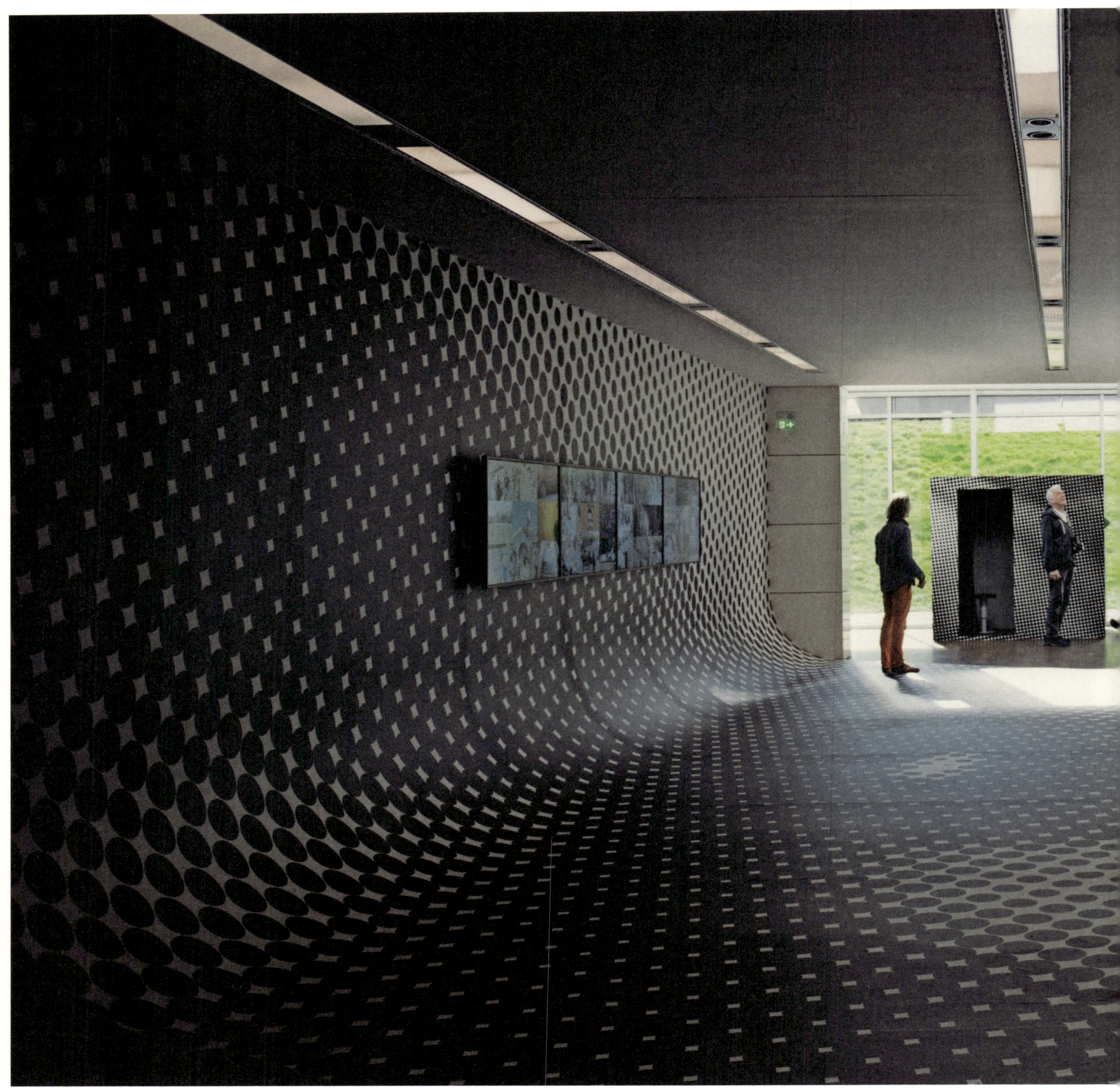

Installation view of *Inside Out* photobooth,
Frieder Burda Museum, Baden Baden, 2014

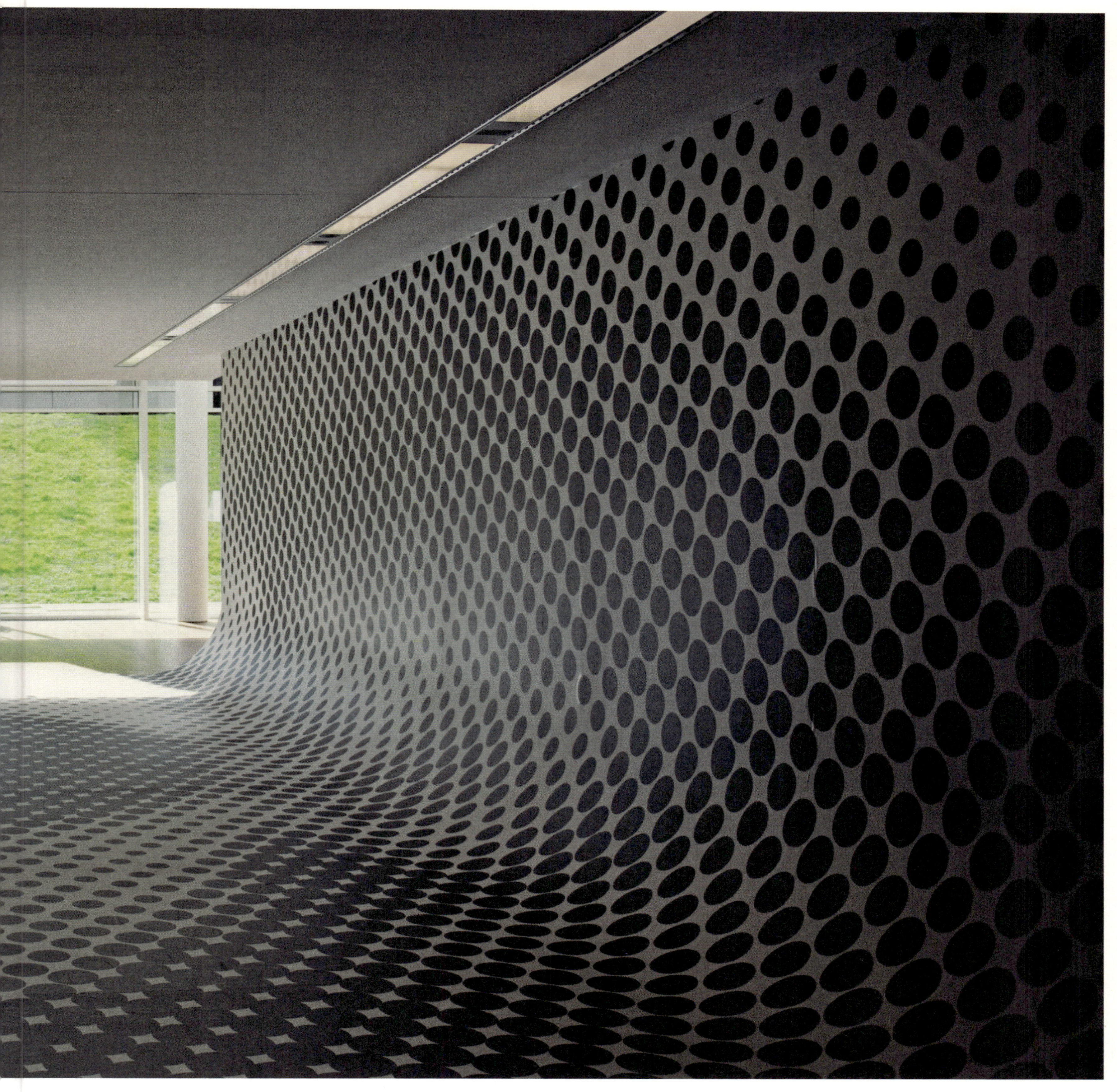

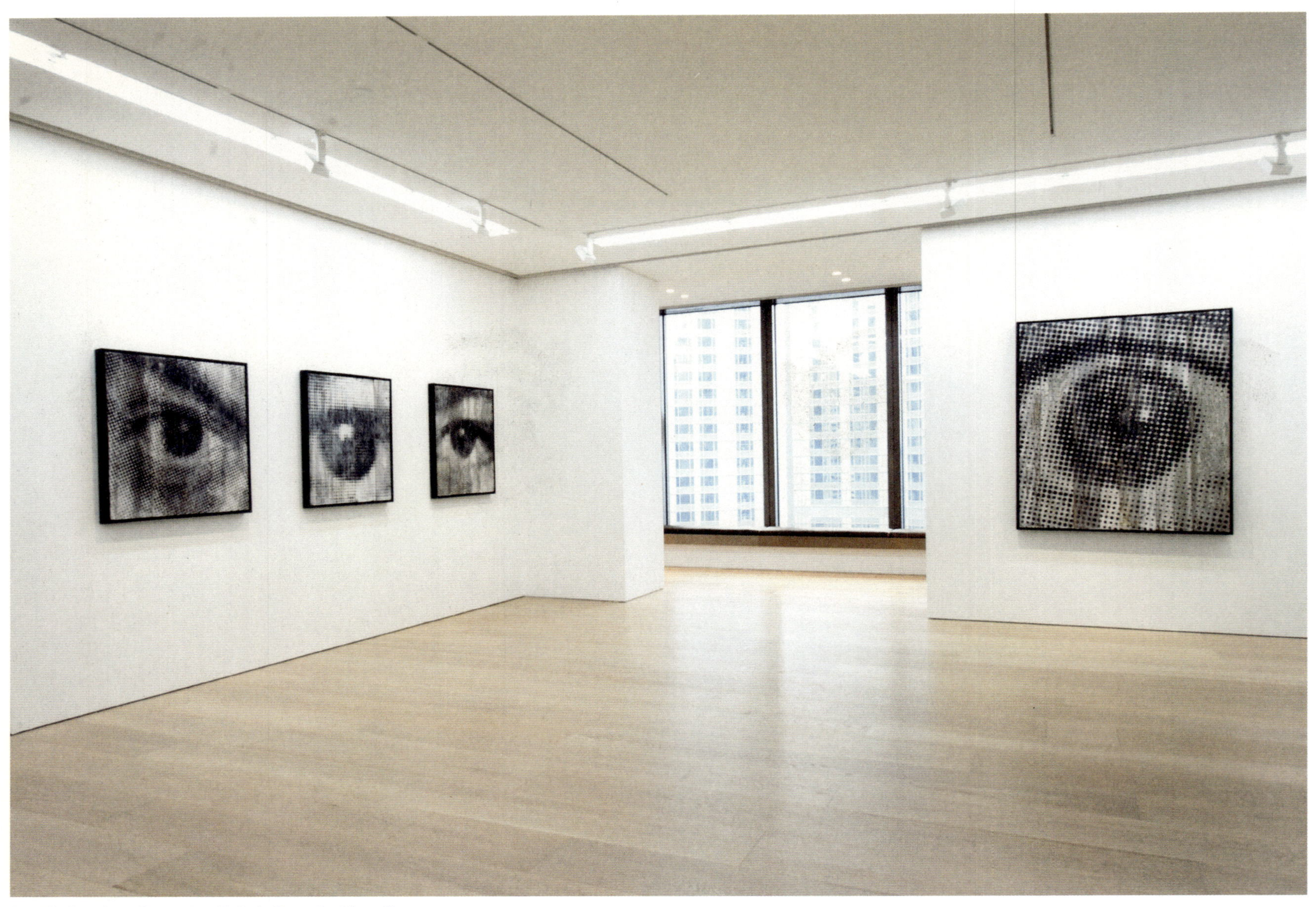

Installation view, 'Pattern' at Galerie Perrotin, Hong Kong, 2012 showing works on wood (from left to right)
Inside Out, 2012 *Oeil Trame #4,*
ink on wood, 91 x 91 cm (35 ¼ x 35 ¼ in);
Inside Out, Oeil Trame #2, 2012
ink on wood, 91 x 91 cm (35 ¼ x 35 ¼ in);
Inside Out, Oeil Trame #3, 2012
ink on wood, 96 x 88 cm (37 ¾ x 34 ½ in);
Inside Out, Oeil Trame #6, 2012
ink on wood, 152 x 152 cm (59 ¾ x 59 ¾ in)

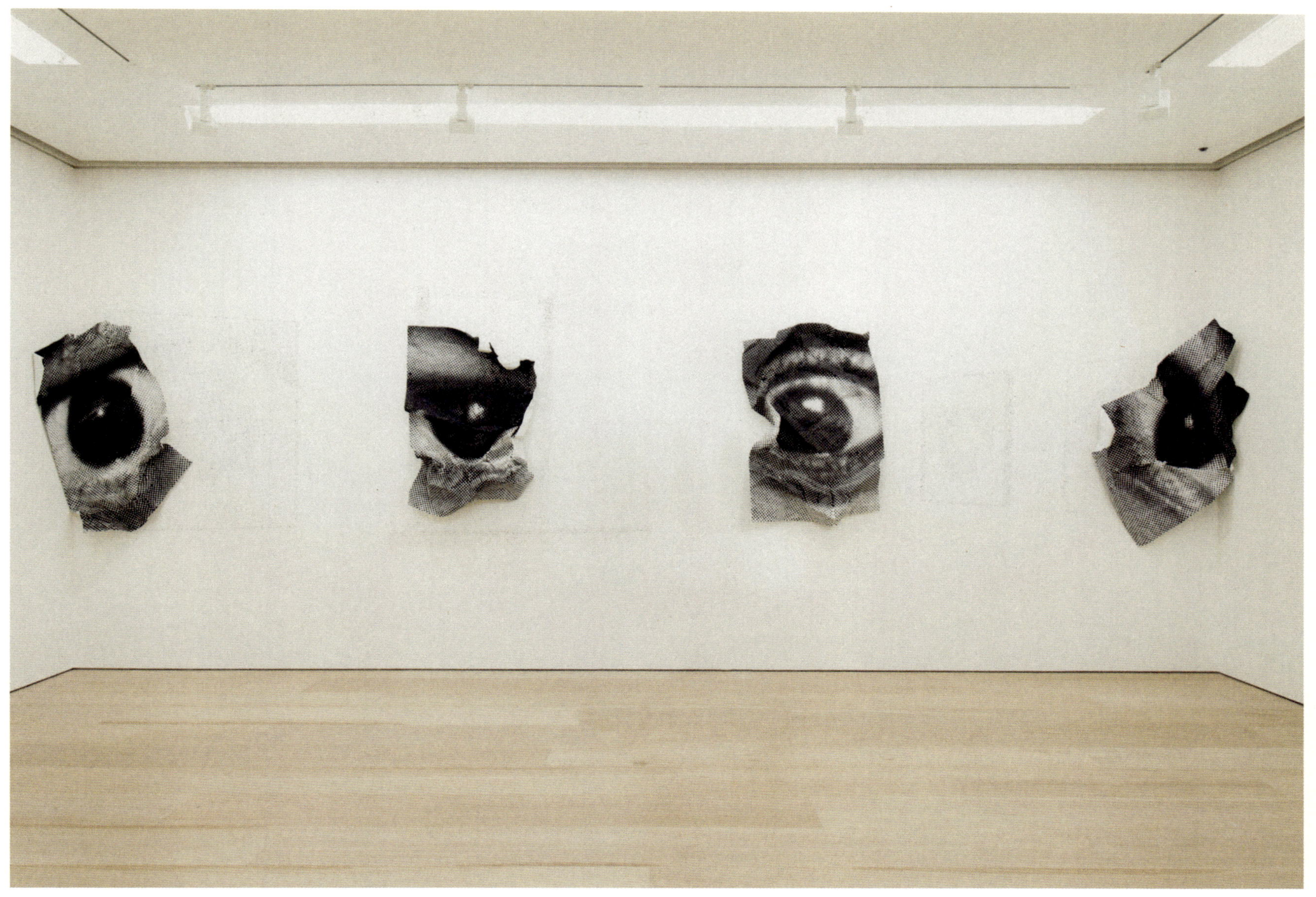

Installation view, 'Pattern' at Galerie Perrotin, Hong Kong, 2012 showing aluminium sculptures (from left to right)
Inside Out Sculpture #4, 2012, aluminium and paint, 130 x 75 x 42 cm (51 x 29½ x 16½ in);
Inside Out Sculpture #1, 2012, aluminium and paint, 120 x 84 x 23 cm (47¼ x 33 x 9 in);
Inside Out Sculpture #2, 2012, aluminium and paint, 125 x 84 x 18 cm (49¼ x 33 x 7 in);
Inside Out Sculpture #3, 2012, aluminium and paint, 146 x 84 x 33 cm (57½ x 33 x 13 in)

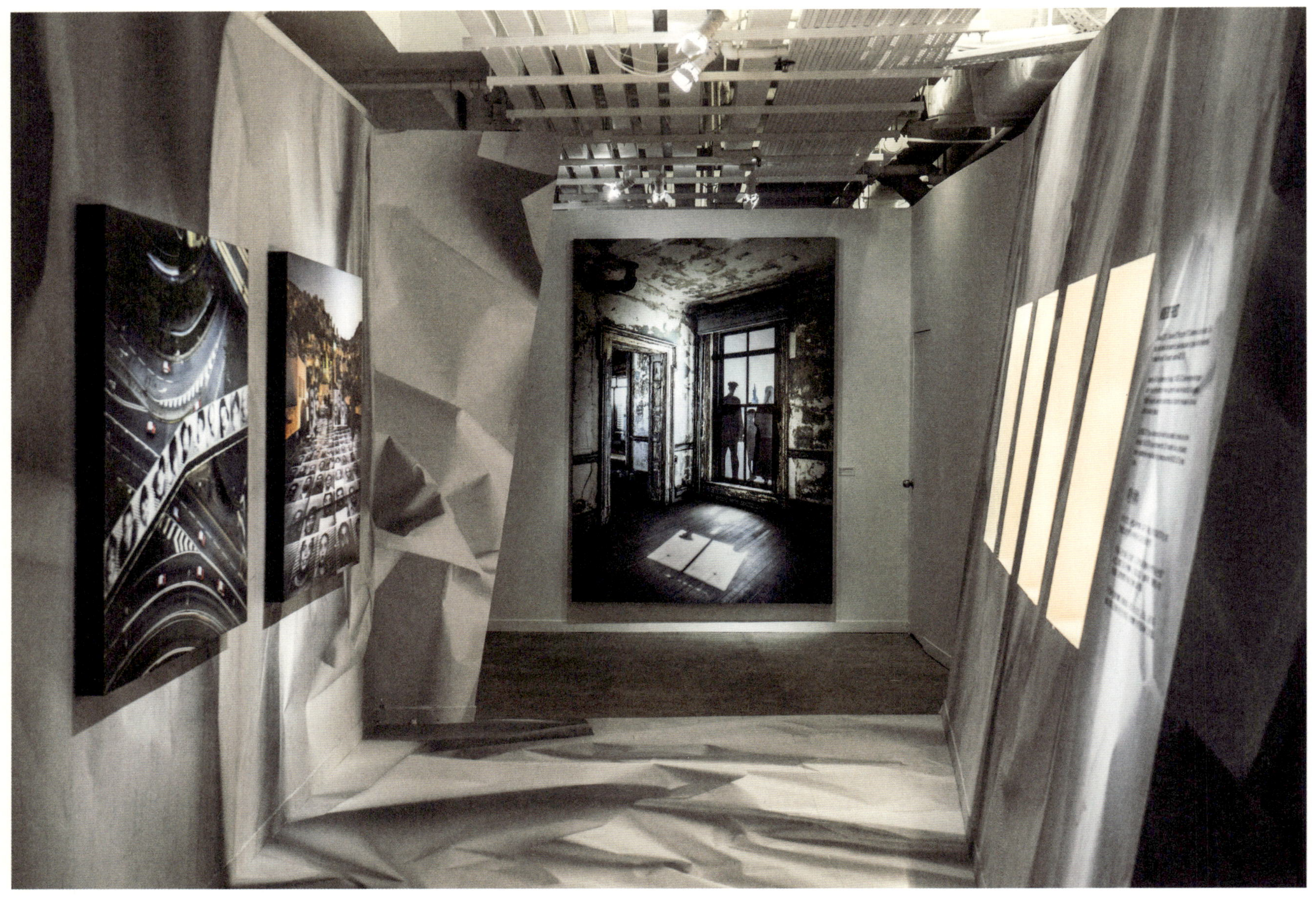

Installation view, 'JR: A Survey Exhibition' at Hong Kong Contemporary Art Foundation, Hong Kong, 2015, showing photographs (from left to right)
Inside Out, Installation in Hong Kong, September, 2012, colour print mounted on aluminium, plexiglas and wood, 125 x 180 cm (49 ¼ x 70 ¾ in);
Inside Out, Naplouse, Palestine, 2011, colour print mounted on aluminium, plexiglas and wood, 125 x 188 cm (49 ¼ x 74 in);
Unframed, An immigrant family views the Statue of Liberty from the Ellis Island Immigration Station dock revu par JR, courtesy of National Park Service, Statue of Liberty National Monument, USA, 2014, colour print mounted on aluminium, plexiglas and wood, 250 x 180 cm (98 ½ x 70 ¾ in)

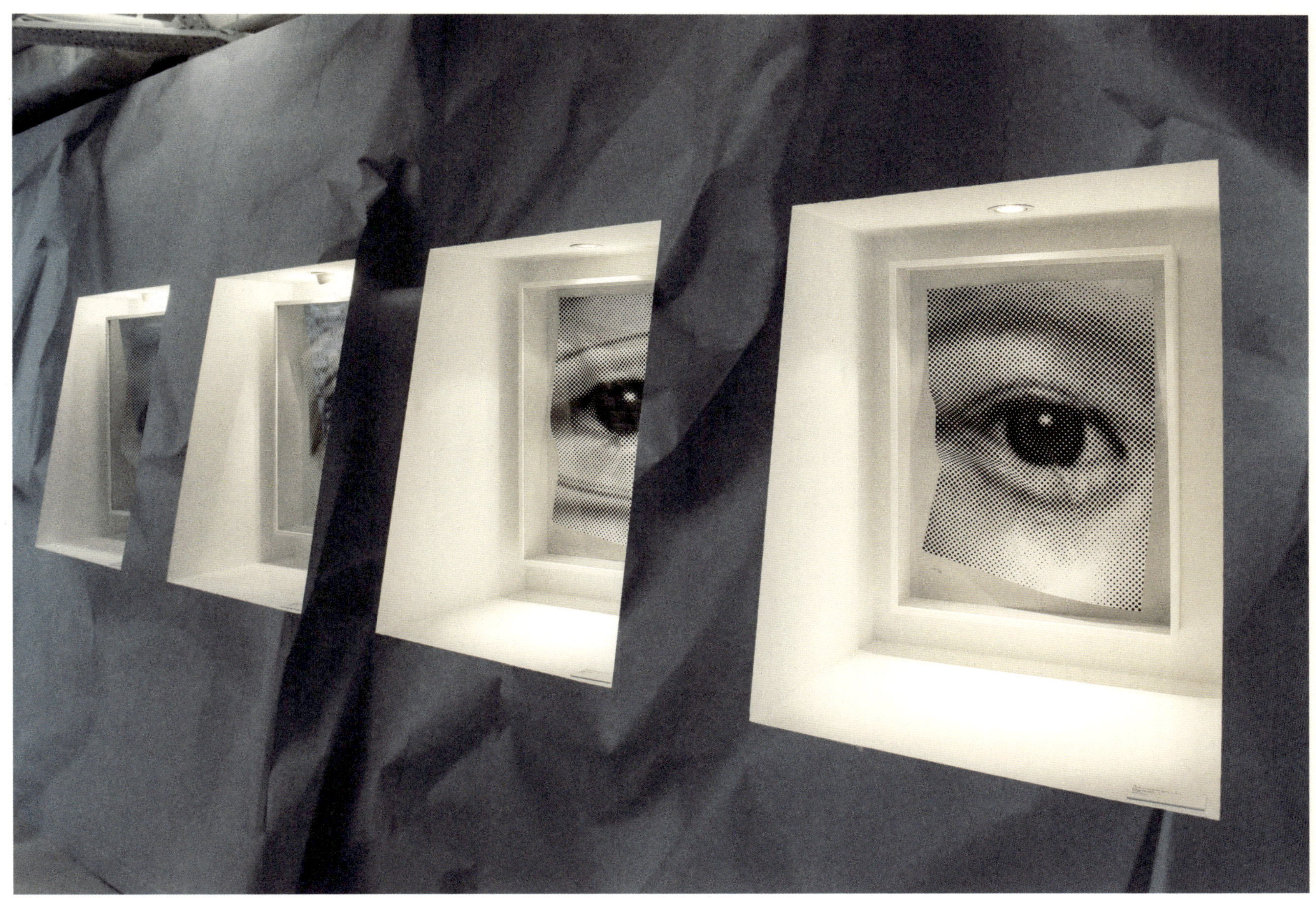

Installation view, 'JR: A Survey Exhibition' at Hong Kong Contemporary Art Foundation, Hong Kong, 2015, showing paper sculptures (from left to right)
Inside Out, Oeil froissé encadré 19, 2014, ink on paper, 86 x 64.5 x 8 cm (33 ¾ x 25 ½ x 3 in);
Inside Out, Oeil froissé encadré 11, 2014, ink on paper, 86 x 64.5 x 8 cm (33 ¾ x 25 ½ x 3 in)

Installation view of JR's pasting of Ladj Ly on the façade of Tate Modern, London, 2008

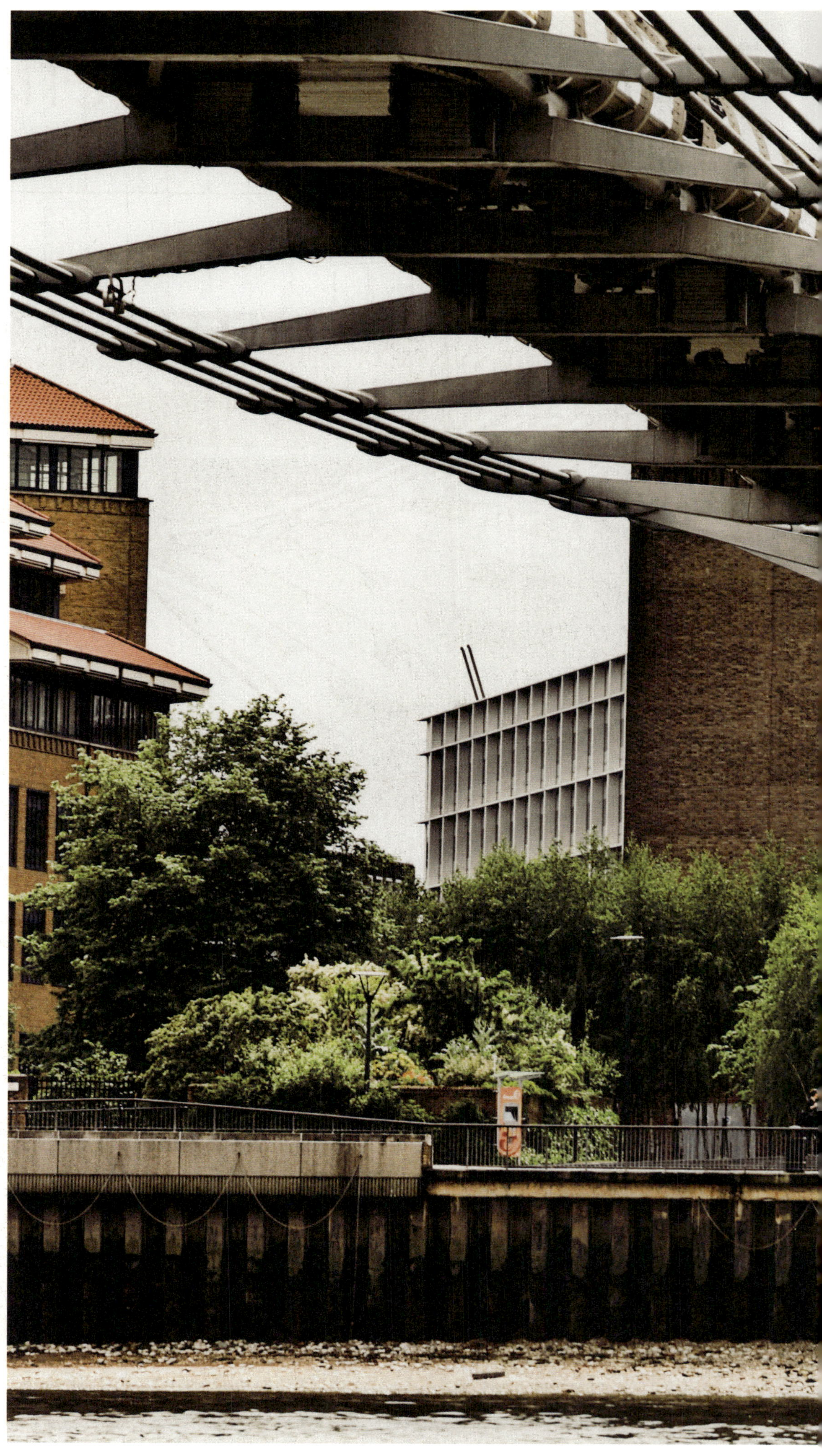

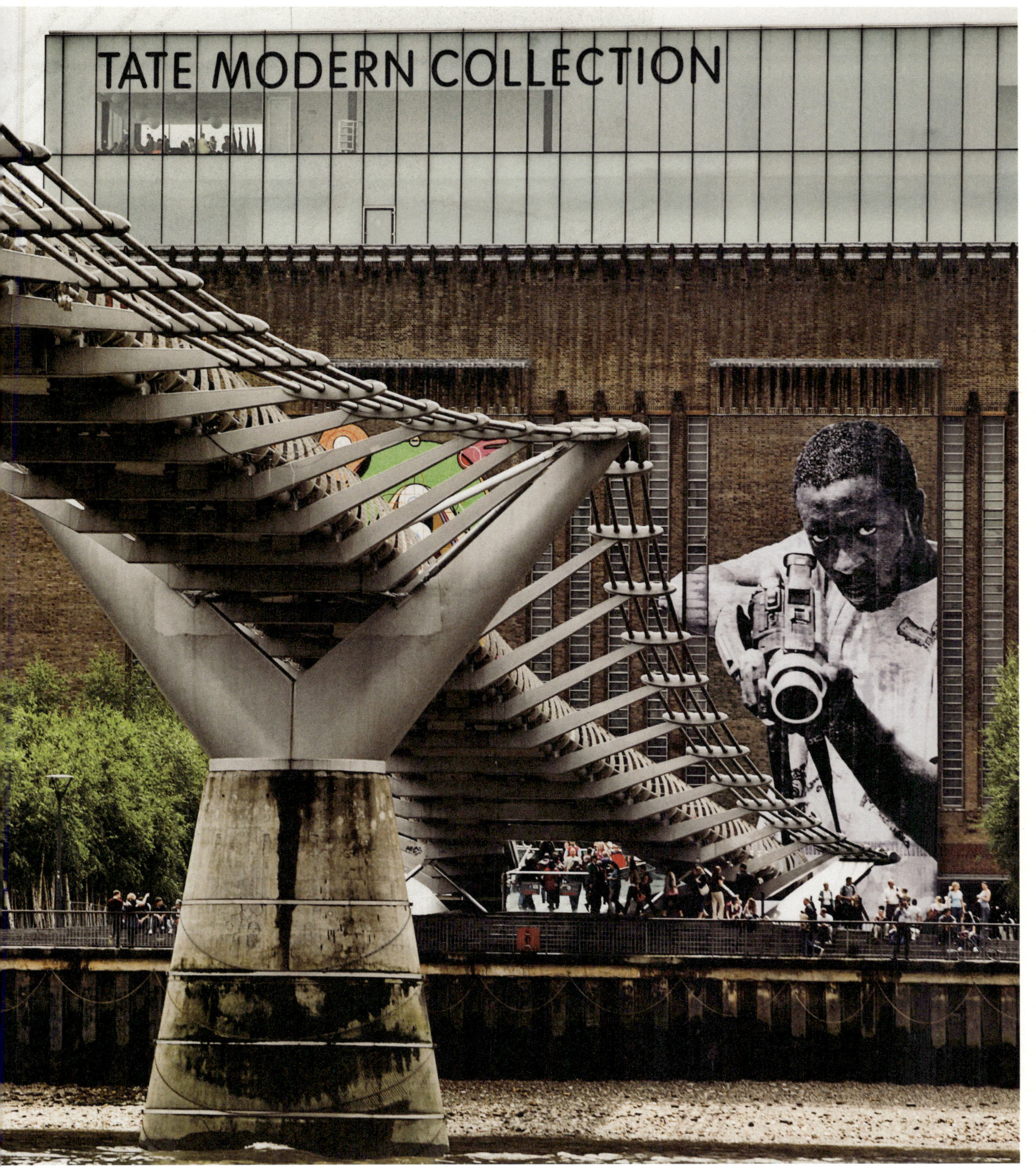
TATE MODERN COLLECTION

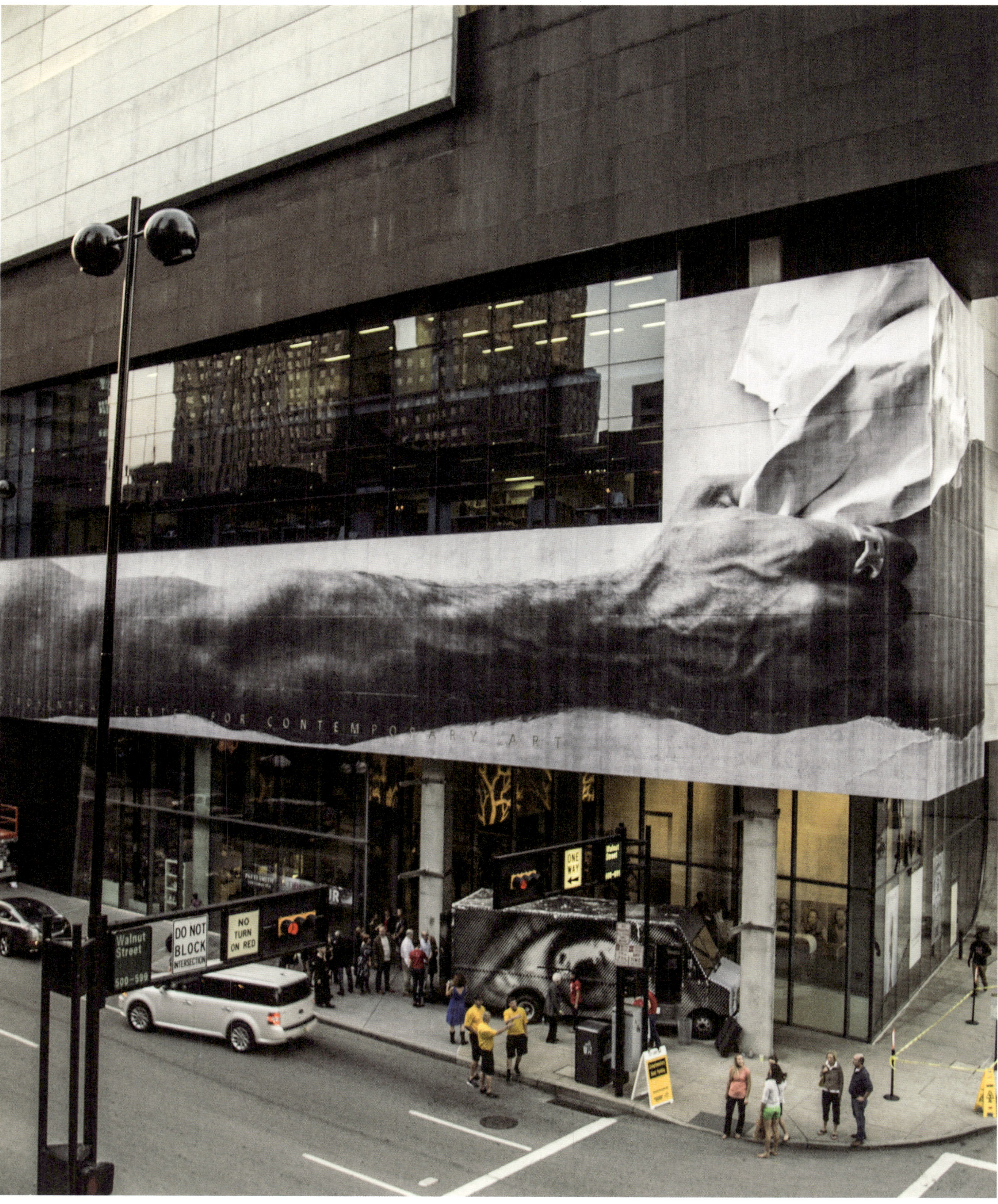
CENTER FOR CONTEMPORARY ART
Walnut Street
500–599
DO NOT BLOCK INTERSECTION
NO TURN ON RED
ONE WAY

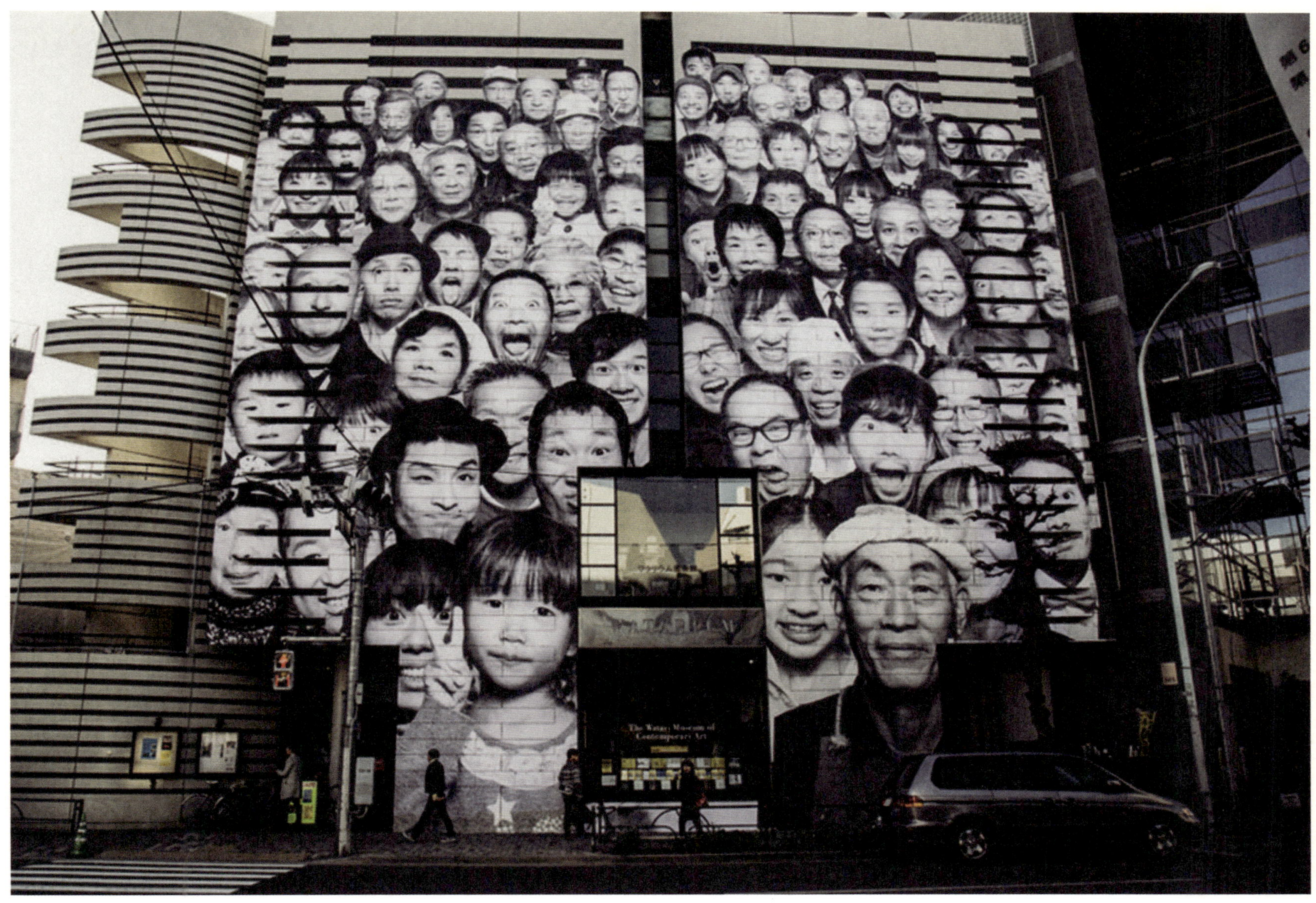

Installation view of the façade of the Watari Museum
of Contemporary Art, Tokyo, 2013
(left) Installation view of the façade of the Contemporary
Arts Center, Cincinnati, 2013

Installation view of the façade of Galerie Perrotin, Paris, for the exhibition, 'Encrages', 2011

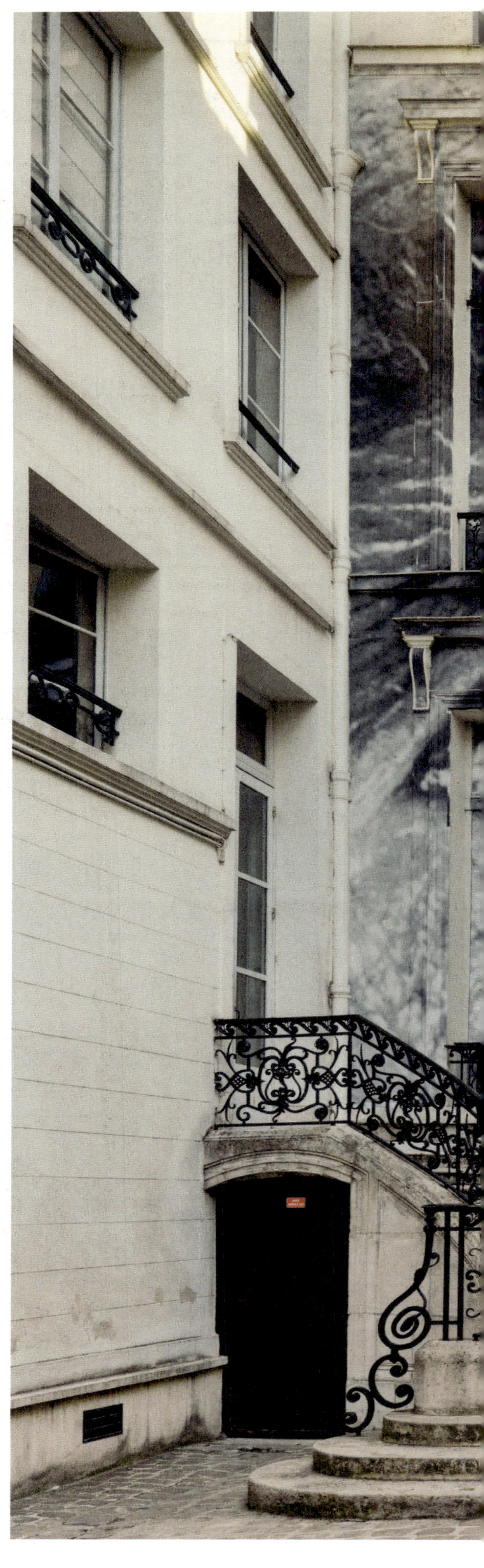

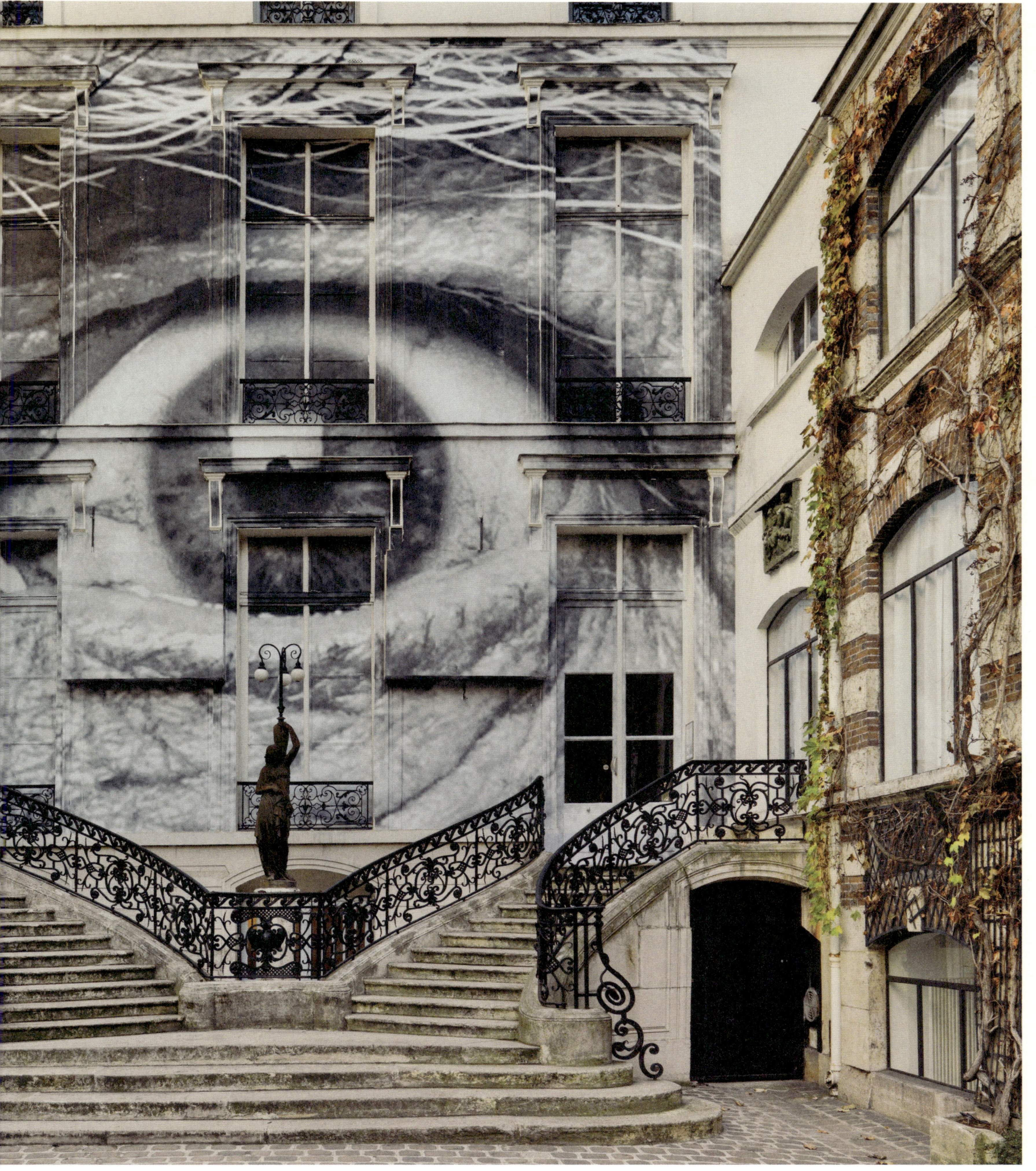

#API

CTURE

A DAY

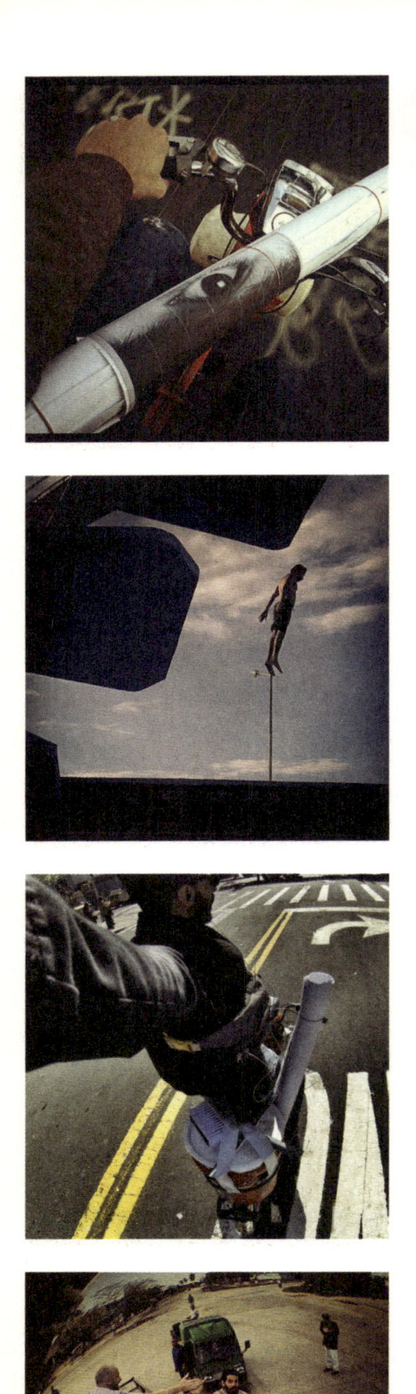

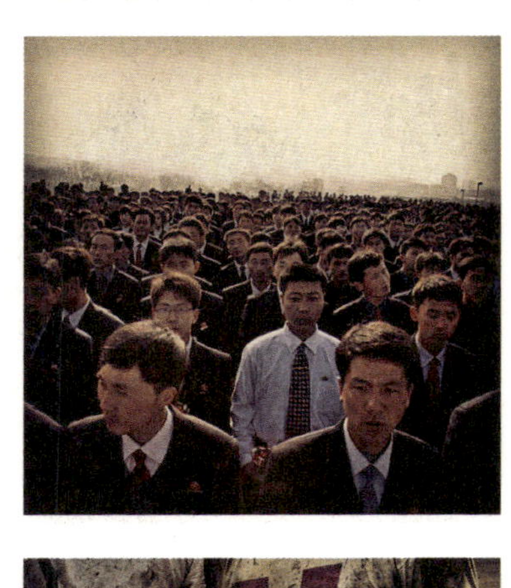

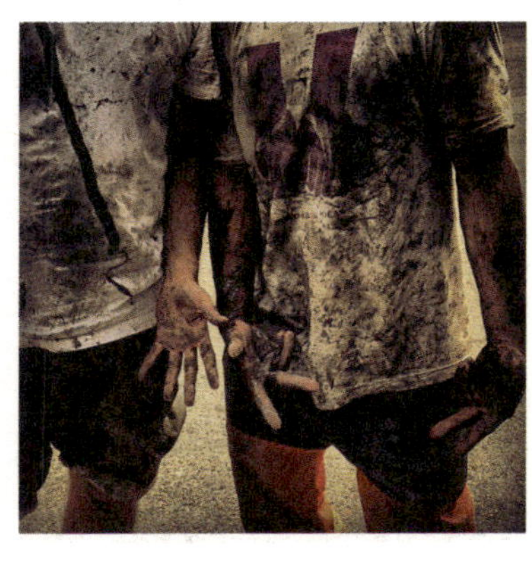

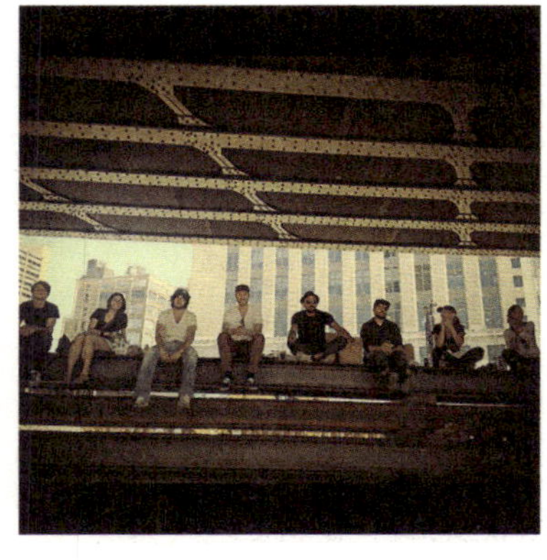

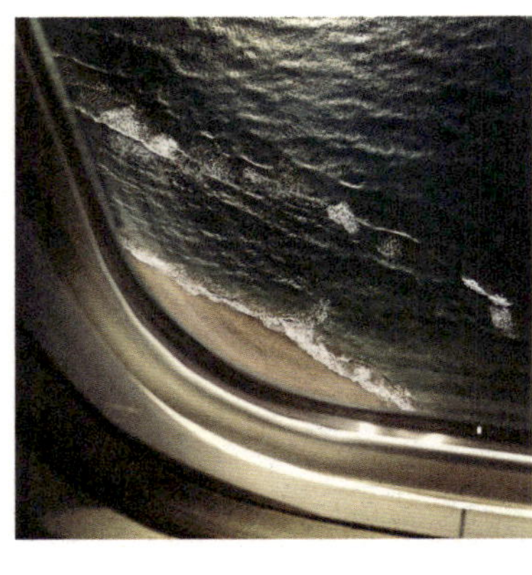

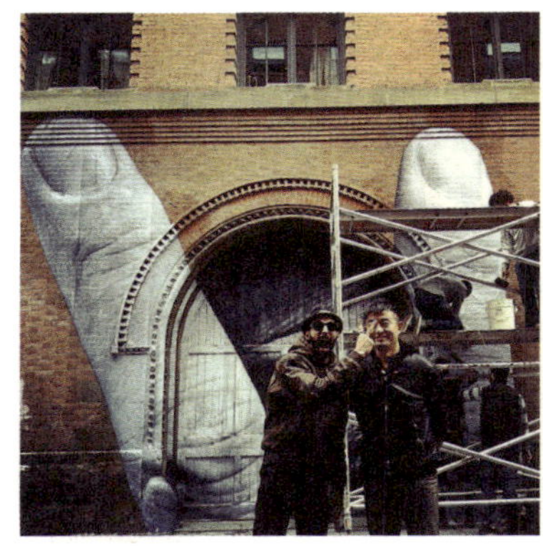

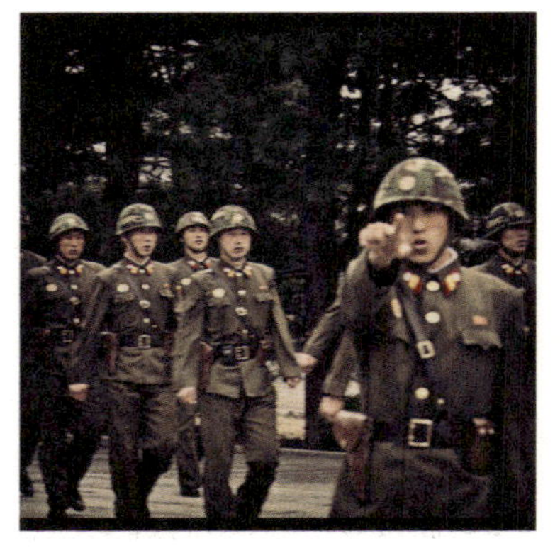

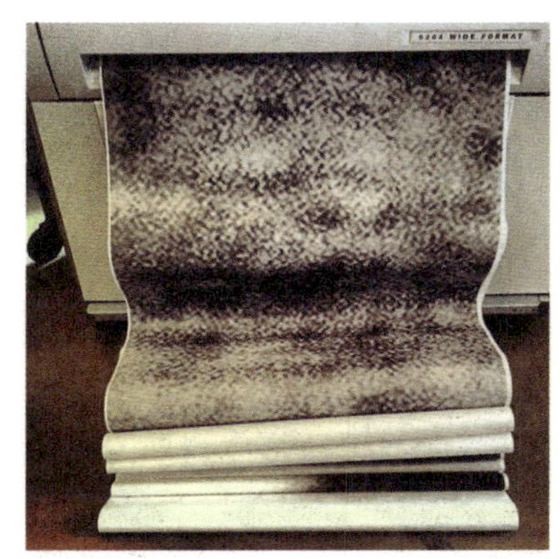

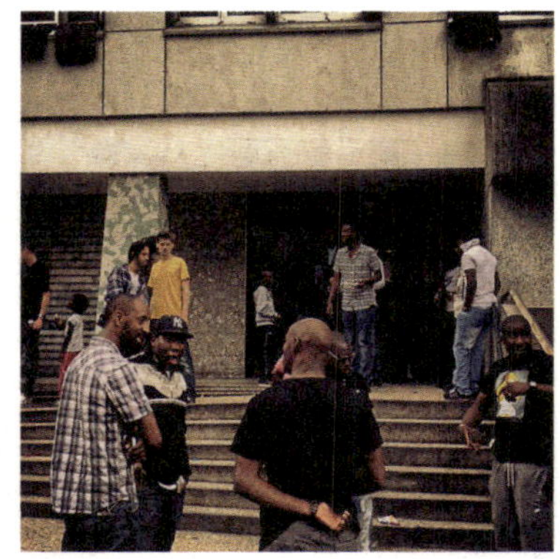

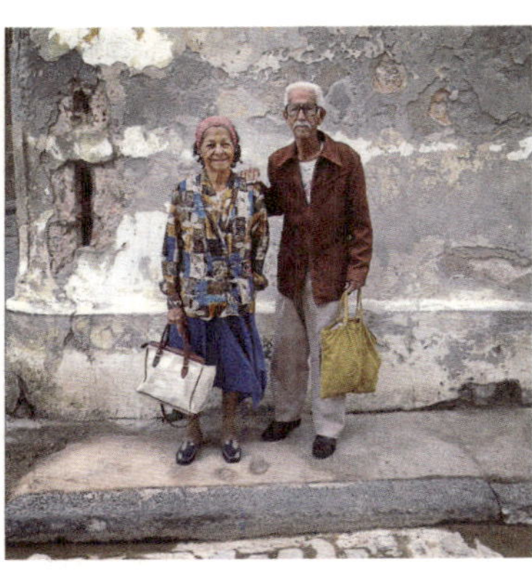

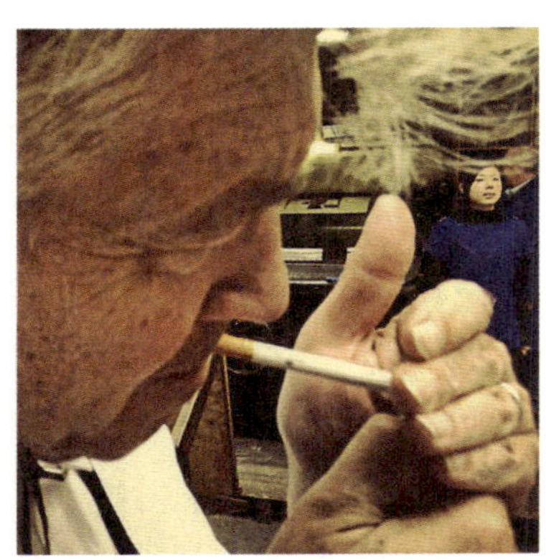

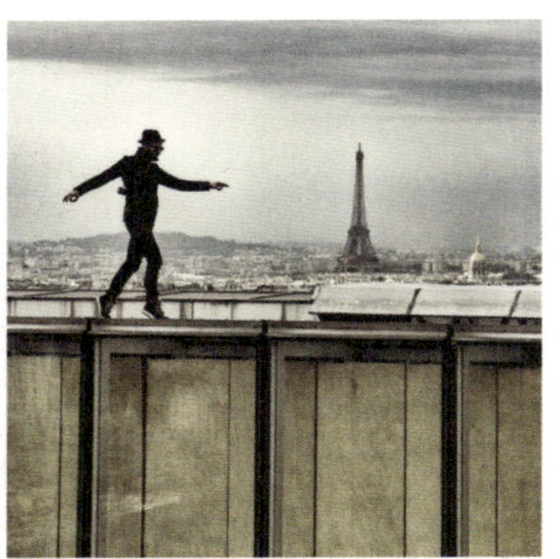

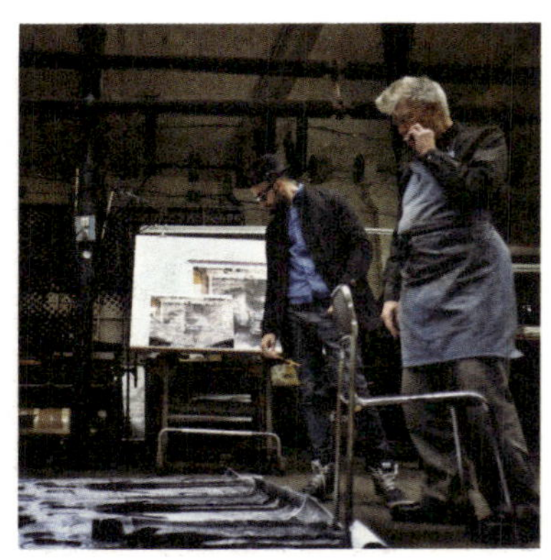

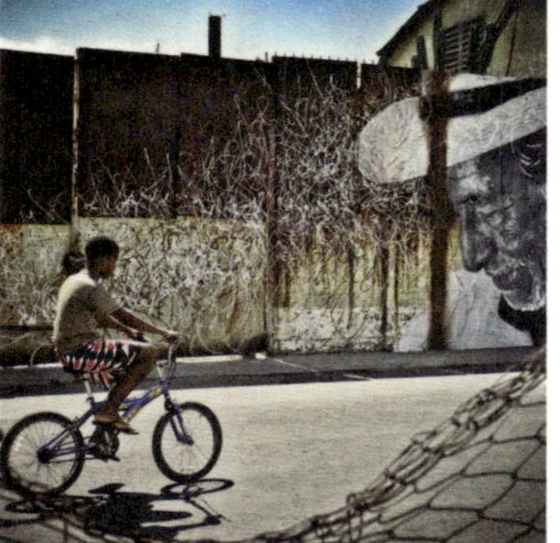

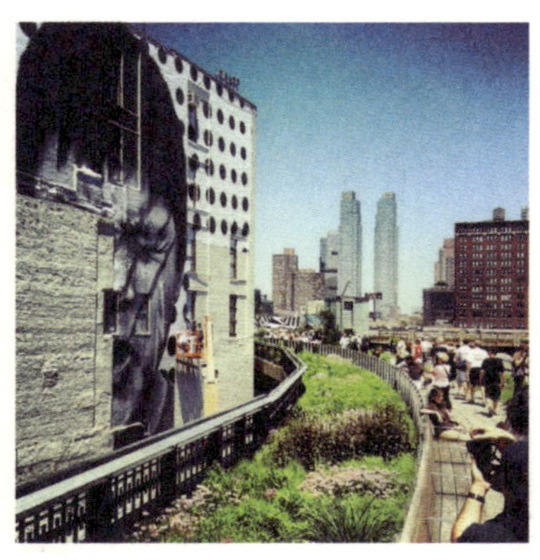

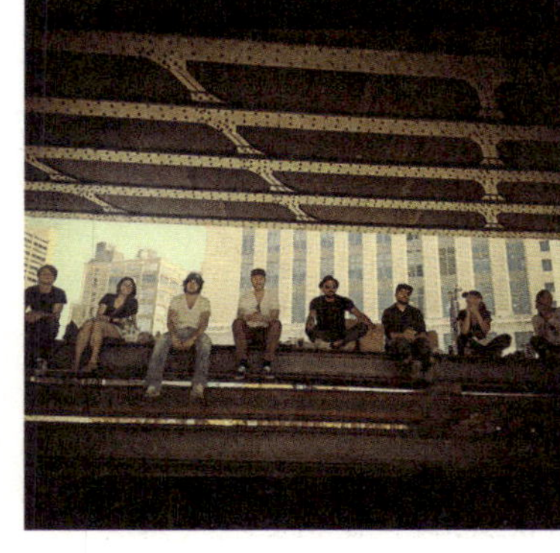

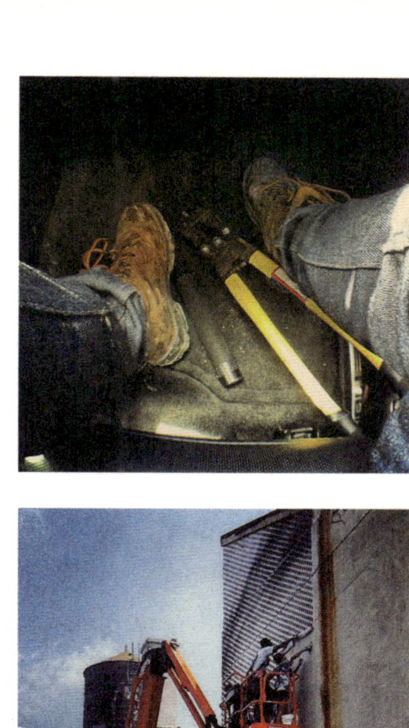
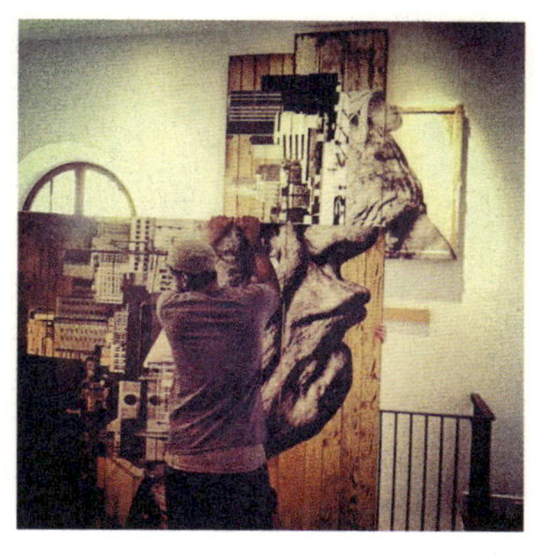
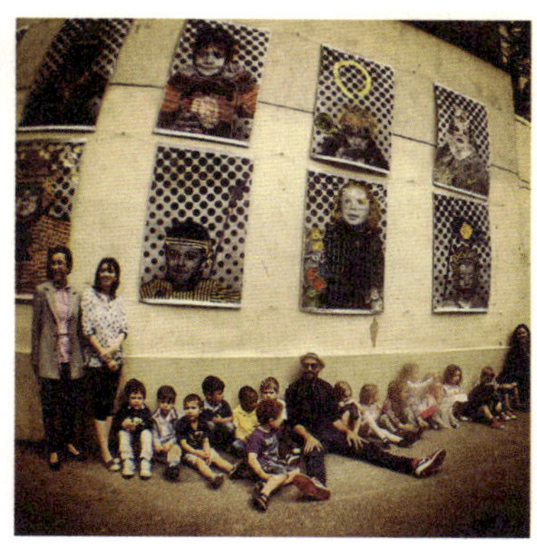
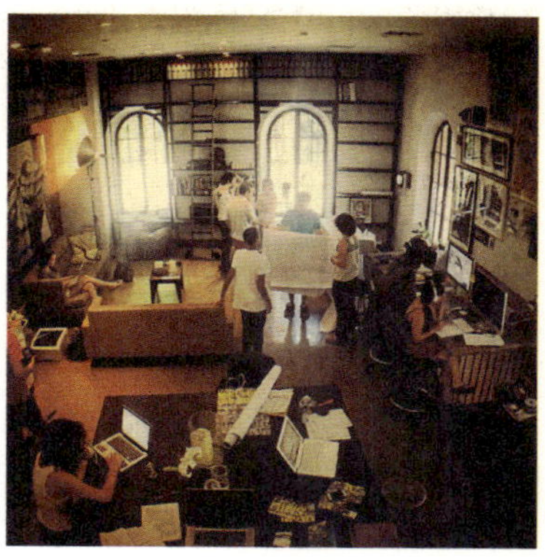
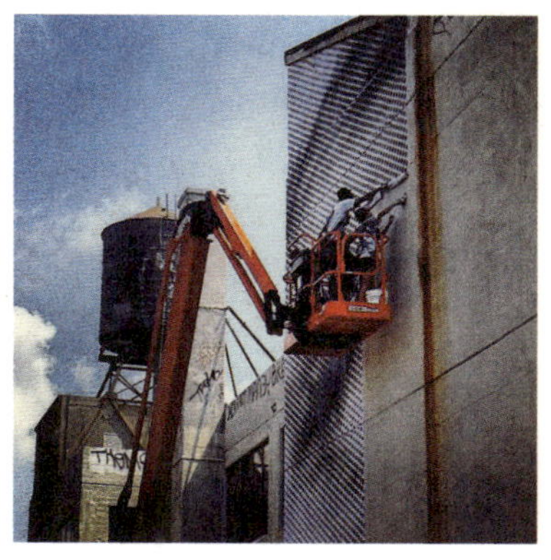
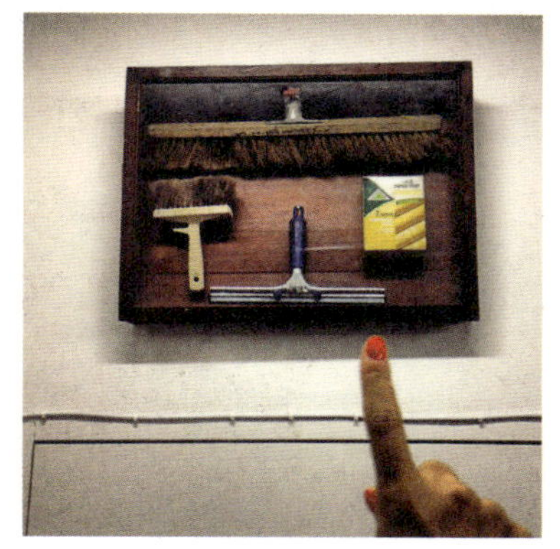
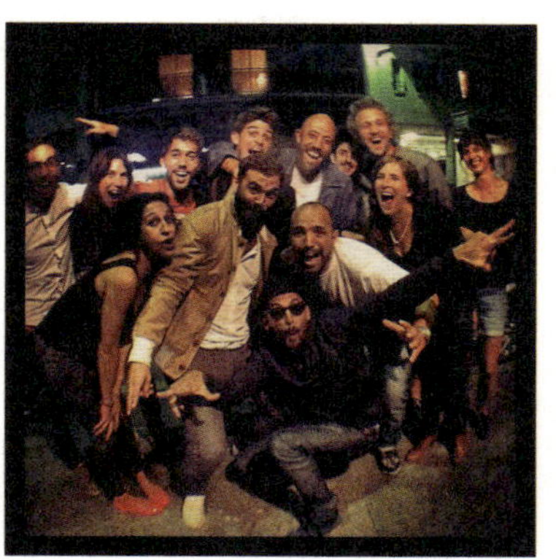
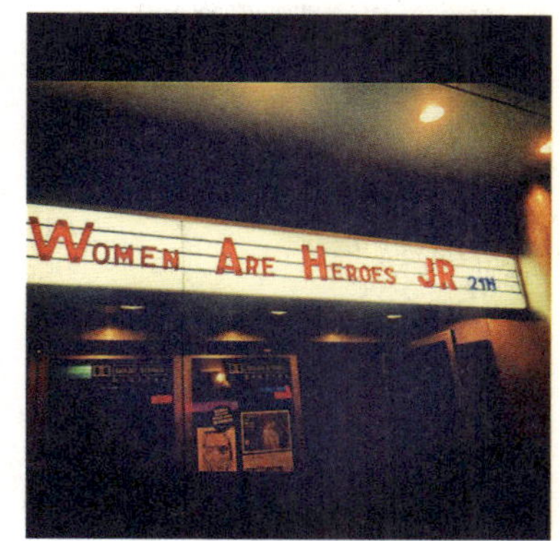
WOMEN ARE HEROES JR
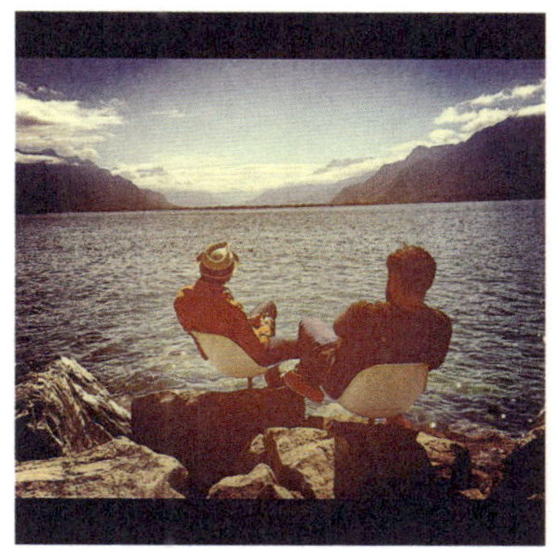
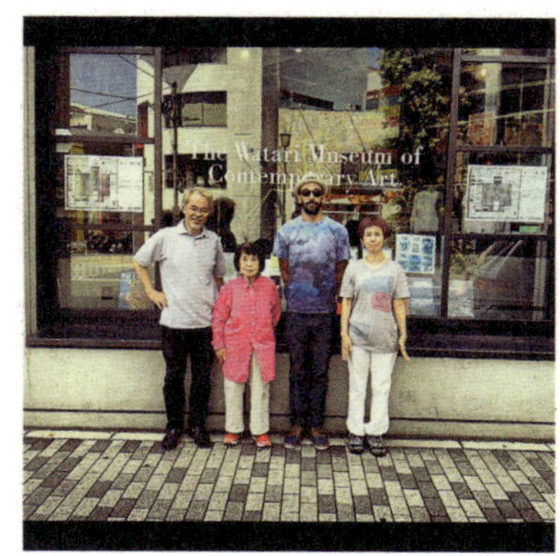
The Watari Museum of
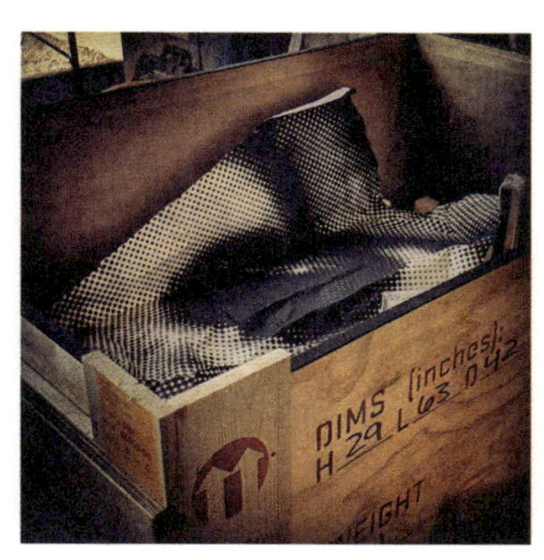
DIMS (inches)
H 29 L 63 D 42
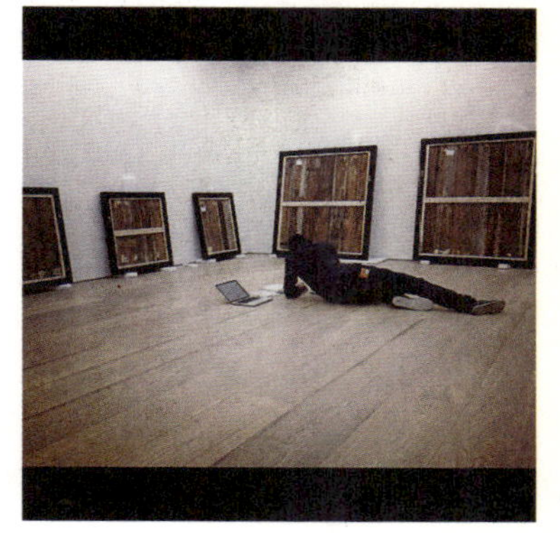
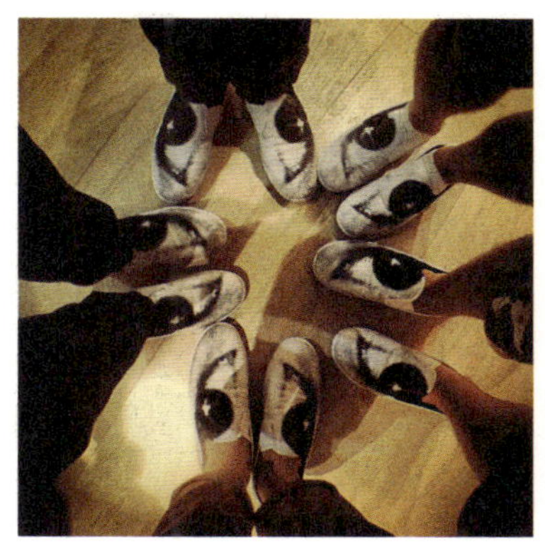
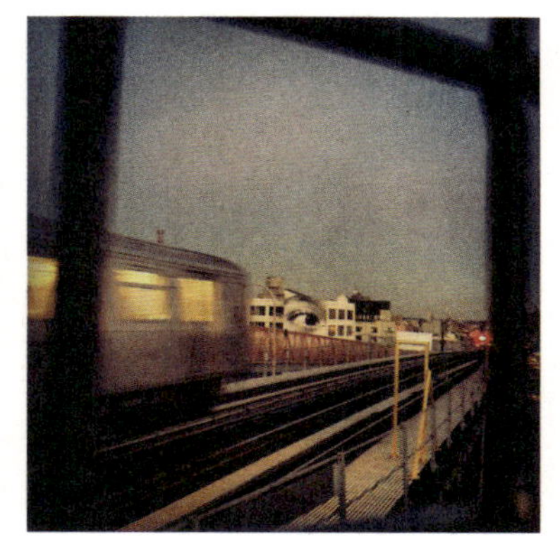
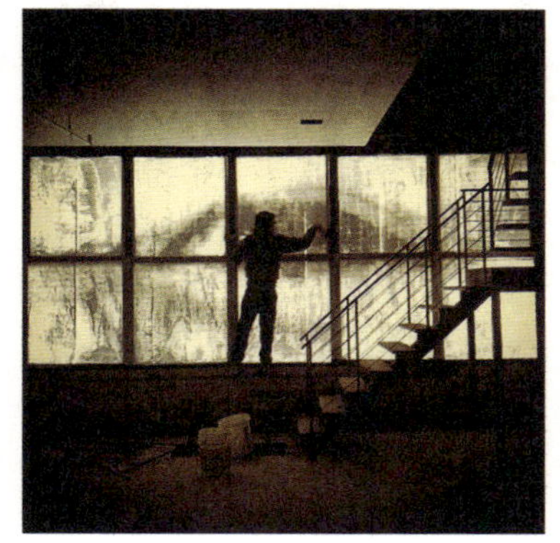
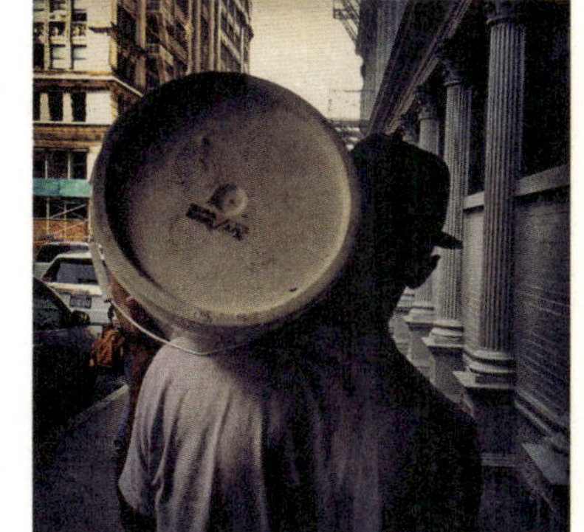
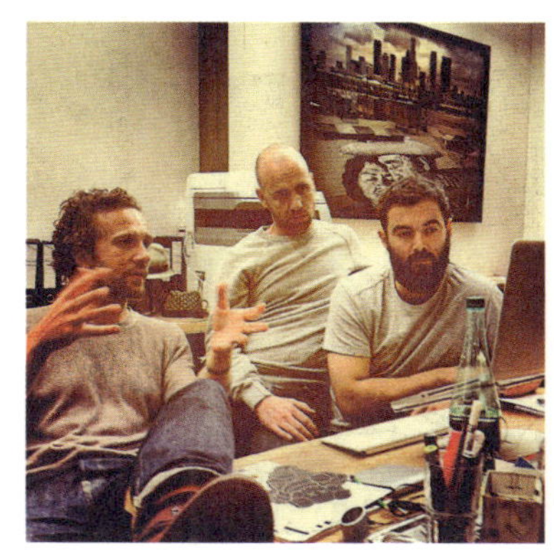
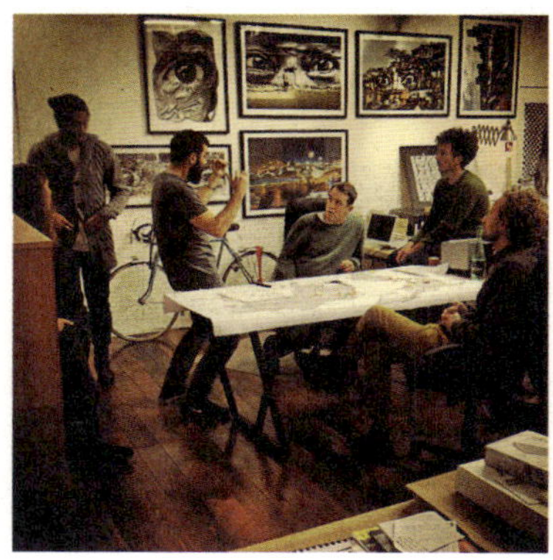
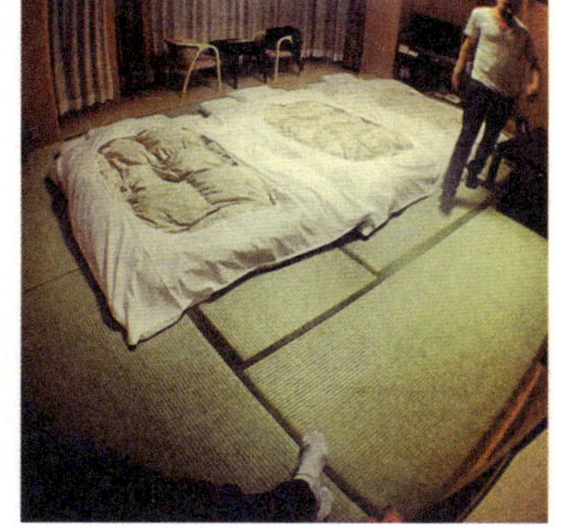
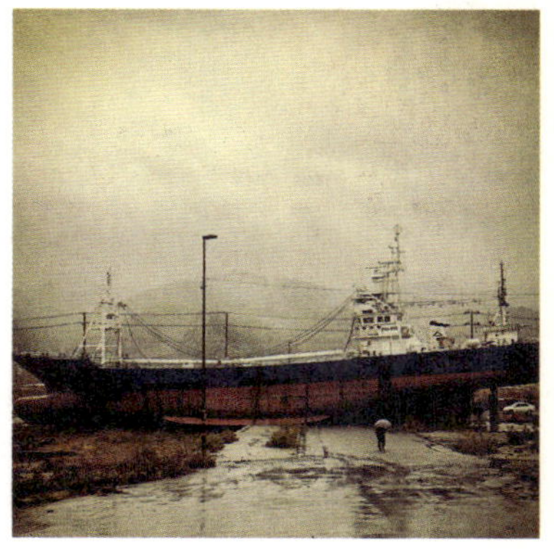

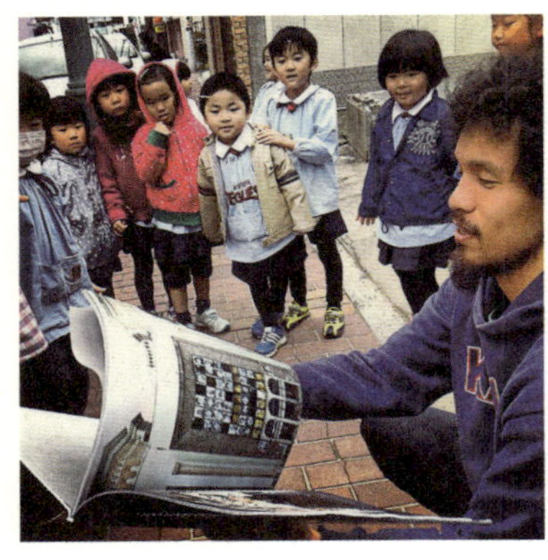
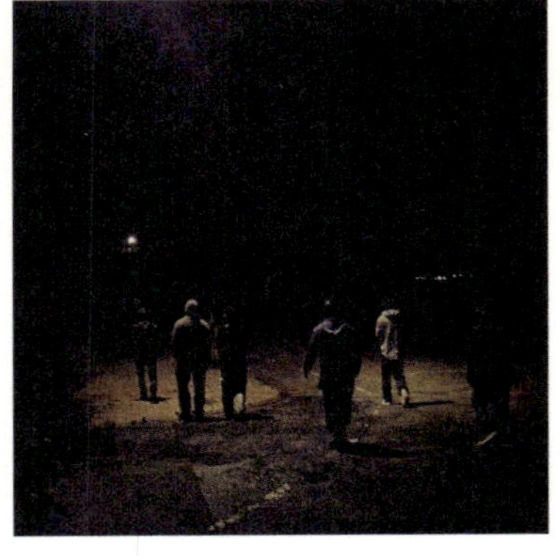
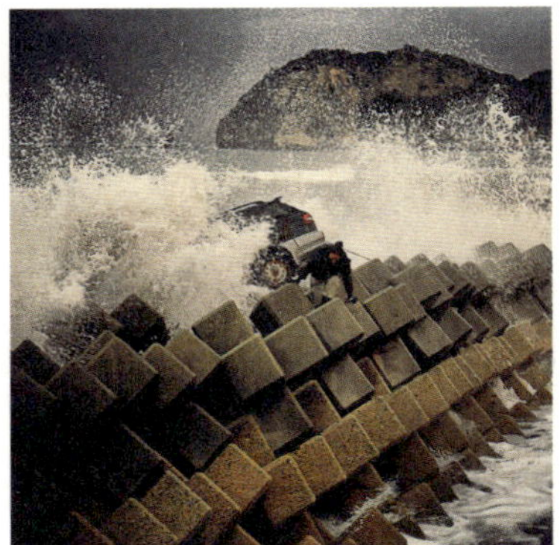
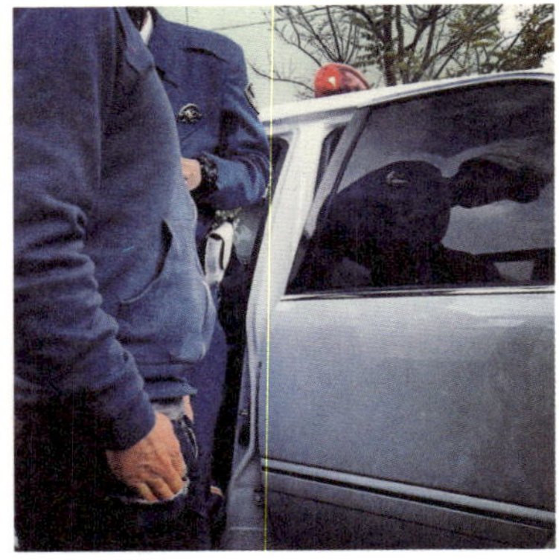
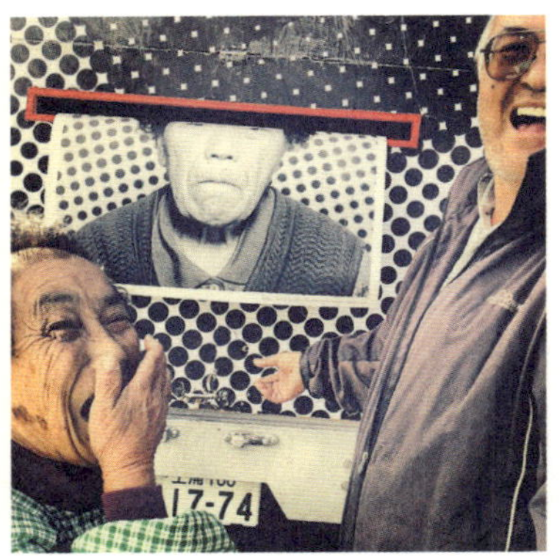
17-74
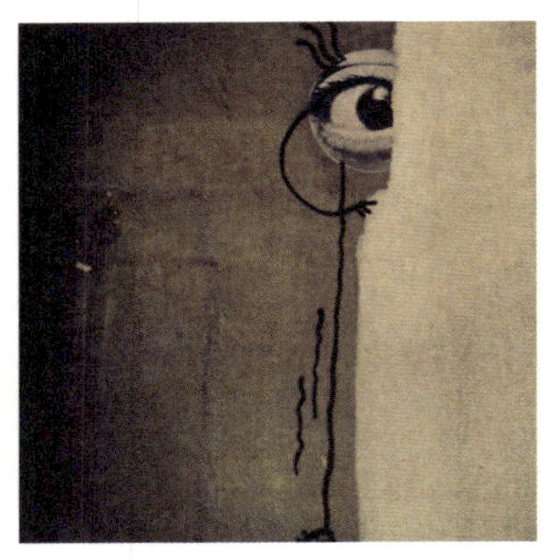
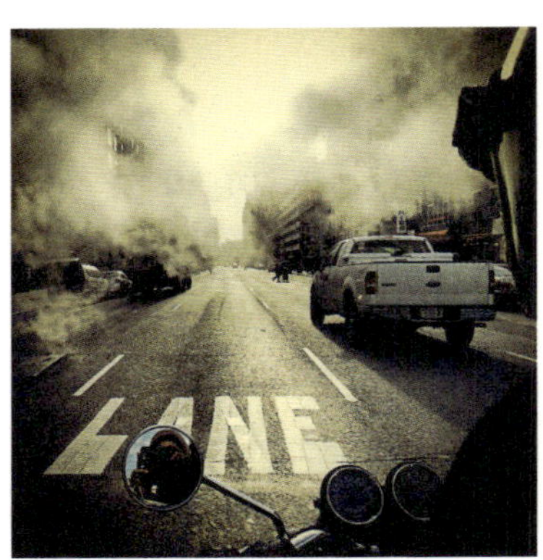
LANE
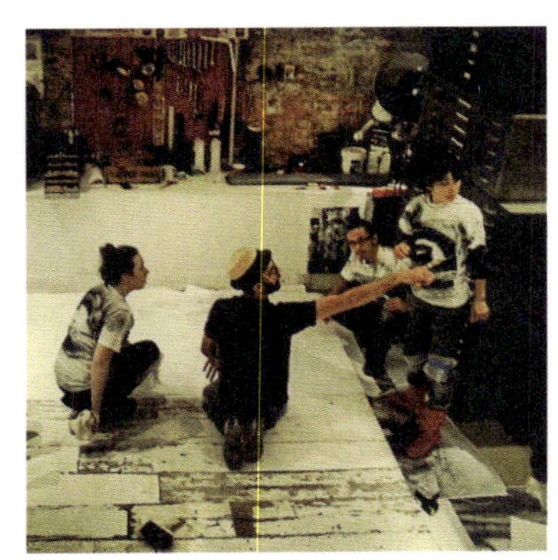
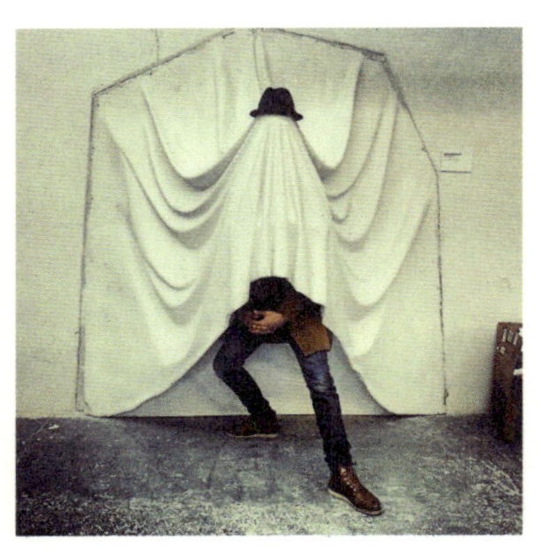
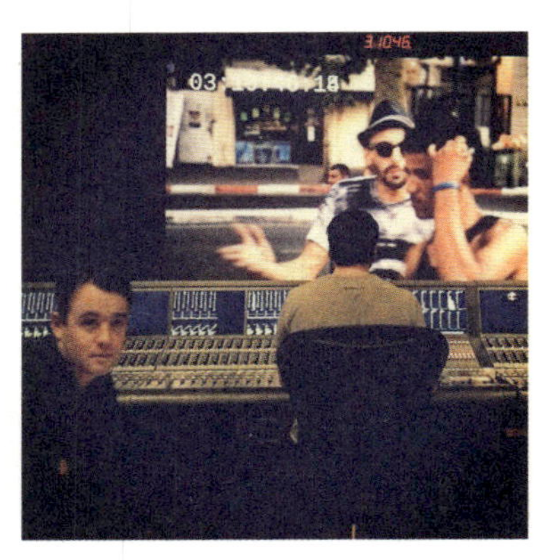
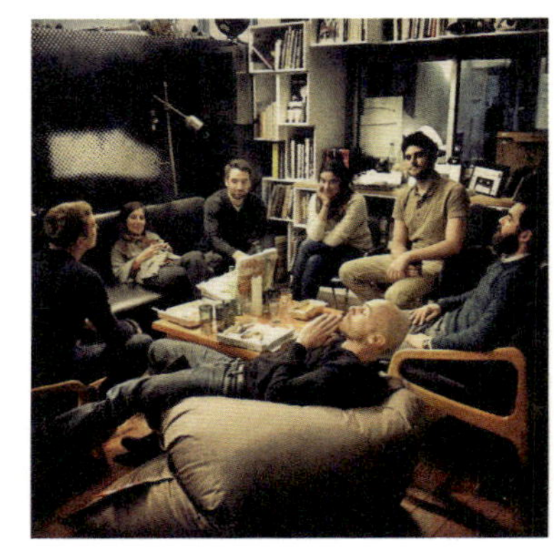
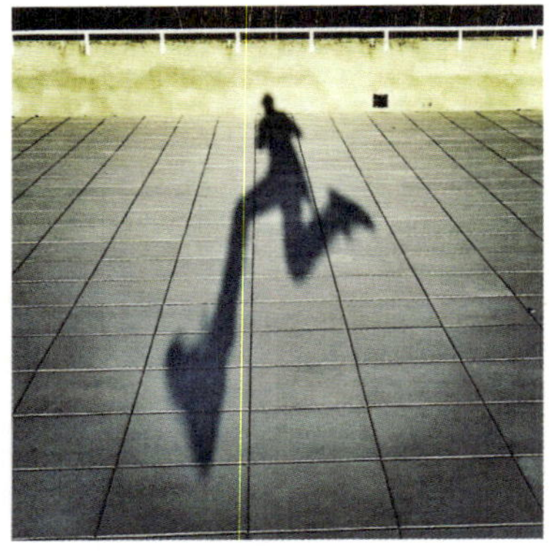
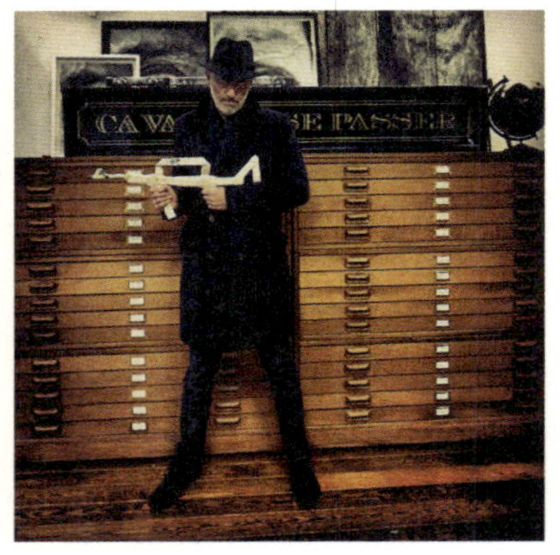
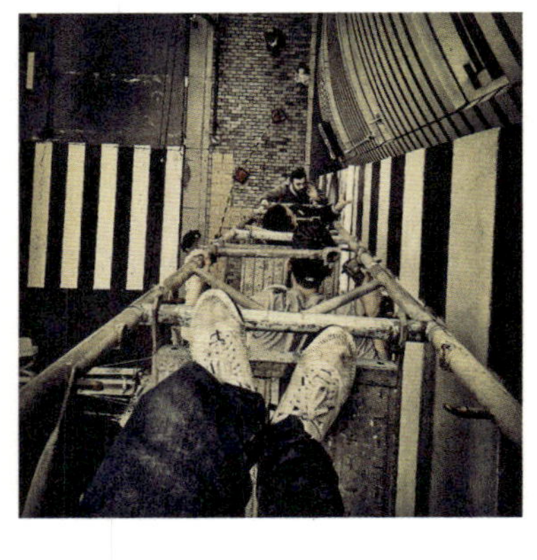
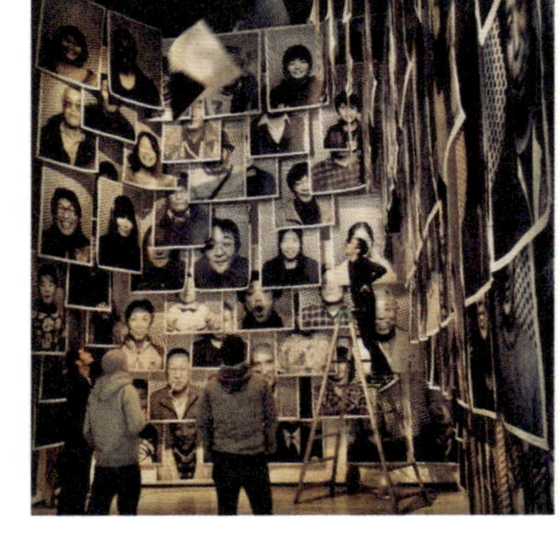
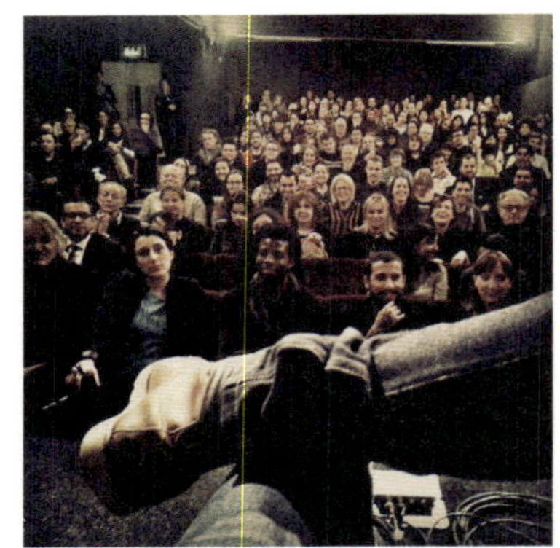
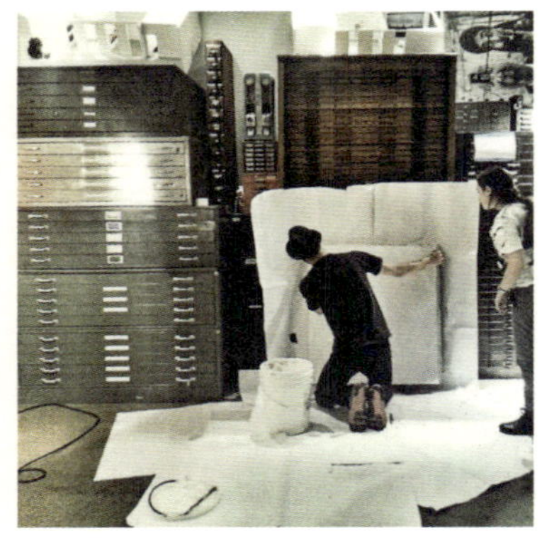
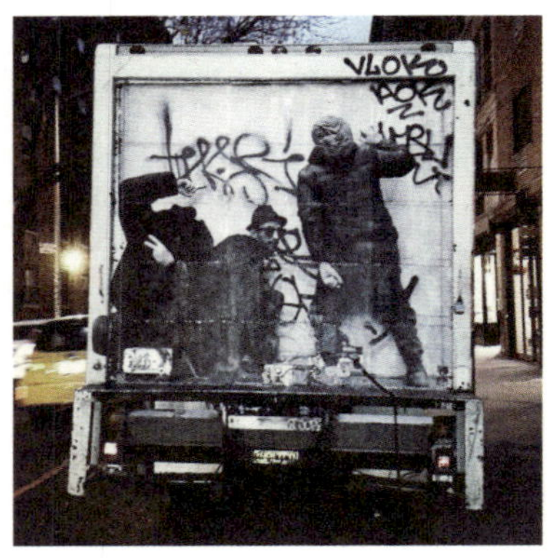
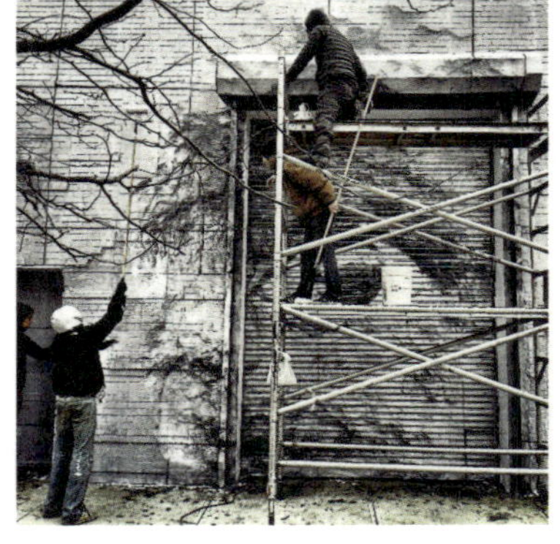
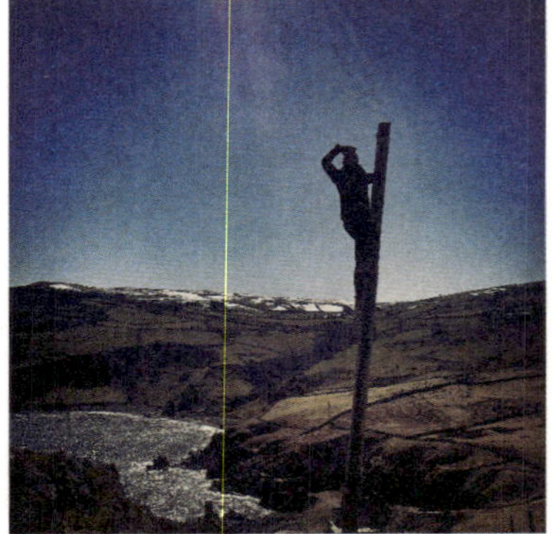

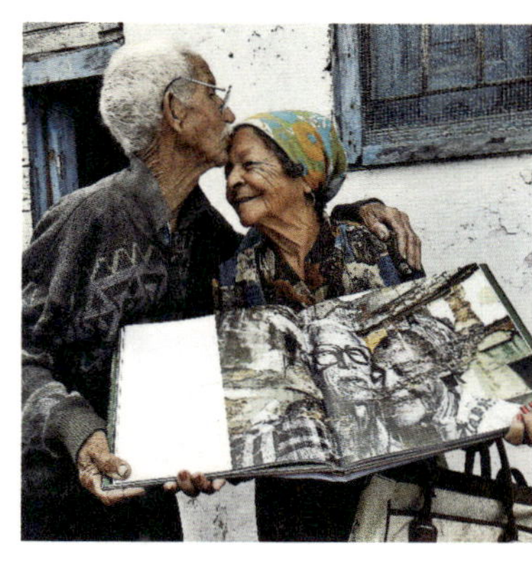
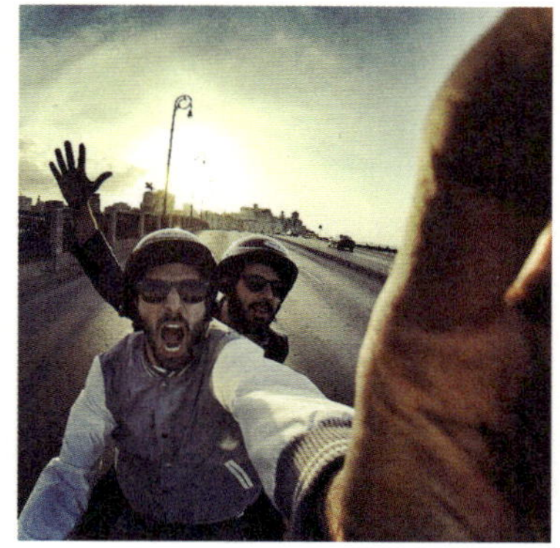
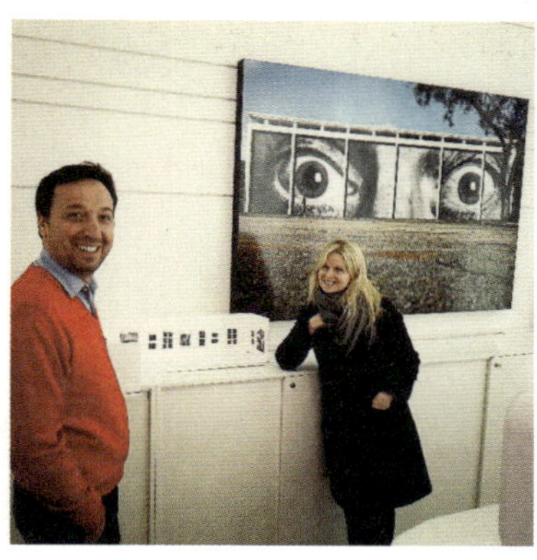
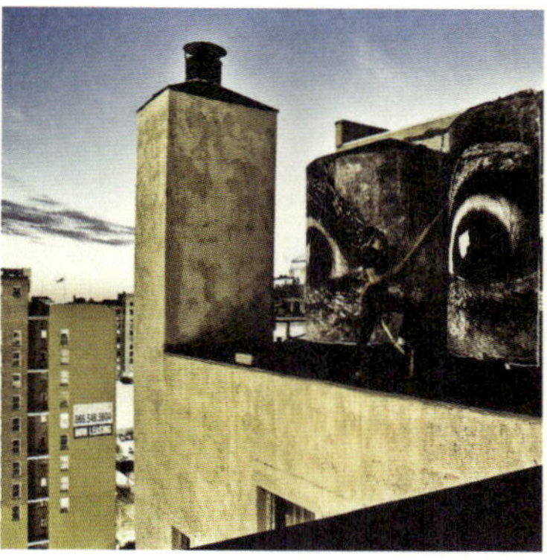
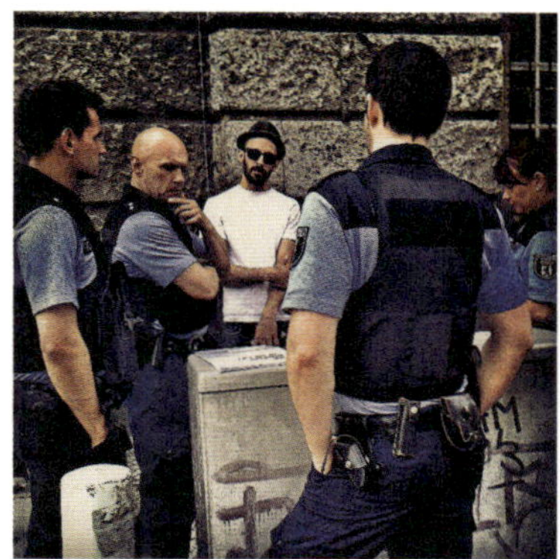
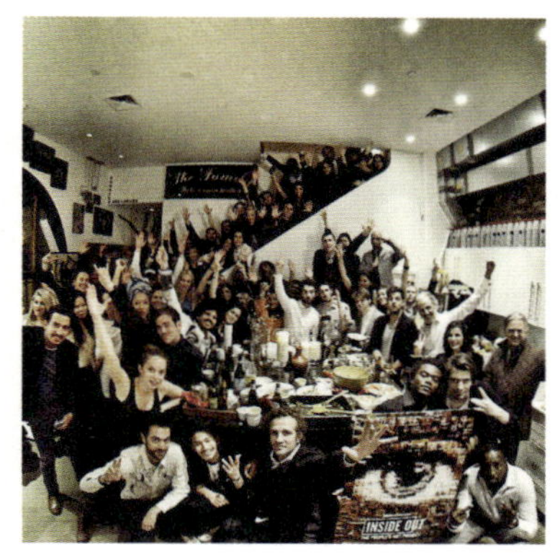
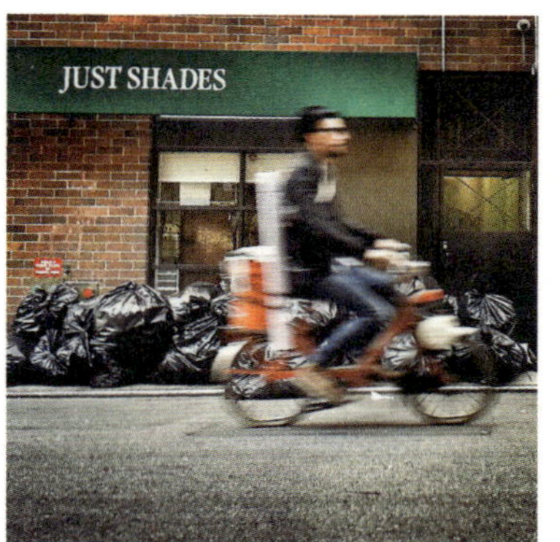
JUST SHADES
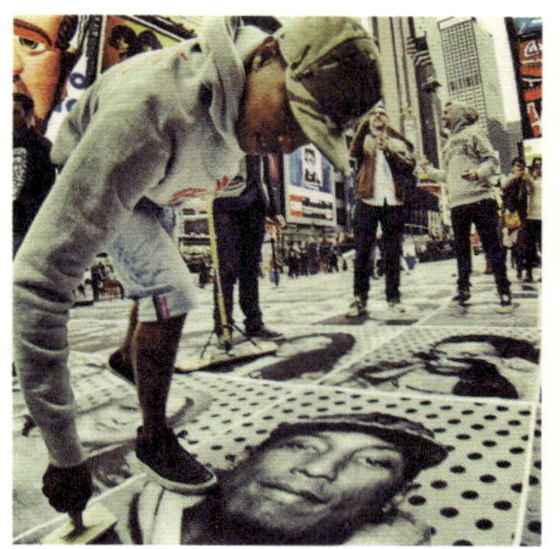
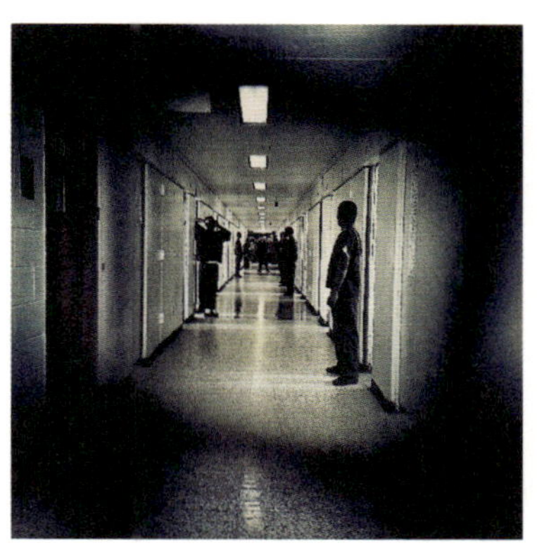
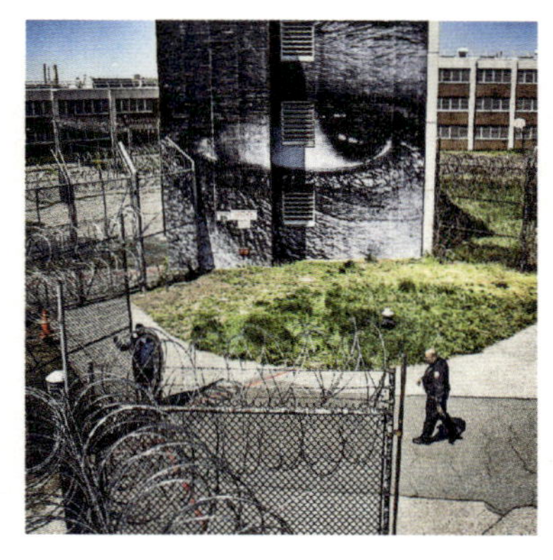
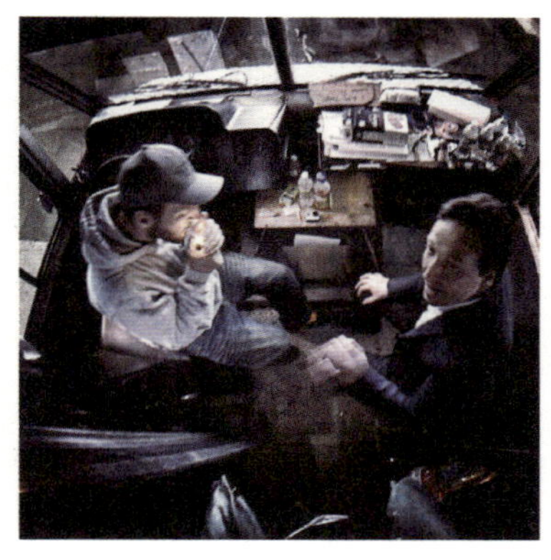
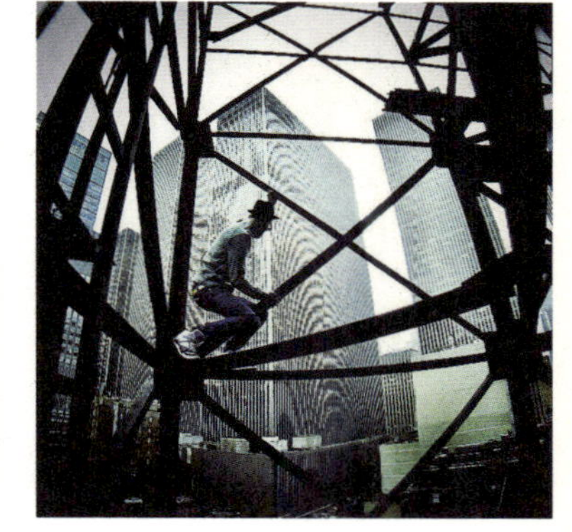
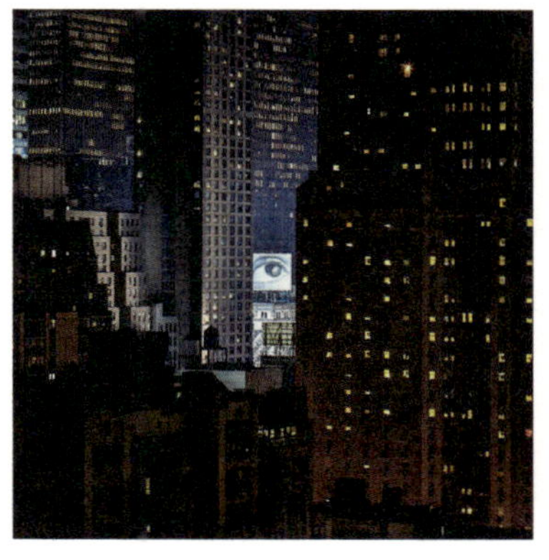
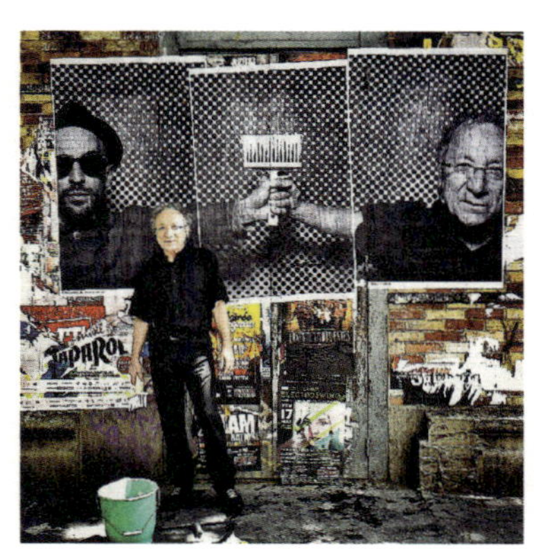
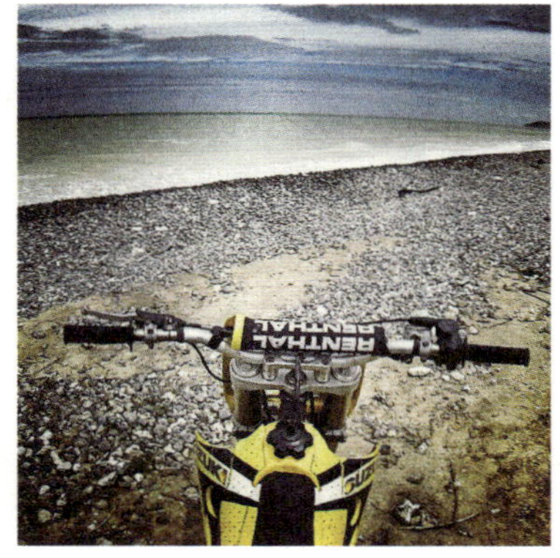
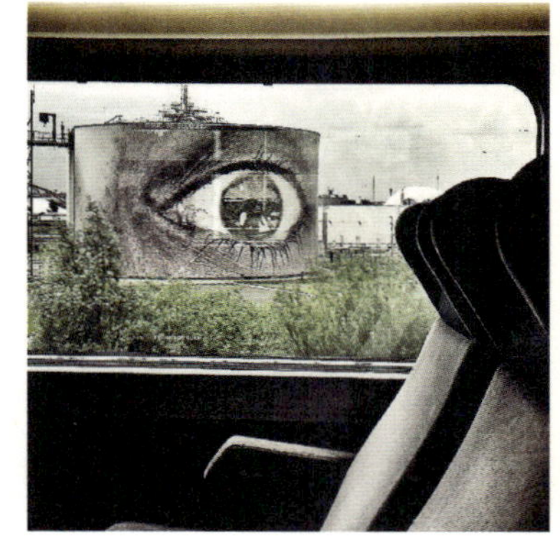
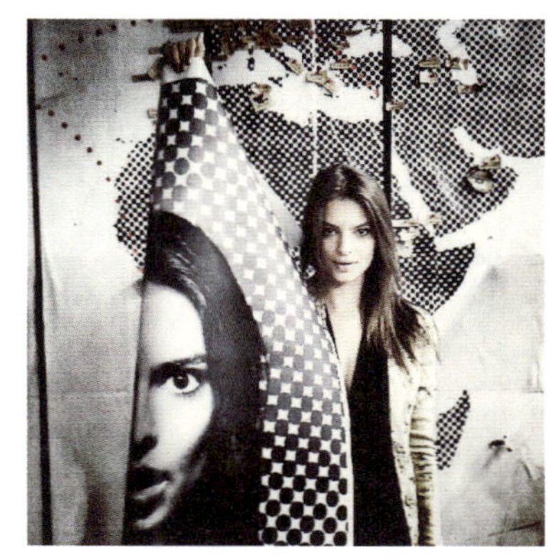
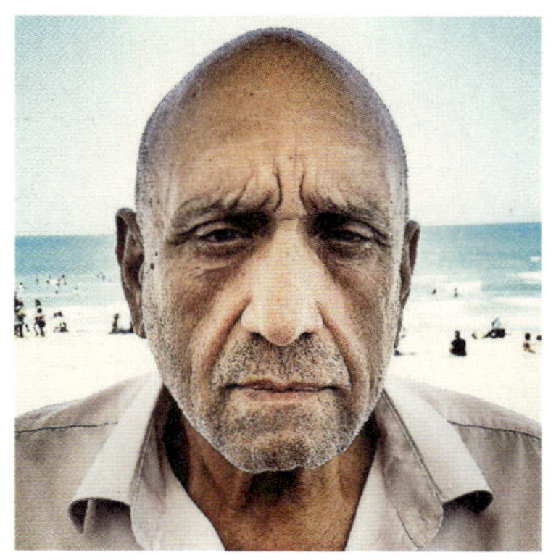
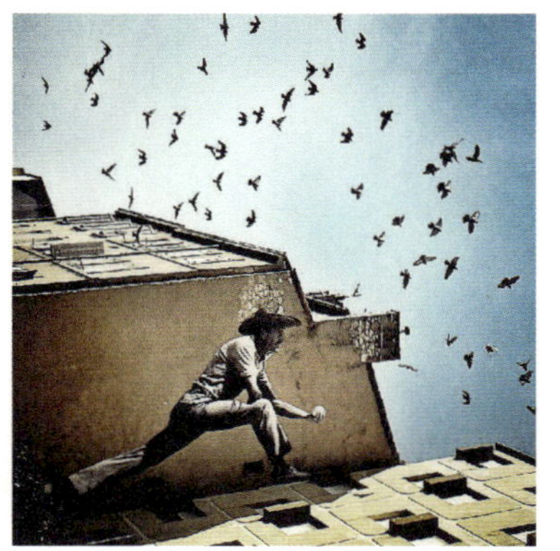
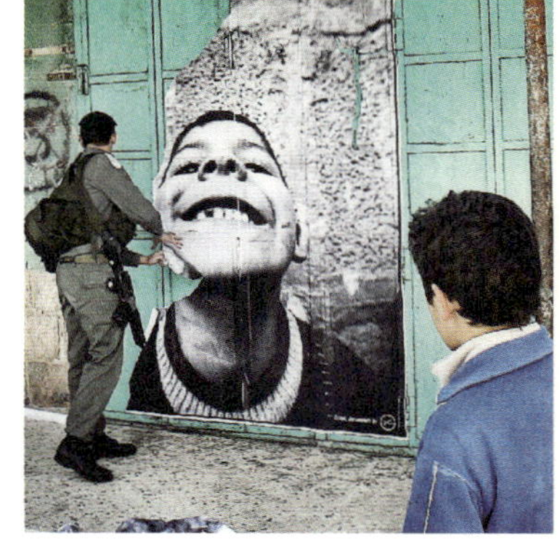

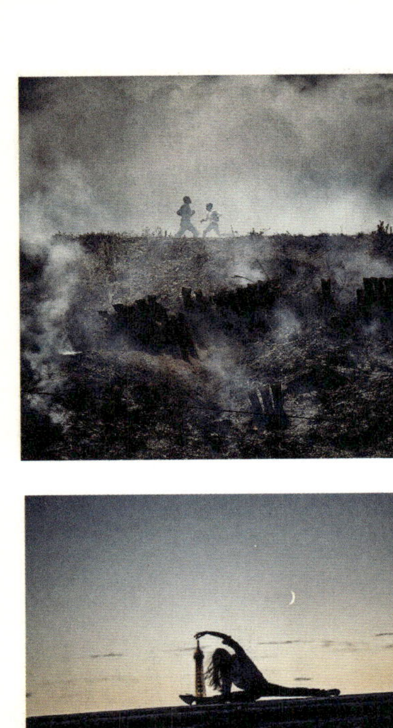
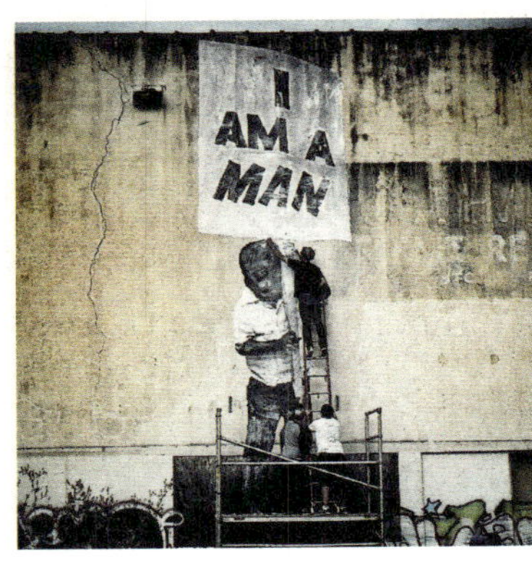
I AM A MAN
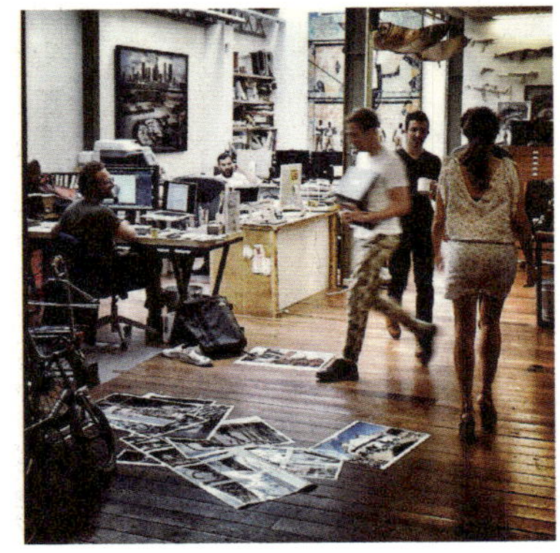
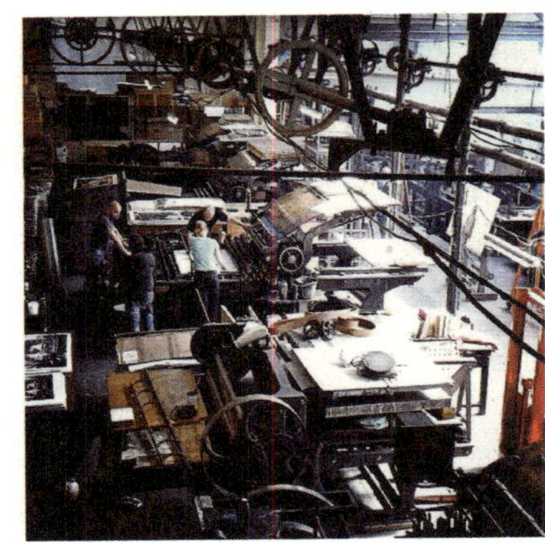
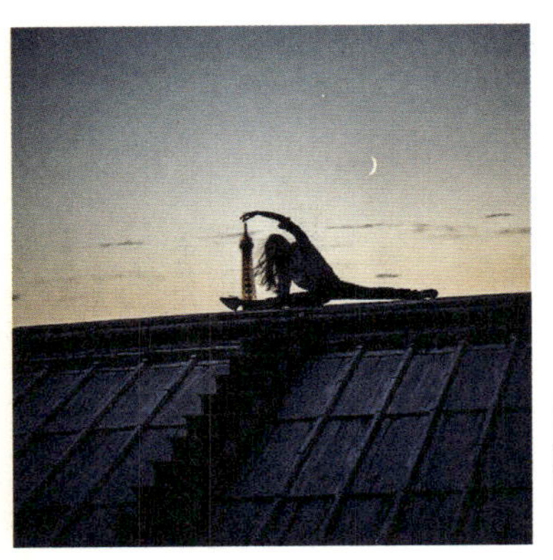
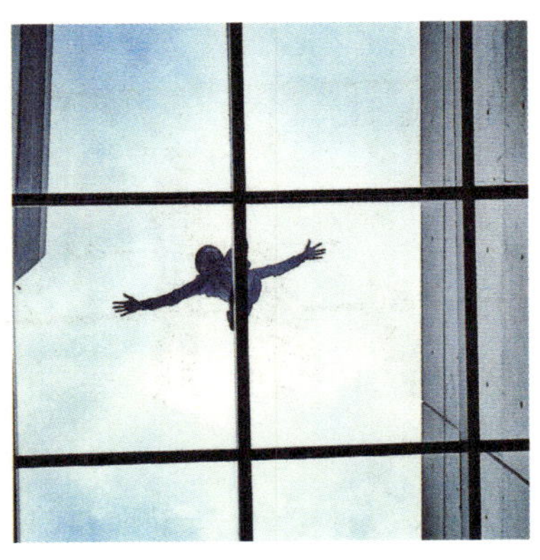
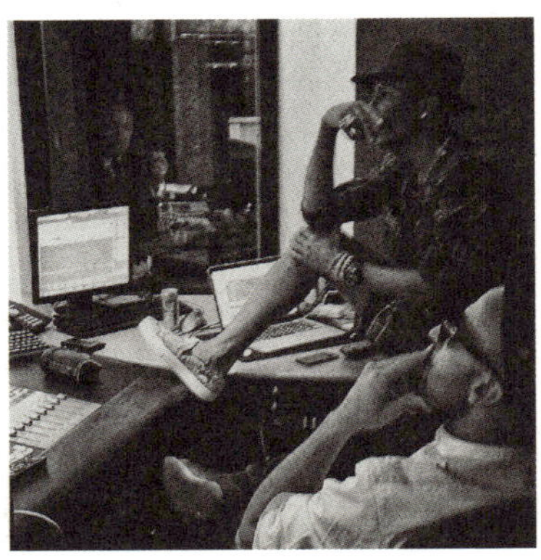
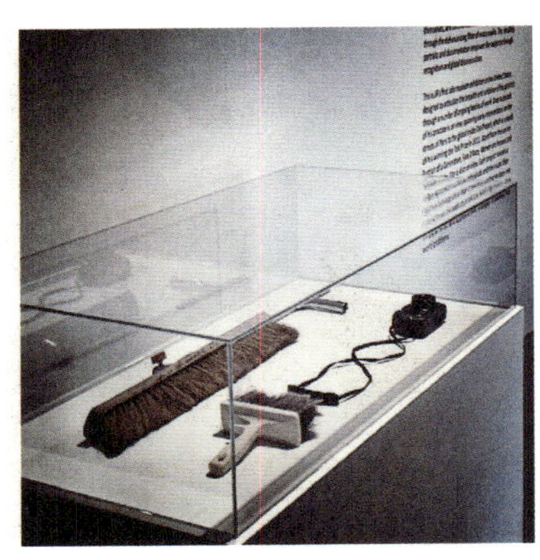
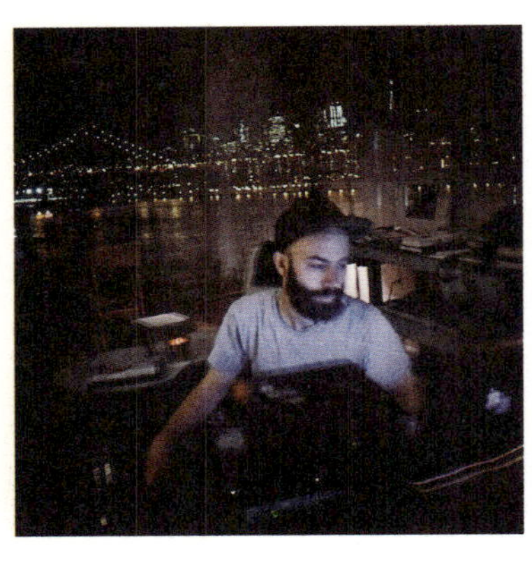
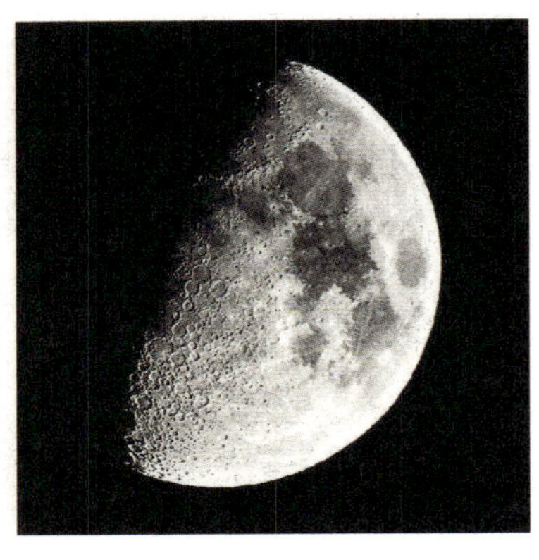
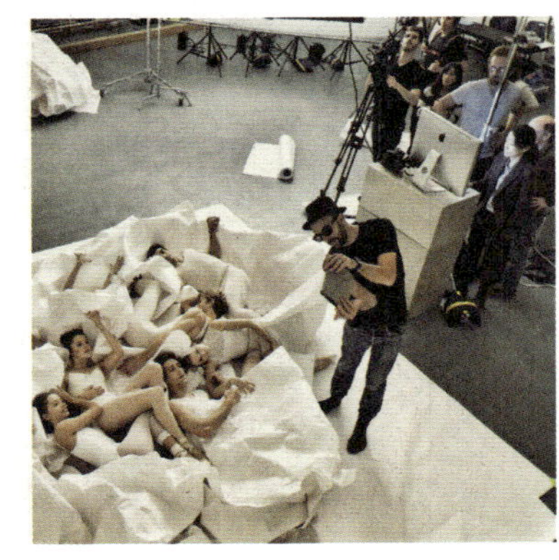
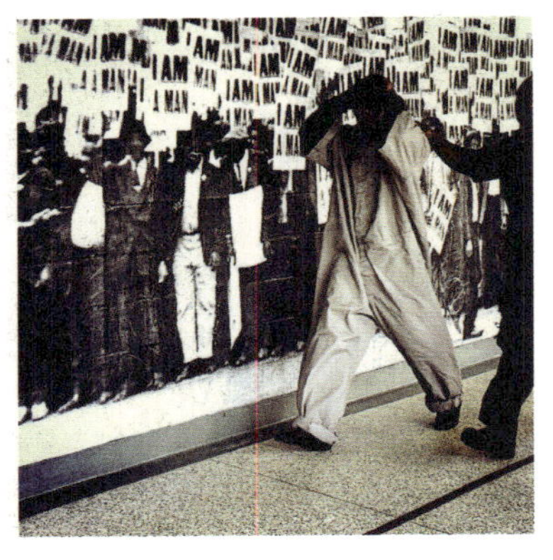
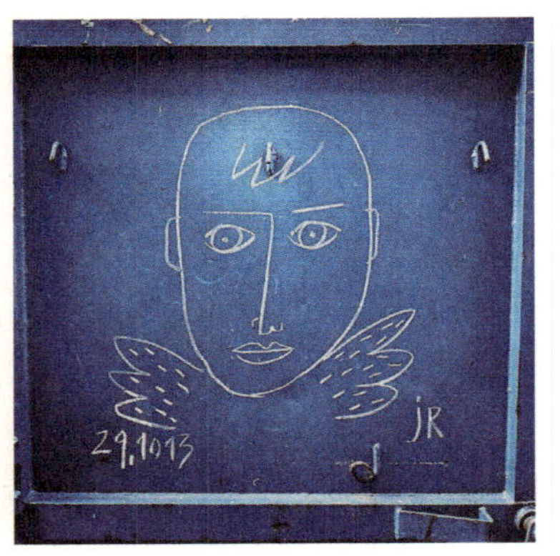
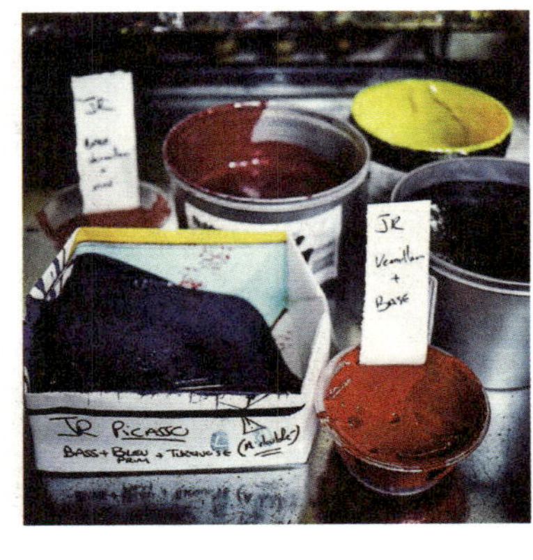
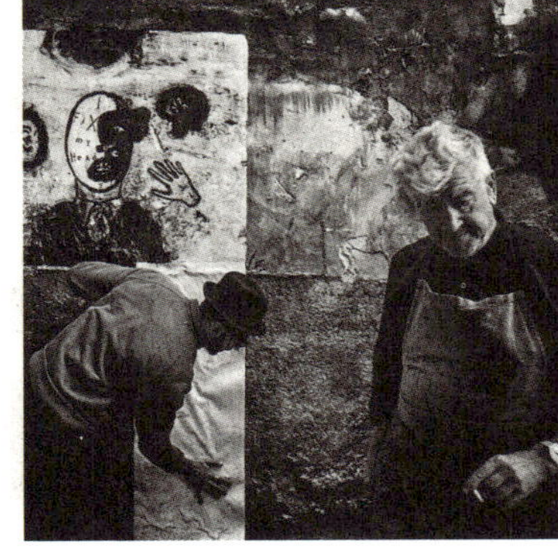
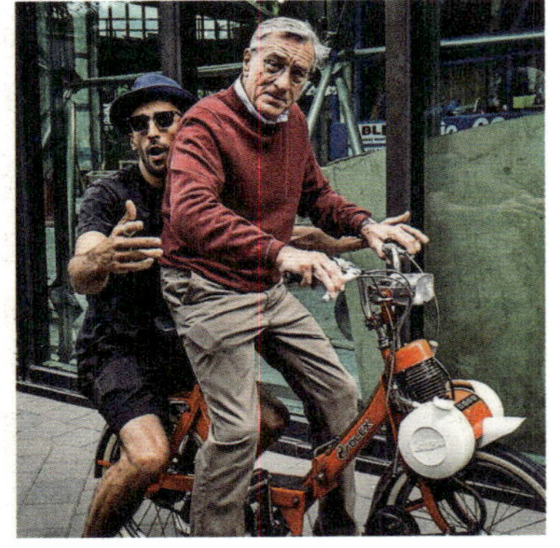
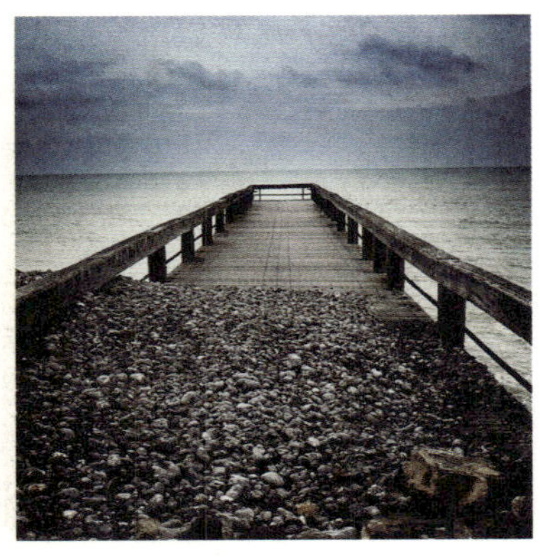
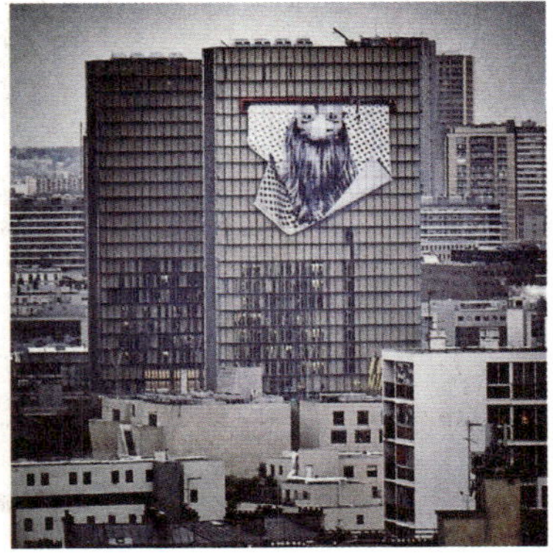
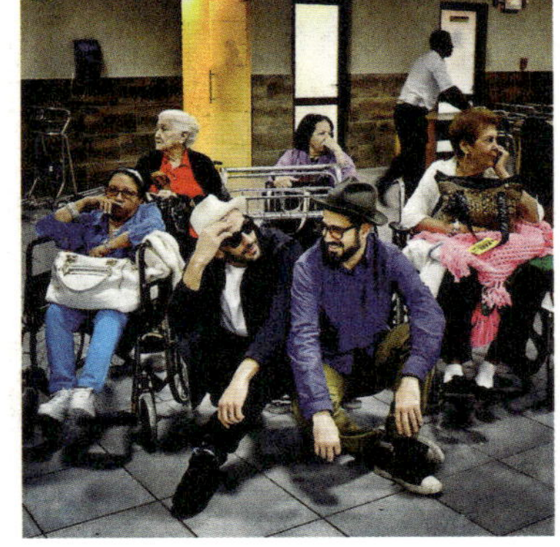
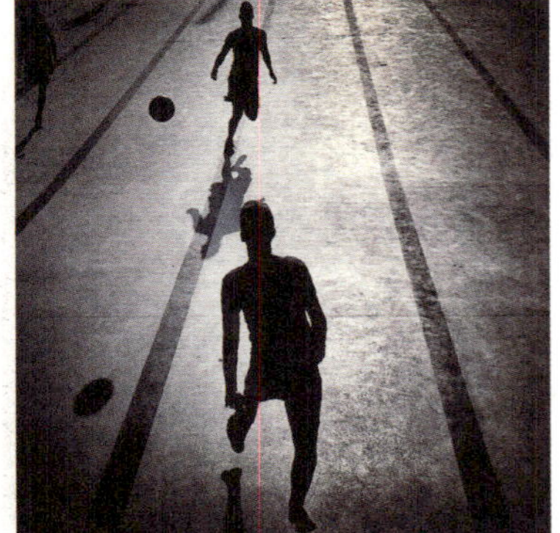

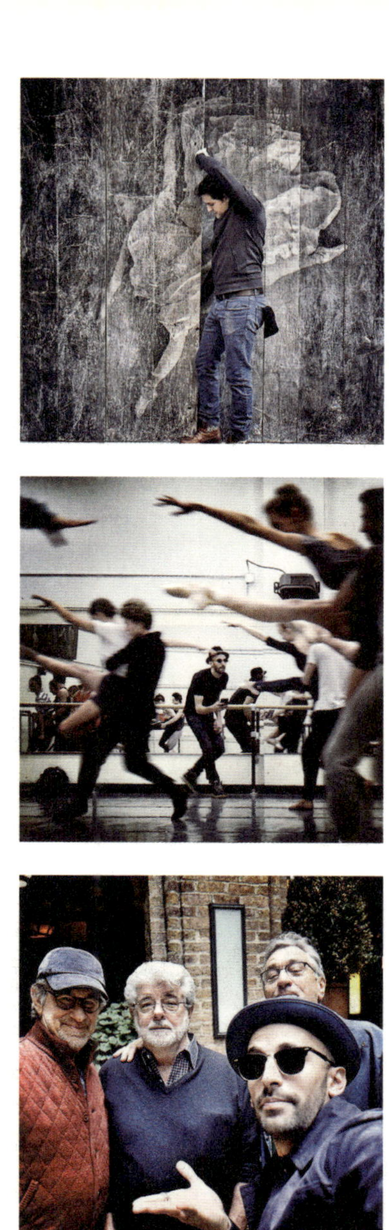

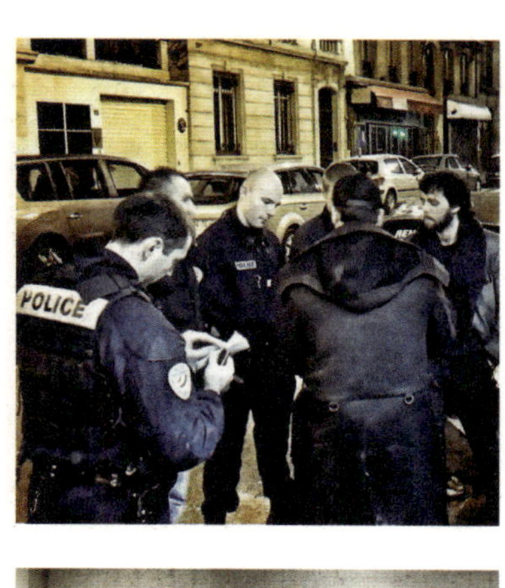

POLICE

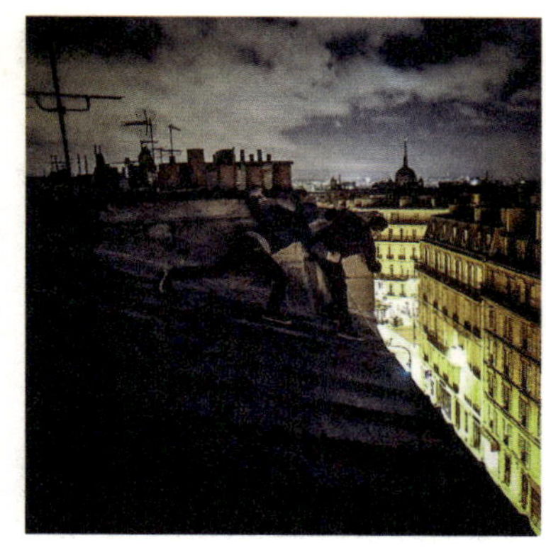

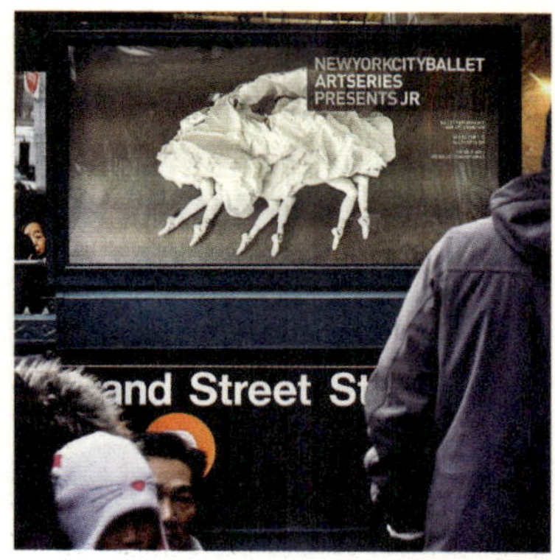

NEWYORKCITYBALLET
ARTSERIES
PRESENTS JR
and Street St

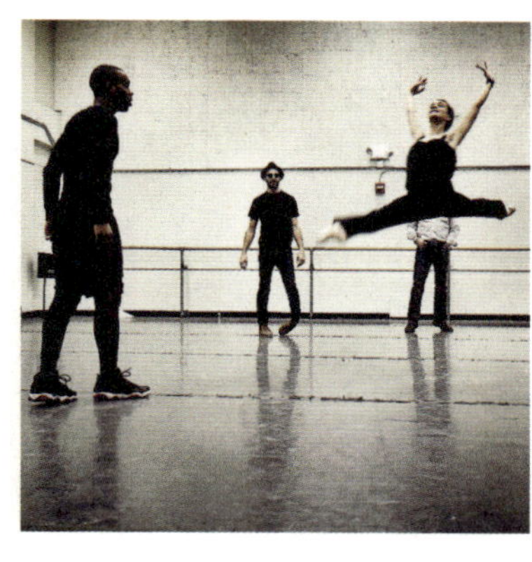

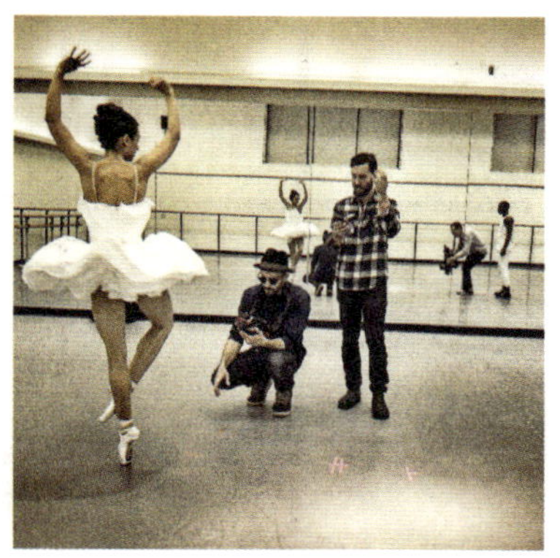

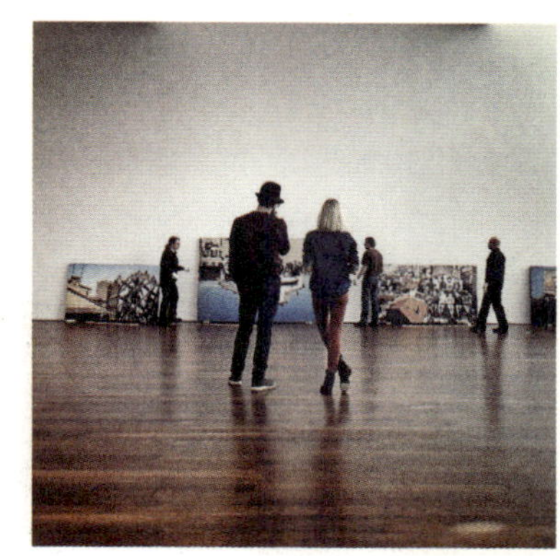

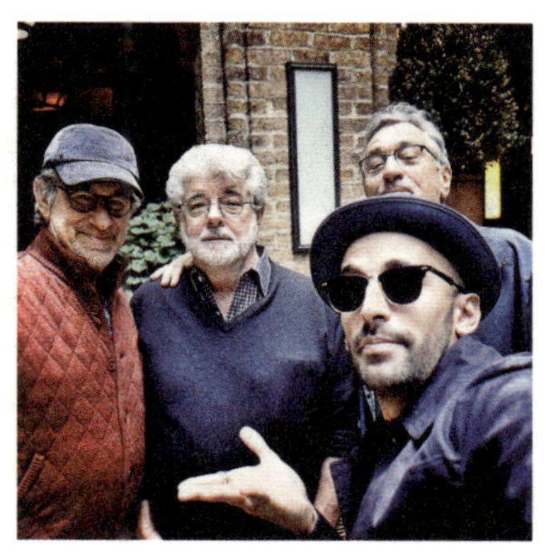

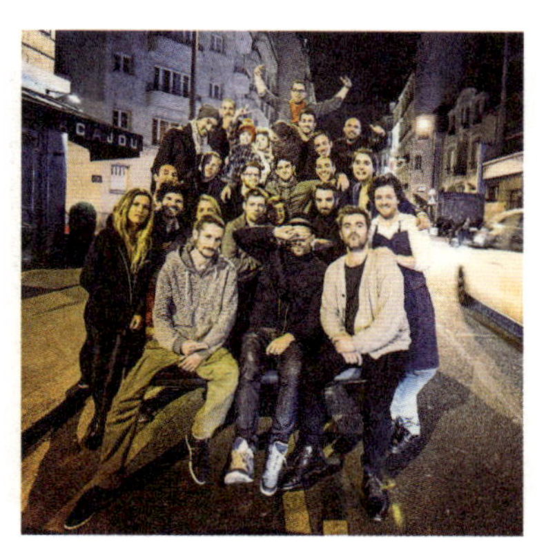

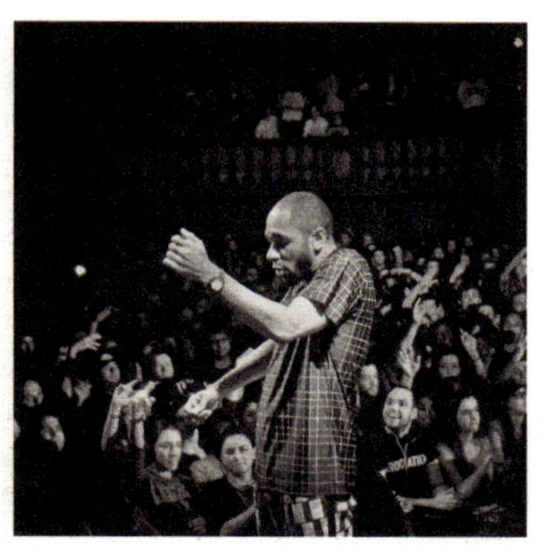

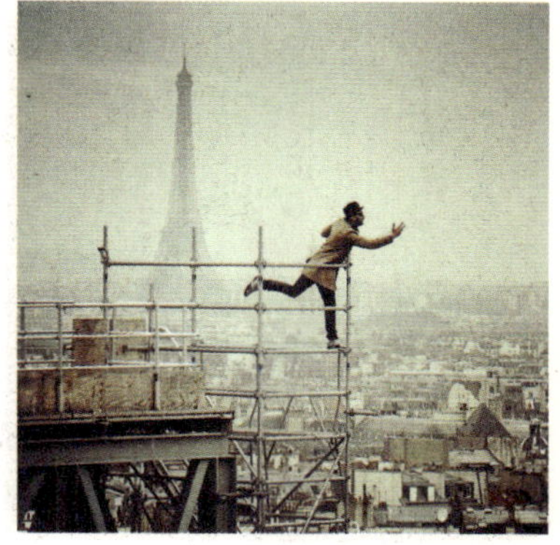

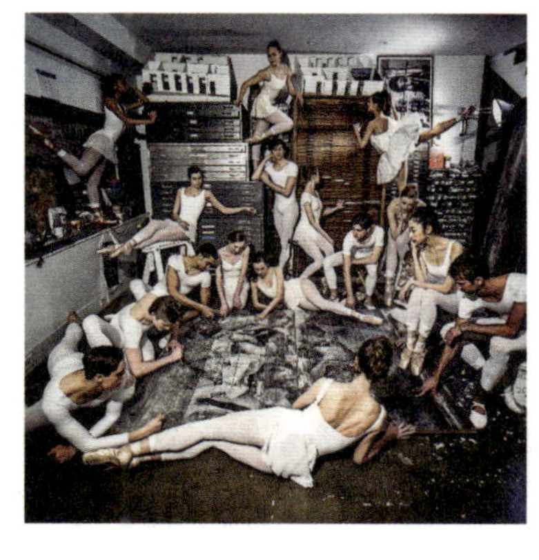

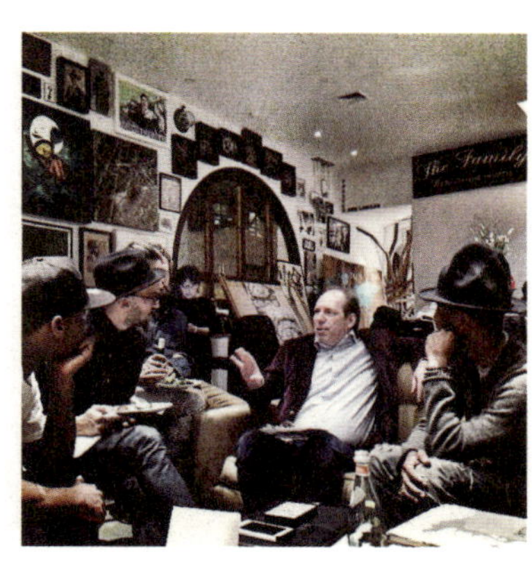

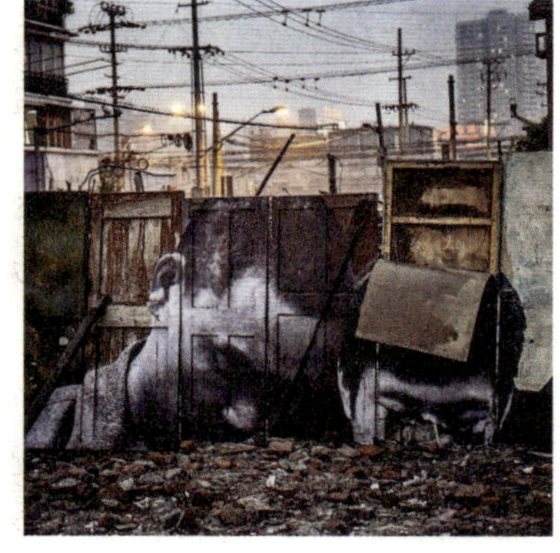

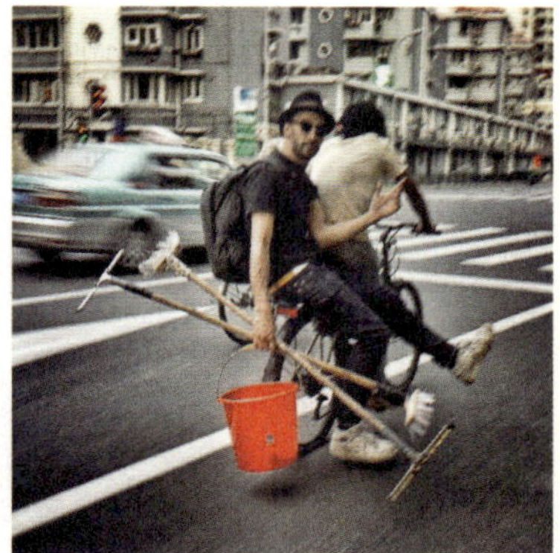

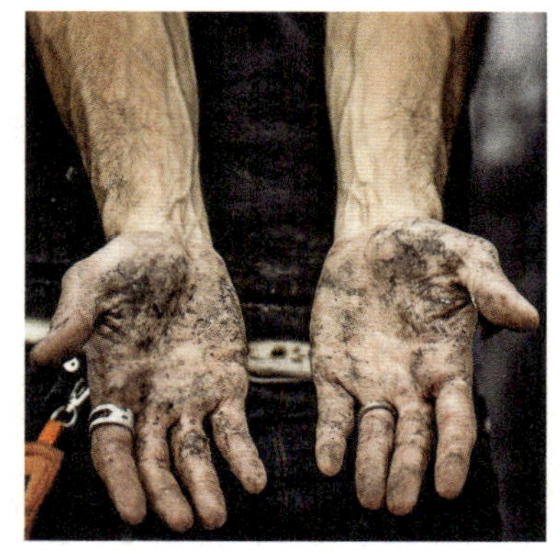

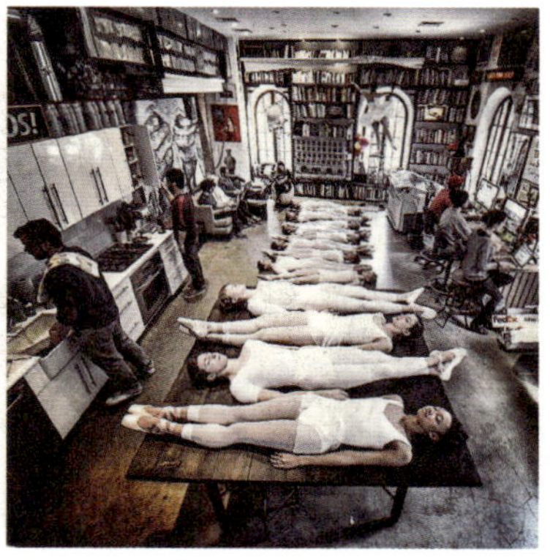

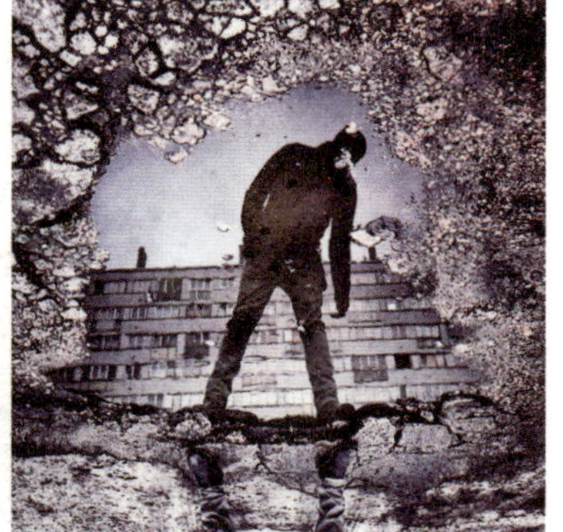

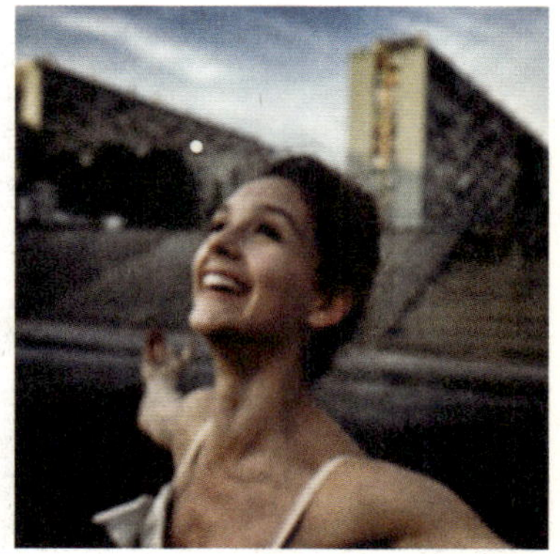

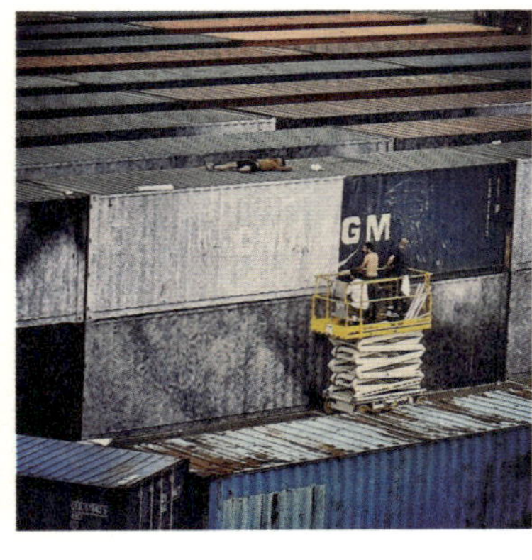
GM
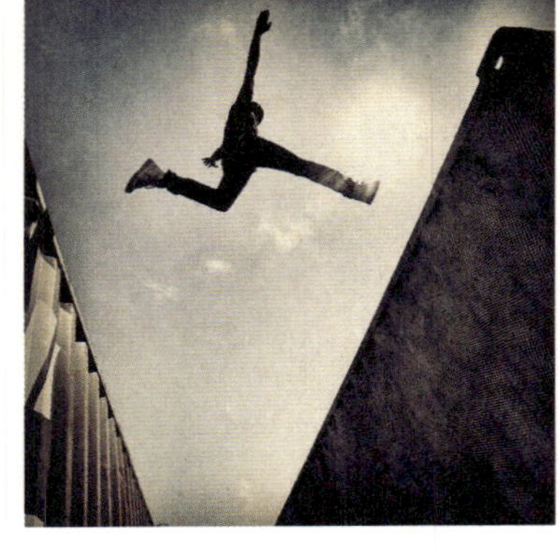
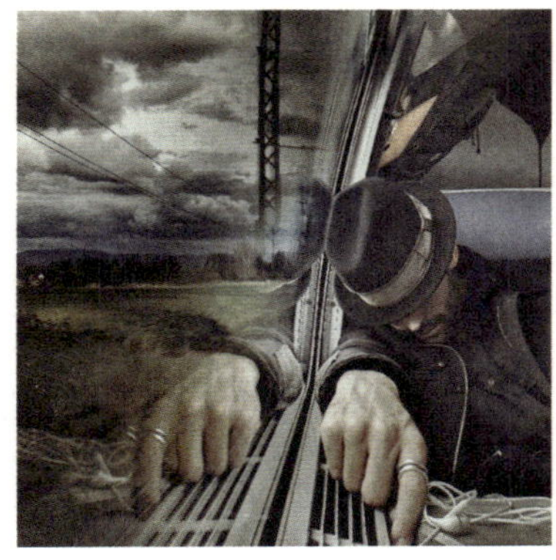
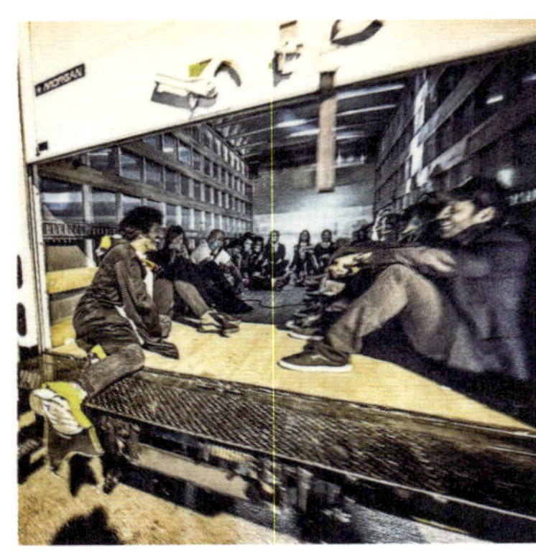
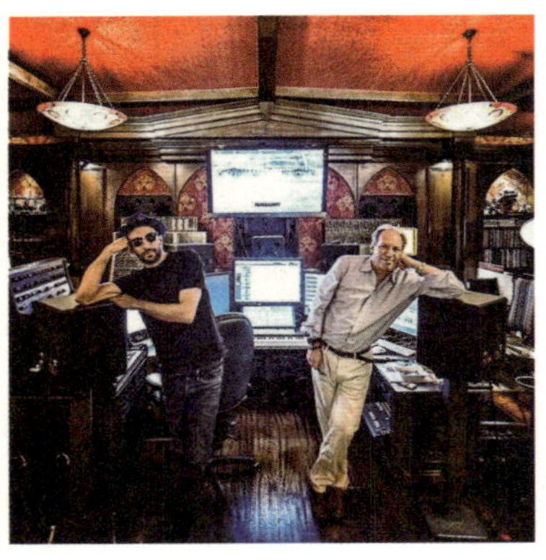
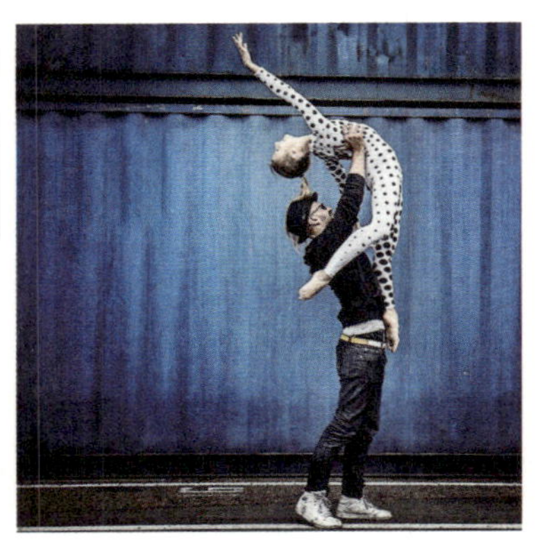
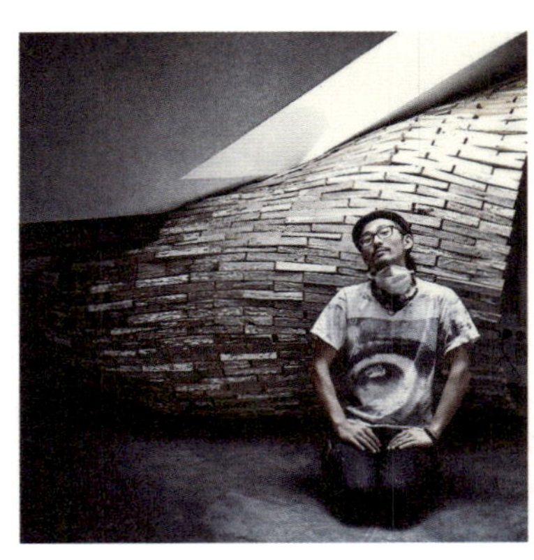
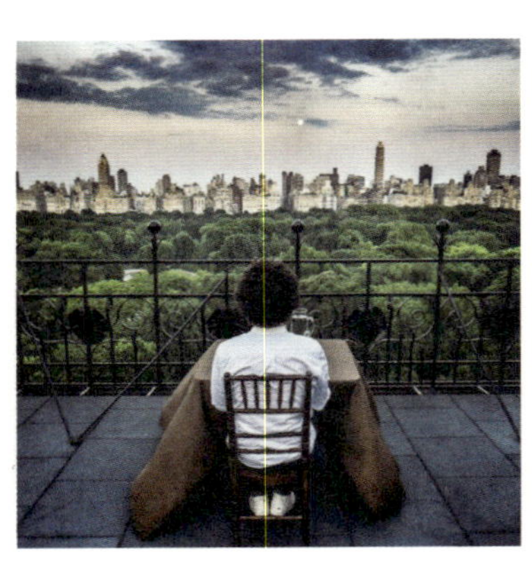
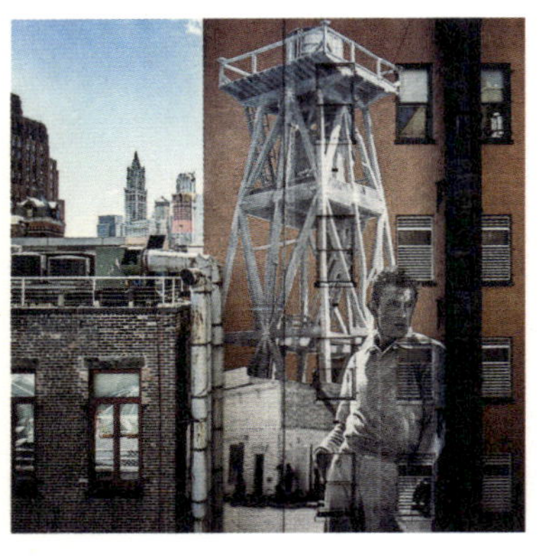
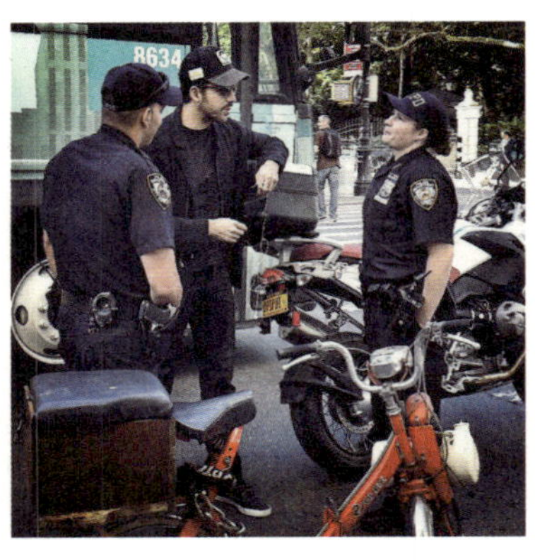
8634
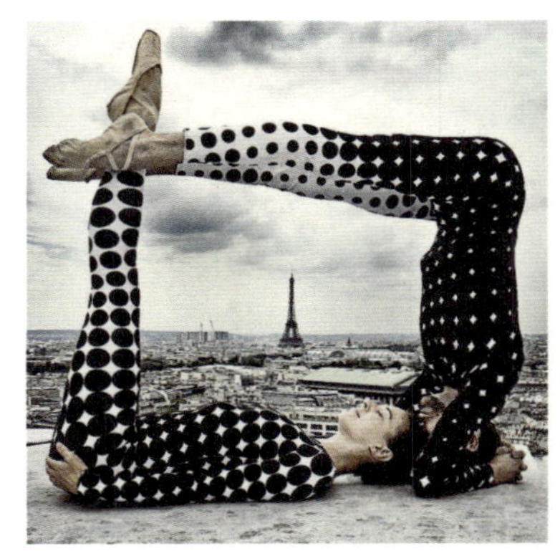
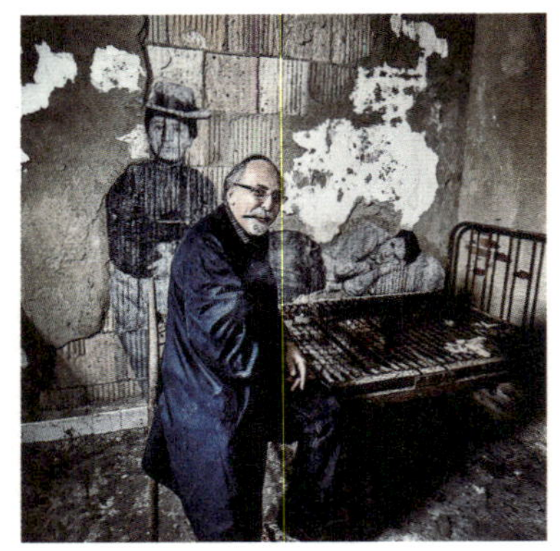
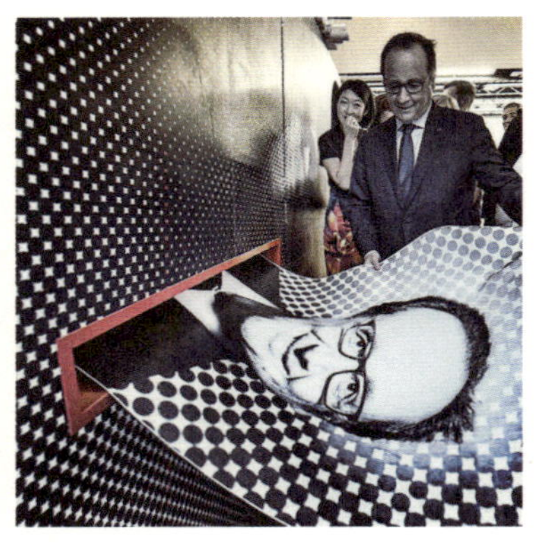
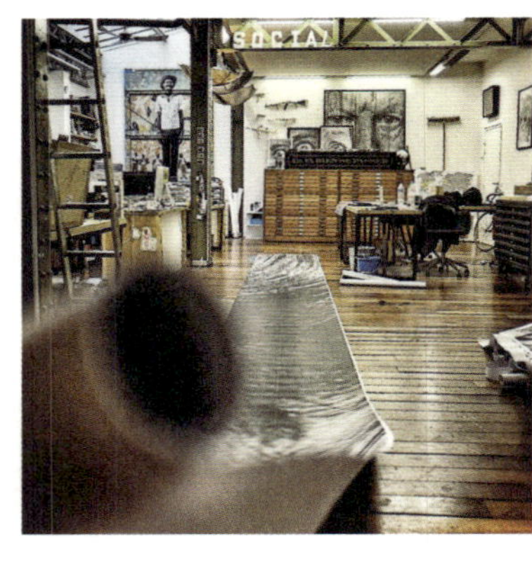
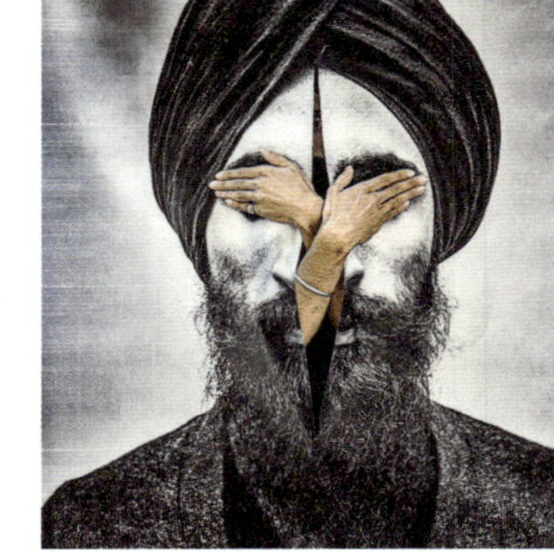
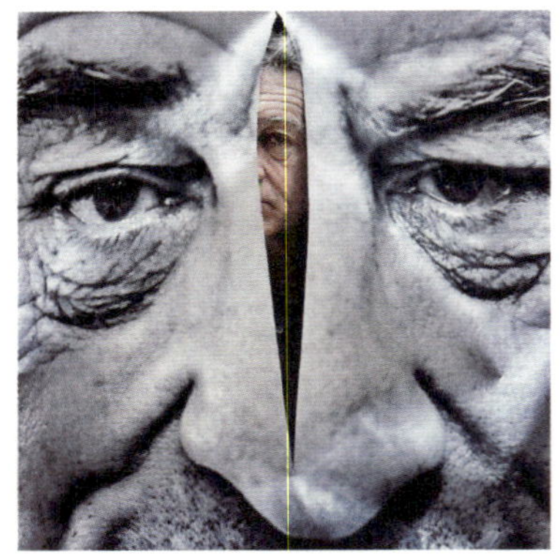
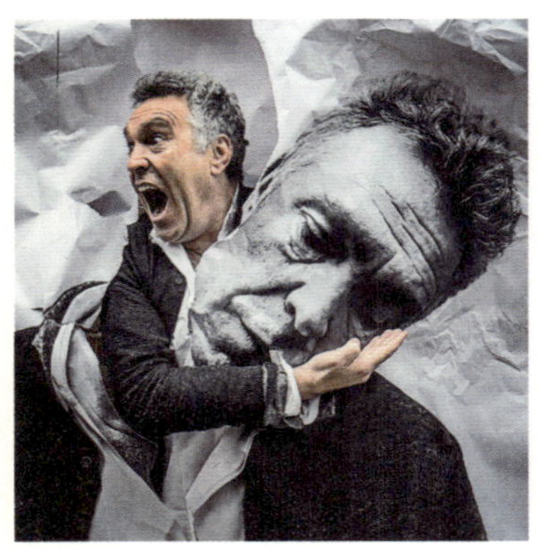
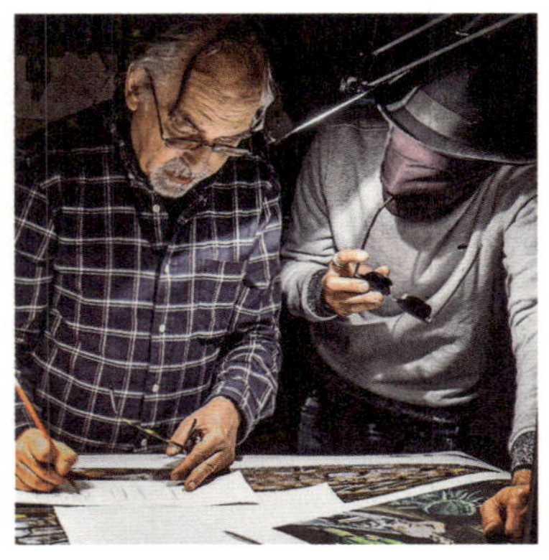
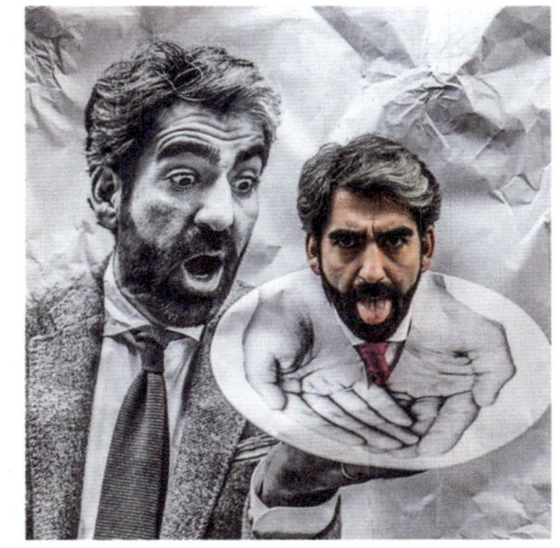
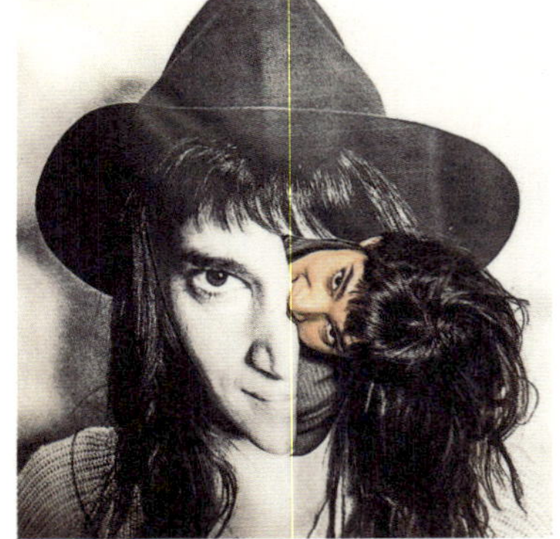

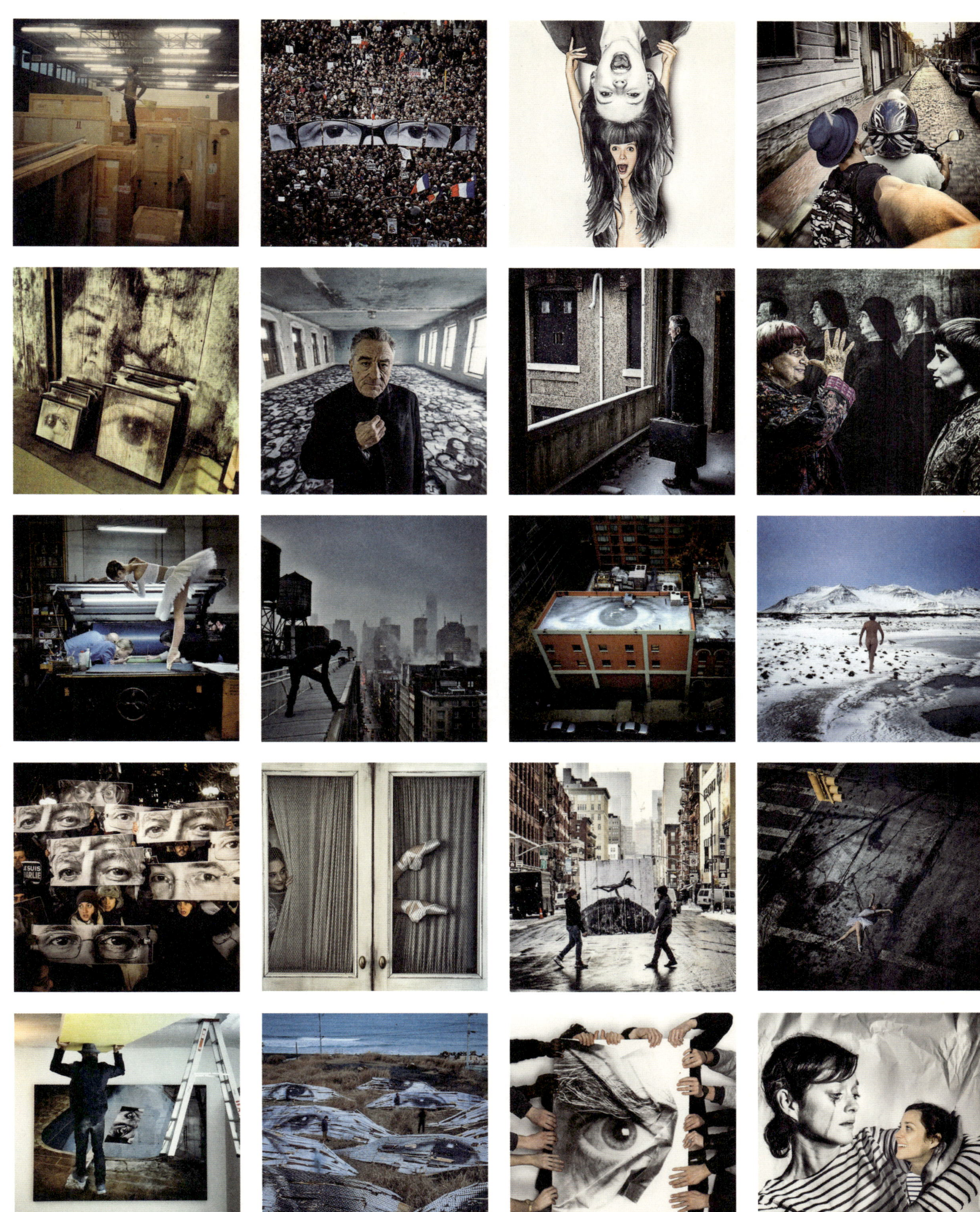

CHRONOLOGY

1983 - 2004

— **1983**
Born in the outskirts of Paris

— **1996**
Starts out as a graffiti tagger using the moniker Face 3

— **2000**
Transitions into photography: finds an old film camera in a Paris Metro station – the Charles de Gaulle – Etoile station of the RER (Paris' suburban railway system) – and starts taking black-and-white photos of his friends while they are tagging

— **2001**
Begins exhibiting his photographs by pasting them on the walls of Paris and in the RER in an ongoing outdoor exhibition, *Expo 2 Rue*, 2001–2004

— **2004**
Begins *Portrait of a Generation*, his first large-scale street pasting project, and makes a short video called 'Clichés de Ghetto' with his friend Ladj Ly

2005

— Self-publishes first publication, *Carnet de Rue (My Street Diary)*, begun in 2004, charting his practice and projects to date. It is a photographic narrative exploring the work of many artists including Blu, Zevs, Banksy, Shepard Fairey, BÄST and FAILE
— Riots break out in the outskirts of Paris in November and JR sees his pastings in Les Bosquets in the backdrop of news reports on the riots in Montfermeil
— JR returns to the *Portrait of a Generation* project – transporting the images of young people out of the *banlieues* of Clichy-sous-Bois and Montfermeil and pasting them in bourgeois areas of Paris

2006

— Covers the walls of the Maison Européenne de la Photographie in Paris with posters from *Portrait of a Generation*
— Pastes *Portrait of a Generation* photos on the outer walls of the Espace des Blancs-Manteaux, Paris
— Invited to paste *Portrait of a Generation* images on the hoardings around the Hotel de Ville in Paris
— Included in group exhibition at Milk Gallery, Saskatoon, Canada
— Travels with his friend Marco Berrebi to Israel and the Palestine to start the project *Face 2 Face*
— Creates a 'Sidewalk Gallery' with images from *Portrait of a Generation* at 11 Spring Street, New York

2007

— *Face 2 Face* actions in Israel and Palestine
— At the 52nd Venice Biennale, pastes *Face 2 Face* images on the front of the Arsenale building
— Outdoor exhibition on the front façade of the FOAM Museum of Photography in Amsterdam and two other sites in the city, along with a video installation
— Outdoor exhibition at the Atelier des Forges during the Rencontres d'Arles in France
— Exhibition on four building fronts and video installation at Artitud, Berlin
— Mural collaboration in Berlin with Italian artist Blu
— Outdoor exhibition on the façade of the Caserne Napoleon, on the Stravinsky square and the Saint-Merri school in Paris
— 17th November: special issue of the French daily newspaper *Libération* devoted to JR
— Gérard Maximin directs a documentary entitled *Faces*, about the *Face 2 Face* project

2008

— Embarks on the *Women Are Heroes* project with the first action in the Morro da Providência favela, Rio de Janeiro, Brazil
— *Women Are Heroes* actions in Freetown and Bo, Sierra Leone; Monrovia, Liberia; and in Sudan
— Participates in a group exhibition at Tate Modern, London, 'Street Art', with an enormous pasting on the façade of the museum and actions around the city
— Solo exhibition entitled '28 Millimetres: Women' at The Outsiders Gallery, London
— Begins the *Wrinkles of the City* project in Cartagena, Spain
— Outdoor exhibition on two building fronts of Geneva during the International Film Festival and Forum on Human Rights, along with a video installation at the Musée Rath, Geneva
— Outdoor exhibition of installations from *Women Are Heroes* around the city of Brussels, Belgium

2009

- *Women Are Heroes* action in Kenya. 2,000 square metres of rooftops are covered with photos of the eyes and faces of the women from the Kibera slum
- *Women Are Heroes* action in Jaipur, India during the Holi festival of colour
- *Women Are Heroes* action in Phnom Penh, Cambodia
- Returns to Brazil to paste images from *Women Are Heroes* in Brazil on the Arcos da Lapa monument. The Casa França Brasil hosted video installations of the project and an opening with the participants from the favela. The Casa Amarela opens, a cultural centre offering photography classes for children and legal counselling for adults in the Morro da Providência favela, where the *Women Are Heroes* action took place
- Participates in the Rencontres d'Arles photo festival, France: exhibiting at the Ateliers SNCF
- Realizes a large-scale exhibition of *Women Are Heroes* on the banks of the Ile-Saint-Louis and the Louis-Philippe Bridge in Paris after being invited by the Pavillon de l'Arsenal, Paris

2010

- *Women Are Heroes* film premieres at the Cannes Film Festival during Critics' Week
- Participates in the Images Festival and the Musée de l'Elysée de Lausanne in Vevey, Switzerland and begins the *Unframed* project
- Participates in the Shanghai Biennale, with *Wrinkles of the City* actions in Shanghai, in collaboration with Magda Danysz Gallery
- Included in group exhibition at Galerie Springmann in Düsseldorf, Germany
- Outdoor exhibition on the façade of the Museum of Contemporary Art, San Diego, and other buildings in San Diego for an exhibition entitled 'Viva la Revolucion: A Dialogue with the Urban Landscape'

2011

- Receives the TED Prize, which offers JR the opportunity to make 'A wish to change the world'. He is the first French person, the first artist and the youngest ever to receive the award
- Initiates *Inside Out*, an international participatory art project that allows people worldwide to get their picture and paste it to support an idea, a project, an action and to share their experience
- First *Inside Out* group action happens in Tunisia, right after the revolution
- *Women Are Heroes* documentary film released in cinemas
- Solo exhibition entitled 'Encrages' at Galerie Perrotin, Paris. Massive Attack opens the exhibition with a concert
- *Inside Out* photobooth installation entitled 'Paris-Delhi-Bombay' in the Centre Pompidou, Paris
- *Wrinkles of the City* action in Los Angeles photographing elderly people
- Participates in 'Art in the Streets' exhibition at Museum of Contemporary Art, Los Angeles
- Builds a photobooth in the foyer of Manarat Al Saadiyat for the opening of the 'Emirati Expressions' exhibition in Abu Dhabi
- Three *Inside Out* photobooths installed in Bethlehem, Ramallah and in Israel

2012

- *Wrinkles of the City* action in Havana, in collaboration with Cuban-American artist José Parlá for the 11th Havana Biennial
- A year after winning the TED Prize, JR gives a TED talk on what has happened in a year of the *Inside Out* project
- *Inside Out* action on the Highline in New York
- Travels to North Korea and captures images of Kim Il Sung's 100th birthday celebrations
- *Inside Out* photobooth installed in Vevey, Switzerland as part of 'Images' festival
- *Inside Out* action in Hong Kong on Connaught Road footbridge in the city centre
- Solo exhibition entitled 'Pattern' at Galerie Perrotin, Hong Kong
- *Unframed* action in Washington, DC, USA using civil rights era photographs
- Initiates a project in the areas of northeast Japan afflicted by the earthquake, tsunami, and the nuclear disaster of Fukushima, and leaves an *Inside Out* photobooth truck to a group of Japanese artists including Takao Shiraishi

2013

- First museum retrospective, 'JR', opens in Tokyo at the Watari Museum of Contemporary Art, with a pasting on the façade representing inhabitants from north east Japan where the tsunami hit in March 2011
- JR and José Parlá return to Havana, Cuba to give books to the participants of the *Wrinkles of the City*, Havana. The film *Wrinkles of the City, Havana* is screened at Centro Cultural Fresa y Chocolate
- JR app for the iPad is released, as well as a *Wrinkles of the City, Los Angeles* iBook for the iPad in English, Spanish and French
- *Wrinkles of the City* action in Berlin and simultaneous exhibition at Galerie Springmann, Berlin
- *Inside Out: The People's Art Project* documentary film directed by Alastair Siddons premieres at the Tribeca Film Festival, New York
- *Wrinkles of the City, Havana* exhibition at Bryce Wolkowitz Gallery, New York
- *Unframed* action at La Belle de Mai in Marseille, France, in which JR asked residents to dig into their personal photo albums and they created a monumental artwork on the walls of the neighbourhood
- *Unframed* action in Atlanta, USA –

pastes civil rights era photographs in the neighbourhood where Martin Luther King grew up in Atlanta, to commemorate the 50th anniversary of the March on Washington

- Returns to Kibera, Kenya for another *Women Art Heroes* action – 4,000 square metres of images representing the faces of women from Kibera are printed on vinyl and installed on roofs to help protect communities from the rain. Since 2010, a team goes back to Kibera regularly to cover more rooftops
- First solo museum exhibition in the USA, 'JR', opens at the Contemporary Arts Center, Cincinnati
- *Inside Out* photobooth truck installed in Times Square. 6,000 people participated and a 3-minute film was shown every night on most Times Square screens for 'Midnight Moment'
- Two *Inside Out* photobooth trucks roam the United States during the summer to show the faces of 11 million illegal immigrants and people pushing for immigration reform
- The first European *Inside Out* photobooth truck travels to Amsterdam for the Unseen Photo Fair. Almost 1,800 posters were printed and pasted in the city
- Solo exhibition 'Actions' at Lazarides gallery, London, featuring work from *Wrinkles of the City* in Berlin; JR's journey to North Korea in 2012; and the 2013 *Portrait of a Generation* action
- *Inside Out* photobooth truck installed at Somerset House, London; the Palais de Tokyo, Paris; and the Bibliotheque Nationale de France, Paris

2014

- *Inside Out* exhibition and photobooth truck at Dallas Contemporary, USA
- 'JR', a major retrospective exhibition at Museum Frieder Burda in Baden Baden, Germany, accompanied with a special *Inside Out* photobooth installation
- *Unframed* action in Baden Baden, Germany, which addresses German-French history using archival photographs from residents' private photo albums
- Massive installation at the Lincoln Center, New York, for 2014 New York City Ballet Art Series: an eye made with the dancers from the company is pasted onto the floor; pasting on the façade of the Lincoln Center
- Creates 'Les Bosquets', a ballet in collaboration with the New York City Ballet, with music by Woodkid, presented at the Lincoln Center during XXIst Century Week
- Major retrospective, 'Close Up' at Power Station of Art, Shanghai
- Solo exhibition showing new photos, wood and paper works at Magda Danysz Gallery, Shanghai
- *Inside Out* photobooth truck travels around Shanghai for two months, with pastings across the city
- *Inside Out* installation, 'Au Panthéon!' opens to the public at the Pantheon, Paris
- *Wrinkles of the City, Havana, Cuba* film released, directed by JR and José Parlá
- *Women Are Heroes* action in Le Havre port outside Paris: 2,600 strips of paper are pasted onto shipping containers in Le Havre with the help of dockers from the port. The containers form a pair of eyes on a 363-metre-long ship leaving Le Havre to Malaysia
- *Unframed* action in the derelict hospital on the south side of Ellis Island, New York, where immigrants to the USA have passed through from 1892 to 1954
- Participates in march against police violence in New York after death of Eric Garner after a police officer put him in a chokehold
- *Rivages*, a film by Guillaume Cagniard, released about JR's pasting on a container ship in Le Havre, France

2015

- JR's eye-strip placards of the contributors of *Charlie Hebdo* killed during the attacks of 11th January appear in the 'Je Suis Charlie' march in Paris
- Coinciding with Art Basel, JR exhibits 'JR: A Survey Exhibition' at the Hong Kong Contemporary Art Foundation and 'Ghosts of Ellis Island' at Galerie Perrotin, Hong Kong
- A short film entitled *Les Bosquets*, featuring ballet dancers from the Paris Opera Ballet, premieres at Tribeca Film Festival, New York
- 26th April: JR creates the cover of 'Walking New York', a special issue of *The New York Times Magazine*. JR releases his first virtual reality short film about the project
- *Wrinkles of the City* action in Istanbul
- A short film, *The Ghosts of Ellis Island*, released, starring Robert De Niro
- Solo exhibition at Galerie Perrotin, Paris
- Solo exhibition at Lazarides Gallery, London
- Exhibition at the Centro de Arte Contemporaneo, CAC Malaga, Spain
- JR is 'Monumental Artist' for the 2015 Toronto Nuit Blanche, Toronto, Canada, and creates an exhibition entitled 'Black and White Night' with multiple projects around the city
- Solo exhibition at the Watari Museum of Contemporary Art, Tokyo, Japan
- Solo exhibition at QM Gallery Katara, Doha, Qatar

BOOKS

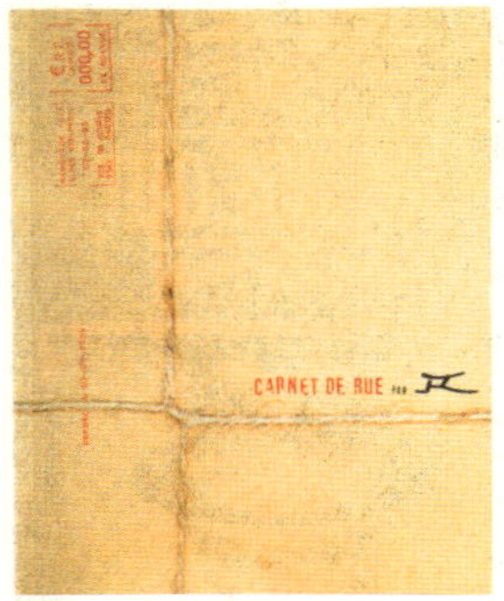

Carnet de Rue par JR
JR, self-published, Paris, 2005, 210x170mm (8¼x6¾in), 114pp, paperback, English and French

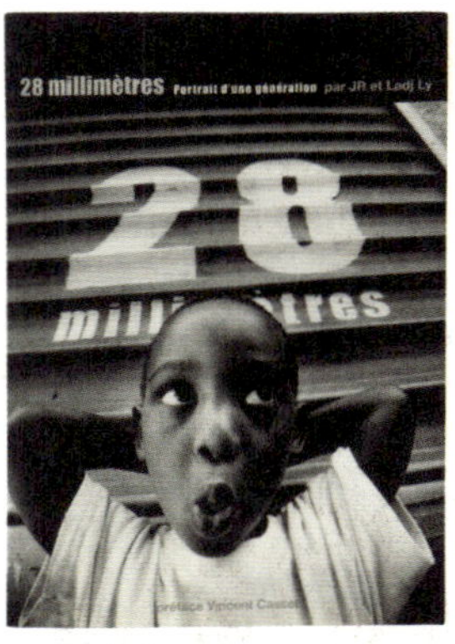

28 Millimètres: Portrait d'une generation
JR and Ladj Ly, with a preface by Vincent Cassel, Éditions Alternatives, Paris, 2006, 340x240mm (13¼x9½in), 96pp, paperback, English and French

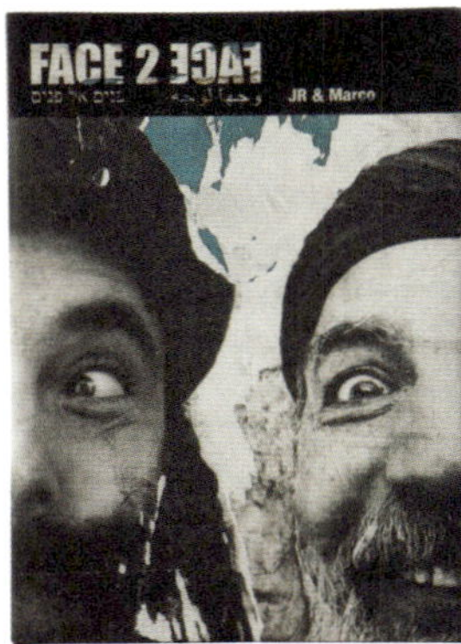

Face 2 Face
JR and Marco Berrebi, Éditions Alternatives, Paris, 2007, 335x235mm (13x9¼in), 144pp, paperback, Arabic, English, French and Hebrew

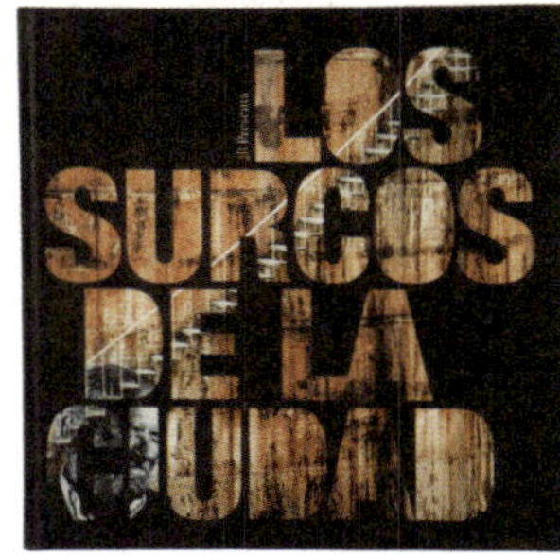

Los Surcos de la Ciudad
JR, Ayuntamiento Cartagena, Murcia, 2008, 300x300mm (11¾x11¾in), 112pp, hardback, English and Spanish

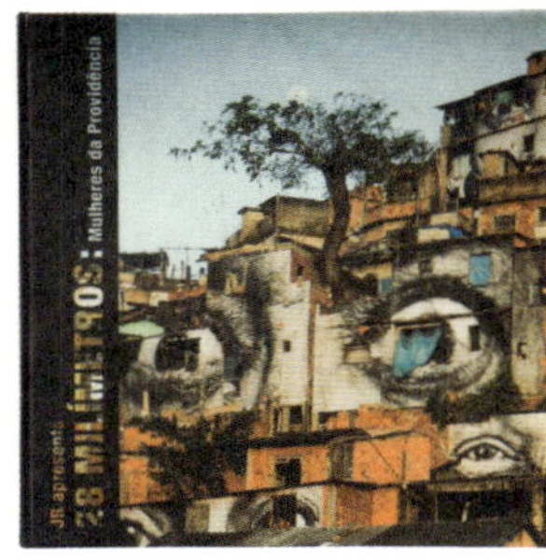

JR, 28 Milímetros: Mulheres da Providência
JR, self-published, 2009, 300x300mm (11¾x11¾in), 144pp, hardback, Portuguese. Not for sale, distributed to project participants only

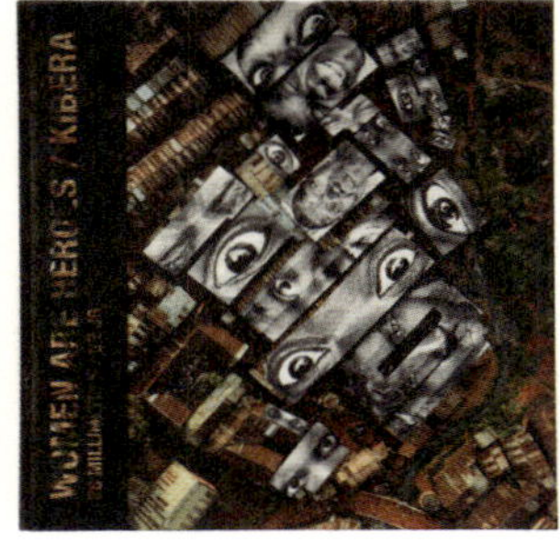

Women Are Heroes / Kibera
JR, self-published, 2009, 300x300mm (11¾x11¾in), 144pp, hardback, English and Swahili. Not for sale, distributed to project participants only

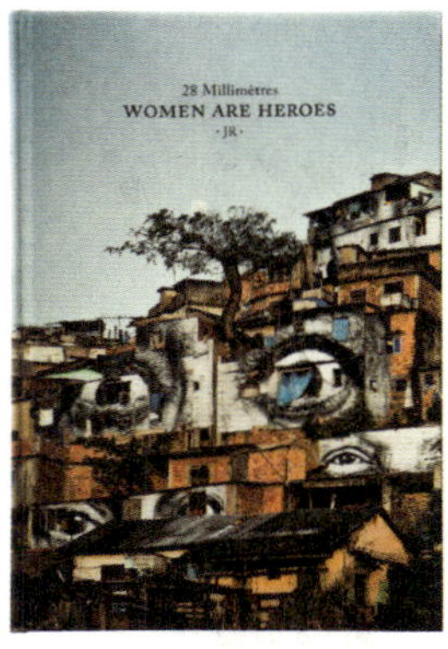

28 Millimètres: Women Are Heroes
JR, Marco Berrebi, Éditions Alternatives, Paris, first edition, 2009, 325x230mm (12¾x9in), 360pp, hardback, English and French

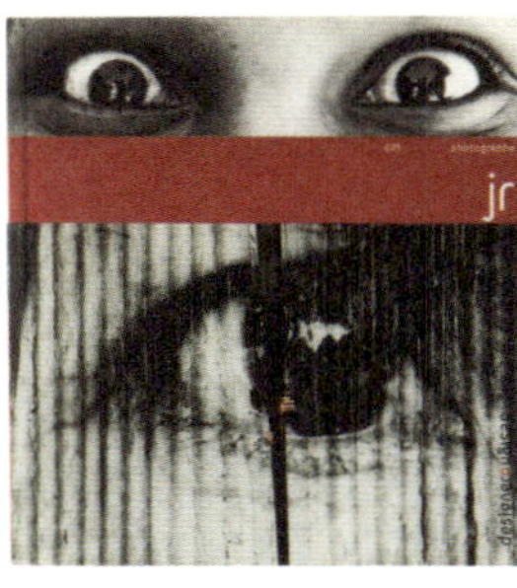

JR – design & designer
Preface by François Hebel, Editions Pyramid, Paris, first edition, 2009, 161x150mm (6¼x6in), 121pp, paperback, English and French

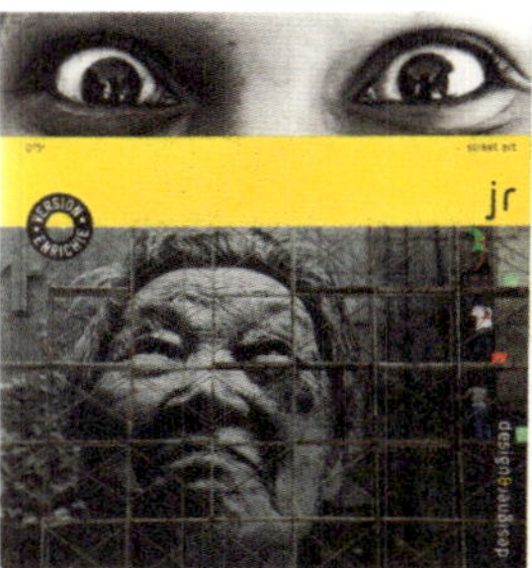

JR – design & designer
Preface by François Hebel, Editions Pyramid, Paris, second edition, 2009, 161x150mm (6¼x6in), 121pp, paperback, English and French

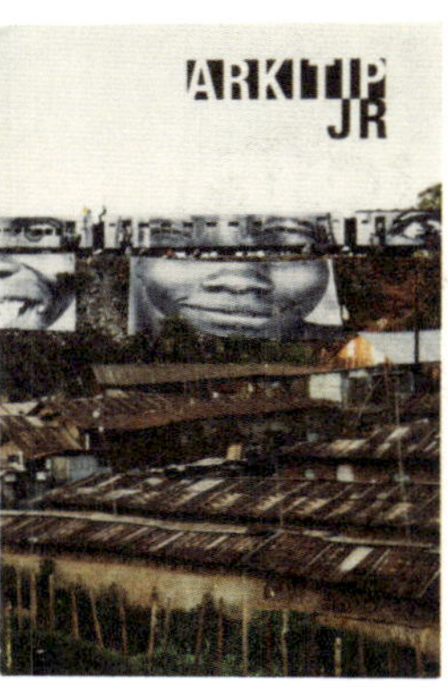

Arkitip: JR
JR, Arkitip, 2011, 241x165mm (9½x6½in), 128pp, paperback, English, hand packaged and numbered limited edition of 1000

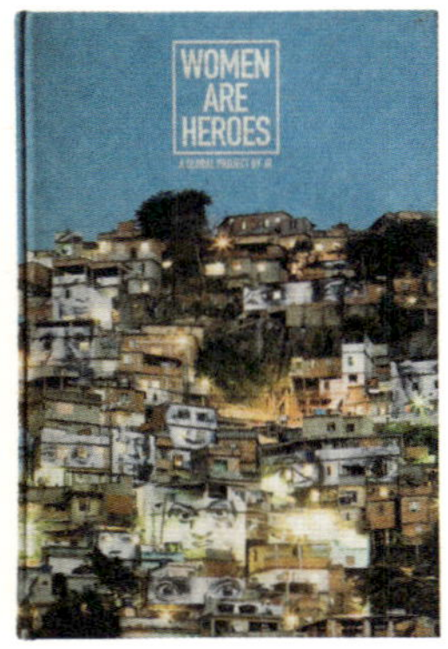

Women Are Heroes: A Global Project by JR
JR, Marco Berrebi, Abrams, New York, 2011, 325x230mm (12¾x9in), 360pp, hardback, English

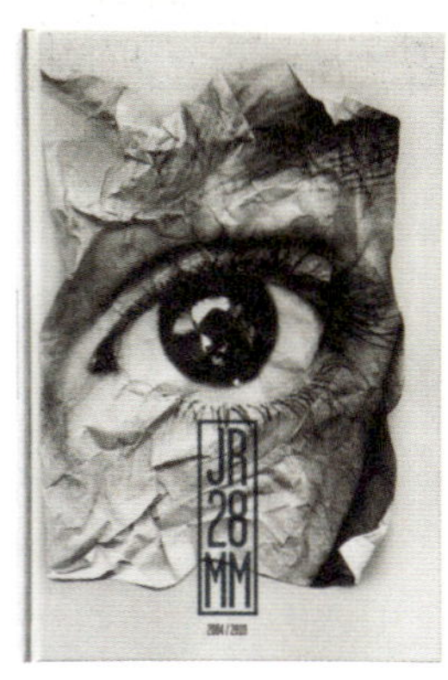

JR: 28MM
JR, Éditions Alternatives, Paris, 2011, 325x220mm (12¾x8¾in), 248pp, hardback, English and French

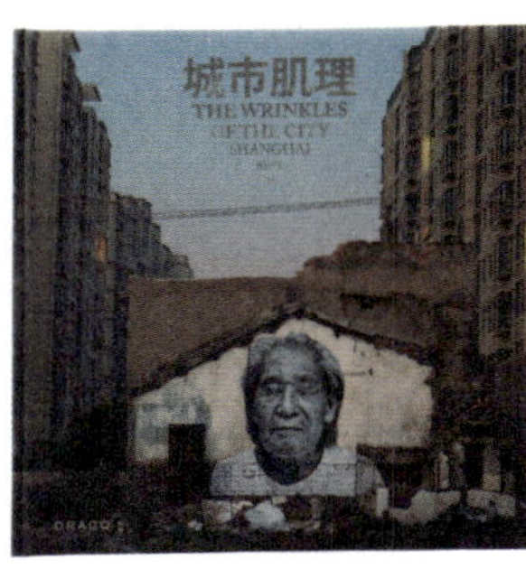

Wrinkles of the City, Shanghai
JR, Drago Editions, 2012, 300x300mm (11¾x11¾in), 144pp, hardback, Chinese and English

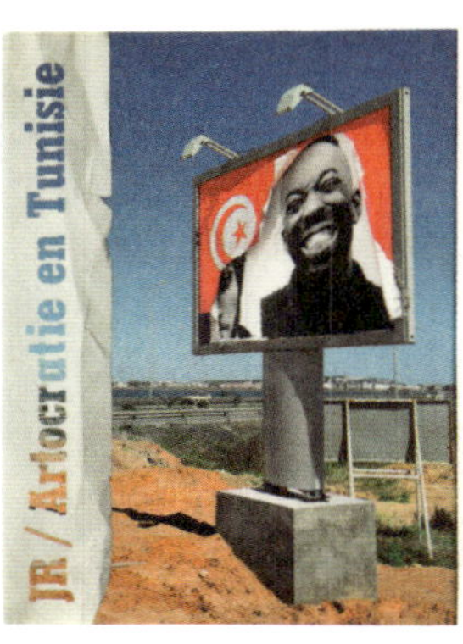

JR / Artocratie en Tunisie
JR and Marco Berrebi, Éditions Alternatives, Paris, 2011, 260x200mm (10¼x8in), 96pp, paperback, English and French

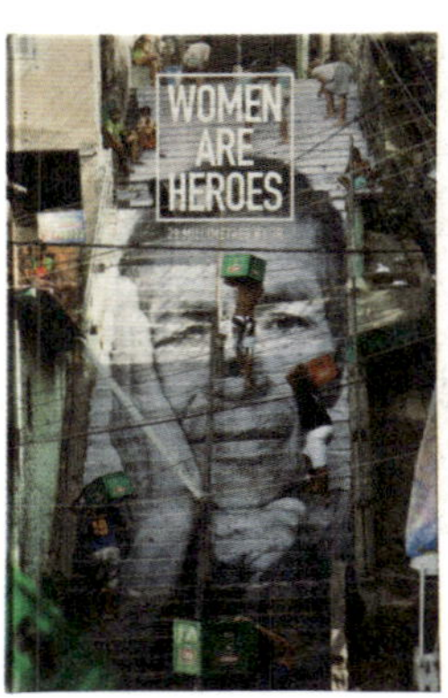

28 Millimètres: Women Are Heroes
JR, Marco Berrebi, Éditions Alternatives, Paris, second edition with an additional 8pp booklet and a new cover, 2011, 325x230mm (12¾x9in), 360pp, hardback, English and French

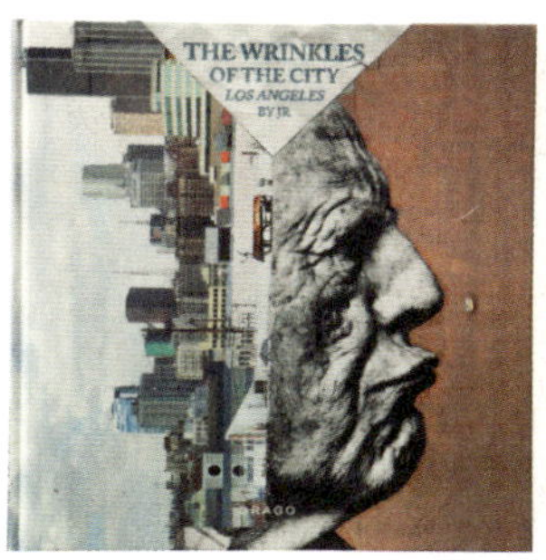

Wrinkles of the City, Los Angeles
JR, Drago Editions, 2012, 300 x 300 mm (11¾ x 11¾ in), 140 pp, hardback, English and Spanish

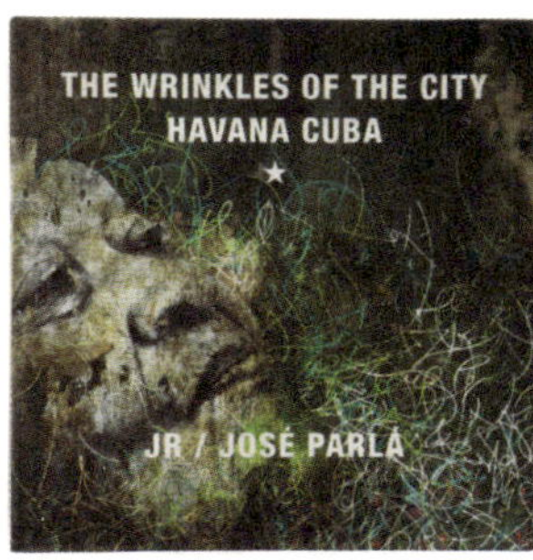

Wrinkles of the City, Havana, Cuba
JR and José Parlá, Damiani, Bologna, 2012, 300 x 300 mm (11¾ x 11¾ in), 158 pp, hardback, English and Spanish

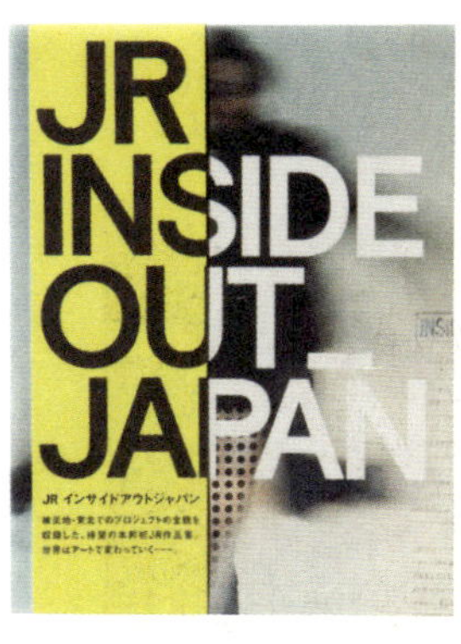

JR: Inside Out Japan
JR, Watari Museum of Contemporary Art, Tokyo, 2012, 206 x 158 mm (8 x 6¼ in), 130 pp, paperback, Japanese

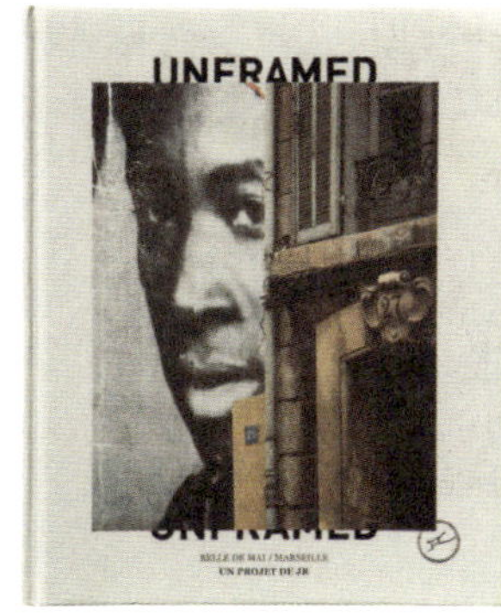

Unframed Marseille
JR, Éditions Alternatives, Paris, 2013, 270 x 220 mm (10½ x 8½ in), 104 pp, hardback, French

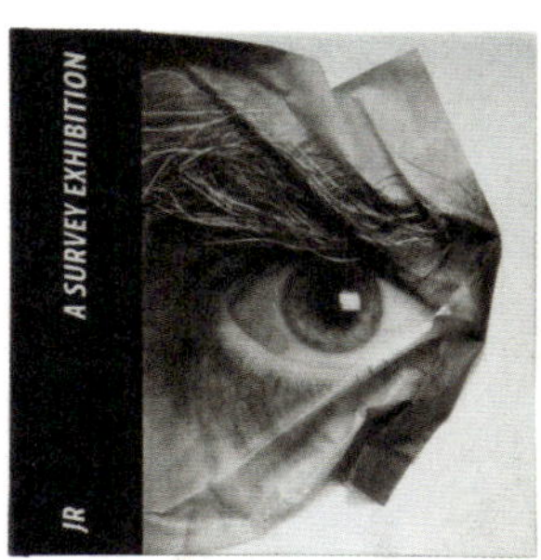

JR: A Survey Exhibition
JR, Contemporary Art Editions Ltd, Hoca Foundation, Hong Kong, 2015, 300 x 300 mm (11¾ x 11¾ in), 96 pp, hardback, English

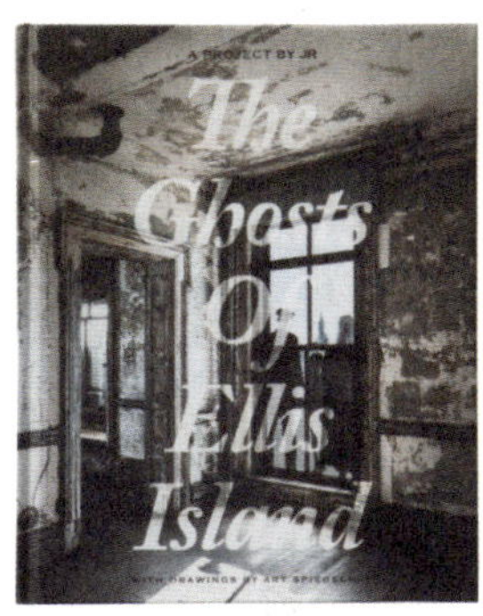

The Ghosts of Ellis Island
JR and Art Spiegelman, Damiani, Bologna, 2015, 277 x 221 mm (11 x 8¼ in), 112pp, hardback, English

FILMS

Faces
2008
76 mins
Directed by GMAX
French, Hebrew and Arabic

Women Are Heroes
2010
80 mins
Directed by JR
English and French

Wrinkles of the City – La Havana
2012
29 mins
Directed by JR and José Parlá
English and Spanish

Inside Out: The People's Art Project
2013
75 mins
Directed by Alastair Siddons
English and French

Rivages
2015
5 mins 53
Directed by Guillaume Cagniard

Les Bosquets
2015
18 mins
Directed by JR
French

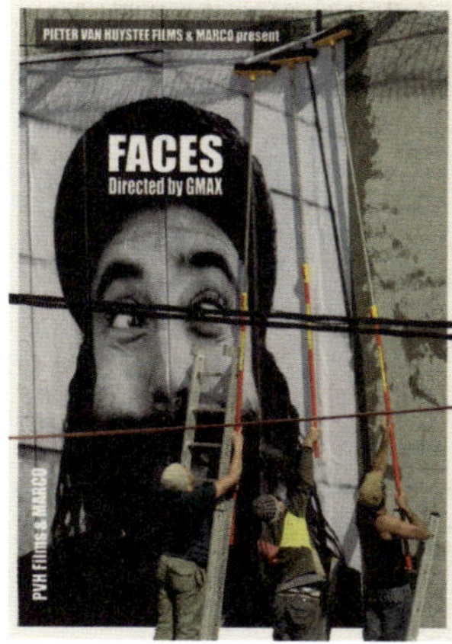

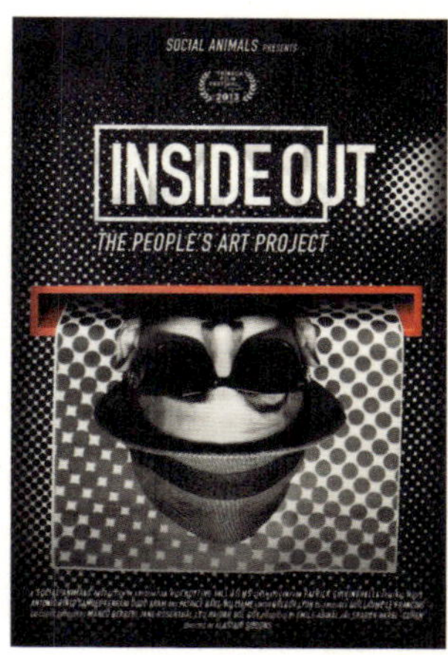

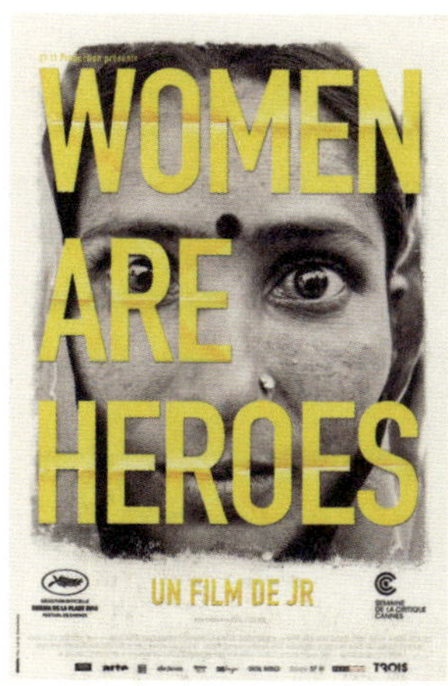

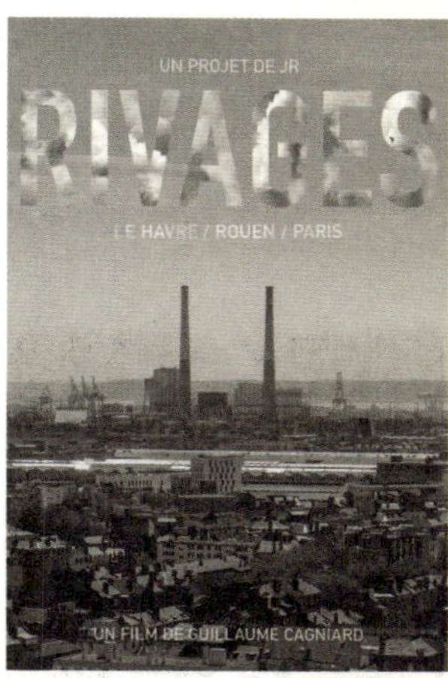

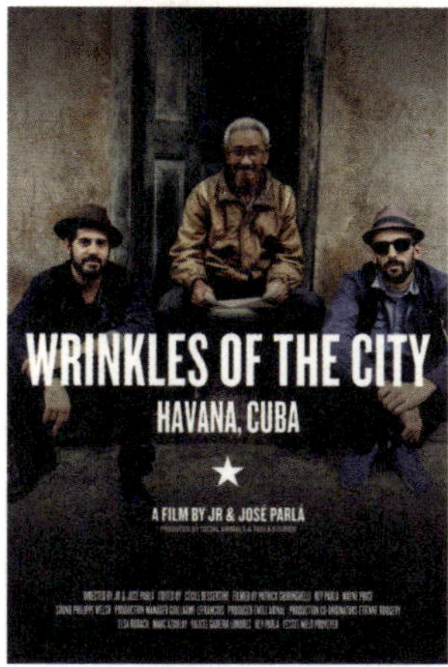

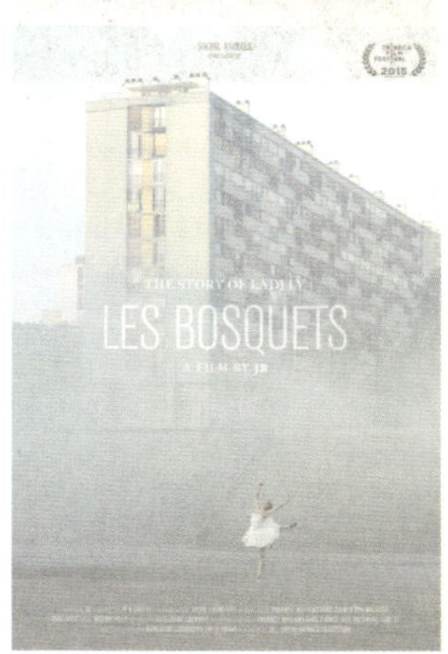

Phaidon Press Limited
Regent's Wharf, All Saints Street
London N1 9PA

Phaidon Press Inc.
65 Bleecker Street
New York, NY 10012

www.phaidon.com

First published 2015

ISBN 978 0 7148 6949 0
A CIP catalogue record for this book is available from the Library of Congress and the British Library.

Design by Sarah Boris
Cover concept by Paul Sahre
Printed in Italy

Picture credits: All artworks ©JR unless otherwise stated. Gerard-Aime/Gamma-Rapho/Getty Images: 33; Christian Aslund: 205; Marc Azoulay: 39l,200,217t; By Afghans for Afghans: 218t; ©Phil Collins. Courtesy Shady Lane Productions, Berlin: 36l,36c,36r; Guillaume Cagniard: 32,58; Mélanie Crépin: 216b; Ellen Doherty: 214t; Romain François: 212; David Gould: 217b; jcLett: 182; Florian Kleinefenn, Courtesy Galerie Perrotin: 39r, 197,279; Charlotte Lebon: 215; Courtesy 唐妮诗 MD Gallery Shanghai: 219; © Maksimka3738|Dreamstime.com: 30,42,50,72,96,138,174,194,224,240,246,280,290; Hyndira Mateta: 213b; Humayun Memon: 211b; Jason Motlagh: 211t; Prune Nourry: 83,90; Camille Pajot: 266,267,268; Ryan Plourde: 212t; Andrew Potoczak: 214b; Ali Rez, Assam Khalid, Saks Afridi, Akash Goel, Insiya Syed, Noor Behram, Jamil Akhtar, Imran Arif Khan, Qasim Nagori, Ovais Suhail: 210; Daniel Schmitt/Spitzlicht: 220t; Laurent Segretier, Courtesy Galerie Perrotin: 2,270,271; ©Zoe Strauss, Photo by C. H. Paquette: 34l,34r; Theonepointeight: 10,158,159; Terry Torok: 213t; Camilla Villa: 216t; Olly Walker: 220b; Guillaume Zicarelli, Courtesy Galerie Perrotin: 263,264. Original artwork credits for *Unframed* (pp177–193): ©Agence FeP/Laget, DR: 177c; ©Collection Archives Municipales de Marseille/19 Fi 2043: 179r,183; Courtesy George Grantham Bain: 193t; Baudelaire ©Fonds Gerard Detaille: 177b; ©Georges Cuny: 177t; ©DR: 178r, 179l,180–181,184; Courtesy Ellis Island Immigration Museum: 190l,192t,192b,193b; ©Man Ray, collection de Musée de l'Elysée, Lausanne, Switzerland: 188; Courtesy National Park Service, Statue of Liberty National Monument: 190r,191; ©Sergei Podiesnov: 186–7; ©Jacqueline Ros, issue du projet Les Chercheurs de Midi, produit par Marseille-Provence 2013, Capitale européenne de la culture: 178l,182; ©Ernest C. Withers. Courtesy the Withers Family Trust: 189.

Huge thanks go to the teams at my studio and Phaidon who made this book possible: Deb Aaronson, Émile Abinal, Marc Azoulay, Sarah Boris, Guillaume Cagniard, Ellen Christie, Victoria Clarke, Julia Hasting, Alenka Oblak and Julie Pugeat. To Melvyn Bonnaffé, Rhea Keller, Camille Pajot, Etienne Rougery-Herbaut and Céline Veyer for pulling together the images, Marc Azoulay and Marco Berrebi for writing the project texts, Agathe Berman for the text on Ballet, Joseph Remnant for his beautiful comics, and Nato Thompson for his insightful essay on my work.

Additional project acknowledgements:
Portrait of a Generation Thank you to: Abdou, Adama, Amad, Araba, Bélé, Blaze, Boulay, Byron, Christophe, Djaize, Goudro, Goune, Jered, Koko, La Tchatche, Lil' Pimp, Malor, Mehdi, Mouloud, Namo, Nico, Omar, Ousse, P'tite Taf, Shone, Younous, Zid. Bouna et Zyed (RIP), Metine, Siaka, Aboud, Alex La Redac, Alex Palu, Al Peco, Alexone, Amada, Amad JP, Anneloes, Asso. AC le feu, Asso. ADM, Athel, B12, Baba et Jean, Bamba, Basskour, Beg, Ben Ichou, Ben, Bens, Boské Zoo, Brigitte C., Bush, Calbo, Chakib, Charly Corporate, Chico, Chiel, Clarck, Claude S, CM Niggaz, Dann, DJ Flex, Dollar, Edou, Emmanuelle C., Eva Gardner, Family Nourry (Marie, Sab. et Olivier), Gangster, Genzu, Fuck Olivier et Tim, H2, Hamid, Harlan, Hitek, Illaria, Jean-Luc Monterosso, Jean-Phi. Et Celine, Jef, Jere, Jeremy Fat, Jess, Julie, Julien London, Kimo, Kourtrajmé Gang (Bart, La Caution, Dimitriu, Franck KT, Kim, Nico, Romain, Tarubi, Toumani), Landry, Loah, Mak, Malam's, Mamie, Marc et Nath, Mare 139, Marianne, Marie-Laure, Marie Rital, Mathieu H2, les Microbes, Nabil et Hakeem, Najib, Nathalie L., Nele, Nick, Nicolas, Niels, Ouriel, Ousmane, Papito, Pax et Babe, Peter Code, Prune, Remi Lazinc, Reurty Reccord, Rim K, Roger, RS4, Sam Roger, Sarah et Sean, Septik, SFG, Sly, Sophie Kulczewski, Steffen Kellner, Sten, Stephen Schuster, Theresa L., The Vicky Hayward, Thomas R., Tim PMH, Vanessa, Vin's de La Haine, Xav Faltot, Xavier, Yassine Belatar, Youssef, Youssouf, Zevs. A tous les Toukos de Clichy-sous-bois et de Montfermeil Les Bosquets, aux mecs du quartier en prison et à tous ceux morts pour rien. *Face 2 Face* Thank you to the F2F team: Marc Berrebi, David Boucris, Youssef Boubekeur, G Max, Prune Nourry, Watan El Kassem, Ouriel Darmon. Thank you to Ayman Abu Azalof, Mars S, Gaby Malka et Mehrav, Gilles Darmon, Ami Bouganim, Sergio Alleyne, Yona, Gérard Aimé, Nathalie, Patrice Aoust, Sabine, Gérard, Maryse, André, Annie, Daniel, Antoinette R, Michèle et Fred, Charly, Farida, Cédric, David C, Philippe et Prisca, Katsumi et Franck, Martin Kann, Steffen et Nele, Steffie, Debora Pill, Dann et Olivia, Zevs, Solal, Elisha, la familly Nourry (Sab, Olivier et Marie), Alex La Redac, Anneloes VanGaalen, Brigitte et Claude, Chakib, Haribo, Jean Phi et Céline, Julien et Nitza, Lunik, Alexandre P., Marie Rital, Nabil et Hakeem, Nadir, Septik, Stephen Schoe, Xav Faltot, Aline et Emmanuel de Nova, Baba et Jean, Jay Smith, Foam Museum, Family Atia et Tuitou, Jacob, Laetitia, Esteban et Ayrton, Lordfunk, Mamies Simone et Nina, Vincent et Squat, Vanessa, Valou, Laurent et Céline, Yaceen, Zinc, Ludivine, Julie et Zaza, Fabien Naudan et Gregory Leroy d'Artcurial, Cheikh Aziz (RIP). *Women Are Heroes* Thank you to: Jessica, Yvette, Alice, Victoria, Emily, Kim, Coralie, Adam, Tom & Alex, Nathalie, Simon, Bilou et Emma, Maryse, Gérard, Julie et Elsa, MSF Belgique, Peter Casaer, Bettina Saerens, Valérie Michaux, Sara Laemens, Sandra Peiffer, Anne Misal, galerie Springmann, Olivier Mouton, Martin Huisman, Patrick Bouton, François Coen, Stéphanie Yvert, Didier Berthelot, Alexandre Labasse, Marion Dambrin, Dominique Albo, le Pavillon de l'Arsenal, Leo Kaneman, Rony Braumann, Laurent Joffrin, Didier Pourquery, Marie-Dominique Arrighi, Marthe Svagelski, Laeticia et Naomie, Canon France, Culturesfrance, l'Agence VU, Sonetrans (Sabine et Patricia), Stephane Schinazi, Tatyana et Alexis, Brigitte Chouet, Edith Bizot, Elle Driver, Vincent Maraval, Thierry Consigny, Marie Bazin et Olvier Dermaux, Sol Guy, Kim Chapiron, Jean-Gabriel Becker, Anthony Cheylan, Géraldine Gomez, Ben Ageorges, Catherine Philippot et Myrtille Beauvert, Rob 3D et Daddy G, Marie Nourry, Catherine Phillipot, Piero Borgel, Farida Cagniard, Thibaut Vieville et Marianne Ratier, Domoina, Steffen et Sophie, Dan et Olivia, Zevs, Blu, Yaze, Os Gemeos, Solal, Evelyne Soullier et Sandrine Debray, Sabine, Olivier, Prune, Marie, Katarina, Fina et Fia, Maurice Grimbaum, Nabil et Hakeem, le Zink et Lisa, Stephen Schuster, Jean Claude et Béatrice, Romain et Ben-j, Lunik, Marc, Sara et Samantha, Xavier Faltot, Sébastien Kopp, Ludivine, Baba et Jean, Jay Smith et Greg, Jacob et Rosine, Mathieu Kassovitz, Laetitia, Esteban et Ayrton, Hélène. Françoise et Thierry, Charlotte Marmian, Iris et Laurent, Marie-Christine et Régis, Vincent et Squat, Patrick Baradel, Yvette Lamy, Christopher Shay, Vanessa, Valou, Timothée, Yvan et Matthieu, Martial & Co, Anthony Cheylan, Jerome Outlines, Olivier Fleurot, Frédéric Rouzaud, Michel Janneau, Dan Lowe, Anthony Dickenson, David Boucris, Patrick Ghiringhelli, Alain Arnaudet, Philong, Youssef Boubekeur. Equipe collage: Christopher Irfane Khan Acito, Patrice Bart Williams, Ulysse Moal, Constance Pentier, Eric Salomon, Caroline Goutal, et Sophie Paumelle. Equipe tournage: Agathe Sofer, Juliette Renaud, Patrick Ghiringhelli, Lazare Pedron, Nathalie Durand, Philippe Welsh, François Hamel, Doctor Flake, Antoine Levi, Romain Alary, Fabrice Rouaud, Guillaume Saignol, Mélanie Karlin. Sierra Leone, Liberia, Soudan: Médecins Sans Frontières/Doctors Without Borders, Cécile et Robert, Karl, Veronica, Barbara, Hiwet, Orange Base et Black Base. Kenya: "Special thanks" to Remy et Isabelle Carrier, la communauté de Kibera, Hussein Musa, Nadir Abdi, Hezron Arunga, Awadh Ibrahim, Cletis Kasanyi, Otieno Goege, Ochieng Onyango, Jirus Agut, Viewfinders, Jean Hartley, Mia Collis, Kenya Grip, Ovidian, l'équipe de MSF Kibera, Monique Tondoi Wanjala, Siama Abraham Musine, Cecilia Magdalene Achieng, Edwin Japaso, Anouk Delafortie, Alinur Adan, Georges Diener, Jesse Karp, Salim Mohamed, Shepard, la coopération culturelle française. Brazil: Mauricio Hora, Rosiete Marinho, Debora Pill, Nele Harlans, Jorg Rohleder, Miliana Nakamura, Marcello Silva, Emmanuelle Boudier, Renato Rangel, Joao Guerreiro, Max Freitas, Pedro Strozenberg, Soluçoes Urbanas, Wallace Cardia, Association Worldbox, Alex Suliano, Romulo Sesh, Tulio Fiuza, Claudio, Baiano, Augusto Alex, Naltitude, Patricia Oliveira. India: Jérôme Bonnafont, ambassadeur de France, Philippe Martinet, Bénédicte Alliot, Nitin Chauhan, Elise Tassin, Marie Berst, Dhritobroto Bhattacharjya 'Tato', Ravi Kumar, Sukhi Singh, Mme Vandan, Sharma (Narirakshak), Aneesha Beri et Subhashree (Khushii), Gauri Chaudhary (Action India), Nandani Rao, Madhu & Sadaf (Jagori), Swami Vishalanand (Divya Jyoti), Yamini Kumar, Shaifali Jetli-Sury et Alain Wuillaume. Cambodia: Alain Arnaudet, Marie de Pibrac, Lucile Charlemagne, Borin Kor, Neang Sam, Navy Tan, Julie Besson, Jean-François Desmazières, ambassadeur de France, Jean-Luc Floch, Paul Ouk & Me Mates Place Gang. *Wrinkles of the City* Cartagena: Antonio Sanchez Ruzafa, Antonio Sánchez Sorroche, Asensio Delgado Sanchez, Carmen Cegarra Gómez, Diego Hernandez Morala, Encarnación García Martínez, Federico Sanchez Sanchez, Francisca Vera Torralba, Julián Jesús Jiménez Fernandez, José Martínez Roca, Juan Garcerán Pedreño, Julian Saura Lucas, Manuel Cos Andreu, Manuel Gómez Aguado, Manuel Gomez Conesa, Manuel Martínez-Illescas, María Corbalán Fernández, Mariano Saura Otón, Martín Fuentes Herrero, Milagros Vallejo Herrero, Pedro Alfaro Leon, Rámon García Pérez y Saturnino Fernandez Sanchez, François et Hélène Meyer, Piero B., Antoinette R, Angèle, Michèle et Fred, Charly, Farida, Cédric, David C, Philippe et Prisca, Katsumi et Franck, Alice Gallery, Johann Circleculture, Martin Kann, Steffen et Nele, Steffie, Debora Pill, Dann et Olivia, Zevs, Solal, Elisha, Ladj Ly, la familly Nourry (Sab, Olivier et Marie), Vicky Hayward and the JaguarShoes Team, Alex Homecore et Alex La Redac, Anneloes VanGaalen, Brigitte et Claude, Chakib, David Walters, Haribo, Graff IT, Henri Thuaud, Jean Phi et Celine, Julien et Nitza, Alex Alabaz, Lunik, Marie Rital, Nabil et Hakeem, Nadir, Septik, Stephen Schoe, Wooster Collective, Xav Faltot, Alastair, Aline et Emmanuel de Nova, Baba et Jean, Jay Smith, Spray, François Hebelle, Foam Museum, Family Atia et Tuitou, Jacob, Laetitia, Esteban et Ayrton, Lordfunk, Mamie Simone et Hania, Os Gemeos et Nina, Vincent et Squat, Vanessa, Valou, Laurent et Celine, Yaceen, Zinc, Julie et Zaza, Sébastien, Emma, Guillaume, Christian et Mme Coler. Shanghai pastings/粘住: JR, Emile Abinal, Christopher Irfane Khan Acito, Léo de Boisgisson, Youssef Boubekeur, Magda Danysz, Sean Hart, Virgile Hermann, Prune Nourry, Sophie Paumelle, Kevin Theraud, Yichen Peng/彭逸晨, Richard Chaoli/李超, Cong Wang/王聪, Aude Quinchon, Xu Linxian, Zhu Lin, Didi, Zko. Thanks to/鸣谢: Magda Danysz, Li Lei/李磊, Vanna Teng/邓懿德, Marc Azoulay, Marc Berrebi, The Shanghai Biennale/上海双年展: Li Lei/李磊, Hua Yi; Shanghai Sculpture Space / 上海城市雕塑中心: Zheng Peiguang/郑培光, Jackie Jiang/姜蕾, Crystal Wang; CGS: Daniel Legendre, Benoit Honnard; Bund18/外滩18号:Vanna Teng/邓懿德, Jill Han/韩雪娇, Kris Yang/楊瑜華; Bérénice Angremy & Léo de Boisgisson, Marion Bertagna, Marie-Laure Lakhdar Bonnet, Li Dandan and the Consulat général de France à Shanghai/李丹丹和法国驻上海领事馆; Culturesfrance Ministère des Affaires Étrangères et Européennes; Otrad Services; Sue Cheng; Han Xiao Gan; Sophie Duhamel, Charity Robertson, Morgane Baer, Clémence Wolff, Marjolaine Moret, Li Sui, Alix Malandain, Shihui Weng/翁诗卉, Léo de Boisgisson, Jolie Pan/潘晨嘉, Cathy Zhu/朱虹, Sabine Friecke. Los Angeles: Jim Budman, Robert Banas, Ramiro Gurrola Ramirez, Maria Antonia Ruiz Gurrola, George Cockfield, Robert Evans, Michael Korhonen, Carl Virden, John Stapp, Jim Hayes, Louis Walden, Burke Armstrong, Oneil Cannon, Jennie Cooper, Jeanne Heimer, Angela Hernandez, Barbara Kaplan, Gerda Maas, Vivien Myerson, Hasmik Simonyan, Rita Guizulfo, Tuangpet Kunavantanit, Ariana Manov, Suriyong Rochanayon, Prapaporn Rochanayon, Cherdchom Sukhom, Hilarie Chan, Maria Chan, Arunee Trunversoo, Gideon Kotzer, Eric Shomof, Daniel Lahoda, Daniel Kotzer, Paul Solomon, Daniel Serfaty, Angel City Brewery, Lee Maen, Miguel Garcia (Barracuda), Fran Camaj, Joel Unangst, Travis Lett, Jim Zafaris, Louise Berrebi, Daniel Salin, Marc Azoulay, Émile Abinal, Guillaume Cagniard, Irfane Khan-Acito, Alexandre Guarneri, Magda Danysz, Greg Hervieux, Jose Lopez, Brian Schmidt, Adrian Avila, Mike Alvarez, Jonathon Jones, Matt Jones, Jenna Wright, Jory Durham, Joy Durham, Justin Polinsky, Micah Mayell, Linsey Romero, David Wittig, Patrick Ghiringhelli, Eden Tyler Banas, Sean Conroy Mehen, Hugo Vitrani, Cecile Dessertine, Carlos Gonzales, Florent Quint, Mathieu Caplanne, Bruce Keen, Jeffrey Deitch, Ethel Seno, Jang Park, Dana Elitches, Michael Nauyok, Stacie London, Carolyn Oakes, David Galligan, Sergio Ramirez, Sunset Hall & seniors participating in Sunset Hall Programs and Wendy Caputo, Prune Nourry, Jane Rosenthal, Sol Guy, Julie Pugeat, Marco Berrebi, Kristine Downing, Thomas Kettig, Leila Cohen, Marilyn Venney, Simon Berrebi, Lucca Dahan, Camille Pajot, Melvyn Bonnaffe, Virginia Cromie, William Hopkins Jr., Gina Pollack, Lola Zajdermann & Natacha Langmantil, Aurélie Sampeur, Kevin Theraud, Guillaume Lefrançois, Etienne Rougery-Herbaut, Philippe Welsh, Alix Malandain, Florence Roudault, Julien Rigoulot, Julien Pasquier, Ashley Lent, Tom Labonge, Kamilla Blanche, Magda Danysz, Juliette Durand, Otrad Services, Hugo Barral, Ashley Lent, Brenda Schmid Sonia Teri, and 'The Audience' team, Juliana Hatkoff, Oliver Luckett. Havana: Rey Parlá & Mika Parlá, Remi Azegami Parlá & Otono Alma Parlá (Alma de Otoño), Dalia Parlá & José Agustín Parlá (RIP), Consuelo y Manolo, Tia Dulce, Clara Astiasarán, Michael Betancourt, Janet Batet, Tio Jesus y Clarita, Claudia Paneca, Claire Darrow & Chris Mosier, Bryce Wolkowitz, Al Moran & Mills Moran OHWOW Gallery, Jorge Fernandez Torres, Yesel Melo Proveyer, Yalicel Gabeira Londres, Luis Gispert, Ella Cisneros Fontanals, Susana Fontanals, Los Van Van, Nila Capetillo Casanova, Geraldo, Miguel y Angel, Adonis Moreno, Ivan Moreno, Chris Mendoza, Magdaley Bellon, Fru Tholstrup, Matt Carey-Williams, Stephanie Schleiffer, Ben Tufnell, Jaurettsi Saisarbitoria, Sade Lythcott, Giada Lumomirski, Latifa, Jane Rosenthal, Robert De Niro, Sean Penn, Sato, Mr. Saeb Eigner and Family, Cristina Grajales, Ramdane Touhami, Jordan Bratman, Yuka Tsuruno, Patrick Ghiringhelli, Philippe Welsh, Marco Berrebi, Scott Landsbaum, Tony Arcabascio, Andrea Albertini, Alexander Galan, Miguel Coyula, Candelario at MACSAN, Matthew Akers, Marina Abromovic, Msc. Karina R. Palacios Sanchez, Ministerio de Cultura de Cuba, Bienal de la Habana, Centro Arte Contemporáneo Wifredo Lam, Manon Slome, No Longer Empty, Holly Block, Bronx Museum, David Harper/BAM, Stefan Ruiz, David Ellis, Sarah Lewis, Harmony Murphy, Rashida Jones, Hakim Bouacha, Heather Graham, David Berliner, David Edgar, Jennifer Justice, Emilia Menocal, Justin Wilkes, Amanda Bhala Wilkes, Jon Kamen, Craig Dykers/Snøhetta, Susan Nutter/NCSU, Enrique (Kiki) Álvarez, Lucca Dahan, Julie Pugeat, Cécile Dessertine, Camille Pajot, Melvyn Bonnaffe, Marc Azoulay, Emile Abinal, Kevin Theraud, Guillaume Lefrançois, Etienne Rougery-Herbaut, Prune Nourry, Virginia Cromie, William Hopkins Jr., Gina Pollack, Lola Zajdermann & Natacha Langmantil, Patrick Ghiringhelli, Camille Barnaud (Ambassade de France à Cuba), Céline Balmelle (Air France), Aurélie Sampeur, Wayne Price, Heather Dell, Jeanne Donovan Fisher, Karen Brooks Hopkins, Joseph V Melillo, Brooklyn Academy of Music, Arnold Lehman, Brooklyn Museum, Gary and Sarah Wolkowitz, Bruce Ratner, Jay Z, Mary Anne Gilmartin, Rebecca D'Eolia, André Balazs, Kay Sides, Darren Romanelli and family, Hiroki Nakamura, Young Kim, Romon Yang, John Jay, Mark Parker, Hiroshi Fujiwara, Carlos Garaicoa, Beth DeWoody, Kyle DeWoody, Manish Vora, Los Carpinteros, Damian Aquiles, Pamela Ruiz, Guerra de la Paz., Sarah @ collete, Adam Glickman, The Dream Team: Geraldo, Miguel, Angel: Vivá Cuba! *Unframed* Marseille: Kasser Korhili, Nabil Allik du Cieres, Fettouma Mehdi, Aramata Traoré, Abdou Kadafi, Ali Ahmad Ahmadi, Amina Abdelmounen, Narimen Chabadi, Stéphanie de Tourris, Noëlle Delcroix, Dominique Tésorière et les élèves du collège de la Belle de Mai, classes de 6e-1, 5e-1 et 3e-5, Marie-France Vollaro, René Fadda, Marie Baglieri, Charles Mourre, Patrick Poiret et le club des Bleus, Raymond Ruot et toute l'équipe des Archives municipales de Marseille, Georges Cuny, Jacques Mollemeyer, Émilie Cester et le CE des Cheminots PACA, Rachid, Cano et toute l'équipe du club des supporters les Winners, la Galerie Detaille et Hélène et Gérard Detaille, Serge Pizzo et le CIQ Belle de Mai, Franck Miguel et la Maison Pour Tous Belle de Mai, Jean-Claude Buguin de l'agence FEP, Simone Uzet, Jacques Roger, Maurice Attias, Olivier Ramon, père Daniel, professeur Yves Baille, Pierre-Emmanuel Danan, Gilbert Donzel et Robert Rossi, Claude Renard, Hélène Boularan, Anne Pfister et le collectif des Brouettes, l'équipe des Proxi-pousse et l'équipe des Têtes de l'Art, Olivier Gorse et Jacqueline Ursch des Archives départementales (13), Corinne Barbereau, Lydie Marchi et Anaïs Launo. M. Allani, M. Vera, Mme Henninot, M. et Mme Naretto-Rosse, M. Tedesco et M. Icard, Jacqueline Ros, Annick Perrot-Bishop, Hervé Jégou, Jean-Pierre Moulères, Alain Pla, les équipes de JC Decaux, Julien Gastaldi, Serge Trigano et Otrad services, Magali Poivert, Marie de Pibrac, Sally-Carol Delay, Fabien Paoli, Christo Ohana et toute l'équipe de la Friche, Anne Loubet, Émile Abinal, Guillaume Cagniard, Étienne Rougery-Herbaut, Caroline Corbal, David Boucris, Natacha Langmantil, Marc Berrebi, Julie Pugeat, Melvyn Bonnafé, Eloi Nourry, Cécile Dessertine, Paul Rougery-Herbaut, David Boucris, Kevin Theraud, Sean Laval Hart, Ales Josifovsky, Rashida Jones, Will McCormack, Felicity Trinet, Victoria Migliore, Priscilla Migliore, Charlotte Dupenloup, Yann Lorteau et Maeva Franceschi, Ziggy Perez et Pauline Exbrayat. Ellis Island pasting team: Prune Nourry, Julie Pugeat, Loic Pugeat, Jaime Scatena, Louise Berrebi, Takao Shiraishi, Andrew Ferguson, Luis Gomez, Tony Herbas, Paola Murillo-Wong, Natalie Eichengreen, Marc Berrebi, Marc Azoulay, Rhea Keller, William Hopkins Jr, Joshua Geyer, Anna Verghese, Cameron Yates. Thank you to Art Spiegelman, Françoise Mouly, John Piltzecker, John Hnedak, Judy Giuriceo, Brent Talbott, George Tselos, Katherine Craine, Diana Pardue, Cherie Butler, Mindi Rambo, Jane Ahern, Paul Roper, Ben Hanslin, Eric Byron, the staff boat operators and all the National Park Service staff of Statue of Liberty National Monument and Ellis Island; Janis Calella, Jessica Cameron-Bush, and all the amazing volunteers of Save Ellis Island; Stephen Wilkes, Philip Engelhorn, Sol Guy, Magda Danysz, Charlotte Lebon, Fabien Barrau, Eric Roth, André Chemetoff, Guillaume Lefrançois, Robert De Niro, Darren Aronofsky, David Blaine, Emmanuel Perrotin, Valentine Blondel, Peggy Leboeuf, Cécile Ktorza, Emmanuelle Orenga de Gaffory, Erin Allweiss, Melena Ryzik, Alessandro Tranchini, Andrea Albertini, Lorenzo Tugnoli, Matt McDonald, Charles Azoulay. *Inside Out* Times Square: the *Inside Out* team: Marc Azoulay, Gina Steffe, William Hopkins Jr, Joshua Geyer, Rhea Keller. Times Square Alliance: Sherry Dobbin, Tim Tompkins, Ka-Man Tse, Gary Winkler, Damian Santucci and all the team of Times Square Arts and Times Square Alliance Truck production team. Guillaume Lefrançois, Camille Pajot, Takao Shiraishi, Alex Alabaz, Jean-Baptiste Le Foll, Guillaume Cagniard.
TED Prize Team: Tom Valentino, Anna Verghese, Erline Maruhom, Sarah Schoengold. Film team: Cédric Klapisch, Mathieu Kassovitz, Marc Azoulay, Espartaco Albornoz Jr, Alexandra Budman, Alexandra Rosenmann, Delphine Diallo, Cécile Dessertine. Special thanks to Philip Engelhorn, Cameron Yates, Kristina Lazarevic, Jane Rosenthal, Sol Guy, Lucien Zayan, Prune Nourry, Marco Berrebi, Emmanuel Perrotin, Bryce Wolkowitz. Thank you to all our volunteers: Adriana Ellermann, Alex Budman Alexa Fábrega, Alexandra Kopanaiko, Andrew Burnett, Andrew Ferguson, Anna Bechtol, Anna Kostuk, Anna Verghese, Annelise Finney, Anthony J. Thomas, Anya Khaoamayzer, Basil Sema, Blair Mikels, Cacy Forgenie, Carolina Pinton, Carolyn Concepcion, Clara Kasser, Clare Bourgeois, Clemence Triffault, Corey Mohr, Cristina Delgado, David Hwang, Debbie Glasserman, Delphine Diallo, Dina Horowitz, Dong Joo Kim, Edward Funes, Ella Saunders-Crivello, Emily Pidgeon, Emmananuel Knight, Erin Loughran, Espartaco Albornoz, Eugenie Rossi, Genia Iartchouk, Hannah Trimble, Heather Phelps-Lipton, Hillary Cutter, Ilsse Garcia, Ingrid Campos, Jaime Scatena, Jamia Wilson, Jarrett Robertson, Jason Maas, Jasper Kerbs, Jessica Edwards, Jocelyne Gilead, Jonathan Pereira, Jordan Reeves, Josefina Lagos, Julien Diggins, Kari Mulholland, Kate Coffey, Keith Rosengarten, Kendra Beitzel, Lauren Gniazdowski, Leo Jimenez, Leora Terzi, Lidia Ferrara, Louise Berrebi, Luisa Calcano, Marie Sicari, Max Collins, Maxime Godenne, Megan Sparkman, Mehdya Belallam, Melissa Sutherland, Michael Burgher, Michael Grammer, Michelle Sordi,Miho Yamagishi, Natalie Almonte, Natalie Eichengreen, Natasha Stragalinou, Northy Chen, Paola Murillo Wong, Patrick D'Arcy, Rhea Keller, Rhynna Santos, Ridah Farooqui, Roman Dzheliiev, Rosanna Bach, Samantha Kelly, Sarah Schoengold, Sarah Workman, Shoham Arad, Shola Owolewa, Skyler Terrell, Sofia Godoy, Stephanie Bruni, Stephanie Londono, Stephanie Mohammed, Stephanie Reyes, Takashi Yagi, Tony Herbas, Tyrone Brown-Osborne, Vashon Watson, Xavier Geinoz. All the *Inside Out* Group Leaders. *Les Bosquets:* André Chemetoff. Original music: Pharrell Williams, Hans Zimmer, Ben Wallfisch, Woodkid. Editor: Maxime Pozzi. Co-editor: Cecile Dessertine. Art director: Guillaume Cagniard. Executive producers: Pharrell Williams, Hans Zimmer, Jane Rosenthal, Ladj Ly. Executive producers: Guillaume Lefrançois, Émile Abinal. Associate producer: New York City Ballet with the dancers of the Paris Opera Ballet. Conducted by Incidence Chorégraphique: Laura Bachman, Marion Barbeau, Sébastien Bertaud, Matthieu Botto, Laure-Adélaïde Boucaud, Bruno Bouche, Alexandre Carniato, Cyril Chokroun, Antonio Conforti, Mathieu Contat, Camille De Bellefon, Yvon Demol, Lucie Fenwick, Letizia Galloni, Claire Gandolfi, Juliette Gernez, Fanny Gorse, Emilie Hasboun, Juliette Hilaire, Aurélien Houette, Axel Ibot, Amélie Joannides, Alexandre Labrot, Mickael Lafon, Pablo Legasa, Erwan Leroux, Laurène Levy, Germain Louvet, Sabrina Mallem, Lucie Matéci, Florent Melac, Antonin Monie, Aubane Philbert, Charlotte Ranson, Alexis Renaud, Caroline Robert, Roxane Stojanov, Daniel Stokes, Simone Valastro, Hugo Vigliotti Et Jennifer Visocchi with the kind permission of Brigitte Lefevre, Director of Paris Opera Ballet & Olivier Aldeano, Dance administrator, the break dancers of Centre Social intercommunal de la Dhuys and Service Municipal de la Jeunesse de Clichy-Sous-Bois, Mehdi Belghanem, Dylan Cordier, Laurenzy Dokossi, Mathieu Goncalves, Faïssoil Hodou, Cherif Kassouri, Sofiane Kissi, Eddie Maurin, Gounedi Traore, Mohamed Zaidou, Nabil Zerfa, Georges Coffi, Guillaume Lapoussiniere. Crew: Guillaume Lefrancois, Michel Barthelemy, Antoine Garceau, Julien Decoin, Clio Nogues, Tommy Kerne, Mohamed Belhamar, Adrien Debackere, Graham Willoughby, Julien Andreetti, Agnès Jeanneau, Sarah Boutin, Manon Sorbier, Camille De Chenay, Nicolas Diaz, Just Meissonnier, Coeurs & Arts, Kim Chapiron, Ladj Ly, Cédric Klapisch, Mohamed Mazouz, David Meignan, Saïd Belktibia, Léo Rougery-Herbaut, Aïssa Lahoucine, dit Sassa, Emmanuel Plumecocq, Stéphane Gauthron, Laurent Coudoux, Yannick Audige, Mickael Wallet, Joël Canard, Jean-Philippe Desfarges, Olivier Martin, Sabrina Perinet, Guillaume Mondin, Frédéric Cantin, Antoine Vidal, Olivier Dubois, Fabien Barrau, Romain Cadilhac, Diego Verastegui, Yann Mégard, Clément Héraut, Jean-Roch Bonnin, Gregory Dauman, Jean-Charles Berlan, Jeremy Scialom, Cyrielle Frauche, Julie Guionneau, Javotte Touret, Arnaud Simon, Jérôme Forge, Mathilde Mallet, Samir Mihi, Oumar Ly, Eléonore Coupry, Natacha Langmantil, Julie Pugeat, Marz Montini, Benoit Talenton, Guillaume Larras, Ronan Chiaradia, Marc Happel, Camille Pajot, Diane Gagnant, Joanna Vainqueur, Stéphanie Selva, Betty Beauchamp, Rémi Canaple, Etienne Rougery-Herbaut, Saïd Belktibia, Melvyn Bonnaffe, Kevin Theraud, Youssef Boubekeur, Charly Bassagal, Eloi Nourry, Adrien Tembremande, Robin Rougery, Agathe Berman, Bruno Bouché, Aurélien Houette, Gounedi Traore, Georges Coffi, Nabil Zerfa, Rhea Keller, Mergui Associes, Haidar, Annette Du Monde, Tombari Sabah, Jean Imbert, Nicolas Guibert, Marco Casanova, Julien Desplanques, Mathieu Hue, Cyril Bordesoulle, Mélanie Teixera, Erwan Quelme, Lorene Ouztric, Maxime Mourey, Thomas Canu, Julien Bonnet, Sébastien Aubert, Clément Papin, Vivien Salvagione, Mathieu Leclercq, Nicolas Daniel, Virginie Seguin, Albin Martinetti, Gilles Marsalet, Antoine Faure, Matthieu Autin, Bruno Bertoli, David Fleming, Czar Russel. JR thanks: Marco & Barbara Caleffi, Nancy & Steve Crown, Caroline & Howard Draft, Hélène & François Meyer, Michal & Guy Meyohas and Pharrell Williams for i am Other Entertainment as well as Marc Azoulay, Marc Berrebi, Julie Pugeat, Loic Villepontoux, Caron Veazey, Mimi Valdes, Peter Martins, Katherine Brown, Karen Girty, Deborah Koolish, Rosemary Dunleavy, Marc Happel, Mark Stanley, Ellen Bar, Lauren Clifford, IATSE Local 1, New York City Ballet, Sol Guy, Perrotin Gallery, Magda Danysz Gallery, Simon Studer Gallery, Springman Gallery, Gilles Kepel and Fabrice Bousteau. Ladj Ly thanks: La Family, Clichy/Montfermeil, Kourtrajme, Lamyia Monkachi, Hamed Bouhout, Olivier Klein, Syaka Traore, Malams Diarra, Boulay Diarra, Samir Mihi, Sami, Karim Asma, Mamadou Kanoté, Hamidou Ly, Moussa Niakaté, Les Daltons, Goune Traore, Nabil Zerf, ma Boulette, Zid 370, Mehdi Bigaderne, Fiston, Doc, Vieux, Zicton, Befa, Namo, Brahim Machalah, Dollar, Cabbo, Chef, Tiga, Fesal, Ousmane, Youssouf, Jef, Las Ly, MBF, Kim Chapiron, Romain Gavras, Toumani et Ben Sangaré, Said Belktibia, Vincent Cassel, Andre Chemetof, Alexi Manenti, Hamed, Mohamed Mazouz, Oxmo Puccino, Momo, Marco Casanova, Mouloud Achour, Karim Boukercha, Mailan, Issa Demba, Marie Joubert. Social Animals thanks: Olivier Klein & mairie de Clichy-sous-Bois, Conseil Général de la Seine Saint-Denis, Direction de l'Eau & de l'Assainissement, Police precinct of Clichy-sous-Bois, Centre d'incendie & de secours de Clichy-Sous-Bois, Centre Social Intercommunal de la Dhuys, the inhabitants & conseil syndical of STAMU II, the inhabitants & conseil syndical of PAMA II, the inhabitants & conseil syndical of Chene Pointus, the inhabitants & conseil syndical of Bois du Temple, Immo de France, AJAssociés, La Soval, Veolia, Vincent Lorca, Ousmane Ly, Pablo Broders, Georges Maubert, Arthur Catton and Ilya Chemetoff, Jean-Marie Lavalou, Jean-Claude Ruellan, Marina, Jego, Sandra Bekkar, Christine Janeau, Fanny Dupuy, Lucile Denéchaud, Ahmed Bouhout, Mamadou Kanouté, Samy Asma, Siaka Traore, Lucca Fletcher Dahan, Katherine Coffey, Charlotte Marmion, Esteban Abinal-Bally, Ayrton Abinal-Bally, Maurice Abinal, Laetitia Bally, Louis Lefrancois and all the mediators and anonymous people who made this film possible on location! *Ellis Island Movie* Roberto De Angelis, Jaime Scatena, Marguerite Espin de la Vega, Louise Prevot, Gary Su, Paul Masmejean, Fred Perret, Quentin Higgins, Marie-Salomé Peyronnel, Noah Neary, Jamel Benabdallah, Matt Mcdonald, Ridah Farooqui, Khadijat Oseni, Basil Sema, Ellen Nelson, Luis Gomez, Tony Herbas, Andrew Ferguson, Edgar Alejandro Garrido, Jahmekya Birhan, Zenat Begum, Khadijat Oseni, Mandy Edgecombe. *Flatiron* project: Marc Azoulay, Rhea Keller, Jaime Scatena, Lucca Fletcher, Louise Prevot, Marguerite Espin de la Vega, Andrew Ferguson, Tony Herbas, Luis Gomez, Kate Coffey, Noah Neary, Josh Geyer, Brandon Bakus, Jamel Benabdallah, Jordan Hewson, Diego Osorio, Leopoldine Despointes, Bryan Meador, Basil Sema, Anya Khalamayzer, Reuben Hernandez, Melvyn Bonnaffe, Elsa Rodach, Joseph Reiver, Alan Reiver, Angèle Arene, Natasha Stragalinou, Sermad, Phrixos, Ariel Agai, Khadijat Oseni, Elodie Villalon, Sam Decker, Angela del Sol, Dirby Luongo, Marta Diego. *Inside Out* the movie: Patrick Ghiringhelli, Antonio Pinto, Samuel Ferrari, Dudu Aram, Patrice Bart-Williams, Gregor Lyon, Sharon Harel-Cohen, Marco Berrebi, Jane Rosenthal, Leo Haidar, Sol Guy, Emile Abinal, Alastair Siddons, Guillaume Lefrançois, Nathalie Durand, Anthony Dalton, Anthony Dickenson, Dan Lowe, James Lovick, William Morisson, Morgan Susser, Neus Olle Soronellas, Pierre Chautard, Pierre Edelmann, Philippe Welsch, Kabe Cornell, Matt Kemp, Andrew Hoare, Fabien Elies, Etienne Rougery-Herbaut, Elsa Rodach, Franck Bonneveau, Natacha Langmantil, Lola Zajdermann, Julie Pugeat, Lucca Fletcher Dahan, Eloi Nourry, Alix Malandain, Maria Bergeaud, Melvyn Bonnafé, Luise Hauschild, Camille Pajot, Tamara Harel-Cohen, Gisela Evert, Katie Bullock-Webster, Sofia Lundberg, Cecile Dessertine, Lisa Forest, Danny Cerqueira, Justine Moreau, Ian Wilson, Steve Single, Paul Ensby, Kim Honeyman, Jean-Pierre Romel, Alex Louis, Mackenley Benoit, Stevens Simeon, Aziz Tnani, Serine Nazer, Sophia Baraket, Frank Etienne, Hichem Driss, Rania Dourai, Chad Agard, Jenny Eagle, Ted Eagle, Abed Abedrabbou, Hela Ammar, Wissal Dargueche, Aden Algazi, Christian Bernard Ricot, Juliana Betancourt Lopex, Rie Nozu, Amel Kissoum, Chibane Hayet, Hoda Fourcade, Shira Legmann, Noémie Dahan, Ranwa Stephan, Marc Azoulay, Guillaume Cagniard, Virginia Cromie, Rhea Keller, Will Hopkins Jr, Joshua Geyer, Gina Pollack, Hillary Cutter, Benton Ferguson, Nina Embiricos, Arani Matti, Nastasia Bach, Emma Berrebi, Jie Xia, Oscar Tine, Julian Bass-Krueger, Noah Domond, Federico Szarfer, Dina Horowitz, Ridah Farooqui, Diana Bejarano, Vivian Wenzler, Natalie Eichengreen, Paola Murillo, Jill Brandwein, Andrew Ferguson, Moira Pernambuco, Mackenley Benoit, Alex Louis, Stevens Simeon, Jean-Pierre Romel, Belle, Tatiana Etienne, Anna Verghese. Merci à Bernard, Massena, Andre Eugène, Atis Rezistans, Thomas Freteur, Dorine Van Ophalvens, Lorraine Silvera, Alessandra Carias Vorbe, Inbal Timor, Veronica Sharon, Louis Albert Leveque Silvera, Marie Arago, Tatiana Mora Liautaud, Kristin Condos, Nicole Letendre, Rachid Ben Smail, Joëlle Vauthier, Serine Nazer, Aziz Tnani, Amina Zeghal, Riadh Kooli, Olfa Khalil Arem, Ali Diouri, Amira Karaoud, Aimara Malika, Omar Bey, Cheikh, Hatem Lahiani, Mylène Salomon. Équipe collage: Amina Abdellatif, Amel Bayrem, Omar Bey, Mehdi Chaker, Hana Cherif, Cyrine Ghannouchi, Ghazi Ghermazi, Malek Hajlaoui, Chiraz Hamdi, Cyrine Hammami, Hager Lakhdher, Myriam Naili, Irane Ouanes, Elyssa Souissi, Emile Abinal, Marc Azoulay, Anne-Sophie Bion, Guillaume Lefrançois, Kevin Theraud, Franck Bonneveau, Anne-Sophie Bion, Moncef Abdelhedi, Azzedine Bachaouch, André Berrebi, Kamel Bjaoui, Brahim, Dalel Drichene, Dora, Azza Filali, Sihem Kallel, Kevin Theraud, DJ 2 Bears, Chase Iron Eyes, Eric Greycloud, Shannon Burnette, Tukilsa, Chase Iron Eyes, Eric Greycloud, Ladonna Brave Bull-Allard, Miles Allard, Rain In The Face, Nicole Thunder Hawk-Archambault, Dave Archambault, Sheridan Seaboy, Max Thunder Hawk, Tomi Cimarosti-Fool Bear, Jodi Lynn Thunder Hawk, Desire Condon Photos, Laurie Running Hawk, Gracey Claymore, Cyprus Nelson, Shaylynn Ramsey, Billi Jo Gravseth, Kenneth Thunder Hawk, Jamie Archambault, Nemo Thunder Hawk. Kevin Theraud, Sitting Bull and all the chiefs and all the families, Jane Rosenthal, Tony Tabatznik, Rebecca Lichtenfeld, Amanda Palmer, Philipp Engelhorn, Cara Mertes, Chris Anderson, Marsha Williams, Mike & Sukey Novogratz, Pablo & Almudena Legorreta et Stuart Davidson, HBO Documentary Films, Sheila Nevins, Sara Bernstein, Geof Bartz A.C.E., Sharon Werner, Barbara Caver, TED, Amy Novogratz, Anna Verghese, Bonnie Calvin, Casson Rosenblatt, Dan Mitchell, Erin Allweiss, Erline Maruhom, Tom Valentino, Jodi Tatum, the TED community et la TED media team, Aashish Gudka, Sirish Malde, Uzma Hasan, Hal Sadoff, Joshua Grode, Maggie Kim, Paul Miller, Khalil Benkirane, Leah Giblin, Adella Ladjevardi, Kristin Feeley, Rahdi Taylor, Hajnal Molnar-Szakacs, Beth Janson, Ryan Harrington, Shoshana Shapiro, Joe Pernice, Elisha Et Marin Karmitz, Juliette Shrameck, Clemence Van Raay, Amel Ourghemmi, Jean-François Rial, Nathalie Belloir, Stephane Even, Olivier Brunisholz, Andrée Lauper, Stephane Stasi, Ladj Ly, Toumani Sangaré, Hadas Kleinemann, Dan Bromfeld, Ayman Abu Al-Zulof, Wissam Salsaa, Matthieu Botrel, Alabaz, Jean-Baptiste Lefoll, Fadi Kattan, Guillaume Tinsel, Sinda Tobni, Ouriel Darmon, Said Belktibia, Youssef Boubakeur, Ulysse Moal, Sean Hart, Charles Azoulay, Noa Magger, Gabriel Malka, Jean-Marc Liling, Mia Dolinger, Eitan Schlesinger, Khalil Hanani, Rémy Cheval, Roi Lind, Yogev Yifat, Ramzi Jaber, Maureen Meyer, Ofer Zalzberg, Tiphaine Guignat, Amira Munther, Gakuranman, Hélène Kelmachter, Julie Le Saos, Liane Khan Acito, Charlotte Marmion, Esteban & Ayrton Abinal-Bally, Laetitia Bally, Claire Rusznievski & Louis Lefrançois, Maria Bergeaud, Craig Hatkoff, Darren Walker, Tracy Chiang, Luis Ubinas, Che Kothari, Chris Haddock, Alex Marshall, Russell & Honor Haidar, Charlotte & Eglantine Haidar-L'Hote, François Choquet, Henriette Chabat-Rivière, Helen Olive et Bianca O'Brien, Lyndsey Marshal, Nelli Turner, Adam Smith, Marley Granville, Sam Turner, Joe Philipps, Nish Panchal, Michael Cutler, Tracey Li Lyon, Prune Nourry, Kevin Konak, Piers Wenger, Anne-Sophie Bion, Cara Mertes, Kristin Feeley Etrahdi Taylor, Joslyn Barnes, Nancy Willen, Bonni Cohen, Elvina Siddons, Jamie Cameron, DJ Two Bears, Alexia Taylor, Sheila Handley, Rachel Sheppard, Tamara Harel Cohen, Anna Verghese, Tatiana Etienne, Max Bygrave, all who worked on the film, everyone on *Inside Out* and JR teams, Serge Alleyne, Thafis Andrea, Rita Aoun, Tanley Arrested Motion, Charly Bassagal, Louise Berrebi, Dominique Bertinotti, Not Blu, Pierre Borgel, Ami Bougamin, Frederic Brenner, Sebastien Breteau, Kim & Mai Lan Chapiron, François Coen, Ronald Cohen, Romain Colin, Phil Cooley, Diana D'arenberg, Roberta Christina Da Silva Gomez, Magda Danysz, Gilles Darmon, Marie De Pibrac, Jeremie Delon, Caroline & Howard Draft, Maurice Ephrati, Roni Eshel, Olivier Fleurot, Edward Fox, Tatyana Franck-Rossignol, Sabine Gabrié, Gael Garcia Bernal, Everardo Gout, Philippe Hadey, Mam Hania, Craig Hatkoff, Alicia Heiniger, Yuta Hirai, Mauricio Hora, Jean Imbert, Tsubasa Japan, Mathieu Kassovitz, Eric Kayser, Sebastien Kopp, Vanessa Laidaoui, Christin Lam, Steve Lazarides, Michel Levy-Provencal, Gabriel Malka, Rosiete Marinho, François, Hélène & Anne Meyer, Merhav Mohar, Etsuko Nakajima, Patrick Newell, Olivier Nourry, José & Rey Parla, Debora Pill, Damian Platt, Gaelle Porte, Paul Ramirez, Anthony Ramirez Ii, Eva Rentsch-Varol, Padre Rodach, Lucie Savarin, Laurent Segretier, Takao Shiraishi, Jay Smith, Henrik et Christine Springmann, Simon Studer, Angelino Studiocromie, Ruuta Ushiro, Stéphanie Vaillant, Selim Varol, Timothée Verrecchia, Vassili Verrecchia, Vhils, David Walters, Ware, Etsuko & Koichi Watari, Cameron Yates, The Bertha Foundation, Sundance Institute Documentary Film Programme, Doha Film Institute, Cinereach.

Thank you to: Emile Abinal, Marc Azoulay, Marco Berrebi, Julie Pugeat, Guillaume Cagniard, Etienne Rougery-Herbaut, Natacha Langmantil, Melvyn Bonnaffé, Cécile Dessertine, Camille Pajot, Alex Alabaz, Guillaume Lefrançois, Lucca Fletcher, Rhea Keller, Andrew Ferguson, Luis Gomez, Tony Herbas, Prune Nourry, Nathalie, Simon, Bilou Et Emma, Maryse, Gérard, Elsa, Sabine, Olivier, Marie, Katarina, Alex Homecore, Jean Baptiste Le Foll, Ladj Ly, David Boucris, Youssef Boubekeur, Charly Bassagal, Saïd Belktibia, Sergio Alleyne, Michèle Mergui, Yael Reinharz-Hazan, David Walters, Alastair Siddons, Anthony Dickenson, Dan Lowe, Fabien Barrau, André Chemetoff, Guillaume Bloch, Patrick Baradel, Paola Murillo Wong, Natalie Eichengreen, Jocelyne Gilead, Jill Brandwein, William Hopkins Jr, Joshua Geyer, Gin Cromie, Eloi Nourry, Patrick Ghiringhelli, Philippe Welsh, Kim Chapiron, Jean-Gabriel Becker, Christopher Irfane, Khan Acito, Patrice Bart Williams, Ulysse Moal, Constance Pentier, Eric Salomon, Caroline Goutal, Sophie Paumelle, Angèle Arène, Caroline And Howard Draft, François et Hélène Meyer, Sir Ronald And Sharon Cohen, Olivier Brunisholz, Maurice Ephrati, Philipp Engelhorn, Cameron Yates, Kristina Lazarevic, Sol Guy, Jane Rosenthal, Robert De Niro, David Blaine, Eric Roth, Anna Verghese, Amy Novogratz, Chris Anderson, Erin Allweiss, Jean-François Rial, Jean Imbert, Timothée Verrecchia, Alireza Niroomand, Jay Smith Et Greg Hervieux, Emmanuel Perrotin, Valentine Blondel, Peggy Leboeuf, Cécile Ktorza, Emmanuelle Orenga De Gaffory, Steve Lazarides, Magda Danysz, Simon Studer, Henrik Springmann Henri Thuaud, Victoria Al Din, Maurice Grimbaum, Ralph Taylor,François Hebel, Fabrice Bousteau, Kathy Ryan, Christine Walsh, Karen Girty, Peter Martins, Sherry Dobbin, Janis Calella, François Sergent, Jean-Baptiste Dumon, Dominique Bertinotti, Pedro Alonzo, Thierry Consigny, Stefano Stoll, Agathe Berman, Mauricio Hora, Rosiete Marinho, Debora Pill, Daniel Salin, Damian Platt, Art Spiegelman, Liu Bolin, \ Os Gemeos, Vhils, José Parlá, Zevs, Blu, Vik Muniz, André, Ernest Pignon Ernest, David Lynch, Agnès Varda, David O Russell, Oliver Jeffers, Lucien Zayan, Lil Buck, Laurent Lovette, all the dancers from the New York City Ballet and the Ballet de l'Opéra de Paris.

All the projects were realized without sponsors or brands. They were made possible by the help of hundreds of volunteers all over the world.